MILESTONES
IN
GLASNOST
AND
PERESTROYKA
THE ECONOMY

MILESTONES

IN

GLASNOST

AND

PERESTROYKA

THE ECONOMY

ED A. HEWETT and **VICTOR H. WINSTON**
Editors

THE BROOKINGS INSTITUTION
Washington, D.C.

About Brookings

The Brookings Institution is a private nonprofit organization devoted to research, education, and publication on important issues of domestic and foreign policy. Its principal purpose is to bring knowledge to bear on the current and emerging policy problems facing the American people.

A board of trustees is responsible for general supervision of the Institution and safeguarding of its independence. The president is the chief administrative officer and bears final responsibility for the decision to publish a manuscript as a Brookings book. Publication of a work signifies that it is deemed a competent treatment worthy of public consideration but does not imply endorsement of conclusions or recommendations. The Institution itself does not take positions on policy issues.

Copyright © 1991

THE BROOKINGS INSTITUTION

1775 Massachusets Avenue, N.W., Washington, D.C. 20036

Library of Congress Cataloging-in-Publication Data:
Milestones in glasnost and perestroyka / Ed A. Hewett and
   Victor H. Winston, editors.
     p.   cm.
    Readings based on contributions to Soviet economy 1985–1991.
    Includes bibliographical references and indexes.
    Contents: v. 1. The economy—v. 2. Politics and people.
    ISBN 0-8157-3622-3 (v. 1 : alk. paper)—ISBN 0-8157-3621-5 (v. 1 : pbk. : alk. paper)—ISBN 0-8157-3624-x (v. 2 : alk. paper)—ISBN 0-8157-3623-1 (v. 2: pbk. : alk. paper)
    1. Soviet Union—Economic policy—1986– . 2. Soviet Union—Economic conditions—1985– . 3. Glasnost. 4. Perestroîka. I. Hewett, Edward A. II. Winston, Victor H., 1925– .
HC336.26.M555   1991
338.947'009'048—dc20

91-15304
CIP

9 8 7 6 5 4 3 2 1

The paper used in this publication meets the minimum requirements of the American National Standard for Information Sciences—Permanence of paper for Printed Library Materials, ANSI Z39.48-1984

Set in Linotron Times Roman
Composition by Harper Graphics
  Waldorf, Maryland
Printed by R.R. Donnelley and Sons Co.
  Harrisonburg, Virginia

Foreword

IN MARCH 1985 Mikhail Gorbachev became General Secretary of the Communist Party and set in motion efforts to open up and restructure Soviet society. *Glasnost'* and *perestroyka* have clearly brought profound changes to the Soviet Union and to the international community. But because of their dizzying pace and uncertain course, these changes have often been as bewildering as they have been dramatic.

Fortunately, also in the spring of 1985 the journal *Soviet Economy* was launched. Introducing the initial volume, the editors recognized that the Soviet economy was "in the early stages of an important transitional period in which the leadership will (and must) introduce significant changes in economic policies and possibly in the fundamentals of the system." They pledged that their journal would present research results and analytic observations concerning those changes as well as essays placing them in historical context. Over the past six years, the journal has indeed offered important research and analysis by Western scholars along with contributions from key Soviet experts and participants in the reform process.

This book on the Soviet economy, and its companion volume on Soviet politics and people, present articles drawn largely from *Soviet Economy*. These readings are intended to offer a valuable chronicle and analysis of the milestones in the reform process. Because *Soviet Economy*, which is published in association with the Joint Committee on Soviet Studies of the American Council of Learned Societies and the Social Science Research Council, is not a Brookings publication, formal review and verification procedures established for the Institution's publications have not been applied in this case.

Ed A. Hewett, founding editor of *Soviet Economy* and a former senior fellow in the Brookings Foreign Policy Studies program, is now Special Assistant to the President on National Security Affairs and Senior Director of Soviet Affairs at the National Security Council. Hewett's work on this book was completed before he joined the National Security Council staff. The views expressed here in his essays and in the introductions he coauthored are his own and not necessarily those of the U.S. Government. Victor H. Winston, the coeditor of *Soviet Economy* and a former head of research at the Mid-European Study Center of Radio Free Europe, is an adjunct professor of international affairs at George Mason University.

The editors are indebted to all the contributors to this volume, but wish to express their particular appreciation to *Soviet Economy*'s coeditor, Professor Gertrude E. Schroeder of the University of Virginia, whose suggestions and comments were of great value. Professional courtesies were also extended by James H. Noren of the Central Intelligence Agency, Julian Cooper of the University of Birmingham, and Andrew R. Bond, the editor of *Soviet Geography*. Andrew Baukol of the Central Intelligence Agency, who compiled the subject index, Hugh Jenkins of the University of Birmingham, who updated the chronology, and Brian W. Hayman of V. H. Winston and Son, Inc., who supervised the flow of manuscripts to Brookings, provided outstanding support. At the Brookings Institution, the publishing effort was in the able hands of Robert Faherty and Norman Turpin. The editors are grateful for their professionalism and assistance.

The views expressed in this book are those of the individual authors and should not be ascribed to the trustees, officers, or staff members of the Brookings Institution.

BRUCE K. MAC LAURY
President

June 1991
Washington, D.C.

Contents

Part I THE EMERGING REFORM

Editors' Introduction   3

1. Gorbachev's Economic Strategy: A Preliminary
   Assessment   5
   Ed A. Hewett
   What Gorbachev Hopes to Achieve *6*
   Strategy for Achieving the Plan Goals *13*
   Feasibility of the Twelfth FYP *18*

2. Gorbachev's Economic Strategy: A Comment   23
   Philip Hanson

3. Gorbachev at Two Years: Perspectives on Economic
   Reforms   30
   Ed A. Hewett

4. Gorbachev: "Radically" Implementing Brezhnev's
   Reforms   36
   Gertrude E. Schroeder

5. The Gorbachev Reform: A Maximal Case   47
   Jerry F. Hough
   Basic Assumptions *48*
   Benchmarks and Standards for Comparison *50*
   Gorbachev's Strategy *52*

6. The Shape of Gorbachev's Economic Reform   57
   Philip Hanson
   An Outline of the Reform *59*
   An Evaluation of the Reform *65*

Part II   THE ARCHITECTS OF CHANGE

Editors' Introduction   71

7. Gorbachev's Economic Advisors   74
   Anders Åslund
   Leading Economic Institutions and Economists   *75*
   Commissions for Economic Reform   *83*
   Economic Advice to Gorbachev   *86*
   Conclusions   *92*

8. Prospects for Change in the Systems of Price
   Formation, Finance, and Credit   95
   Nikolay Ya. Petrakov
   Distortions in the Current Structure of Prices   *95*
   Importance of Change in the Price Structure   *96*
   Objectives for Restructuring the Price System   *97*
   Strategies for Change   *98*
   Links between Price and Financial Reforms   *100*

9. Basic Directions of *Perestroyka*   104
   Abel G. Aganbegyan with *Ed A. Hewett, Abram
   Bergson, Gregory Grossman,* and *Herbert S. Levine*
   The Three Directions   *104*
   Selected Questions and Comments   *110*
   Selected Answers   *115*
   Comments on Competition   *120*

10. The New Model of Economic Management   122
    Leonid I. Abalkin with *Ed A. Hewett, Abram
    Bergson, Gregory Grossman,* and *Jerry F. Hough*
    Economic Model of Soviet Reform   *122*
    Discussion   *126*

11. Socioeconomic Aspects of *Perestroyka*   136
    Tat'yana I. Zaslavskaya with *Abram Bergson,
    Jerry F. Hough,* and *Gregory Grossman*

12. Rethinking Price Reform   153
    Nikolay P. Shmelev
    The Ideal Reform Package   *153*

Complicating Factors *155*
An Alternative Approach *158*

Part III   THE COMPLEXITIES OF TRANSITION

Editors' Introduction   163

13. Price Policies and Comment on Shmelev   167
    Morris Bornstein
    Industrial Wholesale Prices *167*
    Agricultural Purchase Prices *179*
    Retail Prices *186*
    Conclusion *195*
    Comment on Shmelev's Approach *196*

14. Anatomy of Gorbachev's Economic Reform   204
    Gertrude E. Schroeder
    Description of the Reform Package *205*
    Evaluation of the Reform Package *215*
    Outlook *223*

15. The 19th Conference of the CPSU and Its Aftermath   225
    Ed A. Hewett with *Herbert S. Levine,*
    Gertrude E. Schroeder, and *Victor H. Winston*
    Gorbachev's Opening Speech *225*
    Gorbachev and Abalkin *229*
    Gorbachev's Plenum Speech *233*
    The Complexities of Transition *236*
    Concluding Comments *244*

16. Radical Perceptions of *Perestroyka*   246
    Ed A. Hewett with *Yuriy N. Afanas'yev, Pavel G.*
    Bunich, and *Nikolay P. Shmelev*
    The Remonstrations of Pavel Bunich *249*
    A Dialogue with Nikolay Shmelev *252*
    Yuriy Afanas'yev's Retrospective *256*

17. Budget Deficit, Market Disequilibrium, and
    Economic Reforms   263
    Gur Ofer
    Fiscal and Monetary Aspects of a Centrally Planned System *268*

Fiscal Developments: Is the Present Crisis
a Legacy of the Past? *271*
Non-Budgetary Financial Problems *292*
Conclusions: Possible Ways Out *298*
Appendix *305*

18. *Perestroyka* and the Congress of People's Deputies   308
Ed A. Hewett
The Increasingly Sophisticated Debate over *Perestroyka* *309*
Prospects for the Future: The Near Term *313*
Prospects for the Future: The Longer Term *324*

Part IV   ENTERING THE 1990s
Editors' Introduction   331
19. The Making of Economic Policy in 1989 and 1990   335
Anders Åslund
The Legacy of Institutional Changes since 1985 *336*
The New Economic Environment *338*
The Development of Economic Expertise *340*
Transformation of Economic Policy-Making Institutions *347*
The Recent Changes in Perspective *355*
The Aftermath of the 28th Congress of the CPSU *357*

20. The Economic Crisis: Another Perspective   360
James H. Noren
The Reliability of Measures of Performance *361*
Economic Performance under Gorbachev: An Overview *363*
Factors Contributing to the Crisis *376*
Can the Economy Muddle Through? *387*
Outlook *400*

21. "Crisis" in the Consumer Sector: A Comment   408
Gertrude E. Schroeder
The Record for Consumption *408*
Disintegration of the Consumer Market *409*
Resolution of the Paradox *413*

22. Property Rights in the New Phase of Reforms   415
Philip Hanson
Issues in Legislative Reform *415*
The Main Federal Measures *420*

Ownership Elements in the Shatalin Plan *430*
Preliminary Assessment *436*

23. The New Half-Measures 441
Ed A. Hewett
The Initial Blueprints *441*
Half-Measures *443*
The Shatalin Plan *445*
Concluding Comments *455*

24. *Perestroyka* in the Aftermath of 1990 459
Gertrude E. Schroeder
Economic Performance in 1990 *459*
The Radicalization of Economic Reform *461*
Rise of Regional Assertiveness *464*
Entering the 1990s *467*

References 470

Chronology of Major Economic Reform Legislation
in the USSR, April 1985–May 1991 498

Name Index 507

Subject Index 512

Tables

Chapter 1
1. Soviet Economic Performance Indicators and Plans, 1981–1984, and Plans, 1985–2000 8
2. Soviet Investment Variants for the Twelfth Five-Year Plan 20

Chapter 8
1. Revenue Structure in the State Budget of the USSR 101

Chapter 13
1. Indexes of Annual Average Enterprise Wholesale Prices (excluding Turnover Tax) by Industrial Branch, 1981–1985 172
2. Profitability Rates by Industrial Branch, 1980–1985 173
3. Average Annual Production Costs of Collective and State Farms, Selected Products, 1971–1975, 1976–1980, and 1981–1983 181

4. Estimated Additional Sales Revenue of Collective and State Farms from 1983 Agricultural Price Increases and Surcharges for Weak Farms, by Product 183
5. Profitability Rates on Sales to the State by Collective and State Farms, Selected Products, 1982 and 1984 183
6. Subsidies on Selected Agricultural Products, 1965 and 1981–1985 184
7. Indexes of Annual Average State Retail Prices, 1981–1985 188
8. Subsidization of Selected Meat and Dairy Products at 1983 Prices 192

Chapter 15

1. Matrix of Horizontal Interactions in the Soviet Economy, 1977–1978 239
2. Presumed Changes in the Matrix of Horizontal Interactions in the Soviet Economy from 1977–1978 to 1987–1988 240
3. New and Eliminated Horizontal Interactions in the Soviet Economy as Provided by Laws Enacted after 1985 241
4. Additional Cells in the Presumed Matrix of Horizontal Interactions in the Soviet Economy, 1987–1988 242

Chapter 17

1. Soviet State Budget Plans, 1989 and 1990 Reconstructed 266
2. Soviet Budget Deficits and Their Financing, 1971–1990 274
3. Investment in Fixed Capital and Financing Elements, 1971–1990 278
4. Structure of Revenues of the Soviet State Budget, 1971–1990 280
5. Structure of Expenditures of the Soviet State Budget, 1971–1990 282
6. Fiscal Changes, 1981–1985 to 1990 300
A. Soviet State Budget, 1971–1990 306

Chapter 18

1. Soviet Economic Performance, 1981–1990 (Plan) 317

Chapter 20

1. Growth of GNP by Sector of Origin, 1981–1989 365
2. Growth of Fixed Investment and Capital, 1986–1988 367
3. Growth of Consumption, 1981–1988 367
4. Trends in Aggregate Factor Productivity 368
5. Growth of Personal Money Income, 1981–1989 371
6. Changes in Soviet Retail Prices, 1981–1989 371
7. Changes in Economic Aggregates, 1985–1990 373
8. Regular Food Availability, 1987–1989 374
9. Quantities and Prices on Collective Farm Markets, 1988–1989 376

Chapter 21

1. Real Per Capita Consumption in the 1980s 409

Chapter 22

1. Book Value of Fixed Capital Assets in Mid-1990 420
2. Main Federal Laws and Decrees on Property Rights 422
3. Projected Ownership of Industrial Assets in the Shatalin Plan, 1990–2002 433
4. Proposed Legislative Measures in the Shatalin Plan 434

Figures

Chapter 1

1. Incremental Capital-Output Ratio, 1964–1984   11

Chapter 20

1. Economic Performance under Gorbachev and His Predecessors   369
2. Availability of Food Products in State Stores, 1981–1989   374
3. Rationing of Food Products in State Stores, 1987–1990   375
4. Growth in Industrial Production and Transportation, 1987–1990   389
5. Production of Consumer Durables, 1980–1990   391
6. Light Industry Production, 1980–1990   391
7. Production of Processed Foods, 1980–1990   392
8. Consumer Goods Production, 1987–1990 (in Retail Prices and Excluding Alcohol)   393
9. Retail Trade Turnover, 1987–1990   394
10. Average Monthly Earnings of Workers and Employees, 1986–1990   394
11. Housing Commissionings from State Resources, 1987–1990   395
12. Ferrous Metals Production, 1980–1990   395
13. Production of Chemicals, 1980–1990   396
14. Forest Products Production, 1980–1990   396
15. Fuels Production, 1980–1990   397
16. Electric Power Production, 1980–1990   397
17. Volume of Rail Freight Traffic, 1986–1990   398

Contributors

Leonid I. Abalkin Director, Institute of Economics of the Academy of Sciences of the USSR, and advisor to Mikhail Gorbachev

Yuriy N. Afanas'yev Director, Moscow State Institute of Historical Archives, Co-chairman of Inter-Regional Group of Deputies and of Democratic Russia

Abel G. Aganbegyan Rector, Academy of the National Economy, and former advisor to Mikhail Gorbachev

Anders Åslund Director, Stockholm Institute of Soviet and East European Economics

Abram Bergson Professor of Economics, Harvard University

Morris Bornstein Professor of Economics, University of Michigan

Pavel G. Bunich Deputy Rector, Academy of the National Economy, and President, Union of Leaseholders and Entrepreneurs

Gregory Grossman Professor of Economics, University of California, Berkeley

Philip Hanson Professor of Soviet Economics, University of Birmingham

Ed A. Hewett Special Assistant to the President on National Security Affairs, Senior Director of Soviet Affairs at the National Security Council, and founding editor of *Soviet Economy*

Jerry F. Hough Professor of Political Science and Director of the Center on East-West Trade, Investment, and Communications, Duke University, and Senior Fellow, Brookings Institution

Herbert S. Levine Professor of Economics, University of Pennsylvania

James H. Noren Senior Economist, Office of Soviet Analysis, Central Intelligence Agency

Gur Ofer Professor of Economics, Hebrew University of Jerusalem

Nikolay Ya. Petrakov Director, Institute of Market Problems of the Academy of Sciences of the USSR, and former advisor to Mikhail Gorbachev

Gertrude E. Schroeder Professor of Economics, University of Virginia, and coeditor of *Soviet Economy*

Nikolay P. Shmelev   Department Head, Institute of USA and Canada of the Academy of Sciences of the USSR, and advisor to Boris Yel'tsin

Victor H. Winston   Adjunct Professor of International Affairs, George Mason University, and coeditor of *Soviet Economy*

Tat'yana I. Zaslavskaya   Director, All-Union Public Opinion Center, advisor to Boris Yel'tsin, and former advisor to Mikhail Gorbachev.

MILESTONES
IN
GLASNOST
AND
PERESTROYKA

THE ECONOMY

Part I

The Emerging Reform

Editors'
Introduction

To BEGIN this volume's discussion of the economic milestones of recent Soviet history, Part I, entitled "The Emerging Reform," features six papers encompassing the first two years of Mikhail Gorbachev's meandering quest for change. We commence with a look at Gorbachev's economic strategy for the late 1980s, as analyzed by Ed A. Hewett in "Gorbachev's Economic Strategy: A Preliminary Assessment" and by Philip Hanson in his reply to that paper. Both authors focus on the ideas that Gorbachev enumerated during the course of debates surrounding the Twelfth Five-Year Plan.

Gorbachev proceeded to outline his views on the nature of the projected reform soon after ascending to power in March 1985. It was at this time— shortly after the death of Yuriy Andropov, whose influence is clear in some components of the desired reform—that high growth targets, ambitious investment policies biased toward machine building, and an emphasis on the "human factor" assumed a prominent role. Gorbachev's ideas embraced an economic system in which enterprises and local authorities were to participate in decision making and assume greater responsibility commensurate with their increased authority. Production decisions and errors were to generate strictly enforceable rewards or penalties, all predetermined. Individuals who worked hard would earn much more than those who did not. Central authorities were to forgo their commanding role in the general economic environment and shift attention to strategic issues. Control over the country's economy was to be realized primarily through taxes, subsidies, interest rates, and other economic instruments rather than a continuous flow of orders from above.

The general principles enunciated by the summer of 1985 clearly indicated Gorbachev's intention to pursue reforms. But as Hewett and Hanson both point out, they were too vague to guide the actual implementation and too superficial to address the fundamental sources of Soviet economic problems. Pessimism was still rare, but doubts began to surface.

The years 1985 and 1986 saw a flood of new policies and ill-defined res-

3

olutions, some distressingly similar to failed measures attempted in the 1960s and later under Leonid Brezhnev. During this period, Gorbachev appears to have been driven primarily by a desire to score quick political gains, even at the expense of implementing a coherent reform. As a consequence, his rhetoric conflicted with reality and the succession of partial measures began to inflict real damage.

This period is analyzed and debated by Gertrude E. Schroeder, Jerry F. Hough, and again Philip Hanson. Skepticism is very much the substance of Gertrude Schroeder's "Gorbachev: 'Radically' Implementing Brezhnev's Reforms." Prospects for the realization of the reform measures put in place during the course of *perestroyka's* first two years are deflated in light of earlier failed attempts to reverse some of the system's ills. The prognosis is spelled out: Without a radically different blueprint, the system-rooted maladies will continue and so will the treadmill.

Assumptions that a major reform of the Soviet economy cannot materialize are challenged by Jerry Hough. He takes a measured approach toward beliefs that Gorbachev is unable or unwilling to take political risks, that bureaucratic resistance is hardened, and that Communist ideology lacks themes that can be used to mobilize support for innovation. Changes do take place, for in 1986, unlike in 1965, it is no less than the General Secretary of the Communist Party of the Soviet Union, or CPSU, who is behind the reforms. Philip Hanson takes a middle-of-the-road approach in "The Shape of Gorbachev's Economic Reform." Modest reform gains traced to the encouragement of expansion in the legal, private, and cooperative sectors are envisaged in the short term. However, other incompatible policy changes affecting decision making at the enterprise level are regarded as a negative factor in *perestroyka's* chances for survival. In the long term, success is not in sight without a permanent break with the traditions of central planning.

CHAPTER 1

Gorbachev's Economic Strategy: A Preliminary Assessment

Ed A. Hewett

"The course towards intensification is dictated by objective conditions, by the entire development process of the country. There are no alternatives. Only an intensive economy, developing on the basis of the latest science and technology, can serve as a reliable material foundation for raising the welfare of workers, guaranteeing the strengthening of the country in the international arena, allowing it to deservingly enter the new century as a great and prospering power."
—Mikhail S. Gorbachev, December 10, 1984

THREE MONTHS after that speech Mikhail Gorbachev had assumed the post of General Secretary, and along with that, the opportunity and responsibility to formulate and implement his program to reverse the gradual deterioration in economic performance of the last several decades. Since his official appointment, a constant flow of speeches and decrees have begun to give shape to Gorbachev's economic strategy, sufficient shape so that it is now possible to attempt a first, albeit very preliminary, analysis of what he hopes to accomplish, how he expects to do it, and what portion of his goals he is likely to achieve in what time period.

The best indication of what he hopes to accomplish is contained in the draft "Basic Guidelines" for the Twelfth Five-Year Plan (FYPXII), published on November 9, 1985 ("Osnovnyye napravleniya," 1985), which gives targets for many economic variables for the remainder of the 1980s, and key variables to the end of the century. Gorbachev is developing a set of policy and reform measures which he hopes will achieve these goals. FYPXII is particularly informative on the intended policy measures, providing the most specific public statement available on the policy changes Gorbachev is introducing. Economic reforms receive less detailed treatment in the document, but recent decrees,

First published in *Soviet Economy*, 1985, 1, 4, pp. 285–305. [Eds.]

the draft Party Program ("Programma," 1985), and leadership speeches fill in some of the gaps.

This article focuses on the major elements of Gorbachev's economic strategy, not the details. Many of the details are not yet known, and even may not have been decided within the leadership. But the outlines are increasingly clear, sufficiently so, that it is possible not only to describe the strategy, but also to reach a preliminary judgment on the likelihood that it will achieve what Gorbachev hopes it will achieve.

WHAT GORBACHEV HOPES TO ACHIEVE

The document published on November 9, 1985, is the so-called "Basic Guidelines" for FYPXII, not the plan itself. These guidelines are composed of a fairly general discussion accompanied by a highly aggregated set of figures which both reflect and guide the drafting of the actual five-year plan. The public version of the Guidelines is incomplete, omitting all detail on defense and other information regarded as sensitive (for example, details on investment allocations or foreign economic relations). Past experience suggests that the actual five-year plan drawn up on the basis of the Guidelines will not depart from the guidelines on aggregate indicators, but rather will develop a very detailed and comprehensive plan of action to realize them. The actual five-year plan will probably never be published, even in truncated form; therefore the Guidelines, and accompanying commentary, constitute the bulk of publicly available information on the plan. The draft Guidelines published in November will probably be changed somewhat at the time of the February Party Congress, although past experience suggests the changes will not be major or extensive. Because the Guidelines do not provide the aggregate targets, as well as information on key projects, I will follow the convention of referring to them as "the" FYP.[1]

The draft of FYPXII has been the focus of a very heated debate between Gorbachev and the planning bureaucracy which dates back at least until mid-1984, and which basically was resolved in Gorbachev's favor only in the fall of 1985 with the removal of Baybakov and the publication of an ambitious draft. The first important public indication of the debate came in July 1984 (while Chernenko was still General Secretary) when Gorbachev gave a major speech at a meeting in Central Committee Headquarters discussing progress on the drafting of the plan, which was probably already in rough, but fairly complete, form. The text of the speech has not been published, but the brief report of the meeting clearly indicates the general tenor was critical of the conservatively low efficiency (and therefore output) growth rates in the draft; it is quite likely that Gosplan and the ministries were enjoined to produce a

---

1. In recent years, only the 1971–75 (IX) FYP document was published, presumably in truncated form (*Gosudarstvennyy*, 1972). Since then, only the final version of the Basic Guidelines has been published.

new, more ambitious draft (*Ekonomicheskaiya gazeta* [hereafter: *Ekon. gaz.*], No. 31, July 1984, p. 3).

In late January 1985, when Gorbachev was *de facto* in substantial control of the party, the Council of Ministers considered another draft of FYPXII, and sent it back once again for further work, also again emphasizing the need for higher growth rates (*Pravda*, January 24, 1985, p. 2). At the May 24, 1985, Politburo Meeting, 2 months after Gorbachev became General Secretary, Gosplan submitted the redrafted version of FYPXII, which was in essence rejected for a third time.[2] Then, yet one more time in August 1985 (*Sots. ind.*, August 24, 1985), there was a meeting in Central Committee Headquarters involving large elements of the planning hierarchy at which Gorbachev once again spoke (no text was published), reiterating now familiar themes, and criticizing ministries showing reluctance to adopt ambitious targets for FYPXII.

On October 15, Nikolay Baybakov was replaced by Nikolay V. Talyzin as chairman of Gosplan; on November 9, a draft—probably at least the fourth full draft—of FYPXII was published. While the published draft may still not be fully to Gorbachev's liking, it is fair to characterize it as Gorbachev's, not the bureaucracy's, view of what is possible in the second half of the 1980s and—in very broad brushstrokes—in the 1990s. The clearest indication of Gorbachev's influence is in the rapidly accelerating national income growth rates, which are essential to Gorbachev's plans for increasing consumer welfare, the efficiency of the Soviet economy, and the defense capabilities of the Soviet Union.

Overview of Plan Targets

As in past FYPs, FYPXII provides a fairly extensive, but far from comprehensive, set of targets for the 1986–1990 period. In addition, there are a few targets and substantial discussion about the remainder of the century, an improvement on the purely formalistic efforts in previous FYPs to look beyond the five-year period of immediate concern. Table 1 summarizes the key figures, broken down into those for 1986–1990 ("1986–1990 FYP"), and those for 1990–2000 ("1990–2000 FYP"), the latter derived in those few cases where FYPXII gives growth rates for the same indicator for 1986–2000 and 1986–1990.

The acceleration in economic growth which Gorbachev has so consistently called for is clearly evident in the plan for national income. In effect he is proposing to "replay" the national income growth record of the 1970s, but backwards: achieving growth rates characteristic of 1976–1980 during 1986–1990, and then accelerating to growth rates characteristic of the first half of the 1970s in the 1990s.

2. The decision was to go ahead and send the control figures down the hierarchy to the enterprises—a necessary move to allow all levels of the system to make their detailed five-year plans—while at the same time directing Gosplan to "improve" the plan figures, warning all economic units that these were to be taken as a minimum (*Sots. ind.*, May 25, 1985); see also Gorbachev's speech the following month in which he elaborates on his objection to the draft FYPXII (1985b).

Table 1. *Soviet Economic Performance Indicators and Plans, 1981–1984, and Plans, 1985–2000*
(Average annual growth rates)

	1961–65 Actual	1966–70 Actual	1971–75 FYP[a]	1971–75 Actual	1976–80 FYP[a]	1976–80 Actual	1981–85 FYP[a]	1981–84 Actual	1986–90 FYP[a]	1990–2000 FYP[a]
National Income (NMP) Produced	6.5	7.8	6.7	5.7	4.7	4.4		3.6		
National Income (NMP) Utilized	6	7.1		5.1		3.9	3.4	3.2	3.5–4.1	5.0–5.3
GNP (CIA estimate)	5	5.3		3.7		2.7		2.7		
Industrial production	8.8	8.3	8	7.4	6.3	4.5	4.7	3.7	3.9–4.4	4.9–5.1
Machinebuilding & metalworking	12.4	11.8		11.6		8.2	7	6	7.0–7.7	
Agricultural production	2.4	4.3	6.7	.6		1.5	4.7	2.6	2.7–3.0	
Labor productivity										
In all material production	5.5	6.8		4.6		3.3		3.1	3.7–4.2	6.5–7.6
In industry	4.5	5.6	6.8	6	5.5	3.1	3.6	3.1	4.2–4.6	
In agriculture	3.3	6.2		1.4		2.8		2.7	3.9–4.2	
In construction	5.2	4.1	6.5	5.2		1.5		2.7	2.8–3.0	
Gross investment										
Total	6.3	7.2	6.7	7		3.4		3.7		
State and cooperatives[b]	7.3	7.2	6.2	7.1	2.8	3.7	1.1	3.8	3.4–3.8	
Real per capita income	3.9	5.9	5.5	4.4		3.3	3.1	2.2	2.5–2.8	3.2–4.0

Sources: All the data, with the exception of those for GNP, are taken from official Soviet sources. The actual performance data are from *Narkhoz*; the data are from plan documents. The GNP growth rates are CIA estimates from published sources. The figures for 1986–1990 and 1990–2000 are from (or derived from) the first draft of the Twelfth Five-Year Plan (*Sots. ind.*, November 9, 1985), and may be revised before the Party Congress in February 1986.

a. "FYP" refers to planned performance designated in the five-year plan.
b. Excludes collective farm and private investments.

One of the many interesting features of this plan is that the "replay" does not show up consistently in other key indicators. Real per capita income, which grew at 4.4 percent per annum in 1971–1975 and 3.3 percent in 1976–1980, is to grow at no more than 2.8 percent in 1986–1990, and no more than 4 percent in the 1990s, well below the projected growth rate for national income. Investment is also set to grow at rates below those of the 1970s, and below the planned growth rate of national income. Taken together, these targets would seem to imply that during 1986–1990 defense will grow more rapidly than national income.[3]

Despite a strong emphasis on manufacturing, particularly machine building, the planned growth rates for industrial production are far more modest than actual industrial production growth rates in the early 1970s; and, although there are no specific targets given for Machine-building and Metal-working (MBMW) in the 1990s, targets for that sector for 1986–1990 are also somewhat more modest. The apparent intention not to "replay" that part of the 1970s may be a positive sign, since the most serious problem facing Soviet industry is the quality, not the quantity, of output.

Impediments to a Growth Acceleration

In many important ways, the rest of this century will be far less favorable than the 1970s so that Gorbachev's intention to return to growth rates of that earlier period will be difficult to realize. Not only are the growth rates of important factor inputs falling, but so are their productivities, and the international economic environment is likely to be far less hospitable than it was in the 1970s.

The decline in growth rates of productive inputs is a well-known and well-studied phenomenon in the Soviet Union; Gorbachev and his advisors discuss it in public (see, for example, Aganbegyan, 1985a); and the plan implies a recognition of the problem. Labor force growth rates are falling, reflecting a decline in population growth rates. During the 1970s, the labor force was growing at 1.8 percent per annum. By the early 1980s, labor force growth rates had fallen to .5 percent per annum, and they may even fall slightly farther in the late 1980s and early 1990s before rising to .8 percent toward the end of the century (Feshbach, 1983, pp. 94–95).

Growth rates of the capital stock, another key input, are also falling. In the first half of the 1970s, Soviet capital stock—measured by official Soviet data on productive capital—was growing at a rate of 8.7 percent per annum. Falling growth rates for investment, beginning the second half of the 1970s (Table 1), have now begun to have their effect, with a lag, on capital stock growth rates. By the early 1980s, productive capital stock was growing at 6.6 percent per

---

3. If national income is to grow at close to 4 percent in the second half of the decade, while investment grows closer to 3.5 percent and total consumption grows at approximately the same rate (a guess at the rate that total consumption—including social consumption might grow), then that would seem to imply that the residual (including defense) is slated to grow more rapidly than national income.

annum, and in the remainder of this decade the growth rate could fall still further, to approximately 5.5 percent per annum.[4]

*The effect on the economy of the declining growth rate of the capital stock is compounded by a decline in capital productivities. Figure 1 plots a 3-year moving average of the relationship between increments to the capital stock and increments to national income produced.[5] In the last decade and a half, capital productivities have declined by roughly one half, meaning that in the mid-1980s it requires twice as much capital as it did 15 years ago to achieve the same increment to real national income. A fall in capital productivities is hardly surprising for an economy such as the USSR, which has for so many years substituted capital for labor through very high investment growth rates. In addition, the capital costs of Soviet raw materials and fuels have begun to rise very rapidly, particularly in the 1970s as the geographic center of Soviet fuel and raw material production began to shift eastward at an increasing pace, the inevitable consequence of depleting reserves in the European USSR. Clearly, these factors are likely to continue to operate in the remainder of this century, so that capital productivity is, in the absence of dramatic new developments, likely to continue to deteriorate.

One other potentially important impediment relates to the changing international economic situation. During the 1970s, the Soviet Union enjoyed considerable windfall gains as the rise in oil and gold prices so improved their terms of trade that they were able to import significant amounts of goods and services essentially "for free," that is, without exporting additional goods and services. I estimated that just for the 1971–1979 period the improved terms of trade and higher gold prices provided the Soviets with at least an additional $22 billion worth of goods and services, which is double the net debt they incurred during that period, and that is a very conservative estimate of the windfalls.[6] Beginning in the early 1980s, the prices of oil and gold have fallen, and the Soviet economy is now experiencing windfall losses. In the first years of the decade, these declines in prices of key Soviet exportables were counterbalanced by the fact that in its hard-currency trade, Soviet exports were priced in dollars, while imports were priced in other currencies which were

4. The capital stock growth rates are from the series in *Narkhoz (1984*, p. 59; 1975, p. 59) on productive capital stock (which excludes capital not used directly in the production process, for example, housing and health institutions), in 1973 prices. The forecast for the latter half of the 1980s results from an equation explaining the log of the capital stock as a function of the log of total capital investment (in 1969 prices), current and lagged two years back, with weights determined by a third degree polynomial. The equation was estimated using data for 1972–1984; other specifications using shorter and longer time periods were examined, and this specification and time period seemed most sensible. Nevertheless the results are sensitive to the sample period and specification chosen, so the 5.5 percent growth rate should be taken as only a general indication of what might occur.

5. The time-series in Figure 1 is an incremental capital-output ratio in which the numerator is the change in an index (1970 = 100) of the productive capital stock between last period and the period before (K[−1] − K[−2]), and the denominator is the change in an index (1970 = 100) of national income produced between this period and last period (Y − Y[−1]). The lag is necessary because Soviet capital stock data are end-of-year figures; thus capital stock for, say, 1983 is what the economy actually had available for operations in all of 1984. Data for both series are from various issues of *Narkhoz*.

6. The estimates (from Hewett, 1983, p. 289) are for the terms of trade effect just for 1971–1977, but the gold price gains for 1971–1979. An extension of both series into the early 1980s would indicate far larger gains.

Figure 1. *Incremental Capital-Output Ratio, 1964–1984*

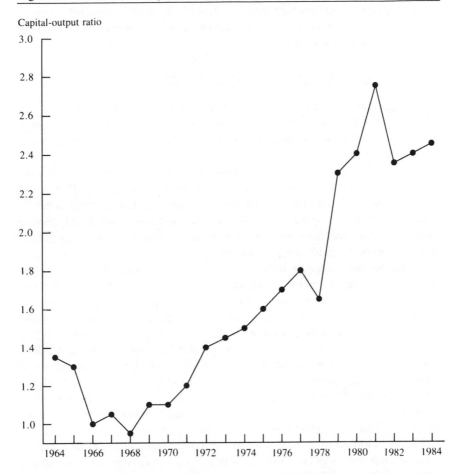

Capital-output ratio

weakening against the dollar. The net effect was virtually no change in the early 1980s in Soviet terms of trade (the ratio of the change in export prices over the change in import prices).[7] But now the dollar is weakening and the Soviet Union is beginning to feel the full effect of the falling oil prices.

The most likely scenario for the latter half of the 1980s is that the Soviet economy will experience significant windfall losses in an unwelcome ''replay'' of that part of the 1970s. And just as the windfall gains allowed increased imports of machinery, equipment, intermediate products, and food without concomitant increases in exports, now even maintaining past levels of imports

7. Soviet terms of trade with non-socialist countries are a decent, although far from perfect, indicator of their terms of trade in dollars (some of their trade with non-socialist LDCs is in clearing currencies; some of their trade with socialist countries is in dollars). Using quantity and value indices out of recent foreign trade year books (*Vneshtorg SSSR*, 1981–1984), it is possible to estimate terms of trade, and they were in fact unchanged during 1980–1984, even though the price of Soviet crude fell almost 20 percent over that period (*Petroleum Intelligence Weekly*, various issues).

of those commodities will require increases in exports. As Gorbachev begins a modernization program which may significantly increase demand for imported technologies, those windfall losses loom as a potentially important impediment to the realization of his plans.

Positive Trends Which Might Ease the Way

This grim recitation of negative trends naturally prompts the question of whether or not there might be some exogenous factors which Gorbachev could count on to make the 1980s easier than the 1970s. In fact, while the list is short, there are possibilities.

First, it is at least conceivable that the run of bad weather with which the Soviets have contended since the late 1970s might turn around. That is not something planners can (or at least should) count on. But if it did occur, it would significantly ease the current squeeze on hard-currency imports, leaving some room for machinery equipment imports without requiring dramatic increases in exports, gold sales, or borrowing.

Gorbachev has apparently fully embraced the policy dating back to the beginning of this decade to improve Soviet terms of trade with Eastern Europe, holding constant or even decreasing fuel and raw material exports, while increasing the quantity and quality of food and manufactures imported from Eastern Europe. And there are clear indications that Gorbachev—along with the leadership in general—expects results from the very tough stand the Soviets took at the June 1984 CMEA summit in the tangible form of significant increases in imports of goods from Eastern Europe during 1986–1990, including presumably a significant jump in imports of machinery and equipment. If this were to succeed—and there are many well-known reasons to be skeptical—then it would also serve to counteract the effects of windfall losses in hard-currency trade.

Finally, Gorbachev's leadership of the party, and the personnel changes flowing from that, may in itself constitute a change in circumstances compared to the stagnation of the 1970s which could enhance his chances for success. This is one component of the "human factor" on which Gorbachev places so much stress, of which more below.

Conclusion: A Very Ambitious Plan

It would go beyond the scope of this paper to undertake a serious effort to quantify the likely net effect of positive and negative factors on Soviet economic growth, assuming no reforms and no changes in policy. Yet it is clear, even in the absence of a major modelling effort, that the net effect of exogenous trends is to push the growth rate downward unless new policies and systemic reforms can manage to reverse the trends. The decline in labor force and capital stock growth rates, and the declining productivity of capital, are the important factors, and those will continue. Changes in the external economic environment will have a particular influence on food and technology imports, but the foreign sector is still a relatively unimportant influence on Soviet economic performance, so that this will act as a marginal, not a fundamental, influence. The only question which a rigorous modelling effort might resolve is how large the decline in growth rates could be in the absence of major policy changes.

Clearly, the architects of this plan understood at least some of the difficulties they faced. As one recent Soviet commentary put it, if the system were to achieve these goals using old ("extensive") strategies, then during the five-year plan capital expenditures would have to grow 30 percent to 40 percent and an additional 8–10 million workers would be required *(Ekon. Gaz.,* No. 47, November 1985, p. 2). In fact, FYPXII calls for capital expenditures to grow by no more than 21 percent over 1986–1990, and the labor force is unlikely to expand by much over 2 million persons (Feshbach, 1983, p. 94).

These facts lead to the inevitable assumptions built into FYPXII that labor productivity in all material production, which has been growing only slightly above 3 percent in the last decade, will grow at close to 4 percent in 1986–1990. Labor productivity in industry, also hovering slightly above 3 percent since the mid 1970s, is now set to grow well above 4 percent, possibly 4.6 percent, during 1986–1990. Within industry, virtually all sectors are scheduled to manage a dramatic turnaround in labor productivities. While this is not an effort to return to the labor productivity growth rates of the early 1970s, it is a very ambitious effort to reverse the clear downward trends of the last decade. FYPXII must also assume that the continued slow growth of investment (compared to the first half of the 1970s) will be accompanied by an acceleration in the growth of capital stock as project completions are accelerated; however, there are no numbers to indicate how rapid that acceleration is to be.

STRATEGY FOR ACHIEVING THE PLAN GOALS

Gorbachev's strategy for achieving the ambitious targets in FYPXII is not yet clear in all of its details, and may not even be fully resolved. Nevertheless, his speeches and FYPXII provide what appears to be a fairly complete outline of how he is approaching the problem. The approach that is emerging is a complicated one, relying primarily on traditional Soviet approaches but with a speed and comprehensiveness which is a significant departure from the Brezhnev years. I will only discuss the highlights here, under two headings: policy changes and economic reforms.

Policy Changes

Policy changes refer to the myriad measures available to the leadership in which they seek to improve performance by using the system, rather than changing the system. Among the policies Gorbachev has introduced, the most visible are probably the broad-based effort to exploit what Gorbachev calls the "human factor." Basically, this seems to refer to the possibility of significantly enhancing economic performance by inducing the labor force to work at rates closer to its potential. An important element of the "human factor" strategy is the entire range of "discipline" measures Gorbachev has introduced, a legacy from Andropov, but one on which Gorbachev has put his own mark. The anti-drunkenness and anti-alcohol campaign begun in the summer of 1985, the general emphasis on discipline at all levels (punctuated by several high-level dismissals related to abuse of office), and the openly tough approach Gorbachev takes to his ministers when they disappoint him, are all parts of an effort to cajole or even force the entire labor force to work harder than they have in the past. The many personnel changes occurring now throughout the system—from top to bottom—are also part of the "human factor" strategy, the theory being that bringing in new people with new ideas will enhance the performance of the system.

Clearly, a lack of enthusiasm and discipline in the work force is not the sole cause of Soviet economic difficulties; even the most enthusiastic workers in a Soviet factory are limited in what they can do if inputs are unavailable, machinery is broken down, or the technology embodied in their products is a quarter century behind the times. But a lack of enthusiasm and discipline is one of the problems with the Soviet economy, and Gorbachev is addressing that problem head on.

Enthusiastic workers need new, modern equipment to manage the productivity turnaround forecast in FYPXII, and modernization of Soviet industry is at the core of Gorbachev's strategy. To realize that goal, FYPXII calls for a dramatic change in most of the important aspects of investment policy. Some of the proposed changes repeat now familiar efforts to introduce policies announced in the past, but not implemented. Once again this time FYPXII places an emphasis on renovation which pays off much more quickly than construction of new factories. Currently approximately one-third of investment in the Soviet Union goes to the renovation of existing factories (Gorbachev, 1985b); FYPXII specifies that one-half of investment will go to renovating existing factories. Gorbachev notes that while this does not imply a total freeze on new project starts, it does mean that some ongoing projects may be cancelled in mid-stream (Gorbachev, 1985b). Once again FYPXII calls for dramatic improvements in the entire construction system so that projects which currently require 8–10 years to get from drawing board to completion (Dyker, 1983, p. 36) can be completed much more rapidly.[8]

Nevertheless, several new themes stand out in investment policy which could have far-reaching implications if implemented. Most notable is the very substantial shift in investment resources to MBMW. In June, Gorbachev called for a "partial redistribution" of investment to MBMW, which currently ac-

8. For example, the plan calls for a shortening by 3–4 times in the period required to design, manufacture, and install new technology in MBMW.

counts for 24 percent of industrial investment and 8.6 percent of total investment (*Narkhoz 1984*, 379, 381). He proposes raising investment there by 1.8–2.0 times, so that MBMW output growth rates could be doubled or tripled. This rapid influx of investment funds and the resulting output expansion are clearly not intended to expand output of existing product lines, but rather to finance the development and rapid expansion in outputs of state-of-the-art technologies dramatically different from current technologies (robots, computer-driven machinery, automatic assembly-lines, products based on new materials, and so on). This is clearly one of the important areas in which Gorbachev and the 11 machine-building ministries have had very serious disagreements.[9]

Where these funds will come from is not completely specified in FYPXII or in Gorbachev's speeches. There was a clear implication in the June speech that agriculture—currently accounting for 17.8 percent of total investment—would pay part of the bill; energy—currently accounting for 35.9 percent of industrial investment and 12.7 percent of total investment—seems a likely candidate for another part (*Narkhoz 1984*, 379, 381). The FYP itself does not specify how large the influx of funds into MBMW is to be, but it clearly calls for a substantial increase in investment; it also calls for an output growth rate of only 7–7.7 percent for MBMW, well short of the doubling or tripling Gorbachev called for (during 1981–1984, MBMW output grew at 6 percent per annum).

Another important element of the modernization program which departs from the past is the announced intention to considerably accelerate replacement of current capital stock, a necessary component of any serious attempt to modernize Soviet industry. The plan calls for one-third of machinery and equipment in the productive capital stock to be replaced during 1985–1990, doubling the retirement rate of obsolete equipment. In MBMW, one-half of the machinery and equipment is to be replaced over the next 5 years.[10] That probably represents a doubling of current actual retirement rates, and will probably take up a considerable portion of gross investment in industry, and particularly in MBMW, even if investment is significantly increased.[11]

9. Since spring 1985, the 11 civilian machine-building ministries have been under constant pressure to accept extremely ambitious plans calling for modernization of their production processes and production profiles; some of the ministries are clearly unwilling to promise what they are being asked to promise, and as a result they have come in for sharp public criticism. Minstankoprom (The Ministry of the Machine-tool and Tool-building Industry), one of the ministries critical to the modernization program, is a good example illustrating the tenor of the public battle (see, for example, the report of a meeting of the Minstankoprom Kollegium in *Sots. Ind.*, June 11, 1985, p. 2; and discussion of a decree concerning shortcomings in the work of Minstankoprom's Party Committee in *Sots. Ind.*, December 13, 1985).

10. The one third figure is given directly in the plan. The one half in MBMW is the implication of a statement in the plan that in MBMW ". . . the active part of productive capital should be turned over at a rate 10–12 percent per annum," which implies approximately half of the machinery and equipment will be replaced during 1986–1990.

11. Rumer (1984) estimates that by 1980 half of gross investment in industry was going simply to replacement when replacement rates were (by his estimate) up to 6 percent. I suspect his estimate was a little high—5 percent seems more likely—but in any event a doubling to 10–12 percent would virtually devote all of gross investment to replacement in industry. Because it is unlikely that investment in industry as a whole will double (it will apparently double only in MBMW), that means that total investment well under half will go to expanding the stock of machinery and equipment if the replacement targets set out here are met.

Economic Reforms

"Reforms" are construed here broadly, including partial as well as comprehensive measures for altering the economic system itself. Gorbachev has remained faithful to standard Soviet (leadership) practice of discussing only a "restructuring" or "further perfection" of the existing system. His speeches contain a rich collection of hints and explicit statements which could add up to a rather far-reaching set of reforms (Gorbachev, 1985a, 1985b), although only the most optimistic reading of those speeches could infer that he intends a radical reform similar to programs in Hungary and China.

The main theme in Gorbachev's statements on reform is the twin desire to enhance central control and to enhance initiative and responsibility at lower levels. He is attempting to redirect the efforts of the central apparatus away from detailed intervention in the daily affairs of economic units to a more general concern with qualitative indicators relating to scientific-technical progress, a heavier reliance on norms set for 5-year periods, and heavier use of financial levers to control lower-level units. To facilitate that redirection in central activities, he intends to streamline the central apparatus, in the process reducing staff. The individual economic units are to be given enhanced rights, but also enhanced responsibility, over their operations. A "more flexible" price system is to facilitate this redistribution of powers and responsibilities.

Decrees already issued, and other measures, are beginning to give substance to this general strategy, and as a result it is now quite clear that Gorbachev has no intention whatsoever of introducing radical reforms in the Soviet economy, at least in this decade. He is apparently convinced that the goals he has set out for the economy can be accomplished with policy changes and partial reforms designed to improve the operation of the existing system. A thorough discussion of the decrees issued to date would require another paper, and in any event such a detailed discussion would be premature before the Party Congress. I will only provide a brief summary of the major measures introduced to date.

On July 22, 1985, the Central Committee and the Council of Ministers issued a joint decree extending the "Andropov Experiments" begun in January 1984, and extended in 1985, to all of industry by January 1, 1987 ("O shirokom," 1985). Some modifications to the experiments are contained in the decree, most notably new targets for enterprises designed to increase their attention to product quality and innovation, but in essence the experiments as they were first conceived are being extended to the entire industrial portion of the economy. Consistent with much commentary now in the Soviet press and academic writings, as well as in leadership speeches, the decree contains strong language forbidding ministries from interfering in the operations of enterprises in areas rightly the purview of the enterprise.

The July decree contains modifications to the price system designed to enhance incentives to enterprises to constantly improve the quality of their output. Most notable in this regard is the new provision that penalties for producing low quality products, and rewards for producing high quality products, are in large part to be taken from or added to the bonus fund of the enterprise.[12] There are also new bonuses for enterprises increasing exports of machinery, equipment, and spare parts for hard currency.

The administrative streamlining Gorbachev intends has so far focused on grouping the ministries into a few entities with as yet uncertain powers which may, in the end, become the "superministries" popular among some Soviet economists. When Nikolay Talyzin was appointed Gosplan Chairman in November 1985, the position was simultaneously upgraded from Deputy to First Deputy Chairman of the Council of Ministers, which presumably was to make room for a new Deputy Chairman to supervise the new groups of ministries. The October 17, 1985, Politburo minutes *(Pravda,* October 18, 1985, p. 1) announced the formation of a "biuro" controlling the 11 machine-building ministries; presumably I. S. Silayev, whose move from Minister of Aviation to Deputy Chairman of the Council of Ministers was announced on November 2, is to be the head of this biuro. It is not clear from the communiqué what the actual powers of this body will be; at the very least, it will be involved in reviewing the plans of the 11 civilian machine-building ministries. It could in fact be determining those plans, but as yet that is unclear.

On November 23, 1985 *(Pravda),* a joint Central Committee-Council of Ministers Decree established a new State Agro-Industrial Committee, amalgamating the old Ministry of Agriculture and four other agro-industrial ministries. This Committee clearly does have the authority of a ministry, and is charged with the task of realizing the long-sought goal of enhancing coordination within the vast agro-industrial complex of the country. V. S. Murakhovskiy has been appointed a First Deputy Chairman of the Council of Ministers and Chairman of this new Committee.

FYPXII indicates that other "groups" of ministries are soon to come— energy and fuels, minerals and raw materials, and construction materials being three likely candidates.[13] It is interesting that so far no overarching conceptual framework seems to be guiding this administrative streamlining. The vague discussion of "groups" of ministries has been followed by the formation of two bodies with different names and possibly with different amounts of au-

---

12. The provision is that enterprises producing new products in the highest quality category may receive up to a 30 percent add-on to the official wholesale price Enterprises whose products are "de-certified" out of the highest quality category will be penalized at 5 percent of the wholesale price the first year (but the price does not change to the purchaser), 10 percent the second year, and 15 percent the third year. Up to 70 percent of the value of this penalty comes out of the enterprise bonus fund as long as it does not reduce the fund by more than 20 percent of its planned value.

13. In this regard, it is interesting to note differences in the format of FYPXII and FYPXI. FYPXI discussed industry in one large section and the agricultural-industrial complex in another. FYPXII divides the discussion of industry up into the machine-building complex, construction materials, the fuel-energy complex, and the minerals-raw materials base. It seems likely that we will soon see "biuros" or state committees with ministerial powers for the latter three groups.

thority. This probably indicates considerable controversy about precisely what new powers these bodies will have, and it seems likely that the issue is not yet resolved.

While this adds a level to the hierarchy, another level is slated to disappear: the all-union industrial associations (VPOs). In the currently popular conventional wisdom that ministries are responsible for a good portion of the current problems with the system, the VPOs are regarded as the real culprit because in fact they are the bodies which intervene most often in the daily operations of enterprises. FYPXII calls for the elimination of these bodies, and the movement towards "primarily" a two-level (ministry-production association/enterprise) system.

Finally, FYPXII explicitly discusses the need to redefine the rights and duties of various central organs. At the same time, it clearly indicates Gorbachev's intention to reduce staff at the central level, but when and how is not indicated.

FEASIBILITY OF THE TWELFTH FYP

Because FYPXII is Gorbachev's plan embodying his goals, the issue of the feasibility of FYPXII is ultimately the issue of the feasibility of Gorbachev's goals for the economy, in light of the strategy he is pursuing. Clearly, this is a very ambitious or "taut" plan. To evaluate just how ambitious it is, and ultimately to reach a judgment on its feasibility, it is useful to consider some of the key interconnections in the plan, focusing on what appear to be the weak links.

The Macro Level

At the macro level, there are several implicit assumptions in this plan which seem very ambitious indeed. One of the fundamental targets in the plan is a dramatic increase in the amount of work and the quality of work out of the entire labor force. The "stick" that will contribute to that is clear in the various components of the discipline campaign; but the "carrot," also important, is not easy to find. On the contrary, this plan seems to assume that workers will increase their work effort even while personal incomes are increasing at a very modest pace, by past standards. The assumption may be that higher quality consumer goods, and more highly differentiated incomes, will be adequate incentives for the work force to work harder, but both of those are very unlikely to occur soon. So in the short run, the discipline campaign seems to carry the formidable burden of stimulating an increase in work effort.

The apparent plan to speed up project completions and the stated goal to focus investments on renovations echo familiar themes in recent Soviet plans. That these goals have generally not been realized in the past is testimony to the complex ways in which the incentives to focus on large new projects, spreading resources over many projects, is built into the core of current Soviet economic institutions, into the Soviet economic system itself. Enterprises operating in an environment in which their main "customer" is their ministry, where the customer wants output growth, and where investment resources are cheap and riskless, naturally attempt to maximize additions to capital stock and minimize replacements. Ministries, under pressure from central authorities to increase output, form natural allies with the enterprises in pushing to maximize investment. Gorbachev proposes to retain the old hierarchy and the incentives within it, yet somehow to alter behavior, essentially through the discipline campaign. In fact, it is even worse than this, because FYPXII places (relatively) more pressure to increase growth rates than this system has felt in the last several decades. Stated so simply, Gorbachev's assumptions concerning the investment process seem unrealistic.

The goal to dramatically increase the quality of goods produced across the board by enterprises is open to criticism for similar reasons. Enterprises in the Soviet Union show little interest in innovation in the products they produce because their "customer" is the ministry, not the final user of their product. And that customer, while under central pressure to increase both quality and quantity, rightly judges that quantity increases are the most important to the center. In any event, increases in quality are very difficult to document, and the tools used in the Soviet Union to measure product quality for plan fulfillment purposes (certification of product quality by quality boards) make it fairly easy to simulate quality increases. Again, Gorbachev intends to retain the existing system essentially as it is, something which is quite clear in the July 12, 1985, decree. He is focusing his efforts on tightening up that system, introducing new quality indicators as obligatory for enterprises (while retaining the old indicators), and tightening up quality certification procedures.

This seems a very weak set of measures for dealing with a problem so deeply intertwined with the essence of a system that provides such extraordinary economic security to enterprises. It might be possible within the traditional system to considerably increase pressure on enterprises to improve the quality of their products if that were made the main indicator, and if simultaneously growth-oriented indicators were dropped. But during FYPXII just the opposite will happen: Enterprises are being asked simultaneously to dramatically increase the quality of their output and grow faster—collectively—than they have in the recent past. When, as is inevitable, many enterprises will be forced to choose between rapid growth and dramatic quality improvements, history and the current make-up of the system suggest that quality will suffer. It is in MBMW where the pressure will be greatest to both grow rapidly and increase quality, and it is precisely here where the efforts to increase quality are likely to most obviously fail.

Another link we can only guess at concerns the plans for hard-currency imports, and their proposed role in the modernization of Soviet industry. The section on foreign economic relations in FYPXII is not more informative than

Table 2. *Soviet Investment Variants for the Twelfth Five-Year Plan*

	1976–80	*1981–85*	*1981–84*	*1980–90 Plan variants*				*Weights*
	Actual	*Plan*	*Actual*	*(A)*	*(B)*	*(C)*	*(D)*	*1981–84*
Total investment	3.4	1.0	3.7	3.4	3.4	3.8	3.8	1.00
Industrial investment	3.7	4.2	4.0	2.5	3.0	3.6	4.1	.35
Energy	7.3	8.9	6.3	7.5	3.0	7.5	3.0	.12
Other	2.3	2.7	2.5	−.2	3.0	1.5	4.7	.23
Agriculture	2.9	1.4	1.0	1.0	1.0	1.0	1.0	.19
Transportation and communications	4.9	5.7	5.7	5.5	4.0	5.5	4.0	.12
Construction, housing, and other	3.0	−1.9	4.3	5.0	5.0	5.0	5.0	.33

Sources: All data are taken from official Soviet sources. The actual performance data are from *Narkhoz*; the plan data are from plan documents. The figures for 1986–1990 are from (or derived from) the first draft of the Twelfth Five-Year Plan (*Sots. ind.*, November 9, 1985), and may be revised before the Party Congress in February 1986.

similar sections in past plans. Nevertheless, the discussion surrounding FYPXII (especially discussion on the modernization program) suggests that hard-currency imports are being given a very modest role in this plan, and that responsibility for the bulk of the modernization program is falling directly on Soviet industry, with some assistance from Eastern Europe. If this is indeed the assumption, then it will be one of the first assumptions of FYPXII to crumble. As soon as it is obvious, say in 1986–1987, that Soviet industry is not capable of a rapid turnaround in the quality of its output, then either the hard currency import plan will have to be dramatically altered or the modernization program will be stretched out, and probably both.

The common thread in all of these ambitious assumptions concerning links assumed in the plan is the critical role of the discipline campaign, and the relatively minor role for systemic reforms. This is clearest in the assumption that the turnaround in performance will be very quick, beginning in 1986. That obviously assumes that whatever measures are to be used will be in place by early 1986, which means essentially the various elements of the discipline campaign and the modest partial reforms discussed above.

The Micro Level

At the micro level, the most obvious problem is in the inconsistency between plans to change the structure of investment and output plans for key sectors, most notably energy. FYPXII calls for total investment to grow at no more than 3.8 percent per annum, but it gives no information on the structure of investment. Nevertheless, Gorbachev's speeches and the commentary make it possible to draw a general picture of what is contemplated, and Table 2 explores the most likely variants. The first three columns contain the recent history of investment growth; the next four columns explore four possible variants of the structure of investment in FYPXII, the first two assuming the low rate of growth for total investment, the latter two the high rate; and the last column gives investment weights for the early 1980s.

All four variants assume that FYPXII calls for a 5 percent rate of growth in construction, housing, and other investment, primarily because of a strong emphasis on housing. Transport and communications are assumed to grow either at 5.5 percent or 4.0 percent, in either case relatively high growth rates for another high priority area. Agriculture is given a relatively low growth rate, consistent with the message Gorbachev seems to have been sending to that sector. Industrial investment is the residual; and within that, a high and a low investment path for energy leaves a residual for other industry, which is where MBMW is.

The planned increase in total investment is not out of line with the recent past, and there is no effort to dramatically cut investment growth rates as there was in FYPXI for 1981–1985. But clearly, if these are indeed to be the growth rates of total investment, and if machine-building is to see a significant influx of new capital, then variant "D" is the only plausible option, which means that energy investment growth rates will have to be about half what they have been over the last decade.

If variant "D" is close to the investment plan in FYPXII, then the targets for energy output are simply unattainable. From the early 1970s to the early 1980s, investment in energy doubled while energy output rose 45 percent (Hewett, 1985b). During 1981–1984, energy investment rose 27.6 percent, while output rose 10.4 percent *(Narkhoz 1984*, pp. 55 and 381). The plan for 1986–1990 calls for energy output to grow about 18 percent (oil, 6–7.6 percent; natural gas, 31–33 percent; nuclear power, 235 percent; and coal, 7.6–10 percent); and it seems to imply a growth in investment of no more than 18 percent. That simply does not add up. Any effort to even sustain oil output at its current 11.9mbd (down from a peak of around 12.4 in early 1984), let alone to increase it, would imply that the incremental capital-output ratio for this critical portion (accounting in 1984 for 45 percent of total energy investment [*Narkhoz 1984*, p. 381]) would rise, not fall. Similarly, the high growth rates for nuclear power shift investment resources in that sector to the most capital intensive power plants. The gas target is probably the only feasible target in this plan, given the likely investment targets. And as a whole, either the investment plan or the energy output plan will have to be scrapped very soon.

The annual plan for 1986 suggests that the moment of truth may have come very soon indeed ("O Gosnarstvennom," 1985). It calls for a rise in total capital investment of 7.6 percent; and for a rise in investment in oil production of 31 percent, in coal production of 27 percent, and in electric power of 24 percent. Simultaneously, investment in MBMW is to rise more than 30 percent. Gorbachev said in his speech before the Supreme Soviet regarding the 1986 plan that they were intentionally "front-loading" the FYP, contrary to previous practice (Gorbachev, 1985c). That probably is the intention, but the fact is that in the first year of the plan investment is exploding in order to make room for both the modernization program and the energy output targets. That investment growth rate is unsustainable over a 5-year period (it may not even be feasible in 1986, unless there is a burst of imports). Barring incredibly good performance in 1986, it is likely that by 1987 Gorbachev shall have to admit (at least privately) that the major FYPXII goals are unattainable, and he shall have to start choosing which targets are the most important to him.

The Twelfth FYP as a Whole

There are sufficient weaknesses in this plan at the macro and micro level to suggest that the major targets in FYPXII cannot be attained. Aside from the obvious wishful thinking built into the investment accounts, the energy plans, and the plans to expand investment in MBMW, there is in general far too much reliance on the discipline campaign. It is one thing to achieve a short burst in output out of increased discipline combined with the rise in enthusiasm following the transition to a new leader. That seemed to work in 1983 for Andropov, and in 1985 for Gorbachev. But it is a totally different matter to count on a discipline campaign to produce the longer-term changes in behavior so critical to the success of a 5-year plan.

The basic behavioral problems of concern to Gorbachev are primarily a reflection of the system itself and the incentives built into it. However important worker attitudes, managerial attitudes, or planners' attitudes may be, they themselves are in part a product of the system, and therefore cannot change unless the system changes.

Yet, so far, the systemic reforms proposed are very minor indeed, comprised of administrative streamlining and a continuation of the very modest Andropov experiments with some minor modifications. No major price reform, no major alteration in the rights and responsibilities of planning authorities, ministries, enterprises or banks, and no shift away from the traditional preoccupation with growth are in sight. And for those reasons, I judge it as highly unlikely that Gorbachev's strategy will work. Growth during 1986–1990 may be satisfactory by recent standards, but it is unlikely to be significantly higher. More important, it is impossible to believe that the modest set of policy measures and reforms Gorbachev has introduced will bring about the technological revolution he is hoping for in MBMW. It is more likely to bring a good deal of simulation (''new'' products which are not new), waste, and quite possibly an acceleration in hidden inflation.

During 1987–1988, as the unattainability of the major targets in FYPXII becomes increasingly evident, the debate over economic reform is likely to once again gather speed. And if Gorbachev is still General Secretary, and if he is as willing to learn from experience (as he seems to be), then in the 1990s, a truly interesting and far-reaching reform is not out of the question.

CHAPTER 2

Gorbachev's Economic Strategy: A Comment

Philip Hanson

IT WOULD be more entertaining for the reader if I could disagree with Dr. Hewett, and present a radically different perspective on current Soviet economic policies and prospects. In fact, I agree with his main conclusions: that there are powerful influences working against an acceleration of Soviet economic growth in the next few years; that the Gorbachev leadership has so far shown no sign of adopting institutional changes that would alter the behavior of Soviet production units; and that the main plan targets for 1986–1990 are ambitious and unlikely to be fulfilled.

A loyal Gorbachevian, I suppose, would say that our agreement on these points merely demonstrates the blinkered vision of Western sovietologists; that we have failed to see a real process of improvement in the Soviet economy because it does not fit our preconceptions of how such an improvement should come about. The loyal Gorbachevian cannot at present be shown conclusively to be wrong, but I think he will be by 1990.

In any event, my comments on Dr. Hewett's paper will consist merely of some differences of judgment over some of the nuances of his account, plus some supplementary remarks on matters that he has not dwelt on. I shall comment briefly on the following: how Gorbachev's strategy is likely to be seen inside the USSR; changes in priorities; the effects of personnel changes; the defense burden; the farm sector; and some puzzles about the implied targets for the 1990s.

Soviet Perceptions of the Gorbachev Strategy

Some Soviet specialists consider that a market reform is necessary to bring about any significant and sustained improvement in the quality of Soviet output and the growth rate of Soviet productivity. A few articles, such as that by

First published in *Soviet Economy*, 1985, 1, 4, pp. 306–312. [Eds.]

Kurashvili (1985), make this clear. There may also be some senior officials who take this view. Such Soviet "marketeers" probably share Hewett's (and my) belief that no serious reform of economic institutions is so far under way, but that there is at least a chance that the Soviet leadership will, under the pressure of continued poor performance, go for decentralization in the 1990s.

My impression is that this is a minority view in the Soviet Union—probably a minority view among academic economists and certainly a minority view (if it is held at all) among policymakers and senior advisers (Hanson, 1985a). Nonetheless, the whole economic strategy being pursued by the new leadership probably appears radical to many Soviet citizens, including many senior officials. This is not just because of discipline and alcohol campaigns, the turnover of top officials, and the shifts in priorities; some of the institutional changes may well seem radical, too.

In particular, the merging of branch ministries and the abolition of industrial associations, described by Hewett, conforms with a characterization of the strategy by Academician Tat'yana Zaslavskaya, the author of the leaked "Novosibirsk Report" of 1983. She described it as a strategy of weakening the middle (branch-ministry) level of the economic hierarchy and strengthening both the central authorities and the production unit (*Izvestiya*, June 1, 1985). The language of Gorbachev's speeches is consistent with this. This strategy is radical in two senses. It can upset a large number of people, and it could yield some improvement in performance.

The logic of the streamlining which Gorbachev is attempting to push through is that a considerable number of middle-to-senior-level officials would be removed from the central branch-ministry apparatus. The logical place for them to go would be the management of the enlarged, inter-branch production associations which Gorbachev advocates (Gorbachev, 1985, p. 15, citing the example of the East German *kombinate*; note also the Politburo's approval of the creation of large inter-branch R and D complexes, *Pravda*, December 13, 1985). Geographically, this would often mean moving from Moscow to the provinces—one of the worst things that can happen to any Soviet citizen who has permission to live in Moscow.

To carry through such streamlining properly would also require severe restriction of ministries' or superministries' powers to impose detailed targets on the enlarged production associations, a genuine devolution of decisions on detail and therefore a clarification of existing legislation about the rights of basic management units. A streamlining systematically carried through in this way should reduce the information overload on central planners and facilitate more coherent and purposeful planning. Insofar as enterprises and associations were continuing to respond to instructions from above and operating with a centralized supply system, their characteristic behavior with respect to costs, quality, and technological change would be unreformed. The possibility, however, of some improvement in economic performance through the reduction of inconsistency in targets and supply allocations cannot be ruled out.

In short, a streamlining type of reorganization may be of some consequence, and is probably what Gorbachev's rhetoric about organic structural change refers to. By the same token, it will not be easy to implement. A crude test of whether or not it is implemented will be whether there actually is an exodus of officials from Moscow to the provinces. The most recent precedent suggests that this is unlikely to happen. The March 1973 decree which *inter alia* abolished branch-ministry main administrations (*Pravda*, April 3, 1973) had a similar logic. The idea was that the old sub-branch *glavki* would be transformed into all-Union industrial associations, which would be Soviet-style profit centers with their head offices located at their centers of productive activity. The Soviet consensus is that by and large the new industrial associations remained just like the old *glavki* but under a different name. Indeed it is these very industrial associations which Gorbachev now seeks to abolish.

Priorities

On the other hand, the power of new Soviet leaders to improve economic performance without radically changing the system should not be underestimated. Hewett's Table 1 shows that there was some acceleration after the removal of Khrushchev. The CIA series of Soviet GNP in 1970 rubles shows an acceleration between Stalin's last years and the first 5 years of the post-Stalin order—from 4.7 percent per annum in 1950–1953 to 6.6 percent in 1953–1958 (U.S. Congress, Joint Economic Committee, 1982, p. 62). And there has been some recovery in industrial growth in the first post-Brezhnev years, 1983–1985 inclusive.

One reason for this is probably that new leaders have made changes in resource allocation priorities which have rectified certain gross policy errors and therefore widened bottlenecks. In this connection, Hewett's analysis of FYPXII investment composition is helpful in clarifying the issues. He argues that the planned reallocation of investment to the MBMW sector would entail a slowdown in energy sector investment that would be incompatible with the ambitious targets for energy output.

I suggest two qualifications to this. First, actual investment growth regularly exceeds FYP planned investment growth. How far the difference is real and how far it arises from unplanned concealed inflation is obscure; but if there is usually some real difference and if the new plan period is not a departure from past practice, total investment resources will in fact be less constrained than the plan implies. Second, it is not clear to me that "construction, housing, and other" are really scheduled to preempt the growing share of total investment that Hewett's Table 2 indicates. New housing floorspace planned for 1986–1990 is 565–570 mn square meters, which means a growth rate of only 0.5–0.7 percent a year between the two 5-year periods.

Hewett notes that a much higher investment growth rate is allowed for in the annual plan for 1986 than in the 1986–1990 plan as a whole. He suggests that the inadequacy of the investment growth planned for FYPXII may have been perceived between the publication dates of the two plans, i.e., between November 9 and 27. That may be the case. Another possibility is that the FYPXII guidelines may be a compromise between Gorbachev allies and more cautious officials, and that the balance of power between the two groups has continued to shift in Gorbachev's favor. It is true that Talyzin had already replaced Baybakov as head of Gosplan in mid-October, but that was still only a very short time before the guidelines were published. In mid-November, the heads of both the Military-Industrial Commission and the State Material-Technical Supply Committee were replaced (*Pravda*, November 16 and 17), and the subsequent flow of ministerial changes has been rapid.

The Effects of Personnel Changes

In general, personnel changes may be another source of the improvements in economic performance that have been obtained under new Soviet leaders. The view that changes of top personnel, combined with labor discipline campaigns, may be able to produce more than merely short-term improvements in performance has been argued by Kontorovich (1985). His careful, detailed assessment of Soviet railroad developments before and after Andropov's sacking of the minister for the railways in late 1982 supports this view.

This change at the top was followed by a ripple of changes of lower-level management personnel, and by some sharp changes in the views publicly expressed about what could be achieved. It is easy to imagine that a personnel shake-up can destroy mutual-protection circles and put everyone on notice that they need to do better to stay in post. Such effects may be medium-term rather than long-term unless a general Stalinist regime of cadres instability is introduced. But it is a medium-term period—namely, 5 years—that is under discussion.

Probably a changing of the guard is now under way, rather than the start of a new era of instability of cadres. One characteristic of many of the men coming into high office is that they have defense industry background. That is consistent with a strategy of diffusing defense-sector management techniques more widely. Some extension of priority treatment to a segment of dual-use industry outside the narrowly defined defense sector may also be intended (a point which has been persuasively argued in a recent talk by my colleague, Julian Cooper).

The Defense Burden

Hewett speculates that Soviet defense spending is planned to rise faster than either consumption or investment. This is plausible enough, given the recent growth in the U.S. military effort. It would be surprising, however, if the

Soviet authorities were supplying us with information on which we could base much arithmetic on this score.

We cannot be sure how defense is treated in the Soviet national income accounts. Gérard Duchêne has provided an interesting reconstruction which yields a defense share in NMP utilized in 1980 of 12.9 percent (Duchêne, 1985). The possibility cannot be ruled out, however, that final-stage assembly of military hardware, say, is simply omitted altogether from published Soviet statistics.

Even if all material expenditure on defense is incorporated in NMP, however, the FYPXII figures are blurred enough to meet the Kremlin's security requirements. The range of investment growth rates and that of NMP utilized growth rates overlap substantially (Table 1). And will not experienced Soviet planners already anticipate that in implementation the former will exceed the latter? The planned growth rates for real per capita incomes (which includes a large part of social consumption) suggest a range of planned growth rates for *total* consumption (allowing for population growth at just under 1 percent a year) which again overlaps substantially with the range for NMP growth. I suggest that the guidelines are giving away very little in the way of sensitive information.

Agriculture

Dr. Hewett judges the targets for labor productivity and for oil production to be implausibly high. The same can be said of some of the agricultural targets. If Western estimates of the 1985 Soviet grain harvest are correct at about 190 mn tons, there was no growth in the grain harvest between 1980 and 1985 but the 1990 target requires growth at 5½–6 percent per annum. Similarly, the target for meat output requires 4.1 percent annual growth in 1986–1990 against 2.6 percent achieved during the last 5 years. (By comparison, milk and egg production targets are modest.)

At the same time, Gorbachev appears to be curbing the flow of investment in agriculture. A great deal is therefore being expected from increased effort and efficiency in the farm sector. It is unlikely that the administrative amalgamation of most of the agro-industrial sector will contribute to this. It is true that, as Hewett notes, there must be a chance of better average weather over the next 5 years than there was over the last. Benefits from this would of course include direct and indirect contributions to total domestic output, as well as the balance of payments effects to which Dr. Hewett specifically draws attention. All the same, Soviet policymakers appear to be expecting rather a lot from acts of God.

The issue of organizational change in agriculture is one on which the apparent conservatism of the new leadership is most striking. The farm sector is a sector in which the returns to serious organizational change would be especially high. Moreover, Gorbachev's past espousal of the small, semi-autonomous contract work groups within the state and collective farms constitutes his only sustainable claim to radicalism about the economic system. Yet he has said next to nothing about the contract brigades since he became party leader. In his major speech in September about agricultural policy, there was nothing, even in the television version, about them or about the private sector (Radio Liberty monitoring report of September 10).

It may be that the contract brigades and an expansion of the private sector are closely linked and are both matters on which opposition to change can be readily mobilized with the use of ideological phrases. Academician Zaslavskaya has said that the organizational experiments she has been supervising have been restricted to collective farms because the ministry bureaucrats had more power to block such experiments on state farms; and in the same interview she observed that the most successful of the small contract work groups in her experiments were based on family units (*Izvestiya*, June 1, 1985). For the time being, at least, the political sensitivity of agricultural reform probably counts for more than its economic attractions.

The 1990s

The few targets that have been given for the year 2000 imply, as Hewett's Table 1 reveals, an expectation of faster growth in the 1990s than in 1986–1990. That is consistent with a scenario sketched out by Academician Aganbegyan, in which an initial improvement in growth is secured by a discipline campaign and more durable and substantial improvement is then obtained by unspecified organizational changes (Aganbegyan, 1985a). For all that, the implicit targets for the 1990s do not appear to be based on systematic calculations.

The numbers in the last column of Hewett's Table 1 are few and odd. They tell us that national income utilized is expected to grow faster than gross industrial output. That—over any substantial period—would be unprecedented. They also seem to imply that labor force in material production is expected to fall significantly, for aggregate labor productivity is to grow 1½–2 percent per annum faster than NMP utilized. Yet the labor force in total will continue to grow, albeit slowly, throughout the period. Various possible explanations of this anomaly all seem untenable. National income produced could hardly grow at a substantially higher rate than national income utilized over an entire decade. A planned reduction in working hours cannot be the answer, for labor productivity is measured per worker, not per worker-hour (*Metodicheskiye ukazaniya*, 1980, p. 53). A shift of labor out of material production into the service sector and/or any unrecorded military activity would have to be implausibly large and sustained to produce this discrepancy.

Probably the labor productivity series is derived from an output series or group of output series that have no close relationship to the NMP series. Nonetheless the lack of any editing of the guidelines to eliminate such oddities suggests that the few aggregate targets given for the entire 15-year period are *ad hoc*, illustrative numbers not derived from a systematically elaborated long-term plan.

Conclusions

I have given three reasons for thinking that the FYPXII targets could be less overambitious than Dr. Hewett suggests. First, it is possible that organizational streamlining can improve central planning. Second, extensive personnel changes probably can and do mobilize more managerial effort for more than a short period of time. Third, better average weather could enable agricultural growth to be higher than in the recent past. None of these additional positive influences, however, can be expected to have a large and reliable effect.

The negative influences listed by Hewett are by contrast substantial and, for the most part, scarcely avoidable: slower capital-stock growth, slower labor-force growth, and increasing costs in the exploitation of natural resources—together with a strong possibility of windfall losses from trade. Hence my agreement with Hewett's main conclusions. In addition, I suggest that the Gorbachev strategy may well include a faster growth of investment than is indicated in the FYPXII guidelines. If this is so, the medium-term growth in per capita consumption will be extremely limited.

CHAPTER 3

Gorbachev at Two Years: Perspectives on Economic Reforms

Ed A. Hewett

MIKHAIL GORBACHEV assumed the post of General Secretary of the CPSU on March 11, 1985, with an apparent mandate to forge a new economic strategy capable of responding to an imposing list of economic problems. By the time of the XXVII Party Congress in March 1986, Gorbachev's strategy was emerging with increasing clarity in his speeches and in the statements of those close to him. He is clearly a man who believes that a sustained improvement in economic performance will only come through a radical systemic reform; and he seems to believe that the measures he is introducing will add up to that radical reform.

Now, two years into his tenure, we are in the midst of an impressive outpouring of decrees, policy changes, and personnel turnover which, when they are completed in 1987–1988, will add up to a definition of the "Gorbachev Reforms." Meanwhile the implementation of the first decrees (dating from 1985) is under way, providing first readings on the resistance which inevitably accompanies such an undertaking.

So much has happened in the last two years, and so very much has been promised that different, even diametrically opposed, interpretations of these developments are to be expected. Indeed such diverse opinions should be cultivated at this early stage in an effort to capture the range of potentialities implicit in the tension between a leader's ambitions for change and a reality so resourceful in its defenses against change. It was the desire to understand those diverse potentialities which led me to invite three of our most distinguished analysts of Soviet affairs—Gertrude Schroeder, Jerry Hough, and Philip Hanson—to write brief essays expressing their views on the course of the reforms and their prospects for the future. The authors did not see each other's essays until their publication.

The authors disagree on many points, with the most fundamental disagreements emerging between Jerry Hough and his two colleagues. My casual em-

First published in *Soviet Economy*, 1986, 2, 4, pp. 283–288. [Eds.]

piricism suggests that this disagreement reflects differences between economists and political scientists in their assessments of the prospects for Gorbachev's economic reform. The differences may be sharper here, particularly between Professors Hough and Schroeder, than among Soviet specialists as a whole. But they do, in my experience, reflect more general differences between the professions in interpreting the significance of these potentially momentous developments.

In this brief introduction I explore the source of these differences in interpretation as they emerge in these essays. I will not present in any detail here my own views on Gorbachev's reforms; those are available elsewhere (Hewett, 1986a, 1988a). Rather, my goal is to understand the nature of the disagreements, and to identify the nature of evidence or further research which would be useful to narrow the differences.

Measuring the "Radicalness" of the Reform: Benchmarks

Soviet economic reforms are destined to be judged according to the standards—or, to use Jerry Hough's term, "benchmarks"—set by reforms in other socialist countries. Hungary and China are generally treated as representatives of a radically reformed system, while the GDR represents a much more conservative variant focused on enhanced control of a highly concentrated economic system. Philip Hanson probably reflects the conventional wisdom among Soviet specialists in his conclusion that while elements of both systems can be found in the Soviet reforms, Gorbachev's preferences seem to lean toward the GDR variant. Professor Hanson sees nothing in the Soviet reforms pointing to the dissolution of the obligatory planning system which occurred in Hungary in 1968.

Jerry Hough sees much more of Hungary and China in Gorbachev's approach, indeed he sees the possibility that within a short time it would be the Soviet Union, not Hungary or China, which is setting the standard for radical reforms. Although Professor Hough does not quite put it this way, his argument essentially is that economists such as Hanson (and for that matter myself) compare Soviet reforms to an idealized version of the Hungarian reforms. In fact, argues Professor Hough, it was not the core of the system, industry, where the Hungarians successfully reformed. It was in agriculture and services, on the "edges" of the system; and that is precisely where Gorbachev can be expected to make his move.

There is a danger of idealizing what has actually transpired in Hungary. While Professor Hanson correctly points to the abolition of obligatory planning in Hungary, it is equally important to note that in fact Hungarian industry still operates in a rarefied, highly protected, environment in which special deals between the center and the enterprise are the norm. In that sense Hungarian industry operates in a system which represents more a variant than a departure from the traditional centrally planned economy.

On the other hand, Professor Hough must realize that the Hungarian experience should give pause to any optimistic assessment of prospects for a Gorbachev economic reform. The Hungarian reforms in the core of industry were in fact far more radical than anything we have yet to see in the USSR, though the ultimate effect on the core of the system was relatively modest. Why should the Soviet experience be different?

The issue of the meaning of East European and Chinese reform experiences for the Soviet reforms deserves much more attention than it has heretofore received, and these essays raise the issue without attempting to resolve it. In the future it would be useful to encourage those who study Eastern European, Soviet, and Chinese reforms to jointly explore the lessons of each for the others.

Gertrude Schroeder uses the past for her benchmark, drawing on her extensive research on previous reform efforts. The point she makes is both inescapable and important: whatever Gorbachev may say of his radical reforms, they are in many ways directly descended from previous reform measures which have failed. Very strong echos of the 1965 reforms and the July 1979 decree, as well as many smaller measures in between show up throughout Gorbachev's reforms. The implication is that the results will show a similar echo, namely, very little, if any, improvement in economic performance.

Those who are more optimistic than Schroeder concerning the prospects for this reform can resort to one of two arguments to buttress their case. First, they may see less similarity than she does between current reforms and past efforts. Here the differences will not focus so much on particular measures but on the judgment of what elements of the current reforms are receiving the most emphasis and how that differs from the past. Stable five-year plans and an accompanying abandonment of "planning from the achieved level" are both features of the current reforms and of previous reforms. But this time the emphasis on enforcing that may be much stronger (or so Professor Hanson suggests) than in the past.

The second possible counter to Professor Schroeder's approach is to argue the existence of important new factors. Professor Hough's argument here is potentially the most telling: this time, unlike 1965, it is the General Secretary who is behind the reforms. These are the *Gorbachev* reforms, not the *Ryzhkov* reforms, and that, says Professor Hough, makes all the difference.

This latter argument probably deserves more attention than it has hitherto received from economists studying the reforms. We have tended to focus on the emerging contradictions in the design of this reform, similar to contradictions characterizing 1965. Those are real, and potentially significant, impediments to the success of the reform. But a powerful General Secretary potentially able to mobilize the system to overcome the problems emerging from such contradictions, and to introduce further change in the system to reduce them, may be able to accomplish things which proved illusive several decades ago. It is an argument about the positive contribution of political power, properly applied, during the transition to a radically reformed system. And economists, who have very little to offer on the theory of politically feasible transitions from traditional to reformed socialist economic systems, should be modest in dismissing such arguments.

The Sources of Evidence

Aside from the issue of the benchmark to apply, a second issue concerns the evidence one can use to identify the nature and direction of a reform. Professors Schroeder and Hanson rely on decrees, giving relatively little, if any, attention to Gorbachev's speeches. Jerry Hough relies much more heavily on the speeches. And at times he uses inference to fill in where specific statements are unavailable. For Professor Hough, the apparent absence of an agricultural reform is a matter of time, not of an absent strategy.

Ultimately decrees and the political will applied to their implementation will be the sole test of the nature of this reform program and its impact. By the early 1990s most of the issues raised in these three essays will be resolved by evidence of what has actually transpired. But in the meantime there is room for argument. My own inclination is to join Professors Schroeder and Hanson in giving much weight to the decrees. Gorbachev is emerging as a superb politician, with all of the accompanying instincts to put a positive gloss on what he does. It remains to be seen if he possesses the ability or the will to completely follow through on his promises.

Yet, a remarkable picture is emerging of Gorbachev as a modern and very tough leader dedicated to reforms as he understands them. The potential Jerry Hough sees in these reforms is real, and those who remain skeptical that Gorbachev can realize that potential must take care that they are not so influenced by past failures that they close their minds to the possibility that this time things will be different. This time words may be a better indicator than in the past of deeds to come.

Judging the Success of Reforms

Ultimately the test of any reform is not whether the majority judges it worthy of the label "radical," but rather whether it makes a difference for economic performance. Problems in economic performance lie at the root of the pressures for reform, and improvements in economic performance are a major consideration in judging the efficacy of a reform.

Gorbachev's standards in this regard are unambiguous. His reform is designed to produce higher economic growth, and a general rise in the quality of goods and services produced throughout the system. For outsiders, and even for Soviets, it will be easier to perceive the change in growth performance than the change in quality. Quality is a subjective judgment, made on a product-by-product basis, and difficult to aggregate. We will surely hear many claims of dramatic quality improvements, but for the most part the evidence will be anecdotal.

The result is a natural tendency to focus on the growth consequences of economic reform. It is here that Jerry Hough reminds us of the important fact that Hungary, regarded by many as a relatively successful case of economic reform, showed very modest growth performance in the post-reform period. To the extent there were significant improvements in Hungarian economic performance, they were in the mix, quality, and availability of goods and services, all variables which the national income accounts were unable to adequately measure. Professor Hough argues, I think legitimately, that the criteria used to judge the success of Soviet reforms should reflect that consideration by devoting serious efforts to measuring improvements in those qualitative factors which national income accounts record only poorly, if at all. This is particularly important for the quality improvements in consumer goods and services, since those directly affect consumer welfare and therefore popular perceptions of the efficacy of the reform.

Issues for Future Research

The issues these reforms present for future research are many, and I will not attempt a list here. But the one set of issues which stands out as possibly the most important involves the economics and politics of the transition from a traditional centrally planned economy to a radically reformed system. The most interesting questions here involve how a political leader wishing to undertake a radical reform, but also wishing to minimize the chaos of the transition, might "partition" the economic system in order to divide up his task into politically managable parts consistent with the economic logic of the system. For example, the Chinese experience suggests that agriculture and rural industry can be reformed before the remainder of the system, providing some foundation for moving ahead, without creating unbearable strains on the remainder of the system. The Hungarian reform suggests it is possible to reform services without simultaneously reforming the core of industry. The question for economists, as Jerry Hough notes, is whether there are feasible piecemeal paths from the current system to a radically reformed system.

For the political scientist the political preconditions for such a transition need to be studied far more deeply than heretofore. The introduction of radical reforms implies reliance on a new system for allocating resources and a subsequent reallocation of resources. Many of those resources are human beings, and their "reallocation" could well lead to political disaster for the regime. The issue for political scientists is whether there are ways a regime can make that transition and survive. Here, again, the Chinese and Hungarian experiences provide some information, although it is not entirely encouraging.

A related issue for political scientists involves the role of the party in the reformed economy. Currently the party is so intertwined with the entire decision-making hierarchy in the Soviet Union, that it is best regarded as an integral part of the entire economy, capable of influencing decisions at any level in the system. A radical reform implies a much different, and seemingly more modest, role for the party. It appears to be that prospect which has slowed progress toward further reform in either Hungary or China, but at this stage that is only a hypothesis that deserves careful scrutiny.

The current developments in the USSR may be no more than another chapter in fruitless efforts to move beyond the traditional centrally planned economy. Or they may prove to be the beginning of a genuine revolution in this system. It is as yet too early to tell.

CHAPTER 4

Gorbachev: "Radically" Implementing Brezhnev's Reforms

Gertrude E. Schroeder

OVER TWENTY years ago, a then-new Soviet leadership launched a program of economic reform that was hailed as the "third great reform" in Soviet history, ranking in importance alongside Lenin's New Economic Policy (NEP) of the early 1920s and Stalin's introduction of central planning toward the end of that decade (*Novyi mir*, December 1965). The multifaceted program attempted to solve four pressing economic problems: a slowing rate of economic growth, a rapidly falling return on investment, a slow rate of improvement in the technological level of the capital stock, and the poor quality and design of products which impeded their sale at home and abroad. Undergirding this program were three basic convictions: that the economic system itself (central planning, allocation, and pricing of resources and state-owned property) was fundamentally sound, that reorganization of the bureaucracies would provide solutions to economic problems, and that state-owned and directed business firms could be made to behave like business firms in a competitive market environment through some use of "economic levers" and curtailment of "administrative methods." In a word, Soviet firms would strive to please customers, cut costs, and be innovative. Thus, the problems would be solved.

As originally outlined by Kosygin, the reform package included such features as the creation of new bureaucracies that would "work in a new way," reduction in the number of plan targets centrally set for firms, and the granting of more "rights" (codified in a statute) and increased autonomy to firms in dealing with labor and investment. In addition, the reforms provided for the establishment of new incentive funds and success indicators based on growth of sales and profits (firms were required to eventually become financially independent of the state budget), extensive use of inter-firm contracts with contractual penalties to enforce compliance, and a gradual transition from central rationing

First published in *Soviet Economy*, 1986, 2, 4, pp. 289–301. The first section is based largely on the author's articles detailing the fate of the 1965 reforms (Schroeder, 1968, 1971, 1979, 1982). [Eds.]

of intermediate and investment goods to free wholesale trade. Finally, the reform package called for the merger of firms into larger associations and the more flexible use of prices to spur efforts to upgrade product quality and modernize the product mix.

Implementation of the program was turned over to the "new" bureaucracy, specifically to a commission created under Gosplan to draft appropriate decrees and monitor the results. The several parts of the program were implemented in varying degrees. In 1966–1967, for instance, a major price revision changed many industrial prices and raised the profit rate included in those prices, although it did not alter the principles on which they were set. Contractual relations among firms were extended slowly, and penalties for non-compliance were raised several times. Although a small experiment with free wholesale trade involving a few products was quickly aborted, a number of small wholesale stores were opened. The new autonomy of enterprises over labor and investment was ultimately withdrawn, both because their actions threatened to upset state investment priorities and because most if not all authorities did not like many of the decisions that were taken. Self-finance was implemented in only a few ministries. Although the new incentive schemes were introduced throughout the industrial sector and in some other sectors, they failed to elicit the desired behavior. Thus, the rules had to be changed several times to add mandatory targets directed at curing specific failures, i.e., to focus on labor productivity, to raise product quality, to fulfill contracts, to reduce labor costs, and to save on raw materials and energy. Much of this was codified anew in a major decree of July 1979, which also specified a bevy of measures to improve planning. The decree emphasized the priority status of contract fulfillment (among others) in the incentive schemes, called for speeding up the merger movement and expansion of self-finance in ministries and firms, and directed the greater use of long-term normatives in planning and regulating enterprise activities. In 1982 industrial prices were once more revised but not reformed.

Meanwhile, economic performance deteriorated. Growth rates slowed, productivity indices worsened dramatically, Soviet manufactures remained largely unsalable in Western markets (and the subject of a continuous tirade of complaints from domestic purchasers), and the technology gap with the West seemed to be widening. At the end of Brezhnev's tenure, the reforms of the reforms had created a situation where enterprises had become mired in a thicket of rules and regulations. And so bureaucracy had proliferated, earnings differentials between blue collar workers and managerial-technical workers had narrowed greatly when compared with 1965, and there was little evidence of a relationship between pertinent plan indicators and incentive funds as well as between effort and reward. Planning had become more centralized and Gosplan intolerably burdened. After Brezhnev, Andropov sought to get out of the seeming morass through firing or threatening to fire officials and by launching a campaign to enforce discipline on one and all. On the reform front, he sanctioned during his brief tenure an experiment in five ministries to test a "new" economic mechanism, which in fact merely implements parts of the 1979 decree (*Pravda*, July 26, 1983). Indeed, in many instances the wording of the two decrees is essentially identical, notably so in respect to success indicators and the use of normatives in planning and regulating. Chernenko's contribution was to endorse the experiment and extend it to 20 ministries beginning in 1985.

Enter Gorbachev

In his nearly two years of tenure, Mikhail Gorbachev has addressed the reform issue vociferously and vigorously. His many speeches have called for "radical" economic reform and "profound restructuring" of the entire economic mechanism and, indeed, of almost everything else. He has declared that the required restructuring amounts to a "revolution" (*Pravda*, August 2, 1986). In addition, Gorbachev has repeatedly lambasted officials at all levels for failure to "restructure" their attitudes and behavior rapidly enough, demanding discipline from one and all and launching vigorous campaigns against drinking of alcoholic beverages (*Pravda*, May 17, 1985) as well as against corruption and other forms of "unearned" incomes (*Pravda*, May 28, 1986). Gorbachev has touted the work ethic, set a high moral tone for his administration, and ordered everyone to fall in line. Finally, through high production targets set for the Twelfth Five-Year Plan and beyond, he is also demanding a speedup in economic activity across the board and a radical improvement in productivity, tangible gains in the quality and design of products, and accomplishments in the modernization of existing capital stock. "Radical reform" of the economic mechanism is a key part of Gorbachev's strategy for achieving such a breakthrough and moving beyond the "turning point" that he declares is imperative.[1]

Actions Speak Louder Than Words

Besides sanctioning a wide-ranging debate on reform-related issues, ceaselessly exhorting one and all, and carping at government and party officials, Gorbachev has presided over a beehive of bureaucratic activity on the reform front that has generated a blitz of decrees and similar issuances. Some 30 of them have been published in the press, and many more have been scheduled to appear in the next few years. Presumably, the melange of directives now in place will fix the rules of the game for the rest of the decade, at least, so it is instructive at this point to outline what Gorbachev has wrought thus far.

Organizational Changes. Several actions address economic problems through changes in organizational structure. Decrees, for example, have established

1. Gorbachev used the term "radical reform" in his speech to the 27th Party Congress in early 1986 (*Pravda*, February 26, 1986).

several new, permanent bodies in the USSR Council of Ministers to oversee related groups of activities, thus implementing an oft-repeated Brezhnev proposal. These bodies include a bureau for social development to oversee consumer-labor welfare programs, a bureau for machinebuilding to oversee the activities of civilian machinery ministries, a bureau for the fuel and energy complex, and the State Foreign Economic Commission (*Izvestiya*, November 2, 1986).[2] Similar coordinating bodies for the agricultural-industrial complex (*Pravda*, November 23, 1985) and for construction (*Pravda*, September 13, 1986) were created in separate reorganizations of those sectors. Besides establishing central coordinating bodies, the decrees on agriculture and construction fundamentally reorganize those bureaucracies, abolishing some ministries and units and creating new ones. Another decree provides for the establishment of inter-branch scientific-technical complexes to develop and diffuse technologies that span ministerial jurisdictions; it lays out a model charter for such a complex.[3] In response to the Chernobyl' disaster, a new ministry charged with production of nuclear power was set up. In January 1986, a Commission to Improve Management, Planning, and the Economic Mechanism was established under the Council of Ministers to draft proposals for, and to monitor the implementation of, the multifaceted program to "restructure" the economic mechanism (V Komissii, 1986a, p. 10). Gosplan Chairman Nikolai Talyzin heads the Commission.[4]

The core of the reform program as it exists to date is contained in a major decree adopted in July 1985 and in more than a dozen follow-up issuances. These extend, with varying detail, the provisions of the so-called "experiment" of 1984–1985, first to a sizable group of ministries as of January 1986 and to the rest of industry and some other sectors as of January 1, 1987 (O shirokom, 1985, pp. 11–14; *Izvestiya*, December 15, 1986). Separate decrees spell out the new working arrangements in agriculture (*Pravda*, March 29, 1986) and construction (*Pravda*, September 13, 1986). Sweeping aside a mass of complexities, we shall try to summarize the essential features of what is being put in place in the industrial sector.

Plan Targets. The number of centrally set plan targets is reduced to several key ones. These include those fixing output in terms of contract obligations and physical units and those setting limits on investment. In addition, targets are to be in place which establish normatives that determine the level of inventories, the wage fund, the three incentive funds, and payments from profits into the state budget and centralized ministerial funds. Probably, there are others, but complete details are lacking on this aspect.

Utilization of Funds. Within the funds available to them, firms are supposed to have a free hand in deciding many matters concerning the size and

2. Although these bodies were established at different times, the source cited provides a complete list.
3. These complexes are described in an interview with G. Marchuk, Chairman of the State Committee on Science and Technology (*Sotsialisticheskaya industriya*, September 2, 1986).
4. This commission presumably absorbed all the duties of the Gosplan commission chaired by Baibakov.

distribution of the workforce, wages and bonuses, and the uses to which the firm's own (decentralized) investment funds are to be put. Even so, these matters are to be specified in plans and collective contracts, and, in the case of investment, the resources required must be detailed far in advance and applied for through the centralized rationing authority (Gossnab). As is the case with earlier reform proposals, ministries are enjoined not to confiscate unused funds or to exercise petty tutelage over the firms. Half a dozen or so variables determine the size of bonus funds in accordance with the now ubiquitous normatives. Managerial bonuses are to depend on several variables to be determined by the ministries (with higher permissible ceilings), but are to be paid only if all contractual obligations for product deliveries are met in full. Except for construction of entirely new production facilities, ministries and firms are required to finance all expenditures internally without budget allocations. Reserve funds set up in the ministries from normative-determined deductions from enterprise funds are to be used to ease the transition to self-finance. Special decrees extend these general principles, with appropriate modifications, to fit the nature of specific activities, e.g., to light industry (*Pravda*, May 6, 1986) and to retail trade (*Pravda*, August 5, 1986). Further, a major decree mandates a fundamental revision of work norms and wage and salary scales that are to be effected in the productive sectors firm by firm. All ensuing increases in wages have to be financed from any extra money in the firm's wage fund that results from reduced employment relative to plan (*Izvestiya*, November 1, 1986; *Sobraniye*, 1986c). Finally, selected firms are being given limited rights to engage directly in foreign trade (*Pravda*, September 24, 1986).

Incentives and Product Quality. To complicate matters further, as of January 1, 1987, four industrial ministries and certain enterprises in other ministries will be operating under rules set forth in a separate set of issuances.[5] The principal distinctive feature seems to be the formation of incentive funds and budget payments as fixed (normative) shares of profits (rather than fixed absolute amounts in the case of profit taxes). These arrangements are patterned after those tried out in the much-touted experiments in the Sumy Science-Production Association Imeni Frunze and the Avto Vaz automobile plant.[6] Meanwhile, the press has provided a stream of both praise and criticism of the results that have been obtained under the assorted "experiments," a critique strongly reminiscent of the press coverage of the early years of the 1965 reforms.[7]

Presumably, the relating of rewards to product quality indicators included in the new incentive arrangements should orient firms toward improvement in

---

5. The Talyzin Commission has approved eight instructions pertaining to this amendment of the standard rules for the experiment (V kommissii, 1986b, p. 17). The text of the instructions on the formation and use of bonus funds is published there (p. 15).

6. For a discussion of these experiments, see *Trud*, May 17, 1986.

7. The following are typical of the large literature critiquing the results of the "experiment": Voronin, 1984, pp. 9–18; Babashkin, 1985, pp. 12–19; Zhelesko et al., 1985, pp. 79–88; Bunich, 1986, pp. 3–20; *Pravda*, September 23, 1986; *Izvestiya*, September 12, 1986; V osnovnom, 1986, pp. 214–232.

that area. Nevertheless, speedy improvement in product quality and modernity of design has become itself a campaign and the subject of separate treatment in decrees. The July 1985 decree that extended the experiment established a specific set of new price markups and discounts and stiffer penalties related to product design and quality. Only one year later a special decree stipulated still one more set of incentives and penalties related to performance on product quality indicators (*Pravda*, July 2, 1986).

Quality Control. Most notable of all, however, was the establishment by special decree of a new system of State acceptance of products (*Gospriyemka*), administered by the State Committee for Standards (Gosstandart) (*Sobraniye*, 1986b, pp. 440–444). The system, to apply to some 1,500 enterprises producing the most important products,[8] provides for the formation in these enterprises of State Acceptance staffs headed by people who are on the local party's nomenklatura list. Members of such staffs are employees of Gosstandart, not of the enterprise. According to its statute, *Gospriyemka*-in-residence has broad powers (for example, unaccepted products cannot be shipped out to customers). The new body also works with the enterprise manager to oversee previously mandated quality control efforts. Among such efforts are state standards, state certification of products, and the Comprehensive Program for Quality Control, which (although declared by one critic to have been ineffective (Popov, 1986, pp. 70–83) is supposed to be in place throughout industry by the end of the Twelfth Five-Year Plan. The inspiration for this latest panacea for the perennial quality and design problems of the economy evidently came by way of analogy with the military representatives (*voyenpredy*) routinely stationed in defense plants to ensure adherence to Ministry of Defense requirements.

Contract Fulfillment. A separate set of decrees attacks anew the seemingly intractable supply problem. A decree adopted in June 1986 addresses the problem on three fronts. First, much earlier deadlines are imposed on Gosplan, ministries, and enterprises for specifying plan targets relating to output and allocations of required materials (defined in physical units) and for the conclusion of the relevant contracts. Second, new rules are enacted which tie contract fulfillment to bonus funds. Finally, penalties are once more stiffened for contract violations (*Sobraniye*, 1986b, pp. 435–439).

"Wholesale Trade." A decree of March 1986 and an instruction issued by Gosplan-Gossnab at about that same time deal with matters that are sometimes referred to as "wholesale trade in the means of production" (Resursy, 1986, p. 23; *Sobraniye*, 1986a, pp. 305–308). The decree lists a number of agencies whose subordinate units, along with most research and design organizations everywhere, are to receive their required materials through the regional divisions of Gossnab. These customers, typically buying in small lots, now may do so without specific higher-level authorizations for their purchases. But their planned requirements must be specified in plans, nonetheless, and the responsible ministries and agencies

---

8. The new system took effect January 1, 1987.

must notify Gossnab, which must then allocate appropriate amounts to its regional units. Essentially the same procedures apply to purchases through such regional units by enterprises using money in their own investment funds and employing in-house construction crews. Gossnab was also directed to increase the number of small wholesale outlets by 30 percent and the number of equipment rental points by 120 percent by 1990.

Related Decrees. Still more decrees deal with other matters related to reform. A decree published in June 1986 purports to give the local Soviets in the republics more authority and responsibility in matters concerning development of local infrastructure and programs to raise living standards (*Pravda*, July 30, 1986). One of the decrees dealing with construction stipulated the transfer of republic-level construction organizations to the jurisdiction of the appropriate union-republic council of ministers. Four issuances deal with the question of the expansion of economic activity by individuals and producer cooperatives. As part of a crackdown on corruption and illegal private economic pursuits, a Supreme Soviet decree adopted in May 1986 sets new penalties for failure to comply with existing laws concerning permissible private activity (*Vedomosti*, 1986a, pp. 369–373). A law adopted by the Supreme Soviet in November 1986 spelled out the kinds of permissible endeavors and the groups that are to be encouraged to engage in them (*Pravda*, November 21, 1986).[9] In August 1986 the Politburo approved some "basic principles for development of cooperative forms of production" (not yet published), which specify that producer cooperatives are to be organized on a voluntary basis "with the participation of ministries, departments, and local Soviets" (*Pravda*, August 16, 1986). Subsequently, the Council of Ministers promulgated a model statute for experimental cooperatives to be engaged in the collection and processing of waste materials (Primernyy, 1986, pp. 15–16).

Upcoming Measures. Finally, in September 1986, the Supreme Soviet and the Council of Ministers published a decree detailing a schedule for drafting a number of new pieces of legislation on economic reform matters during 1986–1988 (*Vedomosti*, 1986b). Most important of these laws-to-be are the Statute on the Socialist Enterprise (Association), proposals concerning material-technical supply, proposals concerning "plan-oriented reform of prices," and regulations concerning USSR ministries and state committees. The first of these, the new Statute on the Socialist Enterprise (to replace the one adopted in 1965), was discussed by the Politburo in early December and remanded for further work (*Pravda*, December 12, 1986). Additional measures envisioned for the period and listed in the decree include regulations concerning intersectoral and industrial-trading associations in light industry, proposals for improving the economic mechanism in agriculture, laws on product quality, and proposals for improving management of the transport sector.

9. These include state employees outside normal working hours, pensioners, housewives, and the handicapped.

What Has Been Learned from Twenty Years of Reforming the 1965 Reforms?

The Gorbachev round of reforms has evoked considerable debate and discussion among academics and officials that is much more lively and far-reaching than that preceding the 1965 reforms, as well as a good deal of soul searching as to why those reforms went awry. A few people seem to have concluded that the failure of the 1965 reforms and their modifications to mitigate the fundamental problems of the economy must be attributed to a failure to marketize the economy. Others seem to have decided that the failure lay in too much decentralization and reliance on value indicators in an attempt to push firms in the desired direction. More significant, however, is the apparent appraisal by Gorbachev and the framers of the reform program actually legislated in the past two years. Their assertion is that the 1965 reform concepts were sound; the failure lay in lack of vigorous implementation.

The program of 1985–1986 shows unequivocally that its framers believe that the principles and philosophy that underlay the 1965 and subsequent legislation were correct. Their actions demonstrate the conviction that reorganizing hierarchical structures will solve deep-rooted economic problems. Central planning in the view of Gorbachev and his advisers is a *sine qua non* of socialism that needs to be "strengthened." The essence of this basic belief is manifest, in turn, in a set of more specific axioms: that the behavior of enterprises can be fundamentally altered by according them more freedom of action; that so-called economic levers are more effective in eliciting this behavior than administrative levers; and that the continued and simultaneous adherence to output targets, centrally set prices, and rationing of material input will not compromise the effectiveness of the first two measures. Thus, by creating accounting conditions and legal forms that resemble those used in market economies, the reformers believe they can induce state-owned firms to respond as do firms in a market environment in regard to attention to customer wants, the mix and quality of products, efficiency in the use of all resources, and innovation.

More specifically, the measures adopted in 1985–1986 actually seek to put into effect several major planks contained in the July 1979 decree. One was the intent ultimately to make ministries and their subordinate firms financially autonomous, covering all current and capital costs from internally generated funds and paying a profit tax to the state. Although this measure is scheduled for implementation with a vengeance in 1987, it is evident that intra-ministry and budget subsidies will have to continue for some time because of the wide variation in profitability among similar firms generated by Soviet methods of price setting.[10] The problems of shifting to self-financed firms, however, will

---

10. Both kinds of subsidies are supposed to be gradually eliminated.

be greatly complicated by a decreed mandate (not part of the 1979 package) that firms must finance a comprehensive revision of wages and salaries designed to improve work incentives. These wage adjustments can be carried out only if internal funds are available.

A related plank of the 1979 decree, now also incorporated into the present reform measures, was the prescription that enterprise and ministerial plans should be established for five years, with annual breakdowns based on stable normatives for various indicators. Plan fulfillment was to be evaluated cumulatively. The intent was to make the five-year plans operational like the annual plans, the stability of which was supposed to be "guaranteed" for the firms by its ministry. Still another element of the 1979 decree scheduled for implementation in the current package of reforms is the establishment of a set of normatives, also to remain stable in five-year and annual plans, to regulate enterprise activities. Most particularly, such normatives have been formulated in respect to formation of the wage funds, the three incentive funds, the level of inventories, and the disposition of profits. Presumably, the normatives in theory should reflect an industry-wide standard of some kind, although the normatives being established by the ministries are in fact firm-specific. Again, this must necessarily be the case, in view of the wide range of economic conditions and profit rates existing among firms producing similar products.

Thus, these normatives would seem to provide fertile ground for bargaining between ministry and firm, a worthy substitute for the specific plan targets they replace. They also provide a convenient device for introducing new regulations, as a recent Council of Ministers decree has done, with respect to inventory levels throughout the economy (*Izvestiya*, December 15, 1986). Although fewer plan targets are supposed to be set for firms by higher authorities, those remaining are the key ones. For example, the centrally set targets for firms in light industry include output of main products in physical units, profits, and commissionings from state centralized investment funds. Also among the targets are normatives for deductions from profits into the budget and ministry reserves, for formation of the three incentive funds, for the allowable growth of the wage fund, and for the permissible increase in the average wage relative to the increase in labor productivity.

Another plank of the 1979 decree, also accorded a key place in the 1985–1986 package, is the role given to inter-firm contracts and their enforcement. As noted previously, the new rules make contract fulfillment the main success indicator, and both bonus funds and managerial bonuses suffer if that criterion is not met. But, as before, firms do not have a free hand in choosing their suppliers, nor do customers have alternative suppliers. For the most part, contracts are arranged through ministries with appropriate units of Gossnab. Thus, a 1985 source states that Gossnab units conclude some 600,000 contracts with suppliers and over 2.5 million contracts with customers, and that "many thousands of contracts" are concluded by other organizations (Shapkina, 1985, p. 19).

Over the years, the drive to increase the role of contracts has resulted in a sharp rise in the share of planned sales effected through formal contracts: "in most branches of industry contracts covered 80 to 90 percent of planned deliveries as of the beginning of 1985 compared with only 50 to 60 percent several years ago" (Shapkina, 1985, p. 19). The aim at present is to complete the process and to increase the share of contracts that are long-term (for five years). To the extent that contracts cover total planned sales, however, their total value becomes equivalent to total sales, which differs little from the much-castigated "val" that has oriented enterprises toward a preference for expensive inputs and for juggling with product mix and prices. The ability of customers to combat these predilections has always been hampered by lack of alternative suppliers and a pervasive sellers' market. The new program's effort to simplify the supply process for small-scale customers is a pale imitation of "wholesale trade in the means of production," the adoption of which would seem to be precluded in any case as long as shortages are widespread.

Upgrading the quality and technological level of products has been the subject of a variety of measures adopted over the past 20 years. A shift, as specified in the 1965 reform decree, to the sales target as a primary success criterion for firms failed to produce the desired results. As a consequence mandatory quality-raising targets were introduced, efforts were made to enforce state standards more strictly, and a system of state certification of products was set up and then tightened. In addition, certain "model" programs for quality control were pushed for universal adoption (the L'vov system, Zero Defects, the Comprehensive Program for Quality Control). The 1985–1986 measures continue these old arrangements in one form or another. The current measures, however, also address the problem through price incentives and financial and legal penalties, and provide for the establishment of a new administrative device—the State Acceptance Service. Thus, government inspectors (and not the customers, as is the case in the defense industries) will now rule on whether or not products conform to all relevant quality and design standards. If the new units carry out their mandate to the letter, this innovation may foul up the supply process, at least temporarily. Alternatively, it may become yet one more bureaucratic formality with which producers must learn to contend or co-opt.

The present round of reforms contains one feature not found in the 1965 decree and related issuances—authorization for expansion of the legal private and cooperative sectors. The law on the private activity, however, sanctions little that is not already legally permissible.[11] Penalties for violations, new reporting requirements, and uncertainty about tax rates, along with the campaign against "unearned incomes," are hardly likely to produce an upsurge in private activity. As of now, the approach to cooperative production endeavors appears similarly cautious.

11. This statement is based on a comparison of the new law with information given in *Argumenty i fakty*, No. 3, January 17, 1984, p. 6.

As a package, the measures effected in 1985–1986 and the rhetoric that has accompanied their adoption and implementation exemplify the thoroughgoing schizophrenia of their framers. The granting of more autonomy to enterprises, for instance, is regarded as good, but only if they use it to make the "correct" decisions. Although enterprises are expected to use their greater autonomy to respond to customers' wants, they remain formally subordinate to, and governed by, the dictates of government agencies. Ministry and party officials are enjoined to eschew petty tutelage over firms, although at the same time they are held "personally" responsible for the results of those firms' activities. Indeed this latter conflict has become even more acute under Gorbachev. In similar fashion, firms that have been accorded greater autonomy, and are now required to finance themselves from their own revenues, are expected to make more efficient decisions about inputs and outputs. Yet the price signals that would show the tradeoffs involved are not provided. Private and cooperative economic endeavors are to be permitted so as to benefit consumers, but rigid regulations are established and campaigns launched against "unearned" incomes, and "abuses." Thus, although "economic methods" are introduced to deal with a given problem, they often are simultaneously supplemented by administrative measures to the same end. The attack on the quality problem is a notable case in point. And, perhaps most contradictory of all, this complicated set of "reforms" intended to achieve a breakthrough in quality and efficiency is being implemented simultaneously with a drive to accelerate the quantity of production! Gorbachev seems to be convinced that by sheer force of will he can have it both ways.

In conclusion, the measures put in place in Gorbachev's nearly two years of tenure are neither radical nor a reform, for they do not re-form (restructure) the economic system in any essential way. Some of the innovations may produce small benefits (along with much else about which to complain), as was the case with the successive sets of measures and revisions thereof promulgated during 1965–1984. But the system-rooted problems will continue. If Mikhail Gorbachev aspires to rank with Vladimir Lenin and Joseph Stalin as great reformers of the Soviet economic system, he will have to come up with a radically different blueprint from that underlying the measures he has sanctioned thus far. As of this writing, the treadmill continues.

CHAPTER 5

The Gorbachev Reform:
A Maximal Case

Jerry F. Hough

FORMER ISRAELI foreign minister Abba Eban once said that every group has its own occupational biases. Lawyers think that everyone is guilty, priests think that everyone is immoral, and experts think that any conceivable change in policy is impossible and won't work.

This general rule is reinforced in the case of Western students of the Soviet economy by a number of specific factors. We have read the same criticisms of the Soviet economy for so long (they are even in the books of David Granick and Joseph Berliner[1] based on information from the 1930s) that we have become extremely cynical about any assertion about reform. The failure of the Kosygin reforms of 1965 had an especially strong impact on our thinking. The Soviet economists with whom we have talked have been disillusioned by the same pattern of events, and none of them more so than the many economists who emigrated in the 1970s.

Yet changes do occur. The Soviet New Economic Policy (NEP) and American prosperity of the 1920s both proved ephemeral. Stalin unexpectedly reversed his Popular Front policy of the 1930s and signed a non-aggression pact with Hitler. Few American specialists on the Soviet Union in 1952 other than Barrington Moore had any sense of an impending de-Stalinization, and he was extraordinarily cautious in his predictions. In fact, the one certain law of history is that the status quo is eventually certain to be transformed in some direction.

The problem with analyzing change is, first of all, determining the direction and speed of change, and, second, predicting its timing. My sense, unlike most other specialists, is that we are now on the brink of major changes in the Soviet economic and political system over the next decade. The purpose of this paper is to try to explain where the assumptions underlying this position are different from those which see little change as likely, and to lay out Gorbachev's strategy as I see it.

First published in *Soviet Economy*, 1986, 2, 4, pp. 302–312. [Eds.]
1. E.g., Granick (1960), Berliner (1957).

BASIC ASSUMPTIONS

The judgment that there will not be major economic reform in the Soviet Union is essentially based on the assumptions that the General Secretary is probably not committed to radical reform and that if he were, he would not be able to overcome resistance to it. The prevailing explanation of the failure of the Kosygin reforms (and the tentativeness of the East European reforms) is that incremental reform permits the bureaucrats to nibble reform to death, i.e., to implement programs so gradually that hopes for substantial change eventually are abandoned. Since Gorbachev is clearly committed, at best, to an incremental reform that stretches over several years, conventional wisdom suggests that he will suffer the same fate.

Whether this judgment is accurate or not, it should be emphasized that it is a political judgment, not an economic one. The economists' own experience is that incremental change may eventually lead to qualitative change.[2] In assuming that the Soviet system is incapable of such evolution, economists are basically accepting the judgment of the majority of political scientists and historians today, rather than drawing a conclusion from developments occurring within their own discipline.

In turn, the majority opinion of the political scientists and historians today is based on very different assumptions than were prevalent a quarter of a century ago. Then the overwhelming majority of the historians saw 19th-century Russia as part of Western Europe and the Bolshevik Revolution as an unnatural break in Russian history, made possible by the accident of World War I. The political scientists saw the Soviet political system as one with an extraordinarily strong General Secretary, with a weak bureaucracy subject to a permanent purge, and with an ideology committed to transformation at home and world domination abroad.

Now these judgments have been reversed. The dominant view of Russian history is that of Richard Pipes (1981), who believes that the Soviet period is the natural continuation of the Tsarist period and that the Russians are naturally xenophobic. Perhaps because of the neo-Marxism of the Vietnam period and the continuing influx of emigres trained as Marxists and not exposed to American scholarly debates of the first half of the 1950s, the dominant view of the Soviet political system has become Marxist (more accurately, Trotskyist): its adherents maintain that power is in the hands of bureaucrats who manage the means of production, the political leadership is a weak "superstructure" comprising a tool of the economic elite, and that ideology is a conservative justification of the privilege of the ruling class.

In my view, the conventional wisdom of the 1950s is closer to the truth than the new orthodoxy. First, the Bolshevik Revolution was an unnatural break with the natural Russian path of integration into the West. It received

---

2. E.g., to the rise of the multinational corporation or the transition of Japan to a high-technology economy.

support among peasants streaming into the city because it provided certain answers for those very insecure about the new urban world into which they were being thrust. A substantial part of the appeal of Bolshevism was precisely that it rejected the Westernized elite, and that it promised a path of development that rejected Western economic and political institutions—the Western values the former peasants associated with the city. In this sense, the Bolshevik revolution was the Khomeini revolution of Russian history.

Today, however, the bureaucrats under 55 years of age are the youth we have seen for the last 30 years, who were not anti-Western but who yearned for Western clothes and music and contact with the West. The economic bureaucrats may fear a change in the planning system, but it is wrong to think that they fear all change. The historical drive for warm water ports has been replaced by a drive for warm water beaches—beaches in the Riviera, in Capri, on Greek islands. Bureaucrats who know that economic reform means an opening to the West will find this a powerful plus to go with the minuses of a more difficult life at work.

Second, the General Secretaryship remains a powerful position. The 1965 reforms failed because they were the *Kosygin, not* the *Brezhnev*, reforms. Brezhnev's first appointments to the Politburo in 1964, Petr Shelest and Aleksandr Shelepin, were surely added as a counterweight to Kosygin and Podgorny, a sign that Brezhnev was skeptical about economic reform from the beginning. Whatever temptation he may have felt at first, he surely became totally negative after the 1968 revolt in Czechoslovakia. Brezhnev had sufficient power to stop economic reform, and the stagnation of the late 1970s was the result of his power to thwart change, not the result of bureaucratic resistance. Now the General Secretary is on the other side of the equation, and the results will be very different than in 1965.

Third, the ideology remains a transforming one, or, to phrase the point more accurately, the stability of the Soviet regime (in comparison with the instability of the regime in a country such as Poland) rests on Communism's tie with Russian nationalism or patriotism. Communism was associated with a restoration of Russian power after the disaster of the Russo-Japanese War and World War I, and with the promise that the Soviet model would lead the world to a higher level of civilization. Thus, if the population comes to associate Communism with permanent technological backwardness and a decline in relative Russian power, then Russia is likely to become as unstable as Poland. The messianic aspects of the ideology are likely to have been inspiring to the Gorbachev generation when they entered politics in the early Khrushchev period, and Gorbachev can use those themes in mobilizing the support of the population (including conservatives) for action that rejuvenates the system.

Finally, I am one political scientist who takes seriously the economists' insight that protectionism is disastrous for technological innovation, quality, and efficiency. Soviet policy has been so protectionist that manufacturers do not lose business when goods are imported, and they have little incentive or pressure to submit themselves to the discipline of the world market with exports. If the pursuit of power and stability drive Soviet leaders to try to bring the level of their technology toward world levels, then the imperatives of the latter will drive them to open their economy (and their society) to the outside world.

As economists observe such fundamental disagreements between historians and political scientists over the driving forces of Russian history and the political system, as described in the preceding paragraphs, their first response may undoubtedly be skepticism about historians and political scientists and their projections. Their professional response should be to develop different economic scenarios based on the different political scenarios. But, as they try to judge between the different historians and political scientists, they might ask themselves whether a young leader such as Gorbachev would be foolish enough to make sweeping promises if he did not intend to put all his power behind them and if he did not think he had a fighting chance to succeed.

BENCHMARKS AND STANDARDS
FOR COMPARISON

If economists do at least accept the possibility that reform will be attempted, then they are in a position to analyze what that reform might be. This is crucial. One of the components of the present skepticism about reform in the Soviet Union has been the establishment of criteria for reform that absolutely cannot be fulfilled and that are inconsistent with the economists' understanding of the complexity of the task.

When we talk about economic reform in the Soviet Union, we usually take the Hungarian and Chinese reforms as benchmarks. Most say that Soviet reform will be less radical than either. My prediction has been an eclectic combination of Hungarian reforms in the services and agricultural sectors with Chinese and East German experiments in attacking protectionism—but, of course, with enough variations in forms that Gorbachev can claim that it is a unique Soviet model. While comparisons may be difficult, I believe that in the seven years from 1986 to 1993 the Soviet Union will go further, and perhaps much further, than China did from 1979 to 1986.

Whether or not these predictions are correct, there is a need to agree on benchmarks and standards for judgment. The Chinese and the Hungarians have implemented relatively marginal reforms in the core of heavy industry, and the failure of the Soviet leaders to introduce fundamental reforms in the core of heavy industry says nothing about Soviet failure to meet the Chinese and Hungarian standards. Nonetheless, economists frequently state flatly that Soviet economic progress will be slower than that of these other Communist systems, even when they speak in specifics only about industrial reform and the obstacles to it.

It is quite possible that Soviet industrial reform by the early 1990s will be more substantial than presently anticipated, but that is not the issue. If the argument is over whether the Soviet Union will reform more or less than China or Hungary over the next seven years or so, then the questions that are asked must be specific—will there be a serious reform of services and agriculture, will there be significant reform in the ties between trade and light industry, will there be the beginnings of an encouragement of foreign investment?

Second, economists need to take more seriously their insights into the difficulties of economic reform and the interconnections among the steps that must be taken. Conceivably incrementalism will permit bureaucrats to sabotage the reform, but, without question, instant radical reform is impossible.

An example of this can be seen in the services sector, probably the realm most amenable to reform. There, legalization of the second economy requires harsh measures against illegal activity, for even if repairmen can buy materials in lumberyards and hardware stores, their profit will be much higher if they continue to steal materials. It also requires generous supplies to new lumberyards (and other supply stores for other services). Prices are an extremely sensitive problem in maintaining political control, especially since early supplies will be erratic and shortages may lead to surges in prices.[3] Hence, some price control is probably necessary at first. Finally, any government will demand its cut from the profits of private economic activity, but the level of taxation is always a contentious question and the establishment of a reliable system of tax collection will be very difficult in a country that has not been relying on individual taxation.

As a consequence, even if Gorbachev were totally committed to thorough reform in trade and the services that was based overwhelmingly on the market, and even if he had a totally united Politburo behind him, such a reform would take several years at best for technical reasons. It seems to me that economists should be using their expertise to develop various possible scenarios of reform. How was the reform in services introduced in Hungary? What was the sequence of steps? Where were the problems? To what extent will the Soviet Union face additional difficulties? Only to the extent that three or four scenarios of reform are developed for the services, three or four in agriculture, three or four in light industry, and three or four in foreign investment will we be able to get some realistic sense of just what Gorbachev is attempting and what his chances of success are.

Finally, economists need to give far more thought to the question of success indicators. The role of growth of GNP is not enough. If GNP indicators do not reveal that life for the consumer in Budapest has become much more pleasant than life for the consumer in a Soviet city, i.e., that real living standards soared during the reform, then something is wrong with the indicator. There have been many attempts to measure hidden inflation, but, to the best of my knowledge, no effort to measure hidden deflation and, consequently, real increases in gross product. If shoddy merchandise is replaced by goods of much higher

---

3. E.g., the campaign against illegal activity in 1986 drove up certain *rynok* prices in a number of northern cities.

quality and nominal prices remain stable, one should price the new high-quality merchandise by what people would have paid in the past, or the old goods by the prices they would command at present. If people value leisure enough to pay higher prices in neighborhood convenience stores instead of spending a few additional minutes at a supermarket, then Soviet consumers would presumably pay more for convenience too, and a reform that saves time has some monetary value. Such factors may be difficult to calculate, but somehow they must be recognized.

Indeed, the problem goes much deeper. If Gorbachev introduced a pell-mell industrialization program that doubled Soviet steel production, it might do wonders for Soviet GNP figures, but it surely would be a disaster for an economy that needs to cut steel production. The enormous number of hospital beds in the Soviet Union is a minus, not a plus. Somehow there must be some way of comparing the mix of products of capitalist and socialist economies in a way that discounts production that fulfills few societal needs. There must be some way of recognizing the rapid progress that is made if and when a socialist society shifts from the production of unwanted and unneeded items to those that are wanted and needed.

GORBACHEV'S STRATEGY

My own sense of Gorbachev's strategy and his scenario of action is, unfortunately, not that of an economist, and hence it remains distressingly vague. Nevertheless, it may be useful to present one political scientist's view of Gorbachev's basic political strategy and the way in which the basic outlines of economic reform are part of it.

The crucial fact about Gorbachev's strategy, as I understand it, is that he has a strategy. He is thinking about what must be done to ensure that the Red Square celebration commemorating the beginning of the 21st century is a triumphal one, with him presiding over it. He has acknowledged that he has no specific "recipe," and in that sense he may have a bit of the Franklin Roosevelt in him, but he does seem to have a general notion of sequences. He told the editors of *Time Magazine*, for example, that he sees foreign policy as a continuation of domestic policy, and plans to conduct a foreign policy that contributes to his understanding of domestic reform.

The first part of the strategy is to use words that make reform irresistible. Gorbachev really has been extraordinarily insistent on the need for reform. In January 1986, Westerners were saying that his failure to use the word "reform" testified to his lack of seriousness, and then in February he used the phrase "radical reform" (*radikal'naya reforma*). "It is impossible to limit ourselves to partial improvements. Radical reform is indispensable" (Gorbachev, 1986b, p. 33). He spoke with contempt about "the peculiar psychology in which it was assumed that things could be improved without changing anything" (Gorbachev, 1986b, p. 4).

Gorbachev was particularly direct at the 27th Party Congress in speaking about a Hungarian-type reform in the services. He promised outright that "the state will facilitate the development of different forms of satisfying [consumer] demand and providing services. It is necessary to give attentive consideration to the proposals to regulate the labor activities of individuals" (Gorbachev, 1986b, p. 47).

Gorbachev did not use the term "market" or "market relations" in any speeches, but at the Party Congress he came extremely close. "It is time," he said, "to overcome the suspicion of money relations and their underestimation in the planned leadership of the economy" (Gorbachev, 1986b, p. 40). He demanded that prices be linked not only with the production costs, but also "with consumer characteristics," and with the degree of balance between the output of the product and the consumer demand and social need for it (Gorbachev, 1986b, p. 35).

By the summer of 1986 the General Secretary's language was even more radical (Gorbachev, 1986a, p. 1):

> I would equate the words "reconstruction" and "revolution." . . . The present reconstruction embraces not only the economy, but all other aspects of social life: social relations, the political system, the spiritual-ideological sphere . . .
>
> Great and urgent work is still before us, comrades . . . We should not be afraid to move boldly forward, to take risks, to take responsibility on ourselves. We will do our reconstruction, as they say, on the march, in the course of the active solution of economic and social tasks.

This language is the first crucial step in Gorbachev's strategy. In part, language is a vehicle used by Gorbachev to present his vision of the future, but it can represent a form of action as well. In the Soviet system, everyone must support his position with quotations from the General Secretary, and a General Secretary who wants to reform must take care to provide the quotations that the most radical reformers can use to advance their arguments.

In addition, Gorbachev's words over the last year have gone so far as to make the issue of economic reform a vote of confidence in his leadership. Gorbachev may end up the target of major popular disillusionment and even ridicule if, like Brezhnev, he does almost nothing. At Khabarovsk his words about taking risks and responsibility made the point explicitly. He was claiming for himself the right to take the steps he thought necessary and conceding that if things worked out badly, the Central Committee could and would change the leader.

In so doing, however, Gorbachev also made opposition to reform risky for its opponents. By linking his personal fate to the success or failure of reform, the General Secretary could demonstrate to potential rivals that major opposition would be treated as a you-or-me test of strength. Opponents know that even the 1981 Central Committee, the Brezhnev officials, selected the youngest member of the Politburo as General Secretary and a man who wanted change. They know as well that the 1986 Central Committee is even more supportive of the General Secretary. It would be extraordinary if any politician wanted to take on the General Secretary in this kind of situation. The normal political response is to give the leader his way and move against him only when and if he fails, rather than risk a test of strength when hopes are high.

The second part of Gorbachev's strategy is to broaden the definition of socialist property. We instinctively accept Stalin's definition of socialism as nationalized property, directly managed by monopolistic ministries. Some Marxists have long derided the Soviet system as "state capitalism," and socialism unquestionably could be defined in different ways. Indeed, in comparison with the individualistic capitalism of the *Communist Manifesto* of 1848, IBM is a socialized enterprise, including workers' pension funds, owned by thousands. "Corporations" and "cooperatives" have much in common. Condominiums or family businesses are cooperatives of more classic types, and franchise operations are an interesting hybrid.

Gorbachev clearly is going to broaden the definition of socialist property. At the Party Congress, he raised the question directly (Gorbachev, 1986b, p. 39):

> Socialist property has a rich content, and includes a variegated system of relations among people, collectives, branches, and regions of the country in using the means and results of production . . . This complex of relations demands a definite harmonizing and constant adjustment, all the more so since it is in motion. If we do not deeply think through these changes on a theoretical plane, we cannot find good practical decisions and, consequently, work out measures for forming a really proprietary relation to socialist property.

In my opinion, Gorbachev's emphasis on the "activization of the human factor" should not be seen simply as an endorsement of moral persuasion. He obviously would like to inspire people to work harder, but I think that the phrase fundamentally refers to the establishment of NEP-like arrangements that unleash the human factor and individual initiative. "It would be naive," he said at the congress, "to imagine that the feeling of being the boss can be instilled by words. The relationship to property is formulated, first of all, by those real conditions in which a person is placed" (Gorbachev, 1986b, p. 39).

The contract with a brigade or subsequently larger units is likely to be the basic strategy for the introduction of market mechanisms and greater enterprise independence into the Soviet economy. If a construction brigade merely includes workers, then it is likely to be little more than a way of stimulating better performance and distributing income. If it includes engineers and managers and works on a contract with a large firm or a private individual, it can have many similarities with a construction contractor in the West. Analogous arrangements in agriculture, trade, the services, and very small-scale industry are easy to imagine. "Cooperative enterprises," Gorbachev said, "should find broad distribution" not only in the services and trade, but also "in production and processing of production, in housing construction" (Gorbachev, 1986b, p. 40).

Novosibirsk has had a major experiment in which shops and even whole enterprises would work on a contract basis. Arrangements such as these could conceivably lead to real enterprise independence if they were carried through to their extreme. And, of course, if the independent collective units could raise their own financing from the banks or the stock or bond market, the line between modern capitalist and modern socialist enterprise would become even more blurred.

The third part of Gorbachev's strategy is to sequence reform in the Hungarian and Chinese pattern, starting with agriculture and the services and then moving out into industry. The outlines of the services reform seem to be in place with the law on unearned income, the explicit legitimization of private labor, the increased attention to individual taxation, and the February 5, 1987, Politburo decision endorsing cooperatives. The agricultural reform remains unclear. Murakhovsky has endorsed family farming in the framework of the collective contract, and apparently the confiscatory taxation on private agriculture earnings has been abolished. However, progress seems rather slow, perhaps because agricultural price reform is considered dangerous.

The Soviet Union is also going to attack protectionism. To some extent, an export strategy will be emerging. Apparently, a number of key manufacturing ministries will have independent foreign currency balances to reward them directly for export earnings. In addition, foreign enterprises, with joint ownership, will be permitted on Soviet soil, and Soviet leaders are talking about joint production arrangements.

The way in which these arrangements work and the extent to which they are carried out remains to be seen. The present incentive system does not give industrial ministries any great incentive to earn foreign currency even if it could be used abroad. The incentive for enterprise managers would soar, on the other hand, if they could use such currency in part to buy equipment for their hospitals and foreign goods for factory stores, or to travel more freely abroad.

The easiest way for industrial and foreign economic reform to be introduced is in conjunction with the reforms in the services and in agriculture. If joint enterprises or cooperative enterprises produce timber for cooperative lumber yards that are supplying cooperative brigades or individual repairmen, the problems of integrating market pricing and irregular supply into the basic planned mechanism are much easier to solve than if an independent Silicon Valley is permitted to supply Soviet heavy industry. Similarly, joint enterprises to supply small tractors or hybrid seed to more independent farms or brigades is a natural way to bring Soviet agricultural machinery plants under the gun of foreign competition.

The fourth part of the Gorbachev strategy apparently is a foreign policy one. If the Soviet Union is going to move beyond the simple importation of technology, then it must break American efforts to impose a technological blockade. Given the extreme reluctance of the United States to supply advanced technology, the Soviet Union must make political concessions to Japan, Europe, China, and major Third World countries in order to induce them to resist American pressure. Since these steps make him look weak at home, Gorbachev has a major domestic need to appear strong in other settings. Standing up to America and emphasizing the defense danger of SDI (and hanging tough on this issue) are good ways of doing this.

As we debate economic reform in public, it seems to me that we should always remember the context of the debate. It is one thing to say that Soviet economic reform is necessary, or to say that the Soviet Union needs to cut military expenditures. It is something else to say that the Soviet Union must make concessions to the United States to achieve reform. That is a political judgment, and economists need at least to reflect on the domestic political problems that a leader faces, especially if economic reform is as difficult as they say.

Economists must also distinguish between their judgments about whether fundamental reform can work (a question on which I myself am agnostic) and about whether Gorbachev will attempt fundamental reform. If he tries reform, then the foreign policy consequences of his actions will be in place long before the reform succeeds or fails. If we tell the political leadership and the population in the United States that Gorbachev will do nothing, that he is compelled to make continual concessions to the United States to survive, that he has no reason or possibility of making major concessions to our allies, the political leadership will draw the conclusion that it can push the Soviet Union around. It may be drawn into unwise actions with Soviet personnel in the United Nations and be forced into humiliating retreats. If that retreat is only on minor issues such as an exchange for Nicholas Daniloff, the cost will be small, if the retreat comes after disaster with Europe and Japan, the costs will be much higher.

CHAPTER 6

The Shape of Gorbachev's Economic Reform

Philip Hanson

IN SEVERAL speeches during 1986 CPSU General Secretary Mikhail S. Gorbachev said that a series of mutually consistent and comprehensive measures were being undertaken—measures which amounted to what he described as a package of radical economic reforms. The main features of such a package are now discernible, and this paper attempts to describe them.[1]

The following excerpts from Gorbachev's more revealing statements on the state of the reform process to date indicate at least the official expectations as to its timing and scope:

> Experiments and discussion in recent years have led to the formation of "an integral concept of economic reform" (speech at the SED Congress in Berlin published in *Pravda*, April 19, 1986).

> The principles of "the improvement (literally, perfecting) of the economic mechanism" are already defined (Plenum speech published in *Izvestiya*, June 17, 1986).

> The reconstruction of the economic mechanism will be "equivalent to a revolution." An integral scheme of economic reform is being worked out by specialist groups (speech in Khabarovsk published in *Izvestiya*, August 3, 1986).

There is an implication that the main elements of a reform are already agreed upon in principle, and that they are now being worked out and implemented in detail. Although these "main elements" could turn out to be no more than a euphemism for stronger central planning and more enterprise autonomy, there are strong indications that considerably more than that has been agreed upon.

First published in *Soviet Economy*, 1986, 2, 4, pp. 313–326. The author is indebted to Ed Hewett, Vladimir Kontorovich, Janos Kornai, Elizabeth Teague, and to participants in a Georgetown University Center for Strategic and International Studies seminar whose helpful suggestions facilitated a revision of an earlier draft. [Eds.]

1. Not considered here are other elements of change in economic policy proper (personnel changes, discipline, and changes in priorities) which may be of equal if not greater importance to future Soviet economic performance in the medium term.

Moreover, there is evidence that some of the elements have already been incorporated in decrees. The main directions that such a program of organizational change might take are listed in several articles by Academician Abel Aganbegyan (e.g., Aganbegyan, 1985a). Another academic economist of some political standing, Leonid Abalkin,[2] has claimed that there is a consensus among Soviet economists on the organizational changes that are needed (interview in *L'Unita*, October 25, 1985).

A high-level commission of several working groups (V komissii, 1986, p. 31) chaired by the USSR Gosplan Chairman Nikolay Talyzin (who is also First Deputy Premier and a candidate member of the Politburo) is now in the process of hammering out the reform details. Aganbegyan is among the commission's advisors, and may have possibly replaced Dzhermen Gvishiani as the chairman of its "scientific council" (i.e., research staff). Gosplan economists have told Western journalists that the reformed economic mechanism is meant to be in place for the start of the 1991–1995 Plan (BBC Radio 4, August 22, 1986), which means that the major decrees issued since early 1985 must be regarded as part of the "radical reform" design. It should be noted that while Gosplan's view of where the reform process will stop might differ from the views of Gorbachev and some of his advisors, there is no clear evidence thus far of such difference.

Another timetable for reform has been presented to an international audience. G. Skorov of the Academy of Sciences' Institute of the USA and Canada stated that reform measures now under discussion will be presented for approval at the next Party Congress, that is, presumably in 1991 (Reuters from Helsinki, November 7, 1986), suggesting a separate, second stage of reform. It is questionable, however, whether Skorov's Institute should be considered an authoritative source on Soviet domestic policy, as distinct from its authoritative position with regard to external public relations.

Regardless of the possible timing of the reform and the personnel involved, the nature of the reform itself (i.e., its major features and the extent to which they will be implemented) must clearly be understood before its ultimate prospects for success can be evaluated. *Is this really a radical reform which will make the Soviet economy more competitive and perhaps more open to the outside world?* Before answering this question, one must consider what is meant by the term "radical reform." One widely accepted definition, and the one adopted as a working model in this paper, is the reorganization thus far achieved in Hungary. It includes the abolition of mandatory targets for state enterprises, abolition of centralized supply allocation, some decontrol of prices, and a significant expansion of the legal private and small-cooperative sectors (which

2. Abalkin, who became the director of the Institute of Economics, USSR Academy of Sciences, was apparently the only economist to speak at an official meeting of senior social scientists addressed by Gorbachev and Ligachev in October 1986 (*Ekon. gaz.*, 1986a, pp. 1–2). He also delivered what appears to have been the introductory report at an Academy of Sciences conference on economic organization in November (Abalkin, 1986a); shortly thereafter, he was in Gorbachev's entourage when the Soviet leader visited India, and spoke with apparent authority about future organizational changes.

are largely unplanned). Kornai has argued, however, that what is described above does not amount to market socialism. Thus, market entry and exit are still tightly controlled; prices are not generally allowed to move to market-clearing levels; state enterprises' profits after taxes and subsidies are only weakly related to performance; industrial concentration and monopoly power remain high; and competition from imports is not allowed to be strong (Kornai, 1986). As a result, Hungarian state enterprises still remain more concerned about their relations with central authorities than about customers and competitors. Such symptoms of central administration as year-end production storming in manufacturing are still strongly in evidence (Rostowski and Auerbach, 1986).

On the other hand, the transmission and use of information in the Hungarian state sector are more decentralized, and concern with customers is somewhat greater than in an unreformed Soviet-type economy. Therefore, product quality, micro-balance in consumer goods markets, and perhaps technological innovation are improved. In Kornai's view, more has been achieved by way of improved product quality and market balance than by the limited decentralization of the state sector (Kornai, 1986). If one accepts this judgment, a Hungarian reform is a source of real economic improvement.[3] This is so, Kornai contends, even though the Hungarian state enterprise is dependent both on the bureaucracy and the market rather than on the market alone.

Will such a Hungarian model be applied in the USSR? The answer must surely be no. There is no evidence to be found either in the measures implemented thus far or in those seemingly planned for implementation by 1991. An evaluation is preceded here by a brief outline of the reform detailing planning in general, the producer-goods sector, the consumer sector, foreign trade, as well as incentives and participation.

AN OUTLINE OF THE REFORM[4]

Planning in General

Enterprise Plans. Plans at both the enterprise and sector level are supposed to be fixed for five years at a time, meaning that the plan for each year of a five-year plan period will be set at the beginning of the five-year period, and not subsequently changed on the basis of performance—at least as a general rule. This is intended to do away with a fundamental defect of the traditional system: the so-called "ratchet" effect of "planning from the achieved level," which forces enterprises to strive to accumulate hidden reserves of inputs (of

3. A crude comparison of Hungarian with other official East European growth statistics sheds no light on this point.
4. The decree on so-called "non-labor incomes" *(Izvestiya*, May 28, 1986) is not included in this summary of organizational changes. It would seem to be better to treat it as part of a separate economic policy program comprising the discipline and anti-corruption campaign. Its possible inconsistency with part of the organization program, however, is discussed in a subsequent section.

sufficient quantity to provide flexibility for meeting output targets) because they believe that next year's target will be set on the basis of this year's achievement. Talyzin claimed that this principle (the fixing of annual targets at the beginning of a five-year plan period) was followed in establishing 1987 annual plan targets (*Pravda*, November 18, 1986). Indeed, it appears that plan output targets for coal and natural gas are described in terms of percentage increases over the 1986 plan, rather than in terms of expected actual output for 1986; these output targets are in line with the 1987 components of the five-year plan. It is even possible that the aggregate national income and industrial output targets for 1987 could be interpreted in this manner, and that more slack is being built into national plans (since many 1986 plan targets were expected to be overfulfilled).

On the other hand, it is worth noting that stable five-year plans for enterprises that were supposed to have been introduced in 1971 did not prove practicable. The imperfect knowledge of the central planners (which gets more imperfect as planning moves from sector to branch to enterprise targets) makes stable five-year enterprise plans a near impossibility unless the great majority of five-year targets are deliberately made very slack at the outset.[5] The difficulty of maintaining this strategy is evidenced by the number of times Talyzin's presentation of the 1987 plan referred to particular targets as being above those originally envisaged for that year in the five-year plan. In other words, Gosplan does not seem to have practiced what its chairman was preaching.

Quality Control. A form of quality testing common in Soviet factories making military equipment is being extended to a substantial part of civilian manufacturing output. Here, conformity with state standards is not assessed primarily by the quality control staffs of the producing organizations, but rather by inspectors of the State Standards Committee located at "important" enterprises. From the beginning of 1987 they have been evaluating product quality without a bias in favor of the producer (interview with G. D. Kolmogorov, Chairman of Gosstandart, in *Izvestiya*, November 23, 1986, p. 2). This centralized quality checking is appropriate to a centralized system with built-in sellers markets. A market reform, however, would make it superfluous.

Territorialization. Some "territorialization" of planning has been announced: for example, the preparation and approval of regional labor balances prior to finalization of economic branch plans in regional detail (decree on the planning powers of regional authorities published in *Izvestiya*, July 30, 1986).

Prices. A general price revision of as yet unspecified character is intended ("0 plan . . . ," 1986).

Material Supply. A reorganization of the centralized supply system has been introduced as of January 1, 1987. It is to apply initially to supplies for all R&D and design organizations and for enterprises for the construction equipment industry. Although it is described as a shift to wholesale trade in

---

5. Slack targets do not seem to have been incorporated in the present five-year plan; on the contrary, the plan is ambitious and affords little flexibility.

producer goods, it is not a shift to a market. Enterprises are to obtain all producer goods (apart from highly specialized equipment) from their local branch of the State Material-Technical Supply Committee (Gossnab) when they are wanted, without the prior issuance of supply allocation certificates and also without the enterprises having to deal with a number of separate authorizing agencies.[6] Conversely, nearly all intermediate products and investment goods are (eventually) to be delivered to Gossnab. Nonetheless, production targets will continue to be centrally set and there will be no choice of supplier (interview with the USSR Gossnab chairman, L. A. Voronin in *Ekon. gaz*) (Snabzheniya, 1986, p. 6).

Producer-Goods Sector[7]

Ministries. Most if not all ministries are being grouped into a small number of "superministries" (a Western term) managing large sectors, for example, machine-building, fuel and energy, construction, etc. Some economists have proposed that these superministries should issue a smaller number of instructions to the next level down the hierarchy than present ministries issue to present enterprises and production associations. They also believed that these instructions should be more highly aggregated, so that more detail is devolved to lower-level decision making (e.g., Aganbegyan, 1985a; Abalkin interview in *l'Unità*, October 25, 1985). The most effective way of ensuring this outcome would be to make the total staff of each superministry significantly smaller than the total staff of the branch ministries it replaces. Then the capability for detailed intervention should be reduced.[8]

So far, no such reduction in staff has been achieved in the producer-goods sector. That is one piece of evidence for the existence of strong and effective resistance to Gorbachev's measures, even when the measures in question are not considered in the West to amount to significant reform. In general, the rigorous delimitation of spheres of authority and responsibility of the different levels in the planning and management hierarchy is a tricky issue. It would call for extensive revision of statutes, and implementation would require an acceptance of the rule of law in disputes between different levels of a single hierarchy.[9]

Enterprises. Another potential reform strategy involves the grouping of existing enterprises and production associations into a considerably smaller number of very large associations, recently referred to as all-Union or regional science-production associations. This looks like an attempt to follow GDR

6. Presumably Gossnab will check that supply requests are in line with the requesting enterprise's plans and with what is available. The role of interenterprise negotiations and of ministries in supply arrangements is planned to decrease while the role of Gossnab is to increase.

7. Refers to production outside of agriculture, food processing, light industry, retail trade, and services.

8. The ministries' intention to intervene can be assumed to be unalterable; they remain responsible, after all, for the performance of "their" branches.

9. For more detail, see Hanson, 1986.

practice whereby 130 industrial *Kombinate* fulfill output and allocation instructions for only 1,150 centrally planned product groups (versus the 18,000 or so product groups at present centrally planned in the USSR). Belousov referred to a desirable total of 500 to 600 large associations (probably in the industrial sector as a whole); he specifically mentioned GDR experience as a guide (Belousov, 1984). The general idea has been echoed by Aganbegyan (1985a). Gorbachev in his June 1985 technology policy speech described this type of structure as desirable, and again referred to GDR experience (Soviet television of June 11, 1985).[10] The same scheme is authoritatively described in two *Izvestiya* interviews, one with deputy premier Ya. P. Ryabov (May 26, 1986) and another with the head of the first All-Union science-production association, V. P. Belyakov (August 19, 1986).

These large, *Kombinat*-like units are to receive "stable five-year plans" incorporating few production targets. Instead, the main indicators are profits and fulfillment of delivery obligations. They are supposed to have a certain share, fixed for five years at a time, of their profits left available to them, with the balance going to the state budget.[11] There is some evidence that stable five-year *Kombinat* plans in the GDR have had some beneficial effects, possibly including the elimination of statistically detectable year-end storming in manufacturing at the branch level; this could mean that the year-on-year ratchet effect of traditional planning has been eliminated (Rostowski and Auerbach, 1986).

That official Soviet intentions run along these lines can be deduced from a number of sources—a combination of the Belyakov interview (Izvestiya, August 19, 1986) and the Politburo decision to extend the VAZ/Sumi experiment (*Izvestiya*, July 19, 1986). Construction-installation organizations as well as manufacturing enterprises are to go on to the "self-financing" regime: their bonuses are to be tied more closely to completion of projects, and both enterprise-retained profits and bank credit are supposed to become somewhat more important in investment finance (decree on the economic mechanism in construction, *Izvestiya*, September 13, 1986).

The Consumer Sector[12]

State Enterprises. New regulations have expanded enterprise-level autonomy in the disposal of above-plan output (decree on the economic mechanism of the agro-industrial sector, *Izvestiya*, March 29, 1986). Broadly similar arrangements are envisaged in the decree on the planning and management of light industry (*Pravda*, May 6, 1986).

---

10. The heavily-edited *Pravda* text omitted the reference to the GDR.
11. These specified arrangements are already (in principle) in effect at the Volga Automobile Works (VAZ) and the Frunze engineering works in Sumy, and are being extended more widely.
12. Refers to branches excluded from the previous section.

Cooperatives. The role of small cooperatives is being expanded (Politburo approval of the preparation of new regulations for cooperatives, *Izvestiya*, August 17, 1986; also the decree on planning powers of territorial authorities, *Izvestiya*, July 30, 1986). According to Abalkin (*Boston Globe*, November 28, 1986), legislation due to be implemented in 1987 will allow small groups of private citizens to form cooperatives for the manufacture of furniture, kitchen utensils, and the like from by-products and waste products produced by local state enterprises. Although the units will not be permitted to hire additional (non-member) labor, Abalkin has predicted that the cooperative sector might account for 10–12 percent of national income within a decade. On the scale of 1985 national income produced in current prices[13] that would amount to some 58–75 billion 1985 rubles value added. Whether Abalkin was including in that assessment the existing cooperatives (consisting almost entirely of the collective farms) is not clear. Agriculture in total contributed 19.4 percent (officially) to 1985 national income produced, or 112.2 billion rubles in 1985 prices (*Narkhoz*, 1986). If the collective farms account for, say, one-third of value added in agriculture, they are generating about 6.5 percent of national income already, and the scale of any *additional* cooperatives (if that was how Abalkin was reckoning his percentage share) would be modest, though not insignificant.

Legal Personal Enterprise. Some extension of legal personal enterprise (self-employed but not employing persons outside the family) was provided for in a law approved by the USSR Supreme Soviet in November 1986, and scheduled to go into effect May 1, 1987.[14] It is intended primarily for pensioners, students, invalids and "housewives" as a full-time activity, and for working-age adults as a secondary activity in addition to a main (and in practice full-time) job in the state or collective-farm sector. However, the law also says, somewhat cryptically (article 3): ". . . in accordance with social needs covered by legislation, persons not engaged in socialized production may also engage in personal labor." The activities allowed include the production of both goods and services: clothing, furniture, carpet-weaving, typing, housing repair and construction, automobile repair, coaching, translating, taxi-driving, and so on.[15] Local authorities can extend the list of allowed activities in their areas. They issue (and can withhold) licenses to set up personal labor enterprises. Income from these activities is to be declared and taxed.

The main change is that what was previously allowed, but with a somewhat uncertain legal status, is now being (in principle) specifically and clearly made legal, and also regulated and taxed for the first time. The intention, according to the official commentaries, is to encourage such activity by clarifying its

---

13. Soviet official figures from *Narkhoz 1985* (1986, p. 409).

14. Summarized by the chairman of the State Committee for Labor and Social Problems in *Pravda*, November 20, 1986, p. 5; published in *Izvestiya*, November 21, p. 2. There were commentaries on it by L. E. Kunel'skiy of the State Committee for Labor and Social Problems in *Izvestiya*, November 25, p. 2, and by the chairman of that committee, Ivan Gladkii, in *Pravda*, November 29, p. 3.

15. Retailing is not specifically listed, which is rather unusual.

legal status. Supplies of materials are supposed to be planned for the newly legalized self-employed, so that the risk of prosecution for obtaining materials illegally should (again, in principle) recede. Abalkin, in the interview already quoted, claims that at present about 2 percent of national income is generated by self-employment, much of which is illegal.[16] Abalkin goes on to forecast a maximum national income share of the newly legal private sector of 4 percent; probably the only basis for this figure is that it is a number significantly smaller than the percentage he envisages for the cooperative sector.

Staff Reductions in Agriculture. An actual reduction in staff numbers at "ministry" level in the new agro-industrial superministry has been announced (Hanson, 1986a).

Foreign Trade

As of January 1, 1987, foreign trade rights are to be initially extended to some 20 production branch ministries and 70 large production associations and enterprises (decree on improving the management of foreign trade, *Pravda*, September 24, 1986). Most likely, the main purpose of this decree is to improve information flows and incentives to domestic organizations producing for export, especially in manufacturing. The decree makes it clear that effective control of import decisions will remain centralized.

There is also a provision for setting up joint ventures with foreign (socialist and capitalist) enterprises. The main aim is probably to improve technology transfers into branches manufacturing for export.

Incentives and Participation

The Brigade System. An attempt is underway to mobilize grass-roots effort and initiative by intraenterprise subcontracting of work to workers on a pay-ment-by-results basis. That is, roughly speaking, the idea behind both the collective brigade or team contracts (including small, family-based teams) within collective farms and the contract brigades in industry and construction. The approach goes beyond a group piece-rate system by delegating some control over organization and input use to the brigades themselves and, in principle, by allowing for some negotiation of terms between them and their farm or enterprise management. Brigade contracts are not one of Gorbachev's inno-vations, but the revival and elaboration of the idea from the late 1970s have been associated with him; also, he seems to treat the "participatory current" in Soviet management thinking (Yanowitch, 1985) more seriously than other Soviet leaders.

---

16. The illegal part is presumably not included in measured national income. Surveys of Soviet emigrees suggest that private economic activity is, in any case, a larger share of true national income than Abalkin acknowledges.

Revisions in the Wage System. A joint decree of September 17, 1986, of the Party Central Committee, the USSR Council of Ministers, and the All-Union Central Council of Trade Unions revises the structure of wage scales and bonuses for some 75 million workers.[17] The general idea is to revise pay differentials and the piece-rate system so as to provide more active encouragement to more industrious workers and more highly qualified personnel. Thus, industrial enterprise directors can have bonuses equivalent to up to 75 percent of their base pay, and differentials between engineers and blue-collar workers are to shift in favor of the former. A revision of the work-rate norms underlying piece rates is part of the exercise, and a general tightening of work norms is apparently envisaged. Officially, the latter is expected to create some superfluous or redundant workers. A temporary statue outlines arrangements for the retraining of redundant workers without loss of pay from their previous jobs, and for severance pay *(vykhodnoye posobiye)*—the latter under existing labor law (Novyye, 1986).

AN EVALUATION OF THE REFORM

The picture presented thus far suggests a system more East German than Hungarian in character. An expansion of the legal private and cooperative sectors would simply be a timid move toward the East European norm.[18] This policy would have to be taken a good deal further before producing the results attained in Hungary. The treatment of the non-consumer sector is more or less an explicit emulation of East German arrangements. There is a deliberate differentiation between the consumer and the non-consumer sectors, but even the former is scarcely Hungarian in character.

The emphasis on small work teams, apparently derived from Gorbachev's long and narrowly specialized experience in agriculture, is the one element that could be said to carry his personal trademark. He has never publicly advanced any radical ideas about economic organization at levels above the intraenterprise units (Weickhardt, 1985). Bialer and Afferica (1986) and Zhores Medvedev (1986) judge Gorbachev to be a politician who believes that the principle of centralized bureaucratic coordination is basically sound. All the economic measures thus far promulgated and foreshadowed at high levels are consistent with that judgment.

That assessment suggests that neither Soviet economic institutions nor Soviet economic performance will change much in the foreseeable future. Four possible developments, however, could upset that prediction.

(1) Persistence or outright deterioration of present levels of economic per-

---

17. See Novyye, 1986, p. 17; interview with B. N. Gavrilov, a deputy chairman of the State Committee for Labor and Social Problems (*Izvestiya*, September 26, 1986).
18. Private entrepreneurs in the GDR, for example, can employ non-family staff.

formance might force reconsideration of basic economic views some time in the 1990s.

(2) On the other hand, it is possible that there are elements in current economic policy which could accelerate growth. Accelerated investment and tighter discipline may both be of some significance.

(3) In addition, it is not inconceivable that present organizational measures themselves might have some power to improve performance.

(4) Nonetheless, and probably most important, the strategies currently envisaged may not prove as politically innocuous as anticipated, and could well encounter substantial resistance. The lack of progress so far in slimming down the ministerial apparatus is a telling example. The rejection of output by the newly invigorated state quality inspectorate at the Kama River truck works apparently caused "stormy protests" (*Izvestiya*, December 4, 1986). Such conflicts might even damage economic performance.

The streamlining of the planning and management hierarchy, through reduction of information overload on central planners and delegation of some detailed decisions to lower levels, could improve the system's information structure and make for better-balanced plans. It is impossible to say *a priori* how large such an effect could possibly be, but it would probably be more than negligible. There are, however, three major obstacles to its realization. First, there is resistance to the formulation of any new decrees and new legislation which embody shifts in the allocation of power in the economy. The creation of mere Council of Ministers *byuros* overseeing groups of ministries, instead of the abolition of ministries and their replacement by leaner and less bureaucratic superministries, is an example of this type of resistance. Second, getting officials to implement whatever is eventually decreed and legislated is problematic. There are, for example, numerous reports of both farms and the distributive system refusing to buy and sell private-plot meat output (e.g., A. Morgachev and V. Ryzhkov in *Sel'skaya zhizn'*, October 26, 1986). It is also unlikely that the local agroindustrial committee officials responsible for procurements will encourage farms to sell a substantial part of their output through cooperative commission trade and the peasant markets. Third, the organizational rationalization which is being attempted requires a suitable environment insofar as economic policy is concerned.

In a word, policy change and organizational change seem to be at odds with one another. The setting of ambitious branch and product-group production targets from now to the end of the century will force plans for individual enterprises to be quite ambitious as well. This will not be compatible with schemes to improve microeconomic balance by encouraging farms and enterprises to make above-plan sales—or rather, it will not be compatible with those above-plan sales being quantitatively significant. The reason, basically, is that the proposed reform does not give ministries and superministries the scope to relax detailed control of subordinate units and substitute fewer, more aggregated targets. Ministries will continue to be apprehensive about plan shortfalls, for which they will be held responsible, and therefore will be more reluctant to forgo detailed control than they would if plans were slack. For the same reason, they will probably want the ability to adjust enterprise annual plans between years and within each year, so that additional output can be extracted from enterprises that are keeping up with their targets and lagging enterprises can thereby be covered. Therefore the stable five-year enterprise plans are likely to continue to prove elusive.

Another source of conflict embedded in the reform is a hostility to any form of private enterprise—a hostility deeply ingrained in the bureaucracy and perhaps quite widespread in the population. The discipline campaign, a policy initiative closely intertwined with the reforms described here as a part of Gorbachev's overall economic strategy, encourages that hostility and thereby hinders moves to activate more legal private initiative.

Altogether, the Gorbachev reorganization package appears to combine streamlining of the traditional hierarchical system with some extension of the legal private and cooperative small-scale sector. From an outsider's perspective, that is quite a reasonable "moderate" strategy.[19] At the same time, it will be a hard strategy to implement, and is to some extent at odds with other elements in current economic policy. The net effect on economic performance in the short or medium term is likely to be small. The improvement that occurred in Soviet economic performance in 1986 can probably be attributed to the discipline campaign, the shake-out of top personnel, the correction of some errors in central resource-allocation policy, and perhaps also some luck with the weather.

The shake-out of senior officials, in particular, has probably had quite an impact on performance. If there is a case in capitalist economies for corporate raiders as stimuli to x-efficiency in industry, there is a case for Gorbachev's kind of shake-up of Soviet economic officials. Corporate raiders, of course, are part of the system in the West, whereas Gorbachev's new-broom effect might be a one-time phenomenon, although it is too soon to determine this with any certainty.

One must refer to politics and history when attempting to explain why gains from organizational change are so problematic in the USSR. Zhores Medvedev argues that the traditional desire by central political authorities to keep political control is still dominant (Medvedev, 1986). Perhaps a difference here between the USSR and both the GDR and Hungary is that Moscow provides the ultimate guarantee of their political status quo.

It may also be important that there is no "reform architect" in the Politburo or Central Committee Secretariat who could play the role for Gorbachev that Reszo Nyers played for Kadar in the early stages of the Hungarian NEM

19. It is close to what Berliner (1983) suggested as a possible "liberal," as distinct from radical, strategy.

reforms. A high official who had a coherent vision of economic reform and economic policy could push for an internally consistent strategy, and perhaps even succeed. It seems, however, that the attitudes of the Soviet political elite exclude people without impeccable party-state apparatus backgrounds from positions of great influence. Perhaps even streetwise academics like Aganbegyan never become full members of the "gang." In Hungary, the reform architect Nyers was a man who had been active as a social democrat before the communist takeover. It is hard to imagine anyone with such an unorthodox background becoming a high official in the USSR, where political "soundness" is narrowly defined. One suspects that top Soviet academics remain on the fringe of the policymaking establishment. If such suspicion is justified, the chances of an effective reform architect emerging at the Politburo or Secretariat level are small.

Finally, the East German economic model may not be in formal terms very remote from the traditional Soviet model, but that does not mean that a Soviet transition to it would be socially painless. An analogy with two Western countries is appropriate in this context. The East German model may be as exportable to the USSR as the West German "economic model," with its more consensual management of labor and income policies, is to the UK. In Britain, nearly two centuries of effortless superiority, inadvertently achieved, have not been good for diligence and social cohesion. Similarly, almost sixty years of being centrally administered, on top of several centuries of being Russian, are not good for discipline. History matters.

Part II

The Architects
of Change

Editors' Introduction

WHO WERE the architects and designers of the change in the Soviet Union that came about in 1985 and then stalled and moved in the opposite direction toward the end of 1990 and in 1991? Mikhail Gorbachev was said to be the champion and evangelist of *perestroyka* but not its architect. And his closest ally, Aleksandr Yakovlev, was not the man at the drafting table, but rather in attendance as the philosopher or theologian of the evolving reformation. One of the first credible answers came in the summer of 1987 from Anders Åslund, at the time a research scholar at the Kennan Institute for Advanced Russian Studies in Washington, D.C., and later director of the Stockholm Institute of Soviet and East European Economics.

Not much was then to be found in the literature and little more had become known to Western students of Soviet affairs exploring the subject with their Soviet colleagues. Professor Åslund's "Gorbachev's Economic Advisors," largely based on extensive personal interviews in Moscow during the course of diplomatic service from 1984 to 1987, traces the activities and environment of Mikhail Gorbachev's intimate advisors through the first quarter of his third year in power.

Academicians Abel G. Aganbegyan, Leonid I. Abalkin, and Tat'yana I. Zaslavskaya, who appear in the following chapters of this volume, are singled out as three of the four members of an informal "economic brain trust," frequently referred to as Gorbachev's "kitchen cabinet." It is they who were the leading architects and designers of the blueprints for *perestroyka*—with Abel Aganbegyan and Leonid Abalkin acting in the role of coordinators and Tat'yana Zaslavskaya and Oleg Bogomolov being responsible for input on social issues and on economic reform in other socialist countries. Åslund leads us through the labyrinth of the country's leading economic institutions, introducing us to Nikolay Petrakov and Stanislav Shatalin—both destined to play a key role in Gorbachev's inner circle some two years later.

Nikolay Petrakov, at the time of Åslund's writing the deputy director of the

71

Central Economic Mathematical Institute (TsEMI) of the Academy of Sciences of the USSR, was, to the best of our knowledge, the first Soviet economist openly to prepare and contribute to a Western journal a highly unorthodox but uncensored paper. In his capacity as chairman of the Interdepartmental Council of Problems of Price Formation of the Academy of Sciences and of the State Committee on Prices, he discusses his blueprint for price reforms in "Prospects for Change in the Systems of Price Formation, Finance, and Credit." Distortions in current price levels and the need to restructure the system had not hitherto been laid bare by the leadership in such professional detail. Petrakov, who not long after became Gorbachev's personal economic advisor, also used the occasion to discuss strategies for change and advance reasonable (at least in 1987) proposals pertaining to the stabilization of prices, circulation of money, and reorganization of banks' structure and credit.

Economists in Gorbachev's entourage gradually began to communicate with unprecedented candor. By the end of 1987, they were reaching out for ideas and, at the least, readily conceding that a fully articulated plan for reforming the system was not in place. The editors of *Soviet Economy* were probably the first American economists to receive an invitation to a joint Soviet-American roundtable conference in Moscow devoted to *perestroyka*.[1] On the agenda was a wide-ranging dialogue and an exchange of views between influential American social scientists committed to a free-market economy and their counterparts in the Soviet Union committed to socialism. Our delegation included Professors Abram Bergson of Harvard University, Gregory Grossman of the University of California at Berkeley, Herbert S. Levine of the University of Pennsylvania, and Jerry Hough of Duke University and the Brookings Institution;[2] their questions, comments, and sharp rejoinders appear in this volume together with the papers by Aganbegyan, Abalkin, and Zaslavskaya.

In the "Basic Directions of *Perestroyka*," Abel Aganbegyan outlines three intertwined precepts molded into the more general concept of *uskoreniye* (acceleration), which was initiated by the CPSU in April 1985 and ratified by its 27th Congress in the beginning of 1986. All are still rooted in the past, even though there is talk that the old system was inappropriate, that a shift to businesslike methods of management is mandatory, and that democratization of the economic environment at the enterprise level would deliver the alleged rewards of *perestroyka* to the deprived populace and consumer. We were confronted with what later was more generally recognized as *perestroyka*'s basic affliction—an addiction to half-measures designed to reconcile socialism with free enterprise.

Somewhat more focused and forthright is Leonid Abalkin's "The New

1. Under the sponsorship of TsEMI, it had at our end the support of the Joint Committee on Soviet Studies of the American Council of Learned Societies and the Social Science Research Council.
2. Only a part of the fascinating discussion is reproduced in this volume. The contributions of other members of our delegation, notably those of Professor Thane Gustafson of Georgetown University, and of Drs. Jan Vanous of PlanEcon, Inc., and Martin N. Baily of the Brookings Institution can be found in Aganbegyan (1987), Zaslavskaya (1987), Panel on Growth (1987), and Reflections on Technology (1987).

Model of Economic Management.'' Here, the architect of *perestroyka*, destined to become one of the most influential government executives in charge of redefining and clarifying *perestroyka*'s objectives, outlined his ''new model'' of economic management. The emphasis is on multiple forms of property ownership as a stimulus to progress. New approaches to private and cooperative activity are seen as a challenge, not a threat, while flexibility in the operation of state enterprises is the imperative for the 1990s.

The last of the three contributions featuring the architects of the reform and change is Tat'yana Zaslavskaya's ''Socioeconomic Aspects of *Perestroyka*.'' More radical than her colleagues, she presented and discussed with us a variety of topics including unemployment, living standards, inequality of income, workers' attitudes, territorial differentiation, the shadow economy, public opinion, adjustments to the anticipated transformation, and democratization of organizational behavior in Soviet society.

The three contributions reflect differences in approach between American and Soviet academics as well as many individual preferences and ways of communicating in a bilingual and potentially contentious atmosphere. As such, they represent a valuable documentary of interaction between both responsible and responsive professionals at a time when the massive rapprochement with America and Americans was yet to emerge.

The sample of contributions by the key architects of change did not appear to be complete without a word from Nikolay P. Shmelev. A pillar of the Academy's Institute of the USA and Canada, renowned journalist and writer, and outspoken proponent of *perestroyka*, he continued to influence the thinking of Gorbachev's economic ''kitchen cabinet'' probably more than any other outsider. That Gorbachev himself was very conscious of Shmelev's radical thinking was evidenced by his sharp polemic with Shmelev in June 1987 (*Izvestiya*, June 26, 1987, p .1). Therefore, disregarding the chronological leap forward, we incorporated ''Rethinking Price Reform'' in this part of the volume.

Shmelev's paper outlines the major components of an ''ideal'' price reform package, before examining its possible difficulties and consequences. But he also tells the reader what he believes is a workable alternative to the official Soviet policy on price reform in the fall of 1988, and supplies a crude timetable for reforms in retail and wholesale prices. His thinking, including the shift in views, is not atypical of the radical Russian intelligentsia—a cultured and educated class with a predisposition to historical determinism, but sometimes given to tinkering with ideas.

CHAPTER 7

Gorbachev's Economic Advisors

Anders Åslund

IT IS difficult to overemphasize the significance of economic reform, quite possibly the most important issue on the Soviet leadership's agenda. General Secretary Mikhail Sergeyevich Gorbachev, without question the most outspoken reformer on the Politburo, enunciated his views in a series of speeches such as the critical pronouncements on June 25, 1987, at the Plenum of the Central Committee (CC) of the CPSU (*Pravda*, June 26, 1987). His orientation largely has been incorporated into a reform program known as "Basic Provisions for Fundamentally Reorganizing Economic Management," which the CC adopted at its June plenum (*Pravda*, June 27, 1987). General Secretary Gorbachev's speeches and the innovative provisions outlined to date reflect a school of economic thought reminiscent of the Hungarian economic reform of 1968.

Both the formal and informal environments of Gorbachev's top-level economic advisors appear to have stabilized after a long period of vacillation. The purpose of this paper is to determine who these major economic advisors are. Their backgrounds and writings indicate the flavor of various ideas that might be presented, although radical and rapid change in the substance and direction of the social sciences in the USSR is the order of the day. Therefore, even recent articles may not give a fully accurate picture of the present position of a particular economist.

Such a state of flux within academic and planning circles requires that I first identify those institutions which have been offering alternative, i.e., competing recommendations to the General Secretary on economic policy, considering in the process any reorganizations or personnel changes at the top of

First published in *Soviet Economy*, 1987, 3. 3, pp. 246–269. The author is greatly indebted to many Soviet economists and officials who were kind enough to share their insights and arrange meetings with knowledgeable interlocutors. He is also grateful to a fairly substantial number of visiting Western scholars as well as diplomats and journalists stationed in Moscow, and lastly but not least to the Kennan Institute's Wilson Center; this paper might not have been written without the aid of a grant as well as research facilities provided by this generous institution. [Eds.]

these bodies. Subsequently, the structure of such advisory bodies (commissions) and their work will be analyzed, inasmuch as they have been transformed repeatedly since Secretary Gorbachev's ascension to power in March 1985. These changes give us a measure of Gorbachev's intentions, as well as a feeling for the relationship between major economic institutes and the dynamics of Soviet economic policy.

Finally, I will attempt to identify Gorbachev's senior economic advisors and economists who appear to have been particularly influential in various aspects of Soviet reform legislation, although it is beyond the scope of this paper to discuss the ideas of many individual economists.[1]

This paper is essentially based on personal interviews and discussions, during the course of the last three years, with as many as a hundred Soviet social scientists (primarily economists) affiliated with 22 Soviet institutes. Information based on oral communications is admittedly somewhat problematic, imprecise in terms of numbers and dates, and for the most part indirect at best. The distinction between substantive facts and superficial, possibly biased, anecdotal evidence is often threadbare. And yet, it did not seem foolhardy to draw on such potentially productive sources of plausible knowledge. The significantly large number of repetitive interviews has made it possible not only to verify the credibility of each source but also to check a sizable range of facts more than once or twice.

The paper's focus is a topic with few, if any, identifiable secrets. Soviet intellectuals talk comparatively freely about the reformers. Most of my interlocutors have been scholars accustomed to sensitive discussions with their Western counterparts in a manner that is not excessively secretive. Characteristically, precise statements or answers to questions were not a rarity. Moreover, I have had many opportunities to compare my information of Soviet origin with that gathered by other Western scholars, diplomats, or journalists who have either interviewed the same individuals or participated in relevant discussions. Because most of my talks and dialogues were off the record, I feel more comfortable about relinquishing the freedom to identify any of my sources unless parallel statements were made in public.

LEADING ECONOMIC INSTITUTIONS
AND ECONOMISTS

Decisions on major economic issues such as the ongoing reform are worked out in three different institutions: (1) Central Committee of the CPSU, (2) Gosplan (the State Planning Committee), and (3) Council of Ministers. Each

---

1. Only passing reference will be made to the positions of these individual economists. Readers interested in details or even minutiae reflecting the leanings and thoughts of these economists may find it useful to consult the references of Soviet origin listed in my original article *Soviet Economy* on pp. 266–269. Apart from these references, I relied more or less frequently on relevant material published by Radio Liberty.

of these organs has affiliated research institutes appropriately equipped to offer economic advice. However, the most prestigious source of such advice is the Academy of Sciences of the USSR. Because the Academy attracts the most qualified specialists and researchers from the university system, all other Soviet institutions of higher learning are of relatively minor significance.

Apparatus of the Party Central Committee

Inasmuch as Gorbachev's principial source of power rests within the CC Secretariat, it is reasonable to initially focus some attention on its economic branch. The executive charged with economic oversight, i.e., CC Secretary for Economic Affairs, has changed repeatedly since Mikhail Gorbachev assumed the reigns of power. In March 1985, Nikolay Ryzhkov occupied this post, simultaneously heading the Economic Department of the CC. However, shortly after his appointment as Prime Minister on September 27, 1985, Ryzhkov had to relinquish the CC Secretaryship at the CC Plenum on October 15, 1985. The former First Deputy Chief of the Economic Department, Boris Gostev, assumed the responsibilities of that top position in August, but stayed only four months through December 14, 1985, when his appointment to head the Ministry of Finance appears to have materialized (*Izvestiya*, December 15, 1985).[2]

The Economic Department functioned without both a Chief and First Deputy Chief for months—a trying period which must have weakened its infuence. In addition, Ryzhkov earlier had taken some aides with him to the chancellery of the Council of Ministers. Finally, it became known in the summer of 1986 that Vladimir Mozhin, previously Chairman of the Council of Productive Forces (a not very prominent institute subordinate to Gosplan) had been appointed First Deputy Chief of the Economic Department. Mozhin is a rather colorless economist, who appears to evade controversial issues and bypass opportunities to disclose his views in publications.

After Ryzhkov's departure from the Secretariat, Lev Zaykov, who became CC Secretary on July 1, 1985, and Politburo member on March 6, 1986, supervised economic reform issues in addition to discharging his primary responsibility for the military-industrial complex. However, Zaykov's presence might have been intended as an interim solution, for he made no impact while serving as the department's *de facto* caretaker Chief. When Nikolay Slyun'kov was elected CC Secretary on January 28, 1987, he took over the responsibilities for reform in the Secretariat from Zaykov and became acting chief of the Economic Department. Slyun'kov's speech at the CC conference on June 8 and 9, 1987, demonstrated considerable involvement in economic reform issues (*Pravda*, June 13, 1987).

2. Here and henceforth I refer to the Moscow evening edition, which, as a rule, is dated one day earlier than other editions.

It is somewhat of a paradox that at the time when the party was gearing up for economic reform, the economic skills and competence of the CC apparatus had been depleted. It was almost as though the CC apparatus was intentionally not equipped to handle economic reform. The main explanation offered by Soviet reformers is that Gorbachev could not secure the appointment of people measuring up to his expectations to the CC apparatus and therefore preferred to emasculate it. At the same time, Prime Minister Ryzhkov wanted to retain ministerial jurisdiction over these issues and Gosplan, in turn, saw them as its responsibility. Meanwhile, the CC Economic Department seems to have been suspended in a vacuum devoid of influence and lacking muscle. Thus far, it has played a remarkably insignificant role in the economic reform process, though it has been reactivated under Slyun'kov.

Certainly Zaykov's failure to contribute to the progress of economic reform, and the tapering of his responsibilities and authority since January 1987 might tell us something about his political standing. One of the most recently elected Politburo members, CC Secretary Aleksandr Yakovlev, who has risen swiftly, became a very powerful politician with the apparent advantage of closeness to Secretary Gorbachev. Though a historian by training, he is a Corresponding Member of the Economic Department of the Academy of Sciences as well. Appearing to be Gorbachev's chief ideologue, Yakovlev will likely influence much work on economic reform, and may assist the Secretary in delegation of authority and selection of economists for major assignments. However, economic reform is not within his formal range of immediate responsibilities.

The Academy of Sciences

By tradition, the bulk of relatively independent scholarly advice in the Soviet Union is forthcoming from the Academy of Sciences. It was therefore hardly surprising that Gorbachev proceeded to rely on this body. The economists best qualified to address issues of economic reform are concentrated essentially in four institutes constituted by the Academy of Sciences. The three located in Moscow are: (1) Central Economics Mathematical Institute (TsEMI), (2) Institute of Economics (IE), and (3) Economics of the World Socialist System Institute (IEMSS), sometimes referred to as Bogomolov's institute, identifying its long-time director. The progressive Institute of Economics and Organization of Industrial Production (IEiOPP) is headquartered in Novosibirsk.

Soviet institutes tend to be capacious, hierarchical bodies. TsEMI, the largest in size, had recently as many as 1,200 employees on its payroll; the smallest, IEMSS about 350; whereas the IE employed approximately 500 people. An institute is governed by its director, as a rule, an Academician or Corresponding Member of the Academy of Sciences who shapes it much to his own liking and imposes his own school of thought. Thus, while there are considerable differences between the institutes, overt disagreements within each are limited.

As a discipline, Soviet economics is in low esteem (Nove, 1987, p. 452), suffering severely from ideological rigidity. Soon after Brezhnev's death, the party began to voice complaints about the lack of creativity and meaningful progress in Soviet economic science. Since the foremost Soviet economists are affiliated with the Academy of Sciences of the USSR, the Academy was directly concerned.

TsEMI. In the 1970s, TsEMI was engaged in a bitter dispute over politics, methodology, and personalities with its orthodox rival the Institute of Economics. The colorful director of TsEMI, Academician Nikolay Fedorenko (born in 1917), was at the time also Academic Secretary of the Economic Department of the Academy of Sciences, i.e., the *de facto* manager of Soviet economic research. TsEMI was reformist and inclined to attract skilled mathematical economists, although a large portion of its work was devoted to elaboration of a "System of the Optimally Functioning Socialist Economy." After the publication of TsEMI's 10th collective volume on that topic, *Pravda's* reviewer commented that the results "are still insufficiently developed for implementation in the national economy" (*Pravda*, February 6, 1986)—a judgment supported by a knowledgeable Western scholar who investigated TsEMI's approach (Sutela, 1984). TsEMI had thus failed, both in theoretical and practical terms, at its main research task.

The Institute's director, Fedorenko, was by Soviet standards a radical reformer with a record of extended skirmishes with orthodox communist economists, Gosplan, and the State Committee on Prices (e.g., Fedorenko, 1984). However, he failed both to produce a blueprint for the improvement of the economy and to inspire Soviet economists to endorse his approach. Among his disadvantages was lack of support from Academician Abel Aganbegyan, whose influence was rapidly increasing. It was therefore not difficult to predict that Fedorenko was destined to fall, even though doubts about his skills as an economist appeared to be only marginally significant (Katsenelinboigen, 1979, pp. 84, 134, 163–164; Hanson, 1985a). At the ideological CC Plenum in June 1983, Secretary Konstantin Chernenko launched a scathing attack against TsEMI, calling attention to its failure to demonstrate tangible results of productive research on current economic problems (Chernenko, 1984, p. 344). Fedorenko's demise appears to have been directly related to Gorbachev's ascent to power. Four days after Mikhail Gorbachev was named General Secretary, Fedorenko was dismissed from his prestigious post of Academic Secretary of the Academy's Economic Department (*Izvestiya*, March 16, 1985). Two months thereafter, he was compelled to relinquish the directorship of TsEMI.

In the summer of 1985, TsEMI spun off a new entity named the Institute for Economic Forecasting of Scientific and Technical Progress. TsEMI's new Director, Corresponding Member of the Academy of Sciences Valeriy Makarov (born in 1937), is a theoretically oriented mathematical economist, a disciple of Novosibirsk's Nobel Prize Laureate Leonid Kantorovich, and a reformist. Highly respected, but not driven to focus on political issues, he appears to have delegated the role of TsEMI's leading spokesman on reform issues to

Fedorenko's protégé, Nikolay Petrakov (born in 1937), also a Corresponding Member of the Academy of Sciences.

The Directorship of the new forecasting institute was entrusted to Academician Aleksandr Anchishkin (born in 1933), another reform-oriented protégé of Fedorenko. The institute's structure rested on a foundation of several departments detached from TsEMI, which he had organized in the past. Reinforced by the reputable economist and reformer Corresponding Member of the Academy of Sciences Stanislav Shatalin (born in 1934) who became his deputy, Anchishkin was gaining influence until his premature death in June 1987, on the eve of the important CC Plenum. All told, the restructuring of TsEMI, far from serving as a move against the talented reform-minded scholars in charge of the parent institute and of its new affiliate, may have actually strengthened their case.

IE. The orthodox Institute of Economics was even more severely criticized than TsEMI for "serious shortcomings" and "creatively fruitless" work in a CC resolution promulgated in February 1984 (*Pravda*, February 24, 1984). It was dominated by old political economists whose poor grasp and somewhat reluctant approach to modern economics was quite apparent. In the spring of 1986, its not overly prominent director, Corresponding Member of the Academy of Sciences Yevgeniy Kapustin, resigned—seemingly voluntarily, but likely under pressure. He was replaced by Corresponding Member of the Academy of Sciences Leonid Abalkin (born in 1931), one of Gorbachev's four intimate economic advisors.

In the process, the old guard of senior economists affiliated with the Institute of Economics lost the remnants of former influence to shape politically oriented economic issues. Having played an important and progressive role durng the period of Kosygin's reforms in the 1960s, the group had turned around, leaning toward and solidifying conservative positions. Its most notable member is Academician Tigran Khachaturov (born in 1906), who continues to hold the honorific position of Editor-in-Chief of *Voprosy Ekonomiki* (the most prestigious Soviet journal in the field), which still toes a rather orthodox communist line.[3]

The Institute's new director proceeded to reorganize its departments, redirecting the emphasis toward the goal of creating a new economic mechanism. Senior conservatives, such as Vasiliy Ivanchenko (formerly IE's Deputy Director) and Anatoliy Deryabin (former Department Chief) were demoted by Abalkin, and the main stronghold of conservative Soviet economists was demolished without much delay. Though many low-ranking conservatives remain in minor positions, the IE's reorganization was both thorough and complete.

The IEiOPP and IEMSS. The Institute of Economics and Organization of Industrial Production (IEiOPP) in Novosibirsk and the Institute of the Eco-

---

3. Of the 20 members of the editorial board of *Vorosy Ekonomiki* named in issue No. 7, 1987, only three are identified reformists (L. I. Abalkin, R. N. Yevstigneyev, and N. Ya. Petrakov). Except for the reform-oriented trio, the board may be viewed as a list of leading orthodox communist politicial economists.

nomics of the World Socialist System (IEMSS) in Moscow are important research centers that managed to survive the purge. Even before March 1985, rumors had it that IEiOPP, then directed by Academician Abel Aganbegyan, would flourish after Gorbachev's ascension to power.

During the period of Academician Aganbegyan's stewardship from 1966 to 1985, the IEiOPP played a role in the formulation of economic policies, particularly those pertaining to the economic development of Siberia. Its reputation was enhanced by such prominent members as Tat'yana Zaslavskaya (born in 1927), as well as publications such as the prestigious *Ekonomika i organizatsiya promyshlennogo proizvodstva (EKO)*.

In the summer of 1985, Aganbegyan moved to Moscow, leaving the Institute's directorship in the hands of Corresponding Member of the Academy of Sciences Aleksandr Granberg.

The IEMSS specializes in the economies of other socialist countries. Headed by Oleg Bogomolov (born in 1927) the institute has a good track record as employer of capable, knowledgeable economists who publish little, implying that they work primarily for the CC apparatus. Two of its political economists (Anatoliy Butenko and Yevgeniy Ambartsumov) were reprimanded by the party for heretical views in 1984, but have since suffered no further mishaps (Ambartsumov, 1984; Butenko, 1982; Teague, 1984a, 1984b).

The Consequences of Reorganization. The demotions of TsEMI's Fedorenko and IE's Kapustin tend to suggest that the new party leadership's involvement in personnel matters of the Academy of Sciences is rather considerable.[4]

Thus, some of the most important positions in the academic economic establishment were vacant due to a shake-up that virtually became a clean sweep. The demoted directors Fedorenko and Kapustin were allowed to stay in their institutes as chiefs of departments and Fedorenko even continues to participate in the debate. But the old guard of economists appears largely to have lost its measure of influence and control of significant events, even though it is difficult to detect any political pattern that promoted the dismissals. The primary focus of the new political leadership seems to have been the need to create a new academic environment in economics.

In the fall of 1986, the economic institutes of the Academy of Sciences had been sufficiently reorganized to satisfy General Secretary Gorbachev's objectives. A new team of leading economists had been installed—all in their fifties, reformers, and better qualified than their predecessors. Their undisputed leaders are Aganbegyan and Abalkin. A persistent argument that seems to haunt them

---

4. Such involvement was highlighted during the election of a new president of the Academy of Sciences in October 1986. Ligachev made a long speech at the general meeting of the Academy, declaring that "the Politburo of the CC recommended" the election of Academcian Guriy Marchuk as President of the Academy of Sciences of the USSR (*Pravda*, October 17, 1986). It was widely rumored that the Academy's former president, the independent-minded Academician A. P. Aleksandrov did not retire (due to advanced age) but was forced to resign. Academician Marchuk, who knew Politburo member Ligachev from Novosibirsk, was Ligachev's candidate, while the runner-up, one of the Academy's Vice-Presidents, Academician Konstantin Frolov, was reportedly the candidate preferred and supported by Ryzhkov.

maintains that they can somehow never agree on an operative reform program. The Economic Department of the Academy of Sciences is attempting to work out a framework of widely acceptable guidelines for the economic reform. Such guidelines reportedly were completed by April 1987, and at the end of June they were adopted by the CC. The leading academic economists succeeded in winning approval for their guidelines due to a combination of unity, competence, and support from Gorbachev.

The Academy of Social Sciences

In the early days of Gorbachev's rule, there was some speculation that the General Secretary would turn to the Academy of Social Sciences of the CC for economic advice. It was related to the Academy's involvement in party affairs as the major institution of higher learning designated to familiarize party officials or train them in economics. Gorbachev's presumed interest in the Academy was to have been based on his consistent record of working within the party apparatus and scant contacts outside the party. Nonetheless, the Academy of Social Sciences has traditionally been identified with orthodox Marxism-Leninism, and thus probably not even adequately prepared to analyze the reform to appeal to Gorbachev. Accordingly, the task of designing a blueprint for the restructuring of the economy was passed on to other academic organizations.

And yet, the Academy employed a number of competent economists with an inclination to favor reform. The Academy's Rector from 1978 to 1983, Corresponding Member of the Academy of Sciences Vadim Medvedev, left his position to head the CC Science and Educational Institutions Department. He is a reform-oriented economist with good credentials and one of the Soviet Union's foremost experts on the economic reform of 1965. However, since March 1986 Medvedev has been CC Secretary and Chief of Liaison with Communist and Workers' Parties of Socialist Countries—a position that appears to have placed him outside of the inner circle of economists discussing the reform. Other promising economists at the Academy included Leonid Abalkin who moved to the IE, and Professors Rem Belousov and Dmitriy Valovoy. Rem Belousov, seemingly a promising reformer (Belousov, 1985), has remained in relative obscurity. Valovoy, on the other hand, turned to journalism and became one of *Pravda's* most vocal and prolific proponents of conservatism in the economic debate (e.g., *Pravda*, June 7, 1985, and July 7, 1986).

Gosplan and Its Economic Research Institute

When Gorbachev became General Secretary, former Chairman Nikolay Baybakov was still in charge of Gosplan. He ruled Gosplan for about 20 years and saw no need for change. On October 14, 1985, he was retired and replaced by Nikolay Talyzin. Baybakov's first deputy for reform issues was Lev Voronin, promoted to the chairmanship of the State Committee for Material and Technical Supply (Gossnab) on November 15, 1985. In the summer of 1985, Academician Dzhermen Gvishiani, Director of the Institute for Systems Analysis and son-in-law of former Premier Alexei Kosygin, became one of Talyzin's deputies. He retained, however, the directorship of his Institute subordinated to both the Academy of Sciences and Gosplan. The Institute thus appeared to be primed to become the center of work on economic reform,[5] and Gvishiani groomed to become one of the reform's major architects. However, in September 1986, in a fall as surprising as his rise, Gvishiani was suddenly removed from his position as Deputy Chairman of Gosplan (*Sobraniye postanovleniy Pezidiyuma Verkhovnogo Soveta SSSR*, No. 33, 1986; Rahr, 1986). Plausible rumors attributed his dismissal by Talyzin to Gvishiani's incompetence and failure to produce plans for the economy's reform. No dispute of substance followed this brief interlude.[6]

After Gvishiani's departure, Stepan Sitaryan (born in 1930), also a Corresponding Member of the Academy of Sciences, inherited the mantle of Gosplan's senior official in charge of economic reform. Sitaryan, a Deputy Chairman of Gosplan since 1983, has been promoted to the position of First Deputy Chairman. Forsaking the good reputation among reformers earned in the past, Sitaryan proceeded to develop his reputation as persuasive spokesman for the vested interests of Gosplan. His orientation may be described as moderately conservative or even reformist, promoting an extended role for the market, though favoring at the same time efforts to preserve material balancing (Sitaryan, 1987).

Leonard Vid, another new Deputy Chairman of Gosplan appointed in 1986, is similarly involved in general issues pertaining to the reform. No changes have occurred, however, at the lower levels of the Gosplan hierarchy. Gosplan's Department for the Improvement of Planning and Economic Stimulation has been headed by Dmitriy Ukrainskiy since the early 1980s. Ukrainskiy's deputy, at least since early 1985, has been Oleg Yun' whose writings suggest a position similar to that of Sitaryan (Yun', 1985, 1986). Gosplan's economic journal, *Planovoye khozyaystvo*, continues to favor solidly conservative views.

The most highly regarded of Gosplan's economic research units is its Economics Scientific Research Institute (NIEI). Until the spring of 1987, it was headed by Professor Vadim Kirichenko (born in 1931). The policy position of this institute may be defined as moderately conservative. After Kirichenko's promotion to a higher position at the Council of Ministers, he was succeeded by one of his two deputies, Vladimir Kostakov, whose writings on prospective problems related to unemployment attracted Western attention. Kostakov's appointment was prompted by pressure exerted by NIEI's employees who were opposed to the candidate supported by Gosplan.

5. Its Deputy Director was at the time Stanislav Shatalin.
6. Gvishiani's rumored inability to resist indulgence in small talk was evident during the course of his appearance on Soviet television on September 26, 1986 (*Summary of World Broadcasts*, SU/8379/C/1-4).

The Council of Ministers and the Academy of the National Economy

When Ryzhkov moved from the Central Committee Secretariat to the Council of Ministers in the fall of 1986, he recruited some people (notably Dr. Melnikov) from the CC Economic Department and placed them in his new domain. A former director of the VAZ automotive plant in Togliatti (Katsura) was appointed as his *chef du cabinet*. In the spring of 1987, Ryzhkov selected and appointed the aforementioned Professor Vadim Kirichenko of Gosplan's Economic Institute to head the Economic Department of the Council of Ministers. It is assumed that Kirichenko is in fact Ryzhkov's main economic counsellor. He managed to stake out a distinct position in the economic debate, opposing superministries and believing that material balancing can be rationalized by reducing the number of balances and intensifying the use of computerized optimization algorithms. Kirichenko's moderately conservative views are not in the mainstream (Kirichenko, 1986).

The principal economic research institution within the Council of Ministers is the Academy of the National Economy, which trains deserving candidates for senior jobs at enterprises and ministries. It seems to have gained strength, and even influence as a source of the Prime Minister's economic advice. Yevgeniy Smirnitskiy was appointed the Academy's Rector soon after Ryzhkov had become the head of the Council of Ministers. Smirnitskiy, who keeps a low public profile, is known as an author of bland and uninspiring general handbooks (Smirnitskiy, 1982, 1986). However, he seems to be prominent within the administration. The Academy's most visible economist is Pavel Bunich, a Corresponding Member of the Academy of Sciences with considerable popular appeal attributed to forceful television appearances in support of the reform and hard-hitting newspaper articles as well (e.g., Bunich, 1986). At the same time, he is also a productive editor of books devoted to studies of the economic mechanism (Bunich, 1984).

Thus, Ryzhkov managed to gather economic advisors from Gosplan and enterprises or organizations attached to the Council of Ministers, though not from the Academy of Sciences. His moderately reformist advisors appear to combine academic training with practical experience.

COMMISSIONS FOR ECONOMIC REFORM

Rather typically, Soviet procedures for preparing major laws or proposals require that a commission or working group be formed to accommodate representatives of various agencies with possibly conflicting interests and independent experts as well. Several commissions have been established to deal with general issues pertaining to the economic reform, and three already existed when Mikhail S. Gorbachev was elected CPSU General Secretary on March 11, 1985.

The first such commission was formed late in 1982, in response to a decree by the 26th Party Congress (1981) calling for the study of attempts to improve the economic mechanism in other socialist countries. It was chaired by then Chairman of Gosplan, Deputy Prime Minister Nikolay Baybakov. Among the other members of that commission were the Prime Minister's deputies Guriy Marchuk (Chairman of the State Committee for Science and Technology) and Nikolay Talyzin (permanent representative to CMEA). The commission's secretary was Academician Oleg Bogomolov, whose institute (IEMSS) served as its secretariat. It appears to have functioned as a superior forum for discussion, examining reports prepared by Bogomolov's aides and meeting once a month until August 1985. In the wake of Baybakov's dismissal as Gosplan's Chairman on October 14, 1985, it was the first commission dissolved *de facto*. No decisions of consequence appear to have emerged from this discussion club, and it became irrelevant when ideas about economic reform began to materialize.

The second commission was more of an earnest undertaking. Called "The Commission for the General Guidance of the Experiment" (*Ekon. gaz.*, No. 1, 1985) and headed by Lev Voronin, First Deputy Chairman of Gosplan, it was to monitor the implementation of the "large-scale economic experiment" in five industrial ministries initiated under Andropov and introduced on January 1, 1984.[7] It consisted of a score of senior economists and convened twice a month. Its work was quite substantive, with a record of new experiments and modifications, both proposed and evaluated. Voronin himself published several articles devoted to that large-scale economic experiment (Voronin, 1984, 1985). However, on November 15, 1985, he advanced to the chairmanship of the State Committee for Material and Technical Supply, and the commission apparently was left hanging in the air.

At the Politburo level, a third commission had been established to supervise the Voronin commission. It was chaired by Prime Minister Nikolay Tikhonov[8] and managed by its secretary, First Deputy Chief of the Economic Department of the CC, Boris Gostev. Little else is known about this commission, which presumably met rarely, inasmuch as its concerns were too minor to command the attention of Politburo members. When Tikhonov was relieved of his duties as Prime Minister on September 27, 1985, this commission most likely ceased to exist.

Thus, in the fall of 1985, the aforementioned three general commissions designed to supervise the economic reform were more or less dissolved, primarly due to changes in personnel. However, instead of making a fresh start, the new leadership opted for a transitional period of adjustment. It was then, prior to Baybakov's dismissal as Gosplan's chairman, that Gvishiani established a working group to design a blueprint for economic reform (based on work at

7. The so-called Five-Ministry Experiment (see Gorbachev's, 1987, pp. 48–49). [Eds.]
8. It was rumored at the time, apparently without justification, that this commission was headed by Gorbachev.

his institute) and present it to the Party Congress in February and March, 1986.

At the same time during the ᴊurse of this transitional period, there was also a commission on the Sumy experiment,[9] established by Ryzhkov not long after he became Prime Minister. It included Pavel Bunich of the Academy of the National Economy, Oleg Yun' of Gosplan, Vladmir Lukyanenko of the Sumy plant (the plant's director and also a Minister appointed in the beginning of 1986), the plant's economic director Dr. Moskalenko, and Dr. Melnikov representing Ryzhkov's staff. At the time, this group appeared to comprise a typical assembly of up-and-coming Soviet reform economists. They may have reached their peak, however, in 1986, since this particular commission has most likely never been mentioned in print and might have been dissolved.

At the end of 1985, a formal structure to develop a blueprint for an economic reform has been put in place by the Council of Ministers. Named the "Commission for the Improvement of Management, Planning, and the Economic Mechanism,"[10] it was constituted to work out and implement measures to modify the management system (*Izvestiya*, January 22, 1986). Its Chairman, Gosplan's Nikolay Talyzin, participated less actively than his First Deputy, Stepan Sitaryan (Gosplan's spokesman on reform issues). The members are essentially functionaries who head economic organs within the Council of Ministers, including the State Committee for Material and Technical Supply, the State Committee on Prices, the Ministry of Finance, the Gosbank, the State Committee for Science and Technology, the State Committee for Labor and Social Problems, and also a few leading economists. The commission has met fairly regularly about once a month (officially 11 times in 1986). The brief bulletin published after each meeting (*Ekon. gaz.*, Nos. 8, 11, 12, 13, 18, 26, 32, 36, 43, 47, 52, 1986), tends to reinforce the impression that it is influential.

The aforementioned commission established a "scientific section" with roughly 15 members—more or less the same group as that which comprised the Voronin commission. At the outset, Gvishiani's empire embraced that section, which he headed prior to his dismissal as Deputy Chairman of Gosplan. Academician Aganbegyan subsequently took over the duties, and later deputized Abalkin to head the scientific section, which presently includes (or included) such prominent economists (primarily institute directors) as Oleg Bogomolov, Valeriy Makarov, Aleksandr Granberg, Aleksandr Anchishkin (until his death), Tat'yana Zaslavskaya, Nikolay Petrakov, Stanislav Shatalin, and Professors Gavriil Popov and Ruben Yevstigneyev of the IEMSS.[11] It

9. The well-known experiment in self-financing which involved the Frunze Engineering Association in the Ukrainian town of Sumy commenced in the beginning of 1985. Soon thereafter, a similar experiment started at the gigantic VAZ automotive works in Toglatti. The experiments were perceived as the second step on the road towards economic reform after the large-scale economic experiment in industry launched by Andropov.

10. Also known as the Talyzin Commission, after its chair. [Eds.]

11. Yevstigneyev specializes in the analysis of economic systems of other communist countries (Yevstigneyev and Senchagov, 1987).

seems to rely on the expertise of other economists on an *ad hoc* basis, i.e., depending on the particular topic under discussion.

A significant number of specialized subcommittees and working groups, reportedly as many as 26 under the section's auspices, develop reform-oriented proposals which are received and passed on to the Talyzin Commission. The Commission then sends these proposals to various government organizations and solicits their counterproposals. Thus, reform-oriented economists from the Academy of Sciences who draft the original proposals have to confront the advocates of the central government represented by the Talyzin Commission.[12] Nonetheless, a coordinated structure for work on economic reform is now in place, while the role of alternative structures is no longer significant.[13]

ECONOMIC ADVICE TO GORBACHEV

Personal Advisors

The General Secretary is traditionally assisted by 5 or 6 personal aides to handle issues of paramount significance. Thus far, Gorbachev has not appointed an economist to a position that would establish him as the Secretary's senior aide. And he is not known to have relied on intimate advice from a functionary in the CC apparatus. However, the General Secretary appears to have gathered a group that is referred to as Gorbachev's informal "kitchen cabinet." During the crucial CC Plenum on June 25 and 26, 1987, Gorbachev was assisted by a group of four senior social scientists: Abel Aganbegyan, Leonid Abalkin, Oleg Bogomolov and Tat'yana Zaslavskaya. The foursome, regarded as his most intimate group of economic advisors, frequently joins the Secretary when he convenes informal meetings to discuss economic affairs.[14]

Academician Aganbegyan. Born in 1932, and director of the IEiOPP since 1966, Academician Abel Gezevich Aganbegyan was involved in efforts to analyze the economic potential of Siberia, and served as editor of *EKO* which gained prestige as the Soviet Union's most popular periodical devoted to economics. With its editorial board representing an almost exclusive group of reform-oriented economists, it functioned in essence as a herald of loyal opposition. Aganbegyan established his position in popular articles that were reformist but not overly ostentatious. In fact, they were even not too critical of the system (*Trud*, November 17, 1981; August 28 and 29, 1984). Typically, Aganbegyan critized the branch ministries, but not the Gosplan, which some

12. The Talyzin Commission became the apex of all reform legislation.
13. There are exceptions such as the State Acceptance Committees for Quality Control, also known as Gospriyemka (1987, pp. 34–37), launched with considerable bravado at the beginning of 1987. They appear to have been designed almost entirely by the State Committee for Standards (Gosstandart SSSR).
14. Our evidence that the foursome functions as an informal economic "brain trust" is fairly solid. Aleksandr Anchishkin was a fifth member of this group prior to his death. Valeriy Makarov of TsEMI is not likely to be one of the frequent participants, even though he directs the Soviet Union's largest economic institute.

economists appeared to view as more of a pragmatic than thorough approach (Katsenelinboigen, 1979, pp. 84–85, 134).

Aganbegyan and Ligachev probably met in 1961 when both resided in Novosibirsk—the former a scholar, and the latter a party official in that Siberian metropolis. Apparently, the academician met Gorbachev only in 1979. Still, there was much evidence to warrant the wide and persistant expectations that Aganbegyan would become Gorbachev's chief economic advisor. His prominence soon became obvious, and it was rumored that Aganbegyan was Gorbachev's main speechwriter who prepared the Secretary's pronouncements on economics. A comparison of Gorbachev's important speech on June 11, 1985, at the CC conference on scientific-technical progress (*Pravda*, June 12, 1985) with Aganbegyan's article in the August 1985 issue of *EKO*, reveals similarities that justify assumptions that Aganbegyan's paper constituted a draft of Gorbachev's speech (Aganbegyan, 1985a).[15] In any event, the source of Gorbachev's inspiration was obvious. Aganbegyan's political preeminence among Soviet economists was in evidence at the CC conference in June 1985, when he was the sole economist with an academic background among the speakers (*Pravda*, June 13, 1985).

While managing the affairs of his institute in Novosibirsk, the academician had no fewer than 42 additional assignments, primarily related to participation in numerous commissions. After his transfer to Moscow in the summer of 1985, Aganbegyan appears to have been somewhat less active, taking his time to establish an institutional base. Rumors abounded about important positions for which he was being considered. Initially, Academician Aganbegyan identified himself as the chair of a small and obscure Commission for the Study of Productive Forces within the Academy of Sciences (Aganbegyan, 1985b), and he was one of the four alternating Deputy Academician Secretaries of the Academy's Economics Department.[16]

In the summer of 1986, Aganbegyan took over the post of Academic Secretary on a permanent basis, though the final election occurred on March 12, 1987—two years after Fedorenko's dismissal from the job (*Pravda*, March 13, 1987). Since his ascension to political prominence in early 1985, Aganbegyan has been very cautious, preferring to deemphasize his own views on what needs to be accomplished, and to follow Gorbachev's line very closely. However, the academician has become more outspoken in his view on the sorry state of Soviet economic affairs (notably, *Ogonek*, Nos. 29 and 30, 1987).

Corresponding Member of the Academy of Sciences Abalkin. When the 56-year old Leonid Ivanovich Abalkin replaced Yevgeniy Kapustin as Director of the Institute of Economics, his transfer in the late spring of 1986 from the Academy of Social Sciences came as no surprise. Abalkin is highly regarded in a number of influential circles, and viewed as one of the most prolific writers and contributors to Soviet economic serials. Many of his papers are devoted

15. It is a common practice in the Soviet Union for speechwriters to publish drafts in their own names.
16. The others were Academicians Aleksandr Anchishkin, Georgiy Arbatov, and Oleg Bogomolov.

to fairly uncomplicated aspects of political economy, such as explaining the reasons why the Stalinist economic model is no longer viable (Abalkin, 1986a, 1986b; Abalkin and Tsakunov, 1986). Nonetheless, he is respected as a competent economist and technician. Although Abalkin is cautious in his writings, which evidence a tendency to evade polemics, his reputation among Soviet reformers is reportedly somewhat higher than Aganbegyan's

This reputation is not apparent when one examines his publications, for Abalkin, unlike Aganbegyan, has prudently avoided setting limits that indicate how far he might be willing to proceed in the reformist direction. In addition, he is a trained party worker and skilled wordsmith with experience in drafting protocols and documents. Partly due to outstanding personal connections within the party, Abalkin seems to be very well qualified to coordinate all work on economic reform. His suitability for such a prospective role is reinforced by observations that Abalkin is more inclined to seek a consensus than fight to advance his own ideas.

Abalkin supervised the editing of the Law on the State Enterprise. In this applied document, however, the influence of opponents representing the government apparatus was strong enough to secure a predictable outcome of half-measures and inconsistencies critized by Aganbegyan at a press conference on June 26, 1987.

Academician Bogomolov. The 60-year-old Oleg Timofeyevich Bogomolov and his Institute of the Economics of the World Socialist System are at the forefront of Soviet research and analysis of the economies of other socialist countries. This knowledge is appropriately useful in the design of the Soviet Union's reform. Bogomolov may owe his career to the fortunate happenstance that he worked under Andropov in the CC Department for Liaison with Communist and Worker's Parties of Socialist Countries in the mid-1960s. During Chernenko's brief rule, not a single one of his papers appeared in print.

Although Bogomolov supports his subordinates at the Institute when necessary, he nonetheless prefers to be cautious in public statements. In recent months, he argued that the experience of economic reform in other communist countries "shows that rapid and most direct effect on the population" is achieved by reforming "agriculture, trade, the light and food-processing industries, and housing construction" (*Pravda*, June 13, 1987).

Academician Zaslavskaya. To a Western audience, the 60-year-old Academician Tat'yana Ivanovna Zaslavskaya of the IEiOPP is probably (together with Aganbegyan) the best-known Soviet social scientist, primarily due to her critical 1983 "Novosibirsk Report" on the state of the Soviet economy leaked to the West by Dusko Doder (*Washington Post*, August 3, 1983). One of the founders of Soviet sociology, she disappeared from print for some time, apparently in disgrace, after the report had been leaked (even though somewhat similar information may have appeared in her own journal *Problemy sotsiologii*). Zaslavskaya surfaced soon after Gorbachev had become General Secretary (*Izvestiya*, May 31, 1985). Today the "Novosibirsk report" represents the mainstream of the debate, and has greatly contributed to Zaslavskaya's reputation. Her frank comments and concrete proposals on social issues (Zaslavskaya, 1986a) continue to attract attention. As an economic sociologist, she is preoccupied with social welfare, and likely is in a position to influence most social issues in the foreseeable future.

Division of Labor and Other Support. There is an obvious division of labor within Gorbachev's group of intimate advisors. Aganbegyan and Abalkin are the coordinators and moderators, while Zaslavskaya specializes in social issues. Bogomolov, who appears to have concentrated on an odd combination of issues such as reform of foreign trade, agriculture and political economy, contributes insights relating to economic reform in other communist countries.

The Secretary's four intimate advisors have close ties with the leading designers of reform proposals who chair the specialized subcommittees of the Talyzin Commission's scientific section. It is not too difficult to deduce who influences thinking in a particular field. Usually, one institute or two is in charge of preliminary work, and it is frequently known which takes the lead to analyze an issue and who directs the work[17]

Gorbachev's economic advisors are essentially Moscovites,[18] though some come from Novosibirsk. Leningrad is still dominated by conservative economists, and the animosity between the new leaders and Politburo member Shcherbitskiy may explain the absence of Ukrainian economists. Estonia, where economists such as Rein Otsason (Director of the Economics Institute of the Estonian Academy of Sciences) and Yu. Sillaste have influenced the design of novel economic experiments in the service sector, is worthy of mention.[19]

Specialized Advice

Specialized advice relating to various sectors of the economy usually comes from relevant institutes and their staff members.

Agriculture. The original design of the agricultural reform based on the decree promulgated by the Party Congress in the spring of 1986 (*Pravda*, March 29, 1986) was drawn up by leading economists affiliated with the Academy of Agricultural Sciences. This group included Agricultural Academicians V. I. Nazarenko and V. R. Boyev (also Director of the Institute of Agricultural Economics). Subsequently, other organizations managed to modify their blueprint during the review process and recommend a less radical reform. After the emphasis shifted toward family farming, the work of Professor Gennadiy Lisichkin of the IEMSS has gained prominence. A noted author of the

17. These scholars frequently publish articles or appear at press conferences to outline their proposals. They perceive themselves as allies of Gorbachev and invariably support more radical reforms than economists employed by the state apparatus.

18. Moscow accounts for roughly one-third of Soviet scientists.

19. They support the development of private enterprise and leasing (Otsason and Raig, 1987).

most market-oriented Soviet book of the 1960s (Lisichkin, 1966), he now appears to be the principal designer of prospective changes in this field.[20]

Foreign Trade. The IEMSS has been in charge of projects designing the changes in foreign trade introduced in 1987 (*Sotsialisticheskaya industriya,* September 23, 1986). The principal coordinator was the institute's Deputy Director Professor Vladimir Shastitko, though Academician Bogomolov has also been deeply involved in the work. Another architect of the reform and coordinator in this area is Professor Ivan Ivanov, Deputy Chairman of the State Commission on Foreign Economic Relations and former Deputy Director of the World Economics and International Relations Institute (IMEMO).[21] As in the case with agriculture, the designers of foreign trade reform have been disappointed by the bureaucratization of their efforts.

Private Enterprise. The "Law on Individual Labor Activity" (*Pravda,* November 21, 1986) was primarily drafted by the Institute of State and Law (IGP) and the Institute of Economics, whose principal spokesman on private enterprise L.V. Nikiforov appeared at two press conferences. Nikiforov is also the most active commentator on new types of cooperatives (*Izvestiya,* October 20, 1986, February 12, 1987; *Pravda,* February 12, 1987; *Sotsialisticheskaya industriya,* February 12, 1987). G. S. Lisichkin, Ye. A. Ambartsumov, and A. P. Butenko of the IEMSS have repeatedly published papers on private enterprise (Tenson, 1983), but their institute has been excluded from the process of drafting legislation on private and cooperative enterprises outside the agricultural sector.

Price Policies. TsEMI is the dominant institute on financial matters and price policy. Nikolay Petrakov, who leads a formidable team of researchers, managed rather impressively to advance his ideas on financial reform (Petrakov and Yasin, 1986; Petrakov and Lvov, 1987; Petrakov 1987a, 1987b, 1987c). When the Economic Department of the Academy of Sciences and th Board of Gosbank held a joint meeting in December 1986 to discuss the reform of the credit system, Petrakov spoke up on behalf of the Academy (*Voprosy ekonomiki,* 59, 8:149, August 1987). Professor Yuriy Borozdin of TsEMI is the major advocate of a far-reaching price reform (Borozdin, 1986), although everyone is concerned and involved with prices and prospects for their revision. The diversity of views in this area is great. The Scientific Research Institute for Prices of the State Committee on Prices offers massive resistance to reform (Chubakov, 1987). Although one of the old conservative spokesmen of the IE, Professor Anatoliy Deryabin, has been demoted by Abalkin, he continues to voice his orthodox views (Deryabin, 1987). Thus, the Academy of Sciences appears to be divided on the issue of pricing (November 1987), and indeed, pricing seems to be the most divisive element of the reform. Professor Vilen Perlamutrov of TsEMI has long advocated a diversification of the banking

20. Lisichkin's relatively high status is evidenced by his press conference devoted to family farming.
21. IMEMO is primarily devoted to international relations.

system, which is presently partly in place (*Pravda,* August 25, 1987); he is most likely the initiator of the banking reform.

Advice on General Issues. Academician Zaslavskaya seems to dominate all general socioeconomic issues (Zaslavskaya, 1986b), although there are many other vocal participants in the debate. Among the most influential people in this area is Stanislav Shatalin, who is mainly interested in problems pertaining to labor incentives (Shatalin, 1986). Equally important is Professor Vladimir Kostakov, the new Director of Gosplan's Economic Research Institute, who has focused his efforts on issues related to employment (Kostakov, 1987).

Most of the aforementioned economists have a coherent, though more or less elaborate general view of the economic reform. But two daring model builders are considered to be particularly important politically. The first is Professor Gavriil Popov of Moscow University, who is known to be close to Academician Aganbegyan. As soon as Chernenko had been placed into his coffin, Popov published two programmatic books advocating radical reform (Popov 1985a, 1985b). Boris Kurashvili of the State and Law Institute appears to be the other most vocal, consistent, and bold reformer. His first fundamental reform article, published in June 1982 when Brezhnev was still in charge (Kurashvili, 1982), was commended by Tat'yana Zaslavskaya in the Novosibirsk Report of 1983. Just after Chernenko's death, Kurashvili developed his ideas about a socialist market economy and the merger of all industrial ministries into one, involving the dismissal of 90 percent of the staff (Kurashvili, 1985). Equally radical thoughts are in evidence in his more recently published book on state management (Kurashvili, 1987). Kurashvili's colleague and friend, Professor Mikhail Piskotin of the Institute of State and Law, should also be mentioned. Piskotin published a similar, though not quite as reform-oriented, book in 1984 (Piskotin, 1984).

Media Support

Virtually all the aforementioned reform-oriented economists frequently publicize their views in the mass media. They receive valuable assistance from a number of well-placed economic editors who tend to champion considerably more radical reform views than academic economists. Among the more important are Vasiliy Parfenov of *Pravda,* Aleksandr Levikov of *Literaturnaya gazeta,* Otto Latsis of *Kommunist,* and A. S. Strelyany of *Novyy mir.* Their outspoken articles allow us to trace the roots of the sudden rise of reformism in the Soviet press. Parfenov and Levikov have held their positions for a long time. Parfenov's writing has become more radical in tandem with the reform movement, while Levikov always championed the most extreme pro-reform views. Latsis, who headed a department at the IEMSS, and Strelyany are newcomers who assumed their editorships in mid-1986 and early 1987, respectively.

In the beginning of 1986, both the *Ekonomicheskaya gazeta* and *Sotsialis-*

ticheskaya industriya had to adjust to new editors. Boris Vladimirov, the editor of the first, once served as an aide to Suslov. Aleksandr Baranov, who now edits the second, toiled as an assistant to the Prime Minister of the RSFSR (Mikhail Solomentsev and later Vitaliy Vorotnikov) for about a decade. Both newspapers adopted pro-reform positions after these appointments.

Other newspapers with recently appointed new editors, frequently from the political apparatus, followed suit. The economic observer of *Sotsialisticheskaya industriya,* Vasiliy Selyunin, is possibly the most persistently radical reformer in the Soviet press. *Izvestiya* has an impressive number of knowledgeable economic journalists who promote the cause of reform as well (for example, V. Romanyuk, V. Tolstov, and Ruslan Lynev). Nonetheless, the major press organs also include important conservative spokesmen, such as Dmitriy Valovoy of *Pravda.* However, a clearly pro-reform bias in the central media is rather obvious. The economic journals, on the other hand, have not changed, retaining their predilection toward conservatism. Thus, the most radicial journal articles on the economy appear primarily in *Novyy mir* and *Literaturnaya gazeta,* although by the summer of 1987 they had also begun to appear in *Ekonomicheskaya gazeta.*

CONCLUSIONS

In the final analysis, a rather clear picture emerges of the social scientists Gorbachev has selected as advisors on economic reform. He has not turned to long-standing acquaintances, possibly because he had no friends among qualified economists. The Secretary seems instead to have relied on a number of different people before settling, perhaps temporarily, on one of several possible arrangements for obtaining economic advice. In essence, Gorbachev has selected the best of what the Academy of Sciences has to offer, avoiding the old, the conservative, and the excessively strident elements of the profession in the process. As a result, he has assembled a coherent team of able economists in their fifties, all party members, and all committed to reforming the Soviet economy, though to varying degrees.

The leading figures are clearly able to chart a course of moderation and, in fact, may be inclined to go too far to reach a compromise. Such tendencies may be responsible for the reform's chronic inconsistencies. Nearly all important advisors work within institutions comprising the Academy of Sciences, where reform economists have long dominated the scene. Although Gosplan and other organs of the Council of Ministers seem to have been circumvented during the initial stage of the effort to design reform measures, they injected themselves into the process (via the Talyzin Commission) soon thereafter and have had success in weakening many proposals. They can, in effect, impede undesirable changes.

Even though reformists called for the establishment of a new independent body to coordinate the work on economic reform, the USSR Council of Ministers, after the June 1987 CC Plenum, decided:

> The coordination of all work on the implementation of the radical reform of the management of the economy is entrusted to the Commission for the Improvement of Management, Planning, and the Economic Mechanism (*Pravda*, July 18, 1987).

The foregoing differences relating to the economic reform suggest a substantial conflict between the General Secretary, on the one hand, and the Prime Minister and the Chairman of Gosplan, on the other. The role of Slyun'kov as CC Secretary for Economic Affairs is certainly important, but remains difficult to define. He served as Deputy Chairman of Gosplan between 1974 and 1983 under Ryzhkov. However, he also facilitated the adoption by the CC of the reform program on June 26, 1987, and his work prior to this CC Plenum was appreciated by leading reform economists.

Ryzhkov's advisors, even Pavel Bunich, are essentially excluded from the main commissions charged with the drafting of blueprints to reform the Soviet economy. The most obvious interpretation of this situation is that Gorbachev is attempting to exclude Ryzhkov's followers from work on the reform. One possible reason might be Ryzhkov's defense of Gosplan, where he worked as First Deputy Chairman from 1979 to 1982, favoring a less radical reform than Gorbachev.[22] The aides of other senior politicians, for example, those advising Zaykov and Slyun'kov, also seem to be virtually absent from the reform process.

Gorbachev's raison d'être for reliance on Academy of Sciences' economists for advice in his ongoing reform effort reflects a number of factors: (1) they are disconnected from the suffocating vested interests of the Soviet economy; (2) they are highly visible in the media and have a strong appeal to the Soviet intelligentsia; and (3) they can rightly be considered the best and brightest of their profession for charting a radical course.

On the other hand, economics in the Soviet Union is more or less a science in disrepute (Selyunin and Khanin, 1987, p. 187). There are reasons to doubt that even the most outstanding Soviet economists are really able to structure and shape an economic reform.

One of the advantages appreciated by Western observers who monitor the reform is access, at least in principle, to all economists affiliated with the Academy of Sciences. Most of the senior economists mentioned have traveled in the West, gaining valuable experience and acquiring a realistic perspective on Soviet economic achievements and failures. Curiously, not even one of Gorbachev's economic advisors has been elected to a political

---

22. See, for example, Gorbachev's and Ryzhkov's pronouncements about the role of Gosplan in *Pravda*, June 26 and 30, 1987.

office. No one is even a Candidate Member of the CC or a deputy of the Supreme Soviet. It appears that Gorbachev has tried to promote Aganbegyan and Abalkin, thus far without success. Accordingly, in spite of their contacts with the General Secretary, Gorbachev's economic advisors lack political status and weight.

CHAPTER 8

Prospects for Change in the Systems of Price Formation, Finance, and Credit

Nikolay Ya. Petrakov

MORRIS BORNSTEIN (1987) has provided a thorough and balanced analysis of the existing price system in the USSR. In this brief comment I discuss how that system should change in the course of the current economic reform. The radical *perestroyka*[1] of the country's economic mechanism outlined by the 27th Party Congress, and discussed in detail at the June 1987 Central Committee Plenum (Osnovnyye, 1987), can be fully realized only through fundamental change in the planning of prices and finances, and enhancement of the role of the banking system in economic management.

DISTORTIONS IN THE CURRENT STRUCTURE OF PRICES

A clearly detectable imbalance is in evidence between prices for manufactured, agricultural, and consumer goods, and also within each price group. Thus, the overall structure of wholesale prices does not correspond to current trends in economic development nor to the cost structure of production. In developed industrial countries, prices of manufactured products are typically low in relation to prices paid for raw materials. The opposite picture emerges, however, in respect to current wholesale prices in the USSR. As a result, profits generated by the high prices of products in machine building exceed that sector's investment demand by nearly a factor of two. On the other hand, investment funds accumulated in the fuel-energy sectors are 25 to 30 percent below the level of investment necessary to achieve growth rates outlined by the last two five-year plans and the State Plan for 1986–1990.

Artificially low prices for raw materials create economic barriers that impede reliance on intensive production methods, limit the wide dissemination of re-

First published in *Soviet Economy*, 1987, 3, 2, pp. 135–144. [Eds.]

1. As used in this chapter, the word *perestroyka* generally conveys the meaning of as well as the focus on the ongoing restructuring of the Soviet economy. [Eds.]

source-saving technologies, and hamper comprehensive utilization of raw materials.

At the same time, prices for products of the machine-building sector are generally set in accordance with an average of actual costs in each branch[2] (plus a normative profit margin), practically ignoring the actual effectiveness of machine tools and related equipment in the economy. Numerous and rather substantial surcharges on wholesale prices (for the highest category of quality, the "N" index, etc.), which have raised the overall price level in machine building, have not proven to be an effective stimulus for rapid renovation of productive capacity, or for the creation and mass assimilation of highly effective types of new equipment. The main problem here is that equipment which has long been fully assimilated, or even become outmoded, continues to be profitable to operate and contributes to the formation of sizeable economic incentive funds.

Relative retail prices among certain food products, and between food products and manufactured goods, have become substantially distorted. Our retail price policy clearly did not provide for enough flexibility to reflect the changing needs of the population.

IMPORTANCE OF CHANGE IN
THE PRICE STRUCTURE

The increased importance of prices in the *perestroyka* of the economic planning system shows up primarily in two areas.

First, the planned system of prices should play an active role in the reconciliation of physical and value flows. The value of material resources, goods, and services circulating in the economy and also delivered to the ultimate consumer should correspond to the amount of money (both cash and financial balances) at the disposal of economic organizations and the population, for the acquisition of products and services on the market. Such balance must be preserved at the aggregate level as well as within each commodity group. In consequence, the social demand for resources and products arising from the proportions fixed in the plan will emerge as effective (money-backed) demand, and price relationships will reflect the balance between that demand and production volumes emerging from the process of plan formulation. If you have equality of supply and demand and price levels correspond to the full economic costs of expanded reproduction,[3] then that will also mean that they represent socially necessary expenditures.

Second, the planned price system performs the important role of reconciling national economic and individual enterprise interests. This function follows

2. It is of note, however, that prices for small production runs and for newly developed equipment are geared to individual costs.

3. Expanded reproduction means that an enterprise or branch has sufficient receipts to cover current costs, real depreciation, and investments to raise output in order to meet increasing demand. [Eds.]

from the two normative functions of prices. First, prices, as economic normatives determined directly by the plan, must preclude (make unprofitable or economically disadvantageous) socially unjustifiable expenditures for production. Second, prices should provide a profit sufficient for the further development of production at planned rates of growth, and the formation of material incentive funds according to plan normatives. Such price structure creates a genuine economic base for the conversion of enterprises and associations to *samoukopayemost*[4] and *samofinansirovaniye* (self-financing).

Therefore, price is destined to play an exceptionally important role in a comprehensive system of management of a socialist economy. It is to become the connecting link between the system of centralized planning and the financially accountable economic activity within individual economic units. That guarantees the commensurability of costs and results in the economy as a whole, and the coordination of economic interests in the achievement of maximum economic efficiency of social production.

OBJECTIVES FOR RESTRUCTURING THE PRICE SYSTEM

With these requirements as a point of departure, the fundamental tasks of *perestroyka* of the price system can be formulated as follows:

A. *Industrial wholesale prices* should reflect the socially essential level of expenditures for the reproduction of output in proportions defined by the national economic plan; they should provide for a balance (in physical and in value terms) of the planned economy in all sectors of social production; and they should create an economic incentive to produce high-efficiency new technology that guarantees real resource savings to users and a lowering of aggregate costs per unit of value.

B. *Agricultural procurement prices* should equalize the economic environment of collective and state farms located in different natural and climatic zones so that the incomes of agricultural enterprises will depend primarily on the effort of labor and on the level at which production is organized in each collective. In addition, procurement prices should encourage an optimal specialization of agricultural production in order to obtain the necessary quantity and variety of agricultural products at the lowest total cost.

C. *Retail prices* should play an active role in the distribution of goods in accordance with the quantity and quality of labor; in achieving a dynamic balance between effective demand and the supply of goods and services; and in stimulating a structure of consumption that corresponds to the socialist ideal of the well-rounded developing personality.

---

4. This term has no precise English-language equivalent, but refers to the requirement that all investments by an enterprise or association, however financed, must generate a profit at least equal to a specified minimum rate of return. [Eds.]

STRATEGIES FOR CHANGE

A look at basic strategies for change in the system of prices designed to resolve the aforementioned problems calls for a focus on price formation from marginal prices and on modification of wholesale prices to stimulate technological progress.

Price Formation from Marginal Prices

The relative prices of products of the economy's extractive and manufacturing sectors must be decisively changed by incorporating differential rent into their structure. It is necessary here to shift from the principle of establishing prices on the basis of average sectoral costs to one that is based on marginal or *closing* prices.[5] Prices in such cases should reflect the additional expenditures which will be borne by the economy in order to obtain an additional million tons of coal or metal, or reflect additional resources it would manage to obtain if such one million tons were to be gained through conservation.

The principle of closing prices is not new. It is based on the theory of differential rent and has long been used in a number of methodological documents regulating Soviet procedures for the selection of rational alternatives in the development of resource-based sectors. However, the application of this principle in price formation has encountered serious objections, which boil down to the fact that the inclusion of rent in the price of raw materials and fuels could lead to the snowballing growth of prices across the entire economy. That argument erroneously assumes that the principle of closing prices will require the setting of prices high enough to cover costs of the most backward, poorly managed, mining-extractive enterprises. On the contrary, these production units should in any case be unprofitable. The price, including rent, is not intended to subsidize lackadaisical managers, but rather to reflect the objective finiteness of natural resources emerging in the process of compiling the national economic plan.

In the current price system rent created in the extractive sectors does not disappear, but shows up as increased profits in manufacturing. In 1985 profit in the fuel industry amounted to 9.5 billion rubles (*Narkhoz*, 1986, p. 550); industry as a whole generated profits equal to 100.6 billion rubles (*Narkhoz*, 1986, p. 550). Capital investment in industry financed from depreciation funds for the same period equalled 30.8 billion rubles (*Narkhoz*, 1986, pp. 367, 558). Material incentive funds, and those for social-cultural objectives, as well as construction of housing, reached 17 billion rubles (*Narkhoz*, 1986, p. 549) amounting to 17 percent of profits. The remaining 52.6 billion, comprising profits in excess of industry's investment and material incentive fund require-

5. These are the *zamykayushchiye zatrary* which are related to shadow prices resulting from a large linear programming model (see Campbell, 1983). [Eds.]

ments, reflect the high prices of manufactured goods relative to those of raw materials and fuel.

This leads us to suggest a clear need to change the structure of prices. Research at TsEMI, using an input-output model of the economy, shows that it is possible to radically alter the relationship between prices of the manufacturing and extractive industries without increasing the overall price level. Such change in the concept of price formation would enable us to take a major step toward bringing price levels closer to socially necessary expenditures, and to streamline planning and administration toward scientific and technical policies prompting conservation of resources.

Changes in Wholesale Prices to Encourage High Technology Production

The role of prices in stimulating technological progress in machine building should be substantially modified. At present the main economic stimulus for such progress at the enterprise (or association) level is the surcharge on wholesale prices for new products receiving the *znak kachestva*[6] rating, with proceeds from such a surcharge going into material stimulation funds.

The main shortcoming of the present system is that the calculated economic effect which is the basis for the surcharge is unrelated to the actual *ex post* economic effect of the new product.

The aforementioned shortcoming is due to the following factors:

(1) The economic effect of new technology is calculated by the producer. Here the control of the consumer is greatly weakened by virtue of such economic factors as: (a) payment for the new technology is to a significant degree made by the consumer, not out of his own funds, but through budgetary financing; (b) the producer has an extreme interest in raising the calculated effect, since the size of the increment to wholesale prices depends on its level.

(2) The increment to the wholesale price is, in essence, an advance to the producer by the consumer, inasmuch as the latter (at the time when new technology is purchased) pays for a part of the effect which will be realized only after the new equipment is in use for some period of time. Accordingly, essentially fictitious incomes enter the accounts of enterprises and the budgets of such enterprises as well.

(3) Inasmuch as part of the calculated effect is already paid at the moment the new item is acquired, almost all incentives for management to monitor the "realization" of the calculated effect (i.e., inspect to make sure that calculated effect is actually realized in practice) automatically disappear.

6. For definition refer to footnote in the *Soviet Economy* Roundtable on Gorbachev's Economic Reform (Gorbachev's, 1987, p. 43). [Eds.]

To eliminate or significantly reduce the effects of the aforementioned short-comings, we recommend as a first step paying for resource-intensive technologies[7] on an installment plan. The essence of this recommendation is that the initial payment to the supplier of the new product is determined by agreement with the consumer on the basis of normative expenditures and profitability. In addition to the wholesale price, the total annual payment to the manufacturer would be defined by agreement based on the estimated effectiveness of the new technology. This total is drawn on the basis of actual performance for the consumer, although it is established on the basis of preliminary estimates in the process of negotiation for the delivery of new technology. This enhances the role of the consumer in evaluating the expected economic effect. It also maximizes his interest in the best use of the new technology, inasmuch as the estimated total increment is paid out of actual profits.[8]

The discount mechanism penalizing enterprises producing obsolete products also needs substantial improvement. It should work automatically so that enterprises that fail to implement an active scientific-technical program will inevitably find themselves in a difficult financial situation as a result of reduced profitability of their products. Clearly, the forgotten idea of "step" prices (in any case for producers) should be put into practice. The period for which each step is in effect and the magnitude of the price reduction during a shift to a new "step" should be determined primarily by normative rates of technical change (specified according to the dynamics of obsolescence), by sector and groups of homogeneous products.

LINKS BETWEEN PRICE AND FINANCIAL REFORMS

One should emphasize that measures for improving the price system (the entire system as well as its individual elements) depend to a great degree on the extent to which such measures will be coordinated with changes in other parts of the socialist economic mechanism. *Perestroyka* of the price system should take place simultaneously with the changes in the fiscal-credit system. Therefore, another problem must be resolved at the same time as such *perestroyka*, namely the problem of essential changes in the system of revenues in the state budget in order to (a) tie the sources of revenue in the budget as closely as possible to the effective use of economic resources in the sphere of material production,[9] and (b) relieve the state budget of the artificial function of compensating for shortcomings in price formation.[10]

---

7. Such as numerical remote control machine tools, flexible automated systems, computers, etc.

8. The proposed method can be modified for large-scale, serial shipment of new technology. The consumer, upon acquiring the new technology, immediately pays the producer in full (or an organ of Gossnab), but must borrow from Gosbank at an increased rate of interest to cover the surcharge.

9. Normatives of payment for productive capital, rates of rent, a progressive tax on profits rather than a free residual of profit, etc.

10. This is now accomplished by budgeting for capital investment in low-profitability sectors which produce vitally needed products for the national economy, and also through a system of normatives for transfers from profit (to the budget) that are specific for each enterprise.

Table 1. *Revenue Structure in the State Budget of the USSR*
(in percent of total)

Source	Income formation	
	Present practice	*Proposed methods*
Turnover tax	27.3	12.9
Payments for productive capital	9.4	21.0
Fees from the free residual of profits	13.1	—
Progressive tax on profit	—	10.5
Fixed (rent) payments	1.5	2.6
Other deductions from profits and miscellaneous payments	6.7	—
Income tax from cooperatives, collective farms, etc.	0.7	6.6
Taxes from the population and state loans	7.9	8.4
State social security funds	6.5	10.5
Other income	26.9	27.5
Total	100.0	100.0

If higher tax rates for social security are incorporated in wholesale prices, and income tax normatives from state and collective farms (depending on appraisal of the land) are included in the procurement price structure, then substantial structural changes will also take place on the revenue side of the budget. Improvement in the practice of applying the turnover tax, the need for which was specifically noted at the 27th Party Congress, is necessary to eliminate distortions on the revenue side of the budget. Methods for including turnover taxes in prices (and subsequently drawing them into the budget) are definitely suitable for financial organizations. But, at the same time, they separate the circulation of the material values from the movement of financial resources. The turnover tax and its application must revert to a narrower economic content. It should take on the role of an excise tax included in the price of a limited group of goods, the consumption of which is economically regulated for special reasons (alcohol, tobacco products, luxury items, etc.).

Our preliminary calculations indicate that the aforementioned measures for modifying the system of price formation will prompt changes in the structure of budget revenues shown in Table 1.

The proposed change in the income structure will not disrupt the overall balance of income and expenditures in the state budget. As before, the total revenue will be sufficient to finance the entire complex of social programs envisioned by the national economic plans, expenditures for basic research, those for defense, etc. The revenue portion of the budget will be reduced only to the degree that budgetary expenditures on subsidies and other forms of budgetary financing, no longer necessary due to *perestroyka* of the price system, are reduced.

Price Stabilization and Money Circulation

While the price system retains the functions of balancing production volumes with effective demand, the problem of price stabilization can be effectively resolved by centralized planned regulation of money in circulation. Therefore, problems related to efforts to improve prices are closely related to the need for normalizing money turnover. In our opinion, this can be resolved as follows:

A. Overall balancing of material and financial resources in the economy. The first step would be a one-time reduction of monetary resources moving through wholesale trade with a simultaneous strengthening of the balance sheets of all enterprises and organizations. This would promote the liquidation of excess inventories and reliance on real monetary valuation of enterprise resources, including valuation of unfinished construction.

B. Strengthening of centralized, long-term financial planning on the basis of a single financial and credit plan with separate treatment of the financial balances of the state and of *khozraschet* organizations. We see the need for a clear delimitation of the resources of enterprises, of the budget, and of banks. Budgetary financing, aside from the nonproductive sectors and other general state needs, should be restricted to a group of high-priority, goal-specific programs on a national scale.

It is also necessary to develop a long-term plan for the circulation of payments, including the circulation of monetary resources both in cash and other forms. The purpose of its development is to balance quantitative indicators of the plan with aggregate monetary resources. Presently the natural indicators of the plan are determined first, and the financial means for their implementation are sought thereafter. Here the role of money and the planned formation of effective demand as a regulator of material flows in production is downgraded. And the strengthening of financial planning and centralized plan guidance of the economy as a whole involves regulation of money flows; such regulation would prompt effective demand and thereby exert pressure on production.

Reorganization of the Bank Credit System

The reorganization of the bank credit system should proceed in the following basic ways.

1. A basic criterion for the granting of credits should be the earnings by enterprises of profits at the level of the planned norm of efficiency to which the bank's interest rate is tied. The rate will differ depending on the financial condition of the enterprise, and also on the amortization period of the loan.

2. All forms of automatic credit are eliminated, including automatic credits to cover payments (for inputs, etc.).

3. The intra-ministerial redistribution of circulating capital, depreciation funds, and profits among enterprises will cease.

4. Payments are introduced both for credit and for deposits, i.e., interest is paid for all types of deposits.

5. The credit resources of the bank are funded by a statutory fund (initial capital), by a part of the bank's profits, by budget allocations, and also fixed liabilities—long- and medium-term deposits and increases of money in circulation (within the limts set by the growth of liquid assets in the economy).

6. The transfer of banking institutions to complete *khozraschet*-oriented financial accountability; the establishment of procedures for allocating the profits of a bank (the difference between the interest received and paid), including the creation of reserve and incentive funds, and creation of incentives for bank personnel to increase the return on credits that are issued.

7. The reorganization of the banking system by creating special *khozraschet*-oriented banks with a defined range of credit resources; such self-supporting banks would work under the principles of complete financial accountability. The measure would enable them to thoroughly analyze the effectiveness of proposed credit allocations, raising the incentive for a better use of credit resources. Needless to say, the leading role of the Gosbank USSR as the administrative body of the banking system, the single center of emission, and a sort of "bank of banks" should be preserved.

CHAPTER 9

Basic Directions of *Perestroyka*

Abel G. Aganbegyan
with *Ed A. Hewett, Abram Bergson, Gregory Grossman,* and
Herbert S. Levine

AGANBEGYAN: I would like to share with you my observations on the initial
results of *perestroyka* as well as discuss some problems precipitated by the
restructuring of the Soviet economy. Conceivably, one might single out three
basic directions of this multiphased, planned process: (1) efforts to enhance
the social orientation of our economic development; (2) commitments to change
the factors and sources of our economic growth to intensify the acceleration
of technological progress; and (3) the radical restructuring of management and
democratization of our economic environment—presently the most significant
direction; in essence, the one that supports the first two.

These three closely intertwined directions fit together into a more general
concept of *uskoreniye* (acceleration) of our country's social and economic
development, initiated by the Plenum of the Central Committee of the Party
in April 1985 (*Materialy*, 1985). Developed and ratified by the 27th Congress
of the Party in the beginning of 1986 (*Materialy*, 1986), *uskoreniye* should be
perceived as a crossover to a new quality of economic growth, rather than
measured, either exclusively or even preferentially, by conventional yardsticks
of economic development (e.g., first 4 and then up to 5 and 5.5 percent per
annum). *Uskoreniye* involves a renewal of our economic environment, and I
should like to emphasize the qualitative aspects of that process.

THE THREE DIRECTIONS

Social Orientation

The raison d'être of *perestroyka* can be traced to the need to resolve social
problems—a need which is no longer obscured—and on orientation to foster

Abbreviated version of a paper first published in *Soviet Economy*, 1987, 3, 4, pp. 277–297. At the time,
Academician Aganbegyan was Academic Secretary in charge of the Economics Department of the Academy of
Sciences of the USSR. As head of the Soviet delegation to the First Joint *Soviet Economy* Roundtable, he
commenced the proceedings on December 14, 1987, by presenting the first part of this chapter. [Eds.]

development for the benefit and well-being of the people. To tell it like it is, the standard of living of our population seriously lags behind our industrial capacity, and one could say that our people deserve a better life. At first, this lag in the social sphere was precipitated by historical determinants known to every student of our difficult beginnings. But later, it began to intensify during the last 10 to 20 years due to negative trends in our economic development, involving redistribution of resources and assignment of priorities to issues involving production, at the expense of goals responsive to needs in the social domain.

And as the so-called principle of residual allocation of resources for social needs became ingrained during the aforementioned 15 to 20 years, we stood still or barely moved forward while the people's wants continued to mount. Hence, the acute discrepancy and the ensuing problems increasingly in evidence and in need of resolution.

Accordingly, the first direction of *perestroyka* is the focus on radical changes in our social policy, promoting the social environment so that its needs are considered on a priority basis, developing appropriate sectors of the economy to satisfy such needs, and redistributing resources in order to raise the standard of living. What has happened during the last two years, in 1986 and 1987, to account for progress in this direction?

Housing and Food Supply. Housing is the most painful social problem. For the first time in 20 years we broke the trend of stagnation in construction, languishing at the average annual level of 2 million new apartment units completed to alleviate the shortage. In 1986, we added 2.2 million new units to the total, and in 1987 one may anticipate as many as 2.4 million new individual apartments. We want to build 3 million every year in the early 1990s and put an end to the shortage by making available an individual apartment or house with appropriate amenities for each family.

Another social problem of similarly immense proportion is the supply of food—primarily the lack of adequate quantities of meat and dairy products. In order to eliminate these deficiencies, we must reverse the trend of stagnation in the development of agriculture. In 1986 and 1987, agricultural output in the USSR increased by 10 percent, i.e., as much as in the preceding 7 years. The output of grain, as compared with the annual average during the preceding five-year period, rose from 180 to 210 million tons, production of meat from 16.2 to 18.7 million tons, and that of milk from about 95 to 102 million tons (*Narkhoz*, 1987, pp. 227, 259, 260). These gains were due to the considerable changes in our investment policy, and to the *perestroyka* of management and economic mechanisms of our agricultural sectors. Regretfully, a significant proportion of the aforementioned gains had to be utilized to lighten the burden of meat and grain imports, so that supplies were not adequately augmented to satisfy demand for deficient products. Thus, much as we wanted them to, many Soviet families did not as yet benefit from *perestroyka* in this domain. We did not manage to cross the threshold of tolerance and must come to terms with the need to increase our efforts. True to our commitment, we are recently expanding facilities to process and store agricultural produce and developing expedients to speed up progress in agriculture.

Health, Education, and Welfare. Health care is our country's third acute problem. During the preceding 20 years, the average life span of our population declined and the death rate increased. This was due to excessive alcohol consumption and inadequate health care. The former doubled, while resources available to the latter were diminishing in accord with the principle of residual allocation. And again we managed to reverse these trends in 1986 and 1987, for the first time in 20 years. The average life span increased from 68 to 70, the death rate dropped from 10.8 to 9.8 per thousand (*Narkhoz*, 1987, pp. 407–409), and infant mortality also decreased.

But even though we demonstrated some progress, these indices are much below those of other developed countries. A radical change is necessary here and an effective program to restructure the health care system servicing the population is in place. An important contribution was made by the struggle against drunkenness and measures to reduce consumption of alcoholic beverages.

However, progress in providing for other social entitlements is also in evidence. We doubled the growth of the service sector, and reforms related to schooling and other aspects of education are on the drawing board. New pension laws to secure significant increases in average retirement benefits, and important measures to alleviate the hardships of manual labor are expected to make a difference. Also, efforts to improve the quality of consumer goods—in effect to fully satisfy the market—are in evidence, though we have not as yet managed to demonstrate radical changes in this area. One can speak only about changes in the direction of vectors relating to the people's standard of living. Surely, the gains attributed to redistribution during the course of the past two years cannot be expected to provide an adequate remedy for all the problems accumulated during the course of decades.

Factors and Sources of Economic Growth

A breakthrough streamlining effective supplies of goods and services cannot materialize overnight, for time is essential to implement a variety of complex measures. And it is precisely toward this end that the second direction of *perestroyka*—to change the factors and sources of economic growth—is shaping up.

We want to accelerate our socio-economic development under conditions that take into account the diminishing supply of resources. In order to attain this goal, it is necessary to increase by as much as one and a half to two times the rate at which effective development of our economy is progressing, and above all, to double growth rates in the productivity of labor. We have quite extensive organizational and social reserves, but the main strategic lever for efficiency is the radical *uskoreniye* of scientific and technological progress.

Our highly developed scientific potential is an asset, and many branches of scientific endeavor can demonstrate advances that are ahead of our times. And yet, we still struggle with problems for which solutions are not at hand, and with a score of disadvantages as well. The main culprit is difficulties in the application of achievements in science and technology, associated, in turn, with inappropriate investment policies that guided the replacement of obsolete machinery and manufacturing equipment in the past.

Much depends on the development of our machine-building industry and particularly of branches manufacturing consumer goods, which are quite backward. Thus, innovative policies to stimulate the redistribution of capital investment in favor of machine building should provide for the radical modernization of all branches at the expense of new construction, which ought to be limited.

In 1985, we modernized 3.1 percent of the variety of equipment produced by the industry. But in 1988, plans call for the modernization of 9.3 percent, and in 1990 for as much as 13 percent. To this end, the rate at which obsolete production equipment in machine building should be replaced must be increased four to five times, and all such renovation calls for substantial capital investment.

During the Twelfth Five-Year Plan period, from 1986 to 1990, investments in machine building are to double, while during the preceding five years they increased by a mere 24 percent. And the basic thrust is to channel investments into technological reconstruction and modernization of existing machine-building plants. In the two years from the beginning of 1986 to the end of 1987, capital investments earmarked for technological reconstruction in machine building were more than one and a half times higher than those allocated to such modernization during the preceding eight-year period.

The tasks are difficult and the solutions no less so, for many branches were not ready to adapt to the changes and reconstruction. In general, painful adjustments to changes in output, coupled with those related to new unfamiliar production equipment, prompted pressures that caused declining rates of output. Moreover, *gospriyemka* derailed a number of machine-building enterprises and retarded development. At this time, the situation is gradually improving, but the Twelfth Five-Year Plan period is the most difficult one to cope with.

Our strategy is to proceed with the *perestroyka* of machine building, commence mass production of new technologies at quality levels that are acceptable throughout the world, and utilize gains from prospective advances in this area to refurbish all other branches of the national economy. All of this calls for economic and social adjustments which the former administrative system of obsolete management served to retard.

Reformed Management and Democratization of the Economy

Because the old system was inappropriate for the new goals of social and economic growth, radical reform of management became the principal direction of *perestroyka*. An expanded concept embracing a new system of management and a program of economic reform was on the drawing board for more than two years. This developmental stage involved many experiments, including some of large scale, as well as studies that scrutinized the experience of other countries. Finally, at the June 1987 Plenum of the Central Committee, the expanded concept and program were duly adopted (Osnovnyye polozheniya, 1987). The Twelfth Five-Year Plan period will be marked by crossovers to the new system of management and new economic mechanism, both to be in place after 1990, when the subsequent five-year plan period is scheduled to begin.

Management. The main point here is the shift to businesslike methods of management. To begin with, it is essential that we expand the independence in economic affairs afforded to enterprises and associations. They are to adapt themselves to a system of complete khozraschet with self-financing and self-management. The foregoing is stipulated in the new Law on the State Enterprise (Zakon, 1987). Also, parallel efforts to establish cooperative enterprises in all branches of the economy are increasingly in evidence. Apparently, 9,000 co-operatives have been created and the number is growing from month to month—a modest beginning for the time being.

A Law on Individual Labor Activity has been adopted (Pravda, November 21, 1986) and more than 200,000 patents issued roughly as of the beginning of November 1987. And the new approach to the economic status of enterprises prompts the reorganization of all aspects of management.

Eleven significant decisions were made in July 1987. These stipulated that perestroyka would affect: (1) the activities of Gosplan; (2) price formation; (3) finance; (4) banking; (5) statistics; (6) activities of the State Committee for Material and Technical Supply; (7) a shift to wholesale trade; (8) activities of the State Committee for Labor and Social Problems; (9) activities of the State Committee for Science and Technology; (10) branch and territorial activities of ministries as well as of republican and local government organizations; and (11) changes in the apparat[1] of the Council of Ministers of the USSR. All of these decisions, except for the last one, have been published in a separate book (O korennoy perestroyke, 1987).

Having just returned from the United States,[2] I should share with you my surprise that many Sovietologists believe that our economic reform came to a halt because the aforementioned decisions have not been adopted. While none were published in the newspapers, 600,000 copies of the book were printed and released for distribution in the summer of 1987. Since that time, formidable work has been done to modify legislation in order to reduce and transform appropriate managerial units in preparation for the change in store on January 1, 1988. And next year, 20 branches of the economy will shift to self-financing. This means that 60 percent of industry, including all modes of transportation,

---

1. Literally apparatus, the term is widely used to denote the network of administrative and political units of an organization. [Eds.]
2. The Academician was among those who accompanied General Secretary Gorbachev to the December 1988 summit meeting in Washington, D.C. [Eds.]

will be converted to this system. Appropriate instructions and decrees have been made available in published form and additional preparations to facilitate conversion to the system are in progress.

The banking system has been transformed. Although in principle the concept of a reform of price formation has been worked out, the methods are being discussed and the reform is scheduled to be in place in 1989 and 1990. The first steps to shift to a wholesale system of trade are in evidence, including a sizable experiment planned for Estonia. Needless to say, there are considerable difficulties, drawbacks, and likely errors, and we are braced to go through a very demanding period of transition from 1988 to 1989, when enterprises will switch to self-financing while prices remain unchanged, and the centralized system of supply predominates. And during the course of that period, the potential benefits of the new economic mechanism will not be overly transparent, particularly because the transition will coincide with the existing Twelfth Five-Year Plan—a plan formulated without due consideration of our new economic mechanism.

The Thirteenth Five-Year Plan period will be different. Its preliminary drafts are inspired by innovation and suitable economic normatives, indices, and measures are being developed to fit *perestroyka*. But during the period of transition, it is nevertheless prudent to preserve adequate measures of centralized control influencing the activities of enterprises and organizations. This will involve greater reliance on state procurement and on differentiation of normatives than the economy will need in the future. And all of this raises doubts in the minds of people who do not deal with this process professionally— doubts and thoughts that things are not working out the way they should. But let me repeat, we are confronting a period of transition.

Democratization. A most important measure—the key to success—is democratization of the economic environment by increasing the role of labor collectives, transferring enterprises to self-management. The law will become effective on the first day of January 1988. Thus far, we have just a few isolated experiments in this field. Nevertheless, democratization is regarded as a main driving force in *perestroyka*, if we are to speak of democratization in the broad sense, including political democratization, as well as of its potential as a source for development. Today we are in the critical, one might say, breakthrough period of moving on from the conceptual and formative stage of *perestroyka*, when the programs and first experimental steps were developed and taken, to the next stage. That stage will incorporate large-scale activities whereby entire branches of the economy would be shifted to new systems of interaction. And the fate of *perestroyka* will depend on the success of the transfer.

We are presently preparing, without sparing any effort, for the All-Union Party Conference, which will take place toward the end of June 1988. This will be a gathering of Communists from the entire country. Similar in significance to that of a party congress, it will assemble in this form for the first time in the last 50 years.[3] The conference will consider the issues of *peres-troyka*—its progress, and its objectives for all aspects of socio-economic life and primarily for the economy. The second item on the agenda is democratization of the society and of the party as well. There is no doubt that decisions reached at this conference will influence and stimulate subsequent developments in *perestroyka*. If we were to trace the evolution from the events of the April 1985 Party Plenum, an honest conclusion that we are proceeding in the direction of strengthening and expanding *perestroyka* is in order. And even though, as we move forward, mounting difficulties such as impatience with the slowness of *perestroyka* are in our way, they are to be expected in light of the complex, revolutionary changes in our economic environment. All told, progress is in evidence and we are determined to follow through, expand, and develop the depth and breadth of *perestroyka*.

SELECTED QUESTIONS AND COMMENTS

HEWETT: Thank you Academician Aganbegyan. We have spent a great deal of time preparing for this roundtable meeting. Indeed, the book of decrees you mentioned was distributed and made available to every member of our delegation three months ago, and we tried to do our homework, read those decrees, and understand them. Moreover, we have done the best we could to follow in the press the enormous amount of material that is now being written about the economic reform in the USSR. It is a job in itself simply to follow Academician Aganbegyan around the world as he talks about that reform. And over the next two days, we hope to have an opportunity to discuss in some detail various aspects and the many questions we have about it.

First of all, you just briefly mentioned American Sovietologists in the context of their view of the economic reform. And let me also just very briefly try to do something very dangerous, namely to characterize our view of this reform process. We are both from countries in which, at least in academia, the democracy is very noisy, and I suspect I will get in trouble doing this, but let me try.

I think the general view in the United States, particularly after the June 1987 Plenum of the Central Committee and publication of the aforementioned decrees (*O korennoy perestroyke*, 1987), is that at least the framework has been constructed for a radical, very interesting, and far-reaching reform of the Soviet economy. And most American Sovietologists, even those who were very skeptical over the last two years, are now simply waiting, watching, and willing to be convinced that indeed, this reform will be implemented. On the other hand, all of us, American as well as Soviet economists who have studied reforms in many countries, are aware of the fact that publication of decrees is only the beginning of a long battle in order to actually implement a reform. We are

3. The last such Party Conference was convened in 1941. [Eds.]

interested observers, but you are the participants, and we know that the battle could take a very long time.

In the process of trying to reach our own opinion on the progress of the war, we have a number of questions which will be raised over the next few days. But for now, I would just raise several questions about the transition period that you, Academician Aganbegyan, discussed in your opening remarks. Obviously, one of the most important issues in a transition period is the sequence within which things are done—the sequence of the many complicated measures that compose a radical, comprehensive economic reform that we see emerging, and what that might mean for its ultimate success. You said it yourself in your opening statement, and we all agree, that the fate of the reform will be determined by the way this transition period is handled.

I would like to raise four questions, of the many that we will hopefully discuss in this first session.

(1) The first question pertains to the sequence of reforming sectors. As we all know, China's economic reform has received much attention. One of the reasons is the fact that the Chinese chose first to reform their rural sectors (not only agriculture but also small industry in rural areas), and then proceeded to reform industry. To a number of Americans who have visited China on more than one occasion and discussed the ''agriculture first'' strategy with the Chinese, that strategy seems to have worked very well.

The move toward a family-contracting system, the elimination of obligatory plan indicators, and measures allowing small business to thrive in the countryside, yielded an expansion in the supply of goods and services in the city as well as in the countryside. This expansion, in turn, created a material basis for a very successful reform in industry. I know that in the Soviet Union Academicians Zaslavskaya and Bogomolov have both recommended a similar strategy. And yet, as far as we can tell, so far that strategy has not been pursued. I am not saying that measures have not been taken to reform agriculture. But they seem to be much more modest and conservative than those taken by the Chinese.

And so my first question is: Why not take the easy and the logical sector first? Why not take agriculture first, instead of starting with industry—the hardest sector of all?

(2) My second question about sequence has to do with price reforms and the interrelationship between these reforms and the new Law on the State Enterprise. That new law, as Academician Aganbegyan emphasized, introduces self-financing, self-management, and operation on full and real *khozraschet*. And yet, without a price reform it is obviously impossible to rely on self-financing and to operate on full *khozraschet*. In fact, it is dangerous.

In a system in which prices are distorted, and in which they are unconnected to demand for the goods in question or to supply, enterprises may see profitable opportunities where they do not exist. On the other hand, opportunities may exist which the price system does not signal.

I am quite puzzled why it has taken so long to decide on a price reform. And indeed, it seems to be taking a very long time. Also, I am particularly puzzled why the issue of changing retail prices and a reform of wholesale prices has become part of a single bundle.

The Hungarians decided early on to reform wholesale prices first, and for obvious and understandable political reasons, to change retail prices and face the effects in the subsidy system later. In the Soviet Union, price reform has come to mean retail price reform, and this is holding up a very important part of the reform. I am deeply concerned that as the new Law on the State Enterprise comes into effect in 1988 and 1989, the distortions during the transition period will call not just for somewhat more government intervention, but for a tremendous amount of such intervention.

(3) The third question about sequencing, or at least about strategy, concerns the reasoning behind the continued emphasis on high growth and improvement in quality at the same time. These are contradictory in the short run, though in the long run they are not. A qualitative improvement in the performance of this economy, of any economy, will eventually bring about an improvement in growth rates. But in the short run an emphasis on quality would lead to temporary shutdowns in factories for retooling, which would be reflected in growth rates.

Currently, it would appear that there is an attempt to maintain high growth rates and improve the quality of goods and services, which inevitably will lead to contradictions at the enterprise level. Enterprises will feel that they must continue to operate, even if in the process they produce goods and services of relatively low quality. At this time the only defense I can see against that is *gospriyemka*. However, *gospriyemka* is an administrative system, and—while it is far more effective than the old quality control system—it is still probably relatively easy for enterprise directors to get around it.

(4) My final question has to do with an issue of strategy and also of sequence in the reform. Obviously, one of the important parts of the reform is that enterprises will henceforth not only have the right to succeed but also the right to fail. Whether or not you call it bankruptcy, although bankruptcy is now a good Russian word, is irrelevant. Enterprises will face the possibility of failure. More important, enterprises will have the right to dismiss labor, or at least they will have that possibility.

I am wondering, though, whether at the same time sufficient attention has been given to creating a set of institutions which will take workers who have been dismissed, retrain them, and move them back into the system? Dr. Vladimir Kostakov has discussed this in some of his work (Kostakov, 1987), and I know that you are thinking about it. But it seems very important, if you are to tell a director of an enterprise relying on self-financing and operating on full *khozraschet* that it has too much labor, then he should have the right to fire some people to reduce the labor force without worrying about finding each former employee another job. That should be the responsibility of society, and not the job of an enterprise director. And yet, as far as I can tell, there is no clear decision on this matter.

These are four questions that I thought might at least be conducive to start the discussion. I emphasize, in my mind they are questions. They may already be resolved in the Soviet Union. And I now invite questions from other members of our American delelgation.

LEVINE: I would like to add a somewhat different dimension to the evolving discussion of transition. It seems that all problems relating to the transition period, the ones Academician Aganbegyan spoke about and those Dr. Hewett has just focused on, should be looked at in a much broader context. It is not only a question of how long it takes to do it well or how long the delay, but really to consider the momentum which is necessary to maintain the process of reform during the transition period. If the momentum is lost, the entire *perestroyka* could be lost.

The problem in managing such an ambitious process of change is one of acquiring and maintaining the support of the people. And such support must be in evidence in an environment where the real fruits of reform will materialize in the very, very long term, and where the costs of reform are immediate. That is the issue Dr. Hewett spoke about. Gaining immediate support for change from something dramatic in agriculture is an important accomplishment, as demonstrated by the Chinese.

The question then, in my mind, is one I actually asked Academician Aganbegyan about a year and a half ago during a previous visit to Moscow,[4] namely: While it is important to get something started, it is also important to make sure that at least a minimum amount of simultaneity in the reform elements is achieved, so that a positive attitude and some successful experience comes early in the process in order to maintain momentum. The Soviet literature from the early stages of the reform is filled with negative comments from Gosplan and Gossnab people and from managers, about the lack of sufficient simultaneity and correspondence. I am just wondering whether it might not have been better to work out more aspects of the necessary simultaneity before starting to introduce measures that may be self-defeating and may lose the momentum of the entire program.

BERGSON: It is more or less implied, but perhaps it is appropriate to be explicit, that all of us here—I am sure I may speak for others, as well as for myself—are greatly impressed with the boldness and novelty of *perestroyka*, and all of us wish the Soviet Union well in its efforts to achieve a more abundant life. If we raise questions, I think it is fair to say that they are not merely motivated by technical concerns. There is a genuine feeling of concern that there be a positive outcome of this process and, to a degree, a certain uneasiness that *perestroyka* may not achieve what the circumstances call for.

Drs. Hewett and Levine have both sagaciously formulated some of the

4. The Eleventh SRI-IMEMO Conference held in Moscow in June 1986. [Eds.]

questions, the specific ones that are before us. I share their uneasiness about
the thrust of the program, particularly the great emphasis that has been placed
on *perestroyka* in industry. I think all of us—again, I believe I am speaking
for others in our delegation as well as for myself—feel that industry is a most
difficult sector for wholesale restructuring and for planning. It has to proceed
in a very empirical manner without the benefit of reliable scientific guidance.
Let's face it, both in the East and in the West, the science of planning economic
reforms is not very well developed.

Since the empirical approach is unavoidable, the question inevitably arises
whether the implementation of such an approach will create very real difficulties. I too wonder if we have to proceed in this manner without scientific
analysis to guide us, whether greater emphasis on agriculture, and I might also
add services, would not be more promising.

I should think that opportunities for an early return to reforms in the service
sector and the household service sector would be greater than in the case of
industry. And the possibilities of reform stressing cooperatives and private
enterprise would perhaps merit more consideration than has been given so far,
although I am aware that attention has been given to these sectors.

In thinking about the period of transition, especially in industry, it may be
a very long one. In Hungary there is still a transition in process that is 19 years
of age. Yes, 19 years since the new economic mechanism was initiated, and
there is still a transition. Moreover, I think it is fair to say that after 19 years
the gains in industry have been modest. I believe it is generally accepted that
there have been gains, especially in regard to the quality and assortment of
goods available to the consumer, but they have not been dramatic and not of
a sort which would galvanize a population in support of a program—support
which Dr. Levine indicates might be politically significant.

HEWETT: I might just add, Professor Bergson is an excellent symbol of
how deep and long our interest has been in the Soviet Union. He first traveled
to your country 50 years ago, in 1937, and we remarked that this is his 50th
anniversary of visiting the USSR.

GROSSMAN: I would like to pick up the term used by Dr. Levine, namely,
momentum, and try to infuse it with some more specific meaning that provides
a lead to my questions. As I see it, momentum is of extreme importance in
any undertaking such as *perestroyka* or economic reform. But momentum under
the present conditions in the Soviet Union means several things. It means a
very rapid and sustained upturn to pull the economy out of the stagnation in
which it existed on the eve of the present administration's advent to power.

Now, in order to do so, it would be necessary to invest enormous amounts
in machine building and, to some extent, in other branches of the economy,
if indeed the state of the capital stock—and I might also add, the degree of
environmental degradation—had reached a point when the loss of one or two
years (or the slowing down of the process of remedial quantitative and qualitative action) would be decisive, or almost decisive for the future (in other

words, if there was no time to waste, which is a possibility). If this is the case, the urgency of rebuilding, modernizing, re-equipping, and reversing some of the trends in both the capital stock and environmental degradation may have been prompted by lack of time. My question is: was there no time to be lost, measured not in years but in months?

The second aspect of momentum is that which assures the viability of institutional changes. Here the comments of my colleagues regarding price reforms, simultaneity, or sequencing are relevant. And the measures taken do not guarantee that continued or even, in some respect, revived administrative intervention will not be requried. Does it mean that some other factors which considerably limit and constrain the reformers' freedom of action are in the picture? And one such factor may be a very large, excessive amount of purchasing power in circulation which weighs heavily on the policy-makers.

There is also need for momentum in convincing the public that something tangible is being done for it, in order to elicit its support, change its psychological outlook, and mobilize it for the task. This, however, seems to be seriously limited by the fact that so much of the available investment has been going into high-priority areas, including such sectors as housing and health care, as we have heard. Accordingly, it is difficult to allocate enough to other areas and thereby convince the public that it is indeed going to benefit tangibly, and benefit soon.

And finally, momentum also refers to efficiency in the static sense, which after all, in the long run, becomes very important. In the short run, it may be less important than the first three, because an economy can perhaps afford to let the improvement of efficiency move more slowly so long as such more immediate and urgent objectives as reinforcing viability, reinforcing the move out of stagnation, and mobilizing public support are at stake.

HEWETT: Thank you very much. Despite the fact that we have only given easy questions to Academician Aganbegyan, let me turn to him for some answers.

SELECTED ANSWERS

I hope you don't expect us to have answers to all your questions. Therefore, I will simply try to discuss some of them and not give you the final answers.

Sequence of Measures in *Perestroyka*

The first question related to the sequence of reforms and to agriculture as a point of departure. We also started with agriculture, and the first measures to reorganize management and our economic mechanism were carried out in 1985 and 1986 in the agricultural sector. And it is only in the beginning of 1988 that such changes in our industry will be initiated. The investment policy changed first in agriculture, prompting the 10 percent growth of that sector in two years; industrial growth is expected to amount to 9 percent.

I agree that in our agriculture the process proceeds more modestly than in China, but our countries are different. Figures show that from 1953 to 1959, we made the same progress as China, even though we were unable to use the kind of reserves available to China (for the most part renting land plots to laborers). Manual labor in agriculture is past history in our system because the equivalent of 40 horsepower per worker is at our disposal in rural areas, and so we had to proceed differently. But I agree that we could do more, that more radical changes are in order, and that it is necessary to advance the pursuit of independence in agriculture. I am confident that we will proceed in this direction, and a new set of rules covering agricultural cooperatives is in preparation. Drastic expansion of the rights of collective farms and revision of the entire system of agricultural procurement prices that fail to stimulate output are thus in sight. Most likely this could be done more efficiently, and there is not enough progress in agriculture and in other branches of the economy as well.

The Price Reform

I agree that it would be prudent to shift to full *khozraschet* and self-financing when a new price system is in place. The question was why does it take us so long to prepare a price reform? It is because we are undertaking such a global reform of prices for the first time in our history. We want to review wholesale prices, fees for services, our tariffs, procurement prices in agriculture, and the system of retail prices. And we want to examine not only the price levels and relative prices, but also make an effort to reform the process of price formation, democratize this domain, reduce reliance on centralized influences on prices, and thus broaden reliance on contractual and unrestricted prices.

And it is a very complicated reform—a key to the intended restructuring of management—that requires careful preparation and calculation as well as publication of lists for centrally determined prices. I trust you appreciate the enormity of our responsibility in this area. Miscalculations can be made if we are not careful, and consequences such as inflation can be bad enough to merit consideration at the expense of all other issues. Essentially, we are opting for a painstakingly thorough approach, for, unlike in Poland and Hungary, there is no one to help us out if we miscalculate. We can only rely on ourselves.

We think two or three years will give us the time to prepare a price reform. A six-month or one-year period is not long enough to accomplish the objective, though one might shave off six months from the total. Perhaps we ought to have started in 1985, but at the time the concept of new price formations was in its infancy. Too dangerous to carry out without the general guidelines of *perestroyka* in place, the price reform had to wait.

Since there were questions with reference to price policies in other socialist countries, I should reiterate that we are not as yet prepared to raise prices of subsidized products. Speaking of meat and milk, I will not stick my neck out and suggest that prices will be doubled. One should not rule out that our leadership may either opt for very limited increases or even decide to leave these prices intact after considering all the advantages and pitfalls. There are various options, though many scientists believe that retail prices of meat and milk should be materially increased. And every advocate of such increases proposes to fully compensate the consumer for all additional expenses related to the price hikes. The advocates suggest that subsidies be withdrawn from meat-packing and dairy industries and transferred to the population.

This would serve to redistribute demand, because the subsidies would not be solely used by the consumer to purchase meat and milk, but partly to acquire manufactured and similar other goods. In any event, the Central Committee's decree pertaining to preliminary measures to reform prices (*O korennoy perestroyke*, 1987, pp. 150–165) states the following:

(1) The reform should follow the most democratic way to implement it, whereby proposals are first published, then debated, and finally decided upon in a manner that reflects the outcome of the debate; and

(2) The reform should be implemented in a manner that protects the living standards of the population which can not be diminished.

Comment on Extended Transition

Needless to say, the *khozraschet* system with old prices will not be all-embracing and real, and self-financing not as efficient as it could have been. But there are several advantages despite the numerous drawbacks. Gradually, we will get business managers to adapt themselves to greater measures of independence. This is a period of transition—a period of adaptation and learning. But, during the transition to the system of self-financing, funds for enterprise development will grow, increasing 3.3 times when compared to their growth in the past. And the social development fund placed at an enterprise's disposal will be increased 4.4 times, while centralized funds will be reduced respectively.

The enterprise will accumulate enormous resources for development. I say this because the expansion of rights to independently use such resources calls for a period of learning. Managers must learn to make independent decisions. And we must make sure that business managers are drawn into the process and procedures of using such independence. The transition period will serve this purpose and it will take time to see it through.

Contradictions in the Pursuit of Quantity and Quality

There were several questions highlighting contradictions between rates of growth and quality of output. Indeed, such contradictions do exist. But increases in rates of development are neither crucial nor a priority from our viewpoint. I did make the point that most important of all is the new quality of growth, and beneficial changes in quality—not in quantity—are more important. Our reasoning is based on the premise that rates of development, when properly calculated, will increase in tandem with improved quality and higher prices, raised in part because such quality more fully satisfies demand (e.g., one unit of a given commodity of superior quality replaces 1.5 units of the same of inferior quality). Accordingly, some of the growth, some but not all, will be due to improvements in the quality of goods.

But we have to admit that contradictions are in evidence. We have to consider, however, that a 4.5 percent growth rate is not a very high one for us, even though you think otherwise. Four to five percent is not a rate at which quality cannot improve, particularly because qualitative improvements will partly influence that rate. I would therefore withhold radical judgments to the effect that quality will remain at a standstill at an annual growth rate of 4 percent. In recent years, production in the U.S. grew at the rate of 4 percent per annum; yet at the same time, improvements in quality have been noted. Also, Japan, while improving the quality of goods, managed quantitative growth rates of 7 or even 8 percent. Hence, rates are not the issue. What matters are sources, factors, and other more serious elements that influence growth.

With regard to quality control, *gospriyemka* is in my opinion a temporary measure of necessity. The user should be the final judge to evaluate eligibility for acceptance. But in order to allow him to do just that, production should be oriented toward the needs of consumers. And this objective can be realized by the new economic mechanism that would incorporate a reform of prices and a shift to wholesale trade. But meanwhile, the struggle against low quality of production justifies the use of administrative levers to improve it.

Allocation of Labor Resources

Labor problems are with us, and I agree that an enterprise should not be burdened by the responsibilities of finding alternative jobs for employees who must be removed from its payroll. Such employees should be guided by state organizations to be found in our cities and in the provinces as well. We should improve their role and activities wherever they are. To some extent the State Committee on Labor and Social Issues deals with the aforementioned problem. The problem of allocating labor is presently easier to resolve due to the demographic consequences of the Second World War. Increments to the labor pool are being reduced 4 to 5 times, a result of the declining growth of the population. Moreover, an important deficiency is our underdeveloped service sector, which should absorb some of the labor force slated for reallocation. And there are job openings to be filled that may be traced to the investment policy pursued in the past—many jobs that were created but not filled, or some filled but not efficiently used (e.g., one shift when two should have been used). All of this is helpful in solving the problem of employment, though structural unemployment due to an inability to satisfy all preferences pertaining to profession, skill, or specialization is a dilemma that needs to be faced.

We have some experience in this area. Our railways are no longer employing as many people as in the past, following the so-called Minsk system of reducing labor force. In 1986, 125,000 people lost their jobs in the railway system, and this year we expect 270,000 people to follow suit. These are reductions in the number of employees—not curtailment by attrition when vacancies are not filled, but contraction. So the problems are quite evident, but solutions are at hand.

However, directors of our enterprises are not in a position to simply discharge the employee. Even in many capitalist countries, management cannot proceed quite so freely. Trade unions will have to be involved and play an important role. In fact, if a Western enterprise director wishes to give notice to 100 people without due consideration of possible objections raised by the trade union committee, and without attempts to explore alternative job opportunities for the same people at the enterprise, he will have to cope with the realities of limited authority.

Comparison with Other Countries

There was a question relating *perestroyka* to the Hungarian reform which commenced in January 1968. Wouldn't it be better to do things simultaneously, as was done in Hungary? The answer is that simultaneous restructuring of the management of our country's economy did not appear to be feasible. But with regard to greater emphasis on the service sector, I agree that we should consider this option more seriously. However, during the preceding five-year plan period, services for fees (*platnyye uslugi*) were slated to increase by 25 percent. The current five-year plan calls for an increase of 50 percent. During the course of its first two years, the rate of growth was 10 percent, and in 1988 it is expected to be 11.8 percent. Accordingly, we should significantly exceed our plan targets, and if more attention is paid to the service sector an increase of 15 to 20 percent is within reach.

I realize, of course, that the more complex the industries, the more effort it takes to make things work. The situation was somewhat different in Hungary, where the economic mechanism, but not the country's economic policy, was expected to change. During their transition to new economic structures, the Hungarians opted for continued reliance on many new large construction projects. Lacking justification, not unlike in Yugoslavia and in Poland as well, most of these inefficient projects proved to be unusable.

They were thus bereft of a strategy for technical reconstruction of the kind that is in evidence here. And our country's approach to *perestroyka* differs, for it undertakes to reform the entire mechanism, as well as all aspects of economic policy, including consumption policy.

Indeed, rather dramatic problems relating to the well-being of the population were surfacing in Hungary and Poland. This was due to their efforts to improve the living standards too rapidly, while the development of productive forces lagged behind, prompting the accumulation of substantial debts. Large indebtedness and radical reduction of net investment rates in Hungary continued during the course of three five-year plan periods.

In the USSR the reverse is true. Our living standards, far from being ahead of the economy, lagged behind. In 1960, many of our indices measuring the well-being of the people were higher than in 1985. Our death rate of 6.7 per 1,000 was the lowest in the world, and the average life expectancy of 70 years in the USSR measured up to that of Japan in the 1960s.

Ours was the best system of secondary school education. In any event, a commission of American educators appointed by your President pointed out that 10 percent of our national income was allocated to education—twice as much as by any other country. And now the U.S. is allocating one and a half times as much as we are. And in those years, we were in a better position to satisfy the demand for food products, etc.

As outlined above, the damaging consequences of trends that persisted in the 1960s and 1970s are reflected in the state of affairs in our social sector. But we now have the room for growth in that sector by relying on redistribution, which the other countries are not in a position to do.

Moreover, our *perestroyka's* main focus is the well-being of the population, and man is at the center of all attention and consideration. Hence, prices for necessities such as meat or milk have to be increased very gradually and not at once as elsewhere.

COMMENTS ON COMPETITION

HEWETT: I have a question I wanted to ask that didn't come up. For those of us who are thinking about price reform and the role of foreign economic relations in *perestroyka*, one of the interesting issues is the role you anticipate for what General Secretary Gorbachev has called economic competition (as opposed to socialist competition). Those of us who wonder how a price reform might work, in particular how contract pricing might be effective, believe that you somehow have to introduce an effective mechanism of competition which will maintain downward pressure on prices to protect society from effective price increases by producers and consumers.

It is a particularly difficult problem in your country, where the concentration of economic power is so great and vested in so few enterprises. And indeed, in his speech at the June Plenum, General Secretary Gorbachev indicated an interest in having even fewer enterprises, something in the order of 2,000 national-level conglomerates producing much of industrial output (*Pravda*, June 26, 1987).

I can think of two forms of economic competition that would be effective.

One of them is imports, which could be used to directly compete with Soviet producers in order to force them to operate more efficiently, to produce higher quality products, or else to have to go out of business. The other possible form of competition would be to encourage Soviet enterprises to compete more with each other. For example, you have approximately 50 industrial ministries supervising enterprises that produce mainly industrial goods. Many of those ministries also supervise production of a broad range of products. Why not encourage enterprises under the jurisdiction of all such ministries to produce any products they wish? Simply advise a director of an enterprise controlled by the Ministry of Metallurgy that he is free to start producing radios, but remind him that there is a bankruptcy law waiting if he makes a mistake. That is, he can fail in light of the all-embracing *khozraschet*. That would produce a form of competition that would seem to be quite useful.

AGANBEGYAN: We must organize competition between enterprises and keep it going under conditions of full *khozraschet* and self-financing, whereby management will select the assortment of products they may wish to produce without approval from ministries. Enterprises have their own resources and freedom to vary production depending on orders from the consumer. Moreover, we are creating cooperatives involving private initiative.

As to the 2,000 conglomerates intended to be under the jurisdiction of ministries while all the relatively small enterprises (judging by the number of employees) would be subordinated to regional or some other provincial organization, it is an idea in very raw form. No one was prepared to limit the number of enterprises to 2,000. The opposite is true. We have as many as 8,000 cooperatives today and hope to create more relatively small enterprises, believing that it is not in our best interests to rely on large enterprises exhibiting signs of hypertrophy. The USSR has only 46,000 enterprises today, not counting collective farm enterprises and cooperatives. But we should have perhaps as many as several hundred thousand.

Imports should be an important component of competition when the process begins to shape up in tandem with progress in the convertibility of our currency. We should at first, however, look forward to convertible currency for the markets of CMEA countries and then consider world markets. But in order to accomplish these objectives, we must first reform prices so as to enhance the ability of our products to compete. And there is also the need to improve technology, and thereby quality, which you appropriately emphasized.

And with regard to some products, for example, turbines, we plan to organize admittedly artificial contests. Also, state procurement orders with competitive bidding, the way it is done in the U.S., are under consideration and are likely in the form of contests as well. In any event, we appreciate the problem and the need to resolve it. It is even possible to consider remedial legislation to curb monopoly in production and in selected sectors of consumption. As Lenin said, any kind of monopoly leads to decomposition, and I too think it does.

CHAPTER 10

The New Model of Economic Management

Leonid I. Abalkin
with *Ed A. Hewett, Abram Bergson, Gregory Grossman*, and
Jerry F. Hough

ABALKIN: I shall address some of the same issues raised by Academician
Aganbegyan in his presentation (Aganbegyan, 1987), but will focus more on
the theoretical aspects of these issues and on the theoretical principles underlying a new model of management which is to be refined and implemented in
the Soviet Union. At the very outset, I would like to stress that it is a complicated
model. Not everyone, even in our own country, has a clear understanding of
what we want and how this management system will function when it is finally
in place. Needless to say, it is even more difficult for foreigners to grasp.

ECONOMIC MODEL OF SOVIET REFORM

About a month ago, for example, I met with an American delegation visiting
our country. I talked with its leader, I believe, a State Department official, for
about an hour on the subject of our reform, and the essence of *perestroyka*.
His reaction at the end of our discussion was a query to the effect that "it will
be something like the reform in Yugoslavia." I tried to explain that *perestroyka*
would not be like that at all.

It seems that attempts are being made to compare the model which is to be
ingrained and established in our country by the beginning of the 1990s with
some standard model or prototype. Such a prototype is then used as a point of
departure to infer what we are trying to accomplish and how far we have
advanced toward that goal. Very often, comparisons are made with a Western,
market-type model, and our progress is viewed and questions are raised in an
effort to measure how closely we approach this model. But this approach reflects
a lack of understanding. We do not intend to evolve into such a model, and
do not consider it to be ideal. Ours is more complex and not a market model.
Nor will it become one in the future. That is why, for example, the role of

First published in *Soviet Economy*, 1987, 3, 4, pp. 298–312. At the time, Academician Abalkin was Director
of the Institute of Economics of the Academy of Sciences of the USSR. [Eds.]

prices is somewhat different here than in a classical model of a market economy. We shall attempt to address many problems (e.g., balance or equilibrium within the market), not only by regulating prices and incomes, but in a number of instances by undertaking a variety of measures, such as those relating to the administration of planning in the economy. All of this contributes to the complexity of our model.

The Radical Character of Change

The next point which needs to be stressed is that today we are speaking about a very profound reform—a reform that is revolutionary in nature—and one that calls for the dismantling of the existing managerial system and the formation of a new system based on principles, ideals, goals, and social maxims considered to be appropriate to socialism. But this raises questions about the character of the existing model. If it is socialist, then why do we have to dismantle it? And if we must discard it, then what compels us to do so?

The answers to these questions have to do with the fact that we had in the past (and still have today) a serious deformation of the principles of socialism in our economic life and in the system of management. It was a deformation of principles yielding a distorted, instead of real, socialism. Our views on socialism today have been substantially reconstituted. They have become more profound, and seem to us more resilient, flexible, and correct, though in many ways also quite different. The reform is called upon to eliminate this deformation and to enable us to freely realize the potentials and advantages that we see in our system.

Our reform has come about as a result of a fundamental change in the objectives that foster the development of the economy. I sometimes ask myself whether *perestroyka* would be necessary if not for the serious economic problems which became apparent during the 1970s and early 1980s. Is *perestroyka* a random occurrence resulting from historical aberrations in our development, without which it would not exist, or is it a natural phenomenon? Is it inevitable?

I am inclined to believe that *perestroyka* is inevitable. It reflects a fundamental change in the very processes we must manage. We now face a different set of technological relationships than in the past, a different scale, a different social situation, and a change in the character of the people who are participating in the process.

Needless to say, if the economic deformations of recent years had not been present, then *perestroyka* would be different in character. Different methods would be used to implement it and, probably, also at another time. Perhaps it would be less difficult to see it through. However, the process of restructuring would still involve efforts to overcome deformation and to combine the renewal and regeneration of socialist principles with the objective logic of economic growth.

Thus, the initial group of reasons for *perestroyka* reflects circumstances specific to the USSR, which may not exist in other countries. A second group of reasons, policies, and trends is more international in character, and not exclusively limited to the USSR. That is why we say that *perestroyka* or a fundamental economic restructuring is not only necessary for the Soviet Union, but for other regions of the world as well—for those located to the east, west, and south of our country.

The Challenge in *Perestroyka*

Many questions have been raised and, for some reason, much attention paid by researchers to the depth of the transformation of our system of property relations, where the main emphasis has been placed on the development of cooperative activity (its current forms, small units, family units, and individual labor activity). This is truly a major step forward and a new approach. We now consider property relations as a multifaceted system combining a multiplicity of large and small forms, each comprising a part of socialism. The matter of cooperatives and private activity, however, is neither the most difficult nor the most important issue involving property relations. It is a relatively simple matter.

The need for progress across a broad front, through a variety of forms of ownership, is quite understandable. It is easy to perceive that these new forms of ownership stimulate an individual to be frugal with property and with production. He is aware of every work hour and every unit of output, and takes care of the tools of his labor. This should be encouraged and, if necessary, regulated by taxes and other means, possibly even including socially unjustified differentiation. There are problems here, but they are not overly complicated dilemmas.

The greatest challenge is how to make production more flexible, capable of rapidly reacting to scientific and technological developments and of adjusting to the perpetually changing requirements of society. How does one make it while maintaining state or socialist property as the dominant form? Is it possible to motivate workers of enterprises based on state property to be more careful when they handle such property? To see to it that they behave and feel like property owners who have a personal stake in their own work, and not like temporary day laborers? Or to eliminate estrangement between management and labor? A candid analysis of our experience embracing the two preceding decades indicates that this problem has not as yet been resolved.

For the present, state property has proven unable to reorganize itself and assimilate new technologies rapidly. And the question should be asked whether it is capable of doing just that and, if so, what should be done about it? That is why our search for answers leads in the direction of full *khozraschet*, self-financing, self-management, and election of enterprise leaders. It is not an effort to increase efficiency by two or three percent, but an answer to the summons of history to prove the ability of socialism to renew itself. We are continuing our search and quest for economic and social progress and are developing new methods and approaches. We shall go forward, but the magnitude of our efforts and the tasks are quite considerable.

About Sequencing and the Need for Decisive Action

Finally, I would like to reiterate that our economic development is on a long and complicated journey. We are now in a period of transition. In China, it was possible to begin with reforms in agriculture, services, and retail trade, and thus accumulate resources for five, six, or eight years, and then to commence the reform of industry. Perhaps China had eight years, but we do not.

We have squandered the time available to us in the past, and we cannot wait another eight years to reorganize industry. If we postpone the matter and lose another eight years, we shall never become a highly developed technological and industrial power. I say this for several reasons.

First, there is the substantial and very rapid progress in science and technology. If we procrastinate and wait eight years before the new technology in industry is mastered and ingrained, an entire generation of equipment, and possibly even two generations, will become obsolete during this period. We will then be behind the state of the art not by one, but by two generations in technology, and be unable to overcome such a gap. It is impossible to leap from a primitive level of technology to one that is up-to-date. An infrastructure and support personnel must be developed. We can reduce the duration of the stages involved, but we cannot skip a stage. Thus, we cannot afford to lag behind. The time is very short, and there is no turning back.

A second reason that we cannot begin in one sector and proceed later on to reform the other has to do with social factors involving attitudes of people. The people are tired of waiting and they are tired of words. This is a serious problem, which reflects an entire complex of social attitudes and the effect of social factors. It cannot be ignored when policy is about to be formulated.

A third reason is that it is very difficult to progress in one area without improvement in the other.[1] We really need a very profound reform in agriculture. But sometimes the matter tends to be viewed somewhat simplistically, e.g.: "Let us tomorrow convert all our collective farms to the family brigade system of organization and we will solve all our problems in a couple of years." And examples are cited to the effect that "this team is using the family contract method, which has doubled their productivity within two or three years." But this approach is bordering on naiveté. We cannot solve these problems simply by turning to the family brigade and produce as much milk per cow as farmers in the United States. Reliance on brigades or on any method, no matter how superior, even if we were in a position to induce American farmers to come here, will not do. We will not be able to achieve this level, because the yield

---

1. In other words, reforms in industry will be difficult without concurrent reforms in agriculture. [Eds.]

of our dairy livestock is not up to par. We must change the breed of our cows and the type of feed, and we must replace outmoded agricultural equipment. But up-to-date agricultural equipment calls for restructuring of technology in agricultural machine building and in the infrastructure—roads, elevators, and warehouses for produce—as well. New technology is not just gigantic crates of the most modern equipment. Therefore, even progress in agriculture in our country within eight years is out of the question if technological progress in industry remains at the level at which it was in the past.

Thus, we are forced to take these partial measures, to go over to full *khozraschet* before the reform in prices is in place. Such half measures will not produce dramatic improvements immediately. Early successes will be quite modest, but will become more substantial as the reform is consolidated and refined by the early 1990s. We have no option here and can no longer postpone these decisions. This reality does not make our lives easier, nor does it facilitate efforts to solve the problem. History has placed us in this situation and we cannot bypass the transitional period.

DISCUSSION

The Role of the Ministry

BERGSON: You have referred to the problems of transition, and suggested, in fact, that the current transition may be followed by another transition. Perhaps it is not appropriate to try to look at what lies further down the road, but I would appreciate it if you could elaborate on at least one aspect. In the reform, as it has thus far been worked out, one gets the impression that economic methods[2] are to be stressed greatly at the enterprise level and the level of the association.

At the same time, one also gets the impression that at the level of the ministry, it is not so clear what the criteria for success are to be, or how extensively financial discipline and controls will operate at that level. In reading the reform documents, I am struck that the ministry is still held accountable for the performance of the enterprise. This raises the question of what will guide the ministry, and to what extent will this influence the behavior of the enterprise in ways that would be in conflict with financial criteria—financial controls and the like?

ABALKIN: There is a problem connected with the role of the ministry in the new system. But we must distinguish between current practices and the model of the new managerial system, which apparently will become a reality only in the beginning of the 1990s.

In principle, ministries should not be responsible for the work of an enter-

---

2. I.e., those methods emphasizing financial discipline and controls, the use of financial criteria to judge and reward success, etc. [Eds.]

prise, but as long as they are, the old bureaucratic mechanism of management will be preserved. It is very difficult to alter the system and to change the psychology of people. But if we don't abandon this idea of the ministry being responsible for the work of the enterprises, then it will be very difficult to change over to new methods.

Moreover, if a ministry retains its original structure and is not transformed into an economic complex,[3] then such a ministry should remain an element of the state apparatus, and economic criteria to evaluate its activity should not apply to it. In other words, if a ministry is not responsible for the work of the enterprises in its branch of activity, say as many as 200 enterprises, if it does not function or take part in the economic activity itself, then financial methods of control are not applicable to it.

What is then the ministry's responsibility? Although 90 percent of our people in the Soviet Union would probably still answer the question that the ministry controls or manages the enterprise, it is in fact in charge of the branch. And a branch of the national economy is more than the sum of its enterprises.

Thus, the question calls for an understanding of fairly complicated theoretical problems. A ministry takes charge of a branch, which comprises an organic system with its own specific characteristics, its own integrity and problems connected with the development of the branch proper. The latter can be illustrated by questions such as what is an above- or below-average number of enterprises within a branch, or what is the appropriate technical approach to the study of social needs, etc. These are functions that an organization that administers the branch must perform—functions of the ministry.

But how can bureaucratic methods and interference by ministries be eliminated? Our new system has its pluses and minuses, but one advantage is the fact that it has been conceived as a holistic or integral organism.[4]

Take the problem of self-management, for instance, and more specifically the election of enterprise directors. Let us assume that a director is summoned by the ministry to be told, as in the past, that he has to shape up, to do "this and that," to correct the plan and change it. The director reacts by suggesting that he intends to discuss the issue with his collective. "I will seek the advice of the council of my labor collective," he will say, "to decide if I should agree with you or not."

The ministry official might respond by intimating that the collective's opinion is irrelevant. "You are ordered to proceed," he is admonished, "and the ministry will dismiss you if you disobey." The director then has the right and authority to remind the official that his ministry did not elect him, did not appoint him, and "you will not dismiss me."

That is what the fully developed system is all about. And if we fail to have

3. It is possible, for instance, that several ministries may be converted into one or more large economic [interbranch] complexes, especially in the republics.
4. What is implied here, as is evident in the following paragraphs, is that the system is sufficiently broad as to incorporate certain checks and balances to authority at any one level of the administrative hierarchy. [Eds.]

it in place, then decisions on financial control, profit, *khozraschet*, and other financial levers will not amount to anything. The system must be finalized to include all decision-making structures, to provide the solution of personnel problems, and to install the financial levers such as profits, *khozraschet*, etc.

There is an additional tool for the restructuring of the decision-making apparatus. In January 1988 we will have to reduce by some 50 percent the number of people employed by the ministries. There are many who claim that this cannot be done—there is a large amount of work to be done and there will only be roughly one-half of the former staff to do the job.[5]

The objective of the prospective curtailment is not confined to saving the funds expended on wages or automobile transportation. Rather, it is intended that with only one-half the staff at their disposal, the ministries will lose the ability to manage by utilizing the old methods. Physically, they will be unable to follow through and thus be compelled to change their style and methods of administration. It is a coercive approach to changes in the approach of ministries to management, but an approach that will make such changes inevitable.

This variety of self-reinforcing measures, then, will have to radically alter the situation: financial methods, the development of democracy in the management of production, a drastic reduction in the number of employees functioning in the administrative apparatus of management, and simplification of its structure.

This is not the ultimate solution, but it is a step that should be taken today. Perhaps another, more radical step will materialize within two or three years in the future. Everything cannot be accomplished all at once. Let us not rush, but see what transpires.

Cooperative Socialism

HOUGH: My question has to do with what General Secretary Gorbachev has to say about cooperative socialism. When you speak of flexibility in state property, about cooperative socialism, are you referring only to the services and agriculture, or does that concept mean that even a very large factory will eventually become some kind of cooperative enterprise? Will the Magnitogorsk Metallurgical Plant become something more than a state enterprise?

ABALKIN: The question is quite interesting. It merits an answer that ought to clarify our understanding of the concept of cooperation. Cooperation, or in this case the adjective "cooperative," has a dual meaning. Traditionally, it is regarded as a form of business management based on cooperative ownership of the means of production. Such ownership was formed by combining properties owned by peasants or artisans, say, in urban areas, whereupon some

---

5. In the Ministry of Education of the Azerbaijan SSR, for example, 52 workers of the original 105 are to remain after the planned staff reduction.

collective form of ownership based on this amalgamation prompted the emergence of cooperation.

Today, our experience shows that the forms of cooperation are much more multifarious and complex. One such form is represented by leasing arrangements involving state property. For example, certain state-owned brick manufacturing plants are leased to cooperatives, and the results turn out to be quite promising. While this arrangement comprises a form of cooperation in ownership, the brick plant continues to be owned by the state. One should note that there is an element of a rental relationship in the aforementioned cooperative arrangement established by agreement to lease the plant. And there are many other forms of cooperative relations. They will be developed in time not only in agriculture, but also in the city, involving retail trade, services, public catering, and some smaller industries. Primarily these will be enterprises of rather local significance, although the possibility of their expansion to form entities of broader significance cannot be ruled out.

There is still another meaning of the term cooperation not directly related to ownership. Cooperation is also a way of organizing communal work, such as a team contract at a state enterprise.[6] It is not cooperation in the sense of cooperative ownership, but rather a form of retaining labor and organizing production on the basis of cooperative principles.

If we then publish data on the share of cooperatives in the national income, not all of the aforementioned forms of cooperative activity will be included in the statistics. The transitional or intermediate forms[7] will appear under the heading of "state enterprises." Therefore, such intermediate forms of cooperative activity will evolve as components within large economic complexes and associations (considered as "state enterprises") and function on the basis of the new Law on the State Enterprise, which will become effective on January 1, 1988. A special law will be adopted to cover the "cooperatives proper," which are neither components of state enterprises nor transitional or intermediate forms of cooperative activity. The law may possibly reflect a different set of principles and a totally different understanding of autonomy.

The State Enterprise under the New Law

GROSSMAN: The following question may be somewhat removed from the extremely interesting topics that we are discussing, but I hope the Academician is willing to answer it. In reading the various documents pertaining to the reforms, such as the Law on the State Enterprise (Zakon 1987), I have been trying to assimilate an understanding of what might be referred to as the objective function (*tselevaya funktsiya*) of the state enterprise. Curiously, there is one kind of state enterprise, the bank, for which the objective function is

---

6. The team or brigade comprises a small collective which controls the production process and allocates wages on the basis of its total earnings.

7. These might include, for example, the brick plant and enterprise team mentioned above. [Eds.]

spelled out unambiguously. Somewhere in the decree pertaining to banking (*O korennoy perestroyke*, 1987), there is a statement that banks will be expected to make profits and, perhaps even by implication, to maximize profits.

When it comes to enterprises in general, on the other hand, there are all kinds of generalized broad, and I would say perhaps sanctimonious, statements, particularly in the Law on the State Enterprise, to the effect that the objective of an enterprise is to serve the needs of society, and that the enterprise must be responsive to the interests of the consumer. But the ultimate purpose of the enterprise expressed in terms of its actual operations is nowhere to be found. In the final analysis, enterprise management is to derive its bonuses largely from the fulfillment of contract obligations, and that presumably will stimulate managers to act accordingly.

Even this, however, is not entirely a satisfactory statement describing the objective of the enterprise. It merely states that contractual obligations of the enterprise must be fulfilled and that management will receive bonuses upon fulfillment. So the question remains: which contractual obligations will the enterprise elect to enter into? There usually is a choice.

Finally, there is the interesting problem of the internal decision-making and power structure in the enterprise, and particularly the role of the collective and that of the workers' council. These bodies have certain decisions to make, which at least by implication will point in the direction of an objective function for the collective and therefore the enterprise.

There has been a plethora of theoretical and empirical research focused on Yugoslav enterprises under similar conditions. Although experts have a variety of opinions about results that have been obtained, the findings have been interesting. A collective, for example, under certain circumstances will resist the hiring of additional labor so as not to share the benefits of production with more workers. Therefore, there may be an economically inefficient tendency to keep the labor force smaller than it otherwise should be.

ABALKIN: In answering your question, I shall proceed to use the currently functioning model as a point of departure, with the understanding that it cannot be fully implemented in 1988, but rather much later. Within the framework of the new model of economic management, an enterprise has two objective functions. It must (1) work for the consumer and (2) make a profit. The idea of working for the consumer is fairly straightforward. Any enterprise works for this purpose, from the store or a dining facility up to the largest *kombinat*. And it should work in a way that reflects satisfactory results requested by the consumer.

The second function, profit, refers to the fact that the enterprise must see to it that state property is used effectively, reflecting a sense of prudence. Some part or segment of state property is set aside for the collective, say one billion rubles worth of fixed assets. That sum is to be utilized efficiently, and the demonstrated efficiency will be expressed in profits.

But why is the draft law (Zakon, 1987) specific with regard to banks, all expected to realize a certain amount of profit, while the term profit is not used in the written document stipulating the law in reference to enterprises? This is a fine point which ought to be clarified. The law provides for two models of *khozraschet*,[8] so the enterprise has a choice between two options—an aspect of the Law on the State Enterprise which I want to emphasize. To a considerable extent, that law is somewhat vague, but this vagueness is one of its great advantages, because the indeterminancy broadens the degree of autonomy available to the enterprise.

Profit does not exist as a category in the second model of *khozraschet*. Cost (*sebestoimost'*), which incidentally is a classical concept in our thinking, also is not mentioned; nor are wages. It is thus a totally different model. It works in accord with the precepts of the residual principle. We take the total revenue, subtract expenditures for the purchase of materials and depreciation, and the residual is considered to be the income. From that we deduct some payments to the budget, and the remainder is *khozraschetnyy dokhod*.[9] Various funds are then created out of that residuum—funds for development, those for technical renovation, and funds for social development. What remains after all these funds are constituted or replenished is the wage fund. And neither profit nor cost is involved in the construct.

This is why we cannot state or express in strictly scientific terms that the objective of a production enterprise is profit. Rather, its objective is this new term, *khozraschetnyy dokhod*, and its objective function is to maximize *khozraschetnyy dokhod*. Thus, there are two interrelated objective functions of the enterprise: satisfaction of the needs of the consumer and an effort to maximize economic efficiency, which shows up either as profit or as *khozraschetnyy dokhod*.

The growth of *khozraschetnyy dokhod* would benefit and thus suitably influence the entire collective. The system would fail if it were to be solely expedient for the manager. Both the manager and the employee have a stake in maximizing *khozraschetnyy dokhod*, and the new economic mechanism anticipates this. With regard to the ability of enterprises to be selective in accepting or rejecting contractual work assignments, we want that to happen. But this calls for an equilibrium in the market, a change in the planning system, as well as for financial and price reforms to create a balance between material and financial resources in the national economy.

Then, as in any civilized economy, we will be able to produce and to manage properly. The customer will not be forced to struggle in pursuit of the producer, but rather the producer will pursue the consumer. Needless to say, the producer will try to secure the most advantageous terms to fulfill the contract, but the

8. One of the models is based on an explicit conception of profit. The other, which is described in the following paragraph, is not. [Eds.]

9. *Khozraschetnyy dokhod*, therefore, refers to the net income of the collective, i.e., the sum of all labor payments and profits retained by the firm. The term is not translated here because there is no analogous English-language term which conveys its specific meaning. See Schroeder (1987, p. 222) for a more detailed explanation. [Eds.]

consumer can determine the price he is ready and willing to pay. Contract prices are a key to the system, without which it will not be able to function. The experience in Yugoslavia and elsewhere as well, demonstrates that such a system will put due pressure on enterprises to limit reliance on hiring additional employees and to reduce the workforce. And we are waiting for this to happen.

We are also aware of the compelling task of motivating and maximizing the desire of enterprise management to reduce the size of the workforce. There will be enough work for everyone in the 1980s and 1990s, above all, due to the major redistribution of labor involving a shift toward the service sector, where we are very much behind the developed countries. This sector will be capable of absorbing both the new workers entering the labor market and those released from, or no longer employed in, industry or other productive branches because of changes prompted by the new mechanism. Again, this is precisely what we wish to accomplish, and the system is directed toward this end. It should lead to the end result of motivating collectives to refrain from hiring new people if they are not absolutely indispensable.

Let us assume that an enterprise faces a need to secure top-quality engineering or management personnel or a skilled procurer (*snabzhenets*). There will have to be an understanding that the person(s) selected will undertake to produce an economic effect that will justify the compensation or wages. Management will seek to pay less than the net effect (profit of *khozraschetnyy dokhod*) provided by the newly hired person to the enterprise. And if the new worker demands more, a wage that is higher than the additional income derived from his work, then the enterprise will not be compelled to hire him. In making the calculation, the enterprise will have to take into account a small fee for each additional worker it hires. For regular workers the fee is 300 rubles per year. But for a specialist with higher education, the enterprise must pay 3,000 rubles to the government when it hires him;[10] thus, a considerable incentive not to employ extra workers will be in the system.

The specialists at our institute regard this as an incorrect solution which will not improve the situation. But, it may be necessary today because 14 percent of our enterprises are operating at a loss, and they cannot pay. And another 20 percent are barely profitable with hardly enough profit even without such payments. But still, let us assume we require a payment not of 300 rubles, but of 3,000 rubles, which we certainly could. Then the barely profitable enterprises could only afford to make the payments if they had a budget subsidy, which they could then return to the budget in the form of payments for labor resources. This is no system.

In reference to your final question, the Law on the State Enterprise does not stipulate how the worker's council should be elected. Nor does it mention an open or secret ballot, or specify who should chair the council. The issue attracted considerable attention and there are two schools of thought. The

---

10. More specifically, the payment is to the higher educational institution that trained the specialist.

proponents of one believe that the enterprise director should be the council's chairman, for there should be no division of power. Their opponents advocate the opposite view, that a director should under no circumstances chair the council—a must, which should be stipulated in the law.

The law, however, provides no answer and I think this to be a great advantage, because it gives a measure of freedom to the collective. In some instances, the first solution will be appropriate, and in others the second. Since the Law on the State Enterprise is designed to promote democracy, it should not regulate every single step that is to be anticipated by a collective.

The Role of Local Party Officials

HEWETT: One issue that has not been discussed thus far is the role of the party in the new reformed economic system, and particularly the role of party first secretaries at the *obkom*[11] level in this system. In the system as it now exists, the *obkom* first secretary plays an important role in the life of the enterprise. On the one hand, the *obkom* secretary acts at times as a supervisor of the work of an enterprise, and on the other, he assists the enterprise in its efforts to acquire resources from the remainder of the system. Thus, the relationship between the manager of a large enterprise and his *obkom* first secretary is very close.

Now, it would seem to me that the logic of the new system, of the reform, would suggest that the local party secretary no longer should interfere in any way in the operation of the enterprise. If you have told an enterprise that its income is what determines its wages and its decisions determine its income, then clearly outside interference restricts the ability of the enterprise to earn income.

Yet, even now we can see in the speeches of the Soviet leaders, in decrees, and in the press ample evidence that the *obkom* first secretarty of the party still plays a critical role and indeed is held responsible for the performance of his enterprises. I recall several years ago a decree was issued about the low quality of radios and television sets (V Tsentral'-nom, 1986). The blame was apportioned between a number of ministries involved in the production of radios and televisions, enterprise directors, and party officials at all levels. They were all held responsible for the quality of the items produced in these ministries.

Now, how can it be the case that, on the one hand, the party secretaries are being told not to interfere in the operation of the enterprise, and, on the other hand, they are still even today being held responsible for what is being done in those enterprises?

ABALKIN: I would begin my answer by emphasizing that our historical experience in comparing this reform with the preceding one, has taught us a great deal. In particular, it is quite clear to us now that radical changes in the

11. Refers to the oblast party committee. [Eds.]

economy and its management are impossible. Such changes cannot demonstrate noticeable results if they occur only in the economic orbit, without similar major changes in the political life of the country, in social relations, and in the spiritual and ideological values. All sustain, supplement, and interact with one another.

It is impossible, for example, to fully implement *khozraschet* without democracy, or more specifically a democratic system of management. Moreover, we will never be able to attain democracy in management without full *khozraschet*. Democracy is presumed to protect the rights of man from interference, and his interests have to be protected. Then he can speak freely without fear. Accordingly, these different aspects of a radical *perestroyka* are interrelated.

Hence, radical changes must take place in the context and within the framework of methods followed by party committees at all levels; at the highest, starting with the Central Committee of the CPSU, and extending down to the primary party organizations in the enterprises, the collective farms, and elsewhere. This is quite clear. Certainly *perestroyka* is complicated, as are the old habits, the inertia, and the difficulties of the transition period. The reform must be protected from attempts to distort it.

Changes, of course, will have to be made. But unless Gosplan reorganizes its operations, unless the ministries restructure themselves, and unless their enterprises start to function within the framework of the new system of management, then it is unthinkable that the first secretaries will have started to pioneer the new methods.

It will certainly take several years, even though we have made several bold moves in this area. We have begun the practice of electing party first secretaries on a competitive basis. The party organization elects its first secretary not by endorsing one candidate, but by voting for one of several candidates and resorting to a secret ballot. The secretaries now are accountable to members who elected them, and such accountability also places certain limits on their activity.

Obviously, when the survival of the collective and its wages depend directly on the quality of its work, when there is no one to help if it performs badly, then economic considerations erect barriers to block interference. Much remains to be done to improve the content, style, and work of the Party committees— one of the central issues on the agenda of the Party Conference next year, noted by Academician Aganbegyan.

Perhaps the following scenario, however, will help place the role of local party officials in proper perspective. A reporter who prepares a critical article for a newspaper, exercising democratic principles and partaking of *glasnost'* to its utmost, boldly expresses his conviction that important officials ought to be purged. What else can he do but identify a local first secretary, enterprise director, or minister by name? That is what *glasnost'* is all about. And while most, if not all, reports tend to reflect the true state of affairs, too much attention appears to be focused on individuals. Not enough is in writing to analyze the essence of the problem, to understand why faulty TV sets are being produced, and to devise measures to correct the situation. It should be understood that even if the enterprise director, the minister, and first secretary end up in prison, the TV sets will not improve solely as a result of exposure. But it is less difficult to expose than to analyze the situation. So returning to what had to be said about the ministries, the matter can be summarized quite succinctly. In order to change the methods of management, the responsibility for plan fulfillment must be removed from the shoulders of party committees and first secretaries. If they continue to be held responsible for the plan of each enterprise, they will interfere as they did in the past. They will have the influence if the responsibility continues to be theirs.

CHAPTER 11

Socioeconomic Aspects of *Perestroyka*

Tat'yana I. Zaslavskaya
with *Abram Bergson, Jerry F. Hough,* and *Gregory Grossman*

ZASLAVSKAYA: My background as an economist and a sociologist leads me to explore a range of issues that involve primarily the social aspects of *perestroyka*. If one were to formulate a social policy, it is important—and perhaps central— to begin by taking full account both of the social aspects of *perestroyka* and of the indirect social consequences that it may produce.

It is abundantly clear that the central framework of the economy defines the system of management. But another dimension of that system is the social structure, bearing in mind that any major change generates corresponding re- verberations in the system's structure. The resonance may be manifested in the formation of some new social groups and the ensuing disappearance, or sub- stantial modification, in a number of other groups.

The main outcome, of course, is the change in the relative status of various groups—improvements for some and setbacks for others. And as various laws are adopted at this planning stage of *perestroyka*, we must clearly understand this social trend. Our literature has not covered it adequately, emphasizing the purely economic approach and tending to abstain from consideration of socio- economic matters. And while the paramount objective of *perestroyka* is to upgrade the efficiency of our economy, it is extremely important to keep in mind the impact that economic relations have on the social sector. Speaking of the social content of *perestroyka* and the measures that have been planned in the economic sector, I would identify the following main elements:

First, democratization of the use and sale of state property, which is a fundamentally important measure at the social level. It affects the interests of a very broad segment of our society.

Second, redistribution of rights and obligations among various administrative

An abbreviated version of this chapter was first published in *Soviet Economy*, 1987, 3, 4, pp. 313–331. Academician Tat'yana Ivanovna Zaslavskaya is one of the founders of Soviet sociology and at the time of writing was president of the Soviet Sociological Association. She is best known in the West as the author of the critical "Novosibirsk Report" (1983). [Eds.]

136

organizations—not a social consequence, but rather an element of *perestroyka*. As you know, we have party, government, and economic organizations that manage the economy. And when *perestroyka* began, the distribution of rights and obligations among these three was extremely uneven. Some have more rights and fewer obligations, while others have many obligations and limited rights. *Perestroyka* seeks a greater balance, whereby every group's rights are commensurate with its obligations. Naturally, this affects group interests. Things get better for some, and for others they deteriorate.

The third is a social diversification expressed in the pluralization of the types of economic entities. When *perestroyka* began, our economy was highly unified, composed of state enterprises plus collective farms, which today are not very different from those enterprises. But currently, the social structure is influenced by the cooperative, contractual, leasing, and other arrangements, which, together with dispersal of the economic activities of local Soviets and public organizations, prompted a substantial pluralization of economic entities; this trend can be traced to the progress of the reform and development of individual activities.

The fourth social trend is an increase in competitiveness in the economic sector, and hence hardened economic relations. This means considerably more variation in the economic positions of enterprises and collectives. It also means possible bankruptcy or liquidation for the least efficient socialist enterprises as well. People in our country are not accustomed to competition; we have a much more easygoing system today. This too comprises a considerable shift in the social system, which may entail some tensions and difficulties.

The fifth element is the inevitable and substantial increase in labor mobility within industries, between and within regions, and between and within enterprises.

We should focus more decisively on the social aspect of *perestroyka* at this stage, because there is some danger that if these elements are not considered in advance, they will have to be considered when they start to materialize. And if there is no strategy for dealing with the resulting difficulties, *perestroyka* itself may be retarded. We see this, for example, in Hungary, when they find it necessary to shut down unprofitable enterprises. The inability to decide what to do with discharged manpower, i.e., a lack of preparation for dealing with social problems, becomes an impediment to the economic reform.

The Problem of Excess Manpower

The social shifts that are intrinsic to *perestroyka* must be considered in conjunction with the likely social consequences that are more indirectly related to it. The changeover of enterprises to the system of self-financing inevitably creates incentives to jettison surplus manpower. The question is, which workers will an enterprise release first? Obviously, not the best ones, but the worst, the least skilled, such as those who have a drinking problem or those whose discipline is not beyond reproach. We must find a solution and make sure that these people are put to work, and we must think about what kind of work to give them.

The second potential problem is discharging workers who are not in a position to compete. In this category are not necessarily the least desirable ones, because they may be very well qualified. I have in mind, for example, women with small children, elderly people, or people in poor health. Managers are usually reluctant to employ them. This problem is also a must on the public agenda, and social guarantees suitable for this group will have to be devised.

The third problem precipitated by release of manpower is vocational rehabilitation. When the economy is restructured, some industries such as mining begin to shrink rather drastically. Thus, miners who seek employment create a new set of problems. Our economists and sociologists see them for what they are, but so far we have tended to define these problems in general terms, focusing on questions of how many people may be released, or attempting to determine where they may be released from. But there is no evidence of a differentiated, qualitative approach, and the effort to solve the dilemma of surplus labor is essentially in its infancy.

Of course, in principle we have a great capacity for dealing with unemployment. However, the issue is not only to have enough jobs for the available manpower, for it also matters where these jobs are located. We are facing the problem of territorial mobility—where are these jobs and who can fill them? There is an obvious requirement for a quantitative, qualitative, and territorial congruity. To sum up, the problem is exceedingly complicated.

The Change in Living Standards

The second consequence that may grow out of *perestroyka*—unless we develop mechanisms for dealing with it beforehand—is the more intensive territorial differentiation in people's living standards with regard to levels of social infrastructure and delivery of various social services. Today, the territorial criterion is the strongest determinant of differences in a person's socioeconomic status. It is not only the well-known difference between the city and countryside; in fact, the distinction there has diminished on the whole. I have in mind the different sizes of cities, towns, and villages (such as district centers, farm centers, and outlying settlements), where conditions vary a great deal.

This also applies, of course, to various regions and republics of the country, where one encounters enormous differences in the level of social infrastructure, way of life, and living conditions.

There is an inherent danger in linking the development of the infrastructure and social services to the economic efficiency of enterprises, because our industries are spread out in a certain geographical pattern. Then, some profitable enterprises will have tens of millions to spend, and their employees will have swimming pools, winter gardens, and a wonderful life to enjoy. Meanwhile, less successful, small enterprises with very meager resources will have very little.

This raises the issue of balancing the industry-by-industry approach with the territorial approach, and of designing a reliable economic mechanism that would provide for both the financial as well as material aspects of development, with more or less uniform, equivalent living standards for various regions.

Differentiated Income

Another problem—an inevitable one—is the prospect of greater income differentiation under the new system. This includes wages, income from individual activities, and family income. A host of factors will work in the direction of greater differentiation, ranging from the right of self-financing enterprises to use additional resources for wages, bonuses, and incentives, to individual activities and the operation of small cooperatives.

These processes are already quite evident today, and one can identify at least two problems, one having to do with people's mentality, and the other with real life. The concepts of wage leveling and the great social value of equality are deeply rooted and ingrained in the minds of our people. We have a relatively small variation in earnings, and there is a clearly pronounced and widespread notion among people (including managers) that making a lot of money is not proper. If some people have a very high income, that in itself is perceived as unfair. It does not matter how one works, because more attention is paid to how much he takes than how much he has given.

This attitude may become, and is already becoming, an obstruction tending to corrode the mechanism of *perestroyka*, because *perestroyka's* aim is to release people's energies, so as to enable people with a great potential to realize that potential. They should have incentives to succeed, and therefore opportunities to increase their income to a very high level. But then roadblocks are immediately in the way, for it is assumed that if a person makes 2,000 rubles a month, it must certainly be unearned income. He can't make that much, it is felt; no one can make more than 500 or 600 rubles.

This is a problem for our mass media to address. A lot of work will be required to overcome such notions and to develop perceptions that if someone demonstrates exceptional results in his work, then he should receive an exceptionally high income. He should have the full legal right to earn it and be proud of it, not ashamed.

The second aspect is that differentiated income should really reflect work and not income from profiteering, which has nothing to do with work. Of course, the development of individual activities and cooperatives will prompt personal income in that sphere to be shaped by the market rather than centrally determined wage scales. That will inevitably lead to wide differentiation, and a part of the income will not fit the prevailing concept of fair compensation. We should consciously proceed and accept this. The only question that arises here is the prospect of progressive taxation, which would remove the most fortuitous income—income that is not appropriately justified, because of the interplay of prices. We have major problems in this area as well.

Workers' Attitudes

HOUGH: We have lively discussions in the United States about not simply the social consequences of *perestroyka*, but also the degree of social support for *perestroyka*, and where the support and opposition would come from. There are two interesting aspects of this question that I am about to raise and look forward to hearing your opinion on.

The first is the attitude of industrial workers to *perestroyka*. In a very real sense, the Soviet Union has been a dictatorship of the proletariat, because social policy very much benefited the industrial workers. But it was the industrial worker in the past whose education tended to be very low. In 1939, for example, 93 percent of those workers had only an elementary education or less. Now one is moving toward a situation where most younger workers—perhaps 70, 80, or 90 percent—have a full secondary education.

The first question is, to what extent do workers today have the same attitudes as those of 20, 30, or 40 years ago? In the West, such workers with at least a secondary education have become members of the middle class. They have wanted what upward mobility gave them—their own shops, or opportunities to become foremen.

So when you are talking about skilled workers under 30, are they people who fear unemployment and who therefore may oppose the reform? Or are they people who are very much interested in that aspect of the reform which involves the creation of cooperative services and individual labor, because this would give them an opportunity to move into the middle class? In any event, is there an age and educational differential in the attitude toward reform?

The second question about support comes from a very famous article that you wrote in 1985 (*Izvestiya*, June 1, 1985), in which you were discussing the three levels of administration and the overconcentration of power in the middle level.

You said nothing about the party in that article, although one certainly can imagine that you were saying that the central as well as the regional party organs—the *obkom*, *gorkom*, and the like—had lost power to the ministries.

One could imagine, therefore, that what you were saying, as part of a political strategy, was that the regional party organs would be a strong ally of General Secretary Gorbachev in any reform that lessened the power of the ministries. But in general, I would be interested in your opinion about whether the regional party organs are natural supporters of the reform against the middle level, or whether they are more natural opponents of reform?

ZASLAVSKAYA: First, there have been very few surveys, so far, focused on people's attitudes toward *perestroyka*, that are sociologically and methodologically reliable. There are fairly good reasons for this lack of information. It is pointless to ask the direct question, "Do you support *perestroyka* or not?" The result will be that 99 or 100 percent will say they support it.

Much more subtle methods of analysis are needed, and they are being developed. We will then be in a position to obtain and analyze results not on attitudes toward *perestroyka*, but on attitudes toward very specific measures. What will emerge is a mixed picture, i.e., a person will support one item, have doubts about another, and disagree with a third.

To answer your general question, therefore, I have to rely on combined knowledge assembled from various sources, including personal observations, rather than final accomplished results.

The strategic objective of *perestroyka* is to speed up economic development and the growth of people's living standards. So in objective terms it is primarily serving the interests of most of the working people, including the working class. The question is the degree to which they realize this.

But in addition to the ultimate goals, *perestroyka* has many tactical aspects that involve efforts to eliminate established attitudes and traditions. When *perestroyka* was just getting under way, a rather large segment of both the working class and the intelligentsia took a wait-and-see position, because they remembered the reforms initiated by Khrushchev that did not always yield positive results.

However, two and a half years have gone by, and major advances have been made, above all in the country's social, psychological, and political climate. The key element here, of course, is *glasnost'*, and the public, including the working class, is reacting by perceiving it simply as the fulfillment of its most pressing need. It prompts most people to support *perestroyka*, and my own observations indicate that it makes them increasingly more active.

In general, the attitude toward *perestroyka* follows a scale, from the negative to positive. But we see the most positive form occurring right before our eyes— supporters rolling up their sleeves and getting down to hard work.

I hear a lot less grumbling lately about various changes. But the working class, after all, is also very diverse. There was a segment of that class that, for various reasons, held a privileged position in the past. For example, workers at enterprises such as meat-packing plants could carry off valuable goods. There was a system under which each worker, when he went home, would grab one or two kilograms of meat for himself. And he was satisfied and content.

Now *perestroyka* has begun, which means order, discipline, and measures to eliminate theft. So one encounters groups of workers, who, of course, are not thrilled, but they have to resign themselves to *perestroyka*. I know people who were unhappy in the beginning about the new order, but now they are gradually becoming accustomed to different arrangements and support *perestroyka*. Apparently, when order is established everywhere, life improves even for those who benefited from certain aspects of the disorder.

On the question about young and old people, the young are clearly among the groups with the greatest interest in *perestroyka*, quite understandably, because *perestroyka* is defining what kind of life these people will live. We older people, after all, have already lived most of our lives. Of course, we would like the remainder to take place under *glasnost'*, democratization, and rapid development.

But the older generation is more conservative. It has established other habits, although one cannot say that the older generation has not supported reform. The young are simply supporting it more actively. They are also the best segment of the working class—the most educated, the most skilled, and physically the strongest and healthiest. In other words, they are the people with the greatest work potential, which they could not fulfill under the old economic system. They would work eight hours, but were not allowed to work more than that limit. They fulfilled a certain amount of the plan, but were not permitted to do more. If they wanted a second job, they were not in a position to secure the required consent.

Under the new system, many say, they can produce ten times as much now as they produced before.

Now about your question on the levels of management and the party. Our party has 19 or 20 million members. To begin with, it is a sizable segment of society, and second, it is the society's most active segment. The people who are most central to *perestroyka* are party members. So the confrontations between supporters and those who try to slow down the reform process take place, as a rule, within the party. The division is not between party and nonparty members but rather between different groups of party members.

The planned decentralization of management works in favor of those who are at the lower levels. The rights of republics are expanded, as are those of *krays, oblasts*, and *rayons*. In other words, to a certain degree, power is being dispersed downward.

But there is much conservatism in the party and government bureaucracies, and I think *perestroyka* is causing changes in the status of these groups in two directions. For example, at the *rayon* level of party administration, rights are being increased along with obligations, and many groups are in this position.

In this regard, individual value systems and personality take on tremendous importance. There are people who prefer to have more rights along with greater responsibility. But there are also people who shirk responsibility and would rather have fewer rights.

This variation of attitudes toward *perestroyka* runs not only through society; even within each group we encounter leaders of various types. And there is a nucleus of leaders or directors who are the driving force of *perestroyka*—its conscious participants, leading managers, innovators, and socioeconomic experimenters.[1]

Then there are much more conservative people with reactionary orientations who, by and large, are thinking, "I will just muddle through the five years

---

1. Our own socioeconomic experiments provide an example. The party secretary of Tret'yakov Rayon of Altay Kray, where we are working, is just the kind of man who is propelling *perestroyka*.

left to retirement, and avoid hard work; then whoever replaces me can do what he wants.''

In addition, any *perestroyka*, even if we are just restructuring our own house, entails inconveniences. Everyone has a certain amount of conservatism in him. There are habits, traditions, and *perestroyka* upsets the routine. New laws are enacted all the time, something has to be changed continuously, people have to work much harder, they have to take on more responsibility, and so on.

In this respect, some managers have a harder time. They will declare themselves in favor of *perestroyka*, but in reality feel rather frigid about it. The only solution here is to replace cadres and let in a new generation of most energetic managers.

Income Inequality and Justice

BERGSON: Academician Zaslavskaya, I have read with much interest your discussions of the social aspects of *perestroyka* which have been made available to us in the West. You touched on one of the themes which you have often discussed, namely the relation between income inequality and justice. I should be glad to hear you elaborate somewhat further on this matter, particularly on the concept of what income is earned and what is unearned and represents a form of injustice.

In the West, I think many observers would agree with you that income inequality does, to a certain degree, proceed so far as to be difficult to justify from a social standpoint.

On the other hand, we have a variety of functions that are performed by the price system, and the performance of these functions generates inequalities that I suspect you might find difficult to accept. And I do wonder just where you might draw the line in this regard and at what cost, in terms of economic performance.

You speak of high incomes being earned by persons with great knowledge and skill. In the West, high incomes are often earned by such people, but they are also often a reward for risk-taking, entrepreneurial activity. This is a very important function of the market and of the high incomes.

The individual takes risks on the assumption that there will be a reward if he succeeds. A risk-averse person usually considers that things might not work out. I just wonder how you might view such earnings.

Beyond that, even where one cannot think of the recipients of the income as necessarily acting in a manner that provides a social justification for their exceptional rewards, the high earnings can serve as a device to induce additional people and additional resources to flow into a certain use. And if one were to try to limit those earnings, such a practice could easily tend to dampen the response of the economy to what is perhaps a very significant social need.

I sometimes wonder whether it will be possible to achieve the kind of results that are widely desired in your country without being more tolerant than you seem to be of various forms of inequality. Sometimes, I think, maybe one has to be more thick-skinned than you seem to be on such matters, in order to push ahead. It is very, very difficult to do these things in a neat way and prevent the kind of, let us say, inequities which concern you.

ZASLAVSKAYA: This is a very complex question, and I cannot answer it for lack of clear-cut definitions of what is earned and unearned income. But I will say something about it.

First, we have to define our main objective in regulating people's income. I think that objective is twofold. On the one hand, and most important today, is the goal to provide incentives for every person to work at his maximum potential. Not in the sense of 14 hours a day, but so that an engineer attempts to design a blueprint with the utmost creativity, a writer makes the effort to write the best book that is in him, and a farmer gathers a harvest five or six times as bountiful as he used to obtain in the past.

It is in step with this process of realizing people's potentials that income differentiation should evolve. And since we want this to happen, we should forthwith proceed toward substantial increases in income differentiation.

A special feature of our wage compensation system is that wages are paid largely for time spent on the job, even though it is not a creative component of labor. The creative component is something that we are in effect unable to either tap or reward.

A senior staff scientist, say, earns 300 or 350 rubles a month. He may be a genius or he may be an average man with little talent. The genius will take home 350 rubles, or maybe much less, because he says things that people are not accustomed to hearing. There really is no opportunity for distinguishing one from the other, and the same is true in production.

We have to get away from this sameness and learn to identify the creative component. In the sector of individual activities and cooperatives, of course, this creative component is showing up more noticeably. And it is precisely the chance for creative self-fulfillment that, most of all, is prodding many people into the cooperative sector. At a state enterprise, no matter how brilliant a design you have produced, there is nothing you can do with it— thousands of people have to review every bit of it. But at a cooperative you may have conceived something yesterday, and you try to implement it today.

Here, of course, the risk factor comes into play. Many people want, and know how, to take risks. So the income in this area depends entirely on the market mechanism. The line should be drawn at income that is totally unnecessary and excessive; such income is parasitic.

To put it into numbers, say, the most skilled creative people, such as highly decorated entertainers,[2] earn roughly 1,000 rubles a month. They are unique

2. People's artists of the USSR (Narodnyye artisty SSSR).

and their work has been recognized throughout the Soviet Union. The so-called *shabashniki*,[3] people without unique talent, make about the same amount. But they toil 14 hours a day, virtually without days off, turning out excellent, high-quality work. Working seven, eight, or nine months a season, they end up making more or less the same amount of money. Roughly speaking, 1,000 rubles a month is the maximum income in the public sector.

Now a few words about the private, individual sector. There the labor-intensiveness is at its maximum, and the creative component is included. People take the risk of spending their own money and failing to realize a return. There is no social security in that sector, no pension, no increments for seniority.

Yet we want this sector to develop and to give it some incentive. Hence we can tolerate earnings in the individual sector that are two to three times as high as those in the public sector. If the most prosperous individuals end up making, say, 2,000 or 3,000 rubles a month, such a sum will be a very powerful incentive to develop similar activities. But there is absolutely no need for individuals to earn 100,000 rubles a month.

So I think the ceiling can be higher than it is, but there should be a ceiling—especially since, under Soviet law, people work in the individual sector in addition to working in the public sector. So they do not run the risk that exists under capitalism, when people can go bankrupt and are left without means of support. But our people have their wages and all the social entitlements. They risk some additional resources, but the risk is not all that enormous.

Why not allow individuals to earn a higher income, reflecting the relationship between demand and supply? And if prices are in fact determined on this basis, then we can recognize a certain fairness in a high income derived from providing a service that is extremely essential and in short supply.

Unfortunately, the prices prevailing today do not reflect demand. Our prices are just about whimsical, and therefore alluring to many people who can simply take advantage of this inadequacy in the system. Under the circumstances, a person should not be entitled to a special reward.

In addition, a whole host of social dangers can be found in this area. Our society is labor-oriented. The worth of labor—one of society's highest values—is unquestioned. Everyone works and lives more or less in proportional conformity to one's work. If someone's income begins to exceed, say, 10,000 to 12,0000 rubles a month, he can very rapidly accumulate a sum of money and just live on the interest, without working. And the fact that such fortunes exist in our country is an outrage in the eyes of our working people. They object to the ostentatious life styles of moneyed people who do not work—an affront considered the worst kind of injustice.

A specific category of people, for whom the life style is a goal in itself, is

3. Seasonal construction workers in the countryside hired on a contractual basis. [Eds.]

visibly taking shape. In this group are small-scale craftsmen, some even with hired labor and private property. If the money was kept in their pockets or stockings, the level of tolerance might have been different. But extraordinary wealth promptly begins to be lavished on extravagant cars and palatial residences, breeding intolerance and resentment.

There is a need for setting a reasonable limit, so that people have an adequately attractive incentive to engage in the aforementioned activities, while the basic values of our society remain intact. I think the idea of instituting a progressive income tax is fully compatible with the notion of cutting off the parasitic layer of wealth.

Since income-equalizing values are so ingrained and widespread among us, bureaucracies actually struggle to limit individual earnings to a much lower level. No one is prepared to discuss whether someone should be permitted to make 2,000 or 10,000 rubles a month; the question on the agenda is whether 600, roughly speaking, is too much. And the economy is now developing so slowly due to such mentality. People are too fearful and reluctant to give some breathing space, lest someone make too much money. I think more latitude with incentives, as well as limits on excessive income, should be put in place.

Territorial Differentiation

In reference to the question pertaining to my work on territorial differentiation and Central Asia,[4] I think my most productive work on the subject is to be found in two books. The first, devoted to the development of rural settlements, was published in 1977. It covered in considerable detail the differentiation of Siberian rural settlements according to a variety of living conditions, and viewed the dynamics of various types of settlements—who makes a lot of money, who does not, and how this differentiation increases.

The second book, which came out three years after the first (Zaslavskaya, 1980), analyzes the social and demographic development of the countryside. It incorporates a typology of oblasts of the Soviet Union, defining 130 units. The book discusses union republics (without subdivision) and oblasts, constructing a typology according to their social and demographic problems pertaining to the rural population.

The differences clearly are infinite. Central Asia, incidentally, emerges as a specific type, where the problems are totally different from those characterizing other regions. Then, of course, Siberia offers a very sharp contrast from the Non-Chernozem Central region. We defined seven or eight major types of

---

4. Posed by Prof. Thane Gusafson. The reference to Central Asia in the question (see Zaslavskaya et al, 1987, p. 324) embraced the following four elements of *perestroyka* that would disfavor the region: potential reallocation of investment for reconstruction of capital stock; tendency to forgo big investment projects; effort to cut back subsidies; and linkage of social spending to profitability of enterprises. [Eds.]

regions with completely distinctive features. The problems of the countryside vary, as do its levels of development, and we proposed guidelines for programs of social development for each type of region.

Although both books investigate the countryside, we also have many devoted to the cities. But I view the first two books as the major samples of our focus.

As for the regional aspect of *perestroyka*, not enough work has been done on its economic relationships. Such paucity is understandable, because until the economic, political, and social aspects were integrated into a fundamental concept of *perestroyka*, it was somewhat too early to apply a differentiated approach to various regions and republics.

Now that the concept has basically evolved—although it needs substantial development—the time is upon us to take a look at the regional breakdown. Here, the principal academic investigators should primarily come from regional rather than central institutions. Nor should a commission on *perestroyka* take charge, for the regional investigator, better than anyone, can apply the general concept and evaluate the outcome on familiar territory.

In reference to Central Asia, I would single out two aspects of the problem— economic and social.

On the economic aspect, if we seek competitiveness and a better life for those who do better work, then we have to begin by creating more or less equal economic conditions. You say that Central Asia receives the most sizable subsidies. Conceivably, these subsidies may have to be incorporated into prices. But normal conditions must be created so that Central Asia can compete and no longer continue in the pitiful position of dependence.

But Central Asia, of course, has a very substantial variety of specific social and demographic features that cannot be rectified or balanced at the level of purely economic measures. Thus, measures such as those that establish prices for cotton within limits to provide support for families with six or seven children, are both unfounded and ill-advised. Social policy must take an active role here. One of its most important functions during the formative stage of *perestroyka* is to conceive and develop safeguards that eliminate, or at least minimize, the anticipated complications of social origin.

Thus far, the social program for *perestroyka* is on the drawing board only for the Soviet Union as a whole, and it is difficult to discuss heterogeneous regions until we decide in what direction the program is headed. Understandably, it must be differentiated by region, while due account is taken of common goals and problems.

Central Asia has its own set of problems, but Siberia with a different set will not necessarily be on the losing end. Priority should be given to reconstruction, of course, but since Siberia is a newly developing region, a host of major new enterprises under construction is there to be seen. It also has objects and structures to rehabilitate, so we don't have the sense that *perestroyka* is in some way disadvantageous to Siberia. Central Asia, on the other hand, has to be dealt with, but efforts will have to emanate from the region rather than from the outside.

The Shadow Economy

GROSSMAN: My question is perhaps not too distant from those already posed, but of a somewhat different nature. All societies have two sets of realities: the formal, official, and legal reality, and the informal reality; the informal society and economy is to be distinguished from the official society and economy. It is true of the United States, Brazil, India; it is, of course, also true of the Soviet Union.

In this conference so far, we have spoken primarily about the formal side of social and economic reality. But I submit that any reform, any *perestroyka* of some significance on the official side of society, by its very nature causes certain adjustments on the informal side, which is inextricably intertwined with the formal.

By informal sides of reality, I mean both horizontal and vertical relations. Horizontal social networks have economic and also other causes and aspects— family, nationality, social group, and so on. And there are horizontal aspects with the same causes and also a presence of family and clan relationships.

What are the changes on the informal side that one might expect in the event that *perestroyka* is realized, bearing in mind that the informal economy is capable of adjusting rather rapidly to changing conditions?

ZASLAVSKAYA: As president of the Soviet Sociological Association, I must express my regrets and assume some responsibility for the paucity of studies focused on the informal side of the Soviet economy, even though we know very well that it exists; it is encountered in our daily lives. I have written on the shadow economy (e.g., *Pravda*, February 6, 1987), not because that economy has been studied, but simply because one cannot get away from it. Moreover, I am directing a research project devoted to the study of the social mechanism of economic development, which is more or less germane to the issue.[5]

The formal economic mechanism is a skeleton, which is not a live organism. It is wrapped in live, concrete social relations, about which we know almost nothing nor have the evidence to identify them in our literature. Yet it is on these very relations that real life is largely focused. Our task is to investigate how the factors of social structure influence the economy. Identified as socio-logical economics—a concept much more specific than working class or in-

---

5. The project is sponsored by the Institute of the Economics and Organization of Industrial Production (IEiOPP) in Novosibirsk. The study examines in detail the social mechanisms functioning in the agrarian sector of Altay Kray. Professor Ryvkin of the IEiOPP is working with a fairly large group that investigates the lives of managers (beginning with brigade leaders, then section heads of kolkhozes and sovkhozes, and managers at higher levels) in light of their informal relations and group interaction.

telligentsia—the field deals with the basic participants in economic life, probing their positions, interests, as well as interaction.[6]

Another element is culture, ethnic or any other, that in part significantly predetermines our actions. The final one is the economic mechanism and its interaction with other elements.

A few points can be made just on the basis of what is known. To begin with, the actual influence of these informal structures on the economy is enormous. It varies a great deal, of course, from region to region. In this respect Transcaucasia, Central Asia, and even the city of Leningrad have a somewhat different economy and different social mechanisms of economic development than even Moscow or other cities.

The field of inquiry here is very large, and lack of insight into this underwater part of the iceberg can lead to very serious consequences due to erroneous administrative measures. I think that the sphere of information relations is precisely the one where the mechanism that impedes *perestroyka* can be located.

We can expect major changes in this informal side, above all because we are fighting to cleanse our society of all afflictions that distort socialism. Such distortions have taken place, and they were particularly evident in the southern republics of our country. Clan and family relationships played a key role there, the status of groups varied widely, and corrupt bureaucracies were present. They represented the shell of formal relations, while the elements inside that shell were completely different.

Now this process of socialist purification, that revitalizes the road followed by the builders of socialism, should sweep away these phenomena—at any rate, it should cast out the large, Mafia-type groups that were able to exercise a leading role. In other words, the goal is to make social relations healthier and to achieve substantial improvement in social justice. Needless to say, one cannot get away from family ties or ethnic relations. These are realities of the culture, and they influence the economy and everything else in life. The point is that they should be manifested at a normal, rather than exaggerated, level.

As for our central regions, informal relations are prevalent—and it is impossible to function without them—when the supply of materials and equipment is at stake. In this area, informal relations play an extremely important, if not a decisive, role.

The resources allocated by central authorities are inadequate, and what is done beyond that channel depends heavily on business managers and other leaders. Transactions take place that are not recorded in the ledger. One man gives another a load of bricks, the other reciprocates by delivering a flock of sheep, and so forth. This is how the shadow part of the economy operates.

If we manage to free ourselves from this process of centralized resource allocation and organize normal procedures for wholesale trade to supply pro-

6. This is in an effort to answer questions relevant to the process, e.g., who deals with whom and why; what items are bartered and how they are obtained; how planning is done; how a less challenging plan is obtained and what was given up in return; and similar ones used in the IEiOPP project.

ducer goods, and particularly eliminate shortages of spare parts, a very important part of the shadow economy will fade away.

There should be room for a vestige of an informal structure, because it also supports the formal system. The point is that it must not be so harmful. I think that informal relations will be squeezed out, and the entire procedure somewhat formalized. It would be especially instructive to identify the informal mechanisms of impairment. They may involve fairly serious relations among groups engaged in various activities—some in the government apparatus, some in the apparatus of the party, some in economic management, and others in commerce.

Informal alliances are formed that wield enormous power. They are not visible on the surface, and from the vantage point of formal management, one would not guess they exist. Yet they are very strong entities, and some articles in our press that have spotlighted cases under investigation or those that have gone to trial underscore the great significance of these mechanisms.

Sociology in our country is unfortunately only taking its first steps to develop the methods to probe the many acute problems that have not been studied by anyone. The field of inquiry is a vast one.

Observations on Public Opinion and Support

In response to a question,[7] I should like to address the security and stability of economic and social life under *perestroyka* in light of prospective changes caused by such factors as bankruptcy and unemployment. These problems are very difficult because we do want to get away from a system that is not dynamic—a system that failed to produce results for the broad public spectrum. On the other hand, it is very lenient and soft on the individual, providing an opportunity to survive with ease and to justify one's labor. Housing is, in effect, free, and prices are low. Food prices are artificially reduced and medical care and education are free as well. Taken together, such entitlements for one's labor secure relative comfort. And one can live without heavy financial burdens and work without taking on great responsibilities. Work is not overly intensive. There are many breaks and periods of idleness, and punishment for tardiness and absenteeism is not too strict. In short, people grow accustomed to a carefree life, albeit not a rich one. And at the same time, they are unaccustomed to tension, to risk, and to danger.

Now it is proposed that they adopt, in essence, a new way of life. This process cannot come into effect without pain—a painful adjustment. But we have a fair number of people who have suffered from constraints on their energies and potential. For them, the change to a new way of life will come without pain. Getting what they wanted, they will at least work as much as they can and as they see fit. It is difficult to estimate the magnitude of the

7. Posed by Prof. Herbert Levine. [Eds.]

population that is prepared, but it is a fairly sizable segment, perhaps as large as 30 percent.

There is probably also an intermediate segment, as well as a segment of people who cannot be retrained. Included in the latter are those who are of preretirement age, those who are about to retire and others who will have to live out their lives in the style of yesteryear.

In this context, social consciousness is extremely important. The mass media can influence it, and today they are doing a great deal to be of help. Accordingly, we now have people who are different than when we started this *perestroyka*.

These past two and a half years have not been in vain. People are much more socially and politically active, much more interested, and even ready to take steps to uphold certain rights. They have, to a much greater degree, become assertive participants, rather than passive objects to be managed from above. They can communicate and one can speak a different language with them.

If people are purely passive objects of management, then they must be promised that tomorrow will be better than today. Because if people only do what they are told and consume as much as they earn, they must be told that tomorrow wages will be higher and there will be more food. Then they may support the steps that are being taken.

But if people become assertive participants and their consciousness is socialized and politicized, then they begin to think in much broader terms—in terms of society, the role of the Soviet Union in the world, and so forth. They begin to think more strategically, and one can already inform them that we want to end up here, on this satisfactory peak, but the road to it runs through a number of obstacles.

Although our mass media are working very actively in this area, I think much more effort needs to be exerted. We probably have to think of new forms of contact, and of new ways to reach out and communicate at the family level. Thus, economists could visit a family to discuss, say, the problem of retail prices, which have been set at an unjustifiably low level.

There is no reason to be delighted when prices are about to be raised—here or in any country. But it is possible to explain, first, why a price hike is necessary and, second, that compensation in the form of higher living standards is in sight. The specific nature and directions of such compensation and the channels through which it will flow can be appropriately demonstrated using examples suitable for an individual family, be it that of a worker, an academician, a pensioner, or a student—it can be shown how the reform will benefit each family.

There is thus a way to influence people to become not only supporters of, but also dedicated participants in, the *perestroyka* of the economy. I think that we can find a common language with the majority of our people—the only possibility to communicate rather than dispense promises that everything will work out, while we really believe that difficulties are inevitable.

Our people are very active contributors of letters to newspapers. Hundreds of thousands, if not millions, are written on issues of concern, so that an ongoing discussion (if not nationwide, then at least on a very broad basis) with the letter writers is already in evidence. In essence, it covers democratization in management, and as a matter of fact, the very concept of *glasnost'* pertains primarily to *glasnost'* in management.

Lastly, a few words on the difference between freedom of the press and *glasnost'*, for I think that the substance here is somewhat different. Freedom of the press is just freedom pertaining to the press, while *glasnost'* is above all not *glasnost'* in literature, opera, or ballet, but *glasnost'* in management. It can be manifested in the press when articles or letters appear in print. However, it can also be manifested in different ways, say, in the distribution of apartments at an enterprise, when it is known who is getting an apartment and why. People must know how management operates and have the answers.

So if we follow through and make management increasingly compatible with *glasnost'*, including the decision-making process itself, then people will perceive managerial decisions as participants—as decisions made together.[8]

By following this course, we can at least substantially reduce the social tension that arises in the process of the radical restructuring—the *perestroyka*—of our social relations. The notion that it could materialize without social tensions is an abstraction incompatible with reality. Democratization of social relations is therefore advanced as a goal on the same level as economic *perestroyka*. Both are viewed as two organically related aspects of the same issue.

---

8. For example, the decision that we must raise retail prices and compensate the consumer in one form or another.

CHAPTER 12

Rethinking Price Reform

Nikolay P. Shmelev

THERE ARE probably few specialists in the Soviet Union today who would deny the necessity of a price reform. Unless objective and sensible (*ratsional'nyye*) price proportions are established and unless the main body of our economy makes the transition to market principles of pricing, the new economic mechanism will not work. The entire issue, however, is what kind of price reform actually will be implemented. Meanwhile, one gets the impression that neither planning agencies, government departments, nor economic scientists have a clear idea today about the purposes of the price reform and about realistic methods of accomplishing it.

THE IDEAL REFORM PACKAGE

What would be necessary in the ideal situation? Ideally, the upcoming price reform would address two objectives and would have to be implemented in two stages. The first goal and first stage would involve smoothing basic price proportions, i.e., between wholesale, purchase (*zakupochnyye*),[1] and retail prices. The second goal and second stage would consist of minimizing centralized intervention in pricing processes and gradually transferring basic pricing functions to the market, i.e., to the relation between effective demand and the supply. The USSR now produces roughly 25 million different products and under a centralized pricing system would thus need 25 million prices. It is

First published in *Soviet Economy*, 1988, 4, 4, pp. 319–327. During the course of our roundtable in Moscow (Supporters, 1988), Nikolay Shmelev made fairly brief but significant comments on the rationale for the current retreat on price reform. This issue is so critical to the reform that we decided a separate and more extensive treatment. We therefore asked Dr. Shmelev to write a piece outlining his views on this issue, and we asked Morris Bornstein to comment (Bornstein, 1988, pp. 328–337). In addition, a rather thorough analysis of Soviet pricing policies appears in the April–June 1987 issue of *Soviet Economy* (Bornstein, 1987), and a discussion of the consequences of procrastination in implementing price reform appears in the *Soviet Economy* Roundtables on the 19th Conference of the CPSU (The 19th, 1988, pp. 123–127; The Aftermath, 1988, pp. 196, 200–202, 204–205). [Eds.]

1. These are the prices at which collective and state farms, for example, sell their output to state procurement organizations. See Bornstein's commentary on Shmelev (Bornstein, 1988, p. 331). [Eds.]

obvious that no central authority will be able, even in purely physical terms, regardless of the circumstances, to calculate this many separate prices. Objectively, there is no other realistic alternative except pricing through the market (centralized controls over several dozens or hundreds of the most important prices would be retained for a rather lengthy period).

The first goal and the first stage of the price reform are the most important at present: establishing in prices objective proportions that correspond to basic world proportions. One of the most serious consequences of the administrative-command system has been the arbitrary deformation of virtually all basic price relations in the economy. As a consequence, prices of raw materials, fuel, food, transportation, housing, and, perhaps most important, manpower, have been depressed artificially at the same time that prices for machines, equipment, and an entire range of industrially produced consumer goods were deliberately elevated. At the present time it is not uncommon for Soviet prices to vary (above or below) world levels by a factor of 3 or more. Up to now this has been the most important obstacle to the economy's transition to intensive and balanced development.

A prestigious member of the Academy of Sciences recently went so far as to say that robots mean only ruination for us. Advantageous to the entire world, but not to us? Why? Well, because at our wage level it is surprising that we have not yet given up the wheel, not to mention robots.

Accordingly, in the ideal situation the first stage of the price reform should comprise elimination of the glaring distortions in prices. At the level of retail prices this would mean, for example, that instead of the present ratio of 2 rubles per kilogram of meat, 50 rubles for a pair of men's shoes, 700 rubles for a color television set, and 9,000 rubles for a car, a more realistic ratio would prevail, in line with actual costs and world trends: 4–4.5 rubles per kilogram of meat, 24–27 rubles for a pair of men's shoes, 250–280 rubles for a color television set, and 4,000 to 4,500 rubles for an automobile. In the USSR we need to come to the sober realization that until such price relations are attained, we will always be living in an economically unreal world, in a kind of "kingdom of distorting mirrors," in which everything is inverted from an economic standpoint.

New price relations, in turn, will bring about a change in the structure of consumer demand. Meat consumption will decline and demand for shoes and television sets will increase. Will this negatively affect retirees and lower-income groups in general, for whom the price of meat is more important in everyday life than the price of shoes, not to mention a television set? It could, unless appropriate compensation is envisaged specifically for them in the course of this reform.

Second, state price subsidies must be eliminated, at the same time that the turnover tax is removed as a source of budget revenues. The resulting losses to individuals from liquidation of price subsidies will be offset almost entirely by elimination of the constant overpayment for goods subject to the turnover tax. Today, the amounts involved in state subsidies to the consumer and turnover tax revenues in the state budget are almost equal. Why must this money be shifted from one pocket to the other? Both phenomena are abnormal and non-economic, and if a normal economy is the objective, then this grievous legacy of the past must be abandoned.[2]

Under present conditions, of course, this will not immediately eliminate food shortages everywhere, not by any means. What is more, at first, no doubt, it will even intensify shortages in the market for industrially produced consumer goods, given the magnitude of deferred demand and limited production capacities for short- and even long-term consumer goods. Lines will be longer for clothing, furniture, television sets, and automobiles, but this is precisely where more rational pricing can help expand imports of industrially produced consumer goods substantially—even though at first there would be no price reduction on imported goods at all.

All the above represents the payment that inevitably must be made to restore the Soviet economy to health—the bill that must be paid for the prolonged domination of the administrative-command system. All mistakes have a cost, including historical mistakes, and we will not manage to avoid the payment. At the same time, this will be an additional incentive for the state to finally make a dramatic change and redistribute capital investments to the consumer goods branches of industry, to purchase several large plants for manufacturing household appliances, to purchase one or two more automobile plants, etc. Of course, the period of transition to normal price relationships in the Soviet economy will not be an easy one. But if the goal of the price reform is specifically to restore the economy to health, and not a primitive plundering of the population, then people will undoubtedly understand it—especially if there are at least some signs of improvement in the consumer goods market.

COMPLICATING FACTORS

The ideal situation described above will be difficult, but attainable. Recent events, however, have prompted fears that the price reform not only will fail to achieve the necessary objectives, but, on the contrary, will compound the current economic situation.

The 19th Party Conference has again confirmed the leadership's intention to implement a retail price reform that will not cause the population to suffer. Most important, certainly, is the leadership's declaration that the state will establish appropriate supplements to wages and pensions, which will return to the population the entire amount added to the budget from the elimination of price subsidies.

2. The above applies, however, only to the turnover tax on industrial goods, and not to the tax on alcoholic beverages and imported consumer goods. Assuming that trade in taxed alcoholic beverages is normalized and consumer imports are expanded considerably, these two legitimate sources of state revenues in and of themselves will be sufficient to offset all costs incurred by the state in price reform, including the essential compensation to pensioners and other low-income groups.

Yet even if this intention is fully realized, it evidently will not be possible to avoid significant damage to the population. At present, as far as is known, Gosplan and Goskomtsen[3] will discuss only two issues—(a) how high prices of basic foodstuffs will be raised and (b) the appropriate size of the corresponding compensation. There is no discussion, however, about what will happen the day after prices are raised and the compensation is paid to the population.

Only one thing can happen (and undoubtedly will): the next cycle in the spiral of rising prices, which will immediately affect all other prices as well. However honest the compensation, the population will inevitably lose on other prices not directly affected by the increase envisaged. What is more, since a corresponding compensation is not foreseen for balances in savings accounts, this will at once sharply diminish their real value.

It cannot be ignored that ordinary consumers by and large are resolutely opposed to higher prices, and even talk of a possible price reform makes them more and more irritated. Unfortunately, there is every basis for such irritation. The ordinary consumer too often has been deceived during the implementation of past reforms for him or her now to suddenly believe that a one-time price increase in basic foodstuffs is in his or her self-interest.

Many remember the 1947 reform, which was accompanied by direct confiscation of individual savings, and the 1962 rise in meat and dairy prices, which were not altogether offset by the drop in prices of industrial goods (and the several subsequent rises of prices and rate schedules for the most varied goods and services, some of which were not even announced). Nor has the recent handling of the "Beryozka" matter strengthened confidence in the state.[4] Aside from everything else, everyone knows that there is always "creeping inflation that is being suppressed"—e.g., the actual rise of prices when labels are changed, which is not recorded by statistics, and the fact that the 2–3 percent annual interest paid on account balances in savings banks by no means covers the "drying up" of savings resulting from such a *de facto* rise in the cost of living.

Social consciousness is sluggish, and the government's reputation is being influenced far more at present by the regrettable experience of past abuses than by the most sincere present intentions to put an end to those abuses once and for all. The population's confidence in the government can be lost in a moment, but it takes years and even decades to win it. And in recent years, unfortunately, nothing has happened in the economy that would increase confidence in the economic policy of the state: the lines are just as long, the shelves are empty just as they were before, and the standard of living is not rising.

Given the situation that has now taken shape, in other words, the leadership

3. The State Planning Commission and State Committee for Prices, respectively. [Eds.]
4. This involved the panic buying spree that followed a government announcement, in late January 1988, of the closing (on July 1, 1988) of the special stores (*Beryozka*) where Soviet citizens possessing hard currency could buy imported goods. [Eds.]

has no realistic possibility of winning the price "campaign." However thoroughly the rise of retail prices might be planned, whatever the explanatory effort that accompanies it, and whatever kind of compensation consumers receive, the majority still end up dissatisfied, and the credit of the new course will be seriously undermined. "So all that restructuring amounted to was a rise of prices," it is easy to predict, will become the typical and predominant opinion after the reform of retail prices.

Nor is everything so simple with the reform of wholesale prices and purchase prices. There already is considerable experience here, and this experience indicates that a short time after the rise, say, of purchase prices for agricultural products, production costs rose in agriculture, so that soon it had become a low-profit operation once again, and then it even began to lose money. As a consequence prices had to be raised once again. That same "profitability cycle" also is observed in other raw materials and fuel and power branches: profitability rises sharply after a one-time rise of wholesale prices; then profitability gradually and continuously drops because of the rise in production costs, so that then a new rise of prices becomes indispensable, and so on.

The cause of this cycle is well-known: branches with a high degree of monopolization of production and a rapidly changing product list (machine building, light industry, construction, etc.) possess the greatest ability to "jack up" the price. In these cases, it is extremely difficult for Goskomtsen to verify the validity of the calculations submitted by the producers. There are many new products, but there is only one Goskomtsen. More often than not, that is why there is "creeping inflation" in such branches—the productivity of the new machine tool or machine increases, say, by 30 percent, but its price rises several times over. Collective self-interest and dishonorable conduct are unfortunately just as distressing a factor of our reality as individual self-interest.

In agriculture, on the other hand, in the fuel industry, and in other raw materials branches where there are a few basic products and they are updated relatively slowly, the monitoring of prices "from above" proves to be relatively effective—which is in fact why these branches periodically fall into the ranks of those with low profitability. After all, the prices of machines and equipment which the branches must purchase are rising continuously, whereas the prices of the products they produce remain stable for long periods of time.

This is why from one five-year plan to another the same thing is repeated in the "price arena"—the prices of finished goods and services run out ahead and the prices of raw materials lag behind, and as a consequence the raw materials branches periodically become low-profit or even unprofitable operations; then, like it or not, large one-time price increases become necessary. One does not have to have the gift of prophecy to predict what will happen in 5 to 10 years after implementation of the "smoothing" of wholesale prices now pending. The same thing will happen that happened earlier—the gap in branch levels of profitability will again widen, so that prices will have to be "smoothed" once again.

A reform of wholesale prices is undoubtedly necessary as a first step, as a starting point. But it would be unrealistic to expect a radical improvement in this area until the market for the means of production (wholesale trade) operates smoothly, until the producer's present monopoly is destroyed, and until competition gets under way.

As for food, the present situation indicates that the present high production cost for agriculture is not so much the result of the poor performance of the farms as of the aggressive pricing policies of planning authorities and the industrial ministries which are monopoly suppliers of equipment, fertilizer, and building materials which agriculture must have. No form of successful performance or kind of reasonable production cost can be expected from the majority of farms as long as they must sell virtually all their grain at a low price and then buy it back, in the form of mixed feeds, at a price that is two to three times higher. What was the rationale that guided the relevant departments in 1988, when they raised fertilizer prices by 1.5–5 times and the prices of thoroughly bad combines threefold? And who is disturbed when all these losses resulting from prices are then written off by the *kolkhozy* and *sovkhozy* or covered with nonrepayable credit? This is charity, and it has nothing to do with the production process.

Herein lie the causes of the "evil endlessness" in the spiral of food prices. Unless this problem is resolved, unless this siphoning of funds out of agriculture through the price mechanism is halted, nothing lasting will ever result from a simple increase in purchase prices, especially one that is passed on to the consumer. Perhaps it would not be so bad if the state derived at least some benefit from that siphoning, but it is just a senseless movement of money back and forth.

AN ALTERNATIVE APPROACH

Is there a workable alternative to present plans for reform of wholesale, purchase, and retail prices? I think so. An alternative version must be based, it seems to me, on three main premises: first, that price reform is necessary and inevitable; second, that this should not be an isolated act, but a gradual and rather slow process which must begin with wholesale prices and end with retail prices; third, that the reform of retail prices must be timed to coincide with the saturation of the consumer goods market as the signs of that saturation become obvious.

Even today the state has a genuine opportunity, without touching retail prices for the present, to extricate itself from most of the food subsidies that have been burdening the state budget. The entire abrupt growth of state subsidies for food (from 20 billion rubles to more than 60 billion rubles over the period 1982–1987) was caused in essence by one thing—raising the purchase price specifically for small farms operating at a loss. The absurdity of this measure is obvious: the end result is that little attention is paid to anyone who performs well and a great deal to those who bungle everything.

It is evident that now the state must give up artificial support to those farms, abandon artifically elevated purchase prices for their products. Today no more than 30 percent of the farms are supplying about 80 percent of all the country's marketable agricultural products (Delegaty, 1988, p. 9). In the future, reliance must be placed on the productive farms, which do not need artifical support from the state, and which at present need only to be freed of the omnipotent administrative layer that has fettered their operations.

The small and unpromising farms should receive their last aid from the state in the form of a write-off of their debt (a sizable portion of which, it should be noted, was not their fault), and hereafter they should be on their own. Let them attach themselves if they can to the stronger farms, let them lease out all their land to small cooperatives and family farms, let them turn their land into parks and hunting grounds; this should not be a concern of the state. The country's guaranteed stock of food does not depend on them. And if those farms are able to get on their feet by their own efforts, without crutches supplied by the state, so much the better.

The possibilities of reducing the cost of agricultural products also are directly related to halting the nonequivalent exchange through the price "scissors" between the products which the state purchases from the farms and the mixed feed, fertilizers, equipment, building materials, repairs, and so on, which are sold to them. The net effect is negligible, inasmuch as everything that the state now receives from that nonequivalent exchange it returns in the form of non-repayable credits to farms which are operating at a loss. Abolishing the principle of compulsory deliveries, allowing the farms to store and process products and sell them as necessary, and the transition from the system of stock allocations to cost-accounting (*khozraschetnyye*) purchases of fertilizers and equipment should also, without a doubt, improve the economic condition of *kolkhozy* and *sovkhozy*. Elimination of the present administrative layer in agriculture, which has outlived its purpose and, according to some estimates, is today devouring between one-seventh and one-eighth of agricultural income, also will improve matters considerably.

In addition, even today it is possible to detect the potential for a sharp reduction in the production cost of agricultural products thanks to the full-fledged development of the collective and family lease. On most family farms, for example, the production cost of pork is in the range of 70 kopecks to 1 ruble per kilogram, and that of beef between 1.5 and 2 rubles per kilogram. However, this potential for saturating the market is only beginning to be utilized. Experience shows that quite often a single family farm yields an output that is five to ten times higher than that obtained from the same number of people working under conventional conditions.

It is also important to emphasize that in this alternative approach the partial restoration of budget equilibrium, about which Gosplan and other departments today are so justifiably concerned, can be achieved under the conditions of (a) a substantial decline in the wholesale prices for much of what is supplied to agriculture,[5] (b) a reduction or stability in the purchase prices of agricultural products, and (c) finally, stability of state retail prices of the principal food-stuffs.[6]

The present seriousness of the problem of the budget deficit depends, of course, on other things besides the food subsidies. But those subsidies are an important factor in the budget imbalance, and I am convinced that its effect can be minimized without damage to the consumer.

It thus would seem that the reform of wholesale prices is most important at present. Its major function would be to level out conditions for the activity of enterprises from branch to branch, safeguard the transition to stable tax relations between the state and enterprises, and create conditions for partial ruble convertibility—without affecting the system of retail prices for some time to come. But the reform of wholesale prices must not be allowed to spill over into a general price increase either: the rise in prices of fuel and raw materials must be balanced by a corresponding reduction of artificially elevated machinery and equipment prices.

There is no need whatsoever to be in a hurry to reform retail prices. Until the market becomes saturated with food and industrially produced consumer goods, until recovery of budget equilibrium is at least partially attained, and until, finally, our workers gain the opportunity to earn as much as they want and can (rather than as much as is allowed them by administrative dictate from above), this action would only undermine the confidence of the people in restructuring. Ultimately a reform of retail prices is unavoidable, as is a change in price ratios for food, housing, transportation, and industrially produced consumer goods. But at present it is both possible and advisable to wait awhile.

Hungary's constructive experience with price reform and Poland's severely adverse experience can serve as precedents. So also can the experience of China, which decided on a reform of retail prices only after the situation with respect to saturation of the consumer goods market had changed radically over a period of 8–9 years. Even in that case the reform was not carried out all at once, but was stretched over a period of five years. The experiences of others in price reform should neither be ignored nor forgotten; they represent an experiment of sorts, performed by other countries, but with potential benefits for the USSR.

5. This would be offset in the budget by the simultaneous elimination of the nonrepayable financing of farms operating at a loss.

6. Subsidies from the budget representing the difference between the purchase price and the retail price will be reimbursed to the state in that the artificially high purchase prices for small farms performing poorly will be abolished.

Part III

The Complexities of Transition

Editors'
Introduction

IT IS difficult to overestimate the significance of Soviet price policies during the time of *perestroyka*'s transition from the relatively mild instability of the first two years to the turbulence of the late 1980s and the chaos that followed. Had the price system been changed, a semblance of a free-market economy might have by now been in place, functioning well enough to justify added faith in Gorbachev's reforms. But the system did not change, and Gorbachev's half-measures merely accelerated the rise of the budget deficit, the market disequilibrium, and the pervasive stagflation.

We begin Part III of this volume with a paper by Professor Morris Bornstein of the University of Michigan. "Price Policies and Comment on Shmelev" takes us back to the pre-*perestroyka* days in an effort to explain why the complexities and contradictions ingrained in the system made it unworkable and in need of reform; the author then moves on to clarify the preceding chapter, which presented the view of Nikolay Shmelev.

In June 30, 1987, the Central Committee of the CPSU approved a package of strong measures designed to change the principles that governed the management of the country's economy. In the past, the economy of the Soviet Union functioned within a system of prices that were set by the central authorities and only changed periodically to reflect fluctuations in costs. Retail prices of most food products and services, as well as those of various consumer goods, were held down by subsidies. Industrial producer prices reflected the cost or supply side, while in agriculture the state effectively subsidized its farms by allowing them to buy industrial materials, fuel, and equipment at prices below the established wholesale norms. All told, because prices were not intended to signal what should be produced, they were not linked to the realities of supply and demand. Because of these contradictions, the price reform envisaged by the measures approved in June 1987 was the most important and difficult part of the proposed transformation.

After walking us through the intricacies of industrial wholesale prices charged by the enterprises, agricultural prices paid to farms by the state, and retail prices at which households bought goods and services, Professor Bornstein reexamines the deficiencies of the system and addresses the reform and solutions proposed by Shmelev.

Gertrude Schroeder addresses the entire package of the radical economic directives adopted in June 1987 in her "Anatomy of Gorbachev's Economic Reform." The areas under her microscope include central planning, the enterprise, territorial versus sectoral management of the economy, the supply system, wages, finance and credit, foreign trade, private and cooperative activity, agriculture, as well as the vital price system. Impressed with the effort of the framers of the reform package, Gertrude Schroeder is nevertheless not prepared to concede that it even approximates the New Economic Policy and market environment created by Lenin in 1921. Gorbachev's eventual disappointment is predicted, because "the reforms do not go nearly far enough" to restructure the economy and create a new mechanism capable of narrowing the country's lag behind the economies of the West.

We move on to the events of 1988, pausing to review the highlights of the 19th Conference of the CPSU with Gertude Schroeder and Herbert Levine. The Conference was a subject of considerable expectations—both here and in the Soviet Union—and is viewed as a watershed event in Gorbachev's *perestroyka*. We first focus on his opening speech delivered on June 28, 1988, and devoted in part to the economic reform. On the positive side, there is candor with regard to things that are going wrong, namely, the supply of food, consumer goods, and housing. But on the negative side, there is a retreat on price reform, which appeared to be advancing after the Central Committee Plenum in June 1987.

In addition to the opening address, special attention in this chapter is devoted to the speech by Leonid Abalkin and to Gorbachev's cryptic reaction to Abalkin's dissertation on the sorry state of the country's economic affairs. Also included is our analysis of the aftermath of the 19th CPSU Conference which concentrated on Gorbachev's speech at the Central Committee Plenum on July 29, 1988, and of selected complexities of the transition; we discuss the undersupplied consumer and horizontal interactions in the open and illegal economies within the array of markets ranging from the formal white to the proverbial black.

Our perceptions of *perestroyka* in mid-1988 were clearly influenced by our commitment to free enterprise, but were also somewhat detached because as outsiders we may not have been as attuned to certain nuances of the process as the participants. Toward the end of that year, we were in search of more meaningful perceptions of *perestroyka*. We were aware of the transparently inaccurate definition of "a carefully prepared program" proffered by no less than Gorbachev himself in his widely distributed English-language book on the subject (Gorbachev, 1988, p. 13). But in Moscow, not far from the seat of power, we heard different accounts of the ongoing reform.

The memorable roundtable in November 1988 with the late Academician Andrey Sakharov gave us an opportunity to probe and explore in depth the views of three prominent CPSU members—two economists and one historian—who were typical representatives of the radical pro-Western Russian intelligentsia. The chapter entitled "Radical Perceptions of *Perestroyka*" features the hitherto unpublished pronouncements of Yuriy Afanas'yev, one of Gorbachev's most prominent detractors at the Congress of People's Deputies in 1991; Pavel Bunich, a relative pragmatist; and Nikolay Shmelev, whose ideas on the price reform have already received attention in this volume. Sharing their thoughts on the cooperatives, pondering the economy's future, and reflecting on Lenin's New Economic Policy, the three intellectuals focus on unresolved issues that are as relevant today as they were in November 1988.

In a more technical chapter, Professor Gur Ofer examines problems within the fiscal and monetary system that was in place in mid-1989. He considers these problems as a function both of past systemic shortcomings and of fiscal developments caused by economic reforms enacted through the end of the year; he also looks at them as obstacles that must be overcome during the transition to a more market-oriented economy. He identifies major sources of the disequilibrium in the Soviet economy through analysis of budgets spanning the reform and pre-reform periods. In a concluding section, Ofer presents policy options for the period of transition to a more radical economic reform, suggesting the "possible ways out." The main thrust on the supply side is a reallocation of resources from defense to consumption—both in light industry and agriculture. On the demand side, the cornerstone is a stabilizing reduction in the size of the budget deficit to restore equilibrium in the market. Also, a critical element and requirement for the reform is a vigorous program designed to eliminate the pervasive monetary overhang—the accumulation of excess rubles chasing increasingly scarce and elusive goods and services.

Finally, Ed Hewett addresses the complexities and contradictions of Gorbachev's reform by focusing on the increasingly sophisticated parliamentary debates over *perestroyka*. A rudimentary, but quite real degree of public accountability had begun to emerge from the deliberations of the Congress of People's Deputies. Many, if not all, deputies were accusing the government of dragging its feet. Still not completely distrusted by the majority, Gorbachev reacted by arranging for the transfer of Leonid Abalkin from his former domicile in academia to an office in the Kremlin.

As head of a newly formed commission, Abalkin was about to propose reforms that would dramatically depart from the past. He would eventually advocate destatization of property over a five-year period with a transition to a market economy in which meaningful competition would be present. Central planning, the rule of the land for seven decades, would be replaced by a policy relying primarily on economic instruments. The price reform would receive the prominence it deserved, while the financial system would be transformed into a Western-type two-tiered banking structure attuned to modern intermediation. The need to move decisively to reduce the budget deficit and expand the output of consumer goods, thus attacking the worsening shortages from the supply side, appears to have been recognized with a sense of urgency. But Abalkin inherited a reform that was going virtually nowhere and an economy that showed it all too clearly. Still salvageable, the economic situation was alarming enough to warrant radically new steps—steps in a direction that would at first be applauded and then, as in the fall of 1990, severely criticized.

CHAPTER 13

Price Policies and Comment on Shmelev

Morris Bornstein

THIS STUDY analyzes and appraises important recent, as well as possible future, developments in the three main parts of the Soviet domestic price system: (1) industrial wholesale prices, at which nonagricultural enterprises sell to other enterprises and organizations; (2) agricultural purchase prices, paid to farms by state procurement organizations; and (3) retail prices, at which households buy goods and services.[1] They are examined in turn in the first, second, and third major parts of the paper, and some general conclusions are presented in a final part.

INDUSTRIAL WHOLESALE PRICES

There are three types of Soviet industrial wholesale prices. (1) The enterprise wholesale price (*optovaya tsena predpriatiya*) is the price at which a producing enterprise sells its output. (2) The industry (i.e., branch of industry) wholesale price (*optovaya tsena promyshlennosti*) is paid by the state-enterprise buyer and may include, in addition to the enterprise wholesale price, one or more of the following: (a) an excise ("turnover") tax on the product; (b) a markup of the branch sales organization; and (c) transportation charges if these are borne

First published in *Soviet Economy*, 1987, 3, 2, pp. 96–134 and 1988, 4, 4, pp. 328–337. This chapter combines two papers. The first part benefitted from financial support provided by the University of Michigan Center for Russian and East European Studies. The second part draws on research supported by several organizations whose assistance is gratefully acknowledged. They are the International Research and Exchanges Board, in connection with a trip to the USSR in 1988, and three units at the University of Michigan: the Office of the Vice-President for Research, the Center for Russian and East European Studies, and the Faculty Research Assistance Fund of the College of Literature, Science, and the Arts. The author also wishes to thank Keely D. Stauter and Michele Smith-Moore for their research assistance and anonymous referees for their helpful comments. The source reference "interview material" is used for statements based on interviews with Soviet pricing specialists. [Eds.]
    1. Space constraints preclude discussion of other types of prices, such as transport rates (see Sagers and Green, 1985; *Spravochnik*, 1985, pp. 357–363 and 369–377), "estimate" prices for construction and installation work (see Deminov, 1984; *Tseny*, 1985, pp. 127–134), and sales organizations' markups (see *Spravochnik*, 1985, pp. 378–387), as well as of administrative arrangements for setting and enforcing prices (see Bornstein, 1978; *Spravochnik*, 1985, pp. 93–140).

by the seller rather than the buyer. (3) A "settlement" or "accounting" price (*raschetnaya tsena*) is used in some branches, such as mining, where production costs diverge widely.[2] Individual enterprises or groups of enterprises receive different settlement prices (rather than a single, uniform enterprise wholesale price) from the branch sales organization. The latter, however, sells to customers of the branch at a single industry wholesale price.

Enterprise wholesale prices are composed of the planned branch average cost of production (*sebestoimost'*) and a profit markup. The former has no exact equivalent in Western cost accounting. It includes direct and indirect labor, materials (including fuel and power), amortization allowances, and various overhead expenses. The profit markup is supposed to provide a "normal" level of profit for the branch as a whole, although the profitability rate may be above or below "normal" for an individual enterprise, depending upon the relationship of the actual cost of its output to the planned branch average cost.

The most important recent changes in regard to industrial wholesale prices are (1) their extensive revision in 1982 and (2) continuing efforts to improve the pricing of new machinery, equipment, and instruments.

The 1982 Industrial Price Revision

The Soviet authorities decided in 1979 to undertake an extensive revision[3] of industrial wholesale prices. Thousands of new price lists were calculated during 1980 and 1981, and the new prices became effective on January 1, 1982. The objectives of the revision and its impact on prices and profits in industry will be discussed in turn.

Objectives. The main aims of the 1982 revision of industrial wholesale prices were (1) to recognize past changes in costs, (2) to reflect costs more accurately, (3) to encourage reduction in the material-intensity of production, and (4) to promote improvement in quality (Bornstein, 1985).

Recognition of Past Changes. Because Soviet industrial producer prices are supposed to be based on planned branch average cost plus a profit markup (rather than on scarcity reflecting supply and demand), at discrete and often long intervals these prices are adjusted with two aims. One is to reflect changes in branch average costs since the preceding price revision. The second is to provide for each branch and most enterprises within it, a "normal" rate of profit (usually 12–15 percent on capital) deemed adequate to cover the various charges against profit (such as taxes, interest, and rent[4]) and still leave the

---

2. On intra-enterprise accounting prices, see *Tsena* (1983, pp. 255–264).

3. In Soviet pricing terminology, a "reform" (*reforma*) refers to a basic change in the way prices are constructed, involves many branches of the economy, and alters significantly the level and the structure of prices. A "revision" (*peresmotr*) does not change the fundamental scheme for price formation, usually covers a smaller set of branches, and modifies the level and structure of prices to a lesser extent. "Changes" (*izmeneniya*) or "corrections" (*popravki*) refer to relatively minor alterations in the prices of particular product groups. By these standards, Soviet industrial producer prices are deemed to have been "reformed" in 1966–1967 but only "revised" in 1982. On the 1966–1967 price reform, see Schroeder (1969).

4. On the calculation of rent charges, see *Spravochnik* (1985, pp. 67–68).

branch a sufficient amount of profit for the three enterprise "economic incentive" funds fed from profits. These funds are the Material Incentive Fund for bonuses; the Social-Cultural and Housing Fund for the construction and operation of housing, child care, health, recreational, and food service facilities; and the Production Development Fund for small investments in production facilities. Price revisions cut the number of enterprises operating at a loss and the number of products produced at a loss. At the same time, these revisions reduce what are judged to be excessive profits for particular branches, specific, product groups, or individual products.

In pursuit of these aims, the 1982 price revision raised the price levels of the extractive branches but essentially maintained the price levels of the processing branches (whose profitability and *relative* prices were thereby reduced).

The 1982 industrial wholesale price revision made all branches profitable with the exception of the coal industry (in which the rate of losses in relation to assets was cut to 3 percent). Also, the price revision reduced, but did not eliminate, planned losses by individual enterprises or for particular products. In both the extractive and the processing branches, some high-cost enterprises still operate at a planned loss in selling their assigned output at prices based on planned branch average cost. Futher, at the new prices individual products are often produced at a loss even though the enterprise achieves "normal" profitability from its entire output.

Treatment of Cost Elements. The 1982 revision sought also to reflect somewhat more accurately costs for labor, natural resources, and the capital stock.

In the Soviet Union, *labor costs* are considered to include wages, bonuses paid from the wage fund (rather than from profits), and social insurance charges on the wage bill.

Social insurance charges are intended to help finance state pension and disability payments. Most of the rates in force before the 1982 price revision were established in 1939. They varied by branch from 4.7 to 9.0 percent of the wage bill, averaging about 7 percent, and generated budget revenues equivalent to approximately 40 percent of social insurance outlays.

In connection with the 1982 price revision, social insurance charges were raised to 14 percent in most branches. The new rates augmented total social insurance charges by about 5 billion rubles, or 70 percent, but they still do not fully cover state social insurance outlays.

To show *natural resource costs* more accurately, the 1982 price revision increased the portion of geological prospecting expenses included in production cost, extended the use of charges for water, and raised forest stumpage taxes.

Before the 1982 price revision, only about half of geological prospecting expenses was charged to production cost, with the remainder covered from the state budget. In 1982 the share of prospecting expenses included in cost was increased in the petroleum, natural gas, and iron ore industries. As a result, about 80 percent of total prospecting outlays are now included in production cost and price. However, such charges are still not counted in production cost in the coal industry and some other extractive branches.

Until the 1982 price revision, industrial enterprises generally used water without charge, although fees were levied for water used by metallurgical plants in the Ukraine and for water taken by enterprises from the Moscow Canal and certain other bodies of water. Effective in 1982, all industrial enterprises have had to pay water charges (to encourage economical use of water) that are included in their cost of production.

Soviet logging enterprises pay a stumpage tax (*popennaya plata*) for the timber they cut, with the revenue used to cover part of the state budget's outlays for reforestation and other types of forest management. The tax rate is differentiated by seven geographical regions, according to the scarcity of timber. The 1982 price revision doubled the stumpage tax rates in an effort to make stumpage tax revenue cover total budget expenditures for forestry.

In regard to a third cost element, *capital costs*, the 1966–1967 price reform established the principle that enterprises should ordinarily pay, out of profit, a 6 percent tax on fixed and working capital. When profitability declined as costs rose after 1967, the tax rate was cut to 4 percent in many industrial branches and was eliminated in branches operating at a loss. Under the 1982 price revision, a standard rate of 6 percent was re-established, and the number of exempted branches and enterprises was cut.

Reduction in Material Intensity. The 1982 price revision sought to encourage reduction in the material-intensity of production by changing the cost base for the profit markup in the price.

Before the revision, the profit markup in a product's price was calculated in relation to (planned branch average) total unit cost. Thus, for any given percentage profit markup, the larger the unit cost of materials (including fuels), depreciation, and labor (including social insurance charges), the larger were the ruble values of the unit profit and of the price composed of unit cost and unit profit. Hence, other things equal, the greater the material intensity of a product, the greater was its contribution to the enterprise's profit, gross value of output, and sales revenue.

To alter this preference for material-intensive products on the part of enterprises in the processing branches, the 1982 revision changed the base for the profit markup in the prices of the output of machine building, the light and food industries, and processing (but not extractive) enterprises in metallurgy. The profit component in their prices is now computed as a percentage of total unit cost minus direct material expenses. These planned profitability percentages are called "profitability normatives." In the machine-building ministries, for example, their average magnitude for the ministry is usually in the range of 40–60 percent.

Soviet pricing and planning agencies recognized that the change in the base for the profit markup from total cost to labor cost (plus depreciation) could cause enterprises to consider labor-intensive rather than material-intensive products the "advantageous" items in their "assortment." Therefore, in some branches the ratio of profit to labor cost was differentiated by products, to encourage enterprises to produce relatively less labor-intensive items. For example, the ratio of profit to labor cost ranges by product from 20 to 70 percent for electrical equipment and from 40 to 150 percent for power machinery.

Quality Improvement. One of the methods used by the Soviet authorities to promote improvement in the quality of industrial output, including through the introduction of new products, is a set of surcharges (*nadbavki*) and discounts (*skidki*).[5] The surcharges increase (or the discounts decrease) the profitabilities and prices of products of higher (lower) quality. Thus they affect a product's relative contribution to an enterprise's gross and net value of output, as well as to its profits.

The 1982 industrial price revision modified the surcharge-discount scheme by applying it to more products and by increasing the size of possible surcharges and discounts. The application and effects of these surcharges and discounts are discussed in detail in a later section.

Impact. The price revision significantly altered the absolute and relative levels of prices, profits, and profitability in Soviet industry. The effects on *prices* are summarized in Table 1, which presents indexes of annual average enterprise wholesale prices (excluding turnover tax) by industrial branches for 1981–1985 in relation to 1980.

Unfortunately, corresponding indexes of industry wholesale prices (including turnover tax) have not been published for years after 1979—an example of the reduction in the disclosure of Soviet official statistics in recent years. Thus, it is not possible to trace the extent to which changes in enterprise wholesale prices were passed along to buyers who pay industry wholesale prices, or were instead offset by changes in turnover taxes. In the 1982 industrial price revision such an offset appears to have occurred, for instance, in the case of petroleum products. Enterprise wholesale prices for petroleum extraction were raised 123 percent, but industry wholesale prices for petroleum products are reported to have increased only 12 percent—because of a substantial reduction in turnover taxes (Nemchinov, 1983, pp. 125–127). Such a compensatory cut in turnover taxes may have been made for other products as well. Total turnover tax revenues grew only 0.2 percent from 1981 to 1982, after a 6.7 percent rise from 1980 to 1981 (*Narkhoz*, 1983, p. 520).

The aggregated indexes in Table 1 show that the 1982 industrial price revision raised enterprise wholesale prices by 11 percent for industry as a whole, 14 percent for heavy industry, and 8 percent for the light and food industries. Within each category, price changes varied widely by product group and individual product and, in extractive branches, by producing area.[6]

Profitability. Table 2 shows how the 1982 price revision affected branch

---

5. Another method is to treat the share of top-quality-grade output in total output as a performance indicator affecting the size of an enterprise's Material Incentive Fund for bonuses.

6. For details, see Bornstein (1985), Chekhlov (1986, p. 182), and Rozenova (1985b, pp. 38–45).

Table 1. *Indexes of Annual Average Enterprise Wholesale Prices (excluding Turnover Tax) by Industrial Branch, 1981–1985*
(1980 = 100)

Category	1981	1982	1983	1984	1985
All industry	100	111	111	111	111
Heavy industry	100	114	114	113	112
Electric power	100	124	124	124	124
Fuel industry	100	162	162	162	162
Petroleum extraction	100	223	223	223	223
Petroleum refining	100	157	157	157	157
Gas	100	128	128	128	128
Coal	100	144	144	144	144
Shale	100	114	114	114	114
Peat	100	117	117	117	116
Ferrous metallurgy	100	123	123	123	123
Chemicals and petrochemicals	100	100	100	100	100
MBMW[a]	100	99	99	98	97
Forest products industry[b]	100	123	123	123	123
Construction materials	100	122	122	122	122
Glassware and pottery[c]	100	98	98	97	97
Light and food industry	100	108	108	108	110
Light	100	112	112	111	111
Food	101	105	105	106	109

Source: *Vestnik statistiki*, 1986, no. 9, p. 79.
a. Machine building and metal working.
b. Includes timber, wood processing, and pulp-paper production.
c. Includes glass, chinaware, and pottery production.

profitability rates in relation to capital.[7] For industry as a whole, profits rose 17 percent, and the profitability rate grew by 1.1 percentage points. In the fuel industry, both profits and the profitability rate more than tripled. Profits and profitability increased sharply in petroleum extraction, but fell markedly in petroleum refining. In natural gas production, profits grew by 72 percent and profitability by 50 percent. In the coal industry, losses were cut by about two-thirds.

However, after 1982, because of cost increases, profitability has been falling in petroleum extraction, logging, and the light and food industries, while losses are growing in the coal industry. In contrast, profitability is rising in the chemical industry and in machine building and metal working.

In 1986, 13 percent of all industrial enterprises operated at a loss. Loss-making enterprises include half of the total in the coal industry and the fertilizer industry, and a fifth of those in the timber, wood-processing, and pulp-paper industry (Chubakov, 1986).

In conclusion, the 1982 revision made some useful alterations in industrial producer prices. For example, it improved price-cost relationships by recognizing past changes in costs in the extractive and processing branches, and by

7. For an explanation of different concepts of profit and profitability, see Smirnitskiy (1980, pp. 380–391).

Table 2. *Profitability Rates by Industrial Branch, 1980–1985*[a]
(percent)

Category	1980	1981	1982	1983	1984	1985
All industry	12.2	11.5	12.6	12.4	12.1	11.7
Heavy industry	10.1	9.5	10.6	10.5	10.5	10.3
Electric power and fuel	6.1	5.2	10.9	9.8	9.1	8.1
Electric power	6.1	5.9	6.9	6.7	6.9	6.9
Fuel	6.2	4.6	15.3	13.1	11.4	9.2
Petroleum extraction	8.6	6.0	27.8	23.5	19.2	b
Petroleum refining	24.1	23.2	16.4	14.5	14.8	b
Gas	15.2	14.4	21.6	20.9	21.3	b
Coal	−7.5	−9.4	−3.2	−4.5	−5.4	b
Peat	−1.5	−2.7	3.1	1.7	0.9	b
Materials and chemicals	9.1	8.3	10.6	10.9	10.8	10.5
Ferrous and non-ferrous metallurgy	8.1	7.0	12.3	12.5	12.1	11.5
Ferrous metallurgy	7.8	7.1	10.5	11.0	10.7	b
Nonferrous metallurgy	b	b	b	b	b	b
Chemicals and petrochemicals	15.2	14.6	8.9	9.4	9.6	9.6
Timber, wood-processing, and pulp-paper	6.1	5.8	12.4	12.3	12.1	12.0
Logging	−2.6	−3.6	9.3	7.5	7.0	b
Pulp-paper production	5.2	4.6	9.3	10.3	10.2	b
Construction materials industry	3.5	3.2	7.3	7.9	7.8	7.5
Cement	7.0	7.0	10.9	11.0	10.7	b
Machine building and metal working	15.8	15.3	11.1	11.6	12.2	13.0
Light industry	24.7	24.7	27.2	25.3	23.2	23.7
Textiles	16.4	16.5	22.3	21.2	19.1	b
Food industry	18.4	18.4	18.5	18.5	16.1	15.1
Meat and dairy	37.2	36.3	32.3	32.1	24.3	24.1
Fish	6.4	6.5	11.0	11.6	11.0	11.1
Other	16.0	16.4	16.2	16.0	15.0	13.4

Sources: *Narkhoz*, 1985, p. 565; *Narkhoz*, 1986, p. 551.
a. Rate of profit on productive assets and inventories. Minus sign denotes rate of loss as percentage of productive assets and inventories.
b. Not available.

more accurately accounting for cost elements such as social insurance, use of water and timber, and geological prospecting expenses. However, the increase in the capital charge (against profit rather than cost) from 4 to 6 percent hardly reflects the scarcity of capital in the Soviet economy. Moreover, industrial producer prices are still set primarily from the cost or supply side and do not usually also reflect demand and scarcity. Hence, enterprise plan assignments must be expressed in physical terms in an effort to secure the desired output of products that price-cost relationships make "disadvantageous" for the enterprise. Also, administrative allocation instead of price rationing must continue to distribute raw, intermediate, and finished goods. Finally, cost and price increases in industry were not passed along in corresponding change in agricultural procurement prices or state retail prices, as explained below.

Pricing New Machinery, Equipment, and Instruments

Soviet economists and administrators consider the pricing of new machinery, equipment, and instruments of cardinal importance in promoting technological progress and the increase of factor productivity that constitutes the "intensive" path of economic development. The challenge in setting prices on these new products is to make substitution of a superior new machine for an existing model attractive to both the producer and the user.

One approach to new product pricing addresses the problem of higher costs for producers through temporary and stepped prices. A second approach, parametric pricing, focuses on product characteristics relevant for users. The third approach seeks to accommodate the interests of producers and their customers by sharing between them the "economic effect" of the new product.

Temporary Prices. A temporary price assigned at the beginning of production is supposed to be high enough to cover all start-up costs plus the prevailing standard profit rate for the product group. After output expands, start-up costs have largely passed, and production cost falls to a normal level, the temporary price is to be replaced by a new, lower, permanent price based on normal cost and profit.

Temporary wholesale prices for producer goods currently are based on the planned unit cost of the first year of production (excluding start-up outlays reimbursed by the ministry's Unified Fund for the Development of Science and Technology) plus the normal profit rate for the product group. These prices are supposed to be used only for "fundamentally new" products (such as those made with foreign licenses and intended to replace imports) which are intended for mass production rather than small or special orders. Temporary prices are approved by producer ministries in agreement with customers. They are to remain in force for two years, after which state pricing agencies are to establish permanent prices.

However, temporary prices are not an important category of new product prices at present for two reasons. First, the list of "fundamentally new" eligible products is rather limited. Second, enterprises find it more attractive to seek surcharges on wholesale prices (discussed below) that cover first-year production costs and provide above-normal profits for a period longer than two years (Komin, 1985, p. 20).

Stepped Prices. Stepped prices involve a schedule of automatic price cuts based on expected cost reductions. When a new product is introduced, it is assigned not a single (temporary or permanent) wholesale price, but instead a set of dated prices. Each price is to be in force for a stated period of time, at the end of which it is to be replaced by the next, lower price. The entire set of prices and their official periods of duration appear in the price catalog or supplements to it (Bornstein, 1976, pp. 33–34).

In principle, stepped prices appear to have several advantages. First, they provide a terminal low profit stage for old products which enterprises might otherwise continue to produce because of their high or comfortable unit profits. Second, scheduled price reductions exert pressure on producers to cut costs. Third, the scheme handles the problem of adjusting profit differentials between older and newer products without requiring price changes not foreseen in annual plans. Instead, planning and financial agencies have in advance the dated set of prices for the product.

However, stepped prices require a forecast of the volume of output for the specific product for each year of its production, an estimate of its cost in each year, and an idea of what its price should be in relation to the prices of whatever its substitutes are in each period. Thus, although stepped prices are advocated by some economists (e.g., Gal'perin, 1986) critical of the "effectiveness" pricing approach discussed below, stepped prices are rarely used because of the difficulty of forecasting cost reductions (Deryabin, 1985, p. 41).

Parametric Prices. Parametric prices are used for "supplementary" products which expand a given product group (such as generators or electric motors) without introducing fundamentally new technical features (Bornstein, 1976, pp. 29–30). In this case, the price of the new product is determined by a "parametric" method which attempts to price the new product properly in relation to the rest of its group through a comparison of performance characteristics.[8]

Several advantages are claimed for parametric methods (Komin, 1986a; Komin, 1986b, pp. 62–63). First, they explicitly consider use characteristics of the product. Second, these methods encourage design organizations and producing enterprises to introduce less costly products of comparable quality. They need not fear that cost reduction will lead to a corresponding decrease in the price, which instead will be kept in the same "parametric" place in relation to the rest of its product group. Third, pricing agencies find that parametric methods simplify price-setting and permit some devolution of this task to lower-level units.

In the 1970s, parametric pricing apparently was the method most commonly authorized by the State Prices Committee for new machinery, equipment, and instruments. It was used for more than half of the new products in these categories. However, the application of "effectiveness" pricing has been increasing, and the share of new machinery, equipment, and instruments priced by this method grew from 23 percent in 1969 to 50 percent in 1981, and it has been rising since then (*Tsena*, 1983, p. 307). This trend corresponds to the reported fall from 60 percent in 1973 to 40 percent in 1983 in the share of new machinery, equipment, and instrument products deemed to "expand the par-

---

8. Different comparison methods are explained in *Spravochnik* (1985, pp. 232–238).

ametric series''—rather than either simply to replace existing models, on the one hand, or to introduce fundamentally new technology, on the other (Rozenova, 1985b, p. 12).

"**Effectiveness Prices.**" The aim of "effectiveness" pricing is to assign a new product a price that is high enough to interest the producer in making it and at the same time low enough to interest the customer in buying it. For this purpose, the "economic effect" to the user from the substitution of the new product for an existing "base" product is calculated, and the gain from this effect is shared between the producer and customer. Methods and results of "effectiveness" pricing will be discussed in turn.

Methods. The current methodology for effectiveness pricing, adopted in 1982 (Metodika, 1983) and modified in 1983 and 1985, is a revision of a 1974 methodology, which in turn revised a 1969 version. (On the earlier versions, see, for example, Berliner, 1976, pp. 308–311; Bornstein, 1976, pp. 28–31; and Pinzenik, 1986.) Briefly, the procedure is as follows (*Spravochnik*, 1985, pp. 221–256).

First, a "lower limit" price for the new product is calculated as the sum of planned unit cost in the first year of mass production (excluding start-up costs reimbursed from the ministry's Unified Fund for the Development of Science and Technology) plus the standard profit markup for the product group.

Second, an analogous current product that the new product might replace is identified and designated as the "base" product for comparative purposes.

Third, an "upper limit" price for the new product is computed by adjusting the price of the base product upward by a formula that calculates the "economic effectiveness" of the new product as the present discounted value of the difference between the new product and base product in regard to annual output, service life, operating costs, and any required supplementary capital investments.

Fourth, the new product should therefore normally be assigned a price no more than 85 percent of the "upper limit" price, in order to make it attractive to the user to purchase the new product rather than the base product. If the new product were priced at the "upper limit," the buyer would see no advantage in buying the new product instead of the base product. The extent of the difference between the new product's price and the calculated "upper limit" price determines how much of the estimated "economic effect" of the new product will go to the user, rather than the producer.

New products are certified according to quality. Products in the "highest" quality category are supposed to meet "international" standards and are awarded the state quality seal (*znak kachestva*). Products in the "first" quality category are deemed to satisfy "contemporary Soviet demand." Products not certified in either of these quality categories are considered obsolete and should be phased out of production.

A product certified in the highest quality category is eligible for an "incentive surcharge" (*pooshchritel'naya nadbavka*) that increases the profit markup, on planned unit cost, above the standard rate for the product group. The size of the surcharge is related to the size of the estimated economic effect according to a specified schedule. The surcharge on the standard profit rate ranges from 50 to 125 percent.[9] The surcharge increases both the profit markup and the price, up to a maximum 30 percent increase in the price above what it would be with only a standard profit markup above planned unit cost.[10]

Up to 70 percent of the additional profit from surcharges is allocated to the economic incentive funds of research and development organizations and producing enterprises involved in the creation and manufacture of the product. Of the remainder, half is allocated to the ministry's Unified Fund for the Development of Science and Technology and half is paid to the state budget.

The counterpart of a surcharge for high quality is a discount (*skidka*) for low quality. A discount of 10–30 percent is applied to the prices of products not certified in the highest or the first quality categories. The price to the buyer is left unchanged, to avoid making the obsolete product cheaper and more attractive than alternative products deemed to meet "contemporary" standards. But the seller's sales revenue and profits are reduced by the ruble amount of the discount, which is paid to the budget.[11]

Experience. In the economic effect calculated for new output of machinery, equipment, and instruments in 1984, the percentage share ascribed to reduction in operating costs and supplementary capital costs was 42.8; to greater productivity, 41.9; and to longer service life, 15.3. The corresponding figures for 1979 were 55.8; 28.9; and 15.3. Soviet price specialists consider the rising importance of productivity, compared to operating costs and supplementary capital costs, a desirable trend, on the ground that productivity should be the decisive criterion (Rozenova, 1985b, pp. 113–115).[12]

The estimated effectiveness of new products is often exaggerated, and thus the resulting prices based on them are too high. According to a recent study, the estimated economic effect was correct in only 20 percent of the calculations reviewed by the State Prices Committee. In 30 percent of the cases, the effect was exaggerated by less than 10 percent. In 20 percent of the cases, the exaggeration ranged from 10 to 30 percent. In another 20 percent of the cases,

9. In exceptional cases involving inventions it can reach 150 percent.

10. The ceiling of 30 percent of the wholesale price applies to products whose calculated effectiveness is at least 50–100 percent above that of the comparable base product; products based on discoveries or interventions; substitutes for convertible-currency imports; and other products of "great national economic significance." In these cases, surcharges can give the producer up to 70 percent of the economic effect. For all other types of machinery, equipment, and instruments, the surcharge should not raise the wholesale price by more than 15 percent and should not include more than half of the estimated economic effect (Prioritet, 1986).

11. Effective January 1, 1986, when goods certified in the highest quality category are recertified into the first quality category, a discount is applied to the wholesale price, in the amount of 5 percent in the first year, 10 percent in the second year, and 15 percent in the third year (Osnovnyye, 1986).

12. At the same time, they note that the figures for service life used in these calculations refer to estimated physical life, say 15–20 years, without regard to likely technological obsolescence much sooner, say in 5–7 years. Also, calculations of economic effect omit some relevant factors, such as improvements in labor productivity due to better working and safety conditions, and benefits in regard to environmental protection. So far, no satisfactory way has been found to include these factors in effectiveness calculations (Komin, 1985, p. 17).

the exaggeration varied from 31 to 50 percent. And in 10 percent of the cases, it exceeded 50 percent. The overstated effects were revised downward by the State Prices Committee, but usually its corrected estimates still proved significantly higher than the actual effect realized when the new product was manufactured and put to use (Shprygin, 1986). The greatest differences between the estimated and actual effects were in productivity, especially reliability (Chekhlov, 1986, p. 187).

There are various reasons for the overstatement of economic effect. First, the effect is calculated at the design stage, rather than after production and use of the new machine, and is at best a probabilistic forecast. Second, actual performance of a new machine depends not only on technical parameters, but also on the specific conditions of its use in particular enterprises—which are not fully known to the unit estimating the economic effect (Gal'perin, 1986). But, third, more important is the interest of the producer in consciously overestimating the effect in order to get a higher price (Deryabin, 1985, p. 45).

Fourth, producers find it easy to get agreement by customers to an overstated economic effect. For many types of machinery of general use (such as metal-cutting machine tools, forge presses, and electric motors), there is no "main" customer qualified to evaluate the economic effect (Rozenova, 1986, p. 35). Customers that could identify overstatement in the economic effect often prefer to leave this task to the review they expect pricing agencies to perform (Komin, 1985, p. 15). Finally, the customer enterprise is not much concerned about higher prices for the new machinery it buys, since it expects its capital investment allocation to cover whatever it pays (*Tsena*, 1983, p. 306).

Each year the State Prices Committee establishes more than 3,000 new incentive surcharges on machinery, equipment, and instruments, and extends 1,500–2,000 surcharges on such products recertified in the highest quality category and rewarded the state quality seal (Rozenova, 1985b, p. 76). The share of new machinery, equipment, and instruments certified in the highest quality category and eligible for surcharges rose from a fourth in 1980 to a half in 1985. The rest of the new products were certified as first quality, ineligible for surcharges (Rozenova, 1985a, p. 116; Rozenova, 1986, p. 30). Yet the operation of the surcharge-discount mechanism has had modest effects on the prices, sales revenue, and profits of the machinery ministries.

The typical surcharge in effect in 1985 added around 10 percent to the wholesale price—triple the typical amount in 1979 and double the typical amount in 1982. In 1985 about 70 percent of the surcharges raised prices by 10 percent or less, about 15 percent of them raised prices by between 11 and 20 percent, and about 15 percent of them raised prices by between 21 and 30 percent (Komin, 1985, p. 14; Chekhlov, 1986, p. 185).

The total value of the surcharges in the sales of the machinery ministries in 1985 was only about 1 billion rubles. The percentage share of profits from surcharge revenue in total profits of these ministries has been small, rising from 1.6 in 1977 to 7.0 in 1985 (Gogoberidze and Lakhov, 1986, p. 93).

In turn, discounts are seldom applied. Producing enterprises and their ministries resist the loss of quality certification that leads to discounts. In 1984, for example, only 413 discounts were established for the output of 11 machinery ministries (Deryabin, 1985, p. 43). In 1985 less than one percent of machinery output was subject to discounts, and their ruble value was insignificant (Komin, 1985, p. 14).

In short, "effectiveness" pricing, currently the principal approach to pricing new machinery, equipment, and instruments, has had limited success in promoting technological progress. Calculations of economic effectiveness are regarded with skepticism by producer enterprises, user enterprises, and pricing agencies. Laxity in quality certification (Sapilov, 1985) places about half of new machinery, equipment, and instruments into the highest quality category, although these products seldom really meet "international" standards—as shown by the small share (20 percent at most) of this highest quality output that is exported (*Tsena*, 1983, p. 324). Surcharges typically raise prices by only about 10 percent, and surcharges make a minor contribution to the profit and bonus funds of enterprises.

AGRICULTURAL PURCHASE PRICES

Collective and state farms sell their output to state procurement organizations at "purchase" prices (*zakupochnyye tseny*). The procurement organizations resell this output at industrial wholesale prices—either to the light and food industries for processing, as in the case of grain and wool, or directly to the trade network when further processing is not needed, as in the case of eggs.

The basic principle is that agricultural procurement prices should cover the costs of farms operating in "normal" conditions and provide them a profit which can be reinvested to expand their capital stock of buildings, equipment, reproductive livestock, and inventories.

Sales assignments for agricultural products are given to large numbers of farms whose production costs vary widely because of differences in natural conditions, such as soil, topography, rainfall, temperature, and length of growing season. Hence, profitability differences would be enormous if a single national purchase price were set for each product at its marginal cost—with differential rents taken away by rental payments, as some Soviet economists have proposed. Instead, Soviet practice is to differentiate the prices of many commodities geographically by price zones, in an effort to capture for the state differential rents arising from more favorable natural conditions. These zonal prices are set with reference to the average costs of production in each zone. The aim is to provide, for each product, lower prices but higher profitability in low-cost areas, and higher prices but lower profitability in high-cost areas.

Major recent developments in Soviet agricultural pricing include (1) a price revision in 1981; (2) a more sweeping price revision in 1983; and (3) new attention to the relationship between the industrial wholesale prices for industrial inputs into agriculture and the purchase prices for agricultural output.

The 1981 Agricultural Price Revision

For many products during 1933–1958 and 1965–1981 farms were paid a base price for deliveries fulfilling plan quotas and a much higher above-quota price for additional quantities. The above-quota price was commonly 50 percent greater than the base price. This two-tier price scheme caused the effective price of a particular product for an individual farm to vary with the skill of its management in securing lower plan quotas, as well as with harvest variations due to managerial and worker effort and weather. The lower the plan quota, the easier it was to surpass it, other things being equal. In turn, in years when the harvest was good, average realized prices were higher because more of the total output was available for above-quota sales. In good weather years, profitability was higher because of larger quantities, higher average prices, and lower unit costs (Borkhunov, Yakovlev, and Kaliman, 1984; Buzdalov, 1985, p. 130; Wyzan, 1985).

The agricultural price revision effective January 1, 1981, altered this scheme of price surchages for additional deliveries above benchmark quantities.[13] First, standard purchase prices were raised through the inclusion in them of the 50 percent surcharge hitherto paid for above-plan sales. Second, a new benchmark was established for price surcharges for above-benchmark deliveries. Instead of the amount specified in the annual plan, the benchmark quantity was to be the average amount actually delivered during the preceding five-year plan period. Thus, average actual deliveries during 1976–1980 became the benchmark quantities for price surcharges on deliveries in 1981–1985 (Kim, 1982, pp. 61–62).

The second change was intended to reduce the farms' incentive to seek lower plan assignments because of a two-tier price system.[14] On the other hand, output growth over the benchmark amount due to the efforts of managers and workers, more material inputs, or better weather would raise average realized prices, sales revenue, and profits.

The scheme for relating price surcharges to average deliveries in the preceding five-year plan period was reiterated but modified in various respects in 1986 (O dal'neyshem, 1986).

The 1983 Agricultural Price Revision

The 1983 agricultural price revision raised the level of prices, altered their structure, modified their zonal differentiation, and introduced special surcharges for weak farms operating with low profitability or losses.[15]

---

13. Also, price differentials for higher quality grades were modified (Krasnopivtsev, 1981). In addition, responsibility for payment of transport costs from farms to procurement points was shifted from the farms to the procurement organizations (Biryukov, 1982, p. 41).

14. However, they might well continue to do so for other reasons, such as the rewards to farm managements for fulfillment and overfulfillment of plan assignments.

15. Also, price differentials for higher quality grades of various products were changed. For detailed discussion of these differentials and conditions of sale for individual products, see Chursin, Kameneva, and Golubitskaya (1984).

Table 3. *Average Annual Production Costs of Collective and State Farms, Selected Products, 1971–1975, 1976–1980, and 1981–1983*[a]

Product	1971–1975	1976–1980	1981–1983	1976–1980 as percent of 1971–1975	1981–1983 as percent of 1976–1980
Grain (excluding corn)	6.15	7.11	8.89	116	125
Sugar beets	2.59	2.98	3.48	115	117
Raw cotton	40.99	46.45	53.61	113	115
Potatoes	8.05	10.34	13.42	128	130
Vegetables	9.58	10.33	11.60	108	112
Milk	20.87	26.49	31.95	127	121
Beef cattle (weight gain)	149.79	209.93	242.90	140	116
Pigs (weight gain)	131.11	167.72	201.24	124	124
Poultry (weight gain)	166.13	173.60	174.57	105	101
Eggs (per thousand)	63.07	63.90	64.77	101	101

Source: Lazutin, 1985, p. 100.
a. Rubles per 100 kilograms unless otherwise noted.

The primary stimulus for the 1983 price revision was the rise in costs of collective and state farms for labor, material inputs, and depreciation (Lazutin, 1985). Table 3 shows cost trends from the early 1970s for 10 important products. Comparison of the figures in the first and third columns reveals the following striking percentage changes in average annual unit costs from 1971–1975 to 1981–1983; beef, 62; pork, 53; milk, 53; grain, 44; and potatoes, 66.[16]

In response, effective January 1, 1983, state purchase prices were raised for virtually all products. Unfortunately, the Soviet authorities do not disclose official indexes for agricultural prices—in contrast to the regularly published aggregate indexes for industrial wholesale prices (Table 1, above) and state retail prices (Table 7, below).[17] However, scattered statements about the increases in base prices report that they averaged 15–17 percent for all products (Borkhunov, Yakovlev, and Kaliman, 1984, p. 42), with the figure for grain about 10 percent and the increase for livestock more than the average (Kufakov, 1984, p. 28).

Purchase prices are differentiated by geographical zones for most, but not all, agricultural products.[18] The boundaries of a zone are supposed to be drawn according to "objective, relatively stable indicators of production" of two types. The first is natural conditions of soil, temperature, relief, etc. The second

16. It would be more appropriate to compare average costs in 1981–1983 with those in 1976–1978, but the corresponding data on the latter are not available.
17. Occasionally Soviet authors provide figures on the average payment per ton (APT) for selected products in particular years (e.g., Nazariyan, 1986, p. 16). The APT for a product appears to be computed as the quotient of (a) total ruble payments by state procurement agencies to farms for the product, divided by (b) the number of tons procured. However, with no changes in the multidimensional agricultural price structure, the APT for a product can vary from year to year because of changes in the shares, within the total quantity of the product procured, of (1) higher quality grades; (2) deliveries from areas with higher zonal prices; (3) above-benchmark-period sales with price surcharges; and (4) deliveries by weak farms receiving price surcharges.
18. They are not zonally differentiated for wool, flax, oilseeds other than sunflowers, maize, groats other than millet, and beans.

is economic indicators, such as specialization of production, yield of plant products, productivity of animals, capital stock, production costs, and profitability of total output. Prices for the same product in adjacent zones should not differ by more than 5–15 percent (*Tseny*, 1985, pp. 106–108).

The 1983 agricultural price revision reduced zonal differentiation by cutting the number of zones and by narrowing the difference in prices across zones.[19]

In addition to zonal differentiation, agricultural purchase prices have also been differentiated within zones around the zonal average price to provide higher prices for weaker farms and lower prices for more successful farms. Intrazonal differentiation was curtailed, and its use within an oblast eliminated, in connection with the adoption in 1983 of a new scheme of price surcharges for weak farms (Yastrebova, 1984, p. 50).

Farms are eligible for these price surcharges if (1) they show profitability (relative to cost) of 10 percent or less, or losses, for their planned deliveries at base purchase prices; and if (2) adverse natural conditions, rather than poor management, are deemed responsible. The surcharge, which can add up to 75 percent to the base price, is differentiated both by products and by groups of farms or even individual farms. The surcharges are intended to raise the farms' profitability to 12–15 percent (Semenov, 1985, pp. 5–6; Kufakov, 1984, p. 28).

The pitfalls of this scheme for individual price surcharges are apparent. In addition to striving for lower plan assignments, farm managements seek higher price surcharges. These surcharges are often awarded when high costs are due to poor management rather than, or as well as, to adverse natural conditions (Okhapkin, 1985, p. 36). In practice, surcharges are granted also to highly profitable farms (Dementsev, 1985, p. 8). Finally, the revenue from surcharges is frequently devoted to wage increases and bonuses, rather than to investment in fixed capital to reduce costs (Borkhunov, Yakovlev, and Kaliman, 1984, p. 46). Nonetheless, in 1986 the price surcharge scheme for weak farms was extended without essential changes through 1990.

Table 4 shows the estimated addition to the sales revenue of collective and state farms from the increase in base prices and the introduction of surcharges for weak farms. The figures in the table refer to the excess of (a) the value of planned 1982 state purchases at 1983 prices and surcharges for weak farms over (b) the value of the same quantities at 1982 prices. Farms' total sales revenue for all products was to increase by 21.0 billion rubles, of which 11.2 billion rubles was due to higher base prices and 9.8 billion rubles to the adoption of price surcharges for weak farms.

The 1983 price changes had striking effects also on the profitability of collective and state farms. In 1982 half of the farms operated at a loss (Semenov, 1985, p. 3). Their combined profits amounted to only 1.3 billion rubles, for a profitability rate of 1.3 percent in relation to cost (Lazutin, 1985, p. 99). In

---

19. For example, in the R.S.F.S.R. the number of zones was reduced from 178 to 78 for milk, from 73 to 53 for wheat, from 40 to 30 for cattle, and from 9 to 6 for sugar beets (Kufakov, 1984, p. 29). However, it was announced in August 1986 that zonal differentiation for grain prices would be increased in 1987.

Table 4. *Estimated Additional Sales Revenue of Collective and State Farms from 1983 Agricultural Price Increases and Surcharges for Weak Farms, by Product*[a]

Product	From price increases		From surcharges for weak farms		Total	
	Billion rubles	Percent of total	Billion rubles	Percent of total	Billion rubles	Percent of total
Cattle and poultry	3.8	33.6	5.1	56.0	8.9	42.6
Milk	2.8	24.6	2.3	23.8	5.1	24.3
Wool	0.4	3.3	0.4	3.9	0.8	3.8
Grain	1.1	9.8	0.8	8.1	1.9	8.6
Sugar beets	1.0	8.5	0.2	2.4	1.2	5.6
Potatoes	0.2	1.5	0.2	1.5	0.4	1.5
Vegetables	0.3	2.5	0.2	2.0	0.5	2.2
Raw cotton	0.6	5.6	0.1	0.9	0.7	3.4
Other products	1.0	10.6	0.5	1.4	1.5	8.0
Total	11.2	100.0	9.8	100.0	21.0	100.0

Source: Semenov, 1983, p.11.
a. Calculated as the excess of the value of planned 1982 state purchases at 1983 prices and surcharges over the value of planned 1982 state purchases at 1982 prices.

Table 5. *Profitability Rates on Sales to the State by Collective and State Farms, Selected Products, 1982 and 1984*[a]

Product	Collective farms		State farms	
	1982	1984	1982	1984
Cattle	−18	9	−9	18
Pigs	−20	−1	1	17
Sheep and goats	−16	−4	−16	−1
Poultry	−14	1	10	14
Milk	−7	23	−8	25
Wool	−15	0.2	−9	7
Sunflowers	118	146	100	112
Sugar beets	6	37	−18	40
Raw cotton	29	38	12	21
Potatoes	11	25	5	20
Vegetables	8	13	8	15
Fruits	57	52	59	49
Wine grapes	58	46	46	52

Source: Bannikov, 1986, p. 10.
a. Profit as a percentage of cost per 100 kilograms. Minus sign denotes rate of loss. Different rounding of figures as presented in source.

1983, combined profitability rose to 24.5 billion rubles, and the profitability rate climbed to 22 percent. The corresponding figures were somewhat lower in 1984 and 1985, when profits in billions of rubles were 20.6 and 21.0, and percentage profitability rates were 19 and 20, respectively.

The effect of the 1983 price changes on the profitability of individual products is shown in Table 5. It compares profitability rates in 1982 and 1984,

Table 6. *Subsidies on Selected Agricultural Products, 1965 and 1981–1985*
(billion rubles)

Product	1965	1981	1982	1983	1984	1985
Meat	2.8	15.2	15.3	21.4	21.0	22.1
Milk	a	8.3	9.0	13.8	14.1	15.2
Grain and oilseed	0.3	1.4	2.0	3.7	3.6	3.6
Potatoes and vegetables	a	1.1	1.7	2.2	2.4	2.4
Other products	0.4	2.8	1.9	4.2	3.8	5.4[b]
Subtotal	3.5	28.8	29.9	45.3	44.9	48.7
Price surcharges for weak farms	a	a	a	9.3	9.8	10.1
Total	3.5	28.8	29.9	54.6	54.7	58.8

Sources: Kufakov, 1986, p. 61; Semenov, 1983, p. 13; and Semenov, 1986b, p. 2.
a. Not applicable.
b. Including agricultural raw materials for light industry, sugar, fruits, and fish meal fodder.

respectively, before and after the 1983 price increases. Despite the growth of unit costs over the two-year period, profitability rates rose sharply for most products, particularly livestock output.[20]

Nevertheless, in 1985, 60–64 percent of the farms delivered pigs, sheep, wool, and eggs at a loss. The respective percentages were 54 for potatoes and 40 for cattle (Kufakov, 1986, p. 60). About 15 percent of the collective farms and 23 percent of the state farms were unprofitable, with combined losses of 3 billion rubles (Semenov, 1985, p. 8; Semenov, 1986a, p. 64). Without surcharges for weak farms, combined profitability of weak farms would have been only about 4 percent, with most of them having lower profitability or losses (Glushkov, 1985, p. 46).

The level of agricultural purchase prices and surcharges on them—and thus farm's profitability—are constrained by the state's unwillingness thus far to pass higher agricultural purchase prices along in higher state retail prices. (See section on retail prices, below). When agricultural purchase prices are raised without a corresponding increase in state retail prices, budget subsidies grow accordingly. Table 6 compares subsidies by product in 1965 and 1981–1985.[21] The data show how subsidies rose because of the 1983 increases in base prices and because of the introduction of price surcharges for weak farms. Meat and milk products are responsible for most of the subsidies of both types. The subsidy bill has been rising slowly since 1984 and is estimated in the 1987 state budget at 58 billion rubles, 13.3 percent of total budget expenditures.

In addition to these subsidies, intended to keep retail prices unaltered when agricultural purchase prices are raised, the state subsidizes farms by selling them industrial inputs at prices below the established industrial wholesale prices, as explained in the next section.

20. Unfortunately, the source for Table 5 does not provide similar data for grain.
21. On subsidies in the 1970s, see Treml (1983).

Prices of Industrial Inputs to Agriculture

One important factor affecting farms' costs and profitability at given agricultural purchase prices (and surcharges on them) is the pricing of industrial inputs to agriculture.

To hold down production costs in agriculture (in order to reduce the size of subsequent agricultural purchase price increases) when higher prices on industrial inputs into agriculture were introduced as a result of the 1967 industrial wholesale price reform, only part of the increase was passed along to the agricultural sector. Farms were charged the new prices for petroleum products, metal products, spare parts, lumber, and construction materials. But in the case of motor vehicles, agricultural equipment, and mineral fertilizer, the price increases were partly offset by budget subsidies, in a "dual-price" scheme. The subsidies, paid to organizations distributing materials and equipment to agriculture, cover the difference between the industrial wholesale prices received by the producer and the lower "release" prices at which the goods are sold to farms. Similarly, sales to farms of electricity and natural gas for hothouses are at preferential rates, with the differences from the normal rates covered by subsidies to the suppliers (Bornstein, 1976, p. 40).

Agriculture was compensated in two ways for the changes in the prices of industrial inputs resulting from the revision of industrial wholesale prices in 1982.[22]

First, about 5 billion rubles of the 21 billion ruble increase in farms' sales revenue due to the 1983 agricultural price revision was intended to enable farms to cover higher prices for their industrial inputs (Kufakov, 1984, p. 27).

Second, subsidies were increased on subsidized goods to avoid passing on to agriculture the full effect of the 1982 industrial price revision. The total amount of subsidies under the "dual-price" system for equipment, vehicles, and fertilizer for agriculture rose from about 4 billion rubles to about 5.2 billion rubles and has remained at about that level. In 1985 subsidies for equipment amounted to 2.6 billion rubles and those for fertilizer and electricity to 2.5 and 2.1 billion rubles, respectively. For equipment, the subsidy averaged about 25 percent of the industrial wholesale price, but ranged from 6.2 percent for motor vehicles to 35.9 percent for agricultural machinery (Glushkov, 1985, p. 48; Semenov, 1986, p. 66).

These subsidies on prices of industrial inputs cause the costs of agricultural production and investment and the subsidies to maintain retail price stability to be understated, and farms' profits and profitability to be overstated.[23] The lower prices for subsidized inputs also encourage inefficient use of mineral fertilizer and the premature write-off of equipment (Semenov, 1983, p. 16).

---

22. Changes in industrial wholesale prices are described in an earlier section of the paper, "The 1982 Industrial Price Revision."

23. Although subsidies reduce the prices of agricultural equipment, farms complain that the prices of new models are too high relative to those of old models, because of exaggerated estimates of new models' comparative economic effectiveness (*Ekonomicheskiy*, 1983, pp. 89–91).

But the Soviet authorities have been unwilling to eliminate the subsidies on industrial inputs to agriculture by raising the "release" prices to farms, agriculture purchase prices, and retail prices (or the subsidies to preserve retail prices).

RETAIL PRICES

There are several types of retail prices in the Soviet Union. Most important are state retail prices (*gosudarstvennyye roznichnyye tseny*) for households at state stores and service establishments such as restaurants, laundries, and theaters, as well as at the stores of consumer cooperatives in rural areas. Households pay collective farm market prices (*tseny kolkhoznogo rynka*) for purchases at those markets. Finally, nonstate prices are paid in various other "second economy" transactions. The following discussion focuses on the most significant category, state retail prices. Collective farm market prices are considered more briefly.

There are three principal components in the state retail price. The first is the producer price, namely the enterprise or industry wholesale price (or, for an unprocessed food product like eggs, the agricultural purchase price plus the markup of the agricultural procurement agency). The second component, covering distribution, includes the wholesale and retail trade margins for planned costs and profits at the respective levels, and transportation charges. The last element is a differentiated excise tax (called the "turnover" tax) or subsidy, if one is applied to the particular commodity. Turnover taxes are levied on alcoholic beverages and many nonfood consumer goods like clothing and appliances. Subsidies are provided primarily for food products and services.[24]

One of the regime's claims for the superiority of the Soviet socialist centrally planned economy over capitalist market economies is the ability to avoid significant inflation by maintaining approximate retail price stability—while money wages and thus real wages rise. However, in practice the regime has so far interpreted price stability not only as the maintenance of the overall level of state retail prices, but also as the rigidity of most individual prices as well.

Also, the regime's policy has been to make the distribution of real income different from (generally, less unequal than) the distribution of money income. This aim is pursued in part by relatively low prices on mass consumption goods (such as basic foodstuffs and standard clothing) which predominate in the budgets of lower-income families, and relatively higher prices for goods (such as luxury foodstuffs and fashionable clothing) which are comparatively more important in the expenditure patterns of higher-income groups.

For many years, many consumer goods and services have been sold at prices below the market-clearing level, as shown by persistent and widespread shortages. Excess demand is common also for services, such as health and post-

---

24. For detailed explanations of state retail prices for goods and services, see, for example, *Spravochnik* (1985, pp. 287–365), and Yezhov and Yershov (1986).

secondary education, provided at no user fee. Hence, various forms of nonprice rationing distribute the available supply. They include administrative allocation (for instance, of housing), access to special stores, queuing both in actual lines and on waiting lists, influence with sales personnel, and black market transactions.

An initial section in the treatment of retail prices considers the extent to which state retail prices are stable (as claimed), followed by analysis of proposals to alter explicitly the traditional policy of stable state retail prices. Finally, collective farm market prices are discussed in a third section.

Extent of Stability of State Retail Prices

The extent of price stability can be assessed from several viewpoints, including official price indexes, changes in effective retail prices not reflected in these indexes, and the use of subsidies to hold down retail prices.

Official Price Indexes. The most comprehensive picture of the evolution of state retail prices for goods in recent years is provided by the data in Table 7. The price level for all products rose only 5 percent from 1980 to 1985.

Price changes were negligible for food products, excluding alcoholic beverages. Retail prices for bread and pasta products, vegetable oil, basic types of fish, and sugar have not been altered since 1954. Prices for most meat and dairy products were last changed in 1962. In contrast, as part of the regime's anti-alcoholism campaign, prices of alcoholic beverages were increased significantly in 1981, 1982, 1983, and 1985. In 1986 there was a further increase in alcoholic beverage prices ranging from 20 to 25 percent. On the other hand, retail prices for fruit juices were cut by an average of 23 percent in 1985.

The overall price level of nonfood products has fluctuated little, although there are noticeable changes for some categories. Prices of wool fabrics rose during 1981–1983 but fell in 1984. In 1981 and especially 1982, prices of tobacco products were increased as part of an antismoking campaign. In 1984, prices on older models of television sets were substantially reduced, as occurred with cameras in 1982 and 1984.

In examining the figures in the table, one should keep in mind that the listings of types of food and nonfood products are not exhaustive. For example, no price indexes are published for furs, jewelry, housewares, and most consumer durables. Also, the coverage of the categories of goods listed in the table is rather broad. Hence, there may be significant price changes for subgroups and for individual products that average out to no, or only a negligible, change for the broader category of the reported index.

Both price decreases and price increases for various nonfood goods are mentioned in official statements about changes in state retail prices. These statements attribute the price reductions to larger production of newer models and the desire to reduce stocks of older models. Price increases are justified as necessary to discourage consumption, for instance, of alcoholic beverages

Table 7. *Indexes of Annual Average State Retail Prices, 1981–1985*[a]
(1980 = 100)

Commodity group	1981	1982	1983	1984	1985
All products	101	105	105	104	105
Food products	102	106	107	107	109
Meat and poultry	100	100	100.5	100.5	100.5
Fish and herring	100	100	100	98	97
Butter	100	100	100	100	100
Vegetable oil	100	100	100	100	100
Sugar	100	100	100	100	100
Confectionery products	100	100	100	100	100
Salt	100	100	100	100	100
Bread and bread products	100	100	100	100	100
Flour	100	100	100	100	100
Groat and bean products	100	100	100	100	100
Pasta products	100	100	100	100	100
Potatoes	108	100.9	102	101	102
Vegetables	99.7	100	100.1	101	103
Alcoholic beverages	105	117	120	120	128
Nonfood products	101	104	104	103	102
Cotton fabrics	100	100	100	100	100
Wool fabrics	104	116	107	103	103
Silk fabrics	99.2	97	97	96	94
Clothing and underwear	100.3	101	100.1	99.2	98
Knit goods	99.6	99	99	98	96
Hosiery	100	100	100	97	91
Leather, cloth, and combination footwear	100	100.1	100.1	100.1	100.1
Rubber footwear	100	100	100	100	100
Haberdashery	100	100	99.8	98	98
Tobacco products	108	127	127	127	127
Matches	100	100	100	100	100
Kerosene	100	100	100	100	100
School notebooks, paper and stationery products	97	96	99.7	100	100
Watches	99	97	97	95	95
Motorcycles	100	100	100	100	100
Bicycles and mopeds	100	100	100	99.3	98
Television sets	100	100	99.3	92	92
Sewing machines	100	100	100	100	100
Cameras	97	91	90	81	81

Source: *Narkhoz*, 1986, pp. 478 and 481.
a. Different rounding of figures as presented in source.

and tobacco, or to cut excess demand in the face of shortages due to limited supplies of raw materials and plant capacity for domestic production, or the limited availability of imports (Glushkov, 1984a).

However, official statements about these periodically announced price changes assure the public that the prices of basic consumption goods are not raised, and that on balance the population gains from the price changes. The latter assurance is based on calculations that household outlays on the price-decrease goods will fall by more (usually 2–3 billion rubles per year) than household outlays on the price-increase goods will rise.

Of course, it is possible for the authorities to change prices without a formal announcement. They are more likely to do so when the change is an increase rather than a decrease.[25]

These kinds of publicized and unpublicized price changes indicate greater flexibility of prices than is conveyed by the behavior of the aggregated indexes in Table 7, which nonetheless incorporate the effects of the changes.

Other Changes in Retail Prices. The published state retail price indexes refer only to changes in the "permanent" state retail prices of goods, in terms of the index sample's coverage and weights. The indexes do not purport to capture explicit or implicit changes in retail prices of five other kinds.

First, the indexes do not cover state sales of services and thus do not provide a comprehensive picture of state retail prices.

Second, the indexes do not encompass legal nonstate sales of goods or services, such as collective farm market sales. The indexes also omit illegal transactions, but such transactions are customarily excluded from official price statistics in other countries because of a lack of data or an unwillingness to acknowledge the extent of illegal activity.

Third, without a modification in the nominal permanent state retail prices of goods, their effective prices can change when quality is altered. Commonly, the effective change is upward due to a reduction in quality, for example, for clothing and electrical appliances (Orlov, 1985, pp. 133–134).

Fourth, without changes in either the permanent state retail prices of goods or their quality, the effective average prices facing households can increase. This occurs when producer enterprises and the trade network alter the product-mix[26] by increasing the share of higher-priced items and decreasing the share of lower-priced items. Such "washing out" of less expensive items from the assortment occurs, for instance, in regard to bread and other baked goods, meat products, clothing, footwear, and furniture (Lokshin, 1981).

Finally, some state retail sales are made at prices different from permanent state retail prices. These alternative prices are not considered in the published indexes for permanent prices (Bornstein, 1976, pp. 50–51). On the one hand,

25. For instance, Western newspaper correspondents in Moscow reported unpublicized price increases, effective February 1, 1983, on various goods, including household utensils, paper products, paint, and bottled soft drinks (Schmemann, 1983; Soviets, 1983).
26. In Soviet terminology, "assortment."

there are seasonal sales of excess stocks at prices below the permanent levels. On the other, new goods may be sold at "temporary" or "contract" prices intended to exceed their permanent levels.

Since 1984 seasonal sales on clothing and footwear have regularly been held twice a year, between February and April for winter goods, and between August and October for summer goods. Sale prices are usually 30–40 percent below the corresponding permanent prices (Akodis, 1985, pp. 65–67; Kurenkov and Zhuravleva, 1985, p. 75).

Temporary prices. The temporary retail price on a new good may include a surcharge, for superior quality, above the corresponding permanent price (*Spravochnik*, 1985, pp. 324–328). The permanent price is set at the same time as the temporary price, which is to be reduced to the permanent price after a designated period, usually 18 months. In principle temporary prices may be established on all nonfood goods, but in practice they are most commonly used for clothing and footwear. To be eligible for a temporary surcharge, a new product should surpass existing counterparts by a combination of criteria, including technical characteristics like capacity and durability as well as fashionability. The size of the surcharge is based on such criteria, rather than additional production cost for the new model. The surcharge can add from 5 to 50 percent of the permanent price. But most surcharges have been set at a rate of 5–10 percent—probably because enterprises and ministries were authorized to establish surcharge rates of up to 10 percent without prior approval by pricing agencies.[27]

Temporary retail prices applied in 1984 to 25 percent of the total output of light industry, with permanent prices covering 74 percent and contract prices (discussed below) 1 percent.[28] Two-thirds of the surcharges were at rates of 10 percent or less (Zhukov, 1985, p. 3). Temporary prices were much less important for consumer durables, covering less than 3 percent of their output in 1983 (Nikitin and Kabankov, 1984, p. 87).

The scheme of temporary retail (and associated wholesale) prices has several deficiencies. Often new products that do not differ significantly from existing products are awarded unjustified surcharges (Yarovikov, 1985, p. 56). Indeed, some of the "fashionable" new goods with temporary price surcharges are of such poor quality that they cannot be sold and instead accumulate in warehouses (Rayevskiy, 1986, p. 8). Even when surcharges are at least partly justified, their use causes higher-priced goods to supplant lower-priced goods, raising

27. In turn, a temporary wholesale price for the product ordinarily is set by the addition, to the permanent wholesale price, of an amount equal to the retail price surcharge minus the wholesale and retail trade margins. The revenue from the temporary surcharge is shared between the producer enterprises and the state budget. Of the total surcharge revenue, 15 percent is allocated to the producer enterprise's material incentive fund and 40 percent is retained by the enterprise to cover additional production costs or provide additional profit. The remaining 45 percent of surcharge revenue is paid to the state budget for a fund to cover subsequent compensation to trade enterprises for reductions of temporary prices to permanent prices on goods in their inventories.

28. Guzhavina (1987) reported respective percentage shares of 27 and 1 for temporary and contract prices, probably in reference to 1986.

the average price of the assortment available to households (Orlov and Fonareva, 1984, p. 36).

Excessive surcharges, and subsequent increases in effective average retail prices not reflected in official indexes, are likely to grow under new regulations issued in 1986. They authorize enterprises and associations to establish surcharges at rates up to 15 percent, and ministries to establish them at rates up to 30 percent, without prior approval by the State Prices Committee (Ob uluchshenii, 1986).

Contract prices. Contract prices provide another method of establishing higher retail prices not reflected in official price indexes. The initial lots of new models of some types of clothing, footwear, and furniture are eligible for contract prices. These prices are set by agreement between producing enterprises and trade organizations, without a requirement for approval by pricing agencies. Contract prices may exceed the permanent prices for counterpart existing goods by up to 50 percent.[29] The contract price may remain in force for six months, during which the initial lot is to be sold. Then, the next lot of the good is to be sold at a temporary retail price 20 percent below the contract price, and subsequent lots at a permanent price not less than 33 percent below the contract price (*Spravochnik*, 1985, pp. 328–330; Akodis, 1985, pp. 54–55; Kurenkov and Zhuravleva, 1985, p. 75).

Two advantages are claimed for contract pricing. One is its recognition of demand (as well as cost) in the negotiations between the trade network and producers about prices. Another is the schedule for price reductions on successive lots.

But so far contract pricing is unimportant, covering only about 1 percent of light industry output. The extent of contract pricing has been restrained by restrictions on the categories of goods and the maximum size of initial lots eligible for these prices, as well as by the lack of materials necessary for product improvements meriting the higher contract (or temporary) retail prices (Salimzhanov and Alpeyev, 1986, p. 21). In 1986 the limits on the size of initial lots were abolished (Ob uluchshenii, 1986), and the use of contract prices may grow as a result. But enterprises generally find it easier to increase prices and profits by the use of temporary retail prices, rather than contract prices (Akodis, 1985, p. 46).

Subsidies. Retail prices of most food products, some nonfood consumer goods, and most services are held down by subsidies.

The growth of total subsidies separating agricultural purchase prices and retail

29. The contract retail price is supposed to cover the following elements: (1) production cost of the new product; (2) a profit markup at the standard rate for the product group; (3) an additional "incentive" profit markup; (4) a turnover tax at the standard rate for the product group; and (5) a trade margin at a rate higher than the standard one for the product group. However, the enterprise retains only half of the extra profit in element (3), with the remainder going to the state budget. Of the enterprise's share, 30 percent goes to the material incentive fund and 70 percent to the social-cultural and housing fund and the production development fund. Thus, elements (1)–(3) address the interests of the producing enterprise; elements (3)–(4), those of the state budget; and element (5), those of the trade network.

Table 8. *Subsidization of Selected Meat and Dairy Products at 1983 Prices*
(rubles per kilogram)

	Beef	Pork	Whole milk	Butter
Average retail price	1.77	1.84	0.24	3.38
Cost to the state for production, transportation, and sale	4.75	3.25	0.42	8.18
Excess of cost over retail price	2.98	1.41	0.18	4.80
Total compensation payments from budget[a]	3.68	1.97	0.29	6.28

Sources: Semenov, 1986a, p. 65.

a. Gross payments from the budget, including payments for an excess of zonal prices over average prices that are offset by payments to the budget for an excess of average prices over zonal prices.

prices on food products was examined in the part of the paper devoted to agricultural purchase prices. Table 8 furnishes additional data for four important food products on the difference in 1983 between the retail price and the cost to the state for their production, transportation, and sale. The retail price as a percentage of the cost to the state was 37 for beef, 56 for pork, 57 for whole milk, and 41 for butter. Essentially the same relationships prevailed in 1986. Unfortunately, similar data are not available for the many other subsidized food products.

Scanty information is published about subsidies for nonfood consumer goods. Prominently mentioned are subsidies in the prices of children's clothing and furniture, amounting to over 1 billion rubles per year. More than half of the medicine produced is distributed without charge at medical institutions (Glushkov, 1984b). Books are often published at a loss (Trotsenko, 1986).

At the beginning of the 1980s, users paid the following percentage shares of the cost of various services: education, 5; health, 6; housing, 37; and cultural, sports, and travel services, 55 (Moskaleva, 1982, p. 39). The current respective shares are probably lower, because in these activities costs have risen without corresponding price increases. Subsidies for housing alone amounted to 9.3 billion rubles in 1985 (*Narkhoz*, 1986, p. 412). It is likely that these subsidies have since grown as a result of cost increases not offset by price increases.

Desirability of Increases in State Retail Prices

For decades, Soviet officials have defended retail prices below costs, as well as retail prices above costs but below market-clearing levels. The official justification for these pricing policies rests primarily on the distributional argument that they make the goods and services available to lower as well as higher income groups (Glushkov, 1984a). This traditional position has recently been challenged on equity, efficiency, and incentive grounds.

The equity objection is that it is "socially unjust" for households to have unequal opportunities to convert into goods and services legitimate money income (and savings) from wages in the socialized sector, transfer payments, and earnings from legal private activity like individual agricultural plots. The effective purchasing power of these rubles varies when households have different possibilities to purchase goods and services at state retail prices. For example, meat and milk products are sold at low state retail prices chiefly in larger cities. In other urban areas and in rural areas, these products usually must be bought at collective farm market prices much higher than state retail prices. Also, some households have preferential access to goods at state retail prices through special stores not open to the general public (Zaslavskaya, 1986b, p. 71).

In regard to efficiency, too much of households' time is devoted to searching and queuing for goods priced below market-clearing levels. In addition, resources are unnecessarily devoted to the redistribution through the black market of scarce goods bought at low state retail prices (Belokh, Petrakov, and Rusakov, 1982; Ayvazyan, 1985, p. 141).

Finally, monetary incentives to the labor force are blunted by shortages of goods and services at below-market clearing prices. Shortages weaken the incentives to respond to wage differentials intended to evoke increases in productivity, and to allocate the labor force by occupation, skill, and geographic area. Workers' interest in earning additional income is reduced when they cannot spend their present money incomes to acquire the goods and services they wish (in the light of their incomes and tastes) at prevailing prices. To some extent they respond by purchasing what is available instead of what they really want. This "forced substitution" reduces their utility from their money incomes and expenditures. Another part of their money incomes is involuntarily saved, accumulating in undesired cash holdings or savings account balances (Belokh and Rusakov, 1984; Volkonskiy and Solov'yev, 1985).

Advocates of a reform in state retail pricing therefore propose that retail prices be increased toward, if not up to, market-clearing levels equating demand and supply. The closer prices approached these levels, the more nearly would be achieved the goal of "equality of all rubles" in purchasing power across goods, across regions, and across households (Zaslavskaya, 1986, p. 71).

Different segments of the population would receive different degrees of "compensation" for such price increases, through changes in wages and transfer payments. A retail price reform therefore should be coordinated with a reform of wages, announced in 1986 and to be gradually implemented over several years, and a corresponding pension reform (Kazakevich, 1986, pp. 38–39; Gladkiy, 1986; Bim and Shokhin, 1986, pp. 67–69).

No similar "compensation" for retail price increases would be provided for savings (in cash holdings and savings bank accounts), and their purchasing power would be decreased accordingly (Shatalin, 1986, p. 66). This result is considered desirable, and deemed better achieved by price increases than by a monetary reform involving the exchange of each present ruble for less than one new ruble (State Bank, 1986).

Increases in state retail food prices, through a reduction in the subsidies separating them from agricultural purchase prices, are proposed for several reasons. The primary one is to reduce excess demand. In addition, a revision of state retail food prices could include adjustment of relative prices within food groups for substitutes, like beef and pork in relation to poultry, and for quality differences (Kalnyn'sh, 1986, p. 70). Higher prices for bread would reduce its use for livestock feed and its waste at food service establishments (Kazakevich, 1986, 36–38).

In the case of nonfood consumer goods, it is suggested that prices could be raised through a widening of the differentials for higher-quality and more fashionable goods, some of which might be sold in separate stores (Levin and Yarkin, 1984, pp. 191–192).

Proposals for price increases for "paid" services include the following, in ascending order of boldness. (1) Time-of-use pricing should be introduced for transportation, telephone, and electricity services (Roze, 1985; Bokov and Shmarov, 1985, p. 21). (2) Rates should be differentiated to include higher prices for greater quality, for example, faster trains, apartments on higher floors, and better hotels (Moskaleva, 1982, pp. 41–42; Ulanovskaya, 1986, p. 94). (3) Low, even subsidized, prices should be charged for minimum quantities considered socially necessary, but higher prices for additional amounts. Housing is the striking example in this category (Kazakevich 1986, pp. 40–41; Ulanovskaya, 1986, pp. 92–93). (4) Prices for some services, such as certain kinds of entertainment, should be raised enough to eliminate subsidies (Rutgayzer, 1985).

In addition, fees might be charged for some education and health services that households now receive free. Tuition could be collected for some specialized advanced courses. The network of optional fee-for-service medical facilities could be expanded (Bim and Shokhin, 1986, p. 73; Ivchenko, 1986).

Thus, proposals for changes in state retail prices that not long ago would have been considered daring have been published recently. They appear not only in "progressive" journals like *Ekonomika i organizatsiya promyshlennogo proizvodstva* (*EKO*), from the Siberian Division of the USSR Academy of Sciences, but also in "conservative" periodicals like *Kommunist*, the Communist Party's leading theoretical journal. These proposals may presage far-reaching changes in retail prices, of two types. One is a substantial initial increase in the prices of important consumer goods and services. The other is subsequent flexibility in pricing, including increases from the new levels, rather than traditional rigidity.

Collective Farm Market Prices

In 1985 collective farm markets accounted for 2.6 percent of total retail sales of all goods at state stores, consumer cooperative stores, and collective farm markets. The markets' percentage shares were 4.9 for total food sales and 9.6 for total sales of the same range of food products (excluding, for example, canned foods not sold at the markets) (*Narkhoz*, 1986, pp. 462–463). But the importance of the markets is greater than these figures suggest. For example, in some cities the markets' share of total food sales is 25 percent

(*Planirovaniye*, 1982, p. 203), and in some cities the markets supply 25–50 percent of the vegetables and 50–75 percent of the fruit (Brovkin and Gorbuntsov, 1986). The four types of sellers had the following percentages of total sales in 1984; individual traders, 85; consumer cooperatives, 10; trade services bureaus, 3; and collective and state farms, 2 (Korovyakovskiy, 1986, p. 89).

The Soviet regime is now seeking to increase the supply and consumption of food through sales of larger quantities, at lower prices, at the collective farm markets. First, it is encouraging production on individual plots, for example, by the provision of more material inputs like feed, as well as by a reaffirmation of the legitimacy of income earned from individual plots. Second, it is extending the activities of consumer cooperatives and trade services bureaus in buying output from individual plots for resale at the markets. Third, it has authorized collective and state farms to count their sales of fruits and vegetables at the markets against the farms' obligations for sales to the state, for up to 30 percent of their sales assignments for the respective products (Korovyakovskiy, 1986, pp. 86–89). Because market prices exceed state agricultural purchase prices, the last measure increases the farms' average selling prices.

CONCLUSION

The Soviet price system has recently been evolving in various respects. A number of constructive changes have been made, and others have been adopted but not yet implemented. However, important deficiencies in the price system remain. Thus, further significant changes are proposed.

Industrial wholesale prices were comprehensively revised in 1982, for the first time since 1967. The new prices acknowledged cost changes over this long interval, and they more accurately account for several types of costs. But industrial producer prices are still set primarily from the cost or supply side and do not usually also reflect demand and scarcity. In prices for new machinery, equipment, and instruments, a greater effort is made to recognize utility to users, through calculations of comparative "economic effectiveness" and price surcharges related to it. Yet the results of this effort have so far been rather modest. Under the recently announced foreign trade reform, domestic prices for exports and imports are to be related more closely to their foreign prices.[30] However, implementation of this approach will be difficult and gradual (Shastiko, 1986). Also, the new domestic prices for traded goods will be compared, in a variety of economic calculations, with nonscarcity industrial wholesale prices for other goods.

Revisions of agricultural purchase prices have established more reasonable relationships between prices and farms' costs. Yet costs are understated because of subsidies for some industrial inputs into agriculture. Also, it is still common for farms to be assigned plans to deliver products at a loss. Finally, for the

---

30. On current arrangements for setting domestic industrial wholesale prices for exported and imported machinery and equipment, see Treml (1981) and Rozenova (1985b, pp. 55–63).

collection of land rent, the regime continues to use zonally differentiated prices, rather than uniform marginal-cost prices with explicit rental payments.

State retail prices for goods and services are often below market-clearing levels, and frequently also below cost. However, bold proposals for price increases to change both the level and the structure of these prices have recently appeared in influential Soviet journals.

In the next few years, the levels and structures of industrial wholesale prices and of agricultural purchase prices may be altered in connection with the preparation of the five-year plan for 1991–1995. In turn, state retail prices of goods and services may be modified in conjunction with changes in industrial wholesale and agricultural purchase prices and wage and pension reforms.

COMMENT ON SHMELEV'S APPROACH

In the preceding chapter, Nikolay Shmelev discussed a number of issues involved in the reform of the Soviet price system (Shmelev, 1988b). Space limitations preclude a thorough analysis of the various facets of this complex economic, social, and political problem. Instead, I shall briefly examine some of the deficiencies of the present Soviet price system, announced official plans for changes, Shmelev's proposals for price reforms, and the views of other Soviet economists who are specialists on pricing. For conciseness, each of the three main components of the Soviet domestic price system is considered in turn: industrial producer prices, agricultural producer prices, and state retail prices.

Industrial Producer Prices

In the USSR industrial producer prices—usually called "industrial wholesale prices" (*optovyye tseny promyshlennosti*)—are based on the branch average cost of production (*sebestoimost'*) and a profit markup. The former includes direct and indirect labor, materials, fuel and power, amortization allowances, and various overhead expenses. The profit markup is supposed to provide a "normal" rate of profit (in relation to capital) for the branch as a whole. But the profitability rate may be above or below "normal" for an individual enterprise, depending upon its product mix and the relationship of the actual cost of its output to the planned branch average cost.

Quality differentials, and the superiority of new products over earlier models, are supposed to be reflected by a set of surcharges (*nadbavki*) and discounts (*skidki*). The surcharges increase (or the discounts decrease) the profitabilities and prices of products of higher (lower) quality. Thus they affect a product's relative contribution to an enterprise's gross and net value of output, as well as to its profits.

Soviet industrial producer prices are set primarily from the cost or supply side and usually do not also reflect demand or scarcity. Surcharges and discounts inadequately reflect differences in quality and technological level. Hence, enterprise plan assignments are often expressed in physical units in an effort to secure the desired output of products that price-cost relationships make "disadvantageous" for the enterprise. Also, administrative allocation, rather than price rationing, is commonly used to distribute raw, intermediate, and finished goods. Finally, cost and price increases in industry often are fully passed along in corresponding changes in agricultural producer prices or state retail prices.[31]

According to official statements, new industrial wholesale prices (and freight rates) are to be introduced on January 1, 1990.[32] It appears that there will be only modest changes in pricing methods. The calculation of costs for the new prices will include higher social insurance rates, additional charges for the use of water, greater rental payments in extractive branches, and charges for environmental protection measures. Also, a labor tax and a larger capital tax will be paid out of profits (Pavlov, 1987, p. 22).

However, no fundamental changes are indicated in the principles for pricing new products of the raw material branches (Metodika, 1988) and new machinery, equipment, and instruments (Vremennaya metodika, 1987). For the latter, there will be greater use of "contract" prices (*dogovornyye tseny*) negotiated between producer and user enterprises, but within the framework of detailed regulations established by the USSR State Committee for Prices (Polozheniye, 1988).

Scattered, often preliminary statements indicate that coal prices will be increased 100 percent and oil and gas prices 100–150 percent (Komin, 1988, p. 113). Electricity rates will rise 45–65 percent (Mayorets, 1988). Similar increases are likely in the prices of metals and petrochemicals. The overall price level for machinery, equipment, and instruments may be approximately unchanged. However, prices of raw-material-intensive output (such as presses) may rise because of higher raw materials prices, and prices of R&D-intensive equipment (e.g., electronics) may fall as a result of the decline in costs resulting from learning and scale effects from the growth of production (interview material). Percentage increases in freight rates, by mode of transport, are to be as follows: rail, 30–35; road, 20–25; river, 30–35; and coastal shipping, 35–45 (Stepanenko, 1988a).[33]

On the whole, the changes envisioned in industrial producer prices correspond more to a "revision" than to a "reform." In Soviet pricing terminology, a reform (*reforma*) refers to a basic change in the way prices are constructed, whereas a revision (*peresmotr*) adjusts many prices without altering the fundamental scheme for price formation. By these standards, Soviet industrial producer prices are deemed to have been "reformed" in 1966–1967 (Schroeder, 1969) but only "revised" in 1982 (Bornstein, 1985).

31. For a more detailed analysis of industrial producer prices, see Bornstein (1987, pp. 96–109).
32. See Pavlov (1987, p. 26) and Rozenova (1988, p. 72). Pavlov and Rozenova are, respectively, Chairman and a Deputy Chairman of the USSR State Committee for Prices (Goskomtsen).
33. For additional details on price changes in individual branches of industry, see Pavlov (1987, pp. 20–23). In 1990 Pavlov became Prime Minister. [Eds.]

Shmelev (1988b, p. 320) endorses increases in prices for fuels and raw materials and decreases in prices for machinery and equipment. He considers these changes desirable to reduce differences across branches in average profitability, and to create conditions for "partial convertibility" of the ruble. The former aim, officially stated, is more obvious.

But Shmelev does not explain how the price changes he favors would contribute to what kind of even limited convertibility of the ruble. For instance, he does not address the relationship of domestic prices for exports and imports to their foreign prices—either through official exchange rates or "differentiated currency coefficients" (*differentsirovannyye valyutnyye koeffitsienty*), now widely discussed in the Soviet technical press (see, for example, Doronin, 1988a; Kuznetsov, 1988). Nor does Shmelev assess the prospects for convertibility of the ruble in terms of the relationship between the Soviet Union's supply of, and demand for, convertible currencies (Doronin, 1988b).

Shmelev asserts that Soviet prices for raw materials, fuels, food, transport, and housing are too low, whereas prices for machinery, equipment, and industrial consumer goods are too high—by a factor of 3 or more, compared to "world" price relationships (Shmelev, 1988b, p. 320). But he does not explain how he reached this conclusion—for example by comparisons of relative prices in the USSR in (domestic) rubles with relative prices in their national currencies in some set of other countries. Nor does he explain why, and how closely, on theoretical grounds relative prices in the USSR should be similar to those in other countries, rather than reflecting different scarcity relationships in the USSR.

Shmelev (1988b, p. 323) is reluctant to let prices be set by market forces in markets in which sellers have a monopolistic position. But he does not offer concrete suggestions to increase competion, for instance, by dissolving associations that group similar enterprises. Nor does he analyze the extent to which sellers' market power is due to excess demand, rather than to concentration of plant capacity and production (Deryabin, 1988a; Yasin, 1988a).

Agricultural Producer Prices

Soviet collective and state farms sell their output to state procurement organizations at "purchase prices" (*zakupochnyye tseny*). The procurement organizations resell this output at industrial wholesale prices—either to the light and food industries for processing, as in the case of grain and wool, or directly to the trade network when further processing is not needed, as is the case of eggs. The basic principle is that agricultural purchase prices should cover the costs of farms operating in "normal" conditions and provide them a profit that can be reinvested to expand their capital stock of buildings, equipment, reproductive livestock, and inventories.

Sales assignments for agricultural products are given to large numbers of farms whose production costs vary widely because of differences in natural conditions, such as soil, topography, rainfall, temperature, and length of growing season. The Soviet practice is to differentiate the prices of many commodities geographically by price zones, in an effort to capture for the state differential rents arising from more favorable natural conditions. These zonal prices are set with reference to the average costs of production in each zone. The aim is to provide, for each product, lower prices but higher profitability in low-cost areas, and higher prices but lower profitability in high-cost areas. In addition, weak farms, with low profitability or losses, receive surcharges on the base zonal prices. Nonetheless, many farms deliver livestock, potatoes, eggs, and other products at a loss.

These losses occur despite the subsidization of industrial inputs to agriculture. Such subsidies cover the difference between the industrial wholesale prices received by the producer and the lower "release" price at which goods and services are sold to farms. This "dual-price" scheme applies, for example, to agricultural equipment, mineral fertilizer, and electricity.

Soviet economists have criticized these pricing arrangements for agriculture. The subsidies on prices of industrial inputs cause the costs of agricultural production and investment to be understated and the farms' profitability to be overstated. Agricultural purchase prices often fail to cover even these understated costs, and to provide necessary funds for investment. Finally, land rent has been collected through zonally differentiated prices, rather than uniform marginal-cost prices with explicit rental payments.[34]

According to official statements, higher agricultural purchase prices are to be introduced January 1, 1991. They are to be based on zonal average costs, although the number of zones will be reduced (and their size thus enlarged). However, explicit rental payments will be collected from farms in more favorable natural conditions. The understatement of farms' costs is to be reduced, through the abolition of subsidies on the prices of industrial inputs and through the introduction of charges for the use of water (Pavlov, 1987, pp. 23–26).

It has been estimated that, at the new prices, farms will receive an additional 30 billion rubles from state procurement agencies. Of this sum, 11.7 billion rubles is to cover the effects of farms' costs from increases in industrial wholesale prices (discussed in the preceding section). The remaining 18.3 billion rubles is to compensate farms for the elimination of subsidies on industrial inputs; the introduction of water charges; higher freight rates (discussed in the preceding section); and higher construction prices to be applied January 1, 1991.[35]

Thus, increases in industrial wholesale prices are to be passed along in higher input and output prices in agriculture. But the Soviet government has not disclosed (or perhaps decided) to what extent it intends to pass such higher agricultural purchase prices along in higher state retail prices. The alternative

34. For a more detailed analysis of the pricing of inputs and outputs of agriculture, see Bornstein (1987, pp. 110–118).
35. See Ayvazov (1987). Ayvazov is a Deputy Chairman of the USSR State Committee for Prices.

is to restrain a rise in retail prices, by increasing the subsidies that now keep retail prices significantly below the agricultural purchase prices for meat, milk, grain, potatoes, and vegetables, and other products.

Shmelev argues that these subsidies can be reduced, without an increase in state retail prices (Shmelev, 1988b, p. 325). He asserts that the primary reason for the subsidies is aid to weak farms and that the solution lies in the write-off of their indebtedness and the termination of assistance to them. He suggests that weak farms might join stronger farms, might lease their land to families or small cooperatives, or might convert their land into parks or hunting preserves.

But Shmelev's proposal seems too facile. More than two-thirds of the state and collective farms now receive price surcharges for weak farms, and even with these subsidies one-third of the farms have a profitability rate (relative to cost) below 10 percent and 13 percent of the farms operate at a loss (Kim, 1988b, p. 30). It is not clear why successful farms would want to incorporate weak farms; how much a change to cooperative or family farming would improve performance; or how present farm personnel would earn a living from parks or hunting preserves. Thus, the government could hardly not worry about the fate of weak farms, as Shmelev advises (Shmelev, 1988b, p. 325).

Hence, rather than maintaining or even reducing agricultural purchase prices, as recommended by Shmelev, the government appears more likely to raise them, in order to improve farms' profitability rates toward the levels of 35–40 percent in relation to cost and 10 percent in relation to capital that Soviet agricultural price specialists deem desirable (Kim, 1988b, p. 30; Lukinov, 1988, p. 22).

State Retail Prices

There are three principal components in the state retail price. The first is the producer price, namely, the industry wholesale price (or, for an unprocessed food product like eggs, the agricultural purchase price plus the markup of the agricultural procurement agency). The second component, covering distribution, includes the wholesale and retail trade margins for planned costs and profits at their respective levels, and transportation charges. The last element is a differentiated excise tax (called the "turnover" tax) or subsidy, if one is applied to the particular commodity. Turnover taxes are levied on alcoholic beverages and many nonfood consumer goods such as clothing and appliances. Subsidies are provided primarily for food products and services.

For many years, many consumer goods and services have been sold at prices below the market-clearing level, as shown by widespread and persistent shortages. Hence various forms of nonprice rationing distribute the available supply. They include administrative allocation (for instance, of housing), coupons, queuing in actual lines or on waiting lists, influence with sales personnel, access to special stores, and black market transactions.

This excess demand is not reflected in official state retail price indexes, which show only a modest rate of inflation of about 1 percent per year from 1980 to 1987 (*Narkhoz*, 1988, p. 434). One explanation is the long-standing official commitment to retail price "stability," understood to mean not only stability of the overall retail level, but also rigidity of many individual prices.

Another explanation is that the published state retail price indexes refer only to changes in the "permanent" state retail prices of goods, in terms of the index sample's coverage and weights. The indexes do not purport to capture changes in retail prices of five other kinds. (1) The indexes do not cover state sales of services. (2) The indexes do not encompass legal nonstate sales of goods or services, such as collective farm market sales and sales by cooperatives. (3) Without a modification in the nominal permanent state retail price of goods, their effective prices can change when quality is reduced. (4) Without changes in either the permanent state retail prices of goods or their quality, the effective average prices facing households can increase. This occurs when the product mix is altered to increase the share of higher-priced items and decrease the share of lower-priced items. (5) Some (at least nominally) "new" goods are sold at "temporary" or "contract" prices intended to exceed their permanent prices. Thus, it is widely recognized, by both professional economists and the general public, that inflationary pressure in the USSR is much more severe than conveyed by official statistics (see, for instance, Rutgayzer et al., 1988, p. 33).

Soviet pricing officials and political leaders now criticize the heavy subsidization of the prices of meat, dairy products, and other foods as economically unsound. They point to the burden of subsidies on the budget on the one hand, and shortages at artificially low prices, on the other.[36] The remedy proposed is increases in state retail prices, accompanied by "compensation" to the population through concurrent increases in wages and transfer payments— "before the start of the next five-year plan" in 1991 (Pavlov, 1987, pp. 24– 26).

Shmelev sketches an "ideal" scenario similar to the above official vision, combining higher prices to reduce excess demand with "compensation" payments, at least to low-income people. A reduction in subsidies for food products would also be offset by a cut in turnover taxes on domestically produced manufactured consumer goods (Shmelev, 1988b, p. 321). He concedes that the latter measure would increase shortages of those goods, but suggests imports of manufactured consumer goods to be sold at present (or higher?) prices. Shmelev does not recommend "compensation" for the loss of purchasing power, when prices rise, of savings in currency or savings bank accounts.

But Shmelev (1988b, pp. 322–323) considers the "ideal" solution politi-

---

36. These shortages have various consequences. (1) The effective purchasing power of money incomes (and savings) varies when households have different possibilities to buy goods and services at state retail prices. (2) Too much of households' time is devoted to searching and queuing for goods. (3) Incentives to the labor force to earn more money are blunted by shortages of goods and services for which they might wish to spend additional income. For further discussion of these issues, see Bornstein (1987, pp. 126–127).

cally infeasible, in view of the population's objections to price increases, even with promises of "compensation." He fears, reasonably enough, that the population will conclude that *perestroyka* means price increases, and therefore will lose faith in *perestroyka*. Instead, Shmelev urges that state retail price increases be deferred until the market is "saturated" with food and nonfood consumer goods. He cites as an example China, where retail price reform was undertaken gradually, after economic reforms and policy changes had increased supplies of consumer goods.

Schmelev endorses "compensation" to (at least part of) the population for retail price increases without analyzing and evaluating proposed compensation schemes. They generally involve two approaches: (1) offsetting increases in food prices by reductions in prices of nonfood consumer goods, and (2) increases in money incomes (Parkhomovskiy, 1987; Chekhlov, 1988; Lopatnikov, 1988).

The problem with the first approach is to identify the appropriate goods. They should be goods for which the price cuts could come out of turnover tax revenues, in order to satisfy the principle that prices should cover costs (and provide "normal" profits) for production and distribution. Also, they should be goods for which supplies are ample to meet greater demand at lower prices, in order to satisfy the principle that prices should clear the market.

In the second approach, if the increment to household money incomes is as large as the increase in the value of retail sales resulting from the price increases, there may be no reduction in the excess aggregate demand of households.[37] Whatever the amount of such compensation payments, their distribution across households must be decided. Presumably the compensation payments should be made to households as consuming units, rather than to individuals as workers. A differentiated scale could provide larger payments per person to households with lower per capita incomes, in an effort to reduce income inequality per capita across households. But such payments would alter the income differentials (from differences in wages by occupation, skill level, and productivity) envisioned by the wage reform (Gladkiy, 1986).

These problems are recognized by some Soviet economists, who question the advisability of "compensation" through (1) reductions in prices of nonfood consumer goods or (2) payments to households (Deryabin, 1988b; Yasin, 1988b). Other Soviet economists consider compensation payments economically undesirable but perhaps politically necessary if retail prices are to be raised (Borozdin, 1988, pp. 55–56).

Finally, some economists share Shmelev's view that retail price increases are so politically sensitive that they threaten *perestroyka* as a whole. According to Academician Shatalin: "The new economic mechanism has not yet been formed. And under the present conditions it is a naive and dangerous undertaking to pull it by such a thin and sensitive thread as retail prices" (Shatalin, 1988).

---

37. Some of the increase in household incomes from compensation payments might be saved voluntarily.

Conclusion

There appears to be considerable uncertainty among Soviet economists, officials, and political leaders about when, how fast, and how far to proceed with the kind of comprehensive reform of the price system envisioned in 1987. The USSR State Committee for Prices has been criticized for calculating new industrial wholesale prices before decisions have been taken on changes in state retail prices—rather than preparing a comprehensive reform encompassing the relationship of all types of prices (Kim, 1988a).

The government may introduce new industrial wholesale prices, and perhaps new agricultural purchase prices, as scheduled. However, it is not clear what all of their key features and magnitudes would be, and the extent to which they would reflect costs and scarcities and the 50-percent devaluation of the ruble (relative to convertible currencies) in regard to export and import transactions scheduled for January 1, 1990 (*Izvestiya*, December 10, 1988, p. 2).

But if industrial wholesale prices and agricultural purchase prices are altered, the government must decide to what extent corresponding adjustments in state retail prices will be made, or will be avoided by an increase in budget subsidies. In the 1989 budget, such subsidies for food alone (excluding subsidies on nonfood consumer goods and services) are planned at 87.9 billion rubles, or 17.8 percent of total budget expenditures (*Pravda*, October 28, 1988, p. 4). Clearly, the decisions on the various facets of price reform will critically affect the nature and fate of *perestroyka*.

CHAPTER 14

Anatomy of Gorbachev's Economic Reform

Gertrude E. Schroeder

ON JUNE 30, 1987, the Supreme Soviet approved by decree a package of measures designed to alter the ways in which the Soviet economy is managed (*Pravda*, July 1, 1987). These measures are set forth in a document approved a few days earlier at a plenum of the Central Committee of the CPSU. The document is entitled "Basic Provisions for the Radical Restructuring of Economic Management" (*Pravda*, June 27, 1987) and is supplemented by 10 decrees subsequently adopted and published (*O Korennoy perestroyke*, 1987).[1] The Supreme Soviet also adopted a new Law on the State Enterprise (Association), which forms a key part of the reform package (*Pravda*, July 1, 1987). Also included in the reform package are the decrees adopted in 1986 mandating an overhaul of the entire wage and salary system, reorganizing the conduct of foreign trade, expanding the rights and responsibilities of regional authorities, sanctioning expansion of the scope of economic activity by private individuals and producer cooperatives, as well as actions taken during 1985–1987 to establish new bureaucracies, reorganize old ones, and reform incentives in agriculture. As a whole, this program provides the present official documents and time schedules for putting into place a "new economic mechanism" that is supposed to be almost fully operational by the start of the 13th Five-Year Plan in 1991.

This paper describes and evaluates the changes laid out in this highly complex set of reform documents. Nine major aspects of the package are considered, in turn: the role of central planning, the status of the firm, the role of central administrative bodies, the system of material/technical supply, prices and wages,

First published in *Soviet Economy*, 1987, 3, 3, pp. 219–241. [Eds.]

1. The decrees, each dealing with a separate aspect of the reforms, were approved by the Central Committee of the CPSU and the Council of Ministers. Each decree is dated July 17, 1987. The 10 decrees deal with the following: the State Planning Committee (Gosplan), the State Committee for Material and Technical Supply (Gossnab), the State Committee for Science and Technology (Gostekhnika), finance, banking, statistics, price formation, responsibilities of regional bodies, the State Committee for Labor and Social Problems (Goskomtrud), and the ministries. An eleventh decree, dealing with the work of the Council of Ministers, has not yet been published.

finance and credit, the conduct of foreign trade, private and cooperative activity, and agricultural reforms. Then, the package is evaluated as a whole, with the focus on the extent to which its provisions as now spelled out alter the basic features of the present economic system. The likely consequences of the concerted attempt to implement those provisions under pressure from a determined leader are assessed as well.

DESCRIPTION OF THE REFORM PACKAGE

The Role of Central Planning

The Basic Provisions stress that the economy shall continue to be planned and managed as "a unified national economic complex" as the principal means for carrying out the Party's economic policies. These policies are to be embodied in a 15-year plan that sets goals and priorities and outlines a program for implementing them. This plan, which is to contain specific targets for the 15-year period, is to be the basis for detailed formulation of the plan for the initial 5-year period, with a breakdown by years. Per the current procedure, this plan will be worked out by Gosplan and sent down to republic Councils of Ministers and to ministries. These bodies, in turn, send "initial planning data" to firms, on the basis of which the latter work out and ratify their own 5-year and annual plans. Plans are reviewed annually and revised if required. Proposals for revisions are submitted to Gosplan, which reviews them, revises the 5-year plan if necessary, and submits a report to the Council of Ministers and to the Central Committee, along with the draft state budget.

The firms receive: (1) "non-binding control figures" that specify the value of output, profit, foreign currency receipts, and major indicators of scientific and technical progress and social development;[2] (2) a mandatory bill of state orders for output that "ensure meeting society's priority needs";[3] (3) limits, which include rationed goods and centralized investment allocations; (4) long-term economic normatives based on a list approved by the Council of Ministers regulating, among other things, growth of total wages, payments for capital and labor, and the allocation of profits among various kinds of taxes and reserve funds set up by ministries and enterprises. Three major funds are the bonus fund, the social development fund, and the fund for financing research and development and investment.

Clearly, the state intends to determine the rate and direction of the bulk of investment. To what extent will depend on how state centralized investment is defined. The state also intends to determine the directions of economic development and to enforce programs of scientific-technical progress that are

2. The list is to be fixed by the USSR Council of Ministers.
3. The bill includes commissionings of facilities financed by state centralized investment and products required to carry out essential state tasks in the areas of social development, scientific-technical progress (including important new products), foreign economic relations, defense, and deliveries of farm products to the state.

worked out from the top. Through the system of state orders the government will continue to dictate production and allocate the requisite materials for some part of total output, but the share of state orders in total output is supposed to gradually decline. Determining the composition of state orders is the "most important task of Gosplan," according to Premier Nikolay Ryzhkov (*Pravda*, June 30, 1987).

Status of the Firm

The new Law on the State Enterprise establishes the intended status of the firm under the reforms in considerable detail. The law takes effect on January 1, 1988, and firms are to be put under its full provisions gradually during 1988 and 1989. As at present, firms, which are founded and liquidated by superior bodies, are accorded legal rights of "possession, use, and disposal" of physical assets, which remain under state ownership, and are formally subordinate to government agencies (ministries or regional bodies).

The Law, which is long on reform rhetoric and short on precise legal language, supposedly greatly expands the decision-making authority of the firm by providing that it "is entitled to make on its own initiative any decisions provided that they do not run counter to existing legislation." The Law endows the firm with "rights whose observance is guaranteed by the state" and provides means by which the firm may obtain redress if superior organs violate such rights. The Law also spells out in considerable detail the rights and obligations of the firm in a number of key areas that are the focus of the reforms and of current policy. Finally, the Law explicitly provides for declaring bankrupt and liquidating firms that persistently make losses. Displaced workers are to be given severance pay and helped to find new jobs.

The firm now "independently" works out and approves its 5-year and annual plans, based on "non-binding" control figures, mandatory state orders, limits, stable economic normatives, and contracts with customers. The Law states, "The enterprise is obligated to strictly observe plan discipline and meet plans and contractual obligations in full." It states further, "Fulfillment of orders and contracts serves as the most important criterion for evaluating the activities of the enterprise and providing material rewards for its employees." Managerial bonuses are fixed by the ministry and paid out of incentive funds formed from enterprise profits; the present "Recommendations," promulgated in implementation of the general wage reform decree of September 1986, link bonuses to 100 percent fulfillment of contracts and other key plan targets and specify ceilings on amounts (*Sotsialisticheskiy trud*, 1987b, pp. 54–66).[4]

4. The criteria and ceilings vary by sector. For industry, the manager may be awarded a monthly bonus of up to 75 percent of his salary for meeting plans for contract deliveries "and the main indicators of production efficiency" and annual bonuses of up to 160 percent of the monthly salary for meeting plan targets "for accelerating scientific-technical progress, assimilation of capacities, production of consumer goods and paid services, and other special bonus systems."

The reform documents require the firm "as a rule" to finance all of its current and capital expenditures from its sales revenues and other internally generated funds—a condition labeled "full economic accountability and self-finance" (*polnyy khozyaystvenniy raschet i samofinansirovaniye*). With its superior organ's approval, the firm may choose one of two approaches to define its "economically accountable income" (*khozraschetnyy dokhod*):

(1) As the sum of the wage fund determined by normatives plus the profit remaining after payment of all taxes, obligatory contributions to ministerial funds, and payments of interest on bank credit. This residual profit is allocated via state-set normatives (percentages) to the three incentive funds— for financing investment and R&D, for financing housing and amenities for workers, and for awarding bonuses.

(2) As the residual that remains after deducting from total revenues the sum of materials and related outlays, taxes, contributions, and interest payments. From this amount are then deducted the payments into the investment and social-cultural funds (determined as prescribed shares) to leave a single fund for remunerating labor.

As of now, the first approach is the usual practice, but the second is a feature of the ongoing wage reform in the retail trade sector. The firm can decide for itself how to spend the money in its three funds within the limits of their use specified in various implementing documents.

Furthering Gorbachev's call for "more democracy," the new Law on the State Enterprise, amending the 1983 Law on the Labor Collective (*Pravda*, June 19, 1983) provides for the establishment of elected enterprise Labor Councils and the election of key managerial personnel. The Council, which must meet at least every quarter, is elected by the workforce by secret or open ballot for 2–3 year terms. No more than one-fourth of the members may be representatives of management. The Council is empowered to decide a variety of matters relating to the use of the enterprise incentive funds and to the pay, discipline, and training of the workforce; its decisions are binding on both the administration and the workforce. According to the new Law, "enterprise managers, heads of divisions of associations, production units, shops, departments, sections, livestock units and links, as well as . . . foremen and brigade leaders" are to be elected by the appropriate workforce. Enterprise managers are elected "as a rule on a competitive basis" at a general meeting of the collective by secret or open ballot for a 5-year term, and the selection must be ratified by the appropriate superior organ. Managers may be removed by vote of the collective. Heads of associations are to be elected at a conference of representatives of the labor collectives of the member firms comprising the associations. The procedure for electing leaders of lower-level bodies is the same, except that election results are ratified by the enterprise manager. The

Basic Provisions recommend that work collectives set up Councils and elect leaders during 1987–1988.

Role of Central and Regional Administrative Bodies

The reform documents make clear the intent to conduct a major overhaul of central and regional bureaucracies, revising their functions, reorganizing their structures, and cutting their staffs. According to Premier Ryzhkov, all this is to take place during 1987–1988. Gosplan, whose staff is to be reorganized to deemphasize sectoral subdivisions in favor of economic complexes, is supposed to concentrate on long-range strategic planning and development of methods for managing the economy through "economic levers"—long-term plans and normatives, finance, prices, and credit (*O korennoy perestroyke*, 1987, pp. 55–90). More specifically, Gosplan is supposed to coordinate the work of all central bodies dealing with the economy, work out 5-year and 15-year plans and transmit them to executants, determine the composition of state orders, and compile material balances and plans of distribution "for the most important types of output." The State Committee for Science and Technology is also to be reorganized to carry out its main functions of working out state scientific and technical (S&T) programs; formation, distribution, and monitoring of the bill of state orders for development of such programs; and guiding the work of intersectoral S&T complexes, whose role is to be expanded (*O korennoy perestroyke*, 1987, pp. 91–105).

Superministries. Superministries—bodies directly subordinate to the USSR Council of Ministers for the oversight of groups of related economic activities— are an ingredient of Gorbachev's reform package. Seven such bodies were established during 1985–1987: (1) State Committee for the Agro-Industrial Complex, (2) State Committee for Construction, (3) State Foreign Economic Commission, (4) Bureau for Machinebuilding, (5) Bureau for the Fuel and Energy Complex, (6) Bureau for the Chemical and Timber Complex, and (7) Bureau for Social Development. The Basic Provisions call for improving the work of such bodies and focusing it on "the tasks of carrying out a radical reform of economic management."

The ministries are to be reorganized to gradually eliminate sectoral subbranches (*glavki*) and to reduce staffs. In place of the *glavki*, the new scheme is to have "several thousand" large associations and enterprises directly subordinated to the ministries (*Pravda*, June 26, 1987).[5] This is to be accomplished by continuing the ongoing process of amalgamating enterprises into production and science-production associations and by creating new groupings called "state production associations," which are supposed to be intersectoral and to integrate all phases of the research-production-marketing chain. Heavy industry is to be

5. In his speech to the June Plenum, Gorbachev said that ultimately "several thousand" large associations could become the objects of management from the center, in place of the 37,000 entities now included in the State Plan.

managed by all-union ministries. To this end, such status has been granted to the union-republic ministries of Coal, Power and Electricity, Ferrous Metallurgy, Nonferrous Metallurgy, Geology, and Petroleum Refining and Petrochemicals (*Pravda*, June 30, 1987).[6] The reorganization of the ministries is supposed to be completed during 1987 and 1988.

The ministries, although relieved of the functions of day-to-day control over firms, are still given enormous responsibility (*O korennoy perestroyke*, 1987, pp. 191–207). According to the Basic Provisions, the ministry "is responsible to the nation for satisfying demand for the branch's product, preventing disproportions, ensuring that the product meets world technical and quality standards, and developing and implementing branch S&T programs." As it does at present, the ministry serves as an intermediate level in the planning and administrative process. While it is enjoined to strictly observe enterprise rights as set forth in the new Law on the State Enterprise, that Law and the subsequent decree on the ministries make clear the large role that the ministry is expected to play vis-a-vis subordinate associations and enterprises. Specifically, the ministry is directed to "counter monopolistic tendencies of firms and to take measures to prevent inflation in costs and prices, stagnation in scientific and technical progress, and restriction of production of goods in demand." Ministries are to create centralized reserve funds financed by deductions from enterprise profits and used to fund ministerial staffs and aid subordinate firms; monitor and conduct annual audits of enterprise activities; guarantee (if appropriate and desirable) the bank loans of firms in trouble, underwrite the expenses of planned-loss firms while working out means to make them profitable, and help out firms temporarily short of cash; define control figures, state orders, limits, and economic normatives for each firm; establish and liquidate firms; "ensure" that the 5-year and annual plans drafted by enterprises are coordinated and consistent; ratify the appointment and dismissal of elected firm directors and administer the awarding of bonuses to them; interact with central and local bodies in carrying out a variety of activities for which all are held mutually responsible.

Regional Bodies. The Basic Provisions and the decrees of July 1986 (*Sobraniye*, 1986a) and July 1987 (*O korennoy perestroyke*, 1987, pp. 208–235) convey the intent to accord the republic Councils of Ministers and their subordinate bodies, notably the local Soviets, a greater role and responsibility for regional economies, especially those aspects relating to the welfare of local populations. These bodies, too, are supposed to be reorganized to improve administration; thus, new "production-economic departments" are to be set up under local Soviets and other regional bodies. Specifically, the Basic Provisions call for: concentrating the administration of enterprises that primarily serve local markets in republic and local bodies; working out 15-year plans for the economic and social development of regions; distributing centralized in-

---

6. This list of ministries was originally given by Premier Ryzhkov in his speech to the Party Plenum in June 1987 (*Izvestiya*, June 30, 1987, pp. 1–4).

vestment among sectors and ensuring that allocations for social development depend on the overall economic performance of regions; making republic Councils of Ministers and their sub-units responsible for coordinating the activities of all enterprises located on their territory in respect to provision of goods and services for the populations; channeling more funds into local budgets through taxes on the profits of local enterprises and granting greater autonomy to local authorities over their budgets; seeing to it that all local enterprises participate actively and cooperate fully with local Soviets in their endeavors on behalf of the local populace, and requiring local Soviets to monitor such enterprise activity.

The Supply System

The Basic Provisions call for a "decisive transition from centralized allocation of material resources and the attachment of users to producers to wholesale trade in the means of production," to be completed in 4 to 5 years. The decree on Gossnab (*O korennoy perestroyke*, 1987, pp. 109–131) charges that body with the task of organizing wholesale trade. The process is to start with "groups of goods of greatest importance for consumer goods production, agriculture, construction, machinery production, and the needs of cooperatives and private producers." Only "particularly scarce" goods will continue to be rationed, but the list includes the allocation of inputs that are required to fulfill mandatory state orders. Wholesale trade, which is to become the main form of supply, is to take the form of "free" purchase and sale under direct contracts between enterprises or with state wholesale organizations, primarily regional bodies, and with manufacturers' direct outlets. Regional units of the State Committee for Material and Technical Supply (Gossnab) are to play the major role in organizing supply. The Law on the State Enterprise gives firms the "preferential right" to retain existing arrangements, expand long-term direct ties, and select the form of supply. That Law, along with existing decrees on product deliveries and contract law, extensively regulates the mutual responsibilities of parties under contracts. Early in 1987, the Supreme Court adopted a law that strengthens the system for settling contract disputes by transferring the State Arbitration Committee from the jurisdiction of the Council of Ministers to the jurisdiction of the court system (*Sobraniye*, 1987c).

According to Ryzhkov, only 5 percent of Gossnab's total deliveries consists of genuine wholesale trade at present, presumably the sales of several hundred wholesale stores in cities and recently permitted unfunded purchases by a variety of small-scale users. A Council of Ministers decree adopted July 17, 1987, (*Pravda*, July 18, 1987), instructs Gossnab to bring the share of wholesale trade in total supply to 60 percent by 1990 and to "complete the transfer" by 1992. That percentage apparently refers to the activities of Gossnab. Other supply networks exist in the agro-industrial complex, the State Committee for Allocation of Petroleum Products, and in the separate supply networks of many ministries. At present, Gossnab sales account for 80 percent of all industrial production that is sold through trading organizations (Solodkov, 1986). Gossnab officials have recently indicated that in 1992 wholesale trade will comprise 75 to 80 percent of Gossnab sales (FBIS, 1987, p. R-6) and two-thirds of total sales (*Ekon. gaz.*, 1987b, p. 6). These officials have stated that wholesale trade will not include electricity, crude oil, gas, metal ores, rolled metal, various kinds of specialized equipment, and products supplied for export, defense, and "market stocks," presumably grain.

Prices and Wages

Prices. The Basic Provisions call for a "radical" reform of prices to be completed by 1990, so that the new prices can be used in developing the 1991–1995 plan. Specifically, the decree on price formation (*O korennoy perestroyke*, 1987, pp. 150–164) states that revised industrial wholesale prices and tariff rates in transportation and communications are to take effect on January 1, 1990, and new construction and agricultural procurement prices are to be introduced on January 1, 1991. No date was set for new retail prices. Unlike its predecessors, this reform is to encompass all forms of prices—wholesale, procurement, and retail prices and rates, with changes in the various sets of prices to be interconnected. Centrally set prices, the share of which is to be "sharply reduced," are to be determined as part of plan formation and, as now, fixed on the basis of "socially necessary expenses of production and sale, utility, quality, and effective demand." They are to take into account the charges for natural resources, capital, and labor, which enterprises will now be required to pay, and the costs of environmental protection. They also will have to incorporate the new amortization rates to take effect on January 1, 1988 (*Sobraniye*, 1985). More specifically, prices of fuels and raw materials are to be raised sharply, so as to ensure "normal profitability" for those branches, and some machinery prices are to be reduced. Contract prices and those set independently by enterprises are to become more common and are to be set on the same basic principles as state-set prices. Those principles and procedures will be specified and all prices closely monitored by state organs, presumably the State Committee on Prices (Goskomtsen), whose membership now includes representatives of Gosplan, the Ministry of Finance, the State Committee on Statistics, and the Central Council of Trade Unions. The Basic Provisions call for the establishment of "a single state system of price control."

The sensitive issue of revising retail prices to conform to the new pricing formula is addressed by calling for a broad public discussion of the price reforms and by stating that changes in retail prices "not only must not reduce living standards of workers, but also must raise them for some groups and more fully promote social justice." At present, some foods and some services are heavily subsidized, costing the state budget 73 billion rubles. Alcoholic beverages, clothing, many durables, and luxury goods are heavily taxed.

Wages. The Basic Provisions, in effect, incorporate as an essential ingredient of the package a major overhaul of the wage and salary structure in the production sectors launched by decree of the CPSU and the Council of Ministers in September 1986 (*Sobraniye*, 1986c). The wage reform is to be carried out branch by branch and firm by firm during 1987–1990. To implement the decree, two lengthy sets of "Recommendations" have been issued under the joint imprimatur of the State Committee for Labor and Social Problems and the All-Union Central Council of Trade Unions (*Sotsialisticheskiy trud*, 1987a, pp. 57–96 and 1987b, pp. 54–66). Differentiated by sector and branch of the economy, this pay reform: (1) establishes new labor grade structures and base rates for production workers, the base rates being raised by an average of 20 to 25 percent; (2) provides for a review of existing assignments of jobs to labor grades and of individuals' assignments to jobs; (3) mandates a revision of work norms and piece rates to make them more "progressive"; (4) establishes new salary scales for white-collar workers, raising the average salary rate by 30–35 percent; (5) gives enterprise managers a variety of options for adjusting job rates and awarding bonuses to encourage efficiency and to ensure that each worker's earnings accord with his productivity; (6) specifies that the reform is to be put into effect in each firm whenever its ministry determines that it can finance any resulting increases in average wages within the limits of the allowed wage fund and some transfers from the bonus fund financed from profits.

The Law on the State Enterprise broadens the rights of directors in matters of labor and wages, in collaboration with the enterprise trade union and the Labor Council. It, as does the Basic Provisions, also specifies that no ceiling shall be put on individual earnings. But the size and growth of the total wage and bonus funds are regulated by various ministry-set normatives.

The intent of this sweeping reform of the pay system is to increase the share of job rates in workers' earnings (to 70–75 percent compared with 50–60 percent at present), make bonuses harder to get and more closely dependent on the efficiency and quality of performance of both the worker and the firm, tighten work norms (which were regularly being overfulfilled by large margins), and contribute to more general reform objectives of enforcing self-financing, eradicating "wage-leveling," and encouraging work effort and the acquisition of job skills by the work-force.

Finance and Credit

This section of the Basic Provisions amounts, in essence, to a demand that the banks and other financial agencies promote the effective implementation of the principle of self-financing by enterprises. Separate decrees spell out the role of the Ministry of Finance and the banks (*O korennoy perestroyke*, 1987, pp. 132–149, 165–177). These agencies are told to put the country's financial house in order by ceasing inflationary practices such as printing money to back up credit. More specifically, as in past reforms, bank credits and interest rates are to serve as important economic levers in promoting efficient resource use in enterprises, and bank credits are to become a more important source of financing investment. The banking system has been reorganized to create six major banks—instead of three as now. The six banks are: the USSR State Bank (Gosbank); Industrial Investment Bank; Bank for the Agro-Industrial Complex; Bank for Housing; Municipal Services and Social Development Savings Bank; and the Bank for Foreign Trade of the USSR. Banks and insurance agencies are supposed to operate on the principles of economic accountability and self-financing. Budget-supported institutions are to be provided with incentives to become more efficient. Finally, enterprise payments for resources are to provide the main source of budget revenues from public sector activities.

Foreign Trade

Gorbachev's reform package also includes an overhaul of the system for conducting foreign trade.[7] A joint CPSU-Council of Ministers decree adopted in August 1986 (*Sobraniye*, 1986b) established the State Foreign Economic Commission as a superministry overseeing all facets of Soviet foreign economic activity; reorganized the Ministry of Foreign Trade to end its monopoly over trade by transferring some of its Foreign Trade Associations to the jurisdiction of ministries and other central bodies; and granted the right as of January 1, 1987 to some 20 ministries and other bodies and 70 selected enterprises to engage directly in importing and exporting activity with appropriate units in foreign countries. In addition, the legislation provided for the establishment of foreign currency funds in exporting enterprises and associations that they can use to finance imports of machinery and equipment; gave firms extensive rights to enage in joint projects with firms in other member countries of the Council for Mutual Economic Assistance (CMEA); and sanctioned joint ventures with firms in capitalist countries. Subsequently, regulations were issued detailing procedures for carrying out such joint projects (*Pravda*, January 13 and 27, 1987).

The Basic Provisions do not include additional foreign trade reforms, merely calling for enhancing the use of financial-credit levers in promoting the expansion and efficient conduct of foreign trade. They do propose implementing a "stage-by-stage" convertibility of the ruble, starting with the CMEA trading system. The Law on the State Enterprise, however, contains a lengthy new section on foreign economic relations, which details the rights accorded to individual firms in the realm of foreign trade by the earlier decree. Emphasis is placed on the development of exports and on arranging mutually beneficial ventures with socialist countries. The firm has the right to keep a part (determined by long-term normatives) of foreign currency earned from exports to

7. Reforms in foreign trade are described in detail in a paper by Ivanov in *Soviet Economy* (Ivanov, 1987). [Eds.]

purchase goods from abroad and is held responsible for the "rational" use of such funds. Higher authorities are forbidden to confiscate unused funds. It seems, however, that firms cannot participate directly in foreign economic activity without the sanction of some higher body, presumably a ministry.

Private and Cooperative Economic Activity

The documents from the June plenum strongly endorse reform measures adopted in 1986 that aim to expand the role of producer cooperatives and private individuals in the economy, particularly in the provision of consumer goods and services. As part of a crackdown on corruption and illegal private economic pursuits, a Supreme Soviet decree adopted in May 1986 set stiff new penalties for failure to comply with existing laws concerning permissible private activity (*Vedomosti*, 1986, pp. 369–373). A law adopted in November 1986 and effective May 1, 1987 (*Pravda*, November 21, 1986), spells out the kinds of permissible endeavors and the groups that are to be encouraged to engage in them.[8] Subsequently, the high tax rates on income from private work were reduced somewhat (*Vedomosti*, 1987, pp. 231–233). In August 1986, the Politburo approved some "basic principles for development of cooperative forms of production," which specify that producer cooperatives are to be organized on a voluntary basis "with the participation of ministries, departments, and local Soviets." Subsequently, the Council of Ministers promulgated decrees and Model Charters for cooperatives to be engaged in the collection and processing of waste materials, in producing consumer goods, and in providing services (*Sobraniye*, 1987a, 1987b, and 1987d; *Ekon. gaz.*, 1987e, pp. 15–16). The decrees on expanding the rights of local Soviets and other regional bodies give them the major role in developing and regulating cooperative and private businesses.

Agricultural Reforms

Besides endorsing the 1982 Food Program, Gorbachev has spelled out his recipe for agricultural reform in two major decrees. The first, adopted in November 1985, established the State Agroindustrial Committee (Gosagroprom), a superministry to manage the production, marketing, and processing of farm products (*Pravda*, November 23, 1985). It was formed through the merger of five ministries and a state committee, but the agencies in charge of grain production and land reclamation remain independent entities. This reorganization also was intended to strengthen the position of the regional agricultural production associations (RAPO) that had been set up at various local levels as part of the 1982 Food Program. The second decree, adopted in March 1986, was directed toward increasing the autonomy of farms and improving

---

8. State employees only outside working hours, pensioners, housewives, and the handicapped.

incentives (*Pravda*, March 29, 1986). The principal provisions of this complex and ambiguous decree are to permit farms to sell a larger share of production at market prices, to introduce measures to market farm products more flexibly, to extend to farms many of the arrangements now being applied in the industrial sector (such as normative planning and self-finance), and to endorse the widespread use of collective contracts. Gosagroprom was instructed to develop further proposals for improving agricultural management in preparation for the drafting of the 1991–1995 plan.

The Basic Provisions and the Law on the State Enterprise apply to agriculture only in a general way. Although there are few specific references to that sector in these documents, Gorbachev addressed agricultural matters at some length in his speech to the June plenum. He stated that the measures already effected had created the potential for a breakthrough in farm output. He strongly endorsed the use of collective contracts, especially brigades using intensive technology and family groups. In late September, a CPSU Central Committee Resolution demanded that all production units adopt contractual forms of labor organization in 1988 and that all agricultural organizations be transferred to full economic accountability and self-financing during 1988–1989 (*Pravda*, September 25, 1987).

EVALUATION OF THE REFORM PACKAGE

The Schedule for Implementation

Mikhail Gorbachev is a man in a hurry. His program of reform, far more than its predecessors, imposes a staggering set of tasks on the central bureaucracies and on the producing units, to be accomplished in the next three years— a period when most of them will be undergoing administrative reorganizations. At its meeting on July 17, 1987, the USSR Council of Ministers excoriated one and all for not moving fast enough on all fronts and imposed some specific tasks and deadlines. The leadership has made it clear that *perestroyka* is to apply to everyone, while simultaneously guaranteeing fulfillment of the demanding plan targets for 1987, 1988, and 1986–1990.

Gosplan, while undergoing an internal reorganization, must work out the plan for 1988 and 1989 for firms and sectors operating under both the new and the old conditions and must begin formulating the plan for 1991–1995 in the reformed format. Two sets of planning and reporting documents will have to be devised for the period 1988–1990 and standard sets worked out for 1991– 1995. One such instruction (on the plan for 1988) was approved in April 1987 (*Ekon. gaz.*, 1987a, p. 14) and already has been revised. Gosplan also must fix the annual bill of state orders to be handed down to ministries and republic councils of ministers. According to a Gosplan official, such orders in 1988 will account for 90 percent of the output of the fuels ministries, 60 percent of that of 9 civilian machinery ministries, 30 groups of chemical and petrochemical products, and 35 products of light oil industry (*Ekon. gaz.*, 1987c, pp. 4, 6). Gosplan will continue to work out material balances and distribution plans for 415 major products—down from about 2,000 (*Pravda*, August 18, 1987).

Gossnab must cope with the inevitable confusion that will ensue from the dual system, whereby state orders and "freely negotiated" contracts with customers and suppliers will be in effect for many firms and the old *modus operandi* in effect for others. The Council of Ministers has instructed Gossnab to raise the share of "wholesale trade" in the total volume of its sales to 60 percent by 1990. Gossnab's role is slated to increase, for, according to its chairman, the wholesale trade market "is not spontaneous, but organized" (*Izvestiya*, August 27, 1987). The agency will also take over from Gosplan the task of compiling material balances and plans of distribution for over 1,500 key products.

Goskomtsen, while meeting its present responsibilities and reorganizing its staff structure, must prepare an overhaul of the entire system of state-set prices and rates, ensuring that changes in the various sets of prices (wholesale, procurement, and retail) are linked together. It must publish lists of the new centrally set prices, prepare instructions for setting contract prices and prices set independently by enterprises, and develop a "unified" system for monitoring all prices. This is a Herculean task, which is to be completed in time for the new prices to be used in the 1991–1995 plan. Since all financial plans depend on these prices, the plan and the reform-related 5-year "stable" normatives cannot be worked out without them.

Ministries. Those ministries operating wholly or partially under self-financing in 1988 will have to plan and conduct their affairs under the new definitions and procedures. Numerous instructions must be formulated to guide enterprises. To carry out the new rules of the game, the ministries will have to define the bill of state orders and establish the many normatives for each enterprise and association individually, because they operate under widely varying levels of profitability and other relevant conditions. Ministries will have to implement the overhaul of wages and salaries by determining when each firm is financially ready to effect it. Simultaneously, they will have to figure out how to manage their branches under the nebulous conditions imposed by the Law on the State Enterprise, which, as noted before, takes effect on January 1, 1988. The minister is held "personally responsible" for expeditious implementation of everything connected with the new order of things, and also is accountable for the current production activities of the branch. Ministries also must amalgamate associations and enterprises into new "state production associations," at the same time reorganizing their own internal structures and reducing staff, and while under constant threat of being abolished, split, or joined with another agency. Already, four machinery ministries have been merged into two (*Pravda*, September 21, 1987) and two State Committees into one (FBIS, 1987, p. R-22).

Regional Bodies. The situation of regional bodies is similar to that of the central ministries. They must handle the new rules of the game for subordinate firms, cope with the new tasks imposed on them, and devise schemes for reorganizing their administrative structures. The USSR Council of Ministers has instructed the republic Councils of Ministers to submit such reorganization plans.

Enterprises. While struggling to carry out the many production and investment tasks imposed by the plans and the new state quality inspectors, the enterprises must figure out how to cope with the intricate new rules of the game that the Law on the State Enterprise imposes on them, with the details of the wage reform, and with the ubiquitous monitors (especially political bodies) determined to see to it that "priority" matters are attended to with dispatch. Enterprises will be under pressure to establish Labor Councils and to hold elections of key managerial officials. The electoral process may well create uncertainty and anxiety among managers and produce considerable turnover in their ranks. Potentially the most disruptive facet of the reforms is the schedule for imposing conditions of full self-financing on enterprises. In 1987, self-financing affected all of the firms within five industrial ministries and 37 entities in various others; all together ministries under self-financing account for over 20 percent of total industrial output and 16 percent of total employment (*Pravda*, July 14, 1987). According to Premier Ryzhkov, self-financed enterprises will account for 60 percent of industrial output in 1988, when the new conditions will also apply to all branches of transportation and a number of other sectors (*Pravda*, June 30, 1987). The process is supposed to be completed in 1989. The new rules already are creating many problems for firms, according to press accounts.

The Total Package

Taken as a whole, the package of reform measures already in place or set in motion through the Basic Provisions (and related decrees) and the Law on the State Enterprise in Gorbachev's two-and-one-half years of tenure is impressive. It is a comprehensive package, embracing nearly every major aspect and sector of the economy. But a major gap in both the 1965 and the present reform package is the failure to provide a mechanism for more efficient allocation of investment among firms and across sectors—a problem that has proved crucial in the reform process in Hungary and Yugoslavia. Although the subjects they address and the direction they take are similar to those of the 1965 reforms, the current reforms add to the major areas addressed in 1965 a complete overhaul of the wage and salary system, a reform of the conduct of foreign trade, measures to expand cooperative and private economic activity, and provisions for the election of enterprise Labor Councils and key managerial personnel by the workforce. Unlike its predecessors, his package spells out the intended changes in fairly explicit terms and sets tight schedules for their implementation.

But one is hard pressed to visualize the nature of the economic system that the framers of this package intend to install, a package variously described as "radical," "revolutionary," and based on the principle of "more socialism, more democracy.'' Its present overall design is not that required for the installation of a system of market socialism or of worker self-management as those terms are usually understood. Despite allusions to the creation of autonomous, competing, self-managed business firms, the reforms do not go nearly far enough to create a market environment, as Lenin did in 1921 with his New Economic Policy (NEP), nor do they allow workers to make the key decisions that determine the outcomes of the firm's activity, as they do in Yugoslavia. Gorbachev's reform documents leave the pillars of the traditional economic system prominently in place—state ownership, central planning (albeit changed in form and reduced in detail), numerous administrative agencies overseeing the activities of firms, rationing of many materials and investment goods, state control over price setting, and enterprise incentives still oriented toward plans and output targets and biased toward dealing with administrative superiors rather than following signals from markets.

Moreover, the package as now spelled out in the relevant laws and decrees contains inconsistencies and contradictions that, if not resolved, will seriously limit its effectiveness. These problems with the design of the reform will be reinforced by some specific policies pursued simultaneously with the implementation of the reforms. The following problems stand out at present:

(1) Ministries and regional bodies are held responsible for production results in their respective areas and for ensuring that subordinate firms act "properly," but simultaneously have been instructed not to interfere in enterprise decision making.

(2) Through the mechanism of self-financing, firms are expected to operate efficiently (to produce goods in demand at least cost), but the price and profit signals needed to assess the tradeoffs are not provided in the price reform now outlined.

(3) The Law on the State Enterprise accords enterprises wide latitude in decision making, but also saddles them with many recipes and expectations inspired from the center, e.g., to introduce multiple shifts, set up brigades, produce a quota of consumer goods and services, set up subsidiary firms, actively support an expansion of private and cooperative activity.

(4) The reforms explicitly require stability (for five years) in a variety of parameters, whereas flexibility is needed to establish markets and make them work effectively.

Key Parts of the Package

Central Planning and Management. The policy statements and specific provisions of the reform program make it clear that central management of the economy is being retained. They display the traditional conviction that economic development—the composition of output and the direction of investment—as well as the broad content and direction of scientific and technological progress must be managed by the center. The framework of mandatory, "stable" five-year plans is retained, along with numerous new and old government bodies to formulate them and monitor their implementation. New forms of central management are to replace the familiar categories.[9] That the center is to slough off a mass of detail is of secondary importance to the fact that the domain of central administration is still so great. Moreover, the central bureaucracies will now have to cope with the confusion and unintended results that will arise in implementing the new rules of the game.

Status of the Firm. The business firm remains subordinate to government agencies, which are to eschew "petty tutelage," while ensuring that the sector's output goals are met and that the firm behaves "properly." Absence of "petty tutelage," if it indeed is realized, may reduce the frustration of managers of firms, but ministerial micro-management, which is often blamed for all sorts of malfunctions, has been a minor factor in the past difficulties of the economy in any case.

On the contrary, under the new arrangements, the firm is likely to be eager for ministerial aid, particularly in respect to the functioning of the many normatives, which undoubtedly will provide a fertile field for bargaining. In fact, the process has already started. Firms are being pushed to "freely" negotiate contracts for much of their output with customers and for the requisite raw materials and capital goods with suppliers in a framework of competition, but are finding that the tissue (information and infrastructure) needed to support competitive sales and purchases is almost totally lacking. A rational (and likely) response on the part of a firm would be to seek to have as much as possible of its product classified as "state orders" backed up with rationed inputs. This, too, is already happening (*Pravda*, August 18, 1987).[10] Portions of its product and raw materials will have rigid state-set prices as they do now, and the prices it may set or negotiate necessarily must take them into account (in addition to the methodological guidelines) and are subject to strict state monitoring. The manager's bonus depends on meeting (planned) contracts for output (little different under universal contracting from gross value of output or sales), and on indicators for several other aspects of performance. Finally, the new deal provides the firm with still another participant in decision making and monitoring (the Labor Council) and subjects key managers to the elective process.

Since all of this does not create a competitive market environment, enterprise strategy likely will continue to emphasize risk avoidance and center orientation. Although the vision—figuring prominently in the reforms—of autonomous, self-financing, socialist business firms threatened with bankruptcy failure conveys an aura of markets and competition, its reality in practice is an artificial accounting construct, both under present Soviet conditions and under those created by the reforms. Because prices of products and material inputs do not

9. Supposedly "non-binding" control figures, state orders and "voluntary" contracts, and long-term, stable normatives.
10. A Gosplan Deputy Chairman complained about such enterprise behavior in connection with formulation of the 1988 plan.

reflect the economic tradeoffs (scarcities), the derivative accounting categories of sales, costs, profits, and returns to capital can be misleading. Managerial decisions based on them do not necessarily result in efficient mixes of inputs and outputs, profits do not indicate relative efficiencies of firms, and failure to earn profits and thus to go bankrupt need not mean that the firm was inefficient. The expectation that large gains in efficiency will accrue from enforcing self-financing is unlikely to be realized.

Supply. The Basic Provisions not only call for a "resolute" shift of the bulk of purchases and sales of intermediate and capital goods from central rationing to "free" wholesale trade between buyers and sellers, but accord Gossnab the key role in the process. The Law on the State Enterprise instructs the firm to arrange for non-rationed supplies "first of all" via contracts with regional divisions of Gossnab. How is this process likely to work out in practice? Contracting is already widespread: in most branches of industry, 80–90 percent or more of total deliveries are now accomplished through formal contracts (*Khozyaystvo i pravo*, 1985, p. 19), the bulk of them with Gossnab units. Five-year contracts (termed "long-term direct ties") have been encouraged and are widely prevalent: in 1986, they comprised 30 percent of total Gossnab sales (*Ekon. gaz.*, 1987e, p. 18). Faced with the need to nail down through contracts their "independently" planned sales and purchases, firms in the near term, aided and abetted by Gossnab, can be expected to scramble to keep existing arrangements and tie up new ones. These arrangements, by and large, are likely to form the basis in the 13th Five-Year Plan for the contracts on which the firms are required to base their plans. All this will make for rigidity and inhibit the competition among firms that the reforms aspire to develop. It certainly does not create a market for raw materials and capital goods.

Even so, the pressure to de-ration goods and enhance the role of wholesale trade organizations should bring some benefits. Above all, elimination of the need for ration coupons will reduce the amount of time and paperwork required to arrange sales and purchases. The drive to shift stocks from enterprise inventories to wholesale bases and to expand manufacturers' direct outlets will make supply more flexible. This process should also benefit to the extent that firms use their greater authority to sell above-plan output and unneeded inventory and equipment.

Prices. Flexible prices that reflect supply and demand reasonably well are crucial to the success of reforms that accord financial autonomy to enterprises. Yet, according to the Basic Provisions and the decree on price reform, the principles on which state-fixed prices are to be set are the same as those now in use—essentially cost-based in the case of wholesale and procurement prices. Although contract prices are to be set by agreement of the parties, they will be heavily influenced by such state-set prices. Contract prices are to be based on so-called "base prices," which may be taken from state price lists, state-set limit prices on new products, and prices on "normative-parametric" price lists (*Pravda*, August 25, 1987). The requirement that state-set prices remain stable for five years and that contract prices be embodied in planned contracts preserves the rigidities now prevailing. Although the intended revision of industrial and procurement prices will bring them once more in line with costs and newly imposed charges for resources, prices will remain poor guides for efficient choices. The removal of producer price subsidies, however, is a rational step toward more efficient use of inputs.

Widespread use of contract prices and prices independently set by firms is likely to produce inflation, unless hard budget constraints are imposed on the firms. But the reforms as now designed include mechanisms that will soften the constraints supposedly imposed on firms by the requirements of self-financing. Clearly, the government intends to monitor contract prices closely, an activity that will require detailed examinations of the books of individual firms. Finally, the declared intent to link the three sets of prices (wholesale, procurement, and retail) involves coming to grips with a major political-economic policy dilemma of what to do about existing large subsidies on food and certain consumer services. Press debate over this issue is gaining momentum, although it remains to be seen whether the requisite political will for dealing with this problem can be mustered.

Worker Incentives. Unlike its predecessor, this round of reforms includes a complete overhaul of the wage and salary structure and of work norms. It also installs new procedures for the formation and use of the enterprise bonus fund. The size of that fund will now depend both on its initial size in the base year and on changes in it which will depend mainly on the level of profits and the fixed percentage (normative) share of profits designated for the fund. To effect the wage reform, the firm must be able to finance the higher rates out of wage and bonus funds that are determined by standard procedures (more normatives). Although the timing of the installation of the new scales is supposed to be determined by the firm, based on when it considers it possible to finance them, considerable pressure is being put on firms to do so with dispatch, and layoffs and morale problems are already arising.

The overhaul of wages and work norms could prove to be highly unpopular. Unlike previous changes in the wage system made in the early 1960s, which offered a large carrot in the form of a substantial reduction in the workweek (from 46 to 41 hours), the current wage reform offers no carrot to rank-and-file production workers; although their base rates will be increased, with the greatest raises going to the more skilled, work norms will be tightened accordingly. Blue collar workers will face layoffs and pressure to redefine and combine jobs and work night shifts. Thus, this reform package, unlike that of 1965, directly and immediately threatens both the job and the pay of every production worker. At the same time, ordinary workers will see the salaries of white collar workers increase sharply and their total earnings rise even more, since bonuses are determined as percentages of base salaries. Thus, the lion's share of wage increases planned for 1986–1990 (15 percent) will accrue to white collar workers, who comprise about one-fifth of the total in the productive sectors. Blue collar workers, long nurtured on egalitarian values, well may consider those developments to be unfair, even though wider differentials may be needed to improve incentives.

Since the wage overhaul is being carried out piecemeal and firm by firm, both between sectors and within sectors, it is likely to result in sizeable differences in wages for similar jobs in the same area and thus violate the socialist principle of equal pay for equal work. Matters will be worsened by the wide variations in the size of bonus and social-cultural funds that will prevail among firms. These inequities will arise because of the highly uneven conditions under which Soviet enterprises operate, which stem from factors over which they have little or no control. For example, profit rates of firms differ widely within industries and among sectors as a result of average cost pricing of products and other peculiarities of price setting. The quality of capital stocks differs greatly because of the vagaries of past investment policy. Thus, the playing field is unequal and in a fundamental sense also unfair.

Managerial Incentives. Salaries for managerial personnel are to be raised substantially as part of the reform of wages and salary scales. In addition, managers are paid bonuses from the firm's new unified bonus fund, which depends on profits and the applicable normative. Ministries or other higher authorities administer the general rules regulating such bonuses. The latest set of rules (recommendations), however, preserve the worst features of the old system. They tie bonuses to meeting a plan for production, now defined as 100 percent fulfillment of contracts for deliveries. In addition to contractual fulfillment, they also tie bonuses to several plan indicators for labor productivity or equivalent measure and for growth of profits or reduction in costs. Bonuses are to be paid for each separate indicator, and half of the total must be paid for meeting contracts. These rules are likely to reinforce the managers' orientation toward meeting production goals, toward pleasing superiors in the administrative hierarchy, and toward avoiding risks. Moreover, a ceiling is placed on managerial earnings. Unless these compensation rules are changed radically, they will frustrate the reform's efforts to create innovative, market-oriented enterprises.

Finance and Credit. Under the reforms, as now, budget income will come almost entirely from various levies on enterprises, with the bulk to come in the form of payments for resources. The charge on capital is retained and will continue to be highly differentiated, as will a new charge on employment to be introduced in 1988. The labor charge is slated to be 300 rubles per year for each list worker for firms in labor deficit regions and 200 rubles per worker per year for those in labor surplus regions (*Ekon. gaz.*, 1987e, p. 8). The size of these payments for resources is necessarily arbitrary in the absence of market prices to establish actual returns to factors. In any case, imposition of a capital charge has proved ineffective in the USSR, according to the repeated assertions of Soviet economists, and charges for capital and/or labor have not proved effective in reforms in Hungary and Yugoslavia.

The reforms, as they did in 1965, are intended to reduce the budget's role in the financing of investment. Until prices are changed in ways that reduce the large variability of profit levels among firms and sectors, however, the budget's share will remain large or funds will have to continue to be redistributed through the ministries. They are authorized to establish several reserve funds financed by deductions from enterprise profits and amortization charges in accordance with state-set normatives.

The reforms create six large banks, an organizational change that amounts to dividing the responsibilities of the present Gosbank and Bank for Financing Capital Investments (Stroybank) among five agencies rather than two. This change does nothing to create a market for investment funds. Although the banks are enjoined to make credit-granting decisions on a more rational basis, they will lack efficient criteria for doing so. In any case, it is clear that the state intends to dictate the sectoral allocation of investment, as it does now. Bank credits and interest rates are supposed to be used as economic levers and normatives to regulate the financial activities of firms, and the banks' role as financial watchdogs is to continue. It seems doubtful that those approaches will work any better than they have in the past 20 years, when similar themes have been in vogue.

OUTLOOK

Although the reform programs adopted thus far under Gorbachev add up to a set of half-measures that retain the pillars of the traditional system, they could produce some positive results. The financial pressures on the enterprise will probably reduce redundant labor and gross waste of materials. Efforts to put producers more closely in touch with their suppliers and customers, aided by the recently introduced system of state inspection (Gospriyemka), should yield higher quality products.

If the go-ahead for private and cooperative endeavors produces strong momentum, it will improve the lot of consumers to some degree. The greater leeway given factories and farms to dispose of their output and unneeded inputs will work mainly to the same end. Paring of government staffs and the consequent forced redistribution of labor will facilitate adjustment to slow growth in the labor force. Relatively higher wages for skilled and efficient workers should improve incentives, provided that supplies of desired consumer goods and services are made available.

At the same time, vigorous implementation of the present reform package has the potential to create serious disruptions in the production process in the next few years. The pressure being exerted on the enterprises simultaneously to meet plan targets and speed up plant modernization, increases the danger. Specifically, the switch to new and unfamiliar supply arrangements may disrupt the flow of materials to firms and create bottlenecks. Changes in the way producer goods are obtained could disrupt the investment process. With unreformed prices, the imposition of self-financing will put many enterprises in severe financial straits, causing them to spend a lot of time and energy negotiating with the banks and with their superiors in the bureaucracy. Because of the vague and ambiguous language of the many relevant laws and decrees, the relationships between enterprises and their supervisory agencies will be confused—a situation hardly conducive to speedy decision making. Matters will be made worse because these agencies themselves will be undergoing reorganization and staff reductions. The combined impact of self-financing and the wage reform certainly will create anxiety among workers, threatened with wage cuts or loss of jobs. The confusion and disarray will be exacerbated because some firms and sectors will be operating under the old rules of the game and others under new ones.

How the leadership will react if production falters or workers protest is a matter of speculation. Although Gorbachev has vowed to keep up the momentum of "restructuring," the leadership may elect to stretch out the schedule for implementing the present reform package: Party Secretary Ligachev has already warned of the perils of undue haste (*Problemy mira*, 1987, p. 6). Alternatively, it could acquiesce to adjustments that would, in effect, preserve the essence of the present *modus operandi*. Gorbachev has already shown a willingness to use administrative methods to resolve problems, as exemplified by the recent decrees mandating state inspection of output, multiple shifts, and inventory reductions. Or he may opt to try to muddle through a period of disruption, in the expectation that economic performance will improve markedly when the reforms are fully in place in the framework of the new five-year plan for 1991–1995. While it seems unlikely that the main parameters of the present reform package will be altered soon, Gorbachev might push through some major changes in agriculture, in the hope of realizing a quick boost in performance there.

In the long run, Gorbachev will be disappointed in the present package of reforms, which do not go nearly far enough to achieve his ambition of creating a dynamic, self-regulating "economic mechanism" capable of narrowing the technological gap with the West. To reach that goal, the leadership will have to make radical changes in the present reform package. If the benefits of a market economy are to be had, markets must be created by getting rid of the elements of central planning still in place, freeing enterprises from subordination to government bureaucracies and allowing them to produce in accord with market forces, and providing the requisite price and profit signals by allowing prices to reflect supply and demand. In addition, a competitive environment must be created by breaking up the present huge amalgamations and permitting competition from abroad, and financial and capital markets must be introduced. These are the lessons learned by Hungary in its 20-year effort to reform its centrally planned economy. Whether any Soviet leadership will opt for such truly "radical" reforms remains to be seen.

CHAPTER 15

The 19th Conference of the CPSU and Its Aftermath

Ed A. Hewett
with *Herbert S. Levine, Gertrude E. Schroeder,*
and *Victor H. Winston*

HEWETT: The 19th Party Conference was a subject of growing expectations. In many ways the event did not disappoint for it served as a platform for the discussion of major political reforms and provided a forum for debates on the economy. But, even a month after the Conference, there is much that remains obscure concerning its ultimate impact on the ongoing reform.

GORBACHEV'S OPENING SPEECH[1]

Gorbachev's opening speech was first and foremost about politics, but in the first two major sections he talked about economics. I would like to summarize the speech and try to draw from it his thinking about economic reform and the economic situation.

Discussion of Speech

Gorbachev started by giving his assessment of how the economy is performing. After some perfunctory positive remarks, he simply said it is not going very well at all. "The situation in the economy is changing quite slowly, and particularly if one judges by the final result—living standards" (*Pravda*, June 29, 1988, p. 2). It was interesting to see why he said this happened.

He said—and this is now a general theme among Soviet economists—that they just didn't understand how bad things were in 1984 and 1985, when they began. Only now is the full depth of the crisis in various spheres of the economy

Excerpts from a transcript of a roundtable on the 19th Conference of the CPSU and its aftermath held on August 11, 1988, at the Brookings Institution in Washington, D.C. under the auspices of the Joint Committee on Soviet Studies of the American Council of Learned Societies and the Social Science Research Council, which provided financial support. Substantially all material in this chapter was first published in *Soviet Economy*, 1988, 4, 2, pp. 103–136 and 3, pp. 181–222. [Eds.]

1. A formal English-language translation of the opening speech has been published in paperback form by the Novosti Press Agency (Documents, 1988). [Eds.]

becoming apparent. Gorbachev emphasizes, in particular, the financial situation, which was worse than he thought it was. Of course, after his alcohol
reform, it was even worse. What was most interesting was his effort to flirt
with something new and quite promising in saying that mistakes were made
in the last three years.

But the mistakes he goes on to talk about were not as interesting as the
statement. More should have been done, he said, to conserve energy. Excessive
capital resources are going into investing and expanding energy supplies, at
the cost of the modernization program. It short, he regrets the results, but not
the approach itself.

Gorbachev dwells in the speech on three traditional areas: food, housing,
and consumer goods. He says none of them is going very well. He plays around
with some formulations for how to deal with them. At a Politburo meeting
immediately after the Party Conference (*Pravda*, July 5, 1988), individual
ministers were given the task of devising ways to accelerate the expansion of
food supplies, consumer goods and housing, and were to report back to the
Politburo.

This is a familiar approach under Gorbachev—people are given clear responsibility for decisions and are held accountable. And it has a role to play
in a bureaucracy. But unfortunately, in this case, Gorbachev simply continues
the pressure on ministries to micro-manage the economy, in contradiction to
the spirit of the reforms, and to specific provisions of the enterprise law.

At the very end of the speech, Gorbachev has a section that literally reads
as though it was tacked on—a discussion of quantity vs. quality. I understand
that this speech was primarily written by Mozhin, Slyun'kov's deputy. Certainly
it is out of the economics department of the Central Committee, and therefore
I presume Mozhin was deeply involved.

But I would not be surprised if this particular part of the speech came from
the academic economists. Just as with the speeches of American presidents,
when people are fighting to get their pages in, someone finally got these pages
to become a part of Gorbachev's speech. At the beginning, he talks about
growth rates as a good sign. At the end of the speech, the same man cautions
against paying so much attention to growth rates. The real problem, he says,
is quality. The need is not for millions of tons of steel or millions of tons of
cement; the need is for higher-quality products. This is something that the
academics can applaud and are discussing more and more.

The section of Gorbachev's speech that dealt with the economic reforms
merits a few additional minutes. First of all, Gorbachev notes that some of the
difficulties with these reforms are the result of their partial nature: some parts
are in place, while others are still being prepared. This is progress over the
way he has talked about the reforms before. Indeed, he says specifically that
because price reform is coming last, it is creating problems with the new
enterprise law; in effect, he says, they have the wrong prices and the right
enterprise law.

But there is a conservative theme about prices in this part that was quite disappointing. What Gorbachev says in the speech is that they have the wrong prices, not the wrong price system. He urges an acceleration of price reform, but he explicitly equates price reform with price revisions. There is nothing about flexible contract pricing in the speech, a major retreat from the June 1987 plenum speech. Alas, he seems to have accepted the position of the State Price Committee that price reform means price revisions.

Gorbachev also emphasizes that one of the problems with the economic reforms is that they were caught in the middle of a five-year plan. Many of you have heard from Soviet economists that because reforms were begun in the middle of the Twelfth Five-Year Plan (1986–1990), it is impossible to introduce some of the more radical measures until the Thirteenth Five-Year Plan. Allocations have already been made, the argument goes, and it is unthinkable to simply stop in midstream and do a new five-year plan, according to new planning procedures.

This is a disingenuous excuse. Five-year plans have always been works of fiction, and Soviet economists know that. Moreover, the current one was Gorbachev's five-year plan, and he can change his mind about his own five-year plan.

LEVINE: The debate about quantity vs. quality is Gorbachev's own doing, because this Twelfth Five-Year Plan is a plan of quantity. The quantitative targets place such pressure on the economy that the Soviet economists have a legitimate argument. It is not just because the reforms began in the middle of *any* five-year plan, but because they began in the middle of *this* plan that they have had such difficulty making headway.

HEWETT: On the contrary. It is precisely because this five-year plan over-emphasizes quantities that it should be scrapped and replaced by, say, an eight-year plan of a much different sort. The Twelfth Five-Year Plan is dead, and was dead on the day it arrived.

Within these constraints, Gorbachev is nevertheless seeking to accelerate parts of his reform program. He did admit that they had not thought through the *goszakazy*[2] and that they were in the middle of drafting a new decree governing *goszakazy* for 1989–1990, which has since been published (*Ekon. gaz.*, No. 31, July 1988, pp. 18–20).

Gorbachev also calls for an acceleration in the introduction of wholesale trade. Alas, he did not make a clear connection between wholesale trade and price reform, and he did not say he is going to speed up price reform. This remains one of the key weaknesses in the entire process, all the more alarming because Gorbachev's support for true price reform seems to be weakening.

I presume that right now the operational timetable for price reform is that

2. An abbreviation derived from *gosudarstvennyye zakazy*, *goszakazy* are orders for the fulfillment of the state's highest-priority needs. A temporary decree on state orders for 1989 and 1990 was promulgated on July 25, 1988. The decree stipulates that the number of *goszakazy* will decline significantly, and they will be issued by Gosplan. It says that ministries may put together proposals that serve as a basis for competitive *goszakazy*, but the ministries themselves are apparently prohibited from issuing *goszakazy* themselves. [Eds.]

of a year ago, which is January 1, 1990, for revisions in wholesale prices. Retail prices are still under consideration; they will be put up for public discussion sometime next year in the form of a proposal to change retail prices and provide income compensation.

LEVINE: Gorbachev really did link wholesale trade and the reform of prices. You are absolutely right that in his discussion of the reform of price formation, he is really talking about revising prices. He talks about the cost and results of production, equivalence in exchange, and not the system of setting the prices. But he does make the link.

HEWETT: He does, but I think when he is talking about the introduction of wholesale trade; he does not also talk about the need to accelerate price reform.

LEVINE: With regard to speeding up the introduction of wholesale trade, he states: "I think that both Gossnab[3] and Gosplan will table concrete proposals on this account." He then continues: "Of course, much now rests on the reform of price formation. By this I mean the review of wholesale procurement and retail prices."

Summary

HEWETT: What I like about the economic part of the speech is that it is very frank. He hasn't pulled back at all from saying that things are not going well. One of the early warning signs that a Soviet reform is dying would be an attempt by the General Secretary to gloss over economic performance. He is not doing that yet. He is spending most of his time talking about things that are going wrong and are important to him. He said from the beginning, food, housing, and consumer goods are important. In each of these areas, he is saying that things are going much worse than he thought they were. To some extent, he is trying to explain it away by saying, for example, that things were worse than anyone understood before he took over. But that is a natural thing for any politician to say. I have some doubts that things were as bad as he says they were. As I've said, I think they are creating such an image of crisis in their minds that they are afraid of doing anything.

Gorbachev's admonition against a focus on growth rates is welcome. That gives reform advocates quotes that they can use in the articles they will write over the next year. And his recognition of contradictions in the reform is quite positive. I have not seen him talk this way before; he admits their problem is that some of the important features of the reform are not in place yet. I presume it is Gorbachev talking and not just his speech writers.

On the negative side, he has retreated on price reform, at least in this speech. This is not the man who was talking in June 1987 primarily about a system of flexible contract prices, with a minimum number of prices centrally set. Now

---

3. The State Committee for Material-Technical Supply. [Eds.]

he is coming back to the State Price Committee position, which is much more conservative. Many Soviet economists say that the supply of goods must be set right first, and then prices can be reformed.

Second, he has this stubborn inclination to hold ministers directly responsible. He says the modernization is not going well and it is the direct responsibility of the Machine-Building Bureau, the State Committee for Science and Technology, and the ministries that are involved.

He is also pushing harder and harder now for a full-scale mobilization of industry to produce consumer goods. This means that the highest-priority state orders—which will remain no matter how low their share of total orders falls—will include state orders to every single industrial enterprise (outside of light industry) to produce consumer goods.

Finally, there is the problem that, while he respects interconnections, he does not mind saying he wants to speed up wholesale trade reform without speeding up price reform.

SCHROEDER: I thought that the Party Conference was terribly significant for *glasnost'* and probably for politics, but not much for economics and the reform of the economy in a formal sense. I was not excited about Gorbachev's opening speech. I did not find anything particularly new or remarkable in it. What struck me most about the Conference was this outpouring of rage, so to speak, by the delegates about state interference in the consumer sector on the one hand and the behavior of bureaucracies on the other.

HEWETT: I will accept the less pessimistic amendments suggested by Thane Gustafson with regard to Gorbachev's references to prospective changes in the financial infrastructure (which Thane sees as a sign of learning) and the guns-vs.-health issue implying possible cuts in military spending that might benefit health care.[4] But on the speech as a whole, I will stick by my commentary—there was good news and bad news in that speech, but it was not as strong a speech as I had hoped for.

GORBACHEV AND ABALKIN

I now want to talk for a minute about the man I regard as the hero for economists at the Party Conference—Leonid Abalkin. Abalkin was the only economist who was a full delegate and the only economist to speak.

Abalkin's Speech[5]

Abalkin chose to use his allotted time to lecture Gorbachev on economics and it was an extraordinary lecture. He started by saying this reform is going

4. Professor Thane Gustafson's comments are published in *Soviet Economy* (The 19th Conference of the CPSU, 1988, pp. 127–128). Those of the other roundtable participants, notably of Professor Gur Ofer of the Brookings Institution and Hebrew University and Jan Vanous of PlanEcon, Inc. appear in two different installments (The 19th Conference of the CPSU, 1988, pp. 107–135; The Aftermath of the 19th Conference of the CPSU, 1988, pp. 182–221).

5. See *Pravda*, June 30, 1988, pp. 3–4. [Eds.]

nowhere, and it is important to emphasize that and not to engage in self-delusion. Then he said: "You cannot really count on success if you are violating the objective logic of life, if you are not taking account of its laws" (*Pravda*, June 30, 1988, p. 3).

Then he goes back to quote Nikolay Turgenev,[6] the early 19th-century Russian economist who said any leadership that ignores, or holds contempt for (*budet prezirat'*), the laws of political economy will bankrupt the nation. He said the years of the last five-year plans are an illustration of that. Then he discusses the Twelfth Five-Year Plan, which is, after all, Gorbachev's plan, and he says this attempt to emphasize quantity and quality at the same time simply will not work.

The most poignant part for me came at the end of this lecture on economics, which is directed straight at the General Secretary. "What we need," he said, "is a totally different system, precisely the one we agreed on a year ago at the June plenum." This is the representative of the economists saying ". . . for God's sake, only a year ago the party plenum decided to adopt an economic system, and it is still in doubt." He has a nice paragraph about the Russian love of decrees, which is a good one for Gorbachev to hear. He says, "We seem to have this notion that decrees fix everything, but experience just doesn't support that idea."

I liked that speech very much. For those of us who are studying Soviet economic reform, it was a very important exchange. My discussions with Soviet economists suggest they feel increasingly shut out of the whole reform discussion with the leadership. To the extent that ideas about reform are being discussed, it is with the economics department of the Central Committee, Slyun'kov and Mozhin. This is not all bad, but most of the academics now have very little direct access to Gorbachev, and they feel that he has, in a sense, turned off the thinking part of the reform and that he now believes it is more an issue of implementation.

What Abalkin is saying on his colleagues' behalf is, ". . . you cannot stop thinking about the principles of economics and political economy; if you do, you are going to lose this reform."

LEVINE: I feel as strongly as Ed does. This speech was very important, very gutsy, and very carefully constructed. His emphasis on the need for economic theory is one of the main threads through all of his work, which you do not find in Aganbegyan, since Abel Aganbegyan is not really a theorist.

Incidently, I think Aganbegyan has passed his peak of influence and is on the way down. Abalkin is taking his place in many ways, not only in public, but in terms of the respect he is getting from other economists. A number of economists in Moscow confirmed to me that, while nothing dramatic is happening, Aganbegyan is indeed losing center stage. His apogee was the June plenum, and since then he has been slipping.

---

6. Nikolay Ivanovich Turgenev (1789–1871), a Decembrist and economist who is considered the founder of the theory of finance in Russia. [Eds.]

Among the many interesting aspects of Abalkin's short speech was the part where he refers to Marxist-Leninist theory. I was at first upset by his reaching for the concept of economic laws. This reminded me of the old reliance on the "laws of socialism" and those other Marxist laws, which do not really comprise economic theory. But then he has this marvelous sentence: "We will not find, even when we read through all the classic works of Marxism-Leninism, ready answers to the questions posed by life; otherwise it would be a religion, not a science."

This sentence sets the tone for his later points, when he says that it is necessary to think about all the alternatives. This is one of his themes: what economists and social scientists should be presenting to decision-makers are options. Later in the speech he says that government can lead the people if it is given options; if it is not given options, then it just amends the recommendations of the bureaucracy. So it is an attempt, it seems to me, to elevate the position of government leaders if they support this development of a true economic science and a true role for the economists.

After his quotation from Turgenev about the responsibility of those governing not to have contempt for political economy, Abalkin follows up with quite a brave thrust at the General Secretary. Gorbachev began his opening speech by criticizing the failure to get *perestroyka* off the ground. Now Abalkin says: "In discussing the reasons [for our failures], we often merely skate over the surface, reducing everything to resistance by the bureaucratic apparatus and certain officials. The causes are considerably deeper and more serious than that. We should start with the fact that when the Twelfth Five-Year Plan was being drawn up, the concept of simultaneously ensuring quantitative growth and qualitative transformations was adopted. From the scientific point of view, these tasks are incompatible."

Now, as Ed Hewett wrote in his account of the development of the Twelfth Five-Year Plan after Gorbachev took power (Hewett, 1988a), there were two, three, or four revisions that Gorbachev insisted on, targeting higher and higher growth rates while relegating the idea of quality to the sidelines. Abalkin's description of this plan as one of quantity and quality is a very pointed, very brave thrust.

Another point that Abalkin seems to be making is that the *osnovnyye polozheniya* (basic principles) from the June 1987 plenum, for example, would serve as a good theoretical foundation for the economic reform. At least it focuses attention in the right place, i.e., on the fact that the scope of interrelated functions in an economy must be addressed with a well-integrated theory. The *polozheniya* serve as useful economic theory, but Abalkin is arguing that they are just the beginning.

I think that as the reform economists—the Abalkins, the Petrakovs, and the Shmelevs—move in and pursue the development of an economic theory of socialism, they are starting to realize how complex this matter is. They are seeing that you cannot elaborate a new theory with just a handful of economists;

you need an entire profession to work on it. So Abalkin's speech is not just saying that things are not moving fast enough. It is saying that the Soviet economics profession does not really know yet exactly what to do, that there have been mistakes because the reforms have not been thought through in a sufficiently scientific, theoretical way.

Gorbachev's Response[7]

I am not a political scientist, but I got the feeling that it was perhaps Abalkin's criticism of the Twelfth Five-Year Plan that prompted Gorbachev's attack on him. Yet Gorbachev chose to direct his response toward the political aspects of Abalkin's speech. Gorbachev begins by quoting Abalkin as saying that it is not important how we elect government officials. Abalkin's actual words were: "I repeat, it is necessary to have a very precise idea of how to elect deputies." He then goes on to say that all this will be for naught if the soviets don't have independence and an independent financial base.

WINSTON: Having compared the FBIS translation to the Russian text of Gorbachev's response to Abalkin's speech (*Pravda*, July 1, 1988, p. 8), I would make a somewhat more optimistic assessment. The original Russian seems softer and not at all belligerent. One might even perceive a measure of covert advocacy. A bit of skillful rhetoric by a lawyer injecting a dose of modified *litotes* to pacify unfriendly jurors—most if not all probably viewing Abalkin's orientation as a Soviet model of voodoo economics.

HEWETT: I disagree with you. First of all, Gorbachev is not a lawyer. He was educated as a lawyer, but never practiced law. Gorbachev is a politician, and remember, he was not just complaining that Abalkin misunderstood the importance of elections. He said Abalkin's problem is that he is an economic determinist, which is not a nice thing to say. Gorbachev's point was really about Abalkin's comment that you can spend all the time you want on elaborate election rules, but if these local authorities have no independent source of revenue, those rules will not matter. You can give them all the powers in the world, but they are deciding without really having any resources to decide about, so why not worry about giving them some resources?

Then Gorbachev shoots back: now, hold it. All that stuff about electing officials *is* important, but he does not want to talk now about how they are going to get money to work with.

---

7. In a speech during the Conference, Gorbachev discussed the failure of the 1965 reform effort. He said, in part: "What went wrong? Everything was based on the political system and the methods of leading society through commands and orders. That is why I tell you frankly that unless we reform the political system, all our undertakings, all of the large-scale projects we have initiated, will be delayed. That is why I disagree with Leonid Ivanovich Abalkin, whose speech smells strongly of economic determinism and, in general, of an underassessment of the superstructure that we have decided to reform. He expressed himself in a spirit suggesting that it is not very important how delegates are selected, how a session is held, or what political institutions there will be. Yet the report did not discuss just any old thing, but the very major reform, which the Conference, our people and indeed the entire world can already see. It is a pity that Comrade Abalkin has not seen this (Applause)" (*Pravda*, June 30, 1988, p. 3). [Eds.]

WINSTON: I do not disagree that elaborate election rules are no substitute for goods and services that are not available. And yes, Gorbachev never practiced law and he is a politician. But since Gorbachev does come through as a politician who says what he means and means what he says, wasn't he entitled to wonder whether a change in political structure might lead to subsequent improvements in the economy? And so he stuck a pin in Abalkin's theoretical doll and diminished his stature a bit while signaling, I think, that Abalkin is still his man. He said: . . . I do not agree with *Leonid Ivanovich* Abalkin— not an insignificant clue. He could have referred to *Comrade* Abalkin as he did to *Comrade* Shmelev when he rejected (though in much milder terms) a challenge from another prominent economist,[8] and as he referred to Abalkin later (see note 7). The word advocacy does seem too strong in this context, Ed. But the eloquence which Gorbachev displayed may be rooted in the legal training which he received. And politics and law are not mutually exclusive.

LEVINE: I see Gorbachev's response differently. If he looks at Abalkin's speech without anger, I can imagine him saying to himself: "Maybe in twenty or thirty years Soviet economic science will produce something usable." And in that context I can't help but recall the experience of Roosevelt and Keynes. The analogy may be strained, but I think it has some substance.

Roosevelt knew almost intuitively what had to be done—that, in a depression, the government should not be pulling revenue out of the economy, as Hoover was doing at the end of the 1920s.

Still, after his famous conversation with Roosevelt, Keynes came away shaking his head and telling himself: "This man really wants to balance the budget; he really doesn't understand what my theory is all about." Roosevelt came out of that meeting regarding Keynes as an abstract economist who would spend the U.S. into chaos (see, for example, Burns, 1956, pp. 328–336).

I have a few other comments on both Abalkin's and Gorbachev's speeches. Why all of this quick judgment about the failure of the economic reforms when everybody is saying that the economic reforms are not really in place yet? What really were their expectations? Did they expect some real effect just from the law on the enterprise, without price changes, without wholesale trade, and from some waving of hands about self-finance? I think there is a problem of credibility here.

GORBACHEV'S PLENUM SPEECH

SCHROEDER: Mikhail Gorbachev's plenum speech followed his pronouncements at the 19th Party Conference which we discussed at some length. After the outpouring of complaints at that conference, it was not by chance that the Politburo met and set up groups to work on four problem areas of the economy: food, consumer goods, construction, and economic reform (*Pravda*, July 5,

---

8. This was a reference to unemployment and Nikolay Shmelev's views on the subject (*Izvestiya*, June 26, 1987, p. 1). [Eds.]

1988, p. 1).[9] These four groups were established to respond to the comments of the delegates to the Party Conference and do something. Apparently they responded with summaries of the delegates' complaints and some remedies. As far as I know, they have not been published. But Gorbachev refers to these papers in his plenum speech and says, "You have these documents in your hands, so I do not have to summarize them in detail" (*Pravda*, July 30, pp. 1–3).

I thought his plenum speech was much more remarkable and hard-hitting than his speeches at the Party Conference. The plenum speech was supposed to deal with political matters, but Gorbachev spoke mainly about economic matters. There seemed to be an emotional, almost desperate, undertone to the speech. But what did he really say?

It seems to me that he went through one gimmicky proposal—I say this advisedly—after another about how to fix everything. On food, well, there is the lease contract, which supersedes other proposals that have been made in the past. But he did hint at the abolition—dare we hope?—of the agricultural bureaucracy, which would be sensational if it came to pass. He talked about getting rid of the RAPOS[10] and replacing them with so-called voluntary unions put together by collective and state farms, which would cooperate at the local level. And he did say it is now known that the steps taken on the agroindustrial complex are bearing fruit. I would not be surprised to see some action on the agricultural front.

On consumer goods, he criticized the poor state of affairs, but I thought his proposed remedies were rather traditional. He indicated that they have increased the planned targets for consumer goods production, and that they have found some reserves. He also said they should be able to increase output by 9 billion rubles above the plan in 1989 and 15 billion above the plan in 1990.

How are they going to do it? Well, he said, everybody has got to get out there and produce consumer goods and capital stock. Then capital stock has to be upgraded in the light and the food industry. But two resolutions already have been passed to that effect; that was not anything new.

Gorbachev then took on retail trade, which is something that did give me a ray of hope. It is one thing to produce all those goods; it is quite another to

---

9. The Politburo, according to *Pravda*, assigned Prime Minister Nikolay Ryzhkov; Party Secretary Viktor Nikonov; Yuriy Maslyukov, Chairman of the Military-Industrial Commission; and Vsevolod Murakhovskiy, Chairman of Gosagroprom (State Agroindustrial Committee), to work on measures to increase food production and supplies. It assigned Nikolay Slyun'kov, Chief of the Central Committee Economic Department; Gosplan Chairman Nikolay Talyzin; Party Secretary Aleksandra Biryukova (as of September 29, 1988, the first woman on the Politburo in 27 years); Shipbuilding Minister Igor' Belousov; and Vladimir Kamentsev, Chairman of the Foreign Economic Commission, to work on measures to increase consumer goods. It designated Ryzhkov, Maslyukov, and Lev Voronin, Chairman of Gossnab (State Committee for Material and Technical Supply), to examine ways to eliminate shortcomings in the implementation of the economic reform. Finally, it assigned Yuriy Batalin, Chairman of Gosstroy (State Construction Committee); Ivan Silayev, Chairman of the Bureau for Machine Building; and Voronin to draw up measures to improve the construction industry. [Eds.]

10. RAPO is the acronym for *rayonnoye agro-promyshlennoye ob"yedineniye*, or rayon agricultural production association. [Eds.]

distribute them. If the distribution system could be made more efficient, the Soviets would be better off—even with the amount of goods they have now.

What were Gorbachev's ideas for improving trade? Well, he said, "some comrades tell us we need more money." "It is true," he agreed, "we could use some more money for trade, but it also requires more space, so we will acquire facilities for trade by taking over the government offices that are being vacated by the bureaucrats."

Incidentally, this remark by Gorbachev cheered me. I was asking a Gosplan official in Moscow whether personnel cuts were really occurring. He assured me that they were. "Then," I said, "you must have surplus space, right?" He said they did, and that the entire fourth floor of Gosplan had been turned over to the Academy of the National Economy.[11] I think they should turn it over to trade.

Then Gorbachev discussed the construction issue. "It is a very difficult problem," he said, "but we have increased the targets for the production of building materials." On economic reform, the General Secretary said, "we have accelerated the pace." "We have to stop the efforts to distort the new economic forms," he declared, and he covered *goszakazy*,[12] but said nothing new. "At the beginning of next year," he continued, "we are going to put all enterprises on full *khozraschet*." "Next year," Gorbachev added, "we will begin reducing the budget deficit." I should think that they would, since by my calculations it has become very large indeed. He also stated that they have to continue to reduce and reorganize the bureaucracy and improve the relationships between the local soviets and enterprises—all of which, I should say, they need to do.

Gorbachev also said something that suggests the Soviets could inherit Yugoslavia's problem. "We need to give the collectives the right," he declared, "to freely choose one or another form of economic accountability and encourage them to choose the *second* model." "This will mean," he said, "renouncing the establishment from above of normatives for the formation of the wage fund and the distribution of profits." In effect, that would introduce the Yugoslav way of accounting, which gives collectives the right to decide how much of the firm's profits to invest and how much to pay out in wages and bonuses (Schroeder, 1987).

Finally, Gorbachev showed that he had discovered the importance of property ownership. How did he reconcile this discovery with the idea that socialist

11. The Academy of the National Economy, affiliated with the USSR Council of Ministers, was founded in 1978, for the purpose of both conducting research on the national economy and training personnel for managerial positions in the economy. According to Åslund (1987, pp. 255–256), it seems to have gained strength, and even influence, as a source of the Prime Minister's economic advice. Yevgeniy Smirnitskiy, appointed the Academy's Rector soon after Ryzhkov had become the head of the Council of Ministers, seems to be prominent within the administration. The Academy's most visible economist was Pavel Bunich, a Corresponding Member of the Academy of Sciences with considerable popular appeal attributed to forceful television appearances in support of Gorbachev's reforms and hardhitting newspaper articles as well (e.g., Bunich, 1986a).

12. *Goszakazy* are orders for the fulfillment of the state's highest-priority needs. [Eds.]

property does not belong to anybody? He said that when leasing contracts begin
to predominate, everybody will feel exactly like an owner.

WINSTON: You did say "gimmicky" in reference to lease contracts intended
to bolster food supplies. Are you inclined to apply the same label to leasing
contracts pertaining to all types of property ownership in the Soviet Union?
To real property as well? If you do, it seems you may have overlooked the
similarity between leaseholds and freeholds in Great Britain. There, a long-
term leasehold by the Crown, say for a period of 99 years, may command
about the same price on the real estate market as a freehold.

SCHROEDER: You may have a point there, Victor, but I qualified my use
of the label with the words "I say it advisedly." I recognize the potential
similarity between residential real estate ownership in the Soviet Union and
ownership by the Crown in Britain. And on the less negative side, Gorbachev's
plenum speech was an interesting and important one—more revealing than his
speech at the Party Conference—because it illustrated Gorbachev's frame of
mind. You might even call it a "counsel of despair"; but he basically offered
all these fairly traditional proposals and said, "fix this, this, and this, and
somehow everything will work out."

Gorbachev's speech said, in effect, "This is what we're going to do, comrades." At the same time, he failed once again—as he has for three and a half
years—to address the policy aspects of the whole reform process. Maybe there
was no other way, but he has pursued a kind of *ad hoc*, poorly thought-out
policy, without any great vision of where he wants the country to be in any
particular year. This approach has led to an economic situation in 1988 that,
to my mind, is fundamentally worse than when he took office. Now, when he
tries to implement the economic reforms from this point, he has to overcome
the legacies of what I think were policy mistakes.

Over the past three and a half years of Gorbachev's policy making, I see
one serious mistake after another: launching an anticorruption drive simultaneously with a law promoting individual business activity; a draconian anti-
drinking campaign; a cutback in imports of consumer goods; and the launching
of a set of economic reforms full of inconsistencies and contradictions.

Then, he threw all his forces at industrial modernization, directing a flood
of rubles at the machinery industries. That turned out to be a mistake, and you
find little mention of modernization in his recent speeches. The latest tack is
to throw masses of rubles at developing consumer infrastructure.

THE COMPLEXITIES OF TRANSITION

HEWETT: One of the critical issues raised by Gorbachev in his plenum
speech is the plight of the consumer. He now realizes, three years later, that
food, housing, and consumer goods are in short supply.

The Undersupplied Consumer

SCHROEDER: True, Gorbachev inherited a consumer sector in great disarray, and he moved quickly with a spate of measures to set things right. But his programs have gotten off to a bad start, and some have misfired. After three years, the state of the consumer sector is as bad as it was before—and in some respects worse. In fact, Western measures of real per capita consumption indicate a small decline over the past three years. Random shortages and queues, along with special distribution systems, have become more prevalent, leading Gorbachev in his plenum speech to lament, "There are lines everywhere."

Plans for substantial gains in retail sales and services have been systematically underfulfilled, mainly because of shortfalls in the production of consumer goods and services and poor agricultural performance in 1985 and 1987. And despite many promises of improvement, Gorbachev has been forced to admit that "there has been hardly any tangible improvement in the quality of consumer goods" (*Pravda*, February 19, 1988).

Unfortunately, Gorbachev has contributed to these difficulties with his own frenetic policies, which have lacked foresight. The antidrinking campaign has resulted in a drastic decline in retail sales of alcoholic beverages, a boom in moonshine production, shortages and rationing of sugar (because of the moonshine boom), and the disappearance from the shelves of a variety of products containing alcohol. Despite concerted efforts, the government has been unable to provide adequate substitutes for the lost alcohol sales. To make matters worse, a decision was made—in response to balance-of-payments problems—to reduce imports of food and manufactured consumer goods in 1986 and 1987.

Meanwhile, the population's incomes have continued to increase appreciably faster than the growth of retail sales and services. As a result, the public added an average of 20 billion rubles a year to savings deposits from 1985 to 1987, compared with an annual average of 11 billion rubles from 1981 to 1984.

A related problem is the budget deficit, which Gorbachev keeps harping on. I have calculated it at around 65 to 70 billion rubles in 1987, which is about 7 or 8 percent of the Soviet Union's GNP and roughly 14 to 15 percent of total budget income. This is a substantial amount, and it is continuing to shoot up. You can calculate it from the skimpy data that we have by making assumptions about the import cutback and its impact on budget funds. You can also estimate the disastrous impact on the consumer-goods sector in a similar way, by calculating the loss in consumer goods that resulted from the cutback in imports.

HEWETT: Let me probe this point a little. Obviously the alcohol campaign caused a macro problem because it had an impact on the budget. It is a supply constraint that is creating involuntary savings. I don't know what the numbers are, but they are large.

You mentioned a cutback in consumer-goods imports; but that is primarily food, and I believe this cutback followed production increases, so the supply was not affected. Accordingly, the question is: aside from alcohol, are things worse than they were in 1985, and if so, how?

SCHROEDER: I don't think you can really abstract the cutback in imports from the alcohol-sales problem. If we assume the traditionally large markups that the Soviets place on the prices of their imports, then I calculate this cutback to mean something like a 7 or 8 billion-ruble reduction in retail sales—both soft goods and food products. So my point is that, with the huge decrease in alcohol sales and the rising incomes of the population, this cutback in consumer imports simply exacerbates the situation.

The New Markets

WINSTON: But the daily problems confronting the undersupplied consumer tend to be resolved outside the markets controlled by the legal system. What is not so apparent outside the Soviet Union is the ongoing shift from the overt and formal economy to the second economy[13] with its dark-colored markets. The leadership is pulling in the opposite direction in an effort to co-opt that economy and its markets. I think the new laws on individual and cooperative activities are designed, in part, to accomplish this objective. But some tend to exacerbate the complexities of the transition by creating new enterprise forms and adding to the variety of interactions within the formal, shadow, and second economies.

In order to take a fresh look at the markets, we may as well depart from the typology refined by Katsenelinboigen and Levine (1977a; 1977b) who developed a matrix of horizontal interactions[14] in the economy which I will present here as Table 1.

That matrix, which now tends to be obsolete, having reflected the state of affairs in the Soviet economy about ten years ago, contained 9 cells in which interacting state enterprises, collective farms, and households were grouped in an array of colored markets, ranging from white to black, as defined by the authors. We now have a new configuration of colors shifting much more in the direction of white markets where consumers' interests are to receive more attention and enterprises more freedom to negotiate prices with consumers. In fact, the new rainbow or mix of markets in 1987–1988 appears to reflect a convergence toward red (i.e., based on prices that are centrally established) and white markets. And even though we do not yet know how all this is going to work out in practice, it may be useful to pause and bring the Katsenelinboigen and Levine matrix up to date.

13. The definition of the term used here is to be found in Grossman (1977, pp. 25–29). [Eds.]
14. Horizontal interactions are characterized by direct interrelations between economic units in which neither unit has administrative authority over the other. In contrast, each unit in vertical interactions possesses administrative authority over the units below it (see Katsenelinboigen and Levine, 1977a, p. 61). [Eds.]

Table 1. *Matrix of Horizontal Interactions in the Soviet Economy, 1977–1978*

Producer \ User	State enterprises	Collective farms	Households
State enterprises	a) Official state supply system (*rationing*) b) Limited redistribution of second-hand machinery and equipment (*red market*-primitive form, seller needs permission for sale) c) Unofficial redistribution of intermediate goods; extensive use of "expediters" (*gray market*)	a) Official state supply system (*rationing*) b) Illegal acquisition of parts, tools, etc. (*brown market*)	a) Most goods and services purchased from state stores at official prices (*red market*) b) Health and education services are primarily distributed free of charge (*free goods*) c) Housing and, during times of crises, other consumer goods distributed through direct allocation (*rationing*) d) Second-hand goods sold on commission by state commission stores (*pink market*) e) Prevalence of "under-the-counter" sales of deficit goods (*brown market*) f) Strictly illegal sales (*black market*)
Collective farms	a) Official state supply system for industrial crops, grain, meat, etc. (*rationing*) b) Sales, at negotiated prices, to the network of cooperative stores, mostly in countryside (*white market*) c) Unauthorized acquisition of industrial crops, etc. (*brown market*) d) Illegal acquisition of materials for production of black market goods (*black market*)	a) Redistribution of equipment and tools at freely negotiated prices (*white market*)	a) Food items sold through collective farm markets (similar to farmers' markets in the West); participants are (usually) free to set prices (*white market*)
Households	a) Workers normally sell labor services to state enterprises at established prices which vary with skills, occupation, industry (*red market*) b) Some direct allocation of labor through compulsory means (*rationing*) c) Under pressure of labor shortage, some violation of established wage rates (*gray market*) d) Illegal kickbacks (*black market*)	a) A person born on a collective does not have right to leave without permission (*rationing*) b) Collectives sometimes purchase labor services from travelling freelance construction teams (*white, gray markets*)	a) Food items sold by individual collective farmers at collective farm markets (*white market*) b) A broad array of goods and services are sold semi-legally: summer homes, building and repair services, tutoring, private medical services (*gray market*) c) Extensive illegal sale of stolen or illegally produced goods for private gain (*black market*)

Source: Katsenelinboigen and Levine, 1977b, p. 190.

Table 2. *Presumed Changes in the Matrix of Horizontal Interactions in the Soviet Economy from 1977–1978 to 1987–1988*[a]

Producer[b] \ User[b]	State enterprises	Collective farms	Households
State enterprises	a) Rationing: −1 b) Red market: −2 c) Gray market: +2	a) Rationing: −1 b) Brown market: +2	a) Red market: 0 b) Free goods: −1 c) Rationing: 0 d) Pink market: 0 e) Brown market: +2 f) Black market: +2
Collective farms	a) Rationing: −1 b) White market: +2 c) Brown market: +1 d) Black market: +1	a) White market: +1	a) White market: +1
Households	a) Red market: 0 b) Rationing: 0 c) Gray market: +2 d) Black market: +1	a) Rationing: −2 b) White, gray markets: +2	a) White market: +2 b) Gray market: +1 c) Black market: +2

a. Excluding new enterprise forms such as producer cooperatives and joint ventures ushered into the Soviet economy in 1986 and thereafter.

b. Positive values on the scale denote increases (+2 substantial and +1 some); zero stands for no charge, and negative values (−2 substantial and −1 some) signify decreases.

In order to facilitate the comparison, Herb Levine and I proceeded to designate a scale ranging from minus 2 to plus 2, whereby minus 2 means substantial decrease, minus 1 some decrease, 0 stands for no change, plus 1 signifies some increase, and plus 2 denotes substantial increase. Applying that scale as a yardstick, we came up with the construct of change given in Table 2.

In addition, Gertrude Schroeder has helpfully incorporated the recent legislation on new enterprise forms (particularly that pertaining to joint ventures and rejuvenated producer cooperatives) into a revised version of the aforementioned matrix. In order to avoid duplication and simplify presentation, I isolated all interactions which Schroeder added to the Katsenelinboigen-Levine matrix as well as those which she eliminated, and arranged them in tabular form. Thus, Table 3 can be viewed as an appendix to Table 1, because each form of interaction has its place in one of the appropriate cells of the 1977–1978 matrix.

I think that it is much too early to contemplate a systematic effort to measure the intended shift from the second economy to the formal economy.[15] Suffice it to say that a new mix of colored markets—a rainbow of markets—is in evidence and that there is another new element of particular interest to Western businessmen and Sovietologists alike. I have in mind the new laws to the effect that all enterprise forms (including new ones such as joint ventures and cooperatives) are accorded, at least potentially, greater access to foreign markets

15 Tat'yana Koryagina, who at the time headed a department at Gosplan's Economics Scientific Research Institute (NIEI), estimated that the magnitude of the illegal and/or semi-legal economy, as reflected in annual turnover, may be as high as 70 billion rubles (Mostovshchikov, 1988). [Eds.]

Table 3. *New and Eliminated Horizontal Interactions in the Soviet Economy as Provided by Laws Enacted after 1985*[a]

		Cell		Change since
Form of interaction	Market	User	Producer	1977–1978
Limited redistribution of second-hand machinery and equipment— primitive form, seller needs permission for sale	Red	State enterprises	State enterprises	Essentially eliminated
Sale of products and surplus equipment at negotiated prices	White	State enterprises	State enterprises	Substantially new
Purchase of products at negotiated prices	White	Collective farms	State enterprises	Substantially new
Purchase of goods and services at prices set by enterprises	White	Households	State enterprises	New
A person born on a collective does not have right to leave without permission	Rationing	Collective farms	Households	Eliminated
Workers are free to join collectives	White	Collective farms	Households	New
Goods and services legally produced by individuals	White	Households	Households	Essentially new[b]

Sources: *Sobraniye*, 1986; *Pravda*, November 21, 1986, July 1, 1987, and June 8, 1988; and other material compiled by Schroeder.

a. An assumption was made that semi-legal and illegal economic activities (gray, brown, and black markets) continued to exist despite the intent of the reform legislation to eliminate them. It was also assumed that all other horizontal interactions (see Table 1 above) continued to play a role in 1987–1988.

b. And expanded.

with opportunities to earn hard currency and retain some for their own use. More specifically, one should bear in mind the law on foreign trade reforms (*Sobraniye*, 1986), that on individual labor activity (*Pravda*, November 21, 1986, pp. 1, 3), the law on the state enterprise (*Pravda*, July 1, 1987, pp. 1–4), that on the cooperative system (*Pravda*, June 8, 1988, pp. 2–5), and finally the principal decrees pertaining to joint ventures that are enumerated in such publications as Braginsky (1988, pp. 4–5). In view of the above, it is possible to visualize 16 rather than 9 cells that group interactions in the Soviet economy at this stage of *perestroyka*. The new cells which represent the two principal new (or rejuvenated) and legal enterprise forms are added to the original ones as shown in Table 4.

It is hardly necessary to note that the admittedly coarse approximations given in Tables 2, 3, and 4 should not be regarded as more than an attempt to systematize a transitional environment—one that is changing rapidly and rather too frequently. It does not even seem to be pausing long enough to allow outside observers to take a second look.

Table 4. *Additional Cells in the Presumed Matrix of Horizontal Interactions in the Soviet Economy, 1987–1988*[a]

Producer \ User	State enterprises	Collective farms	Households	New enterprise forms[b]
State enterprises				Red market White market Rationing[c]
Collective farms				White market
Households				Red market[c] White market
New enterprise forms[b]	Red market White market Rationing[c]	Red market White market	Red market White market	Red market White market

a. Blank cells are identical to those in Table 2 above.
b. Comprising joint ventures and producer cooperatives. Expanded forms of individual enterprises are not addressed.
c. Does not appear to be applicable to joint ventures.

All told, the new forms or ways of transacting business expand the rainbow, which is now reflected more accurately in 16 horizontal interactions between producers and users. By definition, there should be more legality in this mix than in the past. In reality, however, the system is not sanitized but increasingly burdened by the added complexities. Perhaps Mikhail Gorbachev, relying on historical rather than economic determinism, is banking on Russia's proverbial capacity to muddle through the complexities and contradictions of the transition.

A Defense of Gorbachev

HEWETT: Now I am going to make the good case for Gorbachev, because I think we—including myself—are being too hard on him.

Soviet leaders felt that by the end of the 1970s they were moving slowly into a kind of hell in which their society was paralyzed, and Gorbachev believed he would unleash a tremendous burst of productivity just by treating the paralysis. I don't think that is an unreasonable notion.

Try to imagine the state of affairs from Gorbachev's perspective. He has been a regional first secretary in that society, and he has been in Moscow during the worst period. He looks around and thinks, ". . . we cannot always be this bad; we are better than this." In fact, that is one of his themes in his speeches: We are the Soviet Union, we are a superpower, but we are not acting like one.

Forget what has happened the last three years and assume that you are in charge of devising and implementing an economic reform. How would you do it? I think the first answer is, you accept that it is going to take three or four decades, and you will not be in power when it is over. Second, you must start by convincing people that it must be done and that there is no turning back. You must keep moving and looking forward. Gorbachev has done all that.

Then you start a debate about what you are going to do, and you begin to change minds. That is, you have people who lived so much in the old system, they never even thought about another way, and they need to change their entire mindset. He has done that, too. All of us here have benefited from that. Suddenly the USSR is a society of ideas.

It may be that the ideas do not get translated into reality, but you have got to start somewhere. Just the ideas that have been debated over the last three years are remarkable. I daresay, if I had asked people at this table three and a half years ago how many of the items in a typical issue of *Pravda* these days would be publicly discussed in the Soviet Union, in their lifetime, the score would probably have been zero, or perhaps 10 percent.

So let's admit that we are surprised by what is happening—and pleasantly so. But we are maximalists. We say it is not enough—you must do it all in five years. After all, it is not just Gorbachev who is guilty of excessive expectations.

Some have suggested that there is no theoretical foundation for *perestroyka*. But the June 1987 plenum was a very acceptable theoretical foundation for an economic reform. There are currently only two counterparts in the world that I know of: China and Hungary—and very briefly before them, Czechoslovakia. But if you look at the *Osnovnyye polozheniya*, if you look at Gorbachev's speech, they outline a very workable economic reform (*Pravda*, June 26 and 27, 1987).

We have all complained that the reality does not match the theory—but let's not forget the theory. It represented a remarkable victory for the reformers in that society, a victory that Gorbachev engineered by putting Slyun'kov at the head of the Central Committee's Economic Department to break the logjam that had developed in the fall of 1986 and to move reform ahead.

What he has also done is to begin to bring a new breed of people into institutions that are going to have a long-term effect on the system. All the internationalists who were in consequential positions and whom you and I would talk to in the past are now in more consequential positions. And the longer Gorbachev is in power, the more these people begin to come in, and the cadre problem begins to look somewhat more resolvable than it was in the past.

Moreover, his political reform—for all my criticism of it—is important, and it is a way to institutionalize a new kind of politics in the Soviet Union that has potential consequences for the next century more than for this century.

Gorbachev has wrought remarkable changes in Soviet foreign policy, including foreign economic policy, which have directly benefited the rest of the world. When he appointed Shevardnadze as his foreign minister, everyone said, "Who is Shevardnadze and what is he doing in the Foreign Ministry?" Yet, it was a wise decision and we have benefited from those changes. Three

and a half years ago I don't think I could have gotten one out of 100 Sovietologists to agree that it was going to happen.

SCHROEDER: I do not wish to be cast in the role of Gorbachev-basher. I
think that what has been happening in the Soviet Union is the most exciting
development in my whole lifetime, in my more than 30 years of studying the
Soviet economy. Gorbachev has done sensational things. Ed ticked them off,
and I agree with every one. His objective is absolutely right: Given my values,
he should totally marketize and privatize that economy.

CONCLUDING COMMENTS

HEWETT: Is there a crisis? That is what I asked Soviet economists in
Moscow last March. They answered that the crisis is so bad that immediate
action was of the utmost importance. But I think to some extent the crisis is
in their heads.

When you ask them, why not take some logical measures—import consumer
goods, move ahead with price reform—they argue that the crisis is so bad, the
system so fragile, that such drastic measures would threaten the stability of the
system. So they are truly in hell, in the sense that they know they have to
move or they are going to lose control of the system. I think it is because the
"crisis" talk has backfired.

I asked the economists what their evidence was for citing crisis. They did
not give me a complete answer. I think one reason is that there may be some
classified economic information. For example, there may be a lot more information, generated by the KGB, about strikes and worker slowdowns than we
know about. But I believe this is a minor component of what concerns Soviet
economists.

The more significant component is the fact that the General Secretary has
said that they are in a "precrisis" situation. This is still a society where everyone
is pushing a certain line. The line now is, there was a crisis, so even perfectly
good economists are saying without thinking that, of course, there was a crisis.

The most important point is that the level of economic analysis in that
society is low. Many Soviet economists do not necessarily do the analysis
themselves. Rather they simply accept the very poorly documented work of
economists such as Selyunin and Khanin because it conforms to their prejudices.

SCHROEDER: I think the implementation of the reform in the form that it
emerged from the decrees following the June 1987 plenum was a policy mistake
(*O korennoy perestroyke*, 1987). It has led to a situation of total confusion
everywhere. When I was in Moscow just recently, I sensed that everybody
was confused. Policymaking and policy advice were in disarray. People are
simply going to do the same old thing while hoping that the confusion will be
resolved. Also, I think the reason for all this moaning and groaning and gnashing
of teeth at the 19th Conference is related to the confusion and the colossal

mess that has been created in the consumer sector, mostly as a result of Gorbachev's policy.

WINSTON: I think Gorbachev needs to be given the benefit of the doubt, though time does not seem to be on his side. He could be the innovator forever ready to improvise. Thane Gustafson suggested a similarity which implies the frame of mind of a jazz pianist—an analogy which seems appropriate. Gorbachev is attempting to improvise a reconciliation, perhaps blindly, of doctrinaire Marxism with as much laissez-faire capitalism as the system can absorb— a thin line to tread. Hence the colossal confusion.

HEWETT: One of the more obvious problems is the absence of a theory of transition. The Soviets do not have a theory, and I don't think we know much more than they do. Many Western discussions of the reforms in the Soviet Union indicate dissatisfaction with their lack of progress, and implicit in that is a notion that we know what they should have done. In fact, we know they would be much better off at B than A, but we don't know much about how to get there.

They would like to be in an economy that is much more flexible, with a much greater role for prices, and a much more active financial system— wholesale trade, as they call it. Well, there are good ways to get there, bad ways to get there, and ways not to get there at all—by creating such terrible chaos that you have to turn back. That is a theoretical proposition. What is the best way to proceed with an economic reform?

LEVINE: Regarding your point, Ed, about the lack of a theory, it takes a long time to develop a well-grounded one. Yet Gorbachev is in the position of having the political power to move before it is developed. In terms of theory, they are back where they were at the end of the 1920s. You read the textbooks on the theories of economic planning, and you always see that same phrase: practice preceded theory.

To a great extent, unless they just reach for Western theory and take it on almost wholesale, it is not going to be a smooth process, even if they wait until something better is formulated. What comes to mind is the Hungarian experience of putting together at least a new economic mechanism that contained much more detail.

We are all groping for a theory of transition to help us understand the complexities and contradictions of the transition.

CHAPTER 16

Radical Perceptions
of *Perestroyka*

Ed A. Hewett
with *Yuriy N. Afanas'yev, Pavel G. Bunich,* and
Nikolay P. Shmelev

THE COMPANION volume of *Milestones in Glasnost' and Perestroyka* on *Politics and People* features the highlights of a joint Soviet-American roundtable conference in Moscow which included Academician Andrey D. Sakharov and other prominent members of the Moscow intelligentsia whose views on *perestroyka* have become known in the West. We have published an expanded version of the proceedings of that conference in *Soviet Economy* (Supporters, 1988), but delayed publication of material that required clarification and some updating. During the course of 1989—a year that literally overflowed with news and events—we again were compelled to postpone publication, as all efforts to bring the narrative up to date (at best an uphill battle) seemed to have come to naught. Today, the transcript of the unpublished segments of the proceedings is still valuable to the historian investigating the alliance of forces in the Congress of People's Deputies pressing for decisive measures to advance *glasnost'* and free enterprise within *perestroyka*.

Hence, avoiding material that had already appeared in print in the Russian language, we decided to restructure the dialogue involving two economists and one outspoken historian—Pavel Bunich, Nikolay Shmelev, and Yuriy N. Afanas'yev. All are typical representatives of the liberal Russian intelligentsia— passionate radicals nourished by reformist ideas similar to those prevailing in welfare-oriented Western democracies; the historian is a founding member of the so-called Inter-Regional Group of Deputies identified with Andrey Sakharov and Boris Yel'tsin.

Pavel G. Bunich, a Corresponding Member of the Academy of Sciences of the USSR, was born on October 25, 1929. A graduate of Moscow State University in 1952 and of the Moscow Institute of the National Economy in 1955, he earned a doctorate in economic sciences and joined the CPSU in 1956. During 1955–1956, Bunich worked at the Scientific Research Institute of Finance, at TsEMI, and at the Institute of Economics. A prolific writer and television commentator, Pavel Bunich has written extensively on all aspects of the reform. As a deputy to the Supreme Soviet, he was a member of its Committee on Economic Reform as well as of the Constitutional Commission of the Congress of People's Deputies. Bunich has worked on many draft laws, including those dealing with regional economic autonomy, state enterprises, and cooperatives. An expert on *khozraschet*, he chaired the Academy of Sciences' Council on Management and Cost Accounting.[1]

More pragmatic than Yuriy Afanas'yev or Nikolay Shmelev, Bunich nevertheless was actively involved in the advocacy of market-oriented economic reforms during the early stages of *perestroyka*. More recently, in 1990 and 1991, he has become very active in several institutions identified with the political center. Pavel Bunich heads the Union of Leaseholders and Entrepreneurs (*Soyuz Arendatorov i Predprinimateley*), is Vice-Rector of the Academy of National Economy (*Akademiya Narodnogo Khozyaystva*) attached to the Council of Ministers, and serves on the board of the Scientific-Technical Union (*Nauchno-Promyshlennyy Soyuz*) chaired by Arkadiy Vol'skiy. Bunich still functions in a free-market-oriented environment, but in one that can be traced to the military-industrial complex.

Nikolay P. Shmelev, who was born on June 18, 1936, is currently in charge of the Foreign Economic Affairs Department of the Institute of the USA and Canada of the Academy of Sciences of the USSR, he earned a doctorate in economic sciences. Once married to Nikita Khrushchev's youngest daughter, Yelena, Shmelev is one of the Soviet Union's most widely read authors. A former department head at the Institute of Economics of the World Socialist System, he is also a renowned journalist and fiction writer. Among Shmelev's literary works is a novella, *The Pashkov House*, which contains the recollections of a university professor on life in Moscow during the Stalinist period and on political dissent in the 1960s. A deputy of the Congress of People's Deputies, he is a member of the Council of the Union's Budget and Finance Commission.

During the closing days of the Congress's session that ended in August 1989, Shmelev voiced strong disagreement with former Prime Minister Ryzhkov by harshly criticizing the government for minimizing its role in creating their economic crisis. Highly critical of most of Ryzhkov's report to the Congress on June 7, he proposed a bold program of stabilization. While not objecting to the former Prime Minister's neglect of radical price and currency reforms, Shmelev openly rejected Ryzhkov's traditional reliance on increased output to eliminate the accumulated excess of purchasing power in the consumer goods market. His radical program called for: (a) restoration of pre-reform levels of alcoholic beverage production with high sales taxes to augment revenues; (b) immediate purchases of $15 billion worth of consumer goods from the West to be financed by reduction of imports of equipment and agricultural products, curtailment of aid to Latin America (particularly subsidization of Cuba) and borrowing from the West; (c) sale to individuals (for private use

---

1. Pavel Bunich has been affiliated with the Academy's Economics Department since 1970 and with its Far East Scientific Center since 1971. [Eds.]

and ownership) of a broad range of state-owned assets such as apartments, trucks, agricultural machinery, etc., as well as marketing of stocks and bonds that pay relatively high rates of interest; and (d) not unlike elsewhere in the world, substantial and fundamental cuts in the country's budget expenditures.

Toward the end of 1990, while remaining a member of the Congress of People's Deputies, Shmelev began to devote more time to travel abroad, and much less to politics. The exception was Arkadiy Volskiy's Scientific-Technical Union, which listed him as one of its directors. Also, after signing the letter published in *Moscow News* (*Moskovskiye novosti*, January 20, 1991, p. 1) protesting the military assault on Lithuania in January 1991, he joined the group of Yel'tsin's advisors (including Tat'yana Zaslavskaya and Oleg Bogomolov) who had served Gorbachev in the 1980s.

Yuriy N. Afanas'yev, Director of the Moscow State Institute of Historical Archives since January 1987, was born on September 5, 1934. Trained as an archivist-historian, he is known to have specialized in French history. In June 1974, Afanas'yev was identified as Deputy Chief of the Culture Department of the Central Committee of the CPSU. In March 1987, the Western press noted his series of lectures on Stalin, which he appears to have organized to educate Soviet youth. In August 1988, Afanas'yev became an active member of a group dedicated to the construction and maintenance of a memorial to the victims of Stalin's repressions. One of his better known contributions to the literature is the anthology *Inogo ne dano* (Afanas'yev, 1988), which he edited. Devoted to *perestroyka*, it features 35 leaders of the radical intelligentsia as well as progressive scholars including Academicians Sakharov, Zaslavskaya, Ginsburg, and Frank-Kamenetskiy. A deputy in the Congress of People's Deputies, Afanas'yev became one of the five co-chairmen of the Inter-Regional Group at its organizational meeting in the summer of 1989 (*Pravda*, July 31, 1989, p. 2).[2] During the course of that year, he and Boris Yel'tsin helped form the Democratic Platform, an organization intended to remake the CPSU into an "ordinary parliamentary party." Giving up on his efforts to reform the CPSU from within, Afanas'yev finally turned in his resignation and membership card in April 1990. He now cochairs Democratic Russia.

The recurrent theme in the Afanas'yev-Bunich-Shmelev roundtable dialogue is the quest for the reform's success, whether in retrospective analysis as relating to the New Economic Policy or in the future as envisaged by the discussants. Enunciating views that were among some of the most avant garde pronouncements by CPSU members at the time (nine months before the end of the aforementioned meeting of the Congress of People's Deputies) the three radicals

---

2. According to *Pravda*, the July 1989 meeting was attended by 393 deputies of whom 260 became voting members. FBIS, citing TASS (July 30, 1989), reported 316 deputies (including members of the Supreme Soviet) in attendance with an additional 119 absent but communicating their intent to join. In addition to Afanas'yev, the Inter-Regional Group was chaired by Boris Yel'tsin, the late Academician Andrey Sakharov, Gavriil Popov (the noted economist and currently mayor of Moscow), and Academician Victor Palm of the Estonian Academy of Sciences. [Eds.]

focused on the unresolved issues that lie at the heart of economic reform in the USSR. Most remain as relevant today as they were in November 1988 when we heard them, and still shed light on possible solutions suggested by international practice and Soviet history.

THE REMONSTRATIONS OF PAVEL BUNICH

There are three alternative scenarios ahead of us. The first one involves Stalinism. It did not cease to exist, no matter how much one might wish to believe that Stalinism will not be resurrected. The second alternative is to remain where we are by replacing an absolute monarchy with an enlightened one. This is not the best alternative, but in our case the probability that it will develop is high—some believe that it is very high. The third alternative is *perestroyka*, genuine full-scale *perestroyka*.

If we stay with the first two alternatives—and they are very much alike—we will continue to live in a socialist system. Although the third alternative is clearly superior, the most recent surveys show that there are not as many supporters of *perestroyka* as in the past. People are getting tired.

I believe the percentage of supporters declined from about 80 to 70, and it is not at all certain that those included in the 70 percent represent a hard core. The number of opponents increased from 7 to 10 percent, and the remaining 20 percent are undecided. This rising opposition represents a new phenomenon which did not seem to exist before the fall of 1988. It surfaced because the third alternative cannot succeed as long as our leadership fails to demonstrate immediate results. Regretfully, instant results are not possible because the time at our disposal to overcome our fatigue and move ahead is not long enough. And yet, we are not in a position to postpone *perestroyka* for three or four five-year plans.

We are failing. I see no reason to rely on predictions that we might attain the modest growth rates of the current five-year plan. While the targeted four percent increase in national income is not high enough, we are not even near that 4 percent level in 1988. And there is every reason to believe that 1989 will not be a better year. An average growth rate of 3 percent is still possible, but one-third will be traced to increments in population.[3] Hence a mere 2 percent is not *perestroyka*, but simply a poor showing.

Can we count on instant success? The answer is a resounding "no" if the Soviet Union is expected to ascend to the heights of industrialized countries of the West. We might aspire to such goals as the ability to feed and clothe ourselves—in our own homemade garments. But we are not even capable of

3. Goskomstat, the State Committee on Statistics, subsequently reported a 4.4 percent increase in national income in 1988 over the previous year, as compared with a target of 6.6 percent. The average increase for the three years 1986 to 1988 was 3.6 percent. The GNP, which replaced the gross domestic product as a Soviet indicator, was said by Goskomstat to have increased by 5 percent in 1988 (see *Pravda*, January 21, 1989, p. 3). But the CIA estimated Soviet GNP growth in 1988 at only 1.5 percent. In the first quarter of 1989, according to Goskomstat, GNP rose by 5 percent and national income by 4 percent over the same period last year. [Eds.]

managing as little as that. Our plan targets are limited and this *perestroyka* is a tale of tinkering—not of restructuring.

History records two instances of successful drives to reform socialist economies and several efforts marked by questionable achievement. The first clear case of success was our NEP[4] and the second was China. The Chinese Peoples' Republic—a real winner in this case and hardly a paper tiger—demonstrated tangible results within nine years after the beginning of its reform.[5] People who insinuate that the Soviet Union is ahead of China and that the latter will be where we are today in the year 2,000 are not telling the truth. China is probably ahead of our country, moving forward in accord with its reasonable and realistic plan targets, while we are falling behind.

Hungary was successful for about eight years and so was Yugoslavia. And that is about all one has to say about instant success in efforts to restructure socialist economies. Will the Soviet Union manage to survive if the present state of affairs were to continue? Our efforts—superficial tinkering and cosmetic adjustments—tend to convey the answer.

We need a profound, deep reform. Paradoxically, it is the easiest kind to accomplish, for there is no reason to believe that a "slow reform" is possible. History shows that the present state of affairs will lead the country to an explosion. Because nobody knows when the eruption may take place, the reform may as well explode immediately, without further delay. The deeper and more profound the reform, the less painful the rebuilding.

The Cooperatives

What does "deeper" reform really mean? Is there a model to look at and copy? Despite all their shortcomings, cooperatives—an exceptionally solid economic undertaking—provide a reasonable prototype. No one has to be coerced into joining cooperatives, because movers and shakers with skill look forward to becoming a part of that developing sector. Only people without skills and ambition tend to remain in the employ of the state and berate cooperatives. The defection rate from the state sector is very high: 700,000 people during the first year at a time when cooperatives were subjected to abuse; they were nearly strangled and crushed. In other words, it is not unreasonable to predict a shift of as many as 4 to 5 million people to that sector within two years[6]—4 to 5 million of our best people. In the state sector, nobody is forced to work as much as 12 to 14 hours a day. But people employed in a cooperative

4. The New Economic Policy (NEP), instituted by Lenin in 1921, allowed some relaxation of centralized control and doctrinaire socialism. It permitted a generous measure of unrestricted trade within the country, offered incentives to foreign capital, and implicitly recognized private property rights. The dismantling of NEP began in 1927. [Eds.]

5. In 1979, the Chinese government began to introduce a series of economic reforms. A large segment of Chinese agriculture returned to family farming, and some industrial enterprises were given broader managerial power as the role of central planning declined. [Eds.]

6. An accurate prediction. In fact, by 1990 the cooperative sector employed 6.2 million people or 5 percent of the labor force (*Ekonomika i zhizn'*, No. 5, January 1991, p. 5). [Eds.]

do not hesitate to take on a 14-hour shift. They can afford a three-month vacation when there is no work.

An angry factory manager of one of our garment manufacturing enterprises told me a typical story. "I make T-shirts," he complained, "the cooperatives buy them from me, scrawl a word or two and sell them at thrice the price." He was outraged. This intelligent man later explained why the words on the shirts were not stamped in his factory. "Why should I do that? I don't want to." Now that brief statement was a very meaningful reflection of reality. The entire country comprises an army of people who "don't want to." It is a country symbolizing demand rather than supply. "I don't want to" is a way of life for everybody save for the few lease farmers and achievers who move on to join the cooperatives.

Why don't we then convert the entire state sector to the cooperative system? After all, the state sector is clearly collapsing and the bear keeps wasting away, being robbed by the cooperatives which not only take away its best people but also drain state budgets by charging exorbitant prices for services which they perform; reciprocally, the state sector is making things hard on the cooperatives by withholding raw materials.

An example is in order to illustrate the way Soviet cooperatives tend to function around the end of 1988. An economic institute decides to declare itself a "cooperative." It finds an enterprise, talks it into signing a lease contract, and collects 150,000 rubles for the exercise. Moreover, 60,000 of the 150,000 rubles is earmarked for enterprise employees, who purportedly are to work for the institute in the evenings! I would have performed the same "service" for that enterprise for a few rubles. What is then the consideration for the 150,000-ruble payment since, to begin with, the enterprise did not want to sign a lease? Crime prevention, the OBKhSS[7] comes to mind. But our ability to catch so many thieves and profiteers is very limited.

I brought this up because the state sector keeps losing ground to the cooperatives. When there are two distinct categories of rubles in circulation—live and dead ones—only the live ones matter, for the dead ones are on their way out. And if we drag the present ways and means out, we will ruin the state sector more quickly than our leadership managed in the old days when there were no cooperatives. There are additional incentives these days for this ruining process to succeed.

Instead of destroying the state sector, we could convert it. In a healthy system, you tend to freely divide everything you earn. As things stand today, everybody in the state sector receives a small but guaranteed wage, while in the cooperative sector comparable wages are about four times higher. But we keep on doing what we did in the past, stubbornly refusing to introduce the healthy system to our state enterprises. There seem to be no prospects that we will wake up.

7. OBKhSS is the abbreviation for *Otdel bor'by s khishcheniyami sotsialisticheskoy sobstvennosti i spekulyatsiyey* (Department for Combating Thefts of Socialist Property and Profiteering). [Eds.]

Opposition to *Perestroyka*

Opponents of *perestroyka* usually begin their arguments by insisting that a new system would erode capital accumulation and amortization in the state sector in favor of wages. Yet if we were to distribute the state sector's accumulation in the form of stock, people would not oppose the idea of saving. Regretfully, we cannot convince *perestroyka*'s opponents that this would constitute the best lever at our disposal to rescue our accumulations and the state sector as well.

The second argument proffered by the opposition is rooted in ideology. If we give away the accumulations by dividing up the pie so that every shareholder receives a fixed dividend, the state sector will cease to exist. "We will become a huge joint-stock company," they say. And even though this option might tend to cure our chronic inefficiency, the opponents of *perestroyka* nourish their attachment to the state sector in the way they used to place their trust in orthodox Marxism.

The third argument reflects our bleak reality and reconciles the views of Nikolay Shmelev and Leonid Batkin (see Supporters, 1988, pp. 279–280, 282–283). Shmelev saw bureaucracy as a pervasive element which embodies resistance to *perestroyka*. It persists and lives on because bureaucrats at all levels refuse to give up their power. Bureaucracy is thus a pyramid, a monolith, that cannot be abolished from the top. It needs to be eroded by a shift to democracy. The country's central economic agencies must be abolished, and only skillful political maneuvering can be of help to those who may make an attempt to eliminate them.

There are people at the bottom who are willing to accept a change. Putilov is not quite dead in our minds and some genes appear to be intact.[8] Under appropriately favorable circumstances, they might yet develop. Because the principal obstacles reside at the top, we at the bottom will benefit only after someone removes them. The Soviet Union must move in this direction if we truly wish to put behind us the 70 years of life dominated by directives from above.

A DIALOGUE WITH NIKOLAY SHMELEV

HEWETT: As someone who supports *perestroyka* in the Soviet Union and watches it develop from the outside, I am concerned that the conceptual basis for what is happening here is either weak or does not exist at all.

First, putting politics aside, the goals of *perestroyka* are to improve the quality of output, increase labor productivity, and make the Soviet Union a serious industrial force in the world economy—and not just a serious military force. In that case the Soviet Union will become an authentic superpower.

8. A reference to N.I. Putilov, a 19th-century Russian engineer and enterpreneur. [Eds.]

From an economist's viewpoint, we must speak of a full-scale market system, a system that would enable producers to specialize and efficiently produce high-quality output. This kind of institutionalization of the producer's interests is based on the fact that he is a producer and at the same time a consumer as well.

There really must be free-market competition as opposed to socialist competition,[9] with unrestricted setting of prices and free exchange with the rest of the world. What I have in mind is not only the exchange of goods but the internationalization of production and finance. Countries whose economics are successfully developing are not outside the world economy; they are part of it. If you take a look at Britain's banking system, most of the assets there are international, and the banking system operates with foreign currency—hard currency, at any rate. In other words, there is a capital market that is used by many different countries.

Another issue is the rights of the private entrepreneur and the right to private property. Is there anywhere in the Soviet Union—in academic circles, the government, or the party—a conceptual basis or blueprint for what we Americans would call a free market? Are the appropriate institutes working on one?

Looking ahead to the 21st century, when the success of *perestroyka* will be a logical social development, we must differentiate our economy from the Swedish economy or the U.S. economy. What will be special about the Soviet economy? It will be primarily a socialist economy, but I don't know what that is. I read a great deal of Soviet economic literature, and see that people are struggling and fighting over this year's problems, today's problems, trying to avoid something or not do too much. It is, of course, very important to avoid the mistakes of the past. And when we see the past, we notice that it is becoming worse and worse every year. We even joke that it would be nice to publish reports on GNP growth and its fluctuations under Brezhnev. In other words, we focus too much on the past.

My second point is about a theory of transition. Is there such a theory? People are evidently thinking about it. The government is proceeding from some such theory, but it is clearly inadequate. The way *perestroyka* is developing right now—by decrees and resolutions—is a road to disaster, because price reform, as you know, has been put on the back burner, and that is dangerous.

Some people, and Soviet economists in general, are attaching huge importance to cooperatives as a transitional form. That form is expected to grow and the state sector to shrink. That is precisely what occurred in Hungary. Hungarians are expanding the cooperative system, and what is left behind is state-owned industry, which is subsidized by the state. But the process has led to a worsening of the economy, and despite various reforms the situation is deteriorating.

9. Unlike *konkurentsiya* or capitalist-style competition between independent producers, *sorevnovaniye* or socialist competition involves enterprises attempting to meet centrally set plan targets. [Eds.]

Special economic zones are forming, say in the Baltics, but that entails a host of explosive political questions, which are intimidating rather than encouraging. Perhaps the theory could proceed from the premise that we must expand the market, based on a recognition that the government system is bankrupt.

SHMELEV: I think Ed is absolutely right. We do not have a theory of transition. As a result, we are improvising, making mistakes—and sometimes unforgivable ones—and some of those mistakes are due to the lack of a working theory of transition. I will not dwell at length on the mistakes that have been made in the last two or three years. But the anti-alcohol campaign, along with our import problems, the decline in oil prices, and such petty measures as the elimination of certificates to purchase goods in the Beryozkas, brought our budget to the brink of disaster. Most of those events were dictated by ideological considerations, and people with decision-making power failed to think through the consequences of these steps which did not make much sense to professional economists.

What is in store for us? We see many different things, but if one follows the logic of how reforms are developing, the probability is—without ironclad guarantees—that we will have more than one type of ownership. There will be state ownership, but in the form of stockholding[10] with normal capital flow as in a normal market economy. There will be cooperative ownership (small business, family business), provided it survives the next two or three years without being strangled.

Theoretically, I do not reject the notion that we may have private ownership with hired employees—this would be a good catalyst and stimulant for our economy.[11] But I appeal to your sense of realism; for practical purposes, I am convinced that somebody will set fire to the first private enterprise the very night that it is set up. Judging by the reaction to cooperatives, the people on the street will not allow them to open. Seventy years and four generations cannot be erased.

I also visualize mixed forms of ownership: state-cooperative, cooperative-state, and foreign. We have already decided to allow foreign capital to control as much as 80 percent of a joint venture. We have raised this from 49 percent in just one year. I will not rule out that, just like the Chinese on Hunan Island, we may go up to 100 percent for foreign ownership to attract capital. Foreign investors must be able to freely spend their rubles in the Soviet Union and purchase whatever they wish.

Now a few words about economic management. All three historical methods—direct planning, informative planning, and the free market—have their advantages and disadvantages. There is no reason to reject any that perform.

---

10. The labor collective would own the stock of its enterprise, with rights to participate in many other enterprises as well.

11. During the period of NEP, about 20 percent of our industrial production could be attributed to private enterprises with hired labor.

The question is, in what proportion do we apply them to our economy. If everything develops properly without setbacks, I foresee at the end of the next decade the following structure: about 15 percent of our GNP will be managed by direct planning (essentially, the entire defense sector and related civilian enterprises), with the balance by a combination of informative planning and free-market forces.

As for the relationship between direct price setting and market price formation, consider that each year we need to set 25 million prices (for the 25 million products manufactured and produced in the Soviet Union). If several hundred prices are under the government's control, there is nothing wrong with that. It would be especially dangerous now—and will be for another five to seven years—for the government to let prices float freely, because a wave of inflation would devour us instantly. Collective egotism is no easier to deal with than individual egotism. As soon as enterprises receive unrestricted freedom, they begin to strangle the consumer by price increases. We have a complete monopoly, and until some competition is in place the principal prices must not be allowed to change—otherwise enterprises will ruin each other and hurt the consumer as well.

Now, about the prospects for opening up our economy, I think we are all very sincere and there are no opponents. One might question the pace, the methods, or the opportunities for such an open economy. To open it up less than 100 percent, or to do without controls and open up completely?

And there is a heartening point to make. Whereas the average duration of capital construction (i.e., plant construction) was 11.5 years only two years ago (the average in other countries was 1.5 to 2 years), our present average is 8.5 years. This does not mean much to the man on the street, but to a professional economist it represents a fundamental advance and very significant progress.

I recently attended a contentious conference. Significantly, the one issue on which the participants were unified, both leftists and rightists, pertained to attempts by Gosplan and the ministries to manipulate *goszakazy* in order to strangle the Law on the State Enterprise[12] while it was still in its infancy. You know that about 85 percent of industrial production this year followed the route of *goszakazy*—direct planning in another disguise. Significantly, all *obkom* secretaries and others who spoke at the conference were unanimous in suggesting that this is intolerable. And the government is responding by proceeding on the premise that *goszakazy* in 1989 should not amount to more than 40 to 45 percent. This means that we will essentially have a free market, weak and clumsy as it may be. Next year, 60 percent of industrial output may go to the free market. The next step is to accelerate our movement toward wholesale

12. The Law on the State Enterprise, which put enterprises on a self-financing basis and gave them greater managerial autonomy, formally entered into force on January 1, 1988. According to press reports, however, central ministries continued after that date to interfere with the decision-making process of local managers. *Goszakazy* short for *gosudarstvennyye zakazy*, are orders for fulfillment of the state's highest-priority needs. [Eds.]

trade; the pace of that movement has been doubled. After the conference, goals were set so that about 40 percent of our production will be channeled into wholesale trade. In other words, within the next year or two, at most three, we can have a free market in the means of production, and our foreign partners will finally be able to spend their rubles.

HEWETT: But you cannot have a free market with the prices that you now have. I don't know which issue comes first and which comes second, but they are interrelated.

SHMELEV: This is the most frightening issue related to prospects for the economic reform, because it affects the vital interests of people. If we move on prices in a heavy-handed way, it could ruin the entire reform. But there are two aspects here: the reform of wholesale prices and the reform of retail prices. In the past, I believed that retail prices must be reformed, but now I am afraid of such a reform. The Chinese stretched their reform out, taking more than 20 years. We should stretch ours out over 15 years, so that it is completed when the market is saturated. A price reform cannot be carried out when there are no goods for sale on the market. This could cause massive social unrest. First we must achieve some improvement in the market, and then gradually set the reform in motion.

Later, retail prices should be allowed to float and we will have a normal balance between demand and supply. As for wholesale prices, they can be reformed just about painlessly, and this reform is under way. The consumer will not be affected, at least for a while. We must, of course, oppose the objectives of Goskomtsen and the Ministry of Finance. No matter what they say, their aim is to take a little money away from the public, close up the gap in the budget for at least three or four years, and only then take another look. This should not be the case.

Under these promising circumstances we could establish a realistic exchange rate for the ruble. It should not be necessary to wait too long for such an exchange rate. Why not try having two currencies, as was the case during the NEP period in the 1920s? We could have one currency for the time being in the form of old rubles, and a new one, fully convertible from the very beginning (supported, of course, with international credit behind it.) Such a system exists in China, with the gold yuan and the wooden yuan. It is probably premature to talk about opening up our economy, because most, if not all, of our promising new laws serve as organizational blueprints. To sum up, we must solve two issues: wholesale trade in the means of production and convertibility of the ruble.

YURIY AFANAS'YEV'S RETROSPECTIVE

I would classify the opposition to *perestroyka* by distinguishing between "who" and "what." If we look for opponents only among people, it can be very confusing when everyone is "in favor" of *perestroyka* while we sense that this is not the case. The "what" also denotes different things, for it can apply to diverse structures—social, economic, spiritual—that have now become reasonably well established here. It can also apply to dogmas, theories, or myths that have not proven themselves in practice, but stubbornly continue to be implemented. Finally, the "what" can mean simply an unwillingness to face the truth and define the true state of affairs. This can also be a very powerful impediment. Until we accurately perceive the character and essence of the socioeconomic dynamics of our society, I don't think we can understand and persuasively answer the question "who and what opposes *perestroyka*?"

A Look at NEP

Lately, many of our economists, philosophers, and public affairs writers have found it possible to probe the meaning of *perestroyka*, attempting to expose its problems and define them. But as soon as such efforts begin in earnest, hostile forces opposed to *perestroyka* come out of the woodwork. In order to understand the dynamics of the Soviet economy and society, it is necessary to take a closer look at attempts to revise our view of socialism, in 1921 with NEP, in the 1950s with Khrushchev, and now again with Gorbachev. If we try to compare their substance and meaning, we might be able to determine what the three attempts have in common and evaluate the profound differences between them.

In this context, I think we should look at NEP more closely, because when people mention Lenin's NEP, many are inclined to think that everything about it was milk and honey. In fact, NEP also represented an outright contradiction. It contained many elements that were poorly thought through, grossly misinterpreted, and greatly misunderstood. NEP also embodied several alternatives. One could have led to the democratization of Soviet society, while another, destined to materialize, represented Stalinism. Therefore, it is simply impossible to adopt a monochromatic attitude toward that period. I think Pasternak was right when he called NEP the most ambiguous and deceitful of all periods in Soviet history.

Much has been said and written about bureaucratic functionaries and their functions. But I think the real issue before us today is ownership, and we must define it. There are trustworthy documents which infer that the peasant class was liquidated in the 1930s. By way of socialism, we came to a point when we no longer lived in a society that owned property. Members of the bureaucracy, the bureaucratic class, became the property owners. And in the present context, most attempts to develop cooperatives and leasing arrangements, I think, are attempts to take over this ownership under new conditions.

This is what the powerful, tremendous resistance to *perestroyka* is all about. The articles in *Pravda* under the so-called Pravda's Fridays heading[13] simply

---

13. *Pravdinskiye pyatnitsy*, or "Pravda's Fridays," is a regular feature containing historical essays. [Eds.]

mislead the Soviet people and suppress the truth and understanding. They fail to tell us how the peasantry and workers were liquidated as a class, or how ownership changed so that properties proclaimed public became assets belonging to the Party and government bureaucracies. Instead of explaining this transformation, a renewed attempt is in motion to revive the Stalinist concept of what society is about.

It is said that NEP embodied the alternative of introducing Stalinism as a phase, and that NEP was doomed by its intrinsic principles. This is both right and wrong because NEP was a construct of several alternatives, and should be viewed in light of these alternatives as a choice that had been made. Had the democratic principles developed and the persistent efforts to inject planning into the market system (as in NEP) failed, the democratic underpinnings of NEP might have prevailed.

When Lenin attempted to solve NEP's problems, he decided that a mixed system must prevail. And this is what happened at the time. Even at that level, however, everything was done inconsistently and superficially. The peasants used to say, "If they would only allow us to do a little selling on the side." The authorities obliged and allowed them to do "a little selling," but in the spirit that Marx was right in saying that rigid centralized planning rather than a market should govern under socialism. After all, nobody was going to repudiate this Marxist idea outright. They did not repudiate it while carrying out the policies of NEP in the 1920s, and they did not clearly repudiate it up to this very day. The conviction under NEP was that even if a little selling on the side is permitted, it was not a serious, long-term policy, but only a temporary accommodation. The populace may not have been aware of it at the time, but the followers of Marx finally prevailed in the Communist party and the country, and their beliefs materialized in the form of Stalinism.

In the present context, I think the issue of bureaucratic functionaries and functions boils down to ownership by the party-bureaucracy construct. Of course, carrying out the revolution of *perestroyka* is difficult. The Communist party must destroy itself in the form that it always existed, and try to pull itself up by the bootstraps. This is an extremely complicated task, and unless we clarify the economic dynamic and the balance of forces at various stages of *perestroyka*, the most fundamental questions will always remain in the shadows. Democracy without linkage of people to ownership is just empty talk.

Discussion

SHMELEV: I should like to disagree with Yuriy Nikolayevich. Maybe both he and Pasternak are right in saying that NEP was ambiguous in terms of law, ability to survive, and perhaps policy. But from the viewpoint of economics there was nothing ambiguous about that system, which lasted for seven years. It was a pragmatic, successful attempt to construct a viable model of a multisectoral society with a socialist bias. The most important point is that the state sector in this multisectoral model was efficient, competitive, open, and capable of producing results that were not achieved thereafter—in either the 1930s, 1940s, or 1950s—even if one were to use purely statistical yardsticks of measure.

One might speculate that NEP was destroyed by its moral-political ambiguity. But one cannot help but conclude that, after some experience with ideological approaches to reality during the period of War Communism, the major theorists were ready and sufficiently flexible to opt for pragmatism and common sense. They included Lenin, Dzerzhinskiy (who may have played the deciding role with regard to NEP's success), and Bukharin. Why didn't the NEP alternative survive? I am not inclined to agree with some of my colleagues who claim that it was Russia's destiny, that it is our historical misfortune dating back to Ivan the Terrible.[14] I think that there was a conspiracy which succeeded. Soviet history is a tale of such conspiracies.

BUNICH: One should not overemphasize history *per se*. What accounts for official inertia? I think the principal element is the reactionary nature of people who have worked under a system for many years, have grown fat and sluggish, and can no longer absorb anything new. I am on the faculty of the Academy of National Economy where ministers are taught, and I meet them very often. I talk and talk, everyone nods, but as soon as they ask a question it becomes clear that the ministers have not absorbed anything. Not absorbing is the strength of our conservatism.

Second is dogmatism—adherence to the notion that socialism can be feudal and compatible with military force. In many people, this mask has merged with their own face, and they sincerely believe that any other kind of socialism is really revisionism. And only then would I list, far behind, in third place, the historical past of our country. I think that a lot of people exaggerate the degree to which the past exerts pressure on people who live today.

AFANAS'YEV: It may make some sense not to look at the past in very general terms. But in our Soviet context I think it is absolutely necessary to take a look at history in order to answer the most troubling questions of our time. Otherwise the search for an answer to the question of "who" or "what" opposes *perestroyka* will become untenable.

Let me illustrate this by using a suitable example. It is apparent that since last spring the revolution from the top, which began in April 1985 and introduced *glasnost'* with some democracy, has begun to ebb. One can see this, and we can even try to discuss why the decline is happening. But it would be impossible to evaluate this trend in Soviet society without a look at the past. The reason the revolution is declining is related to the relationship between initiatives from the top and from the democratic movements at the bottom. If we return to the 1920s, the NEP was a response to a mass movement that

14. My colleague Igor Klyamkin argues that NEP failed to solve the central problem of injecting competition into industry. But in 1923 there was a market crisis, and in 1924 the market took over after administrative levers were lifted.

spontaneously arose from below—mostly, but not solely, from the peasantry. NEP was a forced response, as Nikolay Shmelev has pointed out, because there was no other way—the peasants of Russia had risen up against Soviet rule and the Bolshevik party. The initial response to this spontaneous mass movement was a specific measure, namely the replacement of *prodrazverstka* with *prodnalog*.[15] As the reaction to the movement from below grew, that measure developed into a system of many measures that began to be called the New Economic Policy. This approach might have constituted an alternative to Stalinism.

But the way things turned out, both in the party and in society, the forces that eventually prevailed obstructed the interests of the spontaneous mass movement. The result was that a movement began from the top, but in a form that destroyed the mass movement from below. The peasantry was, in fact, physically destroyed, and this continued until the mid-1930s. That is one socioeconomic model of Soviet society in its first attempt to revise the view of socialism.

Another model is the Khrushchevian version. I don't think Khrushchev thought very much about democracy; he simply believed that Soviet society could be completely transformed from above. As for the countermovement from below at that time, I think it was weak and not diversified. It began as an attempt to push Khrushchev's reforms along. As they stalled, some people tried to influence the outcome through appeals, petitions, and proposals. But after these efforts failed, the democratic beginning (which mostly involved the intelligentsia) turned into dissidence, and in that form it was destroyed. Again, this dissonance between movements from the top and from below was quite apparent, and it was one of the reasons for the collapse of Khrushchev's reforms—the collapse of the second attempt to reorganize society.

Concluding Comments

What is happening more recently after Mikhail Gorbachev became Secretary General of the CPSU? The movement began from the top, also as a result of listening to dissidents and others say that it had become impossible for the people to live and for society to develop. But all along there was initiative; it seemed to propel the development of society, the democracy and *glasnost'* up to a certain point. But sometime around last spring a downswing became apparent. First, it was manifested in Nina Andreyeva's articles in *Sovetskaya Rossiya* (Andreyeva, 1988) about the restoration of historical truth and in a similar writing in *Pravda* (April 5, 1988, p. 2) aimed at affirming half-truths.

15. *Prodrazverstka*, short for *prodovol'stvennaya razverstka*, or food allotment, was an element of War Communism under which peasants were required to deliver all surplus output to the state at fixed prices. The policy, which lasted from 1919 to 1921, was replaced by *prodnalog*, short for *prodovol'stvennyy nalog*, or food tax. The amount of the tax, which was levied on peasant farms for each crop, depended on local conditions and profitability. [Eds.]

Then came the 19th Conference of the CPSU, which in essence nearly unanimously opposed *glasnost'*. Of course, some people there, including Mikhail Gorbachev, said that if *glasnost'* is done away with, then a funeral can be planned for *perestroyka* as well. But most speakers opposed *glasnost'* at the conference; in fact, the selection of speakers was typically undemocratic.

Then there was the saga of the subscriptions. And the effort to shrink all subscriptions to newspapers and magazines could have succeeded had the powerful voices of protest failed to prevail. But now we have the repressive decrees on demonstrations and internal affairs followed by the proposed changes in the Constitution and the manner in which they are being discussed.[16] I think these measures and facts show a developing downswing, which began in April 1988.

But look at the contrast with what happened under Khrushchev. Now we have a very powerful mass movement which has diversified a great deal of late. First, there is the cooperative movement, which is not developing to the extent that one would wish, but still has become a factor. Second, quite a number of state enterprises are gravitating toward cooperative forms of management, which has never happened before. Third, there is the informal-group movement, which also is expanding and diversifying. Fourth, there are the events in the national republics, above all in the Baltic—the struggle for economic autonomy, sovereignty, etc. Finally, the much less restrained minds of the entire society also are a factor in the countermovement from below.

If we refuse to take into account the specific similarities and differences in the development of our economy since 1921, we may forget that the interrelated movements from the top and from below were ingrained in the various reforms. These movements *are* of paramount significance in determining the success or failure of *perestroyka*, for its outcome depends on what happens when the two movements meet. They may work in unison on behalf of *perestroyka*, or they may end up in a confrontation. Such confrontation would open the way for the other alternatives, either for enlightened absolutism or a form of Stalinism such as military dictatorship. Or it could turn into a disaster for Russia—one of many.

The only thing Stalinism taught Russia and the Soviet Union was how to think and act catastrophically; in other words, to respond to every catastrophe by unleashing a wave of reactionary oppression and increasing the number of prison inmates and death sentences. That is all Stalinism taught Russia. So we must now learn how to respond in a civilized manner to a crisis (i.e., regard a crisis situation as normal for our society) and also how to get out of it in a civilized way. My point about the need to look into the past is justified by the fact that our spiritual and economic structures took shape in the 1930s. We must examine the socioeconomic dynamics of today by analyzing the balance

16. The government issued two decrees on July 29, 1988, pertaining to street demonstrations. One required protesters to obtain advance permission to hold demonstrations, while the other broadened the rights of police to suppress "illegal" protests. The decrees were approved by the Supreme Soviet on October 28, 1988. The reforms were adopted at a session of the Supreme Soviet on December 1, 1988 (*Pravda*, December 2, 1988). [Eds.]

of forces—an effort much too difficult to accomplish without looking into the past.

One more point, regarding the reaction of our intelligentsia to what is happening today and what has happened in the past. I have discerned a dangerous trend, which I would call the time-serving accommodation (*prisposoblenchestvo*) of most of the intelligentsia to official policy. After all, they have not said anything too loudly about what is happening to Armenia or about what has happened to the Crimean Tatars. Now those two decrees on demonstrations and the police have been adopted, and the intelligentsia is still silent. The proposed changes in the Constitution are being discussed—again silence. The experience of decades of totalitarianism and abuse of our intelligentsia left its mark; it still prefers to keep quiet, and that may be the downfall of *glasnost'* and *perestroyka*. We are in favor of *perestroyka*, but in order to be in favor and support Gorbachev, it is necessary to learn how to oppose him as well— argue in his own interests and in the interests of *perestroyka*. We say, yes, we are sure everything will be all right. What makes us so sure after the tragic history of our society?

CHAPTER 17

Budget Deficit, Market Disequilibrium, and Economic Reforms

Gur Ofer

FIVE YEARS into the Gorbachev economic reforms the economic situation in the Soviet Union is deteriorating to a dangerous level. In addition to the various flows of monetary expansion, a decline in the production of a number of industrial goods and growing bottlenecks in transportation and distribution are now contributing to market disequilibrium.[1] Over the last five years the Soviet Union has developed a state budget deficit equal to at least 10 percent of gross domestic product (GDP). This, combined with a monetary overhang, expansion of credits, and cost-push rises in wages and prices, has been a major factor in creating shortages and disequilibria (especially in the consumer goods market) and is blamed for triggering a process of open inflation.[2] Both the leadership and economists in the Soviet Union regard the fiscal crisis as the country's most acutely pressing economic problem, not only because of its effect on the current economic situation, but also because many critical elements of the reforms depend on establishing a solid fiscal and monetary infrastructure.

Most Soviet economists and political leaders believe that under the present conditions of over-monetization and strong inflationary pressures, they cannot risk implementing a badly needed price reform, which would create flexible prices. Price reform, therefore, has been postponed. Without price reform, however, the major Soviet enterprise reform (whereby enterprises are expected to become virtually independent operators and profit maximizers) retains little significance. Inflexible prices frustrate the solving of the budget deficit problem, since about one-fifth of all expenditures goes to subsidizing basic food and housing in order to keep their prices far below cost. Another major element of

First published in *Soviet Economy*, 1989, 5, 2, pp. 107–161. An earlier version of this chapter was presented at the IXth Latin American Meeting of the Econometric Society, Santiago, August 1–3, 1989. The author would like to thank Jim Noren and Jim Millar for helpful comments, Roberta Waxman, Elizabeth Kirkwood, and Gilad Kedmi for research assistance, and Etka Liebowitz and Maggie Eizenstadt for editorial help. [Eds.]

1. Results of 9 months, 11 months, or the entire year.
2. Estimates of the level of inflation in the Soviet Union vary. The highest annual figure cited to date (10–11 percent) was provided by Oleg Bogomolov at a public meeting in 1989. (See also *PlanEcon Report*, September 1 and November 26, 1989; Hanson, 1989; Shmarov and Kirichenko, 1989; Abalkin, 1989b.)

the reforms, and one that should contribute to improved efficiency, is the opening of the economy to external participation and competition. The leaders feel they must postpone this feature also, largely because of the shaky internal financial situation. Unlike China, where financial destabilization was accompanied by very high production growth rates, the Soviet economy is growing very slowly,[3] thus worsening the shortages and disequilibria from the supply side as well.

The new economic reform program presented for discussion by Leonid Abalkin last November thus incorporated a plan for fiscal and monetary stabilization as a pre-condition for further reforms that will come only later (Abalkin, 1989a; Hewett, 1989c). This also is the first priority of Finance Minister Valentin S. Pavlov (Pavlov, 1989) and of Prime Minister Nikolay I. Ryzhkov (Ryzhkov, 1989a). Indeed the five-year plan for 1991–1995 and the annual plan for 1990, presented by Ryzhkov (1989b) last December, mark a substantial retreat from measures to marketize the Soviet economy and reassert the need for central control to assure market equilibrium and increase in the supply of consumer goods.

A number of elements have contributed to the fiscal and monetary disarray. First, there is the legacy of the past, when fiscal and monetary questions played a minor role in the economic system and were almost completely subordinated to central physical planning. In the past, a monetary overhang, repressed inflation, and fiscal deficits could develop without disrupting the system. This is no longer the case under the proposed reforms. In addition to the need to clear up the accumulated problems of the past, the shift from central planning to a more market-oriented economy using monetary instruments requires new systems of budgeting, banking, credit, and fiscal and monetary management. The Soviet Union has almost no experience with such systems, and even less knowledge of how to introduce them as part of a successful reform effort. There also are problems of transition, in which elements of the "old regime" and the new system interact—not always beneficially. There are questions of sequencing, and there is a learning process in which mistakes are made. As a result of this trial-and-error process, the fiscal and monetary situation during the early stages of the reforms may not only deteriorate further, but the economy may become much more dependent on the ordinary functioning of the monetary sector. Finally, a number of exogenous shocks occurred which have fanned the flames of the present crisis.

This paper analyzes the present Soviet fiscal and monetary situation in light of the historic and systemic factors above. After a short description of the main fiscal and monetary characteristics of the old system, the paper surveys the fiscal developments of the Soviet economy before and during the reforms through an analysis of the state budget. There follows a short discussion of additional sources of destabilization stemming from the first steps of the re-

---

3. GDP growth was 1.5 percent in 1988 and probably even less in 1989 (*PlanEcon Report*, November 26, 1989).

forms. The paper concludes with a presentation of several policy options for the period of transition to a more radical economic reform.

A precautionary note on data quality and availability is warranted. With the advance of *glastnost'*, more and more information is being revealed on the structure of the Soviet state budget and the true meaning of various entries. In 1989 the Soviet leadership revealed for the first time a breakdown of the defense budget and its location within the budget, as well as budget revenues and expenditures connected with the external trade aid and debt of the Soviet Union (Gorbachev, 1989; Ryzhkov, 1989a; Yureyev, 1989; Pavlov, 1989). In addition, the government supplied more information on the size of the deficit and the ways in which it had been financed.[4] Table 1 presents a detailed breakdown of the planned Soviet state budgets for 1989 and 1990 and some estimates for the actual budget results for 1989 made by Zoteyev (1989). Since most of the new information does not go back into the past, the rest of the tables in the paper use the old structure but incorporate some new information for 1985–1988 from the above sources, especially Yureyev (1989) and Zoteyev (1989).[5] Note that the present official Soviet defense figures are still considerably below Western estimates (more on this below). The other side of *glasnost'* and the reforms, indeed also of the monetary crisis, is that the quality of the information most likely has deteriorated. Specifically, the unknown rate of inflation obscures the distinction between nominal and real changes, and the relaxation of central control reduced the quality and reliability of reporting. These are added to many uncertainties regarding data for the pre-reform period.

To this day there are no data on the amount of money in the economy or on changes in that amount. Part of the explanation for this scarcity of information is the traditional secretiveness of the Soviet Union, extending far beyond defense matters; part comes from a set of concepts and methodologies different from those commonly used in the West; but part, as is now frequently admitted by Soviet specialists, stems from a lack of relevant information available to the Soviets themselves.

Soviet official data often differ in meaning from comparable series in most Western countries. Prices are determined centrally on the basis of average costing and a different set of cost elements. Having been held constant for long periods, prices gradually deviate more and more from their original cost base. In addition, consumer prices include widely variant tax and subsidy rates. Of special relevance to the present discussion is the fact that profit norms are factored into prices according to a mix of charges to capital and cost, and therefore lose some of their true economic meaning. Accordingly the pricing (and other) authorities possess the power, which they periodically use, to determine the cost, tax, and profit elements of wholesale and retail prices almost at will. This not only distorts the meaning of prices, but also can create arbitrary changes in the budget.

4. In addition to the above, see also Gostev (1988, 1989a) and Zoteyev (1989).
5. See also notes and appendix in Table 1.

Table 1. *Soviet State Budget Plans, 1989 and 1990 Reconstructed*[a]

	1989			1990		
	Billions of rubles	*Percent of total revenues*	*Percent of GDP*	*Billions of rubles*	*Percent of total revenues*	*Percent of GDP*
Revenues						
1. Total	400.2	100.0	43.0	428.2	100.0	42.8
2. Taxes on profits	113.5	28.4	12.2	122.6	28.6	12.3
3. Turnover taxes	113.1	28.3	12.2	121.9	28.5	12.2
4. Alcohol	40.7	11.0	4.4	40.7	9.5	4.1
5. Foreign trade taxes	60.6	15.1	6.5	58.0	13.5	5.8
6. Taxes on individuals	41.7	10.4	4.5	43.5	10.2	4.4
7. Social insurance taxes	33.8	8.4	3.6	40.3	9.4	4.0
8. Taxes on coops and state enterprises	3.0	0.8	0.3	4.0	0.9	0.4
9. Other taxes and revenues	37.5	9.4	4.0	37.9	8.9	3.8
Expenditures		*Percent of expenditures*			*Percent of expenditures*	
10. Total	491.0	100.0	52.8	488.2	100.0	48.8
11. Investment	75.0	15.3	8.1	53.1	10.9	5.3
12. Total ordinary	416.0	84.7	44.7	435.1	89.1	43.5
13. National economy (ordinary)[b]	35.8	7.3	3.8	42.5	8.7	4.3
14. Covering losses[c]	11.0	2.2	1.2	n/a	n/a	n/a
15. Civilian space[d]	3.0	0.6	0.3	n/a	n/a	n/a
16. Other[e]	21.8	4.4	2.3	n/a	n/a	n/a
17. Consumer subsidies	103.0	21.0	11.1	120.0	24.6	12.0

18.	Food subsidies	87.8	17.9	9.4	95.7	19.6	9.6
19.	Public services and transfers	144.2	29.4	15.5	158.8	32.5	15.9
20.	Public services	66.2	13.5	7.1	75.6	15.5	7.6
21.	Transfer payments	78.0	15.9	8.4	93.0	19.0	9.3
22.	Civilian science	7.5	1.5	0.8	11.0	2.3	1.1
22a.	International security	8.6	1.8	0.9	8.8	1.8	0.9
23.	Defense[f]	81.2	16.5	8.7	74.9	15.3	7.5
24.	Operations	20.2	4.1	2.2	19.0	3.9	1.9
25.	Procurement	32.6	6.6	3.5	31.0	6.3	3.1
26.	Construction	4.6	0.9	0.5	3.7	0.8	0.4
27.	Military R&D	15.3	3.1	1.6	13.2	2.7	1.3
28.	Military space	3.9	0.8	0.4	[3.9]	0.8	0.4
29.	Military pensions	2.3	0.5	0.2	2.4	0.5	0.2
30.	Other military	2.3	0.5	0.2	1.3	0.2	0.1
31.	Public administration	2.8	0.6	0.3	2.9	0.6	0.3
32.	Foreign economic activity[e]	29.9	6.1	3.2	26.0	5.3	2.6
33.	Reserves and other	10.9	2.2	1.2	12.9	2.6	1.3
34.	Total deficit	90.8	18.5	9.8	60.0	12.3	6.0
35.	Ordinary deficit	15.8	3.2	1.7	6.9	1.4	0.7
36.	GDP	930.0	189.4	100.0	1,000.0	204.8	100.0

Source: Appendix Table, except as noted.

a. Totals may not add due to rounding.

b. "National economy" from Appendix Table *minus* investment and food subsidies.

c. Gostev, in FBIS, April 4, 1989, p. 109.

d. Ryzhkov, in FBIS, Supplement, June 8, 1989, p. 28.

e. Residual.

f. All the defense entries: for 1989—Ryzkhov, FBIS, Supplement, June 8, 1989; for 1990—Pavlov (1989) and *Argumenty i fakty*, No. 51, December 23–29, 1989, p. 4.

The present analysis nonetheless must rely mainly on Soviet official data in current, established prices. Current prices are essential for the discussion of fiscal and monetary matters, and the Soviets furnish no dependable price indices that could be used to convert budget and other data into constant prices. For these reasons, much of the discussion of fiscal (and even more so, of monetary) matters involves considerable uncertainty.

FISCAL AND MONETARY ASPECTS OF A CENTRALLY PLANNED SYSTEM[6]

Fiscal and monetary matters have only secondary significance in a centrally planned system that uses physical quantities as its main planning tool, utilizes output targets as its main success indicator and generator of incentives, and whose prices are fixed and seldom altered, while interest rates are very low and play an insignificant role. Fiscal tools and the budget are used for purposes of resource allocation, but this is done mainly through the actual transfer of resources rather than via monetary signals and levers. The economy is run by administrative fiat; the main functions of monetary aggregates and flows are in accounting and microeconomic control. The above description of the classical, or pre-reform, system applies somewhat better to the state production sector because money aggregates do play a certain macroeconomic balancing role in the household and collective farm sector.

The production sector is controlled not only by the physical plan, but also through a financial plan formulated by the State Bank (Gosbank), which formerly was practically the sole bank in the country.[7] Gosbank acts as a monobank; it manages the accounts of the enterprises and provides them with "credit" in accordance with the plans. The term credit appears in quotation marks since it is provided in the form of a series of designated, discrete accounts, and is earmarked for specific targets in accordance with the plan: each physical allocation of an input or a supply target to an enterprise is backed by a special bank account. Neither a specific plan's account nor the credits provided can be used for any other than the intended purpose, nor in most cases are any residual balances left in such accounts. All inter-enterprise transactions or transactions with the state are made by transferring balances across accounts, and under the classical system all profits and surpluses not predesignated for enterprise use are transferred to the government. The role of the bank is to make certain that accounts are not overdrawn, that they are used only for the designated purpose, and that no surplus balances remain in the hands of the enterprises. Consumer goods supplied outside the production sector are shipped to various trade organizations according to the same system. Cash is provided

---

6. This section is a concise summary based on Davies (1958), Garvy (1977), Wolf (1985), Bunich (1988), Harrison (1986), Holzman (1975), and Belkin, Medvedev, and Nit (1988).

7. The system also includes an investment bank, a foreign trade bank, and a system of savings banks, the latter fully subordinate to Gosbank.

to enterprises almost solely in order to pay salaries, and the wage bill account has been one of the accounts most closely guarded by the bank.

Disregarding the "informal" activities of enterprises, the production sector may be considered almost money-free—most of the "money" of production enterprises is not fungible. Balances accumulated in a "segregated" account cannot be thrown into the market at large to create a general state of excess demand. But when balances run short and production plans are stalled, credit usually will be provided. The resultant almost permanent prevalence of a seller's market in the production sector can thus be ascribed mainly to the physical plan rather than to monetary control.

The production sector is isolated almost completely from the household sector, as far as monetary transactions are concerned. There are no financial dealings between the two sectors for borrowing money or selling financial or real productive assets. Pressures within the production sector can be shifted to the household sector by failing to meet production targets of consumer goods, by moving production capacity from consumer to producer goods (a rather common practice), or by raising wages above planned levels in an attempt to compensate for shortfalls in other inputs or for unrealistically improved productivity norms (Wolf, 1985; Belkin et al., 1988).

Since wages are paid and consumer goods are purchased with money, the household sector must be kept in some sort of monetary balance in addition to the required physical balance between the volume of work supplied by households (at given fixed wage rates) and the volume of consumer goods produced (also at fixed prices). To the income side of the household sector one should also add pensions, social insurance, and other welfare payments made by the state. A major tool used to reconcile physical production plans and the cost structure with the household balance is the turnover tax.[8] The only legal "money" used in the household sector is cash, which, as noted earlier, is used in the production sector almost exclusively for paying wages. Households are allowed, encouraged, and sometimes even forced to save through the purchase of bonds or by the opening of savings accounts, but consumer access to credit is quite limited.[9]

Disequilibrium[10] in the household sector can emerge when (a) physical production plans for consumer goods are not fulfilled; (b) there are above-plan wage payments; or (c) households change their behavior with respect to work, savings, or money demand. In the absence of government response, such disequilibrium can be channeled into an increased volume of activity in the private farmers' market or in the "second economy," where both supplies and prices are flexible. Other responses could be a decline in the amount of work or of work effort or increased savings. While only the latter two potential

8. This is a form of sales tax, aimed mainly at (almost) balancing the consumer market.

9. Annual consumer credits in 1987 stood at less than 1 billion rubles, i.e., less than 0.25 percent of personal income (CIA, 1989a, p. 15).

10. This always means excess demand in the context of this paper.

effects can reduce the amount of money held by the public, the former absorbs excess money by raising the real volume of transactions (although part of the increase is transferred from the state sector) and by deflating the real value of money balances (and other financial assets). Sometimes, by necessity (in the shorter run), households may accumulate cash or savings balances. Since rates of interest on bonds and savings accounts are very low (2–3 percent), and since accounts are open to government scrutiny, many tend to keep their savings as ready cash. Hence the discussion of an accumulated monetary "overhang" of an unknown quantity threatening equilibrium (Birman, 1980, 1981; Shmelev, 1989a, 1989b; Abalkin, 1989a; and many others). Whenever prices cannot move toward equilibrium, the long lines for consumer goods become supplementary allocative agents.[11]

The collective-farm sector and the adjunct sector of private agriculture operate under a system of monetary transactions somewhere between the state and household sectors. Since food is a major item in short supply, and since prices in the private markets can adjust freely to market conditions, farmers are thought to be among the main holders of surplus rubles.

Under the classical system, all foreign trade is conducted by a state monopoly and the Foreign Trade Bank. All profits and losses arising from differences in prices between internal and foreign markets (calculated at the going official exchange rate) are transferred to the budget. In this way external shocks directly affect the fiscal situation and require a response.[12]

Since Gosbank operates as a department of the Ministry of Finance, the management of the macroeconomic financial apparatus and its steering toward a macroeconomic equilibrium level would not appear to be very difficult tasks. The dichotomy between the production and household sectors, the direct control over enterprises, the existence of only one form of money (cash), the absence of any financial leverages (such as a banking system, a credit market, or a capital market), and the full monopolization and control over external transactions all contribute to the simplification of monetary operations.[13] One problem which remains outside the purview of the monetary and fiscal authorities, however, is the inability to substitute monetary resources for absent real resources.

It is therefore not surprising that most of the sources and some of the tables in this paper indicate a high degree of Soviet budgetary (and presumably also credit) discipline during the entire postwar period (Davies, 1958; Harrison, 1986; Hutchings, 1983; Holzman, 1975; and many others). The main dissenting voice is that of Birman (1980, 1981). The last period of

11. While some lines are the result of the unfulfillment of plans, a certain degree of queuing is "planned" to cover uncertainty at the planning stage and to make sure that planning errors will converge on the excess demand side, thereby reducing waste due to non-purchased goods.

12. Details of the interaction between the outside world and internal monetary and fiscal systems are not addressed here. For a thorough discussion of this topic, see Wolf (1985, 1989).

13. In addition there is the basic fact that the actual planning and balancing of the economy is provided by the administrative planning authorities.

excessive money printing was during World War II, followed in 1947 by a monetary reform and a virtual confiscation of money holdings (Nove, 1972, pp. 308–309).

FISCAL DEVELOPMENTS: IS THE PRESENT CRISIS A LEGACY OF THE PAST?

Budget Deficits

The data in Tables 2–5 analyze the fiscal developments in the Soviet economy since 1971. It is necessary to go this far back in time to capture the fiscal behavior of the system before the energy crisis, when real growth rates still were respectable. The main purpose of this exercise is to investigate the sources of the present problems. Specifically, the paper attempts to discover the extent to which they reflect an accumulation of erroneous past policies and to what degree they represent the outcome of the present reform efforts.

In studying Soviet fiscal policies, the one clear advantage of the budget is that it always is all-inclusive, covering all levels of government. While some incomes and expenditures are under the jurisdiction of the republics and lesser administrative bodies, the Soviet fiscal system always has been highly centralized (Bahry, 1987). Only recently, in connection with the reforms, have there been tendencies toward more economic and political decentralization and local autonomy. One of the main traditional drawbacks of official budgetary data has been the use of the erroneous concept of the deficit (or surplus), where borrowing from a "statewide loan fund" of Gosbank (Gostev, 1988, p. 54) or even sheer money printing were considered legitimate sources of revenue. In this way, and without disclosing any such deficit financing, the finance ministry was able to show budget surpluses for every year until 1989. When V. S. Pavlov[14] first revealed the existence of such a "loan fund," the resources of the fund for the 1989 budget were to cover only part of the planned deficit; indeed, the extent of the deficit was not revealed.[15] Only in later pronouncements was it stated that most of the annual deficit was financed from the "loan fund" (see Yureyev, 1989; Pavlov, 1989; Zoteyev, 1989). Birman (1981) and others discovered this kind of Soviet practice some time ago.

Leaving aside the official Soviet definition of the deficit, basic macroeconomics allows three government deficit concepts to be defined, each with a different effect on the level of aggregate demand and on the money supply:[16]

14. Pavlov, the current Finance Minister, was on the slate of nominees to 70 Council of Ministers posts submitted by N. I. Ryzhkov to the USSR Supreme Soviet in July 1989 (see Hough, 1989a, p. 32). He replaced Boris Ivanovich Gostev. [Eds.]

15. The "loan fund" was supposed to cover a deficit of R 66.4 billion out of a deficit that was later revealed to be R 100 billion, and then R 120 billion. The rest of the financing was not disclosed at the time (Gostev, 1988).

16. See also Harrison (1986).

(a) The ordinary (sometimes current) deficit—the excess of government demand and expenditure for public consumption (Cg) over tax revenues (T). This deficit, or extent of government dissaving, seemingly measures the degree of crowding out of investment (and thereby growth) resulting from the use of national savings for public consumption. It should be noted, however, that in a centrally planned system, where the government finances (or determines) the level of investment directly, "crowding out" is not an appropriate concept; the only relevant question is how investment is financed.

(b) The fiscal deficit—or total government expenditures less tax revenues, $G - T$; where $G = Cg + Ig$, and $Ig =$ government investment. This deficit measures the net effect of the government on the aggregate demand for goods and services in the economy.

(c) The monetary deficit—the extent of monetary expansion caused by the government budget (DM), i.e., the extent to which the fiscal deficit is financed by loans from the central bank or by other money printing devices: $DM = G - T - DB$, where DB is net borrowing from the rest of the economy.

In addition to data problems, fitting these three deficit concepts to the Soviet economic environment raises a number of methodological and structural questions. Since the Soviet government owns all the enterprises in the state sector, to what extent does government budgetary behavior represent pure fiscal policy? To what extent, for example, does it also exhibit features of a large holding company that collects dividends above and beyond government taxes on profits, that makes investment decisions for its enterprises beyond the domain of "government," and that may be allowed to borrow for investment purposes like any other business (with the important difference that only the government can print money)? Ideally, one may attempt to separate out from the budget those government transactions that come under the heading of its role as a holding company, according to behavior patterns of such businesses in other countries. Under a centrally planned system, the government determines the level of investment and finances much of it from the budget. In this way the budget may include the bulk of all investments, and therefore the deficit will be very different from the amount of government savings. The revenues that are earmarked for investment purposes can be included, one way or the other, within the system of taxes. In this way the part of investment that is planned to be financed by the household sector can be taxed away or even netted out when wage rates are determined. With lower (or after-tax) wages, enterprise profits are higher, and they are transferred to the budget. Next, that part of investment that is scheduled to be financed from (undistributed) enterprise profits (the savings of the production sector) can be either taxed away to finance government investment or can be earmarked for specific projects without going through the budget. In both cases the model of the holding company mentioned above applies.

For these reasons, some of the taxes or other sources of government revenues cannot be considered as "ordinary" revenues in the market economy sense, but are part of the would-be savings of households or of enterprises, collected by the government "at the source" to finance its centralized investment plan. The "true" distribution of savings between the three sectors becomes obscure, as does the difference between the ordinary and the fiscal deficits. It is impossible to distinguish between "ordinary" taxes and "forced" savings.

In order to take account of this element (in addition to estimates of the ordinary and fiscal deficit, taking all government revenues as "ordinary") a deficit also has been calculated based on the assumption that all profit taxes in excess of 40 percent of all enterprise profits[17] are collected by the government in its capacity as owner.[18]

Finally, households have the freedom to save out of their disposable income, given any level of taxation. Since these savings cannot be invested productively by either households or enterprises, the government can plan on investing these resources, too. If it borrows the savings from the public, then there is no monetary expansion associated with such investment.

The various estimable figures for the historical development of the Soviet budget revenues, expenditures, and deficit levels are presented in Table 2. For the reasons just mentioned, and owing to other characteristics of socialist economies, the budget's size relative to GDP is substantially higher than in most market economies (Blejer and Szapary, 1989). By 1985 budget expenditures reached a figure almost half of GDP—the relative budget size had been growing over the entire period covered. What is interesting is that it has continued to grow under the reforms, reaching 53 percent of GDP by 1989 (line 15).[19] For 1990 planned expenditures are expected not to rise in current prices so that, given speculations about the rate of inflation and real growth, their share in GDP will drop for the first time. The likelihood of this actually happening is very small. Moreover, while the relative expenditures share in GDP has continued to rise, revenues, the GDP share of which also increased up to 1985, have been dropping in terms of GDP shares since then (line 17). Only the yet provisional figures for 1989 and the plan for 1990 indicate an attempt to halt the decline in revenues.

Until 1984 the simultaneous growth of expenditures and revenues kept the total (fiscal) deficit at between 2–3 percent of GDP (line 13), 4.5–7.5 percent

---

17. As in the U.S. Department of Commerce, *Survey of Current Business*, Vol. 68, July 1988, p. 43.

18. The "norm" of 40 percent appears also as a target for the future reduction of Soviet profit taxes (see Senchagov, 1989, p. 7). Vyacheslav K. Senchagov is the Chairman of the USSR State Committee on Prices.

19. Note that the data for 1989 (plan) and 1990 (plan) are planned magnitudes. Actual expenditures during 1988 were found to be higher than planned and only very drastic measures during 1989 prevented expenditures from rising beyond the *revised* 1989 planned budget. For further discussion of past and present deficits, see Kagalovskiy (1988); Hanson (1989); Gostev (1989a); *PlanEcon Report*, August 19 and November 4, 1988; February 17, April 28, September 1, and November 26, 1989; CIA (1988); Pavlov (1989); and Abalkin (1989a).

Table 2. *Soviet Budget Deficits and Their Financing, 1971–1990*

	1971–1975	1976–1980	1981–1985	1985	1986	1987	1988	1989 (Original plan)	1989 (Revised plan)	1990 (Plan)
		(Annual averages)								
	Billions of nominal rubles									
1. Ordinary revenues	172.6	245.8	336.3	354.5	354.1	362.6	376.9	371.0	400.2	428.2
2. Total expenditures	186.6	260.1	352.9	386.5	417.1	430.9	459.5	494.8	491.0	488.2
3. Investment	44.6	47.7	63.2	70.0	80.0	80.0	69.2	75.0	75.0	53.1
4. Ordinary expenditure	142.0	212.4	289.7	316.5	337.1	350.9	390.3	419.8	416.0	435.1
5. Total (fiscal) deficit[a]	14.0	14.3	16.7	32.0	63.0	68.3	82.6	123.8	90.8	60.0
6. Ordinary deficit[b]	−30.6	−33.4	−46.6	−38.0	−17.0	−11.7	13.4	48.8	15.8	6.9
6a. Ordinary deficit (adjusted)	−7.8	2.0	0.6	14.5	36.4	35.8	45.0	74.0	40.8	26.2
Financing the deficit:										
7. Bond sales to public	0.4	0.6	1.0	1.4	1.9	1.9	2.0	3.0	3.0	3.0
8. "Loan fund" and other sources (5–7)	13.6	13.6	15.7	30.6	61.1	66.4	80.6	120.8	87.8	57.0
9. Soviet reported deficit[c]	−3.1	−5.9	−6.8	−4.1	−2.4	−4.6	n/a	n/a	n/a	n/a
10. GDP	433.7	559.0	712.8	778.3	799.6	825.0	875.0	930.0	930.0	1,000.0
	Percent of total expenditures									
11. Total (fiscal) deficit	7.5	5.5	4.7	8.3	15.1	15.8	18.0	25.0	18.5	12.3
12. Ordinary deficit	−16.4	−12.8	−13.2	−9.8	−4.1	−2.7	2.9	9.9	3.2	1.4
12a. Ordinary deficit (adjusted)	−4.2	0.8	0.2	3.7	8.7	8.3	9.8	15.0	8.3	5.4
	Percent of GDP									
13. Total (fiscal) deficit	3.2	2.6	2.3	4.1	7.9	8.3	9.4	13.3	9.8	6.0
14. Ordinary deficit	−7.1	−6.0	−6.5	−4.9	−2.1	−1.4	1.5	5.2	1.7	0.7
14a. Ordinary deficit (adjusted)	−1.8	0.4	0.1	1.9	4.6	4.3	5.1	8.0	4.4	2.6
15. Total expenditures	43.0	46.5	49.5	49.7	52.2	52.2	52.5	53.2	52.8	48.8
16. Ordinary expenditures	32.7	38.0	40.7	40.7	42.2	42.5	44.6	45.1	44.7	43.5
17. Ordinary revenues	39.8	44.0	47.2	45.5	44.3	43.9	43.1	39.9	43.0	42.8

Source: Appendix Table.

a. Total (Table) deficit in Appendix Table, line 7.

b. Negative saving.

c. As in official Soviet sources (see sources to Appendix Table). For years since 1985 the true level of deficit (as in line 5) is being reported.

of expenditures (line 11). By 1989 it grew to 18.5 percent of expenditures and to almost 10 percent of GDP. The originally proposed budget for 1989 could have brought the deficit up to 23.4 percent of expenditures or 12.5 percent of the GDP. At that time, the end of 1988, the Soviet leadership realized the severity of the situation and started to take measures to reduce the deficit. Accordingly, the 1989 budget may result in a smaller fiscal deficit of "only" R 90.8 billion (Zoteyev, 1989). In addition (as seen from the table), the proposed 1990 budget plans further measures to reduce the deficit to R 60 billion, but execution is not going to be easy. Finally, it should be observed (Appendix Table 1, line 7) that since 1988 there is a sharp jump in residual, unknown sources of revenues; they reach 7–9 percent of all revenues and around 3 percent of GDP. If these revenues are of a temporary nature, or disguised borrowing, then the structural deficit is larger by these amounts or at least by part of them.

It is clear from the above figures that, at least technically, the fiscal deficit is a recent phenomenon—it was created or at least coincided with the reforms. Furthermore, unlike the case of China, the Soviet deficit has widened up to the present with an expanding—not a contracting—budget, having in and of itself a negative impact on the reforms (Blejer and Szapary, 1989).

The pre-reform deficit picture looks even better when it is observed that in none of these years did the government incur negative savings; rather, it sustained a positive savings rate of 5–7 percent of GDP. The ordinary budget surplus (negative deficit, line 6, and in relative terms lines 12 and 14), consistently financed about two-thirds of the government's direct spending on investment. Even when the ordinary deficit is adjusted by taking away from revenues "excess profit taxes" as explained above, there are no ordinary deficits during the pre-reform periods (lines 6a, 12a, 14a). Even with some taxes taken away, the government did not resort to deficit financing of public consumption expenditures.

During the reform years, however, the ordinary budget surplus has declined quite rapidly and turned into a deficit; the government is currently using not only truly ordinary incomes but also part of the excess collection of profits to finance ordinary expenditures. As seen from Table 2 (lines 6, 12, 14), the ordinary deficit for 1989 could have been rather large, but it may actually be substantially smaller. An adjusted ordinary deficit of 4–5 percent of GDP (as in 1988 and 1989, line 14a) is nonetheless still quite large. If some of the undisclosed revenue items (Appendix Table 1, line 7) mentioned above would fit within the definition of the ordinary deficit, then they also should be added to the ordinary deficit figures.

As to the monetary budget deficit, throughout the period only a very small fraction of the fiscal deficit was covered by bonds sold to the public (Table 2, line 7). Most of the financing came from the "loan fund" (Table 2, line 8), calculated here as residual: the difference between ordinary revenues and the official revenue figures. The loan fund (a loan from Gosbank USSR) should technically be considered printing money, but part of it was financed through increasing savings accounts and cash holdings of the population. To the extent that these accounts and cash holdings can be considered non-money, they offset the growth of the money supply. As in the case of the fiscal deficit, here too the budgetary additions to the money supply were relatively small during the pre-reform period, but have been growing very rapidly in recent years (see below).

In assessing the inflationary impact of both the fiscal and the monetary budget deficits, two further qualifications are warranted. First, it is important to know into which part of the economy the excess fiscal demand and the extra "money" created by the monetary deficit is directed: the "monetized" household sector (where it may directly contribute to the inflationary pressure and the monetary overhang) or the business sector (where, until 1985, and to a somewhat lesser extent subsequently, it could still add to unusable enterprise surplus balances). While in any case it is difficult to estimate the distribution of the deficit between the sectors, the initial steps of the reform further blurred the dividing line between them and allowed more spill-overs, mostly from the production into the household sector.

Second, both the fiscal and the monetary deficits are partly offset by the public's accumulations in savings accounts (Table 3, line 8) and in cash holdings. Since these savings accounts are deposited in the same "monobank" system run by the central bank, these savings also could be considered a loan from the banking system drawn against such savings of the public at large. In this case negative government savings are offset by positive household savings, and the monetary expansion equals only the excess of loans over the increase in savings deposits.

The problem is, however, that in the absence of long-term financial savings instruments, both the savings balances and the accumulation of savings as cash (resulting from the unattractiveness of the savings accounts) are high liquid, and therefore increase the volatility of the monetary system as compared with a situation in which long-term savings instruments and real assets are available. What in a "normal" economy would consist of an act of money absorption by the government is not exactly so under the unique Soviet conditions. However, the absence of such instruments does not necessarily eliminate the need and willingness of the public to save.[20] This consideration is more important for the pre-reform period than for recent years, when incremental savings in all forms have been smaller relative to the deficit and when there is much greater doubt as to the voluntary nature of at least some of the additional savings.

In summary, until 1985 formal budget deficits and their inflationary impact tended to be small, given their distribution into the economy, the means of financing, the size of compensating savings, and the restriction of expansion

20. These issues will be addressed in a subsequent section of the paper.

due to unusable balances in the production sector. Only during the first years of the economic reforms did all budget deficits grow to dangerous levels. The inflationary impact of these deficits is even larger, owing to the way in which they were financed and to a partial relaxation of rules restricting the use of money balances by enterprises as part of the reforms.

The Development of Expenditures and Revenues

The development of the large deficits during the reform years is arithmetically the net result of several adverse developments on both the revenue and expenditure sides of the budget. The main structural changes in the budget over the period are analyzed below.[21] Attention will be focused on the effects of these changes on the size of the budget, the size of the deficit, and the mutual relationships between these changes and the reforms. The relevant data are presented in Table 4 (revenues) and Table 5 (expenditures).

Expenditure on Investment and Its Financing by Taxing Profits. A major aspect of the reform involves a retreat by the government, and hence the budget, from direct intervention in the economy. The most significant retreat is the decentralization of investment decisions away from the budget to a newly created and more independent banking system and to the enterprises themselves. The quid pro quo is the release, from the budget, of an increasing proportion of the profit taxes to be used as the main source for financing investment by enterprises.

Table 3 presents supplementary data on the patterns of investment and its financing before and during the first years of the reforms. Only at the beginning of 1988 was the new "USSR Law on State Enterprise," which contains many of the provisions for decentralization, put into operation for part of the economy (USSR Law, 1987); only since the beginning of 1989 has it applied to the entire economy.

The most striking finding from Table 3 is that all along only between one-third and two-fifths of all investment had been financed through the state budget (line 12). This, however, grossly understates the degree of control that the central authorities exercise over investment. First, of the 90 percent or so of total investment concentrated in the state sector,[22] some 90 percent was "centralized" (Tretyakova, 1986). Centralized investment was determined by the plan irrespective of the source of finance. The depreciation funds accumulated by the enterprises were for the most part collected by the relevant ministries and redirected to other enterprises according to the plan for centralized investment. In effect, this is a system of large-scale extra-budgetary discretionary taxation, which should belong to the budget (Tretyakova, 1986; Bunich, 1988, pp. 84–86). Even a considerable proportion of the funds earmarked for in-

---

21. The revenue and expenditure sides are studied not only separately, but also on a net basis, where there is a mutual economic or functional relationship corresponding to specific revenue and expenditure categories.
22. The rest is private investment in housing and investment by collective farms.

Table 3. *Investment in Fixed Capital and Financing Elements, 1971–1990*

	1971–1975	1976–1980	1981–1985	1985	1986	1987	1988	1989 (Original plan)	1990 (Plan)
		(Annual averages)							
		Billions of nominal rubles							
1. Total gross investment in fixed capital[a]	112.6	143.5	168.6	179.5	194.4	205.4	215.3	219.6	199.0
2. State investment[a]	100.1	128.9	152.2	161.6	176.1	186.9	191.4	185.5	178.9
2a. State centralized investment	63.7	121.6	139.1	153.0	166.7	149.7	116.8	99.5	83.5
3. Investment financed from the budget[b]	44.6	47.7	63.3	70.0	80.0	80.0	69.2	75.0	53.1
4. Enterprise profits[c]	97.7	112.2	150.2	167.6	190.9	199.8	220.0	240.5	258.3
5. Profit taxes[d]	61.9	80.3	107.3	119.5	129.8	127.4	119.6	121.2	122.6
6. Above normal profit taxes[e]	22.8	35.4	47.2	52.5	53.4	47.5	31.6	25.2	19.3
7. Depreciation[f]	39.8	63.3	90.4	103.2	110.0	118.1	129.6	136.0	155.0
8. Private savings accounts[g]	8.9	12.1	12.9	18.7	22.0	23.9	29.8	30.3	n/a
		Percent							
9. Profit taxes as percent of profits	63.3	71.5	71.4	71.3	68.0	63.8	54.4	50.4	47.5
10. Profit taxes as percent of investment from the budget	138.8	168.3	169.5	170.7	162.3	159.3	172.8	161.6	230.9
		Percent of total investment							
11. State investment	88.9	89.8	90.2	90.0	90.6	91.0	88.9	84.5	89.9
11a. State centralized investment	n/a	n/a	n/a	n/a	85.8	72.9	54.2	45.3	42.0
12. Investment financed from the budget	39.6	33.2	37.5	39.0	41.2	38.9	32.1	34.2	26.7

13. Enterprise profits	86.8	78.2	89.1	93.4	98.2	97.3	102.2	109.5	129.8
14. Profit taxes	55.0	55.9	63.6	66.6	66.8	62.0	55.6	55.2	61.6
15. Above-normal profit taxes	20.3	24.7	28.0	29.2	27.5	23.1	14.7	11.5	9.7
16. Depreciation	35.4	44.1	53.6	57.5	56.6	57.5	60.2	61.9	77.9
17. Private savings accounts	7.9	9.1	7.6	10.4	11.3	11.6	13.8	13.8	n/a
Percent of GDP									
18. Total gross investment	26.0	25.7	23.7	23.1	24.3	24.9	24.6	23.6	19.9
19. State investment	23.1	23.1	21.3	20.8	22.0	22.7	21.9	19.9	17.9
19a. State centralized investment	n/a	n/a	n/a	n/a	20.8	18.1	13.3	10.7	8.4
20. Investment financed from the budget	10.3	8.5	8.9	9.0	10.0	9.7	7.9	8.1	5.3
21. Enterprise profits	22.5	20.1	21.1	21.5	23.9	24.2	25.1	25.9	25.8
22. Profit taxes	14.3	14.4	15.1	15.4	16.2	15.4	12.9	13.0	12.3
23. Above-normal profit taxes	5.3	6.3	6.6	6.7	6.7	5.8	3.6	2.7	1.9
24. Depreciation	9.2	11.3	12.7	13.3	13.8	14.3	14.8	14.6	15.5
25. Private savings accounts	2.0	2.3	1.8	2.4	2.8	2.9	3.4	3.3	n/a

a. 1971–1987: *Narkhoz*, various years—"kapital'noye vlozheniye." 1988 (gross): *PlanEcon Report* estimate, February 17, 1989, p. 14. Note that *PlanEcon Report*'s measure of gross investment is not exactly comparable with *Narkhoz* figures and tends to run several rubles above *Narkhoz* numbers. 1988 (state): estimate. 1989, 1990: Pavlov (1989).

b. 1975, 1977, 1981: Tretyakova (1986). 1982: Gostev (1988, p. 58). Other years are extrapolated from Tretyakova (1986) and Gostev (1988).

c. *Narkhoz*, various years—"pribyl' predpriyatiy i khozyaystvennykh organizatsiy." 1989, 1990: Pavlov (1989).

d. Appendix Table.

e. Calculated as taxes on profits in excess of 40 percent of enterprise profits (see text).

f. 1971–1987: *Narkhoz*, various years—"amortizatsionnyye otchisleniya predpriatiy i khozyaystvennykh organizatsiy po otraslyam narodnogo khozyaystva." 1988: *PlanEcon Report* estimate, February 17, 1989, p. 14. 1989, 1990: estimates.

g. 1971–1987: CIA (1989a, Table A-4). 1988 and 1989: *PlanEcon Report*, November 24, 1989, pp. 4–6.

Table 4. *Structure of Revenues of the Soviet State Budget, 1971–1990*

	1971–1975	1976–1980 (Annual averages)	1981–1985	1985	1986	1987	1988	1989 (Original plan)	1989 (Revised plan)	1990 (Plan)
	Billions of nominal rubles									
1. Total ordinary revenues	172.6	245.8	336.3	354.5	354.1	362.6	376.9	371.0	400.2	428.2
	Percent of total revenues									
2. Total ordinary revenues	100.0	100.0	100.0	100.0	100.0	100.0	100.0	100.0	100.0	100.0
3. Taxes on profits	35.9	32.7	31.9	33.7	36.7	35.1	31.7	32.7	28.4	38.6
4. Income taxed on coops and state enterprises	0.8	0.7	0.7	0.7	0.7	0.8	0.7	0.8	n/a	0.9
5. Turnover taxes	34.7	33.5	30.0	27.6	25.8	26.0	26.8	28.2	28.3	28.5
6. Alcohol	n/a	n/a	12.2	11.3	9.0	9.0	9.8	11.0	n/a	9.5
7. Income from foreign trade	10.2	15.8	20.2	20.1	18.2	19.1	16.6	16.3	15.1	13.5
8. Taxes on individuals	9.2	9.0	8.2	8.5	8.8	9.0	9.5	9.8	10.4	10.2
9. Social insurance taxes	5.8	5.4	6.6	7.2	7.5	7.7	8.0	8.5	8.4	9.4
10. Other revenues	3.4	3.0	2.4	2.3	2.3	2.2	6.6	3.7	9.4	8.9
	Percent of total expenditures									
11. Total ordinary revenues	92.5	94.5	95.3	91.7	84.9	84.1	82.0	75.0	81.5	87.7
12. Taxes on profits	33.2	30.9	30.4	30.9	31.1	29.6	26.0	24.5	23.1	25.1
13. Income taxes on coops and state enterprises	0.8	0.6	0.6	0.6	0.6	0.6	0.6	0.6	n/a	0.8
14. Turnover taxes	32.1	31.7	28.6	25.3	21.9	21.9	22.0	21.2	23.0	25.0

15. Alcohol	n/a	n/a	11.7	10.3	7.6	7.5	8.1	8.2	n/a	8.3
16. Income from foreign trade	9.4	15.0	19.3	18.4	15.4	16.1	13.6	12.2	12.3	11.9
17. Taxes on individuals	8.6	8.5	7.8	7.8	7.5	7.5	7.8	7.3	8.5	8.9
18. Social insurance taxes	5.3	5.1	6.2	6.6	6.4	6.5	6.6	6.3	6.9	8.3
19. Other revenues	3.2	2.9	2.3	2.1	1.9	1.9	5.4	2.8	7.6	7.8
20. Net taxes on goods and services[a]	32.2	37.3	35.2	29.2	23.5	22.9	21.2	15.7	17.5	17.2
21. Net taxation[b]	67.5	70.2	67.7	62.1	55.8	53.8	58.1	42.8	47.8	51.1
22. Net taxation (adjusted)[b]	55.2	56.7	54.4	48.6	43.0	42.7	45.3	37.8	42.6	45.1
23. Total ordinary revenues	39.8	44.0	47.2	45.5	44.3	44.0	43.1	39.9	43.0	42.8
Percent of GDP										
24. Taxes on profits and income taxes on coops and state enterprises	14.6	14.7	15.4	15.7	16.6	15.8	14.0	13.4	12.2	12.7
25. Turnover taxes	13.8	14.7	14.2	12.6	11.4	11.4	11.5	11.3	12.2	12.2
26. Income from foreign trade	4.0	7.0	9.6	9.1	8.1	8.4	7.2	6.5	6.5	5.8
27. Taxes on individuals	3.7	3.9	3.9	3.9	3.9	3.9	4.1	3.9	4.5	4.4
28. Social insurance taxes	2.3	2.4	3.1	3.3	3.3	3.4	3.4	3.4	3.6	4.0
29. Net taxes on good and services[a]	13.9	17.4	17.4	14.5	12.2	12.0	11.2	8.3	9.2	8.4
30. Net taxation[b]	29.1	32.7	33.5	30.8	29.1	28.1	27.4	22.7	25.2	24.9
31. Net taxation (adjusted)[b]	23.8	26.4	26.9	24.1	22.4	22.3	23.8	20.1	22.5	23.0

Source: Appendix Table.

a. Turnover taxes (Appendix Table, line 1) *plus* foreign trade revenues (line 9) *minus* food subsidies (line 19). Other subsidies (on housing and other goods and services) amount to an additional 2–3 percent of GDP and 4–6 percent of budget expenditures, thereby reducing all estimates of net revenues by the corresponding magnitudes.

b. Ordinary budget revenues (Appendix Table, line 13) *minus* food subsidies (line 19) *minus* transfer payments (line 22). Net taxation (adjusted) is net taxation minus above-normal profit taxes. See discussion on additional subsidies in note *a* above.

Table 5. *Structure of Expenditures of the Soviet State Budget, 1971–1990*

	1971–1975	1976–1980 (Annual averages)	1981–1985	1985	1986	1987	1988	1989 (Original plan)	1989 (Revised plan)	1990 (Plan)
1. Total expenditures	186.7	260.1	353.0	386.5	417.1	430.9	459.5	494.8	491.0	488.2
Billions of rubles										
Percent of total expenditures										
2. Total expenditures	100.0	100.0	100.0	100.0	100.0	100.0	100.0	100.0	100.0	100.0
3. Investment	23.9	18.3	17.9	18.1	19.2	18.6	15.1	15.2	15.3	10.9
4. National economy[a]	16.6	26.1	26.3	24.2	24.2	23.4	21.4	21.4	21.4	21.4
5. Food subsidies	9.3	9.3	12.6	14.5	13.9	15.1	14.4	17.7	17.9	19.6
6. Public services and welfare[b]	32.2	30.8	29.0	29.0	28.6	28.9	29.1	29.0	29.4	32.5
7. Public services	16.5	15.9	14.0	13.9	13.5	13.6	n/a	14.5	n/a	15.5
8. Transfer payments	15.7	15.0	14.9	15.1	15.2	15.3	n/a	14.5	n/a	17.0
9. Science	4.1	3.4	3.5	3.5	3.5	3.6	n/a	1.5	n/a	2.3
10. "Other" defense and public administration	10.6	7.6	5.8	5.7	5.3	5.3	4.7	4.7	n/a	4.7
11. Foreign economic activity and other expenditures	3.2	4.3	5.1	3.9	4.3	5.7	5.7	6.3	6.1	5.3
Percent of GDP										
12. Total expenditures	43.0	46.5	49.5	49.7	52.2	52.2	52.5	53.2	52.8	48.8
13. Investment	10.3	8.5	8.9	9.0	10.0	9.7	7.9	8.1	8.1	5.3
14. National economy[a]	7.2	12.2	12.9	12.0	12.6	12.2	11.6	11.6	11.6	11.6
15. Food subsidies	4.0	4.3	6.3	7.2	7.3	7.9	7.5	9.4	9.4	9.6
16. Public services and welfare[b]	13.9	14.3	14.3	14.4	14.9	15.1	15.3	15.4	15.5	15.9
17. Public services	7.1	7.4	6.9	6.9	7.0	7.1	n/a	7.7	7.1	7.6
18. Transfer payments	6.8	7.0	7.4	7.5	7.9	8.0	n/a	7.7	8.4	8.3
19. Science	1.7	1.6	1.7	1.7	1.8	1.9	n/a	0.8	n/a	1.1
20. "Other" defense and public administration	4.5	3.5	2.9	2.9	2.8	2.8	2.5	2.5	n/a	2.5
21. Foreign economic activity and other expenditures	1.4	2.0	2.5	1.9	2.3	3.0	3.0	3.4	3.2	2.6

Source: Appendix Table.
a. Does not include investment or food subsidies. Includes enterprise losses, payments to enterprises, civilian space, various military, and other expenditures.
b. Does not include science.

vestment by enterprises out of depreciation and retained profits had traditionally been part of centralized investment. Finally, some centralized investment has always been authorized through bank credits, and it is not always clear either whether this investment is included in the budget entry for investment or how it is financed.[23] Before the reforms, such credits financed about 5 percent of total investment. Under the reforms, both of these extra-budgetary practices are to be gradually discontinued and replaced on a voluntary basis by the banking system and the enterprises themselves. In addition to changes in the structure of investments in the state sector, the proportion of investments in the cooperative and private sectors will rise.

According to data presented in Table 3, the proportion of non-state investments, 10 percent or less until very recently, was scheduled to grow to 15 percent of the total in 1989 (line 11), but this tendency is apparently being halted, at least for now (see the 1990 budget). Within the state sector centralized investment started to decline in absolute terms since 1987, and according to the plan for 1990 it will fall to about half the 1986 level (line 2a). In relative terms, centralized investment has been declining, from the bulk of the state investment up to 1986, down to less than one-half of total investment in fixed capital, even below one-half of investments in the state sectors (line 11a).

Turning to that part of investment included in the budget, the investment burden on the expenditure side of the budget declined from 24 percent in 1971–1975 to 18.6 percent in 1987 (Table 5, line 3). This was more the outcome of a rise in the relative volume of the budget to GDP (Table 5, line 12) than of a drop in investment's share in GDP (which hardly declined at all) (see Table 5, line 2). The relative budgetary burden of financing investment was nearly as high in 1987 as in the early 1970s. But since 1985 and 1986, when it reached a very high level of 40 percent, it has been declining, and according to the plan for 1990 it is scheduled to decline further to about one-quarter of the total (Table 3, line 12). Budget-financed investment as a percentage of GDP also appears to have declined during this period (Table 5, line 20).[24] Since traditional investment plans in the Soviet Union had been over- rather than underfulfilled, it remains to be seen how the present plans are going to be kept.

The decentralization and destatization of more investment decisions to the enterprises and to the new branch banks created under the banking reform have reduced the expenditure burden and deficit potential of the budget. However, the behavior of enterprises and the banks with the released funds may be creating even stronger inflationary pressures.

The economic reform, in addition to containing provisions designed to redistribute the responsibility for the financing of investments, also aims to reduce

23. According to Tretyakova (1986), centralized investment finance through bank credits is not included in the investment budget entry.

24. See notes and sources to Table 3. On plans to reduce centralized investments of all kinds, see Gostev (1989a), Ryzhkov (1989a, 1989b), Selyunin (1989), and Pavlov (1989).

the share of investment in GDP. This planned change in resource allocation, in addition to easing the general pressure on resources, can support and facilitate the decentralization trend. The traditionally high rate of investment concentrated in construction and other, less technology-intensive projects has contributed to a sharp decline in capital productivity, a constantly increasing stockpile of unfinished projects, and the crowding out of consumption. Upon assuming power in 1985, the new leadership quickly discovered that no renewed economic growth would be possible without accelerating the rate of investment in certain key areas, notably the machine-building industry, housing, etc. The result was internally inconsistent, rapid growth in investment during the early years of the current five-year plan 1986–1990, with the hope of eventually achieving a long-term reduction in the rate of investment. Without attempting to pass judgment on the merits of this decision, it should be noted that the new leadership undoubtedly faced a difficult dilemma caused by the long period of faulty investment policies. The backlogs and neglect that developed in many central spheres make the problem of reducing the share of investment in the central budget an even more difficult task (Hewett, Roberts, and Vanous, 1987; *PlanEcon Report*, February 17, 1989, pp. 20–23; November 24, pp. 3–5; Ofer, 1987, pp. 1824–1825; Maslyukov, 1989; Ryzhkov, 1989).

Relieving the budget from part of the responsibility for investment helps to reduce the size of the budget, but not necessarily the size of the deficit. This depends on the extent of the compensating decline in budgetary incomes from profit taxes. In China, for example, a similar reform resulted in an increase in the deficit because of a sharper drop in profit taxes than in investment expenditures (Blejer and Szapary, 1989).

Taxes on profits, together with turnover taxes, are the two major sources of revenue. Traditionally, profit taxes comprised about one-third of all budgetary revenues, but their share increased even further during the first years of the reform when other sources of income declined (Table 4, line 3). Their share was scheduled to grow to an all-time high according to plans for 1988, but in effect it subsequently declined to 32 percent in 1988 and to 28 percent in 1989, which is also their planned level for 1990 (line 3). It may be interesting to note that in both 1988 and 1989 the proposed budgets included significantly higher figures for profit taxes than the actual realized amounts (line 3). Given the development of the budget deficit, profit taxes had been covering about 30 percent of all expenditures, but with the more recent rise in the deficit their share declined to around one-quarter of all expenditures (line 12). Profit taxes have tended to increase as a percent of GDP, including during the early reform years (up to 16 percent in 1987) with a downturn since then which also is apparent in plans for 1990 (line 21).

The base for profit taxes, i.e., enterprise profits, had been growing over the period at higher rates than GDP (Table 3, line 21) and those of the state budget, increasing the enterprises' "ability to pay" into the budget. It is interesting that enterprise profits did not decline at the introduction of the reforms and are expected to continue to grow into the near future, both absolutely and relative to both the budget and GDP. This seems to contradict one of the main tenets of the reform, namely to impose a hard budget constraint on enterprises, as indeed happened in China (Blejer and Szapary, 1989). Quite clearly the reform did not yet start to bite. The continuation of a seller's market and the piecemeal nature of the reforms probably contributed to this result.

On top of an expanded tax base, the effective tax rate on profits also increased during the pre-reform period, peaking in 1985 at 71.3 percent of all profits.[25] The rate subsequently has declined quite sharply, and it is scheduled to fall below 50 percent in 1990 (Table 3, line 9).[26]

Over most of the period, budget investment "used" only about 60 percent of profit tax revenues (Table 3, line 10). Only lately has this proportion risen somewhat, though plans for 1990 are not only to sharply reduce investments from the budget, but to keep the amount of profit taxes unchanged (both in current prices). It seems that the government plans to continue to impose relatively high profit tax rates, while sharply reducing investment expenditures. Under this policy, profit taxes are considered mainly as a major source of revenue for all purposes, including that of narrowing the deficit.

While only a small part of enterprise profits have been released from the budgets back to the enterprises, the release by the ministries of control over the depreciation funds of the enterprises, at least, has proceeded more rapidly. Of the more than R 80 billion that would be transferred on an annual basis from centralized to non-centralized investment by 1990, compared with 1986, more than two-thirds seems to be coming from the depreciation funds (Table 3, lines 7, 2a). The extent to which enterprises have gained complete control over their depreciation deductions remains unclear (Bunich, 1988).

Table 3 (lines 3 and 6) also shows the extent of government financing of budgetary investment out of "above-normal" profit taxes. Since 1975 above-normal profit taxes have indeed been financing between two-thirds and three-quarters of total budgetary investment, but this proportion has tended to decline under the reforms, as above-normal profit taxes tend to decline at a faster rate than budget-financed investment. Since 1985 above-normal profit taxes declined by half (1989) or by two-thirds (plan for 1990). Investment financed from the budget declined over the same period, up to 1989, only marginally. However, it is planned to decline in 1990 by one-third. Thus the separation of profit taxes into two segments results in a more rapid decline in the relevant part of profit taxes than in investment expenditures, with at least a temporary "deficit" on this account being created during the transition period.

Indirect Taxes and Subsidies.[27] Second only to profit taxes as a source of budgetary revenues are turnover taxes, most of which are levied between

25. This does not include further "taxation" of the depreciation funds discussed above.
26. Offsetting some of the profit taxes are losses of enterprises which are covered by the budget. As of late these losses stood at R 10–11 billion (Gostev, 1989a). See, in addition to the sources for the Tables, also Organizatsiya (1989), Vid (1988), Maslyukov (1989), and Ryzhkov (1989a).
27. For a recent article on Soviet turnover taxes, see Senchagov (1989).

the factory and the wholesaler at different rates on different goods. In addition
to their fiscal function, these taxes are designed to adjust demand in specific
consumer markets (and in the consumer market as a whole) so that it matches
the planned supply of consumer goods. There is at least some degree of substitution between turnover taxes and profits and also between profits, turnover
taxes, and prices, at the discretion of both the planning and the pricing authorities. A second major indirect "tax" is the revenue derived by the government from foreign trade. These revenues consist of the price differentials,
calculated in rubles, between domestic and foreign trade prices at the highly
over-valued official exchange rate. Traditionally most of this revenue was
derived from imports, similar to customs duties in other countries, but since
the rise in energy prices in 1973, government profits on exports of oil and gas
also have become a sizable source of income. Foreign trade revenues are partly
offset by foreign trade subsidies paid by the state to support most other exports.[28]

Until 1985 there was a decline in the relative contribution of the turnover
tax to the budget, but a slight rise in the share of the turnover tax in GDP
(Table 4, lines 5 and 25). Incomes from foreign trade, however, rose very
rapidly over the same period, more than compensating for the decline of the
turnover tax in the budget and reinforcing its growing share in GDP. This rapid
growth in foreign trade revenues was the combined outcome of trade expansion
and a rise in energy prices. These two sources of revenue combined rose by
1981–1985 from less than half to more than half of all revenues, and from 17
to 23 percent of GDP (Table 4, lines 5, 7, 25, and 26).

Two exogenous forces damaged these revenue sources in the mid-1980s.
First, to inaugurate the reforms, Gorbachev introduced an antidrinking campaign, slashing state production of alcohol. Second, the sharp decline in energy
prices, starting already in the early 1980s, affected foreign trade revenues on
two counts: directly, through lower revenues from oil exports, and indirectly,
through a drop in import taxes stemming from the need to reduce imports,
especially of consumer goods. These tax losses, compared with the peak income
years, run at an annual level of about R 10 billion for each source (for the
turnover tax by 1986 and for foreign trade revenues by 1988 and beyond—
Appendix Table 1, lines 1, 9). As a result, the share of taxation of domestic
and foreign goods and services declined by 1988 from over half of all revenues
(1981–1985) to 43.4 percent, from nearly half of all expenditures to 35.5
percent, and from almost one-quarter of GDP to 18.7 percent (Table 4). The
1988 lower figures already represent an almost full restoration in the production
and taxation of alcohol, and an effort to raise turnover taxes on other goods,
efforts that are intended to intensify in the immediate future (see the plan for
1990 in Appendix Table 1). But even these lower figures are quite high (especially the share in GDP) compared with industrial countries, and even with
industrializing ones (Blejer and Szapary, 1989, Table 2). It may be difficult

---

28. Prices of trade between socialist countries are determined at average, estimated world price levels.
Soviet exports to these countries also need support.

to sustain them under any scheme of price reform and/or under even a partial opening of the economy.

While these two sources of lost revenue are definitely exogenous to the reforms, their coincidence is highly detrimental to them. One wonders how the fiscal authorities in the past tolerated the increased dependency on one undesirable and another temporary source of finance. In this respect, some of the blame for the present deficit can legitimately be shifted to past behavior, even though the budgets of the past were basically balanced.

The converse of taxes on goods and services are expenditures on subsidies. Most subsidies in the Soviet Union are for basic foods. They are employed mostly in order to keep consumer prices at a low and constant level, but at the same time they are meant to compensate farmers for production costs, thereby assuring supplies. Other subsidies are for rent, clothing for children and the elderly, and a few other items. As shown in Table 5, food subsidies (and probably all subsidies) have been the fastest-growing expenditure item in the Soviet budget. In absolute terms, food subsidies grew almost fivefold, from R 17.3 billion in 1971–1975 to R 87.9 billion (planned) in 1989.[29] Over the period, total subsidies increased from about 10 percent of total expenditures to over 20 percent, and from about 4 percent to 11 percent of GDP. This is a very high figure by any standard, and a truly formidable burden. The rise in subsidies was fairly monotonic, with a planned leap for 1989 and for 1990 in response to more rapidly rising costs and reflecting a renewed effort to motivate an improvement in food supplies.

When all positive and negative taxes on goods and services are combined, the net budget revenue from domestic taxation goes down over the period from nearly R 40 billion, or two-thirds of turnover tax revenues in the early 1970s, to probably negligible amounts by the late 1980s (Table 4, lines 20, 29; see note 1 to Table 4).[30] Given the limited potential of raising more sales tax revenues in the near future, especially under any kind of price reform, and the certain need to further raise the subsidy bill at an accelerated rate, the outlook for amelioration of the budget deficit from this segment is not very promising. Indeed, this segment of budget elements will threaten the stability of the system unless a radical change takes place.

In addition to the high fiscal burden of both taxes and subsidies on goods and services, these taxes and subsidies also introduce serious microeconomic distortions. The tax rates vary quite extremely among different goods and services, and the subsidies are concentrated heavily in grain, meat, and dairy products. Both contribute significantly to the highly distorted price structure. A price reform would probably include a change in tax rates to a more uniform scale across different groups of products and a sharp reduction in subsidies. But the price reform has been put off in view of the unstable monetary situation

29. Total subsidies grew from about R 20 billion to R 103 billion.

30. In other words, all these tax revenues are consumed by subsidies to other goods and services. This leaves only the presently declining revenues from foreign trade for other uses.

and for fear of the social consequences of raising retail prices (as experienced in many other countries). The question is whether continued postponement of the necessary steps will further aggravate the situation. The present leaders clearly have a justified grievance against the previous regime for not addressing the subsidy problem earlier. Should they wait any longer?

Taxes on Individuals. Taxes on individuals have always played a minor role in the fiscal history of the Soviet Union. Since wages are paid by the state, and since wage scales can take into account considerations of social justice, wages and salaries could be determined and paid net of imaginary taxes to begin with. Nonetheless, a single-rate income tax of 13 percent was established and imposed on all salaries, wages, and other incomes above a certain minimum. In addition, a small social security levy is collected from all employers as a percent of wages. To date, both taxes together have accounted for 14–16 percent of all revenues and 2–6 percent of GDP, a very low proportion by any comparison (Blejer and Szapary, 1989; Table 2). The legalization under the reforms of private and cooperative activity, the opening of wider wage gaps as an economic stimulant, and fiscal needs all have combined to bring about the institution of a more progressive income tax law. The law also covers non-state enterprises and may eventually (although not in the near future) provide more income (Tedstrom, 1989). There should be no problem in deducting such taxes from the wages of employees of state enterprises, but it will be a formidable problem to collect them from the private sector, with its lack of infrastructure or experience and its strong tendency to avoid payments. The absence of a tradition of direct taxation is clearly a serious fiscal handicap.

Social Services, Social Insurance, and Welfare.[31] Included in the budget under this category are expenditures on education and health services (public services), provided almost free of charge, and social insurance and welfare transfers, including most pension payments (transfers).[32] The share of social services in the budget declined slowly over the period under review and their share in GDP increased only minimally (Table 5, lines 6–8, 16–18). The same is true for each of the two main subdivisions (public services and transfer payments) which share the social budget almost equally. In contrast, in most other countries these categories exploded as a share of the budget. Also, the relative level of these services in the USSR is low by international standards (OECD, 1985, Table 1, p. 21). Only if expenditures on subsidies are added to the social budget is it possible to estimate the overall increase in social expenditures' share of the budget. At the same time, relative decline in social

---

31. A more detailed discussion of the welfare state aspects of the budget is included in Ofer (1989c). A survey of recent Soviet measures in the field is included in Chapman (1989).

32. We have removed from the Soviet entry on social services all expenditures on "science," three-quarters of which are devoted to the military (see Table 1 and notes there for details). In addition, note that some social and welfare services are provided by enterprises to their employees. In 1987, expenses in these fields outside the budget amounted to R 38 billion on top of R 140 billion included in the budget (*Narkhoz*, 1987, pp. 588, 591; see also Ofer, 1989c).

services and transfers is more than compensated by the sharp increase in subsidies.

The neglect in social areas—in education, health services, housing, and pensions and other welfare support—occurred in the past twenty years or so. With respect to social services, this neglect is the result of increasing resource constraints in the Soviet economy attributable to declining growth rates and to an increased defense burden. As for transfers, the neglect resulted from a secular decline in the real value of nominal payments and, in a more fundamental way, from the concentration of welfare in work-related (pensions and disability) payments and a relative neglect of the needs of large and single-parent families (Ofer and Vinokur, 1988). The neglect in social areas is now fully recognized in the Soviet Union, and steps are being taken to correct some of the most urgent needs (Feshbach, 1982; Kagalovskiy, 1988; Ryzhkov, 1989a; Gorbachev, 1989; Pavlov, 1989; Voronin, 1989). The financing of some of these measures through the budget already shows in the rising shares of social services in the budget results for 1988 and the revised plan for 1989. The rather ambitious plans for 1990 will bring this category of expenditures to almost one-third (Table 5, lines 6–8). Needless to say, it will aggravate the budget situation beyond its present state (Ryzhkov, 1989a; Pavlov, 1989). The minimum amount needed to make up for the long neglect is enormous, and it is quite clear that under present arrangements the budget will not be able to handle it. The need will be even larger if enterprises are relieved of the burden of providing services they shoulder at present. This is another major example of how a balanced budget was secured in the past by imposing a very high burden on the future. The "future" is now here.

Net Taxation. Two conventional criteria for evaluating the budgetary situation are the levels and the trends of "net taxation" (total taxes less transfer payments and subsidies). For the Soviet budget two measures of net taxation have been computed—one that includes all taxes and another that excludes what we previously termed "above-normal" profits. The figures for the more inclusive concept were 29 percent of GDP for 1971–1975; 33.5 percent for 1981–1985; and 25.2 percent of the revised 1989 planned budget. The corresponding figures for the second, more exclusive concept are 23.8, 26.9, and 14 percent, respectively (Table 4, lines 30, 31).[33] The combined loss of revenues and the rise in subsidies caused a severe decline in net taxation over the period, despite the only moderate increase in transfer payments. One way to describe the current Soviet fiscal problem is as a need to raise net taxation of the public without upsetting the delicate social balance.

Defense and Other Expenditures. Table 1 includes a rearrangement of the Soviet state budget in which elements of defense expenditures, which appear

33. As indicated in the notes to Table 4, the above figures should be lower by 2–3 GDP percentage points when all subsidies, rather than only food subsidies, are included in the calculations. See the guesstimates for the entire subsidy bill in Appendix Table 1, and calculations based on them in Table 6.

in the official budget under various non-defense headings, are grouped together. While the rearrangement is the author's, the figures are those recently disclosed by Soviet officials. Accordingly, the Soviet defense budget for 1989 is R 81.2 billion, or 16.4 percent of expenditures and 8.9 percent of GDP. The announced figure for 1990 is R 74.8 billion and 7.5 percent of GNP (Pavlov, 1989).[34] The author has added outlays on procurement and construction from the official entry of "expenditures on the national economy," R&D expenditures (which make up most of the official entry of "science"), and military pensions from the official entry on "social transfers" to the official defense entry in the budget of R 20.2 billion.

But even after the disclosure of these defense figures (and perhaps because of them) a number of questions are raised in relation to the extent of the true budget deficit. The main problem is that the CIA, which has been estimating the Soviet defense budget for many years, uses an alternative estimate for recent years: R 140–150 billion (CIA and DIA, 1989, p. 5). Another estimate, still much higher than the Soviet figure, is provided by Vanous (*PlanEcon Report*, 1989). This is not the place for a detailed comparison among the figures, but if the CIA estimate is reasonably correct, or even close to the truth, there is very little leeway in the present reported budget for significant additional outlays. This means that there may be extra, unreported budgetary expenses for the military, with possible additional deficit financing of one sort or another. Another possibility is that the higher CIA figure takes into account higher prices for military procurement and other expenses, reflecting "true" production costs rather than the lower subsidized prices actually paid by the Defense Ministry. If such low prices do exist, they may cause losses to the producing enterprises, thereby reducing their profits and profit-tax payments, or forcing the government to subsidize them. If this is the case, then at least part of the higher CIA estimates of defense expenditures already are accurately reflected in the evaluation of the budget deficit. Alternatively, the low prices paid for military equipment could be compensated for by higher prices to consumers.[35] Such a practice would amount to an additional hidden tax. It would cover extra budgetary expenses with extra budgetary taxes without an increase in the deficit. The price differences could also be paid to the ministry as a subsidy.

While the present paper cannot settle the debate over the true size of the defense budget, the discussion illustrates, first, the range of possibilities of substitution among prices, taxes, and subsidies under Soviet conditions. Second, it reflects the remaining uncertainty in estimating the true size of the deficit.

Even the official Soviet estimate of the level of the military budget implies an exceptionally heavy burden on the economy and a heavier burden still on

---

34. To the officially announced figure of R 77.3 billion, R 3.9 billion has been added for expenditures on military space programs. See notes to Table 1 for further details on the reconstruction of the budget.

35. Ministries that produce for the military produce on average 40 percent of their output for civilian use (Ryzhkov, 1989a, p. 28).

the state budget. However, if the CIA estimate is close to the truth, then both burdens become almost unbearable, and it is hard to see a way out, either for the budget or for the economy as a whole, without a sharp reduction in military expenditures.

As for temporal trends in Soviet defense spending, reliance must be placed on CIA estimates in the absence of credible Soviet information. These estimates show a fairly consistent rise in the relative burden of defense as a percentage of GDP over the period covered in this paper. Over the entire period, real defense expenditures grew at similar or higher rates than real GDP and there seems to have been a faster increase in defense prices (as estimated by the CIA) than in the general price level. As a result, the share of defense spending in GDP rose from about 12–13 percent in 1970 to 15–17 percent in the mid-1980s (CIA and DIA, 1989, p. 5). Extrapolating this growth in the dynamics of the budget, it follows that defense spending was growing only very slowly as a share of total expenditures, but it did grow faster than available revenues, thus increasing the pressure on the budget.

Reducing the defense burden is a major ingredient in the Soviet reform effort. According to official statements, defense expenditures were already frozen at the 1986 level for both 1987 and 1988, and may not have risen (or may have even declined) in 1989.[36] A crude calculation reveals that if these statements are correct, and given the Soviet figures for the level of defense spending, defense expenditures may not have grown at all since 1986. According to official pronouncements, there will be a real cut in the defense budget, from R 81.4 billion in 1989 to R 74.8 billion in 1990. If this is true, it is a major achievement, but it makes the present deficit, which would already incorporate the cuts, look even more threatening.[37]

The breakdown of the residual category of the budget expenditures is now given in Yureyev (1989) and Pavlov (1989) and the entry for foreign economic activity includes three items: the servicing of foreign debt, the foreign aid bill, and a hard currency reserve. There seems to be a renewed effort to cut the aid bill, but under any kind of reform scenario, the servicing of foreign debt, mostly to the West, is expected to rise substantially.

Although the present regime did not inherit a large accumulation of fiscal deficits, it did inherit a legacy of rapidly growing expenditure elements, such as consumption subsidies, payments to prop up weak enterprises, and an increasingly heavy defense burden. The regime also inherited a legacy of neglect in a number of key areas, including public services, social transfers, housing, infrastructure, and other fields; and a legacy of growing dependency on unstable and conjectural, even speculative, sources of revenue, such as profits from oil exports. Lacking also is a solid infrastructure necessary for modern tax collection, especially in the sphere of individual income taxes.

---

36. This would provide a total "saving" of about R 30 billion over 1986–1990, as compared with spending levels planned in 1985.

37. This calculation is based on a statement by Ryzhkov (1989a).

A serious policy error related to alcohol production (now being reversed), the coincidence of the decline in world oil prices, and the temporal proximity of several very costly disasters (Chernobyl, the Armenian earthquake), and more recently the spread of strikes and the ethnic turmoil added to the acuteness of the budgetary situation at the worst possible time. At least some of these events belong in principle, even to some extent in timing, to past neglect.

The main direct effect of early reform measures on the budget is in the area of decentralization of investment. More investment has been shifted from the budget and away from central determination, and rates or amounts of profit taxes reduced. At this stage it is not yet clear how this balance between the two policies will affect the deficit, but there is a real danger that with growing enterprise independence, income from profit taxes could fall faster than investment financed from the budget. In any case it is not clear whether or not the substitute investment process will be even more inflationary than deficit financing.

Most other fiscal implications of the reforms are indirect, in the sense that they may influence the level of profits and thereby affect the extent of the deficit. Still other aspects of the reforms may have monetary implications without affecting the budget. These non-budget elements are discussed below.

NON-BUDGETARY FINANCIAL PROBLEMS

The paper now addresses, in summary fashion, two non-budgetary sources of monetary pressure related to the reforms:[38] (1) the newly created flows of liquidity or potential liquidity caused by the relaxation of central planning and the increased independence of enterprises to use funds, to determine wages and prices, and to receive credit; the establishment of a new banking and credit system; and the activities of cooperative and private entrepreneurs; (2) the accumulated monetary "overhang," of savings and cash balances in the household sector, created over the years as a result of budget deficits and net liquidity flows from the production sector. Some Western scholars have estimated that the entire accumulation of liquid assets at the hands of households, including cash and savings account balances, stood at about R 225 billion by 1985 and reached approximately R 445 billion by the end of 1989 (CIA, 1989; *PlanEcon Report*, November 24–25, 1989; Ofer, 1990; Table 3). These accumulations consisted of approximately 80 percent of disposable household income in 1985 and nearly 100 percent in 1989.

Inflationary Pressures in the Production Sector

The Monetization of Enterprise Accounts and Credit Expansion. The increase in the monetary means available to enterprises comes from a number

---

38. A more detailed discussion and analysis of the non-budgetary inflationary pressures and of the overhang are included in Ofer (1990).

of sources. First, some of the previously segmented credit accounts or balances that corresponded almost exactly to the physical plan but could not be used as money have been "monetized" as all-purpose credits. Second, since the banking and credit reform of 1987 (Basic Provisions, 1987, pp. R12–14) new public and cooperative banks have sprung up with broad powers to grant credits beyond the plans. Such credits have partially replaced budgetary allocations and central credits substituted for institutional (planned) credit, and have also provided additional credit not always drawn from funds within the system. Since, with the exception of the cooperative banks, interest rates have usually remained very low (2–4 percent), the brief experience since 1987 suggests that credit expansion has raised the liquidity of the system beyond safe levels, especially in the production sector (Bochkov, 1989). With access to cheap credit, enterprises prefer to use their own funds to raise wages and related services, relying more heavily on credit to finance investment and expansion (Bunich, 1988). Finally, inter-enterprise commercial credit, banned in the past, is starting to develop into another expansionary source (Bunich, 1988).[39]

The macroeconomic destabilization created by the expansion of credit is aggravated because the monetization of accounts is not accompanied by sufficient decentralization of input resources and the creation of free wholesale trade. Most producers' goods are kept within the planning system to assure the fulfillment of state orders. This results in a considerable bidding up of prices within the very limited market, for state enterprises and cooperatives alike.

At the microeconomic level, the granting of credit has failed thus far to improve economic efficiency and to create the desired supply response. There is a large amount of bureaucratic direction and discretion in the granting of credit, with the result that much credit is granted to less productive enterprises and many loans are not repaid (Levchuk, 1989). Neither the banks nor the enterprises are utilizing the credit within a framework of a hard budget constraint. Rates of interest charged still are very low, with the exception of some cooperative banks; even the higher rates fail to keep pace with the growing inflation.

Despite the fact that credit systems are highly decentralized in market economies, they are also tightly controlled by central banks. An ironic aspect of the situation in the Soviet Union and the East European countries is that in the name of decentralization central authorities loosen macroeconomic control over credit expansion but do not achieve the microeconomic benefits of such a decentralized system (Bochkov, 1989). While a higher rate of interest is very important for enhanced economic discipline, a stronger resource constraint on both lenders and borrowers is even more important. Regardless of whether this is a temporary problem of the transition phase, or a more pervasive phenomenon inherent in the emergent mixed system, as claimed by Kornai, its occurrence

39. For further discussion on the expansion of credits, see Levchuk (1989).

at this initial stage of the reforms is unfortunate (Bunich, 1988; Levchuk, 1989; Wolf, 1985, 1989; Tardos, 1989; Kornai, 1989).

Wage Policy of Enterprises. One persistent source of cost-push inflation in many market economies is the upward movement of wages caused by imperfections, unionization, and other organizational peculiarities of labor markets. Wage growth also is the factor that many countries find the most difficult to contain and control—much more so, it seems, during the early phases of decentralization in socialist countries. Under the reforms, managers in the Soviet Union are allowed to raise wages above the centrally determined rates in a variety of ways, provided all increases fully correspond to "increases in productivity." The official figures for both 1988 and 1989 show that wages (and the wage fund) have been rising at rates considerably faster than productivity growth, which in itself is most likely an overestimate (*PlanEcon Report*, February 17, 1989, pp. 8–9; April 28, 1989, pp. 3, 14–16; Maslyukov, 1989, p. 40). Most observers see the excessive rise in wages as a more serious destabilizing factor than the budget deficit (Gostev, 1989a; Ryzhkov, 1989a; but see also Shmelev, 1989b).

As in other countries, the pressure to raise wages is an important initiator of cost-push inflation. Much of the inflationary pressures thus created are shifted to the consumer sector which receives the higher wages but fails to receive an accompanying increased supply of consumer goods.

Price Increases by Enterprises. To be sure, an increase in prices, all other things being equal, is a cure for the disequilibria of markets discussed here. It would reduce excess demand by cutting real incomes and reduce the value of all nominal assets. Price inflexibility is the "original sin" underlying many of the imbalances, and price flexibility is important not only for macroeconomic balance, but equally as a microeconomic allocation tool. In response to the above, but mainly in order to create a supply response, the early steps of the reform provided for some independent price changes by enterprises, some freedom to set prices for "new" products, and for above-plan and direct contract sales. All prices in the newly created private and cooperative sectors were to be freely determined.

However, due to the state of market imbalance, the monopolistic structure of the Soviet production sector, and the lack of hard budget constraints for buyers, prices did rise and the production of less expensive, "unprofitable" goods has been discontinued. Relatively little increase in suppliers resulted, however. Instead, the limited liberalization of price determination set the stage for a cost-push inflationary process, with all the necessary conditions, including the probability that it would be enhanced by an accommodating policy of monetary expansion. A very important condition, in addition to those mentioned above, is the long tradition of full employment and the strong resistance against bankruptcy and unemployment. Finally, price increases have been resisted strongly by the public, especially the very high prices developed in the private sector; thus there is a significant degree of sensitivity to the possible social response.

The problem with all these decentralization and enhanced-flexibility steps lies, as Tom Wolf (1989, p. 17) put it, in wrong sequencing.[40] The steps taken can only produce the right responses in an economic environment that is consistent with their function. Enterprises will use their increased independence productively only when pressed against a wall of hard budget constraints and faced with real competition from alternative suppliers. As long as losses can be reclaimed from or bargained away with the government, as long as credit is obtained at less than its real price, and as long as prices are increased and wages are raised without increased productivity, such measures cannot do much good. Indeed, they may be corrupting as well as counterproductive. The questions raised are whether this phenomenon of "softness" is temporary, for the duration of the transition period, or will last longer as part of the new system; whether a different sequencing can proceed better; and especially, whether the only promising sequencing is a "Big Bang"—installing the entire new system in one swoop. The present response of the Soviet authorities to the problems created by the various liberalizations of credit, wage, and price policies is to retighten control, in effect retracting some of the reforms (Ryzhkov, 1989b; On Measures, 1989).[41]

The Consumer Sector and the Monetary Overhang

Consistent with the dichotomized monetary system, there are also two separate stocks of accumulated financial assets: one in the form of various bank balances of enterprises in the production sector, the other mostly in the form of savings accounts, government bonds, and cash held by the public. The inflationary potential of the first stock of financial assets depends to a large extent on the degree to which the government allows enterprise reserves to be turned into real money—that is, to be used by the enterprises as they wish. In the past, the government tended to liquidate such surplus balances rather than liquefy them; this gradually is being changed with liberalization. Observers already perceive that enterprises have accumulated substantial amounts of fungible reserves and that these reserves are playing an inflationary role (Bunich, 1988; Belkin et al., 1988; Bochkov, 1989; *PlanEcon Report*, August 19, 1988, pp. 79–80; Levchuk, 1989).

The amount of monetary assets in the household sector by the end of 1988 is estimated at about R 450 billion, composed mainly of R 327 billion in savings account balances, and about R 120 billion in cash holdings (CIA, 1989a, p. 6; Pavlov, 1989; see also *PlanEcon Report*, September 1, 1989, p. 17; November

---

40. It also can be called "lopsided" reform.

41. A discussion of reform options, both theoretical and those actually implemented, can be found in the concluding section.

26, 1989). This financial stock has been growing during the past two or three years at a substantially faster rate and, given present imbalances, is likely to accelerate further. The stock of monetary assets is approximately equal in value to one full year of private consumption by the populace or to the annual value of its disposable income (see above sources; Ofer, 1990; Table 3).

The extent of the inflationary thrust of the monetary assets in the household sector—the "overhang" or "hot" money, money held involuntarily—has been estimated by Bogomolov (*Argumenty i facty*, No. 3, 1989) at R 80 billion, and more recently by Abalkin (1989b) at R 100 billion.[42] Repressed inflation and considerable excess liquidity unquestionably exist in the Soviet Union. It is, however, a grave mistake to include the entire stock of financial assets held by the population (and enterprises) in the category of "hot" money, if only for the fact that these liquid assets are almost the only ones that most Soviet citizens can legally own. In a system where cash and savings accounts are virtually the only assets available, the demand for holding total financial assets approaches the demand for "money" and the demand for savings approximates the flow demand for money.[43]

According to the classical theory of centrally planned systems, and during the early Soviet period, with its very low levels of personal income, the question of savings rarely arose.[44] Both planners and economists were taken by surprise when voluntary savings balances started to grow in the late 1950s and early 1960s. Indeed, many viewed them as forced savings right from the start. The naive theory seems to have been that since the state takes care of most (or all) of the life-cycle needs of families (education, health care, pensions, housing) and since people are not allowed to own real assets, there is neither the need nor the desire to save. The state simply withholds the savings component of income from wages and provides the necessary services. These conditions, combined with the very low interest rates paid on savings and the social resentment and fear of political sanctions against both hoarders of wealth and conspicuous consumers, lead to a lower level of voluntary saving in comparison with market economies.

Between the 1950s and the 1980s, however, some of the above conditions have changed in the USSR: incomes increased by a factor of three; more opportunities developed to purchase cooperative (private) apartments, private cars, and household appliances, and to spend more money on vacations; both the need and the ability to provide more for retirements grew substantially;[45] and the development of the second economy and the spread of corruption created new opportunities to buy better health care and education and even to invest.

42. See also Shmelev (1989a, 1989b).
43. Defined as cash and savings balances. The demand for savings includes the demand for additional cash and additional savings accounts. Investment in government bonds in recent years has been very limited (CIA, 1989a, p. 4). In addition, people can legally own homes, dachas, and cars and also tend to hold jewelry or foreign currency.
44. In 1955 the outstanding stock of savings accounts stood at less than 10 percent of disposable income and the average propensity to save was 1.6 percent (CIA, 1989a, Tables 3, 4, and 5).
45. The relative value of pensions declined significantly (see Vinokur and Ofer, 1988; Table 19).

All these factors should have increased the propensity to save. In addition, conditions of extreme uncertainty as to the timing of the availability of goods and very limited opportunities for consumer credit increased the need for savings and the demand for money. In 1984, the stock of savings balances stood at 58 percent of disposable income, and the flow demand, the average propensity to save, grew to 4.55 percent (CIA, 1989a, Table 3). The balance figure will be higher by about one-third if cash holdings are added. Although these figures probably include at least some forced accumulation, they are not exceptionally high in comparison with other countries.[46]

The economic reforms of marketization and changing property relations should have a converging (to normal market economy functions) effect on the demand functions for assets, money, and savings. There should be a rise in the demand for assets and savings to accommodate greater life-cycle needs, higher short-term risks, opportunities to earn higher rates of return, and requirements to diversify asset holdings, including productive assets. The propensity for saving should decrease with the development of a modern consumer credit system. While in the longer run the availability of alternative assets should reduce the demand for cash and savings accounts, this demand may rise in anticipation of the opening up of opportunities to buy such assets. A credible government pronouncement on the direction of change (including postponement of the development of a consumer credit system) can provide a strong incentive for accumulation of financial assets and prove of great assistance to stabilization efforts. Such credibility can be enhanced by actually starting such a program. The evidence of a rather skewed distribution of savings and of the concentraction of most of these balances in relatively few hands (Organizatsiya, 1989; Vid, 1988; Vinokur and Ofer, 1987, p. 196; Ofer and Pickersgill, 1980) enhances the prospects of a shift in these directions. Finally, the anticipation for improved consumption opportunities in the future is an additional incentive to save.

In the shorter term, anticipation of price increases (or even of open inflation) and the fear of a monetary reform, together with uncertainty as to the real intentions of the government concerning the reform in the longer run, work in the opposite direction. They reduce the demand for monetary assets, thereby exacerbating the imbalances. Disillusionment over prospects of improved conditions also have the same effect.

The observed increased propensities to save and the higher proportion of accumulation to income during the last few years (mentioned above) seem to reflect forced savings and disequilibrium rather than positive expectations for successful reforms. With correct policies the motivation for such accumulation can change and thereby contribute to stabilization.

---

46. A review of the question of savings and the nature of disequilibria in the consumer markets of the Soviet Union can be found in Wolf (1985), van Brabant (1988), Nuti (1985), Ofer and Pickersgill (1980), and Pickersgill (1980).

CONCLUSIONS: POSSIBLE WAYS OUT

The Soviet leadership has no easy way out of the present fiscal and monetary crisis. In addition to its quite horrifying dimensions, it is connected strongly with structural reform. Fiscal and monetary reform has to be implemented at a time when the economy lacks reserves (mainly due to past irresponsibility and heavy "borrowing" from the future) and when almost every aspect of the reform is deeply involved in delicate social and political issues. Nineteen eighty-nine was the year when many of these longer term problems surfaced in the form of the very wide budget deficit, and when they coincided with and were reinforced by the negative macro consequences of the partial decentralization reforms in the production sector. The extent of market disequilibrium and the clear trend of its further widening has forced the leadership to take immediate ameliorating steps in the short run, and to go back to the drawing board to rethink and redesign the entire reform program from the start. In the short run the 1989 budget was resubmitted with a smaller planned deficit (R 92 billion, instead of R 120 billion), and with various additional measures taken to curb the expansion of credit and the rise in wages. Various committees, mostly under the supervision of Abalkin, the newly appointed chairman of the State Commission on Economic Reform and deputy to Ryzhkov, came up toward the end of the year with a more rounded plan of action (including guidelines for the new five-year plan).

The revamped strategy basically contains three interrelated and mutually reinforcing elements (Abalkin, 1989a; Ryzhkov, 1989b; see also Maslyukov, 1989; Voronin, 1989; Yureyev, 1989). First, the government is to reallocate resources from investment and defense to consumption both in light industry and agriculture. This is the main thrust, though not the only one on the supply side. The reallocation will be carried out mainly via the old methods of central planning and direction, with a considerable restoration of binding state orders for both inputs and outputs. Second, a macroeconomic stabilization program will be carried out in order to restore market equilibrium on the demand side. The cornerstone of the stabilization program is the reduction of the size of the government budget deficit to 2–2.5 percent of GDP by 1993, but it includes also other steps to control wage and price hikes, rationalize the credit system, and further attempts to harden the budget constraints on enterprises. These two elements of the program are the main agenda for action during 1990 and 1991. The more radical aspects of the reform—price reform (even price changes), true marketization of input and output markets, denationalization and/or des-tatization of enterprises—are being postponed for the most part until 1992 or later. By this time, the proper legislation is to be prepared, macroeconomic equilibrium is to be restored, and the proper infrastructure and budget instru-ments in the sphere of social and welfare policy are to be put in place to cushion the economic impact of the reforms (price reform, inflation, unemployment, etc.). On the one hand, the program presented by the economic leadership looks to be more organized and well conceived than the set of partial steps taken so far. Indeed it is presented as the moderate variant between conservative and radical alternatives. Critics, on the other hand, see in the program a clear retreat, at least for two years, especially in the restoration of central control and in avoidance of the critical issues of price restructuring (if not price reform) and marketization in the broad sense.

The main justification for the new sequencing of the reforms is the need for a stabilization program to create a solid foundation for the real reforms. The following discussion identifies some of the difficulties in achieving stabilization[47] with the kind of program that is offered. Balancing the budget will be very difficult without due treatment of the growing subsidy bill. Under the present arrangements there is a danger that steps that balance the budget may simply shift inflationary pressures outside of the budget, and the postponement of the real reforms may prevent the development of expectations that would ameliorate the "overhang" problem.

The stabilization program first needs to address the monetary flows into the economy[48] and the accumulated monetary overhang. Table 6 summarizes the main features of the deterioration of the budget situation between 1981–1985 and the first draft of the 1989 budget, and then the efforts to reverse the trend as part of the stabilization program. All the figures are in percentages of GDP. Column 2 shows the deterioration of the budget situation, column 4 the planned correction through 1990, and column 5 the entire 1981–1985 to 1990 change.[49]

Of all the budget categories discussed in this paper, it is least necessary to reiterate the issue of reducing direct budgetary involvement in most investment. A combination of a general cut in investment levels and further transfer of the responsibility for investments to the enterprises (and perhaps to the banks) in exchange for the release of some profit taxes[50] may be feasible. Fiscal considerations demand that profit taxes go down at a slower rate than investment. The plan for 1990 calls for a slightly larger cut in investment, but a smaller cut in above-normal profits. There are two serious uncertainties here: (a) whether the plan for investment will be overfulfilled and/or the plan for profits and profit taxes will be underfulfilled; and (b) whether decentralized investments will create more inflationary pressures than centralized ones. In any case, very little potential exists for balancing the budget in the investment sphere, even according to plans. A related plan is to cut the government expenditure on enterprise losses by the sale or lease of loss-making enterprises to cooperatives by the end of 1990 (industrial) and 1991 (agricultural) (figures included in line 7). There is good reason to believe that, at least in the short run, the operation

47. This pertains especially to balancing the budget, but applies on other fronts as well.
48. One flow results from the budget deficit and a second from the partial decentralization steps summarized earlier.
49. Note that in this table the entry for "national economy" is for ordinary civilian expenditures only. An estimate for total defense (with the possible exception of military construction—see *PlanEcon Report*, Vol. 5, Nos. 24–25, 1989) has been transferred to line 7 and investment expenditures were taken out.
50. This might include the part above normal profits, for example.

Table 6. *Fiscal Changes, 1981–1985 to 1990*
(percent of GDP)

	1981–1985 (1)	1989 Original plan (2)	Changes (2)-(1) (3)	Changes 1990-(2) (4)	Changes 1990-(1) (5)
1. Total expenditures	49.5	53.2	3.7	−4.4	−0.7
2. Investment	8.9	8.7	−0.2	−3.4	−3.6
3. Ordinary expenditures	40.6	44.4	3.7	−0.9	2.9
4. National economy[a]	12.6	14.7	2.1	−1.3	0.9
5. Subsidies[b]	9.1	11.1	2.0	0.9	2.9
6. Social welfare	14.3	15.3	0.9	0.6	1.5
7. Defense[c]	9.1	8.3	−0.8	−1.2	−2.0
8. External expenditures[d]	2.5	3.8	1.3	−1.2	0.1
11. Total revenues	47.2	39.9	2.1	−6.5	−4.4
12. Profit taxes	15.1	13.0	−2.0	−0.8	−2.8
13. Above-normal profit taxes[e]	6.6	2.7	−3.9	−0.8	−4.7
14. Turnover taxes	14.1	11.2	−3.0	1.0	−2.0
15. Foreign trade revenues	9.5	6.5	−3.1	−0.6	−3.7
16. Taxes on individuals	4.2	4.6	0.5	0.2	0.5
17. Social security taxes[d]	3.1	3.4	0.3	0.6	0.9
19. Total fiscal deficit	2.3	13.5	11.2	−7.5	3.7
20. Ordinary deficit	−6.5	4.7	11.2	−4.0	7.2
21. Ordinary deficit (adjusted)	0.1	7.4	7.3	−4.8	2.5

Sources: Based on Appendix Table.
a. Excluding expenditures on investment and defense.
b. The figure for 1981–1985 is estimated by applying the same ratio between food and total subsidies as in 1989.
c. The figure for defense in 1981–1985 was estimated by assuming real annual growth of 3 percent between 1983 and 1989.
d. The numbering of lines is not sequential.
e. As in Table 2.

involves at least some compensating expenses and expansion of credits. On a higher level, the economic meaning of losses becomes uncertain under conditions of extremely distorted prices, as does the prudence of taking such steps before the price reform.

There is a plan and even larger potential for cutting the defense budget, especially if one believes in much higher figures than those revealed so far. However, the quid pro quo for reducing the size of the military establishment is a promise for modernization of the armed forces that may prove very costly.

Thus far, taxes on foreign trade are expected to fall, both gross (line 15) and even more so net of foreign obligations (line 15 *minus* line 8). By 1990 there is a planned loss of about 4 percent of GDP. There are those (Shmelev, the most notable) who advocate an increase in imports of consumer goods, not only as a means of increasing supplies, but also as a tax-collecting device. This option is discussed below.

Thus far there are only moderate plans to raise personal taxes. Social security taxes will rise somewhat (line 17), and the taxation of the increased volume of cooperative and private activity is still in its infancy.

Two additional points should be made in reference to planned fiscal changes. First, despite much talk and pressure, the entire budget for social welfare (a main target for improvement of past neglect) grew by only 1.5 percent of GDP since 1985.[51] Second, the net taxation of goods and services (turnover taxes and customs, minus subsidies, Table 4, line 29) fell over the period since 1981–1985 by more than 9 GDP points, to less than half of its original size. This second calculation already includes plans for 1989 and 1990 to raise income from turnover taxes because of the shift toward consumption where these taxes are imposed and the restoration of alcohol production nearly to its original level. In addition to the decline in foreign trade taxes, this is the outcome of the constantly increasing subsidy bill. Furthermore, efforts to shift resources toward consumption are double-edged as far as taxes are concerned: tax revenues on industrial goods will go up, but at the same time subsidies for agricultural and food products will rise as well, as indeed has happened during the last few years.

Given the high level of skepticism as to the feasibility of achieving the budget targets with the means prescribed above (and the still remaining substantial budget deficit), given urgent needs in the welfare system and other infrastructure investments, and given the highly distorting tax system on goods and services (Senchagov, 1989), a reform in this system of taxes is called for that will attend to some of these problems. It involves a basic price revision that at the minimum will eliminate most food and housing subsidies and at the maximum will also establish a more uniform and rational sales (or value-added) tax system. This has been advocated strongly on a number of grounds by McKinnon (1989a, 1989b). Such a revision would involve both rationalization of relative prices and an increase in *net* taxation. It would go a long way toward closing the budget deficit. Part of the money saved should be used to compensate low-income families and in general to revamp the social welfare system, especially the pension, disability, and child support programs. The improvement in the welfare support system would result from the release of resources from a universal welfare program that is only mildly progressive and the direction of the subsidies into more targeted programs for the weakest households: the retired, one-parent families, and households with many children. Additional support for poor working families (which do exist) can be achieved by raising the minimum wage to the long-promised level of R 80 per month. Estimates show that subsidies in the Soviet Union are distributed about equally, in absolute amounts, across different income groups (Vinokur and Ofer, 1988). Even with full compensation for the weakest third of the population, a total saving of R 70 billion will be realized, which can be used as suggested above.[52] The efforts made to improve the quality of social services may also benefit from some of the privatization or cost-sharing schemes now popular in the West.

---

51. This was mostly financed by increased social security taxes, lines 6 and 17.

52. The assumption of full compensation for everyone is what causes Kagalovskiy (1988, p. 7) and others to downgrade the fiscal significance of the elimination of subsidies.

There is some discussion along these lines in the Soviet Union (Zaslavskaya, 1986a, 1986b). The creation of a sound base for income taxation and a gradual rise in social security taxes also are a part of the social and welfare package. Other indirectly related benefits of the proposed price revision would be the removal of some major relative price distortions, a higher level of rationalization of decision making, a price structure more compatible with international markets, and the elimination of some of the monetary overhang through a partial monetary reform.

The general benefits of potential price revision are not lost on most economists inside and outside the Soviet Union. However, in view of the deteriorating economic environment, most of them, if not all (including Shmelev, 1989b), support the postponement of this step until after some improvements are achieved. If price reform comes with an adequate and credible compensation scheme and an increased supply of consumer goods, obtained initially from imports, it may have a quick effect on both the consumer markets and the deficit, thereby cutting the politically risky period. Furthermore, when the political risks are considered, the hazards involved in the alternative—an intensifying crisis—should also be taken into account. In a paradoxical way, the deeper the crisis, the better the chances that the population will appreciate, after a while, the benefits of equilibrium, even when achieved at higher prices (that many of them pay anyhow).

The second major source of monetary flows and inflationary pressures comes from the production sector as a result of the various decentralization measures in the decision-making process of enterprises and the creation of a market-like credit system. While both, as has been demonstrated, have important monetary aspects, they also are at the core of the economic reforms—the transformation of the production sector from one run by administrative methods to one that is directed by the market mechanism, with the conversion of the soft budget constraint into a hard one. If and when enterprises and banks get to this position and a reasonable degree of market competition is assured (by breaking the present monopolistic ministries), then sound macroeconomic management of money and credit can provide the needed solid monetary infrastructure. But the really crucial problem of the reforms remains how to turn state enterprises operating under soft constraints into self-reliant ones. Following unsuccessful attempts to achieve exactly this during twenty years of reform in Hungary, Kornai (1986 and 1989) appears to reach the conclusion that the goal is almost unachievable under conditions of state or public-sector ownership of enterprises. It is too late to discuss this issue in this paper. Some of the pros and cons of a gradual versus a one-shot approach have been mentioned, however—the first is full of contradictions that may make it counterproductive; the second is very risky. While more and more stabilization programs in inflation-ridden countries are taking the latter approach, some of them fail, and only seldom do the programs succeed in penetrating the sphere of the soft budget constraint of enterprises, the public sector, or even consumers.

Between the two approaches described above are those who seek solutions which will avoid some of the drawbacks of the two extremes. One such intermediate approach is offered by Belkin et al. (1988), in which individual enterprises or sectors, when ready, will move in one leap from the hothouse of the government sector to the market environment. For the conversion of the entire economy such a process may take quite a few years. In this specific scheme, the authors advocate beginning with light industry and agriculture, which sell directly to the household sector, thereby assuring the hardness of the budget constraint. The process will then proceed to sectors that channel supplies to light industry and agriculture and continue backward in this fashion, always depending on the money balances of the household sector. The advantage of this approach is that it achieves a full shift of regime for the enterprises involved without imposing it on the entire economy at once. Weaker enterprises have more time to prepare or to go under. The drawback lies in the creation of two discrete but concurrent economic regimes in one country, with the attendant difficulties entailed in the relationship between them (see McKinnon, 1989a). McKinnon, who prefers a one-time reform to a gradual one, proposes to impose a temporary constraint in the form of a ban on credit. During the transition period, which may be long, enterprises would have to survive, and invest, on the basis of their own earned funds (McKinnon, 1989a, pp. 28–35). This draconic rule helps to underline the perceived danger of the establishment of any credit system in the early stages of the transition.[53]

During 1989, and in the plans presented for the following years, the Soviet leadership has taken a number of steps to tighten control over credits. These include raising the interest rate and restricting the right of enterprises to raise wages and prices. With a few exceptions the new steps point backward, toward the kind of controls common under central planning. This may be justified as a temporary measure, but it appears, especially when reading Ryzhkov's December 1989 speech (Ryzhkov, 1989b), as though the retreat is of longer duration. Earlier it was pointed out that a major imbalance in the reforms in the production sectors was that monetary expansion far exceeded the opening of goods markets where this money could be used. For the next three years, at least, it appears that the amount of money in the production sector will be restricted to an even narrower segment of that market. State orders are to be increased rather than reduced.

A third critical element of needed reform is reduction of the monetary overhang. A combination of an offer to sell state-owned production and housing assets, the measured use of imports of consumer goods, a substantial increase in the interest rate, and a one-shot price adjustment (as part of the budget package, see below), should reduce the size of the overhang to a manageable level. The offer to sell state-owned production assets should be combined with the release of enough corresponding property rights to make

---

53. It should, however, be remembered that self-financing of investment is only rational when the prices are correct and when private profits (and losses) more or less reflect social ones.

the offer attractive. In order for state apartments to be sold to their tenants, the level of state rents must be raised. The stock of government-owned assets is one of the major reserves in the hands of the state, and the transfer of part of this stock is motivated, in the first place, by efficiency considerations. Along the way, it can help solve the overhang problem. This approach is being advocated by a number of Soviet economists (Bogomolov, 1989, pp. 5–6; Shmelev, 1989b, pp. 28–29; and many others). A particularly interesting scheme has been proposed by Belkin et al. (1988), in which all the monetary reserves of the enterprises would be confiscated and replaced by cash balances held by the household sector. Enterprises will have to earn these balances by selling directly or indirectly to the household sector.

A one-time resort to imports of consumer goods, sold at a profit to the state of 800–1000 percent, has been advocated by Shmelev for some time as a means of absorbing excess purchasing power in the very short run and of raising public morale.[54] The one-time, large-scale import should be followed by a much smaller flow of imports for a few more years. This is a stop-gap, short-term solution. In the longer run, the margin of profits on imports would go down, both as a result of the price reform and reduced customs barriers. There is some discussion on whether the Soviet Union can afford to spend the needed foreign currency (but see Ryzhkov, 1989a, p. 23). The most serious objection, however, seems to be the futility of such a policy unless the state is set for sustained increases in the domestic production of consumer goods—a far more difficult target. In addition, real interest rates must go up: cooperative banks are already offering 5–7 percent for deposits (*New Times*, 1989), but more should be done across the board.

In view of the present acute and accelerating overhang crisis, the budget deficit, and the flow of liquidity from the reformed credit system and the enterprise sector (combined with the long-term nature of the transformation of the Soviet production sector to a profit-maximization footing), it seems reasonable to address the problem piecemeal. A "stabilization program" could be introduced first, to absorb excess liquidity in the very short run through a one-time price revision and a significant cut in subsidies. It might also include a short-term plan to balance the budget, some importation of consumer goods, and a moderate version of "monetary reform" in both the household and production sectors, including severe restrictions on the volume of credit and much higher interest rates. As part of the monetary reform, as well as of longer-term reforms, the stabilization stage could make a start on sales of apartments and sales and long-term leases of productive assets and land to cooperatives and to private parties. This, in the short run, will be the main contribution of the long-term reform to the stabilization effort. But, as argued before, the commitment for a massive transfer of assets from the government to individuals and small groups must be firmly established. For a short period of "stabili-

54. Gorbachev (1989, p. 50) seems to agree (see also Shmelev, 1989a).

zation'' there would be a freeze on wages and on the (revised) prices. The stabilization would be accompanied by reform in transfer payments as described earlier. The present enterprise reform would go on, with the above temporary restrictions, and the proportion of goods freed from planning should continue to increase and help soak up excess money. It also will serve as a longer term educational process to managers.

If successful, the relief created in the consumer goods market might stimulate enhanced work effort and more support for the reforms. To be sure, the initial stage of the stabilization would involve economic sacrifices by the population and therefore would entail considerable political risks. However, if it is true that people spend long hours in lines, end up paying much higher prices than the official ones, or are unable to get basic goods at all, then they may appreciate the changes rather quickly.

The true enterprise reform that is conditioned upon a true price reform— the only way to create real markets—would follow gradually a year or two later. This would be the real start of a long, uphill struggle to impose the hard budget constraint on the economy. There are two main differences between the framework suggested here and the content of the Abalkin papers, or the much more conservative Ryzhkov plan. First, price revisions are put up front. This will assure stabilization and shorten the duration of this stage. Second, the outlook of the plan presented here is forward, toward radical reform, rather than backward, as under Ryzhkov. It allows people to form positive expectations toward the new economic structure and the new property relations. This will push their demand for assets, savings, and money in stabilizing rather than destabilizing directions, thereby helping the program.

The separation of the reform into two stages by postponing the price reform until after stabilization is secured is necessary in order to spare the Soviet Union the need to go through a stage of uncontrolled inflation (currently happening in Poland). Under conditions of high inflation, relative prices have little meaning in any case, but the additional costs to the economy and the price of correcting it are very high. Today it may still be possible to have stabilization before rather than after a phase of uncontrolled inflation.

APPENDIX

Because the following table is cited throughout the paper, it appears as an appendix at the end.

Appendix Table. Soviet State Budget, 1971–1990
(billions of nominal rubles)

	1971–1975 (Annual averages)	1976–1980	1981–1985	1985	1986	1987	1988	1989 (Original plan)	1989 (Revised plan)	1990 (Plan)
Revenues										
1. Turnover tax	59.9	82.4	100.9	97.7	91.5	94.4	101.0	104.8	113.1	121.9
2. Alcohol	n/a	n/a	41.1	39.9	31.7	32.5	37.0	40.7	n/a	40.7
3. Taxes on profits	61.9	80.3	107.3	119.5	129.8	127.4	119.6	121.2	113.5	122.6
4. Taxes on individuals	16.0	22.0	27.7	30.0	31.2	32.5	35.9	36.3	41.7	43.5
5. Social insurance taxes	10.0	13.2	22.1	25.4	26.5	28.1	30.1	31.4	33.8	40.3
6. Income taxes paid by coops and public enterprises	1.4	1.6	2.2	2.5	2.6	2.8	2.8	3.0	n/a	4.0
7. Other revenues	5.9	7.5	8.1	8.3	8.1	8.1	24.9	13.7	37.5	37.9
8. Total revenues from domestic sources	155.1	206.9	268.2	283.4	289.7	293.3	314.3	310.4	339.6	370.2
9. Foreign trade taxes	17.5	38.9	68.1	71.1	64.4	69.3	62.6	60.6	60.6	58.0
10. Total ordinary revenues	172.6	245.8	336.3	354.5	354.1	362.6	376.9	371.0	400.2	428.2
11. Soviet total reported revenues	189.8	266.0	359.8	390.6	419.5	435.5	469.0	374.0	408.0	428.2
12. Public bond sales	0.4	0.6	1.0	1.4	1.9	1.9	2.0	3.0	3.0	3.0
Expenditures										
13. National economy	93.4	140.4	200.0	209.1	226.3	226.9	242.8	199.4	198.6	187.4
14. Investment	44.6	47.7	63.3	70.0	80.0	80.0	69.2	82.1	75.0	53.1
15. Consumer subsidies	n/a	n/a	65.0	n/a	n/a	n/a	90.0	103.0	103.0	120.0
16. Food subsidies	17.3	24.2	44.5	56.0	58.0	64.9	66.0	87.8	87.8	95.7
17. Public services and welfare	60.1	80.2	102.2	112.0	119.3	124.4	133.5	143.4	144.2	158.8
18. Public services	30.8	41.2	49.5	53.6	56.1	58.6	n/a	71.8	66.2	75.6
19. Transfer payments	29.3	39.0	52.7	58.4	63.2	65.8	n/a	71.6	78.0	83.2
20. Science	7.6	8.9	12.4	13.6	14.4	15.6	n/a	7.5	n/a	11.0
21. "Defense"	17.8	17.2	17.5	19.1	19.1	20.0	20.2	77.3	n/a	70.9
22. Internal security	n/a	n/a	n/a	n/a	n/a	n/a	n/a	8.6	n/a	8.5
23. Public administration	1.9	2.3	2.8	3.0	3.0	2.9	3.0	2.8	n/a	2.9
24. Foreign economic activity and other expenditures	5.9	11.1	18.0	15.1	18.0	24.6	26.0	31.4	29.9	26.0

	Col 1	Col 2	Col 3	Col 4	Col 5	Col 6	Col 7	Col 8	Col 9	Col 10
25. Debt service (internal) and reserve	n/a	n/a	n/a	n/a	n/a	n/a	n/a	10.9	n/a	12.9
26. Other expenditures	n/a	n/a	n/a	14.6	17.0	16.5	34.0	13.5	n/a	9.8
27. Total expenditures	186.7	260.1	353.0	386.5	417.1	430.9	459.5	494.8	491.0	488.2
28. Ordinary expenditures	142.0	212.4	289.7	316.5	337.1	350.9	390.3	419.8	416.0	435.1
Deficit										
29. Table deficit (27–13)	14.0	14.3	16.7	32.0	63.0	68.3	82.6	123.8	90.8	60.0
30. *PlanEcon Report* estimate	n/a	n/a	17.6	20.6	51.9	66.2	98.7	120.0	92.0	60.0
31. Ordinary deficit	-30.6	-33.4	-46.6	-38.0	-17.0	-11.7	13.4	48.8	15.8	6.9
32. Soviet reported deficit	n/a	n/a	n/a	18.0	47.9	57.1	90.1	121.0	92.0	60.0
33. GDP (nominal)	433.7	559.0	712.8	778.3	799.6	825.0	875.0	930.0	930.0	1,000.0

Sources: Data taken from *Gosudarstvennyy byudzhet SSSR i byudzhety soyuznykh respublik*, and *Narodnoye khozyaystvo SSSR*, various years, unless otherwise specified; 1985–1988 are based on the above but updated on the basis of Yureyev (1989); 1988 (plan) are also from CIA (1988, p. 18); 1989: data for 1989 (plan), 1989, and 1990 (plan) are based on Pavlov (1989) and Zoteyev (1989) (only 1989), some figures for 1989 (plan) are from Gostev (1988).

Other specific notes and sources:

Lines:

2. Alcohol, 1971–1988: *PlanEcon Report*, November 4, 1988, p. 10.
9. Estimated foreign trade revenues:
   1971–1980: CIA (1988, p. 16).
   1981–1984: Calculated from CIA (1988, pp. 16–19) and revised CIA estimates of deficit (May 1989), assuming that the entire change in CIA estimates of deficits reflects a decline in export revenues.
12. Public bond sales: 1988 and 1989: *PlanEcon Report*, November 4, 1988, p. 10.
14. Investment: 1975, 1977, 1981: Tretyakova (1986). Others years are extrapolated from Tretyakova and Pavlov (1989).
15. Consumer subsidies:
   1988: *PlanEcon Report*, November 4, 1988, p. 10.
   1989: Gostev, in FBIS, October 28, 1988, p. 56; other years, guesstimates, based on extrapolations and on information on the extent of housing subsidies (*Narkhoz*, various years).
16. Food subsidies:
   1971–1975: Treml (1978, p. 9).
   1976–1979 (average), 1982 and 1983: Gray and Markish (1987, p. 26).
   1980 and 1986: CIA (1985, p. 2).
   1985 and 1988: Kagalovskiy (1988, p. 6).
   1987: USDA (1989, p. 80).
   1981 and 1984: calculated as average of preceding and following years.
21. "Defense": 1989: Gostev (1988, p. 56).
24. 25, 26. Foreign economic activity and other expenditures: 1971–1975: unidentified residual of "total expenditures." Since 1985 there is data in Yureyev (1989) and Pavlov (1989) on some breakdown of the above. In these cases line 24 does not include "other."
28. Ordinary expenditures: calculated as "Total expenditures" minus "Investment."
30. *PlanEcon* estimate: *PlanEcon Report*, November 4, 1988, p. 10.
31. Ordinary deficit: calculated as "Total deficit (line 29) minus "Investment" (line 17).
33. GDP (nominal):
   1971–1985: extrapolated from GDP figures for 1970, 1975, 1980, and 1985 reported in Zoteyev (1987, p. 10).
   1986–1989: *PlanEcon Report*, February 17, 1989, p. 14, and Zoteyev (1989).
   1990: estimate.

CHAPTER 18

Perestroyka and the Congress of People's Deputies

Ed A. Hewett

THE POLITICAL drama of the summer of 1989 in the USSR has captured our attention and imagination in the West, and rightfully so. The Congress of People's Deputies, the two houses of the Supreme Soviet, and their commissions have changed the political and social landscape in the USSR in a way that was unimaginable a few years ago. A rudimentary, but quite real, degree of public accountability emerged from the operation of the new Congress which, if it continues to develop, will profoundly alter the way the Soviet people are governed.

That rudimentary public accountability may have been most evident in economic affairs. From the first day of the Congress to the last day of the first Supreme Soviet session there was almost constant debate, sometimes savage criticism, even ridicule, of the state of the economy and the inability of the government to come up with a credible approach to remedy the situation. This fall those ministers in the new government who survived what Prime Minister Ryzhkov called the "purgatory" of the confirmation process are left with no doubts that they must do something dramatic, that they must follow through, and that the commissions of the Supreme Soviet will be following their actions very closely.

Whether this means that, finally, a truly radical economic reform will emerge in the USSR is not yet clear. It depends on the new government—in particular, on its ability to develop a coherent reform concept, combined with a strong stabilization program, which together form a credible response to the deteriorating economic situation, and on the skill and determination with which it approaches the implementation. It also depends on political developments, most notably the direction of republican self-finance, which could stall the reform process if it degenerates into the segmentation of the Soviet Union into increasingly autarkic regional markets. Finally, it depends on how the government

First published in *Soviet Economy*, 1989, 5, 1, pp. 47–69. [Eds.]

responds to the inevitable populist pressures emanating from a Congress of People's Deputies in the form of demands for higher living standards, job security, and price stability, when in fact economic reform will initially mean a deterioration in all three.

These are formidable challenges, and it would be naive to suppose that Soviet leaders will be able to respond to them unflinchingly, avoiding mistakes and setbacks. Even those of us in the West who follow Soviet developments closely, and frequently criticize particular measures, would find it very difficult to change places with Soviet leaders and come up with a practical strategy to manage the creation of a socialist market system. Certainly existing economic theory offers very little guidance for Soviet reformers outside of common sense and a promise that they will be much better off if, and when, they figure out how to create a market system (Hewett, 1989b).

There are, nevertheless, reasons to believe that the prognosis for economic reform has generally improved over the last few years, but in particular as a result of the summer of 1989. The debate over economics and economic policy is much more sophisticated than it was even two years ago, which enhances the support for radical reforms. The government has moved to build new, unprecedented ties between policy makers and economists through Deputy Prime Minister Leonid Abalkin's newly created Commission on Economic Reform, and that enhances the chances for a comprehensive reform blueprint. Finally, the rapid deterioration in the economy, a frank admission by Soviet leaders that little they have done these last few years has had any effect on the economy, and the government's efforts to implement a major stabilization program, all suggest that the time is ripe for a radical reform.

THE INCREASINGLY SOPHISTICATED DEBATE OVER *PERESTROYKA*

The debate over *perestroyka* has proven to be an extraordinary public process of "consciousness-raising," in which a deteriorating economic situation, a blizzard of poorly prepared half-measures, and the glaring light of day provided by *glasnost'* have melded into a force pushing the debate, and economic policy, in more radical directions. The *Osnovnyye polozheniya* of June 1987 constituted a reform program, radical by past standards, but primarily focused on the devolution of decision-making powers to state-owned enterprises in the context of a vaguely defined combination of central planning and market (Hewett, 1988a, Ch. 7). The underlying assumption was that workers could be induced to work efficiently for managers who in turn would be stimulated by the new system to produce high-quality products consumers actually wanted. That such an outcome would only result if there were a truly competitive environment in which property rights were significantly "democratized" received only marginal attention. Now, two years later, the debate has taken on a much more pragmatic and radical tone, while moving the issue of property rights to center stage, where it belongs.

Property Rights

Academician Leonid I. Abalkin—Director of the Institute of Economics, and recently appointed to an additional post as Deputy Prime Minister and Chairman of the newly created State Commission on Economic Reform of the USSR Council of Ministers—has done much to set that pragmatic tone and to stimulate the debate on property rights. In a November 1988 article reporting on a project in the Institute of Economics on property rights under socialism, he sets out his own very practical views on what forms of property rights might be desirable under socialism. His view is that socialism should be able to accommodate a multiplicity of property forms, but, more important, that ". . . if property nominally appears to be state[-owned], but it is operated uneconomically and with low efficiency, then it cannot be considered to be socialist" (Abalkin, 1988, p. 10). In other words, unprofitable enterprises are not socialist enterprises!

Since then a fascinating debate has emerged, especially on the pages of *Ekonomicheskaya gazeta*, which is essentially about "privatization," the term in the Soviet context being *"razgosudarstvleniye,"* or "de-statization" of assets.[1] In this debate the favored form of privatization is the long-term leasing of state assets to groups of workers, usually in a cooperative. Such leases already exist in the USSR—2,000 enterprises of all sorts were operating under leases on July 1, 1989 (Maslyukov, 1989, p. 3)—but they are fairly tame arrangements in which the leasee has very limited rights. The academic advocates of leasing have a much stronger form of leasing in mind, in which leasees would enjoy considerable control over their assets, and considerable income over and above a reasonable lease payment. In addition, there are advocates for partial public ownership of companies through shares, and some who argue for the direct sale of state enterprises to workers (Rutgayzer, 1989; Aleksashenko, 1989). The idea of selling enterprises to workers—inconceivable a few years ago—has been formally endorsed by Gosplan chairman Yuriy Maslyukov (1989, p. 3).

Possibly more important is the fact that Academician Abalkin's Reform Commission now has the task of elaborating principles governing a multiplicity of property arrangements and the creation of equal conditions for all forms of property in the economic system ("O Gosudarstvennoy," 1989). It would not be at all surprising if someone, possibly Abalkin's Commission, takes the next step of proposing the sale of enterprises to foreign buyers, something which is already legal in Poland and Hungary.

1. See, for example, Seleznev (1989). Other interesting contributions to the debate include Sorokin (1988), Gribanov and Sukhanov (1989), and Khubiyev (1989).

Whether or not that next step is taken, much remains to be worked out:

- the procedure for valuing assets designated for lease or sale in the absence of a capital market (and in the presence of disequilibrium prices);
- the creation of an economic environment which will allow cooperative or private leasees (effectively owners) sufficient leeway and incentive to seek out and pursue economic opportunities;
- the establishment of a legal framework providing a "level playing field" for the various forms of ownership.

Moreover, very difficult issues are involved in specifying which state bodies now effectively control the assets, and therefore can negotiate their sale or lease. The inclination thus far has been to leave leasing arrangements to ministries, but they obviously have a severe conflict of interest that militates against such a role. It would make much more sense to temporarily shift "ownership" of all or part of the enterprises in selected ministries to a special body charged with negotiating lease contracts on behalf of the state. But that would confer complete economic independence to the leasees—no state orders; no norms; no administrative controls over the enterprises. And that in turn assumes the reform moves ahead quickly, and that most ministries are disbanded.

Competition (*Konkurentsiya*)

A similar, although less pronounced, change is occurring in the tone of the debate over the role of competition in a socialist market economy. Early on in the reform debate one could find little discussion about the importance of competition (including import competition) as a mechanism for institutionalizing pressure on enterprises to lower costs and raise quality. Indeed the word for the kind of competition needed to make Soviet reform work—*konkurentsiya*—was almost never uttered outside of its normal use to describe the unforgiving and supposedly wasteful operation of capitalist market economies. Socialism, as I learned several years ago in discussion with a high Soviet economic official, would never have a place for *konkurentsiya*.

More recently the economics literature and popular press have carried an increasing number of articles railing against the evils of monopoly, in particular the high concentration of economic power in the USSR, and extolling the potential benefits from *konkurentsiya* as a mechanism to control costs and stimulate the production of goods and services consumers want (Simakov, 1988; Simonyan, 1988, Telen', 1988; Yasin, 1988a).

The impact of this debate on government leaders is most apparent in the increased attention to the need to break up large enterprises and protect the economy against monopolies. At a special meeting of the Council of Ministers Presidium in January 1989, where Leonid Abalkin presented the Institute of Economic's program for stabilizing the economy and moving ahead with reform, Georgiy Arbatov's Institute for the USA and Canada was asked to produce within 2–3 months a draft anti-monopoly law ("V presidiume," 1989, p. 4). Almost certainly, a later product of that effort was the recommendation of an inter-governmental group to the government for the adoption of a set of laws ". . . on anti-monopoly policy and the development of competition," which was openly linked to U.S. anti-trust legislation ("Nachalo," 1989).

To be certain, this debate still has a long way to go. There is still little support for the notion that import competition can be important even in a country the size of the USSR, and even with the balance of payments pressures the country is under. But as with the debate on property rights, there is a logic to this process, and it is pushing the consensus in the right direction.

Social Guarantees

If the USSR is to move to a market system allowing a multiplicity of forms of property ownership in a competitive environment where there are real losers, then it will have to totally redefine its approach to social welfare. Mikhail Gorbachev inherited a situation in which Soviet socialism constituted an entitlement of Soviet citizens to a job and to wage and fringe benefits, even when their work produced no socially useful goods. If a reformed system is to work at all, then job and income entitlements will have to be replaced by a more general promise of jobs for those who wish to work, and incomes commensurate with worker productivity. But, as a practical matter, it is unclear how such a potentially unpopular change in social guarantees can be "sold" to the population, and how it can be implemented in a way which minimizes disruption. Right now the Soviet Union does not have even a minimally acceptable system for assisting those who are unemployed and in need of retraining, a situation which must be rectified before the reform goes much further. In addition, the strong focus of the Congress of People's Deputies on social welfare issues— particularly living conditions in the countryside, and poverty among pensioners—indicates areas which require redress before the reform moves ahead.[2]

Public debate is only beginning to address this question, primarily over the issue of whether or not unemployment is "necessary" for the successful functioning of a socialist market economy. Clearly this touches on the nature of basic differences between the "new" socialism, to which the USSR is trying to move, and capitalism as it now exists in the industrialized West. Some Soviets see no major differences between the system they would like to introduce and that of, say, Sweden; others see fundamental differences, among which would be job guarantees. This debate has scarcely begun, and its outcome will be one of the important determinants of where the reform itself eventually leads. Until and if the government has in place a credible safety net to protect the population from the excesses of which a market is

2. For a summary of the Congress's concerns on social welfare issues, see "Ob osnovnykh," 1989.

capable, there is little chance that a radical reform of the sort that is necessary can be introduced.

Unresolved Issues

There is much that remains to be resolved, which is not surprising given the fact that serious debate on the total transformation of this system is only several years old. If a radical reform is to be implemented, it will be necessary first to forge a much firmer consensus than now exists on the points discussed here. Without a consensus, especially among the professional economists, government and party officials will find it easy to postpone radical reforms, indeed they may find it necessary in light of the lack of agreement among their professional advisors.

Moreover, the focus of the debate will have shifted more to the pure transition issues raised by an effort to reform a system. It is fine to say, for example, that in the new system all enterprises will have to sink or swim on the basis of their profitability in a fair price system. But how should one deal with the not unusual situation of a socialist enterprise with capital stock so old that it probably will never survive in a truly competitive environment? It is not fair to simply cut it off from all subsidies overnight, since the inefficiency of that enterprise is not so much its own doing as it is a legacy of an inefficient system. On the other hand, too generous a subsidy would eliminate any incentive to adjust. There are many questions of this sort regarding the transition per se, involving tradeoffs between fair social guarantees and economic incentives, which need to be much more carefully addressed than they have been to date in the Soviet debate.

The new Commission on Economic Reform chaired by Academician Abalkin will have to play a crucial role in forging the consensus and focusing on the right issues. If that Commission performs well, moving quickly but with care to forge a new reform program, then there is a chance the reform will finally assume the coherence it has lacked so far. If, on the other hand, the Commission simply turns into yet another forum for discussion and endless bureaucratic wrangling, or if it is undercut through lack of support from Prime Minister Ryzhkov and President Gorbachev on critical issues, then the reform will continue the disorganized and basically inconsequential path it has traced over the last few years.

PROSPECTS FOR THE FUTURE: THE NEAR TERM

Although it is possible to make a respectable case that in the end the effort to reform this system will fail, there is also a case to be made that prospects are decent for significant progress on economic reform and economic performance. Since the arguments against success are far easier to see than those favoring prospects for considerable progress, I shall focus on the latter.

The Reform Commission[3]

The creation of the Reform Commission, and its composition, are both very hopeful signs. To be sure, this is not a totally new entity. It is rather an upgraded and expanded version of the Commission on the Improvement of Management, Planning and the Economic Mechanism, formerly chaired by the Gosplan chairman.[4] But the new status signalled by its chairman's rank as deputy prime minister, and the fact that Abalkin will lead it, are both hopeful signs. Academician Abalkin, one of the most respected figures in Soviet economics today, has proven his willingness to tell the leadership what it might not like to hear, and to do so even in the most intimidating of circumstances.[5] Moreover, Abalkin has been at the forefront in pushing for pragmatic approaches to the economy, and he will most assuredly continue to do so in his current position.

In addition to Abalkin, the new Commission includes in its 22 members all of the ministerial apparatus responsible for overall management of the economy. To mention the most important ones:

- S. A. Sitaryan, First Deputy Chairman of Gosplan, and also one of the Deputy Chairmen of the Reform Commission;
- The Minister of Finance (V. S. Pavlov);
- The Chairmen of the Committees on Prices (V. K. Senchagov), Labor (V. I. Shcherbakov), Statistics (V. N. Kirichenko), and Construction (V. M. Serov);
- First Deputy Chairman of the State Committees for Material-Technical Supply (Yu. P. Boyev), and Science and Technology (I. M. Bortnik);
- a Deputy Chairman of the State Foreign Economic Commission (I. D. Ivanov).

These are the top economic policy makers in the USSR, and if a consensus can be achieved here, it is sufficient for the reform to move ahead rapidly.

Moreover, the Commission gives prominence to links with the academic specialists, thus providing them a formal role in designing the reform policy. Abel Aganbegyan is a member of the Commission and chairman of its Scientific Council (a role he also played on the Commission's predecessor). Representatives of major academic institutions sit on the Commission, and presumably the Scientific Council will involve many more academics. Furthermore, the Institute of Economics (at which Abalkin continues as chairman) is virtually

---

3. "O Gosudarstvennoy" (1989) is the source for this section.
4. Hewett (1988a, pp. 111–112) provides a brief account of this earlier commission.
5. I am thinking most notably of Abalkin's public disagreement with Mikhail Gorbachev at the 19th Party Conference (Hewett, 1988b).

serving as staff for the Commission, along with the Council of Ministers' Academy of Economics, which is now directly subordinated to the Commission.

Finally, the Commission has several powers which, if they are supported by the leadership, will provide it with significant influence on the entire reform process. It directly leads (*rukovodit*) the work of the State Bank and the State Committees on Prices, Labor and Social Questions, and Statistics. Abalkin's control over the State Prices Committee, combined with the influence of its new, pro-reform chairman, V. K. Senchagov, suggest that the committee could begin to take more seriously its part in the reform process. In addition, the Commission has the legal right to rescind any normative or methodological document relating to reform issued by any ministry, department, or republican commission if that document contradicts current law, decrees of the Council of Ministers, or decrees of the Commission.

This is precisely the sort of entity Mikhail Gorbachev should have created in 1985, focusing in one place the authority, the mission, and the wherewithal to forge a consensus on a reform strategy and see it through. It is a pity that it took him four years to accomplish this, but at least he finally has recognized what needs to be done. Whether or not the Reform Commission will succeed in its daunting task will depend on many factors. It will have to produce quickly a coherent reform package and work with the remainder of the apparatus to implement a credible short-term stabilization program. The governmental and party structures are likely to offer rhetorical support but *de facto* opposition, and if the Commission is doing its job well, there should be some nasty arguments beginning in the fall of 1989. Complete harmony, at least at the beginning, will be a sign that things are going badly.

For the academic specialists this Commission represents an enormous challenge. Many of the most prominent economists have criticized the course of economic reform, and now they are being asked to be part of the solution. There is a very real danger that they will fail—possibly through no fault of their own—or at least that they will be drawn into supporting insignificant variations on the approaches they have criticized. But they have a chance in the current environment to make a difference.

Academician Abalkin inherits a reform which has gone virtually nowhere and an economy that shows it. By many measures the economic situation has deteriorated since 1988, and the likelihood is high of further deterioration over the near term. The question, both for Soviet leaders and for those who analyze developments in the USSR, is just how serious the situation is, and what can be done about it? The Reform Commission will focus primarily on medium- to long-term measures, but in the meantime it will be critical to introduce a stabilization program to prepare the way for, and support, the reform. Such a program seems to be in the works for 1990, judging from Gosplan Chairman Maslyukov's speech in August to the Supreme Soviet (Maslyukov, 1989). In order to evaluate that program, it is necessary first of all to review briefly the economic situation as of the summer of 1989.

The Economic Situation at Mid-1989

There is no simple set of economic indicators that summarizes the current state of the Soviet economy. Some traditional quantitative indicators are of questionable quality in the Soviet case (national income statistics, for example), while some simply do not exist (price deflators). Moreover, there are no useful time series on shortages, so anecdotal evidence is frequently all that is available, but that is notoriously difficult to evaluate.

It is, nevertheless, possible to gather a servicable, if incomplete, impression of the current situation, and in particular of trends, by drawing on both quantitative and qualitative information. Some of the relevant quantitative indicators are assembled in Table 1, which describes actual performance through the first half of 1989, and provides statistics on plans for the second half of the 1980s (the Twelfth Five-Year Plan) and on the annual plans for 1989 and (very preliminary figures) for 1990. I will set aside for the moment the matter of the 1990 plan, focusing on the period from 1986 through mid-1989.

The first four rows contain three official Soviet, and one CIA-estimated, measures of economic activity. The Soviet figures are higher, presumably because they include inflation expunged from the CIA estimates.[6] Whichever indices one uses, it is clear that average national income growth will come out well below the Twelfth Five-Year Plan. More important, the trend seems to be downward: the CIA estimate for 1989 will most likely be less than 1 percent per annum, while the 1990 official plan figure of 2 percent for produced national income suggests the possibility that, if the plan is realized, the CIA estimates will show zero GNP growth that year.

Labor productivity in the material sectors is running above plan, which—given the fact that national income is growing more slowly than planned—would suggest that labor productivity in the "non-productive" sectors (primarily services) must be growing considerably more slowly than planned. It is also possible that hidden inflation is focused disproportionately on the "productive" sectors, since it is probably easier to realize hidden inflation through new products than through new services.

Gross state investment was "front-loaded" the way Soviet planners said it would be, but on a higher plateau than anticipated, so that average actual growth has been well above the 4.3 percent target for the Twelfth Five-Year Plan. This is the normal pattern for five-year plan investment targets, as is the fact that the effort to accelerate commissionings ahead of investment growth rates (to shorten gestation periods) has been a failure. During 1986–1988, while investment grew at an average of 6.3 percent, new commissionings grew at 4.5 percent, a less favorable relationship between investments and commissionings than in recent five-year plans (*Tsifrakh*, p. 246).[7]

---

6. Part of the problem here is the comparable price method used to derive official Soviet quantity indices (Kushnirsky, 1985; CIA, 1987).

7. For the sake of comparison, during 1981–85, when investment grew at 3.5 percent, new commissionings grew at 3.0 percent, below the 1986–88 rate but relatively close to the investment growth rate.

Table 1. *Soviet Economic Performance, 1981–1990 (Plan)*
(percent per annum unless otherwise indicated)

	1981–85 actual (a)	1986–90 plan (b)	1986–88 actual (c)	1986 actual (d)	1987 actual (e)	1988 actual (f)	1989 plan (g)	1989 Ja-Jn (h)	1990 plan (i)
National income utilized* (1)	3.1%	4.1%	3.0%	3.4%	1.5%	4.2%	3.4%	n.a.	n.a.
National income produced* (2)	3.6%	n.a.	3.6%	4.1%	2.3%	4.4%	3.8%	2.5%	2.0%
GNP (official Soviet*) (3)	4.1%	n.a.	4.1%	4.1%	3.1%	5.0%	4.5%	3.5%	n.a.
GNP (CIA estimate**) (4)	1.9%	n.a.	2.2%	4.0%	1.3%	1.5%	n.a.	2.8%	n.a.
Labor productivity in material sectors* (5)	3.1%	4.2%	3.8%	3.8%	2.4%	5.1%	4.4%	3.0%	n.a.
Gross state investment* (6)	3.5%	4.3%	6.3%	8.3%	5.7%	4.8%	2.3%	3.0%	n.a.
Per capita income (official Soviet*) (7)	2.1%	2.7%	2.7%	2.5%	2.0%	2.5%	3.1%	n.a.	n.a.
Per capita consumption (CIA est.**) (8)	0.8%	n.a.	0.3%	-1.5%	1.0%	1.5%	n.a.	n.a.	n.a.
Budget deficit (billion rubles) (9)	R17.6	n.a.	R65.7	R51.9	R66.2	R79.0	R120.0	n.a.	R60.0
Savings deposits (10)	7.1%	n.a.	10.5%	10.0%	9.9%	11.5%	n.a.	12.3%	n.a.
Net HC debt (billion dollars) (11)	$12.6	n.a.	$26.6	$21.5	$27.1	$28.2	n.a.	n.a.	n.a.
Debt service ratio (12)	.13	n.a.	.18	.17	.18	.20	n.a.	n.a.	n.a.

Sources: For columns: b) Ryzhkov, 1986; c) Average of d, e, f; g) (except 9-g) Maslyukov, 1988; h) (except 10-h) Goskomstat 1989b; i) Maslyukov, 1989. For rows: 4) CIA-DIA, 1989, Table B-4;
8) CIA-DIA, 1989 Table B-3; 11–12) *PETFR-SU*, July 1989, pages 25, 27. Remaining entries (row number-column letter):

1-a) *Narkhoz 1987*, 388; 1-d, e) *Narkhoz 1987*, 8; 1-f) Goskomstat 1989a.
2-a) *Narkhoz 1987*, 7; 2-d, e) *Narkhoz 1987*, 8; 2-f) Goskomstat 1989a.
3-a) *Narkhoz 1987*, 15; 3-d, e) *Narkhoz 1987*, 14; 3-f) Goskomstat 1989a.
5-a) *Narkhoz 1987*, 7; 5-d, e) *Narkhoz 1987*, 8; 5-f) Goskomstat 1989a.
6-a) *Narkhoz 1987*, 293; 6-d, e) *Narkhoz 1987*, 8; 6-f) Goskomstat 1989a.
7-a) *Narkhoz 1987*, 7; 7-d, e) *Narkhoz 1987*, 8; 7-f) Goskomstat 1989b.
9-a, d, e, f) *PER*, 41: November 4, 1988; 9-g) Maslyukov, 1989; 9-i) Maslyukov, 1989 (where he says the deficit will be cut by about one-half in 1990 over 1989).
10-a, d, e) *Narkhoz 1987*, -406; 10-f) Goskomstat 1989a and *Narkhoz 1987*, 406; 10-h) First half of 1989 from Goskomstat 1989b divided by first half of 1988 from Goskomstat 1988.

*In Soviet "comparable prices" of 1973 (for 1981–1985 data, and of 1983 for data after 1986.
**In fixed, 1982, prices.
act.—actual.
n.a.—Data not available.
HC—hard currency.

Despite the fact that investment was growing above plan, and defense was most likely growing on plan for these years, there is no indication in Soviet official figures of any shortfall in the growth of per capita real income. That seems implausible. The CIA data tell a more believable story, indicating a virtual stagnation in per capita consumption.

What is most interesting about these data—even those from the CIA—is that, in isolation, they indicate an economy in decent shape. GNP growth rates in the 2-percent range are considered quite respectable in Western countries. The per capita consumption growth rates are low, but hardly consistent with the "crisis" which many inside and outside the USSR see.

But if one looks a little deeper, the signs of trouble are unmistakable. The budget deficit has exploded under Gorbachev, rising from an annual average of R17.6 billion in 1981–1985 (2.4 percent of GNP) to R79 billion in 1988 (9.1 percent of GNP), and an estimated R120 billion (13.7 percent of GNP) in 1989.[8] Prime Minister Ryzhkov made it clear during the Congress of People's Deputies that this deficit was unanticipated, and that it reflected in large part, although not exclusively, the impact of exogenous events (Ryzhkov, 1989, pp. 2–3):

- an unanticipated decline in the terms of trade (primarily due to declining oil prices) led to an estimated R30 billion loss (presumably in government receipts from foreign trade);

- R8 billion for Chernobyl';

- R10 billion in unanticipated additional expenditures for agriculture;

- R21 in unanticipated additional expenditures for reforming the health services, general and higher education, increasing pensions to various groups, improving assistance to children in low-income families, and improving living conditions for orphans;

- unspecified expenditures for clean-up from the Armenian earthquake;

- unspecified cost of the anti-alcohol campaign, which probably amounted to approximately R15 billion in lost tax receipts in 1988.[9]

In addition, Ryzhkov mentioned a R5 billion cost per year for Afghanistan, but that cannot be regarded as unanticipated.

The total, not counting Armenia, is R84 billion, which more than covers the 1988 deficit. Armenia would surely bring the total above R90 billion. But

8. The GNP estimates are from *PER*, 6–7: February 17, 1989, pp. 14–15. The 1989 GNP is a guesstimate, 1 percent above 1988. Gur Ofer (Ofer, 1989) has a preliminary estimate of R125 billion in 1989, or 13.8 percent of GNP.

9. During 1980–1984, turnover tax receipts from alcohol sales were growing at 3.5 percent per annum, having reached R43.6 billion in 1984. In 1986 they bottomed out at R31.7 billion; by 1988 they were back up approximately to R35 billion (*PER*, 41: November 4, 1988, p. 10). Assuming the 3.5 percent growth had continued through 1988, turnover tax receipts from alcohol would have been R50 billion.

some of Ryzhkov's figures may be too high. For example, the budgetary impact of the terms-of-trade loss was probably closer to R20 billion than R30 billion.[10] In general it would be necessary to see the analysis behind the figures before taking them seriously as indicators of the sources of the deficit explosion. But even in their current form, they do make the important point that roughly half of the unanticipated deficit is attributable to factors totally beyond the control of Gorbachev-era leaders: the oil price decline (R20–R30 billion); Chernobyl' (R8 billion); Armenia (at least R5 billion). The biggest self-inflicted wound was the anti-alcohol campaign, costing about R15 billion.

The deficit is not directly comparable to that of a Western country, primarily because state centralized investment is an on-budget item, accounting for approximately R82 billion in 1989. Taking that out, the Soviet budgetary deficit as a percent of GNP drops from 13.7 percent to 4.8 percent (Ofer, 1989c, Table 1), which is roughly comparable to similar figures for Western countries, and far less alarming than the unadjusted figure.[11] What is alarming is the rate at which that deficit has risen over the last few years. In 1981—1985 that budget deficit, excluding centralized investment expenditures, was in surplus, averaging R46.6 billion, or 6.5 percent of GNP (Ofer, 1989, Table 2).

Another alarming indicator of strong and growing inflationary pressures can be found in the rapidly expanding gap between productivity and wage growth. In 1986–1988, when productivity grew an average of 3.1 percent per annum, the wage "fund" in the economy grew an average of 3.7 percent (*Narkhoz*, 1989, p. 10), clearly an undesirable and, in the long run, untenable relationship, but not something requiring immediate action given the fairly tight control over prices. But in 1988, apparently as a result of the new freedom in wage-setting given to enterprises under the Enterprise Law, matters began to get out of hand. In a year when productivity grew an average of 5.1 percent, the wage fund grew an average of 5.5 percent in the first half of the year, and 6.5 percent during the second half (the third quarter being the worst at 8.2 percent) (*PER*, 6–7: February 17, 1989, p. 12). In the first half of 1989 wages exploded, growing 9.5 percent (relative to the first half of 1988), while productivity grew only 2.8 percent (Goskomstat, 1989b).

Because prices are still under relatively tight control in the USSR, these inflationary pressures are likely to spill over into a combination of shortages and involuntary saving, although one would also expect hidden inflation to accelerate. One Soviet economist has estimated that mostly hidden inflation averaged 2 percent per annum during 1971–1987, then doubled to 4 percent

10. Net foreign trade taxes (primarily the difference between export receipts converted to domestic rubles and the wholesale price of export goods) were contributing approximately R86 billion to the budget at their peak in 1985, on the eve of the decline in oil prices. By 1988 Vanous estimates they had fallen to R67 billion (*PER*, 41: November 4, 1988, p. 10).

11. This is one of the most important conclusions from Gur Ofer's (1989) excellent analysis of the Soviet budget. Another way to think about this is that if Soviet leaders decided tomorrow to take all R82 billion in centralized investment off budget, and at the same time to divert the R63.4 billion in funds from the state savings bank (Ofer, 1989, Table 1) directly to finance the projects, with the remainder coming through the commerical banking system, then the deficit would fall to 4.8 percent of GNP.

per annum in 1988. Some Soviet and Western economists estimate the 1988–1989 inflation rate to be in the 6 percent to 9 percent range.[12]

Moreover, it is generally recognized now by Soviet leaders that shortages have worsened for many goods, including the most common commodities needed for everyday life; for example, sugar and soap are now rationed. Growth rates for savings deposits also are accelerating, reflecting growth in involuntary savings. Recorded savings (in the State Savings Bank), which grew at 7.1 percent during 1981–1985, grew at an average of 10.5 percent during 1986–1988, and 12.3 percent during the first half of 1989 (relative to the first half of 1988). Because savings deposit rates average 2–3 percent, and the rate of inflation (open and hidden) is surely higher, cash "under mattresses" may be growing even more rapidly.

The growing imbalance in the system also has spilled over into the balance of payments, although not in sufficient magnitude to threaten the USSR's excellent credit rating. Average net hard-currency debt doubled during 1986–1988 relative to 1981–1985, bringing debt service (interest on all debt, repayments of principal on medium and long-term debt) up from 13 percent of hard-currency exports in 1981–1985 to 20 percent of the estimated $34 billion in 1988 hard-currency receipts (*PETFR-SU*, July 1989, p. 27). For an economy with the raw material and fuel deposits of the USSR, with $15 billion in known dollar assets and a $32 billion gold stock (*Ibid.*, p. 26), this is a totally acceptable debt-servicing burden, offering considerable room for further borrowing.

The Congress of People's Deputies provided vivid testimony to the anger the population now feels over a deteriorating economic situation, all the more disappointing because Gorbachev and Ryzhkov promised in 1985–1986 a rapid improvement during the course of the Twelfth Five-Year Plan. One only needs to recall the hubris with which Soviet leaders projected that by 1990, 80–95 percent of Soviet serially produced manufactured goods would meet "world standards" (Hewett, 1988a, pp. 307–308). The current popular view of the Twelfth Five-Year Plan was probably best summarized by N. A. Nazarbayev, Chairman of the Kazakh SSR Council of Ministers and a delegate to the Congress of People's Deputies, who complained bitterly that it was just another example of an ill-fated plan drawn up in the old way, with an emphasis on quantity rather than quality. For him, and for many, the plan is dead. But for Nazarbayev that is not the end of it:

. . . [I]f someone introduces a proposal and manages to have it accepted—and . . . if it turns out in fact to be bankrupt, a bust—the authors are retired. And so we too, deputies, ought to know who in fact drew up such a five-

12. The latter figure is from Abel Aganbegyan, and refers to a rate for 1989 (*New York Times*, June 8, 1989, p. D9). PlanEcon estimates inflation in the range of 6–8 percent in 1988 (*PER*, 6–7: February 17, 1989, p. 9).

year plan, and whose ideas are being carried out in the course of restructuring. (FBIS-SU, June 28, 1989, p. 11)

The main author of that plan was Mikhail Gorbachev (Hewett, 1985a, p. 287).

The 1990 Emergency Plan

Without quick and resolute action to stabilize the economy, the situation will become truly dangerous, both for the reform and for the general political-economic situation. It was only toward the end of 1988 that Soviet leaders began to understand that not only were they not fulfilling the qualitative expectations of the Twelfth Five-Year Plan, but in fact that economic performance was beginning to deteriorate. That was the background for the Council of Ministers' Presidium meeting in January ("V presidiume," 1989), discussed earlier, and the February 16 Politburo meeting in which the first topic on the agenda was restoring the "financial health" (*finansovoye ozdovovleniye*) of the economy, which means a stabilization program. But, at least through the first half of 1989, there was no evidence of any serious effort to deal with the growing signs of disequilibrium, with the exception of an apparent decision to raise interest rates charged to farms and enterprises to 15 percent, approximately tripling their costs for short-term credits.[13]

Out of that has come a stabilization program for 1989–1990, which includes an effort to reduce subsidies to loss-making enterprises, cuts in defense spending (relative to the plan), and economies in central administrative costs. Nikolay Ryzhkov has promised that these measures will cut the deficit by R29 billion in 1989 and R34 billion in 1990 (Ryzhkov, 1989, p. 3). The particulars of how this will be accomplished, and the specific linkage between these budget reduction targets and Yuriy Maslyukov's promise to halve what he estimated to be a R120-billion 1989 deficit by 1990, are not clear. In fact, the scant available evidence suggests that the government began this summer concerned about the economy, and in particular the deficit, desirous of doing something about it, but not terribly clear what it should do.

Certainly the Congress of People's Deputies thought that the government was dragging its feet. Their first and most urgent goal was to attack inequities revealed over the last few years. With support (and pressure) from the Congress, the government acted to increase pensions for various classes of workers, increase payments to war veterans and widows of servicemen, and increase payments to invalids. The new measures, which Nikolay Ryzhkov estimates will cost R6 billion (Ryzhkov, 1989, p. 2), will be financed through increased enterprise payments for social insurance and taxes based on the size of administrative staff ("Zakon," 1989). These measures are a first response to

---

13. Although the decree has not been published, there are several references to it. See, for example, the speech to the May 31, 1989, session of the Congress by V. A. Starodubtsev (FBIS-SU Supplement, June 2, 1989, p. 6), and an interview with former Minister of Finance, Boris Gostev (Gonzal'yez, 1989).

some of the shocking revelations over the last several years of the scale of poverty in the USSR, and its concentration among pensioners, in particular those living in the countryside.[14]

The Resolution of the Congress on domestic and foreign policy clearly signals an intention to keep up the pressure on equity issues, and at the same time to push the government for quick and resolute action on the economy with a goal of dramatically improving living standards, particularly in the country-side, while addressing long-standing issues concerning the environment, working conditions, the role of women, the impact of inflation on fixed incomes (pensions in particular), and the issue of equitable access to all services ("Ob osnovnykh," 1989). The labor strikes during the summer of 1989 beginning in the Kuzbass, but spreading to other areas, simply underlined the urgency of these goals.

The government has begun to respond in what can only be called an emergency plan for 1990, outlined in a preliminary draft form to the Supreme Soviet on August 5 (Maslyukov, 1989). The plan was far from complete as of then, one of the major unresolved issues being the level of imports (probably of consumer goods), but the major contours are clear and rather remarkable.

The Twelfth Five-Year Plan targets have been abandoned. National income is to grow by only 2 percent per annum, a welcome retreat from the preoccupation with growth rates. The focus has shifted from high growth to the restoration of balance in the financial system, and in the market for consumer goods.

The commitment to restore financial balance is symbolized by a commitment to cut the deficit in half in one year, apparently primarily through expenditure reductions:

- Capital expenditures in the productive sphere (approximately three-quarters of all investment) are to be cut 30 percent, with 40 percent cuts in the fuel-energy and metallurgical complexes.

- Defense expenditures are to be cut, but the amount is not given.

- Further cuts are planned in the size of the central apparatus.

- Subsidies are to be cut to enterprises operating at a loss, although no figure is given.

No specific measures are mentioned to raise revenue, although Maslyukov does mention that he expects the push for higher efficiency will raise profits, and therefore receipts from profits taxes.

These are demand-side measures designed to cut the hemorrhage in the money supply. The new wage tax which comes into effect on October 1, 1989, should be considered part of this package ("O nalogooblozhenii," 1989).

---

14. The general figure the Congress worked with was approximately 43 million Soviet living on less than R75 per month, which is the official poverty line. See, for example, Ryzhkov's statement before the Congress (FBIS-SU, June 9, 1989, p. 4).

According to this decree, any increase in the wage fund above 3 percent per annum will be taxed at a progressive rate:

- a 50 percent tax rate on increments to wage funds in the range of 3 percent to 5 percent growth;
- a 66.7 percent tax rate on increments to wage funds in the range of 5 percent to 7 percent;
- a 75 percent tax rate on increments to wage funds above 7 percent.

Unfortunately, there is an exception granted for wages devoted to the production of consumer goods and services, which inevitably will set the stage for complex games between enterprises and authorities. Moreover, the decree calls on re-publican Councils of Ministers to devise mechanisms for controlling wage payments in cooperatives, which could simply turn into another restriction on cooperatives. In addition, the decree calls on the Council of Ministers to present to the Supreme Soviet a plan to eliminate unjustified price increases (presumably through simulations of new products, and other devices), which could provide a rationale for a new effort at administrative control over prices.

The government also is searching for ways to soak up the accumulated excess purchasing power in savings accounts and household cash reserves. Maslyukov indicated that Gosplan is working on proposals for raising savings deposit rates to attract savings and for issuing bonds which offer high interest rates. He also encourages republics to think of schemes in which loans are solicited from the population in exchange for guaranteed access to scarce goods and services.

In addition to these financial measures, the 1990 plan signals an all-out effort to dramatically expand the supply of consumer goods, primarily through extraordinarily high rates of increase in their production. The preliminary 1990 targets call for the production of all consumer goods to increase by 12 percent; the production of non-food consumer goods to rise by 18 percent; and the production of durables to rise 24 percent. All of this is designed to flood the market with consumer goods in an effort to reduce shortages or at least, as Maslyukov says, to arrest the deterioration in the economy.

In support of this policy—but also in an effort to improve the balance of payments—imports of heavy industrial products will be cut substantially.[15] Investments in consumer goods industries and imports of heavy industrial prod-ucts for consumer goods will be shielded from the cuts. Defense conversion will be accelerated to support expanded supplies of consumer goods. Imports of consumer goods will rise, although by how much is not clear.

The effort to expand the supply of consumer goods, and to soak up excess purchasing power, would both obviously be served by a program to import consumer goods, pricing them at whatever the market will bear. Maslyukov indicates a serious disagreement within the leadership on the "foreign trade

---

15. Rolled ferrous metals, including cold-rolled steel, for example.

variants'' in the plan, meaning presumably the level of consumer goods imports. He told the Congress that there was no way of getting around the need to export raw materials and fuels in the near term, and that even then hard-currency debt would rise in 1990. The problem seems to be the level of consumer goods imports.

Presumably, there is some support for Shmelev's proposal of large consumer goods imports, say in the range of $15 billion, to be sold at R10 = $1 ("Obmenyayemsya," 1989).[16] The problem is that the leadership is generally much more concerned about the Soviet international financial position than its actual situation would seem to warrant. Ryzhkov has strongly opposed consumer goods imports and, in a strange episode during the Congress, he dramatically overstated Soviet hard-currency debt-service, implying it was something like 75 percent of hard-currency receipts, when in fact it is in the range of 20 percent.[17] Part of the problem here was surely that Ryzhkov was given some bad numbers. But, in addition, he was reflecting a strong consensus among top leaders that this is not the time to borrow for consumers, mainly because there is no guarantee that as a result exports will improve sufficiently to service the new debt.

PROSPECTS FOR THE FUTURE: THE LONGER TERM

Right now the top priority in the USSR must be to arrest the decline in the economy, stabilize the situation, and then as quickly as possible get on with the reform. The policy mistakes of the last four years, most notably the terribly weak control over monetary aggregates in 1988–1989, have led to a deterioration in the economy which many Soviets associate with *perestroyka*, and which as a consequence is threatening support for further reforms. That has also led to a decline in the credibility of the Soviet leadership. For that reason it is critical that the next reform package be well considered—radical but feasible. And then Soviet leaders must make certain they follow through. If the leadership repeats the exercise in fantasy which accompanied the Twelfth Five-Year Plan, they will lose whatever remaining credibility they have with the population.

Oversimplifying, a successful package must have two parts—a short-term stabilization component and a longer-term reform program—and inevitably there will be tension between the two. In the stabilization program there will be a constant temptation to go back to familiar administrative approaches as a "temporary" response to a deteriorating situation. Those "temporary" solu-

16. Nikolay Shmelev has done quite well with his proposals. He has suggested a one-third cut in investment expenditures, and has gotten that from Maslyukov. He has proposed that farmers be paid in hard currency, possibly at one-half to one-third the world price (at the official exchange rate), and has gotten that. Now he has apparently triggered serious consideration of a proposal for massive consumer goods imports. For all of these proposals, see, for example, "Obmenyayemsya," 1989.

17. For a discussion see *PETFR-SU*, July 1989.

tions may actually worsen the situation, which will in turn lead to a tendency for the "temporary" approaches to become permanent.

On the other hand, there will be strong voices in the government, in the Congress, and among the specialists, who will make the case that administrative measures got them where they are, and can be of only limited utility in improving matters. The urge to fall back on what is familiar but ineffective, and the rational realization that such a course is self-destructive, will provide a constant source of tension in the foreseeable future in the USSR, even under the best of circumstances.

Simultaneously with the introduction of an effective stabilization program, Soviet leaders will have to develop a coherent strategy (of which the stabilization package will be only one part) for the economic reform, reflecting a social and political consensus. Without a well thought-through, and radical, reform strategy, the stabilization package will only provide, at best, short-lived relief. Without a stabilization package the reforms will never get off the ground, because it is impossible to "monetize" an economy in this state of monetary disequilibrium. The stabilization package and the reform package are mutually indispensable, the two legs on which a successful economic strategy must rest.

Soviet leaders made significant progress in assembling a stabilization package during the summer of 1989. The government is taking inflationary pressures seriously now, and it has discarded the Twelfth Five-Year Plan. Both developments are very good news for the economy. But there is much more work to be done if the 1990 plan is to be turned into a credible stabilization package. The target of a R60-billion reduction in the deficit looks, on the surface, like little more than a wish. To give it credibility, and to actually achieve it, the government will have to put together a set of realistic expenditure reductions and revenue increases. Investment cuts will be part of the package, and here the government will have to make sure that the cuts are handled in a way which minimizes disruption in what will be inevitably a disruptive period, while maximizing the likelihood that salable goods are produced for domestic and foreign customers.

The planned increases in consumer goods production (the major supply-side component of the 1990 plan) will be one of several focal points in the tension between administrative and economic methods. Some resort to administrative measures is inevitable in the quick turnaround Soviet planners are seeking to engineer. But, if the longer-term goal is a radical reform, they will have to try to maximize the use of tax incentives and prices instead of brute-force decrees via *goszakazy*. Coops, and leased enterprises, operating under minimal restrictions in an economic environment where consumer rubles mean something, could go a long way to meet consumer needs quickly without resorting to old planning and management techniques. This is one way in which the new approach to property rights, which must play a central role in the radical reform, could also be part of the stabilization process setting the stage for the reform.

The 1990 plan focuses primarily on stemming the imbalance between the flows of money and goods. It discusses possibilities for dealing with the equally important threat from the monetary "overhang," representing accumulated excess purchasing power, but there are very few specifics. This overhang might decline somewhat if there were a successful stabilization program which reduced inflationary expections (and therefore increased the appeal of holding money), but that is some way off. For now the government will have to be very creative, not only raising interest rates, or permitting bond sales for high rates, but also contemplating the sale of apartments, possibly issuing bonds with interest paid in hard currency, and possibly permitting the sale of small enterprises to private entrepreneurs. In addition, this is obviously where consumer goods imports could be immensely helpful.

The new wage tax is a move in the right direction and of the right sort, similar to systems tried with some success in Hungary. It does not order enterprises to cut back wage increases; rather it penalizes them for excessive wage increases. The 3 percent wage increase limit, beyond which taxes are collective at a progressively higher rate, is a reasonable estimate of real productivity growth in this system. A highly progressive income tax would do the same thing, but this is probably better as a temporary solution since it appears to place the tax burden on the enterprises, not individuals—admittedly an illusion—and it allows individual wage differentiation for incentive purposes. If the stabilization program were successful, and Soviet workers discovered that, say, a 3 percent increase in wages meant a 3 percent increase in real goods, that would be a major improvement over the current situation.

The most critical determinant of the fate of the reform itself is the Reform Commission. Its brief includes the important reform issues; on paper it has sufficient powers; and it has the best economic policy team yet assembled in a Soviet government. That would be sufficient to provide a decent chance for success if it were not for the daunting political, social, and economic challenges facing the USSR in the foreseeable future.

The Commission will have to serve as an honest broker in the burgeoning debate on economics, encouraging that debate, drawing on the best ideas, and bringing them into the mainstream policy-making process as soon as possible. It will be critical for this commission to support and elaborate a conception of *de facto* privatization (or *razgosudarstvleniye*) in a competitive environment where entry is easy, unfettered by national or local bureaucrats. If that can be accepted in principle by Soviet leaders, and then codified into law, and if the stabilization program takes hold, then it will be easier to move ahead with price and banking reforms so important to the long-term future of the reform.

All of this takes place in the midst of tremendous pressures from a difficult economic situation, and in the context of increasing demands from republics for increased autonomy. If the Reform Commission is sufficiently committed to its task, then both of these situations work to its advantage. The deteriorating economic situation is an argument for more, and more radical, reform, not less, a point which even the conservative Maslyukov made in his discussion of the 1990 plan (Maslyukov, 1989). The push for greater republican autonomy is also an opportunity if it is used to broaden property rights and to monetize relations in the economy.

But both the deteriorating economic situation and the drive for increased regional autonomy have their dangers for the reform process. If Soviet leaders continue to dwell on the dangers of the current economic situation, without looking for opportunities, they may panic, leading to a reversal of the reforms. And, if republican self-finance degenerates into republican autarky, where republican bureaucrats replace all-union bureaucrats in the over-centralized administration of the economy, then matters could grow worse, not better.

This next year will be critical. If by early next year there is a consensus on a credible reform program to be implemented in the early 1990s, beginning with a well thought-through stabilization package; if the work for the Thirteenth Five-Year Plan truly reflects a radically new, economically oriented approach to economic policy; if the reform of the administrative apparatus gathers momentum; and if somehow with luck and political skill Soviet leaders can cope with the tremendous social forces unleashed by *glasnost'*, then the USSR will be on the right track for the reform so many Soviets wish for.

As it is, all that can be said now is that, with luck and determination, the economic situation and the economic reform are both still salvageable, and the economic situation is alarming enough that the political elite is ready to contemplate radical changes. Time will tell whether or not this government is actually able to seize the opportunity.

Part IV

Entering the
1990s

Editors'
Introduction

THE FIRST chapter of the final part of this volume brings another encounter with the bureaucratic labyrinth, highlighting the maneuvering and infighting within the new economic environment. Presenting a comprehensive survey of policymaking from the summer of 1989 through September 1990, Anders Åslund leads us to the 1990s by discussing the political and institutional dissonance at the top. Again, there is a focus on such key architects of the foundering *perestroyka* as Leonid Abalkin, Abel Aganbegyan, Oleg Bogomolov, Nikolay Petrakov, and Stanislav Shatalin, the only economist on the now-defunct Presidential Council and the one responsible for drafting the so-called 500-Day Plan. "The Making of Economic Policy in 1989 and 1990" is in fact a sequel to Chapter 7, equally balanced in its assessment of the state of the economy but more outspoken about the need to abandon the past and thus prevent the rapidly approaching breakdown of the mechanism.

By 1990 the economy was in deep recession with every prospect that 1991 would be worse. The apparent failure of measures designed to make *perestroyka* a promising path to prosperity coalesced with the already explosive political climate to create a sense of lost direction and impending chaos. Was Gorbachev aware of the crisis? And what measures, if any, led this once functioning economy to the brink of anticipated disaster? A grasp for words to answer these uneasy questions is evident in Yevgeny Yevtushenko's poem "Half-measures," which is presented in the companion volume, *Milestones in Glasnost' and Perestroyka: Politics and People*.

After the events of the remarkable summer of 1989, with televised debates denouncing the state of the economy and the first massive labor strikes in modern Soviet history, came the irreversible collapse of communism and central planning in Eastern Europe in the fall of that year.

The Abalkin reform proposals—a brief hopeful sign—fared poorly, encountering a generally hostile reception from economic officials, CPSU apparatchiks, and other bureaucrats and politicians. Both the then Prime Minster

Ryzhkov and, to some extent, Gorbachev distanced themselves from Abalkin's measures, though their impact was clear in subsequent reform plans. In December 1989, Ryzhkov came to the Supreme Soviet with plans for 1990 and the 1991–1995 period that paid lip-service to many of Abalkin's specific recommendations. In May 1990, Ryzhkov's government outlined yet another more comprehensive plan for moving to a regulated market system. But while these plans were debated, the economic decline continued. And while the government seemed capable of deliberating endlessly, it appeared more able to talk than act. In May 1990, Ryzhkov again made a bad mistake by proposing a dramatic increase in retail prices, while also proposing to compensate the consumer almost fully by increasing personal incomes. Confidence in the government had fallen so low that the proposal was bluntly rejected. Ryzhkov was ordered to come back to the Supreme Soviet with a new panacea by September 1990.

"The Economic Crisis: Another Perspective," by Dr. James H. Noren of the Central Intelligence Agency, is an attempt to analyze factors contributing to that crisis by providing an overview of economic performance from March 1985 to September 1990. An effort to assess the economy's ability to recover is followed by an outline of near-term prospects. Can the country's economy muddle through? Not surprisingly, part of the answer is to be found in such preconditions for a regulated market economy as curbing excess demand for consumer goods, reducing the budget deficit, rationing credit, and decontrolling prices. However, because experience with successful reforming of centrally planned economies is so limited, Dr. Noren is not in favor of pedantic recommendations—be they in the form of remedial measures themselves or in the sequencing of such measures.

In "'Crisis' in the Consumer Sector: A Comment," Gertrude Schroeder echoes Noren's reluctance to rely on the flow of alarming news and is reinforced by statistical data of Soviet origin that is no less pessimistic. She analyzes the seeming contradiction between observations of empty shelves in stores, which have fueled perceptions of deteriorating living standards since the beginning of *perestroyka*, and the fact that CIA and Soviet statistical measures show increases in real consumption. She notes that goods have been diverted on a large scale into household hoards, sales through workplaces, and black market channels. The growing difficulties in obtaining consumer goods in the face of rapidly rising money incomes, along with accelerating inflation, have reduced the quality of life and people's welfare.

By far the most disruptive element in the country's economy as it was entering the 1990s was the debate over the nature of the Union. The election of Boris Yel'tsin in May 1990 to the chairmanship of the Supreme Soviet of the RSFSR strengthened the assertiveness of other republics, energized those seeking independence, and encouraged all to demand a share in a variety of Union resources. After declaring sovereignty and supremacy of Russian over Soviet law in June 1990, Russia's Supreme Soviet proposed to curtail the economic empire of the bureaucratic center. Only the defense industry, transport and communications, and energy distribution were to continue in the center's domain. The remainder, including all property within Russia's borders, would come under the jurisdiction of its republican apparatus, which lost no time in attempting to take over Gosbank and the ministry that controls the oil and gas industries. By the summer of 1990, it was clear to virtually everyone that the country within the borders of the USSR was in the midst of profound crisis corroding the economy and burdening the leadership beyond the limits of political endurance. Unmistakable signs of deepening recession and accelerating inflation were in abundance. Meanwhile, the government of Nikolay Ryzhkov was making no headway on the new version of its plan for economic stabilization that was commissioned for September.

Boris Yel'tsin, the focal point of the crisis, made clear from the very beginning his commitment to Russia's transformation into a market economy, whether or not Mikhail Gorbachev was ready to go along. His government, announced in July, was headed by several of the most articulate advocates of Western-style economies, including Grigoriy Yavlinskiy, Boris Fedorov, and Mikhail Bocharov. The team quickly set out to design a plan for rapid reform in the Russian republic, while at the same time Yel'tsin kept up the public pressure on Gorbachev to restructure all republics and the entire Union into a market economy. Engaged in an increasingly acrimonious and damaging struggle for control, the two leaders and their institutions imposed on the economy and the populace the stress of conflicting measures that began to paralyze the country.

By July 1990, the pressure became strong enough for Gorbachev to consider a blueprint for action that he and Yel'tsin could both support. The 500-Day Plan and the two competing alternatives came out of this brief period when the two rivals for the coveted seat of power were said to be at peace.

The 500-Day Plan, also known as the Shatalin Plan, was in many ways a logical outgrowth of the aspirations of the republics for genuine sovereignty in a viable system. It proposed that the USSR reconstitute itself as a confederation governed through an Interrepublican Economic Committee on which each republic would be represented equally. With power flowing from the republics, the Committee would be in charge of all-Union authorities set up to handle defense, foreign policy, pricing of key commodities, and environmental protection. The core of the economy, however, including tax collection and the power to spend, would rest with the republics. The newly formed confederation would then move within "500 days" to install the infrastructure of a free market economy and dismantle the old administrative system

The all-important issue of property rights—a key element in the dismantling of state monopolies, destatization, and eventual privatization—is reviewed and analyzed in light of the 500-Day Plan by Philip Hanson. "Property Rights in the New Phase of Reforms" details the essence of federal laws on leasing land, joint-stock companies, small business enterprises, and other forms of ownership, which are then compared with relevant provisions of the Shatalin Plan. Included in the chapter is a discussion and assessment of the process of privatization as it appeared to develop in early December 1990.

"The New Half-Measures," written by Ed Hewett at roughly the same time, looks at the Shatalin Plan, the resuscitated plan proffered by Nikolay Ryzhkov, and the "compromise" pasted up in apparent haste by Abel Aganbegyan. Many of the ideas in the 500-Day Plan could be traced to Abalkin and most were in evidence in the last moribund program supported by Ryzhkov, which, among other shortcomings, lacked the commitment to privatization of state-owned enterprises.

But the most striking, albeit understandable, difference between the two conflicting half-measures, the one advocated by Ryzhkov and the other by Shatalin, was the latter's commitment to confederation. Under Shatalin's 500-Day Plan, the Ryzhkov government would have disappeared, the ministries would have been eliminated, while the Presidency and the Supreme Soviet of the country within the present boundaries of the USSR would have faced a dramatic reduction in their powers.

The unveiling of the Shatalin Plan set off a chain reaction of competing efforts to assert decisive authority. Boris Yel'tsin accepted the plan immediately, seeing it through approval and ratification by Russia's Supreme Soviet. Mikhail Gorbachev, however, wavered. After a period of hesitation and confusion, he turned to the somewhat tarnished talents and services of Abel Aganbegyan, who promptly proceeded to "reconcile" Shatalin's plan with Ryzhkov's resuscitated proposal. The result, known as the "Presidential Plan" approved by the Supreme Soviet in mid-October 1990, was a vaguely worded half-measure rhetorically committed to stabilize the economy without the confederation, the privatization, or the liberal price reforms featured in the 500-Day Plan.

The failure of the 500-Day Plan led to a political and economic crisis of enormous dimensions, whose consequences are yet to become fully apparent. Gertrude Schroeder, in *"Perestroyka* in the Aftermath of 1990," tells us that the year 1990—an economic milestone—was both the worst and in a way the best since the Second World War. While total output declined and consumer problems worsened, laws and economic reform programs that would have been unthinkable five years earlier were at least put on the books. Written in early 1991, her concise study embraces a discussion of efforts by republic and lower-level administrative territorial units to exert greater control over economic activity within their borders, over trade relations with other regions, and over budget allocations to the center. No fewer than six republics and the center are now engaged in an increasingly grim struggle for power. And the March 1991 referendum does not augur a lasting respite from the confrontation. Hence the resolution of the crisis of governance becomes the single most important objective while the economy struggles to stay alive. Will it disintegrate before we determine who ultimately remains in charge? And if so, when? In the words of a radical legislator interviewed by David Remnick of the *Washington Post* in mid-March, "It depends on your definition of time."

CHAPTER 19

The Making of Economic Policy in 1989 and 1990

Anders Åslund

THE PURPOSE of this chapter is to trace changes in the system of economic policy making in the Soviet Union from the summer of 1989 up to the 28th Congress of the CPSU in July 1990.[1] The emphasis will rest on the role of institutions and their interaction, but important individuals also will be highlighted. It focuses on attempts at fundamental economic reform, at the central level, undertaken by consecutive reform commissions of the USSR Council of Ministers, with the exception of agricultural reform, which has been discussed in other forums. Current economic policy is the exclusive domain of the government and the narrative here examines the institutions and people who make policy, rather than what they decide. Thus, the substance of economic reform is not covered in this discussion.

The paper first summarizes the system of economic policy making established during the second half of 1985, and then proceeds to analyze the new economic and political environment that emerged during the period from 1986 to 1989. This is followed by a review of economic expertise. The main thrust of the paper scrutinizes, to the extent of their relevancy, the changes in economic policy making in the Politburo and the Central Committee (CC) of the CPSU, the government, the legislature, the Presidential Council, and the economic brain trust. The paper also examines the role of Mikhail Gorbachev in 1989 and 1990. Finally, an afterword, written in September 1990 following the 28th Congress of the CPSU held that July, provides an update to the material presented in earlier parts of the paper.

First published in *Soviet Economy*, 1990, 6, 1, pp. 65–94. The author would like to thank each of the 34 Soviet economists and officials mentioned in this chapter for useful talks related to this topic in 1989 or 1990. Also, Sten Luthman and Marion Cutting were of assistance in many ways. [Eds.]

1. This chapter constitutes a sequel to Åslund (1987), published in *Soviet Economy*.

335

THE LEGACY OF INSTITUTIONAL CHANGES
SINCE 1985[2]

During the last four months of 1985, important personnel changes took place in the Soviet government, allowing it to expand its policy-making powers at the expense of the CC of the CPSU. Upon becoming Prime Minister, Nikolay Ryzhkov saw to it that the Chancellery of the Council of Ministers had a policy-making apparatus. Dr. Pyotr Katsura was appointed to head a new department devoted to the "economic mechanism" and Professor Anatoliy Milyukov became his deputy. In the spring of 1987, Professor Vadim Kirichenko became the head of a new department on economic policy.[3] All three were professional economists.

Reform issues were to be sorted out in the Commission for the Improvement of Management, Planning and the Economic Mechanism established as an appendage of the Council of Ministers in December 1985. Although this commission was directly subordinated to the Council of Ministers, it was in fact controlled by the State Planning Committee (Gosplan). Its first chairman was First Deputy Prime Minister Nikolay Talyzin, at the time also Chairman of Gosplan.[4] Gosplan was responsible for staffing the commission's secretariat. However, because its scientific section was controlled by reform economists from the academic community, the two—the commission and its scientific section—were locked in a continuous tug of war. Moreover, after the introduction of the reform in 1988, the staff of Gosplan was reduced by one-third, to a total of 2,000 people.

The Economic Department of the Academy of Sciences and its main economic institutes, all subjected to considerable reorganizations in 1985 and 1986, were intended to be the main sources of external economic advice. Academician Abel Aganbegyan emerged as the country's chief economist, heading the Economic Department of the Academy of Sciences from the summer of 1985. The second politically influential economist was the then Corresponding Member of the Academy, Leonid Abalkin. He became director of the Institute of Economics in Moscow in the spring of 1986. Not unexpectedly, a scientific section attached to the Talyzin Commission was headed by Aganbegyan as chairman and Abalkin as his deputy.

The two other politically active and influential academic economists were Academicians Oleg Bogomolov (Director of the Institute of the Economics of the World Socialist System, IEMSS) and Tat'yana Zaslavskaya from Novosibirsk. Next in political importance were Nikolay Petrakov and Stanislav

2. This section is based on Åslund (1987).

3. Previously Pyotr Katsura served as economic director of the Avtovaz car works in Togliatti, Anatoliy Milyukov had worked for the State Committee for Labor and Social Affairs, and Vadim Kirichenko previously served as the director of Gosplan's Economics Research Institute. Katsura's department employed some 10 professionals, and Kirichenko's about 20.

4. This commission will be referred to as the Talyzin Commission. However, Stepan Sitaryan, First Deputy Chairman of Gosplan, seems to have been in charge of its work.

Shatalin, both corresponding members of the Academy of Sciences and deputy directors of major economic institutes located in Moscow. The rise of reform-minded professors of economics was very much in evidence, and the Academy of Sciences was revitalized.

Not much transpired in the Politburo or in the CC of the CPSU. The CC Economic Department, with some 100 professionals, remained static. In January 1987, Nikolay Slyun'kov assumed the posts of CC Secretary for Economic Affairs and head of the CC Economic Department. By June 1987, he was elected a voting member of the Politburo. One of Aganbegyan's associates from Novosibirsk, Professor Vladimir Mozhin, was promoted to become first deputy chief of the CC Economic Department. Before Slyun'kov's and Mozhin's appointments to that department, their posts had remained vacant for one year and one-half year, respectively. These protracted vacancies at a time when the Council of Ministers was strengthening its role indicated that the power of the CC Economic Department was meant to decline.

During the first half of 1987, work on economic reform was pursued with some vigor. At the time, General Secretary Gorbachev participated actively in the work, especially inviting the leading reform economists (Aganbegyan, Abalkin, Bogomolov, and Zaslavskaya) to participate in long informal discussions. Traditionally, the General Secretary of the CPSU has had a personal aide for economic affairs. Even Konstantin Chernenko appointed an economic aide (Arkadiy Volskiy). But Gorbachev transferred Volskiy, without naming a replacement, relying instead on informal advisors on economic affairs. The more operative (day-to-day) work was directed by Nikolay Slyun'kov, who presented the reform proposals to a key CC conference in June 1987. The Talyzin Commission seems to have played a secondary role, acting on commands from the CPSU in the traditional manner.

In effect, the Talyzin Commission, Gosplan, and the central economic organizations were outranked by the scientific section. Aganbegyan (1989b, p. 21) reinforces this contention by stating that "the country's leading economists were engaged in the development and refinement of basic laws and also in the preparation of materials for the June 1987 Plenum." However, the central economic organs recovered their power when the issue became one of their application. At the same time, eleven applied decrees were developed and, according to Aganbegyan, "prepared by the apparatus of Gosplan, the Ministry of Finance, and Gosbank, in fact, without involving the scholars" (Aganbegyan, 1989b, p. 21).

The first reform wave culminated in the June 1987 CC Plenum and the subsequent adoption of the Law on the State Enterprise by the USSR Supreme Soviet. Two other important legal guidelines for reform were the Law on Individual Labor Activity of November 1986 and the Law on Cooperatives of May 1988. For the sake of brevity, references to reform in this paper essentially are limited to the Law on State Enterprise, which went into effect on January 1, 1988.

THE NEW ECONOMIC ENVIRONMENT

It did not take much time for the effects of the Law on the State Enterprise to be recognized as being virtually catastrophic. Initially, the public discussion focused on the so-called state orders that were supposed to regulate public purchases from enterprises. In fact, these state orders turned out to be the same as the old commands, so that in this regard little had changed. The outcome was blamed on Talyzin. He was perceived as an ineffective leader of Gosplan who failed both to comprehend reform and to carry out the orders of the Prime Minister. Reportedly, a direct clash between Talyzin and his protector, Ryzhkov, forced the former's removal (Åslund, 1989, pp. 124–126).

In February 1988, Yuriy Maslyukov replaced Talyzin as Gosplan's Chairman. Presumably, Maslyukov took over the chairmanship of the reform commission at about the same time. He seems to have managed to recover some of the powers that Gosplan lost under Talyzin's inept leadership, which Maslyukov himself continues to criticize (*Pravda*, July 5, 1990). He was well assisted by his deputies Stepan Sitaryan (elected an Academician in December 1987) and Leonard Vid, who were responsible for economic reform issues within Gosplan.

Soon enough it became apparent that the major change wrought by the reform in the economy was that wages and monetary incomes of the population had gone out of control. In 1988, average state wages increased by 8.3 percent—more than twice as fast as planned (*Narkhoz*, 1989, p. 77; *Pravda*, October 20, 1987). In 1989, this process accelerated in spite of several attempts to impede wage increases, both by administrative means and punitive taxes on wage increases. The monetary incomes of the population rose by 12.9 percent (*Pravda*, January 28, 1990). Wages had been more deregulated than prices by the reform, and major financial imbalances had been created.

In principle, prices remained fixed, but enterprises were allowed to adjust their assortments rather freely. As a result, cheap commodities vanished from production, while expensive products (convenient for the producers) became increasingly popular with manufacturers. Frequently, the physical volume of production declined, while value targets were attained. In time, all signs of a severe crisis had become very apparent (*PlanEcon Report*, February 2, 1990).

Because of the massive imbalances, most markets were demonetarized and virtually ceased to function. Barter trade, which is far less efficient than a command economy, proliferated. At the same time, reform legislation explicitly prohibited the central administration from interfering in the work of enterprises. In addition, the apparatus of the central economic bodies and ministries had been reduced by one-third, from 1.6 million people in 1986 to 1.1 million in 1988 (*Narkhoz*, 1989, p. 36).

The economy was stalemated. The old command structure no longer functioned, while no preconditions for a market economy had been created. Gross macroimbalances prevailed, plans for marketization had failed, and the old system was collapsing. In Maslyukov's words: "As a result [of the reform] the state management structures practically lost control over many of the most important aspects of economic development, including the regulation of monetary incomes of the population . . ." (*Pravda*, July 5, 1990).

Political responses to the alarming situation that was gaining momentum were not adequate. The 19th Party Conference in June–July 1988 focused on political reform. The financial crisis was properly noted in the fall of 1988, as the Minister of Finance revealed that the budget for 1989 contained a substantial deficit, soon assessed at 100 billion rubles (*Izvestiya*, October 28, 1988).

Gorbachev turned away from economic issues altogether, with the exception of agricultural reforms discussed with little success at the long-awaited CC Plenum in March 1989. Instead, he concentrated on domestic politics, as evidenced by the proceedings at the 19th Party Conference, and on reform of both the party and the political system. Gorbachev also devoted a great deal of his time to foreign policy, strangely, not dealing with economic reform from the summer of 1987 until the fall of 1989. The alienation between Gorbachev and the economists came into the open at the 19th Party Conference. One of its major highlights was a sharp attack by Leonid Abalkin on Soviet economic policy, which Gorbachev personally refuted (*Pravda*, June 30, 1988; July 1, 1988).

While Gorbachev turned his back on reform issues, Gosplan and other central organs of the Council of Ministers proceeded to consolidate control of the reform commission. On January 5, 1989, the Council of Ministers issued a decree on the "Commission for the Improvement of the Economic Mechanism at the USSR Council of Ministers," as the reform commission of December 1985 was renamed. Maslyukov also chaired that new commission, while Sitaryan acted as his deputy. Out of 28 members of this body, no fewer than four were functionaries of Gosplan and an additional 14 of the Council of Ministers. Gosplan staffed the secretariat serving both the Commission and its scientific section, still headed by Aganbegyan (*Sobraniye*, 1989a). A consecutive decree of March 31, 1989, substantiated assumptions that the Commission was to have very limited rights (*Sobraniye*, 1989b), leaving most responsibilities to the conventional line organization. Gosplan and the central organs of the Council of Ministers had reinforced their already strong control over meaningful efforts to promote reform.

By 1989, the reform had turned out to be no less than an economic failure. Popular pressures for improvements in the standard of living were rising, fomented by ever-worsening shortages and the advent of political liberalization. At the same time, while a decisive push for radicalized economic reform was badly needed, conservative forces of the government apparatus mounted an effort to organize their opposition. In the summer of 1989, after the first session of the Congress of People's Deputies, Gorbachev finally clearly demonstrated resolve to do something about economic reform.

THE DEVELOPMENT OF ECONOMIC EXPERTISE[5]

Surprisingly, few institutional changes occurred within the field of economic science after the first year of *perestroyka*. The predominance of the Academy of Sciences and Moscow continued. A few new institutes were established. Academician Tat'yana Zaslavskaya became the director of the new Center of the Study of Public Opinion in Moscow, and Professor Natalya M. Rimashevskaya of the new Institute of Socio-Economic Problems of the Population, formed by parts of the Institute of Economics and TsEMI (the Central Economics-Mathematical Institute) of the Academy of Sciences. Toward the end of 1989, the Institute of the Market was formed out of parts of TsEMI under the leadership of TsEMI's deputy director, Nikolay Petrakov. The system of antiquated hierarchical institutes persisted.

All leading economists, as well as senior economic officials, began to travel quite frequently abroad, gaining experience which widened their horizons. Exchanges with foreign economists developed on a large scale. Gradually, the vestiges of ideology withered and few, if any, inhibitions survived. Domestic pluralism is impressive and economists who advance these days tend to be among the most solid or eloquent individuals. Still, their basic competence remains low and little has been done to change it. There are many economic researchers but not much formal economics in the USSR. Few Soviet students or young researchers go abroad to study economics. In the words of Academician Stanislav Shatalin: "What worries me? First of all, the extremely low level of our economic science and economic education in general" (*Ogonyok*, No. 20, 1990, p. 24).

Most top economists have become politicians and adjust their statements to what sounds and appears politically convenient. Many have become too preoccupied with political tactics after at long last gaining freedom of expression. As time is in short supply and the discussions heated, many top economists indulge in economic journalism, devoting less to research. The field of economics in the Soviet Union, not unlike the country's economy, cries out for reform. Outside Moscow, particularly in the Russian and Ukrainian provinces, exegesis tends to prevail under the label of political economy. In many cases, reform-minded Soviet economic journalists seem to understand that a market

---

5. Much of the evidence in this section has been gathered during the course of conversations with the 34 economists and officials mentioned above.

economy represents something better than old-fashioned Soviet thinking and the professors of economics of yesteryear.

At the top of the professional pyramid, the most significant change is the replacement of Aganbegyan by Abalkin, who is now perceived as the chief economist, and the marked advancement of Shatalin and Petrakov. Reform economists became more or less distinctly divided, between those who want to influence the government from within and those who prefer to stand in opposition. Political divisions between liberals and social democrats have emerged as well (e.g., *Izvestiya*, March 1, 1990). Seemingly everywhere, new independent economists have emerged from the ranks, as well as from relative obscurity.

Abel G. Aganbegyan. After the CC of the CPSU approved the first reform program at its plenum in June 1987, it was unveiled at a press conference by Academician Aganbegyan, even though he was not a member of the CC.[6] This event highlighted Aganbegyan's standing as Gorbachev's chief economic advisor—an informal position which he was soon to lose. In June 1988, at the 19th Party Conference, it was Academician Leonid Abalkin who spoke as the top economist, and it was not Aganbegyan but Abalkin who became Chairman of the government's Reform Commission in July 1989. At about the same time, Aganbegyan became the Rector of the Economic Academy of the Council of Ministers, the foremost management training institution in the USSR. He soon resigned as head of the Economic Department of the Academy of Sciences, and was replaced by Academician Stanislav Shatalin who later joined Gorbachev's all-important Presidential Council. In January 1990, Nikolay Petrakov was appointed by Gorbachev to serve as his personal economic aide. Aganbegyan did not lose all that much ground, but he was no longer the top economist of the land.

There were many reasons for Aganbegyan's demotion. For quite a while, he began to project the impression of a tired man. He simply exposed himself on the political firing line for a period much too long to endure and seems to prefer a less visible and vulnerable position. He is widely and correctly blamed for Gorbachev's first and unfortunate economic slogan *uskoreniye* (acceleration).[7] In a combative article, Aganbegyan does not refute this charge, but denies many other charges (Aganbegyan, 1989b). He attacks the government for deficient work routines, whereby professional economic expertise becomes involved only at the stage when key strategies are developed and refined. Typical decisions made without economic consultations included the campaign against alcohol and the reduction of consumer goods imports in 1987. Notably, Ryzhkov himself worked through the eleven applied reform decrees of July 1987 without seeking advice from any economist outside his own apparatus.

6. For biographical details, see Admirin (1989).

7. Indirectly, Maslyukov criticizes this concept (*Pravda*, July 5, 1990). Gennadiy Zoteyev, deputy director of Gosplan's Economic Research Institute, has criticized Aganbegyan straightforwardly (see Rumer, 1990). Public strictures were launched both by the liberal Vasiliy Selyunin and the reactionary Mikhail Antonov.

Aganbegyan also points out that an article he wrote for *Pravda* in July 1988 was not published until February 1989—an example of inability to make his voice heard (Aganbegyan, 1989b). However, his successor as head of the Economic Department of the Academy of Sciences of the USSR (Stanislav Shatalin) stated that it was the considerable neglect of the Economic Department which resulted in the absence of its own alternative program for radical reform, clearly blaming Aganbegyan (*Argumenty i fakty*, No. 13, 1990).

Aganbegyan seems to have been finally broken by a political incident. In December 1987, he incautiously spoke in London and Paris about a commission concerned with the possible change of status of the disputed province of Nagorno-Karabakh. This news item was broadcast, reaching the media in the USSR. Two months later, the conflict between Armenia and Azerbaijan flared up and Aganbegyan was partly blamed. Unlike most leading economists, he did not appear on the ballot as a candidate in the many recent political elections.

But Aganbegyan's views are not submerged, for he has written and published rather extensively. Because such expressions of views are strongly restricted by his official positions, he does not stand out as a very controversial (nor particularly outspoken) writer, and it is often unclear if Aganbegyan really enunciates his own views. He appears in print as a sensible, mainstream, market-oriented reform economist.[8] However, on behalf of the Economic Department of the Academy of Sciences, Aganbegyan has rather strangely argued in favor of a reform of retail prices *after* the stabilization of the market (Aganbegyan, No. 4, 1990).[9] Aganbegyan's old institute in Novosibirsk has lost much of its previous high profile since Aleksandr G. Granberg took over. In Moscow, Aganbegyan's closest collaborator is Viktor D. Belkin.

Leonid I. Abalkin. Leonid Abalkin has risen rapidly under *perestroyka*, becoming the natural leader reflected in his personality. There are many positive things to say about Abalkin. He is extremely hard-working, a prolific speaker, and skilled writer. Few people have such a sense of duty and destiny, seemingly carrying the fate of the Russian people on his back. A characteristic statement of his admonishes: "But somebody must work. Somebody must save the country. There is still a chance to pull it out of the crisis" (*Ekon. gaz.*, No. 27, 1989).[10] Abalkin tends to work for consensus, often devoting a great amount of time to convince people. He displays the rare habit of not telling lies, which frequently gets him into tedious elaborations to avoid political embarrassment. Abalkin's behavior has earned him few enemies and much respect, making it fairly self-evident that his candidacy for top jobs is logical and sound.

Criticism against Abalkin centers on the fact that he is very much a political economist. On the other hand, this is why he realized the paramount importance of pluralism of ownership at an early stage. Abalkin is one of the main advocates of the Swedish model for the USSR, implying that no system more socialist

8. Aganbegyan recently has published two books in English (Aganbegyan, 1988, 1989a).
9. Unfortunately, this is a frequent, possibly even predominant, view expressed by Soviet economists.
10. The statement is quoted in Rumer (1990, p. 76).

than the Swedish is likely to work.[11] For him, the best socialism is clearly social democracy. Thus, Abalkin favors far-reaching marketization and denationalization, though avoiding the term "private property." While his approach is complex, Abalkin is intellectually open and curious.

Many critics say that Abalkin has become too conservative after joining the government, but he never sounded overly radical. At an early phase of the reform, he realized how very poor the state of the Soviet economy really was and that the crisis had deepened. But Abalkin has a strong sense of loyalty. Strangely, he long favored the concept that reform should start in industry and not in agriculture. Skeptical of free economic zones, Abalkin opposed proposals for currency reform or the introduction of a parallel currency. On nationality issues, he has provoked the anger of the Balts for defending the preeminence of Moscow. Few people have made so many speeches, given as many interviews, and published as many articles in the last two years as has Leonid Abalkin.[12]

Abalkin retained the directorship of the Institute of Economics which serves as his think tank. Boris Z. Milner, his immediate deputy at that institute, has a major share of responsibility for the organization of the government's economic schemes.[13] Abalkin's point man on his favorite issue—"ownership"— is Lev. V. Nikiforov, also a senior professional on the staff of that institute.[14] Still, the formerly conservative Institute of Economics has not fully recovered under Abalkin's leadership and continues to be viewed as somewhat of a mediocre center of study.

Oleg T. Bogomolov. Academician Oleg Bogomolov has long been known as director of the Institute of the Economics of the Socialist World System and for more than two decades as the USSR's official spokesman on economic relations with other socialist countries. He was one of Andropov's protégés with a background in the CC apparatus. Even during the course of the most severe periods of what is now referred to as stagnation. Bogomolov stood out as a protector of heretic researchers in various social sciences and his institute became the principal employer of stimulating intellectuals during *perestroyka*. To name a few: Anatoliy Butenko, Yevgeniy Ambartsumov, and Aleksandr Tsipko have critically scrutinized the ideology.[15] Professor Gennadiy Lisichkin has long been known as an outstanding vocal proponent of market economy (e.g., Lisichkin, 1989, 1990). Professor Vyacheslav Dashishev advocated German unification in a paper written as early as April 1989 (*Der Spiegel*, No. 6, 1990). Otto R. Latsis, first deputy editor of the journal *Kommunist*, also was shielded by Bogomolov. Moreover, the Institute commanded the best Soviet

11. Abalkin visited Sweden extensively in both 1987 and 1988 to investigate the Swedish model.
12. A few have been published in *Pravda*, August 4 and 11, 1989; November 14 and December 16, 1989; March 30, June 4, and July 17, 1990; *Izvestiya*, September 22 and December 18, 1989; *Rabochaya tribuna*, May 26, 1990; *Ekonomicheskaya gazeta*, Nos. 21 and 17, 1990; *Newsweek*, January 1990. See also Rumer (1990) for further comments on Abalkin's program and additional references.
13. For ideas on this topic, see Milner (1989).
14. On leaseholding see Nikiforov (1989); on ownership in general (O variantnosti, 1990).
15. The outstanding piece is Tsipko (1988, 1989).

expertise on other socialist countries and their economic systems, particularly when represented by the likes of Professor Ruben N. Yevstigneyev.

After many years of caution, Bogomolov came out of the closet in 1987 and began to show his true colors in public (most notably, Bogomolov, 1987a). He distanced himself from the party apparatus and joined forces with the rapidly radicalizing collective of his Institute, which became the most forward-looking institution and a center of unofficial opposition movements. Drawing on his knowledge of reform in China, Hungary, and Poland, Bogomolov advocated a free market economy and massive privatization (see *Ogonyok*, No. 23, 1990). He favors an initial reform in agriculture, free economic zones, the introduction of a parallel hard currency, and general distribution of shares.

On all these points, Bogomolov opposes Abalkin's ideas, even though the two men do not stand far apart on basic principles. After elections to the Congress of People's Deputies in the spring of 1989, Bogomolov became a deputy, winning a popular vote against the reformist party secretary in a district of Moscow. His support came from informal organizations and a coalition with Boris Yel'tsin. Abalkin supported Bogomolov's opponent. Thus, Bogomolov opted for the political opposition critical of the government in the Congress, remaining outside much of the committee work in which previously he had been involved, but developing increasingly intimate ties with the leadership of the Inter-regional Group of deputies.

Stanislav Shatalin. More than others, Academician Stanislav Shatalin surged from relative obscurity to the heights of prominence in the center of power (eroding though it may be). He is one of the most highly respected Soviet economists and a long-standing proponent of the market. Coming from TsEMI after several years at the Institute for Systems Analysis (whose significance declined with the political demotion of its director, Dzhermen Gvishiani), he became deputy director of the new Institute of Economic Forecasting and Scientific and Technical progress, which was formed in 1985 on the basis of roughly one quarter of TsEMI.[16] Shatalin tends to be controversial in his statements. Recently, he emphatically advocated private ownership on a large scale (*Ogonyok*, No. 20, 1990; *Delovyye lyudi*, May 1990). In 1986, he came out in favor of reforms in prices, wages, as well as currency, for which he was criticized severely (Shatalin, 1986). Battered, he returned two years later to this theme, retracting his formerly expressed views and stating that retail prices should remain intact under any circumstances (*Sotsialisticheskaya industriya*, October 30, 1988). Shatalin's new arguments did not make economic sense and he appeared to act as a professional giving in to populist pressures.

In December 1987, Shatalin was among those elected to become Academicians (together with Abalkin and Sitaryan) and in the fall of 1989 he succeeded Aganbegyan as head of the Economic Department of the Academy of

---

16. This institute has not really taken off. It was created for Academician Aleksandr Anchishkin, who died prematurely in June 1987. Its new director, Yuriy V. Yaremenko, Corresponding Member of the Academy of Sciences, is neither particularly prominent nor clear-sighted on reform issues (see *Izvestiya*, June 19, 1990).

Sciences. He has since given a large number of interviews professing the need for a market economy and private ownership, but sharply opposing those who wish to move more rapidly or choose a more radical route to a liberal economy. In particular, Shatalin argues strongly against a Polish type of transition (*Literaturnaya gazeta*, May 2, 1990; *Izvestiya*, April 21, 1990). Still, he probably is the most progressive member of the Presidential Council.

Nikolay Ya. Petrakov. Another academic reform economist who advanced during the recent period is Corresponding Member of the Academy of Sciences Nikolay Petrakov. Long the top Soviet specialist on finance, pricing, and money, his advice was in great demand when the financial crisis grew from bad to worse. Furthermore, he has a long history of ardent struggle for promarket ideas since the 1960s, and a record evidencing concentration on systemic issues.[17] Like Bogomolov, Petrakov has argued for the introduction of a parallel hard currency (Petrakov, 1987c). As deputy director of TsEMI, he benefited from reliance on a solid group of knowledgeable collaborators, such as Professors Yevgeniy Yasin, Dmitriy L'vov,[18] Boris Rakitskiy,[19] Yuriy Borozdin,[20] Vilen Perlamutrov[21] and Lev Braginskiy. The director of TsEMI, Valeriy M. Makarov, also Corresponding Member of the Academy of Sciences, has kept a low public profile.

In effect, a trio of leading economists—Leonid Abalkin, Stanislav Shatalin, and Nikolay Petrakov—has emerged at the top of the federal structure. All three profess rather similar views, but their public posture is very different. Abalkin appears as the loyal servant of the government, Petrakov as the assiduous critic, while Shatalin uneasily criticizes both the government and its radical critics. Clearly, Abalkin is more of a politician and leader, while Petrakov and Shatalin have more credibility among radical reform economists. With regard to views, Petrakov and Bogomolov stand close to one another, but each opted for a different political strategy.

Other Participants. Unlike the others in the informal foursome of Gorbachev's economic advisors (Åslund, 1987, pp. 259–262), Academician Tat'yana Zaslavskaya is really a sociologist. As the head of the most important Soviet center of opinion polls and with a busy agenda, she probably never considered herself an economist. Her emergence as one of the leading economic advisors in the late 1980s evidences the shortage of professionals trained in economics. Since others have come to the fore, Academician Zaslavskaya appears to have voluntarily stepped aside from direct work on the economic reform. Poor health also contributed to that shift in her activities.

With *glasnost'* and democratic elections, a number of economists have risen to prominence because of their strongly critical views and staunch advocacy of market economy and private ownership. Pavel G. Bunich, Corresponding

17. For a recent review of his thinking, see *Rabochaya tribuna*, April 24, 1990.
18. For views on the market economy, see L'vov (1990).
19. For views on bureaucracy, see Rakitskiy (1989).
20. Borozdin is primarily a specialist on pricing (see Borozdin, 1989).
21. Perlamutrov specializes in banking.

Member of the Academy of Sciences, is a splendid orator and prolific writer.[22] He enjoys great popularity, but for personal reasons is not among the top economists. Bunich seems to be a politician with considerable potential.

Professor Gavriil Popov of Moscow University attracted a lot of attention for his many imaginative publications on reform at the outset of *perestroyka* (e.g., Popov, 1985a, 1987). In the spring of 1988, he became editor-in-chief of the main economic journal *Voprosy ekonomiki*, which he swiftly transformed into an interesting reformist publication. As of this writing, Popov is one of the country's leading democratic politicians and mayor of Moscow. Two other reformist professors of economics at Moscow University who managed to surface politically are Gevork A. Yegyazaryan and Aleksey M. Yemelyanov.

Professor Nikolay P. Shmelev of the Academy's Institute of the USA and Canada has played an outstanding role in the promotion of *glasnost'*. As no one else, he continued to expose the economic crisis and uselessness of the command reform. His voice aroused reactions which prompted Gorbachev to come out in his support (*Pravda*, June 22, 1987). Shmelev's base of operations, the USA and Canada Institute, known for its primary focus on foreign policy, recently began to play an important role (not unlike IMEMO) in bringing home economic experience from the West.

Somewhat surprisingly, Gosplan's Economic Research Institute also turned radical. In the spring of 1987, Professor Vladimir Kostakov, who dealt with the specter of unemployment, became its director, elected by the staff against the wishes of Gosplan's leadership. Kostakov's deputy, Gennadiy Zoteyev, is an economist with a reputation for broad competence who specializes in long-term planning. Professor Tat'yana Koryagina emerged as the main expert on the underground economy (e.g., Koryagina, 1989, 1990). Other radical economists who ascended to political prominence with appropriate visibility include Academician Vladimir Tikhonov of the Economic Academy and Professor Ruslan I. Khasbulatov of the Plekhanov Institute of Economics in Moscow.[23]

While progressive thoughts flourished, *glasnost'* also has allowed a number of reactionary economists to rise to the fore. Mikhail Antonov of IMEMO attacks economic progress as such in Russophile journals, and Aleksey A. Sergeyev of the Higher School of the Trade Unions stands out as a leading dogmatist (*Pravda*, July 8, 1990). Even the extreme anti-Semitic organization *Pamyat'* heralds an economist, Mikhail Lemeshev of TsEMI.

A new occurrence is the appearance of purely liberal economists with no pretension to profess socialist ideas. On March 1, 1990, *Izvestiya* published a letter by Dr. Larisa Piyasheva in which she states: "According to my conviction, I am a consistent liberal by principle in the European sense and a conservative in the American [sense]."[24] Other prominent liberals are the

22. His latest book on reform is Bunich (1989).

23. Khasbulatov was elected First Deputy Chairman of the RSFSR Supreme Soviet as Yel'tsin's candidate in June 1990.

24. Larisa Piyasheva wrote a letter under a pseudonym that was published as early as May 1987, in which

economic journalist Vasiliy Selyunin, Dr. Grigoriy I. Khanin of Novosibirsk, and Oleg Pinsker. In a multitude of articles, Selyunin and Khanin have pioneered investigations into the dark depths of the Soviet economy and the effects of the malfunctioning of the system.[25]

A large number of Soviet economists have by now become well-known political figures, winning one political office after the other. It is as though they need to acquire political power before they can achieve much change. Still, for the future, the dismal level of competence of the economists, even of those at the top, is worrisome.

TRANSFORMATION OF ECONOMIC POLICY-MAKING INSTITUTIONS

In 1989 and 1990, the institutions responsible for making economic policy were completely revamped. Most changes were derived from the decisions of the 19th Party Congress in June–July 1988. Its resolution "On the Democratization of Soviet Society and Reform of the Political System" and the resolution "On the Struggle with Bureaucracy" contained stipulations of considerable importance (*Pravda*, July 5, 1988). First, the role of the party apparatus was to be checked. Large CC commissions were to be set up, in fact replacing the CC secretariat and dissipating its powers. The CC apparatus was sharply reduced, and subsequent demarcation of the functions of party and state organs further reduced the influence of the CPSU. Second, the Soviet legislature was strengthened by the establishment of an elected Congress of People's Deputies, which in turn elected a Supreme Soviet as a standing legislative, administrative, and monitoring body. Third, implicitly the government was to lose power resulting from monitoring by the soviets at all levels, and its staff was to be trimmed. Fourth, the groundwork was laid for a strong presidency, or initially chairmanship of the Supreme Soviet, a move obviously intended to increase Gorbachev's power.

The 1988 Party Conference seemed astoundingly unaware of the approaching economic havoc. Its main resolution read: "The country's slide toward economic and sociopolitical crisis has been halted" (*Pravda*, July 5, 1988). Apparently, the Soviet leadership thought it had time to concentrate on political reform and downgrade economic concerns, but economic priorities changed. The main resolution stated: "The most important task in the socioeconomic sphere is to accelerate the solution of the urgent problems of the people's prosperity" (*Pravda*, July 5, 1988). This was the time when engineering and heavy industry lost their longstanding top priority.

In both September 1988 and September 1989, Gorbachev managed to implement considerable personnel changes in the Politburo and the CC secretariat.

she argued against social democracy from a liberal point of view, with the argument that you cannot be "half-pregnant" (Popkova, 1987).

25. Their pioneering article was Selyunin and Khanin (1987).

Several of the most conservative communists were retired. However, remarkably little happened to appointments that had a bearing on economic reform. Prime Minister Ryzhkov and CC Secretary Slyun'kov retained their posts, and Gosplan Chairman Maslyukov was elevated to a voting member of the Politburo in September 1989—an unprecedented event. Moreover, the reactionary communist Yegor Ligachev became CC Secretary for agriculture and Chairman of the new CC Commission on Agrarian Policy in September 1988. Thus, moderate or hesitant reformers maintained their grip on economic reform issues in the CPSU.

The power of the CPSU was effectively undermined by the decisions of the 19th Party Conference. A CC Commission on Socioeconomic Policy was established in September 1988, with Nikolay Slyun'kov as its chairman. These commissions have only met about once each quarter and their meetings appear to have been of a rather formal nature. Politburo meetings have become even more infrequent and limited in scope. The CC secretariat ceased to function altogether.[26]

In a parallel development, the number of CC departments was reduced from 20 to nine, and all CC departments responsible for particular industries, apart from the defense industry and agriculture, were abolished. No less than seven branch departments have disappeared (*Izvestiya TsK KPSS*, No. 1, 1989, pp. 81–88) and most of the functionaries[27] transferred to the provinces. Essentially, departments in the economic sphere were abolished, and the CC apparatus lost more power in matters related to the economy than in any other field. A number of special Politburo commissions were established, but apparently none specifically for economic affairs.

The CC Socioeconomic Department was assigned a new head, Vladimir Shimko, an engineer who previously had headed a ministry in the military-industrial complex. However, he did not stay on and was replaced within months by his first deputy, Professor Vladimir Mozhin. Nikolay Slyun'kov remained at the helm as CC Secretary for Economic Affairs, and Anatoliy Milyukov became deputy head of the Socioeconomic Department and the CC's troubleshooter on economic reform issues. However, CC jobs no longer looked like good career opportunities for aspiring professionals.

Thus, the powers of the CPSU were weakened. The CC staff was probably slightly more reformist than that at the Council of Ministers, but their agenda was put on a back burner. Although the power of the CC apparatus declined in general, it lost most substance in the economic area. One reason was that economic matters comprised the most typical business of the government, but it was equally apparent that the powers of Prime Minister Ryzhkov and of Gosplan's Chairman Maslyukov grew at the expense of CC Secretary Slyun'kov. An extensive interview with Slyun'kov before the 28th Party Congress clarifies that he had not really been involved in the work on reform during the past year

26. According to Yegor Ligachev (*Pravda*, July 5, 1990).
27. Many of the heads of the disbanded departments were Ligachev's protégés.

(*Pravda*, June 25, 1990). The contrast with agrarian issues is striking. There, Yegor Ligachev held his own and maintained CC control over policy making.

Elections to the new Congress of People's Deputies were held in the spring of 1989, and the Congress convened on May 25, 1989. Its first session changed the Soviet political landscape. An exciting fortnight of televised democratic debate on all diverse issues brought about a complete breakthrough for open discussion. Reform economists were prominent among the deputies and they made frequent public appearances. Among the leading economists who became deputies were Leonid Abalkin, Oleg Bogomolov, Nikolay Petrakov, Pavel Bunich, Gavriil Popov, Vladimir Tikhonov, Gennadiy Lisichkin, Nikolay Shmelev, and Aleksey Yemelyanov (all from Moscow), Rein Otsason from Estonia and Edvardas Vilkas from Lithuania. The Congress of People's Deputies and the Supreme Soviet became important popular tribunes. Gradually, their members grew more radical and increasingly independent. Characteristically, Prime Minister Ryzhkov had his economic program approved by the Congress in December 1989, but was told to refine it by the Supreme Soviet in June 1990.

A score of committees of the Supreme Soviet were established. Several dealt with economic issues (for example, finance and budget as well as regional economics). One committee specifically concentrated on economic reform. It was chaired by a reformist, V. M. Vologzhin, who served as director general of an enterprise in L'vov which had been the first to set up a joint-stock company (see *Izvestiya*, April 1, 1990; Vologzhin, 1989). However, these committees were not really effective. Usually only a few members of a committee had the professional insight to understand the issues, while the staffs were meager. Because alternative proposals were rarely at hand, the committees could do little more than amend or block governmental proposals (*Izvestiya*, June 12, 1990).[28]

On the government side, the central economic bodies held their own. Gosplan had marked its strong position through the reconstitution of the reform commission in early 1989 and the promotion of Maslyukov to voting membership of the then still-powerful Politburo in September 1989. At the confirmations of ministers in the summer of 1989, the USSR Supreme Soviet blocked several nominations made by Ryzhkov. The new appointees were probably more qualified. Academic merits were highly rated. Notably, Stepan Sitaryan became Deputy Prime Minister and Chairman of the State Foreign Economic Commission, Vyacheslav Senchagov (Deputy Minister of Finance) took over the chairmanship of the State Price Committee, Valentin Pavlov, Chairman of Goskomtsen (the State Price Committee), moved to become Minister of Finance, and Vadim Kirichenko became Chairman of Goskomstat (the State Committee on Statistics). While these men were highly qualified economists, all were connected with Gosplan and the Ministry of Finance, where each rose

28. For a description of the work of a Committee of the Supreme Soviet, see Tsypkin (1990).

from the ranks. On the one hand, they possessed the economic know-how and competence to understand reform and kept pace with the radicalization of society. On the other, by orientation they were close to the central economic bureaucracies and therefore tended to impede reform. Their promotions showed how the economists advanced at the expense of engineers in the central economic entities in the wake of economic reform.[29]

In spite of the aggravated economic crisis, Prime Minister Ryzhkov emerged with more strength as the leading politician alongside Gorbachev. The memorable visit to earthquake-ridden Armenia in December 1988 served to enhance his prestige and fairly substantial popularity. Remarkably, at a CC meeting on July 18, 1989, Ryzhkov criticized Gorbachev all but by name, complaining that the General Secretary did not devote enough of his time to the party (*Pravda*, July 21, 1989). Never before had such a clear rift between Gorbachev and Ryzhkov surfaced in public. One reason for Ryzhkov's manifestation of dissatisfaction might have been a major political decision made just before the event.

On July 5, 1989, a new State Commission of the USSR Council of Ministers on Economic Reform was formed by a decree of the USSR Council of Ministers (*Ekon. gaz.*, No. 31, July 1989, pp. 16–17; *Sobraniye*, 1989c), replacing the Maslyukov Commission. It differed from the former in several important ways. First, its chairman was not Maslyukov but the leading reform economist, Academician Leonid Abalkin, who was appointed Deputy Prime Minister for the purpose. Second, its status was much higher because the commission was a permanent body of the Council of Ministers. Third, it was to have an independent apparatus. Fourth, its tasks were broad, and it was given substantial powers. For instance, it was to report directly to the Council of Ministers, and it could give orders to other central economic organizations.

Finally, the composition of this new Commission was completely different from the former reform commission. It was highly professional, with only one of the 27 members representing Gosplan (Sitaryan). As many as nine were academic economists—all outspoken reformers.[30] Of the others, 14 represented organizations subordinated to the Council of Ministers, but not all were in charge of these bureaucracies. It was very evident that a selection had been made to appoint officials who were also competent economists.[31] Two progressive enterprise directors were included, as well as a reactionary secretary of the Central Council of Trade Unions, K. Turysov, who had also served as a member of the former reform commission.

Still, an ominous feature was that its nascent apparatus was based on the

29. This phenomenon is discussed in Åslund (1989, pp. 145–146).

30. In addition to Abalkin, the reformers included Aganbegyan, Shatalin, Professor Ruben N. Yevstigneyev of Bogomolov's Institute, V. A. Martynov (Director of IMEMO), Boris Z. Milner (Deputy Director of Abalkin's Institute of Economics), Professor Tat'yana I. Koryagina of Gosplan's Economic Research Institute, Professor G. A. Yegyazaryan of Moscow University, and A. P. Vladislavlev.

31. Notably, these included Sitaryan of Gosplan (who is not among the fourteen), Minister of Finance Valentin S. Pavlov, Vyacheslav K. Senchagov of the State Price Committee, Vadim N. Kirichenko of Goskomstat, and Ivan D. Ivanov of the State Foreign Economic Commission.

Department on the Economic Mechanism at the Council of Ministers, headed by Pyotr Katsura, who became First Deputy Chairman of the Reform Commission. His immediate subordinates, S. V. Assekritov and A. V. Orlov, were deputies together with Sitaryan.[32] Katsura and his group had increasingly evidenced conservative leanings. Abalkin had little opportunity to choose his own staff and his subordinates who worked for a time for his superior, Ryzhkov, were conditioned by the Prime Minister's inadequate grasp of economic reform. Lastly, officials of the Council of Ministers still formed the majority of the Reform Commission.[33]

The CC of the CPSU had been represented on the Maslyukov Commission (by Anatoliy Milyukov), but more recently the party was excluded when it was to be separated from the government. Similarly, leading economists who won elections to become deputies of the Congress of People's Deputies were not included in the Reform Commission.[34] In any event, the new Reform Commission constituted a great step forward for the group of academic reform economists. The main losers were Gosplan, as well as Ryzhkov and the CC of the CPSU.

In spite of the open dispute between Gorbachev and Abalkin at the 19th Party Conference a year earlier, the new initiative obviously came from Gorbachev. At the same time, it was rumored that Gorbachev had offered Oleg Bogomolov the chairmanship of Gosplan and Nikolay Petrakov the chairmanship of Goskomtsen, but both have reportedly turned down his offer.[35] In September 1989 (after his summer vacation), Gorbachev gathered most leading reform economists and told them to work out a comprehensive reform proposal as rapidly as possible. The result, promptly published in early October, was the first comprehensive proposal to switch to a market economy, marking a radical departure from all former documents. This new proposal clearly expressed the ideas cherished by Abalkin, including an unambiguous denunciation of central planning in favor of the market, an advocacy of pluralism in ownership, and a radical shift in the economic system. It envisaged a step-by-step introduction of a market economy from 1991 onward (*Ekon. gaz.*, No. 43, 1989, pp. 4–7).

Gorbachev emphasized his personal involvement in this reform program by chairing no fewer than three publicly reported meetings on October 23, November 1, and November 13 through 15 (*Pravda*, October 24, 1989 and November 2, 6, 11, and 14, 1989; *Ekon. gaz.*, No. 47, November 1989; Hewett,

32. Orlov frequently appeared in the press with substantive and reasonably reform-oriented statements (*Izvestiya*, April 2 and 3, 1990; June 8, 1990); Katsura maintained a rather low profile. In September 1989, the apparatus comprised some 30 professionals. By March 1990, the number had grown to 50–60. Moreover, the Abalkin Commission set up a considerable number of working groups, involving many officials and academics.
33. One of the few early Abalkin appointments was Yevgeniy Yasin, who became head of a department.
34. Economists who otherwise presumably would have been chosen include Oleg Bogomolov, Tat'yana Zaslavskaya, Nikolay Petrakov, Gavriil Popov, and Pavel Bunich. Abalkin was a deputy (elected on the CC list), but resigned after appointment as Deputy Prime Minister.
35. This came from reliable sources in Moscow in June 1989. The offer to Petrakov is almost beyond doubt.

1989c, p. 11). At the large economic conference with 1400 participants from November 13 to 15, both the opening and concluding speeches were delivered by CC Secretary Slyun'kov, even though Ryzhkov was present (*Ekon. gaz.*, No. 47, November 1989). However, that conference backfired. Much to his surprise, Abalkin encountered pressures from the conservative forces (*International Herald Tribune*, November 16, 1989). As Ed A. Hewett reported: "it was shocking to sit through speeches on the need for better planning, and strictly controlled markets, without any obvious sign of understanding by the majority in the auditorium that this neo-conservative approach to the economy has no more hope of working now than it did under Brezhnev" (Hewett, 1989c, p. 13). This conference marked the political resurrection of substandard dogmatic communist economists. One outstanding example was Professor A. A. Sergeyev, backed by the reactionary official trade unions.

As a follow-up, the second session of the Congress of People's Deputies in December 1989 was expected to receive a more specific blueprint for reform. Instead, Prime Minister Ryzhkov unveiled a completely different proposal. The transition to a market economy was postponed until 1993. In the meantime (1990–1992), a stabilization was to be undertaken through recentralization (*Pravda*, December 14, 1989).

This amounted to a total rejection of Abalkin's program. It is worth noting that it had been promoted by Abalkin with support from Gorbachev and Slyun'kov, while Ryzhkov had not been visibly involved in the process. At the time when Abalkin's program was published, Ryzhkov delivered a major speech on the same topic to the Supreme Soviet. It did not contradict Abalkin directly, but rather ignored his program and commission by neglecting to acknowledge their existence. Ryzhkov's speech was focused on five draft laws dealing with property, land, the socialist enterprise, taxation, and leaseholds (*Pravda*, October 3, 1989). Gorbachev kept an uncharacteristically low profile during the December 1989 session of the Congress of People's Deputies. Abalkin's statements were somewhat ambiguous (*Izvestiya*, December 18, 1989), and at a press conference he evaded the direct question asking whether he supported Ryzhkov's program.

There is evidence to suggest that Ryzhkov was neither involved with, nor supportive of, the Abalkin Commission. Presumably, his own program was worked out by Gosplan. The discussion at the Congress left no doubt that First Deputy Prime Ministers Yuriy Maslyukov and Lev Voronin, who were not members of the Abalkin Commission, stood by Ryzhkov (*Izvestiya*, December 16 and 18, 1989).[36] Later on, Maslyukov emphatically assumed the responsibility for the Ryzhkov program, leaving little doubt that he was a prime mover behind it (*Pravda*, June 30, 1990).

The Abalkin Commission had suffered a serious setback and was effectively defeated by an alliance between Ryzhkov and Gosplan, backed by other central

---

36. Voronin was long the First Deputy Chairman of Gosplan.

economic bureaucracies of the government. Abalkin did not come out in the open to voice his opposition, thus becoming widely identified by the public with the Ryzhkov-Maslyukov program. Liberal members of his Commission grew increasingly dissatisfied with the lack of radicalism, influence, and action. Initially, the most radical member, Tat'yana Koryagina, stated that Abalkin had made clear that "there can be no limitations on the expression of individual viewpoints, no matter how disturbing they may be. There also can be no limitations as far as our contacts with the mass media are concerned" (*Moscow News*, No. 37, 1989). But at the beginning of 1990, after she criticized Ryzhkov in the press, Koryagina no longer received invitations to attend the meetings of the Commission.

In early January 1990, Gorbachev appointed one of the most prominent Soviet advocates of a market economy as his personal aide for economic affairs. By selecting Nikolay Petrakov, he distanced himself from Ryzhkov's program and began to spend much time with his aide and other reform economists discussing the ways and means of radicalizing the economic reform.[37]

On March 15, 1990, Gorbachev was elected President. In his first speech to the Presidential Council on March 27 he concentrated on "the development of concrete measures to radicalize economic reform." He advocated "the formation of a normal full-blooded market" (*Pravda*, March 28, 1990). It looked as if at long last Gorbachev could disregard the predominantly conservative Politburo and carry out his own program (Mann, 1990; Teague, 1990).

The new Presidential Council was created to replace the Politburo as the major policy-making body. However, its composition, presumably fully reflecting Gorbachev's own choice, attracted considerable criticism. Academician Stanislav Shatalin was the Council's single reform economist, and it included Ryzhkov and Maslyukov as well as more reactionary opponents of economic reform such as the nationalistic writer Valentin Rasputin and one of the cochairmen of United Workers' Front of Russia, Venyamin Yarin (Rahr, 1990). The council did not represent a reformist majority, but rather suggested that Yel'tsin was on the right track by criticizing Gorbachev's preference for half-measures and compromises (Yel'tsin, 1990). Did Gorbahev fail to grasp the essence of the economic reform? His close adviser Shatalin saw it as follows:

> . . . I understand that even [Gorbachev and Ryzhkov], who started *perestroyka*, are not able to, if you wish, do not have the biological facilities to, change their philosophy instantly, to move from the existing way of thinking to the new realities. As everyone, they have been fed for decades with the ideas of a strict plan and a technocratic approach to the solution of economic questions. (*Izvestiya*, April 21, 1990)

At the first session of the Presidential Council, many reform economists, including Academicians Aganbegyan and Bogomolov, were invited to speak.

---

37. Personal communication from Ed A. Hewett.

They criticized the government for considering Ryzhkov's program unveiled in December 1989. At the second session of the Presidential Council in late April 1990, not one of the critical outsiders was asked to be there to speak up, even though the topic was economic reform. Morever, Abalkin was sent away to Cuba on a routine bilateral mission—a task which could have been handled by any of the other deputy ministers. The only participant in attendance who criticized the government's policy at the time was Petrakov, while Shatalin maintained a silence.[38] The President and his council missed their chances to radicalize economic reform. The Presidential Council appeared barely more reformist than the soon-to-be emasculated Politburo. In effect, then, the new institutional setting failed to achieve the goal designed for it by Mikhail Gorbachev.

Again, in a parallel effort, a new government commission on "the acceleration of the transition to a planned market economy" was formed by a decree issued by the Council of Ministers on March 11, 1990.[39] Both its tasks and its membership clearly indicate that it superseded the Abalkin Commission, though it did not replace it. Reminiscent of the Maslyukov Commission in composition, it was chaired by Ryzhkov himself, with Maslyukov and Abalkin as his deputies. Of its 20 members, no fewer than ten owed their allegiance to the Presidium of the Council of Ministers. Among the top economists, only Shatalin and Aganbegyan were included. Abalkin's diminished authority was further emphasized by his appointment to a new working group in the Commission assigned the unrealistic task of completing a proposal on transition to "a planned market economy" to be embodied in 27 drafts of laws and decrees by May 1, 1990.

Needless to say, such a deadline could not be met, though several draft laws emerged in the spring; the main program was presented by Ryzhkov to the Supreme Soviet on May 24. However, from the very outset Maslyukov seems to have been in charge, taking over the chairmanship of the commission and becoming Abalkin's superior.[40] This role was defined by Maslyukov as follows: "Being deeply convinced that the state can in no way rely on automatic functioning of the spontaneous market, I was the initiator and direct leader of the work on and assembly of documents presented to the third session of the USSR Supreme Soviet" [in May and June 1990] (*Pravda*, July 5, 1990).

On June 13, 1990, the Supreme Soviet adopted a decree "On the Concept of Transition to a Regulated Market Economy in the USSR" (*Pravda*, June 16, 1990), ordering the Council of Ministers to prepare a new program by September 1, 1990, which promptly established yet another new special commission headed by Maslyukov to accomplish the objective (*Izvestiya*, June 22, 1990).

38. Personal communication from two senior Soviet reform economists.
39. "O podgotovke materrialov, neobkhodimykh dlya osushchestvleniya perekhoda k planovo-ryochnoy ekonomike (On the Preparation of Materials Necessary for Transition to a Planned Market Economy)," Decree No. 257. This unpublished decree was supplied by Peter Rutland (1990).
40. Personal communications from senior Soviet officials.

Thus, after one year of intense maneuvering, Maslyukov formally took over the ranking reform commission. Again, reform economists were outwitted by Gosplan and the apparatus of central economic bureaucracies of the Council of Ministers. Still, Abalkin managed to put together an apparatus with the singular task of promoting reform, and his Commission has not been disbanded. During the past year, Abalkin lost much public acclaim because he seemed responsible for the government's failing policies. However, both in December 1989 and May 1990, it was Ryzhkov who found himself on the firing line, for the public perceived him as the main culprit. As time marches on and Maslyukov's profile is increasingly in the news, he is likely to become more vulnerable as well as exposed to public scorn. The three men at the top of the government pyramid who more than other people shape and adjust the inner workings of the Soviet economy (Ryzhkov, Maslyukov, and Abalkin), have much in common. But the common denominator of undisputed merit is the consensus that each is a workaholic.

THE RECENT CHANGES IN PERSPECTIVE

The period from 1989 through the first half of 1990 was marked by a very conspicuous transformation of the economic policy-making apparatus. There is little doubt that the hand behind that transformation was Mikhail Gorbachev's, particularly because most changes have been directed against Nikolay Ryzhkov, Nikolay Slyun'kov, and Yuriy Maslyukov—the three members of the weakening Politburo in charge of economic affairs.

Gorbachev was clearly motivated by the need to strengthen the reformers. Institutionally, this course of action involved efforts to gradually diminish the commanding influence of the Politburo and Central Committee apparatus, while a number of other entities such as the Reform Commission of the Council of Ministers, the Congress of People's Deputies, the Supreme Soviet, the Presidency, and the Presidential Council gained a goodly measure of power. Most of these institutional changes served to enhance the influence and political prominence of academic economists. In the end, an even more complex balance of power had developed, whereby the new institutions (Congress of People's Deputies with its many committees and the Presidency with its council) and political activism at the grass roots level undermined the once mighty leadership of the CPSU apparatus, sapped the strength of the central economic bodies and Gosplan, and tipped the scales in favor of the Presidency.

On the personal level, Gorbachev solicited support from Leonid Abalkin, Nikolay Petrakov, and Stanislav Shatalin, while demoting the former leading reform economist, Abel Aganbegyan. Gorbachev tried to finesse Nikolay Slyun'kov and Yuriy Maslyukov, while containing Nikolay Ryzhkov in a somewhat ambiguous manner. He succeeded in reducing the influence of Slyun'kov as well as that of his bureaucratic domain at the CC, but Maslyukov and Gosplan fought back. By June 1990, Gosplan recovered most of the power lost to the Abalkin Commission.

The many changes in institutional and personal setting lead us to believe that the apparent attempt to accomplish a fundamental break with the old institutional powers and economic system did not succeed up to this time. The Abalkin Commission, with a precarious balance of forces prompting a series of inconsistent compromises, ran out of steam because of the conservative apparatus inherited from Ryzhkov on which it had to rely. His virtual demise allowed Maslyukov to take over the reform work in June 1990. Contrary to expectations that Gorbachev's newly restated goal to radicalize reform[41] within the new organizational framework of the presidency and its council will materialize, it was evident within a month (around the end of April 1990) that the conservatives on the Council had managed to slow down the reformers.

And while the Congress of People's Deputies and the Supreme Soviet tend to be reform-oriented, though somewhat populist in outlook, they are not at this time in the mainstream of economic policy decision making and therefore decelerate rather than promote radical reform. Thus, surprisingly little came out of the succession of institutional changes during the period discussed in this chapter. On the eve of the 28th Congress of the CPSU one is very much aware of the intense struggle between the upper crust of the Council of Ministers (Ryzhkov, Maslyukov, Voronin, and Sitaryan) and the reform economists, both within and outside the government. Abalkin is the point man, while Gorbachev—the initiator and the evangelist—continues to play an impassive and hesitant role.[42]

The disappointing outcome can be dissected into two components. First, thus far a comprehensive package of economic reforms is not in evidence, not even on paper, though the agenda has been in place and substantial work and effort (hopefully of some usefulness for the future) expended. The demands emanating from the leadership, prompting a full load of comprehensive economic reforms, came much too quickly. None were in fact realistic, especially in light of the lingering political and ideological hangovers from the past. Moreover, constructive work could hardly succeed when so many representatives of the old vested interests were allowed to influence the drafting of reform legislation.

Second, Mikhail Gorbachev and the Soviet leadership failed to make the radical decisions not only to implement, but even to structure, a reliable blueprint for economic reform. Gorbachev might have been compelled to assign top priority to political issues on the agenda of the 28th Party Congress or possibly have lacked the time or stamina to deal with more than immediate concerns such as the nationality conflicts and related centrifugal pressures. Whatever the reason, he did not manage to carry out his original design to

---

41. In his first speech as President on March 27, 1990 (*Pravda*, March 28, 1990).

42. I see much more of a distinction between the Ryzhkov-Maslyukov and the Abalkin side than does, for example, Boris Rumer (1990), whose article reflects the standard view expressed by economists in Moscow.

radicalize the economic reform promulgated in the summer of 1989, though the road may have been prepared and paved for a more forceful reform in the near future.

THE AFTERMATH OF THE 28TH CONGRESS OF THE CPSU

This final section of the chapter, written during the third week of September 1990, updates the preceding narrative. What were the changes in economic policy making following the reorganization of the Politburo, by now virtually devoid of its consequential authority prevailing since the days of Vladimir Lenin? And those in the air after Boris Yel'tsin's enhanced proximity to substantive power?

The 28th Party Congress which commenced on July 2, 1990, yielded changes which President Gorbachev managed to convert into a number of major successes. The most important outcome was the effective transfer of most of the CPSU's powers to the presidency. The Politburo was transformed into a larger, weakened body which included the first party secretaries of all republics. The country's top politicians were divided into two groups. In the smaller one were those compelled to retire because Gorbachev saw little need for their services. Those transferred to the new Presidential Council largely managed to retain most of their power. Similarly, competent reformists in the CC apparatus were transferred to the new apparatus of the Presidential Council. Thus, Nikolay Petrakov became the personal economic aide of the President rather than of the General Secretary of the CPSU, even though Gorbachev held both positions. Anatoliy Milyukov moved to the presidential apparatus to head a newly formed Socioeconomic Department, while Nikolay Slyun'kov retired, together with Lev Zaykov and Yegor Ligachev. A power vacuum which emerged in the wake of the CPSU's withdrawal became increasingly evident.

The man who seems to have decided to fill that vacuum was Boris Yel'tsin, the Chairman of the Supreme Soviet of the RSFSR since the end of May. He left the CPSU toward the end of its congress, which adjourned on July 13, 1990. About a month before Yel'tsin's dramatic resignation, a radical reform plan (the so-called 500-day program) was presented to the Supreme Soviet of the RSFSR by one of his men, Mikhail Bocharov (*Sovetskaya Rossiya*, June 16, 1990). Its essence was to switch to a market economy in 500 days, with massive privatization to take place before prices were freed from control and in the aftermath of a severe stabilization policy (*Izvestiya*, August 16, 1990, p. 1). The principal author of the 500-day program was Grigoriy A. Yavlinskiy, who had previously worked in the Abalkin commission.[43] Now he has become

---

43. The program appeared in print under the title of "400 days of trust" (Yavlinskiy, Mikhaylov, and Zadornov, 1990). Its three authors are very young—Yavlinskiy is 38 years old and Mikhaylov only 27. Originally designed for 400 days, the program was allegedly changed to 500 by Mikhail Bocharov, who appeared to be motivated by political considerations (caution) and metaphor.

Deputy Prime Minister of the RSFSR in charge of economic reform. Yel'tsin gathered a number of highly educated and youngish professionals (several in their thirties), who as his ministers of economic affairs became the driving force stimulating the economic reform. After the 500-day program was formally presented, it became the main plank on the reformist agenda.

Gorbachev seemed to have little choice but to accommodate Yel'tsin and adjust to the thrust. At the end of July, Gorbachev and Yel'tsin agreed to set up a common "working group for the preparation of a conception of a union program of transition to market economy as a basis of a Union treaty" (*Izvestiya*, August 2, 1990, p. 2). It was headed by Stanislav Shatalin and included the brightest reform economists surrounding Gorbachev and Yel'tsin. All members of the group were prominent reformers. But, unlike other commissions, it was reasonably small—with only 13 members, including Leonid Abalkin (who soon dropped out), Nikolay Petrakov, Nikolay Shmelev, Yevgeniy Yasin, and Yel'tsin's men Grigoriy Yavlinskiy and Boris G. Fedorov (*Sovetskaya Rossiya*, August 5, 1990).[44] Fedorov was the 32-year-old Minister of Finance of the RSFSR, previously employed in the CC's Socioeconomic Department. In fact, the Yel'tsin and Gorbachev economists comprised more or less the same group and had much more in common with the academic reformers than with the economists supporting Ryzhkov and Maslyukov. It soon became very clear that this group was to be the one to present the real program of systematic change. Its work, based on the 500-day program, needed a rather substantial amount of refinement.

Simultaneously, a parallel commission established by the Council of Ministers was directed to evaluate alternative proposals on the transition to a market economy, with a focus on the least social and economic costs. Headed by Abel Aganbegyan, it comprised 23 members, mostly directors of economics institutes. Unlike Shatalin's group, its composition was very traditional (*Economika i zhizn'*, No. 28, 1990, p. 2). The commission succeeded in meeting its deadline in the middle of August. However, it did not develop a distinct program, but rather systematized the available proposals. In fact, it seems to have been designed to make sure that the authorities could not be blamed for neglect of, or failure to identify and utilize, any of the ideas.

On September 4, 1990, the Shatalin group (as the presidential group began to be known in the West) unveiled its program in considerable detail (*Izvestiya*, September 4, 1990, p. 3). It appeared in print (*Perekhod*, 1990a; *Perekhod*, 1990b) in the form of two volumes,[45] which will be studied and debated both in the East and West for some weeks to come. Comprising a clean break with the past, it focused on *razgosudarstvleniye* (destatization)—the key part of the strategy to win the confidence of the Soviet population.[46]

44. The remaining six were Sergey Aleksashenko, Andrey Vavilov, Leonid Grigor'yev, Mikhail Zadornov, Vladimir Mashchits, and Aleksey Mikhaylov.
45. Notably absent from the roster of authors were Leonid Abalkin and Nikolay Shmelev. But while Shmelev's contributions were acknowledged (as were Aganbegyan's), Abalkin's were not. According to Yavlinskiy (*Soyuz*, No. 37, 1990, p. 3), while Shmelev was abroad, "L. I. Abalkin did not work with us because he had a different point of view and adhered to another concept."

Not surprisingly, the two groups—the one headed by Shatalin and the more traditional one sponsored by, and in reality responsive to, Ryzhkov and Maslyukov—began to compete. Initially, Leonid Abalkin found himself in the uncomfortable position as a member of both groups as well as of his own commission; the latter probably organized most of the actual work and data pertaining to the reform plans. Soon, however, Abalkin made a clean break and at last fully joined Ryzhkov, just as Ryzhkov looked like an obvious loser. Thus, a major opponent of the Ryzhkov camp at the end of 1989 was eventually coopted by that camp.

There seem to have been many reasons for Abalkin's switch. He was gradually absorbed by the government's concerns while working in a Kremlin office. Abalkin saw no possibility of reducing the budget deficit quickly and urged early price rises, sharing Ryzhkov's anxiety about strong central power and feeling obliged to remain committed to the premise that the Soviet Union should not disintegrate. Moreover, Abalkin objected to any kind of imposed privatization. Finally, his personal relations with the radical economists in the Shatalin group had grown too strained during the last year. At the same time, the government's policy was radicalized and began to approach Abalkin's ideas.

All told, Gorbachev's options in mid-September 1990 were reduced to a clear choice between Shatalin's 500-day program or some revised plan promoted by Ryzhkov. It was a choice that should have been made without hesitation, but Gorbachev seemed to have a problem in making it. By September 13, for example, conventional wisdom in the West was about to dismiss Ryzhkov as the loser.[47] Within a day, however, Gorbachev revised the radical plan in an effort to retain control over monetary policy and taxation (*The Washington Post*, September 15, 1990). In a speech delivered to his colleagues at the Supreme Soviet, Leonid Abalkin suggested that the differences between Shatalin's and Ryzhkov's approaches were probably insurmountable. Describing the former as unworkable, he was particularly opposed to immediate destatization. When the two competing programs were ready, President Gorbachev gave Abel Aganbegyan the task of combining them. Aganbegyan was equally convinced that they were incompatible. He predicted that the country's leadership will have to bite the bullet and make an unequivocal choice between the two rival options (*The Washington Post*, September 15, 1990, pp. A13–A14). Essentially, Abel Aganbegyan came out in support of the Shatalin program.

Around the end of September 1990 it is quite evident that a break with the past had become a must. But the outcome is just too difficult to predict in light of the increasingly unsettled state of affairs in what is still the Union of Soviet Socialist Republics.

---

46. See especially *Perekhod* (1990a, pp. 57–69) and the table on p. 208 appraising the economic aggregates slated for privatization.

47. At a press conference, Gorbachev's presidential aide Nikolay Petrakov scarcely objected when a journalist suggested that the Soviet Union was abandoning socialism (*The Washington Post*, September 14, 1990, p. A1).

CHAPTER 20

The Economic Crisis:
Another Perspective

James H. Noren

As of September 1990, the future of the Soviet economy is much discussed
and its ability to muddle through much in doubt. Soviet officials and members
of the academic community describe an economy in crisis, deteriorating rapidly,
or on the verge of a severe depression on the scale of the Polish crisis of 1980–
1981. The December 1989 program of stabilization and delayed reform soon
was overtaken by an attempt to accelerate the introduction of a "regulated
market." Groups of experts, notably those guided by Leonid Abalkin, devised
a new reform plan which was reviewed and initially favored by the Presidential
Council in mid-April 1990. When Prime Minister Nikolay Ryzhkov presented
the government's proposal for economic reform to the Supreme Soviet in May,
however, its content was different from that discussed in April. Meanwhile,
13 republics have declared their sovereignty, an all-Union treaty is being negotiated in an attempt to ascertain what kind of union will remain, and (as of
this writing) a reform commission co-sponsored by President Mikhail Gorbachev and RSFSR President Boris Yel'tsin is striving to reach agreement on
a reform blueprint that may render the central government's program obsolete.

    The growing sense of panic within the Soviet leadership can be attributed
partly to perceptions that time is running out. Whereas optimists wonder whether
Gorbachev has time to reform the economy, pessimists are confident that he
does not. To express it differently, most, if not all, members of the leadership
seem convinced that the economy will collapse unless a market economy is

First published in *Soviet Economy*, 1990, 6, 1, pp. 3–55. The author is a senior analyst at the Central
Intelligence Agency. Whereas the views expressed in this chapter do not necessarily represent those of the
Agency, selected statistics in the text, tables, and figures (specifically those not attributed to sources listed in
the reference section of the *Soviet Economy* article) are based on CIA estimates and calculations cleared for
publication. The methodology underlying these estimates is explained in JEC (1982) and Kurtzweg (1987). It
should be noted that no attempt has been made to systematically identify CIA data, particularly those pertaining
to statistics preceding 1990 and some based on earlier versions appearing in CIA (SOV 88–10049), 1988 and
CIA/DIA, 1986; CIA/DIA (DDB-1900–140–87), 1987; CIA/DIA (DDB-1900–187–88), 1988; CIA/DIA (DDB-
1900–155–99), 1989; and CIA/DIA (DDB-1900–161–90), 1990. The contribution of Bruce Lawrence, who
adapted Western methods of seasonal adjustment to the Soviet problem, calculated the series used in this paper,
and wrote the explanation in note 28 below, is gratefully acknowledged. [Eds.]

introduced without delay. Much of the leadership also appears to believe that the population will not accept market reforms unless certain social guarantees are first put in place, and even then only after an intensive and prolonged period of education. Hence, the vacillation in economic policy as President Gorbachev and his advisors confront the dilemma they seem to have accepted as real—collapse without reform and revolt with reform.

The purpose of this paper is to review the performance of the Soviet economy in an effort to determine whether Gorbachev's options are as stark as they have been depicted. In order to accomplish this objective, it is essential to identify reasons for the stagnation and growing disorder in the economy, so that the policy responses by the government can be evaluated. Also, it is prudent to examine certain trends in the economy over the past year and a half to determine how much progress has been made in implementing the decisions on restructuring and stabilization adopted in 1988 and early 1989.

This examination will then provide a basis for assessing the central government's economic reform proposals on May 1990, as well as possible alternative programs and measures such as the just-published "500 days" drafted by the committee headed by Stanislav Shatalin (*Perekhod*, 1990a; *Perekhod*, 1990b).[1]

Soviet economic performance is still quite frequently judged on the basis of statistics published by the State Committee for Statistics (Goskomstat). However, I will tend to base my analysis on one of the alternative measures— namely, on that developed by the U.S. Central Intelligence Agency. Because the adequacy of these measures for assessing recent performance is critical to this or, for that matter, to any analysis of the Soviet economy, the issue is addressed in the beginning.

THE RELIABILITY OF MEASURES OF PERFORMANCE

Both the Goskomstat and CIA figures show a decline in growth rates during the Gorbachev years, but some Soviet as well as Western analysts and politicians claim that the country's economic performance was even worse than that estimated by the CIA. Whether the CIA estimates overstate or understate growth is a complicated question, and one that is not central to the purpose of this paper. What is important is whether the degree of any bias in CIA's estimates has changed since 1985.[2] For this paper, then, the question is whether the CIA indexes of GNP are adequate measures of the change in Soviet economic output between the early 1980s (before Gorbachev) and the late 1980s. This reduces to the question of whether the accuracy of published statistics on physical production, on which the CIA indexes are based, has varied over time. The

---

1. Because of the timing of the original publication of this article in *Soviet Economy*, only brief mention is made of Shatalin's program.
2. Is it plausible, for example, that GNP and consumption dropped sharply in 1988 or 1989 and that CIA estimates did not capture the sudden decline in economic performance?

share of products or activities measured in physical units in the total sample used in estimating Soviet GNP by sector of origin is so large (90 percent in the base year 1982) that GNP growth estimates are not much affected by assumed changes to the value series in the sample to correct for inflation.[3] The relative accuracy of these physical series is at issue.[4]

No definitive answer is possible because no one has yet tried to quantify the forces that may be at work. Overreporting of physical output may have declined since 1985 because:

(1) The abandonment of fixed production targets reduced the enterprise's incentive to overstate production.

(2) The substitution of profits for fulfillment of the production plan as the basis for bonuses reduces the incentive to overstate production.

(3) The introduction of tighter quality control (e.g., *gospriyemka*) may have raised the average quality of a given product.

(4) The unraveling of the state supply system and the increasing resort to barter probably inclined enterprises to underreport production so as to have some goods to trade.

(5) In an effort to increase profits, some enterprises shifted their production assortment toward higher-priced models. The CIA production categories are in some instances too aggregated to reflect the increase in average value per unit of output.

(6) Statistical authorities at all levels were under considerable pressure to wage war on falsification, and prosecutions for wrongful reporting have increased during the Gorbachev years.

Overreporting of physical output, on the other hand, may have increased during certain periods because:

(1) The introduction of self-financing in 1988 encouraged firms to relax quality standards where they could in order to increase profits.[5]

(2) During the high-level emphasis on acceleration (1985–1987) and the campaign to produce more consumer goods and carry out conversion in the defense industry (1988–1990) enterprises would have had an incentive to overreport physical production in these areas if they could get away with it.

To the extent that these tendencies were realized, CIA indexes would overstate the level of real production relative to that in other periods.

It is very difficult to strike a balance among these opposing factors. My sense

---

3. See the sensitivity tests carried out on CIA estimates of Soviet GNP in Noren (1988).

4. For example, if padding of reported production (*pripiski*) amounts to 3 percent every year for one product and 1 percent for another, the indexes of real and reported growth will be the same, and it is these indexes that are used to move the base-year sector-of-origin value-added weights over time.

5. Examples might include more rock in the coal shipped, more water in the milk, and cheaper assortment in the production of fabrics.

is that because of changes in incentives and stricter supervision of reporting, padding or outright falsification has declined in relative importance. As shortages proliferated in producer and consumer markets and the role of enterprise profits increased, however, the seller had the motive and the opportunity to deliver products that were of lower quality than those shipped earlier. Customer complaints in the Soviet Union, however, have centered on irregular deliveries, failure to deliver all that was ordered, and delivering an assortment different from the original order. All of the aforementioned shortfalls will have an impact on production, but in a way that the CIA indexes would capture.[6]

At any rate, relying on the official Soviet statistics on physical production, my perspective on the possibilities for the future differs from the views of many observers and students of the Soviet economy simply because my analysis of recent developments is different. Instead of imminent collapse, certain signs of progress can be detected in implementing a wrenching restructuring of the economy. I also believe that by continuing to correct some of the mistakes that are responsible for today's dismal economic scene, the Soviet leadership could gain the time to design and win support for a workable program for systemic reform.

ECONOMIC PERFORMANCE UNDER GORBACHEV: AN OVERVIEW

Economic policy under Gorbachev's rule can be described and assessed in three phases without excessive distortion of the facts: (1) acceleration and modernization (1985–1986), (2) initial attempts at reform (1987–1988), and (3) reorientation and stabilization (1989–1990).

Acceleration and Modernization

In the beginning, Gorbachev organized his efforts to revive the economy under the broad umbrella of *perestroyka*, a term that included three major economic elements—tighter discipline, industrial modernization, and economic reform. He characterized his program as "a genuine revolution in the entire system of relations in society" (*Pravda*, August 2, 1986, p. 1) and justified the need for such professedly radical measures by claiming that by the time he came to power the Soviet economy had reached a "pre-crisis" stage (*Ekonomicheskaya gazeta*, No. 27, July 1987, pp. 2, 6).

According to CIA calculations, the Five-Year Plan for 1986–1990, together with guidelines announced to the year 2000, called for an acceleration of GNP growth from about 2 percent per year in 1981–1985 to 4 percent in 1986–1990 and then to more than 5 percent per year in the 1990s. Gorbachev declared that such an acceleration (*uskoreniye*) was necessary if the USSR was to achieve

---

6. The evidence is not at hand to determine with adequate certainty whether the quality of individual products is declining on a scale sufficient to offset or more than offset a possible reduction in *pripiski*.

its primary economic objectives—to create a modern industrial base equal to any in the West, raise living standards, and provide for the country's defense during a period of extremely rapid technological change.

To achieve this acceleration, the Soviet government at first pursued a two-tiered strategy featuring near-term reliance on the "human factor" and longer-term dependence on restructuring and modernization of the economy. The human factors encompassed remedies traditionally applied when the economy needed a quick boost. They included measures intended to instill more initiative in workers and managers, purge economic life of so-called negative phenomena (e.g., corruption, drunkenness, illegal economic activity), and enforce greater discipline in the work force. The limits to reliance on human factors were recognized, however. As Leonid Abalkin then stated, even the full utilization of existing potential is "unable to guarantee a radical rise in labor productivity, product quality, and production efficiency" (Abalkin, 1986a, p. 13). Or, as two of the leading advocates of an acceleration in investment argued:

> During 1983–1984 it was mainly organizational-economic and social reserves of growth that were mobilized. But it is inevitable that they are quickly exhausted since their effect is impeded by the fact that a number of basic problems in economic development are not resolved. One of these problems under modern conditions is the need to overcome the technical backwardness of the production apparatus and the disproportions that have come to exist in it (Val'tukh and Lavrovskiy, 1986, p. 19).

After the evaporation of the productivity gains associated with the human factor, the leadership relied on continuing growth in efficiency spurred by improvements in organization and planning and primarily by modernization of industry and the economy as a whole.

While modifications in the economic mechanism were still under discussion, Gorbachev concluded that the USSR must embark upon a comprehensive renewal of the country's fixed capital stock. Retirements of low-productivity capital stock were to be accelerated, and new stock was to be substantially more productive than the capital it replaced. In the words of the then new Chairman of the Council of Ministers, Nikolay Ryzhkov, "we can no longer tolerate the situation where only 29 percent of series-produced machine-building output conforms to world standards" (*Pravda*, June 19, 1986, p. 2).

The formulation of this program, however, was no easy matter. The draft five-year plan repeatedly was returned to planners on the grounds that it was not sufficiently strenuous. Politburo member and CPSU Secretary Lev Zaykov explained the situation as follows:

> It must be said that in the course of preparations for the Central Committee April Plenum, not only economic leaders but also certain theorists of the political economy of socialism expressed ideas to the effect that it is necessary to wait a while, to pull up the rear ground, to gather strength, to

Table 1. *Growth of GNP by Sector of Origin, 1981–1989*[a]

Sector	1981–1984[b]	1985	1986	1987	1988	1989
GNP	2.0	0.9	4.1	1.3	2.2	1.4
Industry	1.9	2.2	2.5	3.1	2.9	0.2
Construction	0.8	2.3	3.7	2.5	2.5	0.1
Agriculture	2.4	−3.9	11.0	−3.9	−0.6	3.4
Transportation and communications	2.3	2.4	3.2	1.7	2.8	0.6
Services	2.2	2.4	2.3	3.2	3.0	2.7

a. Annual percentage change based on 1982 rubles at factor cost.
b. Annual average.

await a more favorable demographic situation, and only then to make a rapid spurt along the path of building Communism (*Pravda*, April 30, 1986, p. 2).

In June 1986, Gorbachev described the Plan as having a "difficult birth," noting that "for a whole year we persistently sought new approaches that would create conditions for deepening efforts to intensify production and ensure an increase in the rates of assimilation of the achievements of science and technology" (*Pravda*, June 17, 1986, p. 1).

After nearly two years in charge of the Soviet Union, Gorbachev could derive some encouragement from developments in the country's economy. Following a poor performance in 1985, it improved somewhat in 1986, sparked by an enormous turnaround in agricultural output, as shown in Table 1. Industrial production also increased, as did output in every major sector of origin except domestic trade and services. An increasing share of production went to new fixed investment, however, because of Gorbachev's initial strategy favoring investment and the delayed effects on consumption of poor harvests in 1984 and 1985 as well as drastic cutbacks in production and consumption of alcoholic beverages.

Even the meager results of 1985 were not attributed to the new leadership. Instead, Gorbachev was given credit for reviving the economy after an extremely poor showing in the first quarter of 1985, when the coldest winter in 20 years snarled rail traffic and the industrial supply system (CIA/DIA, 1986, p. 13). Gorbachev, of course, had nothing to do with the better weather that resolved the transportation problems in his first months in office. But his campaigns for greater labor discipline, a vigorous assault on drunkenness, and his firing during the year of one-third of all industrial ministers undoubtedly played a substantial role in elevating the rate of growth of industrial production during the year.

Initial Attempts at Reform

With his acceleration and modernization program in place, Gorbachev turned to the country's "economic mechanism." Before the June 1987 Central Committee plenum, it was not even clear that he had a blueprint for economic reform. Gorbachev had started by extending Andropov's and Chernenko's reforms in the industrial sector on planning and finance, and introducing self-financing, wage reform, and planning reform on a small scale. In addition, he had established a commission in January 1986 to develop a program of reform legislation, and had sanctioned an unprecedented, wide-ranging debate on economic reform. This discussion reached a crescendo just before the Central Committee plenum in June 1987, which was called to ratify the new program.

In any event, the June plenum approved guidelines for a "new economic mechanism," which was to be "almost fully" implemented by the start of the Thirteenth Five-Year Plan in 1991 (*Pravda*, June 27, 1987, pp. 2–3). Ten decrees devoted to different parts of the reform were issued later, and the Supreme Soviet passed a Law on the State Enterprise, which was to give greater scope to decision making at the enterprise level.[7] On January 1, 1988, these reforms were introduced in or extended to a large portion of the economy. The measures included self-financing, new planning practices, wholesale trade, changes in the banking and credit system, wage reforms, new foreign trade procedures, and reorganization of the production and foreign trade ministries. With the adoption of these decrees, Gorbachev hoped to replace his predecessors' piecemeal approach to reform with a considerably more comprehensive program.[8]

If fully implemented, this reform package promised to greatly modify the economic structure of the USSR. The role of Gosplan and other national planning organizations was to be limited to long-range national planning, while the day-to-day operation of the economy would be handled largely at the enterprise and local levels.

The Soviet leadership expected the year 1987 to mark an important stage in the effort to revitalize the country's economy. The growth targets in the annual economic plan were extremely ambitious, and Gorbachev decided to press ahead with a number of new economic and administrative reforms. At the beginning of 1987, a new quality-control regime, *Gospriyemka*, was introduced in 1,508 enterprises accounting for roughly 20 percent of industrial output and 60 percent of civil machine-building production. Under this system state inspectors directly responsible to the Committee on State Standards (Gosstandart) were stationed at the enterprises. They had the right to inspect products at any stage of the production process for adherence to state technical standards. *Gospriyemka* was extended to another 732 enterprises in January 1988 (Matosich and Matosich, 1988).[9]

---

7. The collection of guidelines, decrees, and legislation is described and assessed in detail in Schroeder (1987).

8. At the same time, Gorbachev's views as to what socialism should be were evolving. Writing in the spring of 1990, he said "there is much that we still do not know about the society toward which we are striving. We have determined the general direction. We know what kind of socialism we would like to see. However, only time, experience, and practice will show what kind of socialism it will be" (Gorbachev, 1990).

9. It was to include food processing and construction for the first time.

Table 2. *Growth of Fixed Investment and Capital, 1986–1988*
(percent)

Category	1986	1987	1988
New fixed investment[a]	8.3	5.7	6.2
Commissionings of fixed capital	5.8	6.8	−2.6

a. New fixed investment as reported by Goskomstat in order to ensure consistency with Soviet statistics on commissionings.

Table 3. *Growth of Consumption, 1981–1988*
(percent)

Category	1981–1984[a]	1985–1986[a]	1987	1988
Food	0.2	−5.3	−0.9	3.0
Soft goods	0.8	2.7	0.5	3.1
Durables	2.7	3.3	0.3	3.1
Services[b]	2.2	2.5	3.5	3.7
Total	0.9	−1.3	0.2	3.1

a. Annual average.
b. Consumer goods and household services (excluding communally provided health and education services).

Instead of the acceleration anticipated by planners, the Soviet economy stalled in 1987–1988 and some worrisome new problems began to surface. After 4 percent growth in 1986, GNP increased by an average of 1.7 percent in the following two years (Table 1). Successive declines in farm output accounted for much of the slump in growth, but industrial growth leveled off and output in the construction and transportation sectors declined substantially. Civil machine building fell far short of plan, and the resulting shortages of equipment for investment severely constrained Gorbachev's modernization goals. The growth of new fixed investment slowed somewhat in 1987 and 1988 as planned. Nevertheless, the investment front broadened to such an extent that by 1988 commissionings of new fixed capital were declining while new fixed investment was still increasing at a healthy rate as shown in Table 2.

The Soviet consumer fared better in 1987–1988 than in the first two years of Gorbachev's tenure, but the forward progress in 1987–1988 did little more than restore the 1984 level of per capita consumption (Table 3). The situation with respect to food and soft goods, especially fabrics and clothing, was especially disappointing, but not unexpected given the setbacks in agriculture and the effect of reductions in alcoholic beverage production.

Progress toward the goals of stimulating productivity and modernizing the economy was at best inconclusive. The anti-alcohol drive and the administration reorganization apparently arrested the decline in aggregate factor productivity that had set in after the mid-1970s in both the nonagricultural nonservice sector and in industry as shown in Table 4.[10] It is unlikely, however, that the improvements in factor productivity were to any large extent related to accelerated

10. Agriculture and services are excluded from GNP in estimating factor productivity in order to avoid the random effects of weather on GNP and to remove the elements of GNP growth that cannot reflect productivity changes because they are measured by inputs rather than output.

Table 4. *Trends in Aggregate Factor Productivity*[a]
(percent)

Economic aggregate	1981–1984	1985–1986	1987–1988
Nonagricultural, nonservice GNP	1.8	2.2	2.6
Inputs			
Manhours	0.6	0.6	−0.7
Capital	5.4	4.3	3.0
Labor and capital	3.1	2.5	1.2
Factor productivity	−1.2	−0.3	1.4
Industrial output	1.9	2.3	3.0
Inputs			
Manhours	0.6	0.4	−1.0
Capital	5.6	4.4	2.9
Labor and capital	3.3	2.6	1.1
Factor productivity	−1.4	−0.3	1.8

a. Average annual rate of growth.

technical progress due to more rapid assimilation and diffusion of new technology. The leadership experimented with various methods of improving the rate of innovation under Gorbachev, but none seems to have had an appreciable impact. Twenty-three interbranch scientific-technical complexes were established in 1986–1987 to foster research and development on key technologies, but they were unable to overcome institutional barriers and the disinterest of industrial enterprises, which felt little pressure to introduce new technology because they could readily sell what they were already manufacturing. The centrally directed programs promoting high-technology machine-building output were ill-conceived in that they directed producing enterprises to shift their product assortment much too rapidly, leaving customers struggling to find uses for machinery that they often had not ordered.

In sum, by 1989, the Gorbachev economic program was essentially moribund. Figure 1 illustrates rather clearly that, since coming to power, the new economic team had not improved aggregate economic performance. The rates of growth of GNP, industry, and agriculture during Gorbachev's first five years were no better than they were during the last years of Brezhnev's reign or in the brief Andropov-Chernenko interlude. In other words, there was no evidence of *uskoreniye*.

Official Soviet statistics present much the same picture—a steady decline in national income growth during the Brezhnev years. The average annual rate of increase appears to have remained about the same in both the Andropov-Chernenko and Gorbachev eras—about 3.75 percent annually. These rates, however, are slightly less than the 4 percent average growth claimed in 1976–1982, the last years of Brezhnev's rule. The Soviet leadership also has complained increasingly about the lack of improvement in the quality of manufactured goods generally and the slow rate of improvement in their technical characteristics.

While registering no progress in elevating growth rates and very little on

Figure 1. *Economic Performance under Gorbachev and His Predecessors*

Average annual growth rates

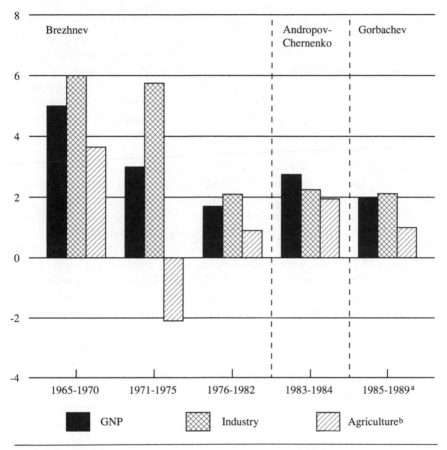

a. 1989 data are preliminary.
b. Excludes farm products used within agriculture and purchases by agriculture from other sectors.

the industrial modernization front, the leadership gradually and belatedly realized that the macroeconomic balance that was for the most part preserved
under the old system of central planning and administrative controls was eroding
quite rapidly. The proximate and interrelated causes of this erosion were a
soaring state budget deficit, loss of control over enterprise deposits in a state
bank settlement accounts and over the volume of inter-enterprise credit, new
independence granted to enterprises in setting prices, and a sharp acceleration
in the growth of money flowing to the population in the form of incomes.

The Budget Deficit. The first large state budget deficits in the postwar
years appeared under Gorbachev. In 1984, the excess of budget outlays over
revenues (excluding borrowing from Gosbank and the population) was negli-

gible. Thereafter, the deficit increased sharply, particularly in 1986 and 1988. By 1989 it had reached 95 billion rubles, or 19 percent of budget outlays and 10 percent of GNP. Stagnation in revenues was the principal reason for the deficit; expenditures increased more slowly from 1985 to 1988 than during the period from 1981 to 1984 (5.5 percent compared with 6.0 percent annually).

By borrowing from the state banking system (namely, by printing money) rather than from the population or enterprises, the Soviet economic leadership pumped a river of additional rubles into the hands of the population, which accumulated either as cash in hand or as savings deposits. At the same time, enterprise funds were accumulating because of weakened constraints on prices charged by enterprises and the policy of allowing enterprises to keep a greater share of their profits to finance investment in both productive capital stock and social-cultural amenities.

Loss of Control over Enterprise Bank Balances. In an earlier issue of this journal, Gur Ofer described the monetization of enterprise bank balances that formerly had been strictly controlled (Ofer, 1989b). As a result of past experience with high rates of inflation and extreme macroeconomic imbalance, the controls over enterprise finances had been tightened considerably. An enterprise was to deposit expeditiously all currency that it managed to obtain in the branch of Gosbank with which it dealt. The management of such an enterprise could draw currency out of the bank to pay wages, but only in amounts approved in its plan. It could augment its balances through deposits from its current revenue stream, by short-term borrowing from Gosbank for working capital needs, by long-term borrowing from specialized banks to finance investment, and by acquiring allocations from the state budget for financing investment in fixed and working capital. But transfers from one enterprise's account to that of another could only be carried out if they were in line with the production and development plan established for the enterprise. In order to prevent the evasion of Gosbank controls, lending by one firm to another was not permitted, and the time taken to settle accounts payable was monitored closely.

These controls began to disintegrate during the initial introduction of economic reform (Ofer, 1989b, pp. 140–141). Given new freedom to devise their production plans and encouraged to finance their own investment, enterprises could now use their balances to finance wage increases and bid for material supplies and investment goods. They also could borrow from the new commercial and cooperative banks as an alternative to banks in the state system. Meanwhile, the barriers to inter-enterprise credit beyond specified time limits appear to have been lowered. Accounts receivable increased by 21.0 billion rubles, or 18 percent during 1988.[11]

Flow of Money Incomes to the Population. While supplies of consumer goods and services barely grew, the rise in the population's money income

11. A new statistical handbook provides data on enterprise balance sheets for January 1, 1988, and January 1, 1989 (*Finansy*, 1989, p. 52).

Table 5. *Growth of Personal Money Income, 1981–1989*
(percent)

Year	Total	Disposable
1981–1984[a]	4.0	4.0
1985–1986[a]	4.0	3.9
1987	3.4	3.4
1988	8.0	8.0
1989	12.9	n.a.

a. Annual average.

Table 6. *Changes in Soviet Retail Prices, 1981–1989*
(percent)

Year	CIA[a]	Goskomstat[b]	Gosplan[c] Open inflation	Gosplan[c] Repressed inflation
1981–1985[d]	2.2	1.0	1.6	4.1
1986	4.4	2.0	3.0	3.2
1987	2.2	1.7	3.1	4.2
1988	3.1	0.3	4.1	4.3
1989	6.0	2.0	5.0	5.5

a. Calculated by dividing official Soviet estimates of retail sales of consumer goods in state stores and collective farm markets in current prices by corresponding CIA estimates in constant prices.

b. For 1989 only, Goskomstat's estimate includes sales on collective farm markets and sales by individuals and cooperatives, in addition to state retail sales. Goskomstat has also acknowledged that repressed inflation is running at 5.5 percent per year (Gur'yev and Zaytseva, 1990, p. 28).

c. Estimates for 1981–1988 as presented in Shmarov and Kirichenko (1989).

d. Annual average.

began to accelerate. The growth of such personal income was practically constant from 1981 to 1987. In 1988, however, personal incomes began to rise at a much faster rate, as shown in Table 5.

Inflationary pressures and weakening of control over prices were in evidence. Weakened controls over incomes and the money supply, coupled with the greater freedom granted to enterprises in setting prices, inevitably generated both open and repressed inflation. Although judgments about the extent of inflation vary quite widely, three agencies, as shown in Table 6, have compiled estimates supported by more or less plausible arguments to defend them. According to Goskomstat, it has reviewed and revised its procedures for estimating open price inflation in 1989 (Kirichenko, 1990). Still, Goskomstat figures seem low when compared with those of the other two agencies. Gosplan's calculation of repressed inflation is an imaginative attempt to estimate how much retail prices would have to rise to increase consumer spending by an amount equal to their forced savings during the year—the savings that would not have been made if consumer goods and services had not been in such short supply (Shmarov and Kirichenko, 1989, pp. 27–28).

These estimates of retail price inflation suggest that the USSR is far from experiencing the kind of inflation characteristic of many developing countries. But for families who could not find goods and services at state outlets and had to pay much higher prices for purchases from cooperatives or from those in the black on collective farm markets, a weighted average of price changes on these markets does not reflect the real situation. Those most disadvantaged were pensioners, students, and workers employed by enterprises and organizations that did not offer food and other consumer goods through special distribution channels.

Reorientation and Stabilization

New Policies. At least midway through 1988 the Soviet leadership realized that new economic policies were absolutely necessary. Gorbachev, addressing the CPSU Party Congress in June, stated that "we underestimated the whole depth and weight of the deformations during the past years of stagnation" (*Pravda*, June 29, 1988, p. 2). He cited the serious financial situation, failure to meet targets for conserving resources, and slow progress in developing high-technology sectors. A "common view (was) forming" in the party and the government that the "social reorientation of our economy must be more strongly and consistently pursued" (*Pravda*, June 29, 1988, p. 3). The focus was on a shift to increasing supplies of food and consumer goods, services, and housing; to improving health, education, and culture; and to addressing environmental issues. This reorientation toward raising the share of consumption in national income "must become the pivot and the keystone for shaping the pace and proportions of the economy" (*Pravda*, June 29, 1988, p. 3).

The 1989 economic plan reflected the shift in priorities by calling for extraordinarily large increases in the output of consumer goods (CIA/DIA, 1989, p. 9). More important, the December 1988 and January 1989 announcements of cuts in military forces and defense spending indicated strongly that there was now some substance in the intended shift in priorities.[12] During 1987 and in early 1988, the demands became more insistent, and in 1988 the Ministry of Machine Building for Light and Food Industry and Household Appliances was abolished and its plants allocated to various defense-industrial ministries (CIA/DIA, 1988, pp. 8, 12–14). However, the response was still anemic: military production was more profitable than production of consumer durables, and Ministry of Defense orders received priority attention. The leadership apparently finally concluded that civilian production in the defense industry could be raised substantially only if room were made for it. When Gorbachev declared that military production would be reduced by 19.5 percent over two years (*Financial Times*, January 19, 1989, p. 32), the basis for the conversion program was established.

Results. According to usual Soviet or Western aggregate measures, restructuring and stabilization was a failure in 1989, and continued to be in 1990, as indicated in Table 7. But the evidence is not to be found in the production

---

12. Since Khrushchev's time, the defense industry has been exhorted to manufacture more consumer goods.

Table 7. *Changes in Economic Aggregates, 1985–1990*

Economic aggregate	1985–1986[a]	1987–1988[a]	1989	First Q 1990 / First Q 1989	First H 1990 / First H 1989
GNP					
• CIA	2.5	1.7	1.4	n.a.	n.a.
• Goskomstat	2.8	4.2	3.0	− 1.0	− 1.0
National income produced					
• CIA	n.a.	n.a.	n.a.	n.a.	n.a.
• Goskomstat	2.9	3.0	2.4	− 2.0	− 2.0
Industrial output					
• CIA (value added)	2.3	3.0	0.2	n.a.	n.a.
• Goskomstat (gross output)	4.3	3.5	1.7	− 1.2	− 0.7
Agricultural output					
• CIA (value added)	3.2	− 2.2	3.4	n.a.	n.a.
• Goskomstat (gross output)	2.7	0.6	1.0	n.a.	n.a.

Sources: CIA/DIA, 1990; *SSSR v tsifrakh*, 1990, p. 9; *Ekonomika i zhizn,*' No. 18, April 1990, pp. 15–18; and first quarter and first half 1990 plan fulfillment reports.

a. Annual average.

figures. Although they show a continued decline in the growth of GNP and industrial output in 1989 and an absolute fall in the first half of 1990, as compared with the first half of 1989, low or even negative rates of growth could be expected and accepted if a genuine restructuring were under way and inflationary pressures were subsiding.[13] In its annual plan fulfillment report, however, Goskomstat revealed that money incomes of the population had increased by almost 13 percent in 1989 and later said that in the first half of 1990 they were 12.9 percent higher than in January–June 1989, a rate almost twice as high as the 7.1 percent rise planned for 1990 (*Ekonomika i zhizn'*, No. 32, April 1990, p. 15). Since during most of this period the supply of goods and services to the population was rising at a slower pace, shortages became more pervasive, and inflationary pressures mounted rather than declined.

Although assessing the extent of the shortages and the inflation in consumer markets is extremely difficult, some useful indicators are available. One valuable measure is based on responses of 5,000 emigrants who left the Soviet Union in 1981–1989.[14] From these data, a rough index of the availability in state stores and collective farm markets of 22 basic food items can be calculated.[15] The index can, in turn, be disaggregated by region and city size. The percentage of respondents reporting regular availability of the 22 foods in 1981–1989 is shown in Figure 2. In no year did the Soviet shopper have an easy time. After 1985, however, the curve turns downward and falls particularly

13. The case for accepting the CIA estimates as reflecting real trends in output in the Gorbachev era is presented in the introduction.

14. The results of these surveys are reported in RFE/RL series of reports on food supplies in the USSR.

15. The 22 items were grouped in five categories: meat, chicken, and fish—beef, pork, canned fish, mutton, chicken sausage; dairy products, eggs, and margarine—milk, butter, cheese, eggs, margarine; vegatables and fruit—beets, cabbage, tomatoes, apples, oranges; staples—bread, flour, potatoes, rice, sugar; and vodka.

Figure 2. *Availability of Food Products in State Stores, 1981–1989*

Percent

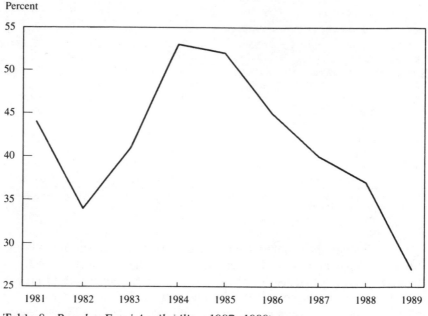

Table 8. *Regular Food Availability, 1987–1989*[a]
(percent)

Region	1987	1988	1989
Baltic Republics	51.4	53.6	36.2
Transcaucasus	42.8	40.6	24.2
Eastern RSFSR	20.7	36.7	19.8
Kazakhstan and Central Asia	35.7	38.0	23.1
Ukraine and Moldavia	40.0	34.7	23.6
Western RSFSR and Belorussia	41.1	36.8	24.9

a. Based on survey respondents.

steeply in 1989. Over the last few years, food availability declined appreciably in all regions except the Eastern RSFSR, where availability already was poor, as shown in Table 8.

When they could not keep the shelves stocked, local authorities often rationed foods—generally by giving local residents coupons granting them the right to buy a certain quantity. By the end of 1989, according to the respondent reporting depicted in Figure 3, 97 percent of the localities rationed sugar; 62 percent rationed butter; and almost 40 percent, beef.[16]

The demand for food products that could not be satisfied in state stores at state-controlled prices was to some extent diverted to collective farm markets. The émigré responses indicated that most food products regularly were available in

16. Additional discussion of the consumer market is given in Schroeder (1990).

Figure 3. *Rationing of Food Products in State Stores, 1987–1989*

Percent

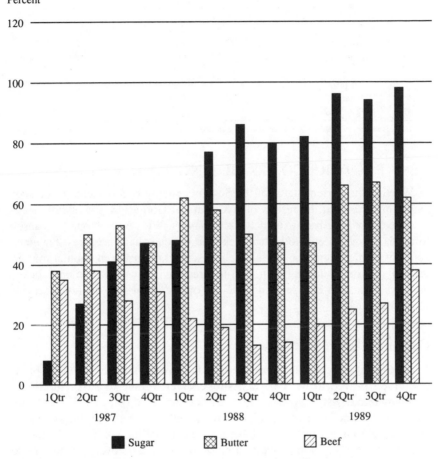

collective farm markets throughout the period 1981–1989, although consumers did have to pay higher prices at these markets (two to five times higher). Surprisingly, as shown in Table 9, the excess demand for food indicated by surveys of availability and an abundance of anecdotal evidence is not reflected in rising prices on collective farm markets until 1989—even though supplies to these markets did not increase. Moreover, the reports on availability in state stores are not always consistent with Soviet estimates of the monetary overhang and the behavior of collective farm market prices. For example, meat was reported to be in extremely short supply in state stores in 1989, but its price in collective farm markets rose by little more than 4 percent. This lack of an appreciable response suggests, perhaps, that a large part of the population was obtaining meat through alternative channels (workplace distribution, for example) at prices lower than, or at least competitive with, collective farm market prices.

Table 9. *Quantities and Prices on Collective Farm Markets, 1988–1989*[a]
(1987 = 100)

		1988	1989
Quantities			
	All products	97.8	99.3
	Meat	96.4	92.7
	Fruit and vegetables	98.4	99.4
Prices			
	All products	101.2	114.8
	Meat	103.6	108.0
	Fruit and vegetables	100.7	117.3

a. Derived from data published by Goskomstat on sales and prices of 17 products sold in collective farm markets in 264 cities.

FACTORS CONTRIBUTING TO THE CRISIS

Whether the current status of the Soviet economy is considered to be stagnation or recession, the results of five years of Gorbachev's economic stewardship clearly have been extremely disappointing. What went wrong? In capsule form, the answer seems to be bad luck, bad policies, half measures, the emergence of ethnic turmoil on an unimagined scale, an erosion in popular morale, the initial costs of dealing with long-ignored environmental problems, developments in Eastern Europe, and tenacious opposition within the lower reaches of the bureaucracy.

Calamities and Misfortune

In terms of its economic consequences, the downturn in world energy prices after 1985 proved to be the worst stroke of ill fortune to strike the Soviet economy in the past five years. If these prices had held firm, the Soviet Union would have gained perhaps an additional $24 billion in hard-currency earnings, and the state budget would not have lost tens of billions of rubles in foreign trade revenue. The drop in hard-currency receipts, moreover, led the Soviet government to curtail imports of consumer goods and machinery, which in turn was responsible for some of the growing tension on consumer markets and in the modernization campaign.

Additional calamities were Chernobyl' and the Armenian earthquake. Aside from the enormous human suffering, the USSR has already spent 9.2 billion rubles on coping with the consequences of Chernobyl'. Premier Ryzhkov has said that another 16 billion rubles will be required in the future (*Moskovskaya pravda*, April 26, 1990, p. 3). The Shatalin group reported in September 1990 that the cost of the cleanup would mount to 25 billion rubles by 1991 (*Perekhod*, 1990a, p. 177).

The earthquake that devasted northern Armenia on December 7, 1988, resulted in the deaths of 25,000 people, left 530,000 homeless, and caused damage that will take an estimated 13 billion rubles to repair—a figure that

Abel Aganbegyan says is too low (*Moscow TASS in English*, August 9, 1989). Ten percent of Armenia's industrial base and 11 percent of its housing stock were destroyed, and schools, hospitals, and transportation facilities also sustained heavy damage. The two-year schedule for construction in the aftermath of the earthquake is not being met, and most of the people left without shelter still are living in temporary housing, ranging from tents to empty railroad cars. In February 1989, TASS reported that the earthquake had caused 10 billion rubles of damage. In addition, monetary compensation to victims by the state, trade unions, and the CPSU probably will amount to more than 2 billion rubles. The reconstruction effort is a particular strain on the construction resources of the country and is setting back housing programs in other republics.

Gorbachev's plan to focus on modernizing the economy also was severely compromised by failures in agriculture, in which bad weather played an important role. Using regression analysis, Kellogg (1988) estimated weather-related losses in 1984–1987. He reports that "two of the years—1985 and 1987—were among the three coldest winters in the last 20 years, and the two remaining years (1984 and 1986) were among the five years with the hottest and driest conditions during spring and early summer" (Kellogg, 1988, p.10). By comparing model predictions of output using alternative "average" weather data and actual weather data, Kellogg calculates farm losses resulting from worse-than-average weather at 30 billion rubles during those four years, or 6 percent of actual output.

Faulty Policies and Bad Assumptions

While misfortune has played a role in deteriorating Soviet economic performance over the past five years, the country's present economic difficulties remain largely the consequence of bad policies grounded on bad assumptions.

Overly Ambitious Plans. Gorbachev set the tone for economic policy when he forced Gosplan to ratchet upward the targets for investment in the 1986–1990 plan. In the end, the plan called for new fixed investment over this period to rise by 24 percent over the 1981–1985 level. At the time, this target seemed daunting enough (CIA/DIA, 1986, pp. 15–18), but during the past year both Ryzhkov and Gorbachev have revealed that defense spending was scheduled to increase at very high rates as well. According to Ryzhkov, the original plan called for defense spending to increase faster than national income—that is, by more than 4 percent per year (*Izvestiya*, June 1989, p. 3).[17] Then in April 1990, Gorbachev (in a speech at Nizhniy Tagil) claimed that outlays on defense programs had at first been scheduled to rise by 45 percent, or almost 8 percent per year in 1986–1990 (*Pravda*, April 29, 1990, p. 2). The investment and defense plans, taken together,

17. In an initial evaluation of the 1986–1990 plan, Ed A. Hewett noted that national income utilized was to increase more than either real incomes or state and cooperative investment and that this seemed to "imply that the residual (including defense) is stated to grow more rapidly than national income" (Hewett, 1985a, p. 288).

placed an especially large burden on the machine-building sector, which was burdened with the task of producing all of the producer durables and military hardware required by the plans. Moreover, the sector was charged with meeting these targets while implementing a comprehensive transformation of its production profile and improving the quality of its products.

The feasibility of the 1986–1990 plan production goals from the beginning was, at best, doubtful. During the plan period, for example, labor force growth would be low. Although the investment plan counted on an acceleration in the rate of increase in productive fixed capital available to the economy, the discrepancy between the projected growth in output and the supply of combined inputs of labor and capital was startling, especially when viewed in light of past productivity trends (Table 4).[18] At the time the five-year plan was compiled, nothing was in place to support a revival in productivity except for the discipline campaign in the early years and some hoped-for return from the modernization campaign toward the end of the plan period. As indicated earlier, the impetus provided by the discipline campaign was transitory, and the modernization campaign never gained the necessary momentum.

The dependence of Gorbachev's economic program on unrealistic goals for productivity was paralleled by its dependence on accelerated conservation of energy, metal, and other industrial materials. To the extent that these plans for materials saving had a basis, however, they required drastic shifts in production toward more energy-efficient and materials-conserving equipment. The machinery sector proved unequal to the task. In addition, a revision of wholesale prices to raise the cost of energy and basic industrial materials might have provided some incentives for conservation in a regime of enterprise self-financing, but wholesale price reform was deferred. Before long, the inconsistency between the plans for the production of energy and basic raw materials and the levels of activity projected for sectors using energy and materials became apparent. Shortages of fuel, metals, and construction materials plagued construction, machine-building, agriculture, and transportation.

The leaders in charge of the economy, moreover, compounded the mistakes inherent in the initial formulation of the five-year plan by failing to adjust. Despite the shortfalls accumulating through 1986 and 1987, these officials continued to hold to the original five-year plan targets. Thus, annual plan goals for growth in industrial production and investment were based on the original goals for the preceding year. When compared with actual production levels of each preceding year, the successive annual plans implied increasingly unrealistic targets for increases in production. The plan, therefore, became more and

18. Many commentators expressed skepticism about the efficiency assumption of the plan. The Central Intelligence Agency estimated that to meet the goals for growth in GNP in 1986–1990, aggregate factor productivity in the economy would have to increase by 0.8 percent per year in 1981–1985 (CIA/DIA, 1986, p. 17ff). Hewett (1985a) advanced a series of reasons why the productivity goals probably would not be met (for example, rising incremental capital/output ratios for fuels and raw materials, a likely deterioration in Soviet terms of trade because of falling energy prices, and an investment plan that did not allocate enough money to the energy sector).

more fictional in character, although its distortions played a very real role in creating or amplifying imbalances in the economy.

As one economist complained, ". . . strenuous plans will reproduce as before the present situation in which the accumulation of outdated machines and equipment, diverting to themselves substantial amounts of material and labor resources (including resources to carry out major repairs), are combined with a less than full load on new capacities" (Zhuravlev, 1989, p. 37).

The Anti-Alcohol Campaign. Although now almost universally condemned, Gorbachev's campaign against alcohol was a key feature of the effort to strengthen discipline in the work force and probably had some initial positive impact on labor productivity. Within a year, however, the effects on state finances and consumer markets were becoming apparent; the fall in turnover tax on alcohol sales amounted to eight billion rubles in 1986 (Ofer, 1989, p. 125). By 1988 the government had reversed itself, and alcohol sales and tax collections began to climb. Nevertheless, the sobriety campaign added about 20 billion rubles to the state budget deficits in 1986–1988, and contributed indirectly to growth in the money supply.[19]

Another important consequence of the anti-alcohol campaign was its effect on excess demand in consumer markets. Retail sales of alcohol through state trade declined in consumer markets. Retail sales of alcohol through state trade declined by 10.2 billion rubles in 1986, and by another one-half billion rubles in 1987.[20] The economy was not in a position to provide the additional consumer goods and services to offset the declining sales, so shortages in consumer markets became more acute. Within a year or two, home distillers filled part of the void. In the process, however, the state lost tax revenue, and sugar rationing became the rule, as private entrepreneurs emptied the stores in search of supplies for their operations.

Administered Technical Progress. The ambitious plans to accelerate the rate of technical progress in the Soviet Union, as already noted, came to naught. Assignments to raise the quality of new machinery and the productivity of research and development were passed down from above. In an overheated market where enterprises could sell almost anything they produced, and where most investment funds were still provided as budget grants or supplied in the form of low-cost credits, the reluctance to innovate—even to take advantage of already available technology—effectively neutralized the campaign to upgrade the country's fixed capital and its manufactures.

The tension between quality objectives and production goals was well illustrated by the history of *gospriyemka*. When introduced in early 1987, the enforcement of stricter quality standards by independent state inspectors did raise the rejection rate (on substandard goods) and contributed to improvements in quality. It also halted the growth of civil machine-building output. Release

19. Abel Aganbegyan, however, has assessed the losses stemming from the cutback in state sales of alcohol at 20 billion rubles per year (*Die Welt*, October 31, 1989, p. 22). The difference remains unexplained.

20. This amounted to roughly 3 percent of the population's total spending in 1985.

of the plan fulfillment report for the first quarter showed output in the machine-building complex up only 1.3 percent over first quarter 1986, compared with planned growth of 5.5 percent (*Ekonomicheskaya gazeta*, No. 18, April 1987a, p. 8). With production of producer and consumer durables lagging badly, the government relaxed enforcement, and *gospriyemka* was for all practical purposes dismantled before it had ever attained its intended scope. For the entire year of 1987, gross output in the machine-building complex reportedly increased by 5.5. percent, the planned rate (*Narkhoz*, 1988, p. 332). In principle, the objective was impractical because, as enterprises justifiably claimed, high-quality output depends on the availability of high-quality inputs and decent machinery. The army of inspectors that would be required to attack the problem as a whole, as well as the degree of coordination in their actions, was clearly infeasible. The seller's market again had prevailed against an administrative approach to improving quality.

Partial Reforms. Soviet leaders and economic specialists agree that the partial and contradictory nature of the reforms introduced in 1988 and 1989 are largely responsible for the sharp deterioration in the USSR's economic situation in those years. Indeed, Gorbachev, in remarks to a conference of economists in October 1989, declared that "all today's difficulty resides in the fact that constituents of and stages in our entry to the new economic system have not been fully thought through and elaborated" (*Pravda*, November 6, 1989, p. 2). Stepan Sitaryan, Deputy Chairman of the Council of Ministers, highlighted the problem as follows:

> We have embarked on dismantling the edict system without backing up this work with the introduction of an appropriate set of new tools. This dismantling has basically affected the circulation and use of monetary resources. But the flow of material resources is still in the grip of rigid state regulation (*Pravda*, November 6, 1989, p. 1).

Until this contradiction is resolved, Sitaryan indicated, no future reforms—including the development of new ownership forms—will make any difference.

The effect of the 1988 and 1989 reforms on money circulation already has been described. The relaxation of central controls over some prices and enterprise funds led to explosive growth in wages. According to V. I. Shcherbakov, Chairman of the USSR State Committee for Labor and Social Problems, "we expanded enterprises' rights not in the earning but in the spending of money. We made it possible to artificially raise prices and pay out all kinds of money" (*Pravda*, November 6, 1989, p. 1). But Yevgeniy Primakov maintains that when the government gave more freedom to the enterprises, it made a "deliberate decision" to allow higher incomes to enterprises and workers, suggesting that not all of the consequences were unexpected (Primakov, 1989). Otto Latsis cites the "fantastic growth in state centralized investments" as a primary culprit in the growing macroeconomic imbalance in 1988 (*Rabochaya tribuna*, March

27, 1990, p. 2). These investments were financed both through the old ministerial channels and from the now unfrozen enterprise funds. Meanwhile, outlays on social programs were beginning to rise more rapidly, without offsetting reductions in other areas. Nikolay Shmelev rhetorically asked a June 1989 meeting of the Congress of Peoples' Deputies where the money would come from. "The printing press, of course . . ." was his answer. "But do we have central authority or not? Ryzhkov and Gostev could have said, 'No, there is no money' " (*Izvestiya*, June 9, 1989, p. 9).

When, under the reforms, enterprises no longer received detailed production plans from their ministries, the old supply and distribution system began to erode. The number of products distributed centrally by Gosplan and Gossnab in 1990 (610) was lower than in 1987 by a factor of 14. Of these, 360 were included in the state order and 250 in control figures (Malakhov, 1989). Enterprises, guided by "control figures," were to plan their output and find customers for that part of it not covered by state orders. This direct contracting proceeded slowly, however. Although enterprises were to conclude contracts before the beginning of the year which, together with state orders, would commit their capacities fully, they in fact began 1988, 1989, and 1990 without knowledge of what to do with part of their capacity. The then Deputy Chairman of the Belorussian Council of Ministers, Vyacheslav Kebich, told the Supreme Soviet in October 1989 that the "experience of this year" had shown the danger "of satisfying so-called non-priority areas"[21] by transferring to direct ties" (*Moscow Domestic Service in Russian*, 1300 GMT, October 31, 1989). He said the result had been a rash of unjustified price increases and a rising incidence of what could not be called anything other than "industrial speculation" because of the "expanding diktat of the suppliers." A related common complaint was that enterprises, now seriously interested in profits as a result of the transition to self-financing, stopped producing unprofitable items. In consumer goods production, the inexpensive items in a given category tended to be less profitable, so the assortment shifted toward the high end of the range as the supply of cheaper brands of shoes, clothing, and the like declined markedly.

As difficulties in finding suppliers mounted, the utility of ruble holdings dissipated in wholesale trade, as it had done in retail trade. Local and ministerial interests attempted to "take care of their own" by enforcing preferential treatment in deliveries by enterprises under their control. Enterprises, in turn, attempted to protect themselves through barter, usually a sort of tie-in sale in which part of the condition of sale of some product in short supply was the reciprocal delivery of an item needed by the seller. The authorities railed against the practice,[22] but in

---

21. Areas not covered by state orders.

22. Pavel Mostovoy, Chairman of the State Committee for Material and Technical Supply, blamed monopoly enterprises for propagating barter trade. He cited a Riga enterprise manufacturing buses for demanding that buyers of its vans build housing for the bus collective. (More recently, the Tyumen' oil men have been insisting on the same kind of arrangement.) Mostovoy complained that "this is not a market, but rather a caricature of it" (*Rabochaya tribuna*, June 13, 1990, p. 1). Another report called this kind of "industrial racket" a fact of

the absence of genuine wholesale trade and a realignment of prices, the trend toward the use of a barter arrangement was a step toward marketization.

The partial reforms introduced in the foreign trade sector also had their unanticipated and negative consequences. Selected organizations were given the right to deal directly with foreign firms and to keep a portion of the foreign currency that they earned. Again, however, the relaxation of central controls was not counterbalanced by the strengthening of financial constraints. Foreign firms found it hard to work in a new bureaucratic setting, but they persevered. In an effort to earn hard currency, Soviet enterprises began to sell finished steel as scrap and, in one notorious episode, arranged the export of tanks.[23] Other enterprises were making purchases, taking advantage of supplier's credits. Most, however, did not have sufficient amounts of foreign exchange to repay the credits, and when they turned to the central authorities, they often found them less than accommodating.

In March 1989, the government issued a decree that dampened some of the spontaneity that had developed in Soviet foreign trade.[24] It ordered the registration of all participants in external economic relations, required that all property crossing Soviet borders be declared in a cargo customs declaration, and established lists of products or work which could be exported or imported under licenses issued by the USSR Ministry of Foreign Economic Relations, designated ministries and state committees, or the Councils of Ministers of union republics. The list focused on energy products, metals, chemical products, grain, and food—products in short supply on the domestic market. More than 90 percent of the USSR's trade in hard-currency markets was subject to license. To curb the burgeoning intermediary role played by cooperatives, paragraph 8 of the decree stipulates that production cooperatives and their associations can export only those goods and services that they produced. "They shall have no right to engage in buying goods with the object of their resale for export, in importing goods for their subsequent resale on the USSR's home market and mediation in external economic transactions as a form of activity" (On Measures, 1989, p. 2).

Despite the stricter regulation of trade, reports of Soviet nonpayment of trade debts proliferated. By mid-1990, Soviet officials put the value of overdue foreign trade bills at $2 billion (*Wall Street Journal*, June 21, 1990, p. A1). Precisely what happened is still unclear. It is known that the reorganization of foreign trade in the Soviet Union directed foreign trade earnings into new channels. Exporters kept some of their hard currency to pay for imports of machinery, materials, or even consumer goods for their employees. The central

life in dealing with metallurgical plants, which demand "sausage, wood products, plumbing equipment, and convertible currency" in exchange for metal (*Sel'skaya zhizn'*, February 25, 1990, p. 2).

23. The industrial state-cooperative association involved was ANT (the Automatic Equipment, Science and Technology Association). It had been given broad rights to export without obtaining licenses and had been buying defense-industrial enterprises who were in part looking for hard currency to finance the import of machinery needed to meet their new targets for the production of consumer goods (see A. Protsenko's *Izvestiya* interview with Minister of the Aviation Industry A. S. Systov (March 28, 1990) and the attack on "the state cooperative monster" by L. Kislinskaya in *Sovetskaya Rossiya* (May 4, 1990)).

24. Decree of the USSR Council of Ministers (On Measures, 1989).

government no longer controlled all hard-currency receipts and could not finance all of the imports of those sectors that did not earn foreign currency. Nevertheless, the government agencies in charge of imports continued to make their purchases. Then in late 1989 and in 1990 the government's decision to accelerate imports of consumer goods placed an additional strain on the diminished foreign-exchange reserves available to the central government.

Demoralization of the Party

The Communist Party always has played a vital role in managing the Soviet economy. Besides having the power to make major decisions on economic policy, CPSU representatives at both the national and local levels served as troubleshooters in the informal administration of the economy. They marshalled labor and resources to deal with bottlenecks in the economy and monitored closely the performance of the enterprises under their functional and geographic jurisdiction. *Perestroyka*, with its call to remove the party from the process of management of the economy, changed the rules of the game, and the gradual demoralization of the party under *glasnost'* and democratization sapped its incentive to intervene in economic affairs.

A Ministry of Railways official pointed to the change in the party's role in discussing the reasons for the buildup in the number of railcars waiting to be unloaded in late 1989:

> What's happening? In this matter railroad specialists are unanimous; Party organs have stopped handling economic matters, while the introduction of economic arrangements which would replace the command method of management has been dangerously delayed (*Gudok*, October 21, 1989, p. 1).

Party apathy extended throughout the economy. Lev Zaykov, the now retired CPSU Politburo member and secretary in charge of defense matters, declared at a defense conversion meeting that "the conversion of the defense industry is purely a party matter, and it is the party committees that are called upon to head this work." Zaykov indicated, however, that party organizations at all levels were withdrawing from "direct participation in solving economic problems" (*Moskovskaya pravda*, October 24, 1989, p. 2). Zakhov's statement illustrates the ambivalence of the leadership toward the CPSU's role in the economy. At times, party organizations were told that they were responsible for the success of Gorbachev's economic program. At other times, however, local soviets were said to be the inheritors of those party responsibilities that had not devolved to enterprise management.

The Shift Toward the Consumer

The difficulties of the past three years also can be traced in part to the sudden shift in economic policy in favor of the consumer, in the middle of the

Twelfth Five-Year Plan. By its very nature, the new consumer program represented yet another campaign, directed from above and spawning a large number of centrally imposed production targets. It thus violated the spirit of the economic reform being introduced concurrently. Under the reform, for example, a gradual reduction of the share of state orders in total industrial production had been contemplated. The consumer program, on the other hand, relied on an expansion of state orders. Instead of making their own decisions regarding what to produce, enterprise managers again found the government making the decisions for them.

Moreover, the suddenness of the shift in resource allocation policy generated considerable dislocation. Gorbachev's defense conversion plan is a prime example. Very high targets for the production of consumer durables and equipment for consumer industries were formulated in Moscow. The assignments then were parceled out to enterprises by the defense industrial ministries with very little deliberation. As a result, some of the most sophisticated manufacturing plants in the USSR found themselves producing low-tech products far removed from their production profile.[25]

In addition, production planning was uncoordinated. Some enterprises learned in the first quarter of 1989 that orders for their military production for that year had been cut, but were not told what new products they were to begin producing. By late 1989, the general praise of the defense conversion program had changed to mostly criticism. In response, the government promised to prepare by the end of the year a detailed blueprint for conversion that addressed some of the complaints directed against the original program. As of September 1990, a new conversion program still had not been adopted.

The decision to undertake emergency imports of consumer goods in 1989 provided another example of the negative consequences of sudden policy shifts. Transportation workers were not prepared to deal with the surge in imports which began in mid-September, and reacted slowly to the situation: sufficient railcars were not released to the ports and imports were trapped in the congested ports. The timing of the purchases was sometimes unfortunate—for example, the decision to buy potatoes from East Germany at the same time that railroads and trucks were trying to cope with the harvest in the USSR (*Izvestiya*, November 3, 1989, p. 3).

The Impact of Ethnic Unrest

The Soviet leadership did not (and could not have been expected to) foresee the ethnic unrest that the relaxation of controls on dissent would spark. Demonstrations, strikes, blockades, and armed clashes all took their toll on production and distribution, as well as on the integrity of the Soviet state. By mid-

25. Sometimes defense-industrial enterprises deliberately chose to manufacture pots and pans and samovars, because they could do so in auxiliary workshops using scrap without interfering with their main lines of production.

1990, the central government could expect to deal with at least one major ethnic eruption in any given month.

Assessing the impact of ethnic troubles on the economy is not a straightforward exercise, however. One way of approaching the problem is to estimate how much higher the USSR's industrial production would have been in 1988–1989 if industrial output in Georgia, Armenia, and Azerbaijan had grown at the same rate as that of other republics. The effect would have been small. The USSR's gross industrial output (the Soviet measure) would have increased by 5.9 percent per year instead of 5.7 percent per year. The rise in nationalism probably contributed more importantly to the deterioration in the distribution system. It reinforced the autarkic tendencies that led local and republic authorities to limit the export of consumer goods and scarce industrial supplies.

By 1990, frustration with the lack of economic progress under *perestroyka* had led most republics to assert their independence. After Premier Ryzhkov presented his revised reform program[26] with its planned steep increase in retail prices, the RSFSR, Ukraine, Belorussia, and Uzbekistan reserved the right to pass on new economic reform measures. By the late summer of 1990, 13 republics had declared their economic sovereignty, buttressed by assertions that republic laws would prevail when they conflicted with all-Union legislation.

The Cost of Environmental Policies

Over the past few years, the burgeoning political influence of the environmental movement in the USSR has placed a serious constraint on economic development. By the first quarter of 1990 more than 1,000 facilities had been shut down at the insistence of local environmental groups (Kirichenko, 1990, p. 3). The chemical and forest products complexes were affected especially strongly. Although Soviet leaders are asking that more attention be paid to the economic implications of such closings, the backlog of polluting facilities is large enough to maintain the past rate of closings, given continued public pressure. The future of electric power supplies is particularly in doubt. Popular opposition in the aftermath of Chernobyl' already has led to the cancellation or halted construction of 40–50 nuclear power plants that had been approved by the beginning of the 1986–1990 plan.

Revolution in Eastern Europe

The Soviet Union counted heavily on imports of East European machinery to support its modernization program and on purchases of East European consumer goods to ease the tension in retail markets. As energy prices fell, the terms of trade shifted in favor of Eastern Europe and resulted in the USSR running import surpluses with these countries. But the "domino effect" of

26. This was in May 1990 (*Moscow Domestic Service in Russian*, 1100 GMT, May 29, 1990).

falling communist regimes in Eastern Europe altered the trade picture drastically. In the first quarter of 1990, Soviet exports to Eastern Europe were down 9.7 percent compared with the first quarter of 1989, as a result of the failure to conclude trade agreements and lower prices for Soviet energy and goods. For a sputtering Soviet economy, the 11 percent decline in imports from Eastern Europe was a significant blow (*Ekonomika i zhizn'*, No. 18, April 1990, p. 18). The other CMEA countries were no longer willing (or in some cases able) to maintain an export surplus in their trade with the USSR. Thus, in Eastern Europe, Soviet pressure on governments to reform (in a manner consistent with Gorbachev's domestic *perestroyka*) had unfavorable consequences in the economic sphere.

Erosion of Popular Morale

The cumulative impact of natural and man-made disasters, feverish shifts in policy, and the untoward effects of economic reforms on consumer markets brought about a sea change in popular attitudes toward Gorbachev and his economic policies. By mid-1989 Soviet citizens no longer expected to see an improvement in their situation in the near term. The mood of pessimism was only partly inspired by developments in the economy. Political and societal change was challenging and destroying old beliefs and values as well. The population also had been frightened by an incidence of crime that in other countries would not have been considered extraordinary. Enmity among the nationalities poisoned the atmosphere in many enterprises in non-Russian republics, and the rise of republican independence movements and the loss of Eastern Europe only added to the general perception that the Soviet Union was adrift, with no clear course and no certain destination.

The effect of declining morale on production cannot be discerned in the statistics on labor productivity. Too much else was transpiring in the economy that interfered with the rhythm of production (notably, the economic reform). The rash of strikes in 1989 was more important as a signal of worker discontent than for its effect on output. Goskomstat, for example, estimates that in first quarter 1990 about 130,000 workers were absent on average each working day because of strikes or absenteeism related to ethnic conflict. The direct cost in lost output, according to the State Committee, was 820 million rubles. In comparison, it reported that an average of 100,000 workers were absent each work day last September, the worst month in 1989 (*Ekonomika i zhizn'*, No. 18, April 1990, p. 15).[27] As shortages of consumer goods intensified, more workers left their workplaces on an informal basis to shop. But far more important, though impossible to quantify, is the effort put forth while at work. Work effort very likely declined as general frustration with the economy in-

27. The lost work time in September amounted to 0.2 percent of total man days worked. By way of comparison, time lost to strikes in the United States in 1988 (4,364,000 work days) amounted to 0.02 percent of all working days (United, 1989).

creased. Nonetheless, in view of all of the other negative influences at work, there is no convincing indication that it played a pronounced role in constraining production.

CAN THE ECONOMY MUDDLE THROUGH?

Premise of the Question

The experience with the economic reforms announced in 1987, the mid-1990 debate over the future direction of economic reform in the USSR, and the history of reform in Eastern Europe and China suggest that economic reform in the Soviet Union will be a long, uncertain, trial-and-error process. At best, the timetable might be similar to that described by Ryzhkov in May 1990 (*Moscow Domestic Service in Russian*, 1100 GMT, May 29, 1990), with the transition to a market economy delayed until the mid-1990s.

So, will the economy perform well enough to keep the reform process alive? The prevailing commentary on the condition of the Soviet economy would suggest not. For example, *The Washington Post*'s Moscow correspondent, Michael Dobbs, reported in the aftermath of the 28th CPSU Congress that the "main problem facing Gorbachev today is precisely the same one he faced before the Congress started: his apparent inability to stop the collapse of the Soviet economy" (*Washington Post*, July 15, 1990, p. A25). According to many writers, the "collapse" (rarely defined) has been imminent or under way for more than a year. I would define a collapse as a pronounced and sustained decline in GNP—perhaps accumulating to 20 percent or more. As noted earlier, the dominant view seems to be that the economy is going to collapse if far-reaching reforms are not implemented rapidly. To assess the likelihood that this would occur, a reexamination of the record of the past 18 months is in order.

Another Perspective on Recent Economic Performance

The Goals of the Government's Program. Since late 1988 and early 1989, the government's objectives, as elaborated in the 1989 and 1990 annual economic plans and state budgets (and in adjustments to them), have been to rearrange overall economic priorities and restore macroeconomic balance. The government declared that it would cut defense spending and focus on the conversion of the defense-industrial complex, so that by 1995 civilian products would represent 60 percent of total production (a goal recently raised to 65 percent), compared with 40 percent in 1989 (*Pravitel'stvennyy vestnik*, No. 18, September 1989, p. 11). It said it would reduce both state investment financed by the budget and total state investment as well. These savings, together with other reductions in expenditures and additions to revenue, would lower the budget deficit to 60 billion rubles in 1990 and to 20–25 billion rubles in 1993 (*Izvestiya*, December 14, 1989, p. 3).

The reduction in demand for investment and defense goods was expected to release resources for the production of consumer goods and moderate some of the excess demand for industrial materials. At the same time, the government hoped to curb the growth of the money income of the population by curbing the increase in wages—first by Gosbank monitoring of the relationship between wage and productivity increases and, in late 1989, by imposing a punitive tax on wage increases greater than three percent.

The Official Record. When the economic results of the first quarter and then first half of 1990 were announced, there was much wringing of hands. As Figure 4 shows, industrial production as reported by Goskomstat was down, and the announcement that money incomes in first half 1990 were 13 percent higher than in January–June of 1989 indicated failure on that front as well (*Ekonomika i zhizn'*, No. 32, August 1990, p. 15).

There is a problem with the official statistics, however. Goskomstat now provides quarterly statistics on industrial production, retail sales, earnings, employment, and other similar indices. They are presented in a cumulative progression: first quarter over first quarter of the preceding year, January–June over January–June (preceding year), January–September over January–September (preceding year), and finally year over year. Goskomstat and those who calculate independent indices of Soviet economic activity can make use of these comparisons or through subtraction can compare, for example, statistics for first quarter 1989 with those for first quarter 1988, results for second quarter 1989 with those for second quarter 1988, etc. The problem with these comparisons is that they leave out information necessary to identify turning points in production, incomes, and consumption. They indicate, for example, that steel production was 2 percent lower in first quarter 1990 than in first quarter 1989, but do not indicate what happened in the interim.

An alternative approach is to compare statistics in a given quarter with those of all preceding quarters. Economic activity, however, is almost always affected by seasonal factors, so direct comparisons between quarters can be quite misleading. Fortunately, the quarterly data can be (and have been) adjusted to remove their seasonal components, and the so-called seasonally adjusted data can be compared in order to analyze trends and turning points.[28]

28. Variations in time series data are traditionally attributed to four separable components: (1) a long-term secular trend, (2) wave-like cyclical movements, (3) annual seasonal patterns, and (4) irregular or residual fluctuations—that is, everything not accounted for by the preceding three factors. The first two components often are combined in a singe "trend/cycle component." Efforts to describe and explain movements in time series data have centered on separating the variation of a series into these components. Seasonal analysis involves isolating the third component—annual seasonal patterns—from the others. Many different phenomena contribute to patterns in time series data within a year: (1) Seasonal changes in weather affect production, transportation, and energy usage (in winter, for example, electric power generation rises to meet heating needs; in summer, cows produce more milk); (2) holidays reduce the number of working days and may increase the demand for products associated with the holiday, such as toys at Christmas time; (3) the number of scheduled working days varies both from month to month and from year to year; (4) periodic occurrences such as shutdowns for retooling or inventory can cause temporary downswings each year; and (5) in planned economies, storming to meet

Figure 4. *Growth in Industrial Production and Transportation, 1987–1990*

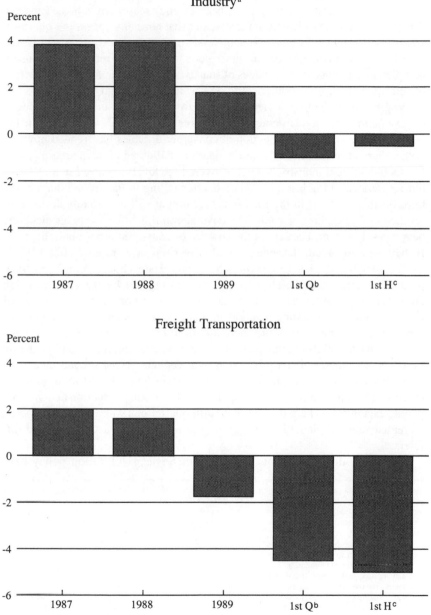

Industry[a]

Percent

Freight Transportation

Percent

a. Goskomstat plan fulfillment reports for first quarter and first half.
b. First quarter 1990 over first quarter 1989.
c. First half 1990 over first half 1989.

Some Seasonally Adjusted Statistics for the USSR. The derivation of seasonal adjustments requires a complete and fairly lengthy series of data. Because Goskomstat's reporting has been erratic, seasonally adjusted indices can be calculated for only part of the statistics that normally appear in a quarterly Goskomstat statistical report. Nonetheless, reasonably good series can be estimated for the production of consumer goods in industry; retail sales; housing completions; average money wages of state workers and employees; production of ferrous metals, fuels, and electric power; and rail freight traffic.

Progress in reorienting Soviet production toward the consumer can be gauged by examining the trends depicted in Figures 5, 6, and 7. Beginning in the second quarter of 1988, production of consumer durables has trended upward, with a sharp acceleration in the fourth quarter of 1989 and first quarter of 1990. Production in light industry has not recovered the levels achieved in mid-1988, but accelerated in the last three quarters after falling in the second quarter and third quarter of 1989. In the food industry, output still is basically at the level reached in first quarter of 1988. The coverage of this index excludes alcoholic beverages, however, because of the absence of consistent reporting in the past. If they were included, the index would have risen more rapidly after 1987.

The statistics depicted in Figures 5, 6, and 7 are almost entirely physical production series and therefore are not biased upward by the price inflation embodied in value series. Goskomstat, however, reports total production of consumer goods (excluding alcohol) in retail prices which, even allowing for some inflation, shows an appreciable upturn in the fourth quarter of 1989 and the first quarter of 1990 after seasonal influences are removed, as indicated in Figure 8. Consumer goods production then declines in the second quarter of 1990, but remains above the fourth quarter 1989 level. Retail trade turnover (Figure 9) has, in turn, risen more rapidly than domestic production of consumer goods, except for a sharp drop in the fourth quarter of 1989. Growing imports, increased sales of alcoholic beverages, and rising prices account for the difference.

The major disappointments of the recent Soviet stabilization policy have

---

quarterly plan targets can cause an upswing in production late in each quarter and particularly at the end of the year. The concept of seasonality is sometimes misunderstood. In the case of weather, for instance, it often is assumed that seasonality should account for the effects of unusually harsh or mild winters, but this is incorrect. Seasonality accounts for annual variations, and, while winter is an annual occurrence, exceptional winters are not.

The seasonal component of a time series is usually not examined as an end in and of itself but, rather, is treated as a problem to be eliminated or circumvented. When, as is typically the case, an analyst wants to look at the trend and cycle component, he or she must first account for the seasonal component. Short-term seasonal fluctuations may make more subtle changes in trend and cycle. Deseasonalization, or seasonal adjustment, attempts to remove seasonality from the data to provide a clearer picture of the underlying trend, cycle, and residual components. This is typically done by determining an "average" trend/cycle and computing seasonal factors as "average" deviations from it. The most common methods of seasonal adjustment use the ratio-to-trend approach, which establishes a trend by any of various methods—including freehand drawing, polynomial functions, and moving averages—and then removes the trend by division or subtraction, leaving only the seasonal and irregular patterns. The most widely used seasonal adjustment technique today, and the one used in this article, is the X-11 method developed by the U.S. Bureau of Census. X-11 employs moving averages to estimate the trend/cycle and includes features that moderate the influence of outliers and allow for gradually changing seasonality.

Figure 5. *Production of Consumer Durables, 1980–1990*

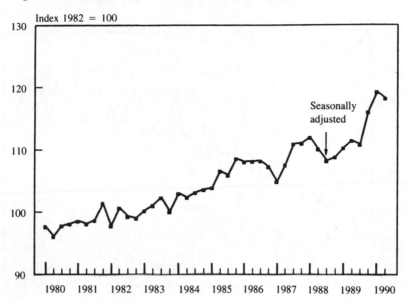

Figure 6. *Light Industry Production, 1980–1990*

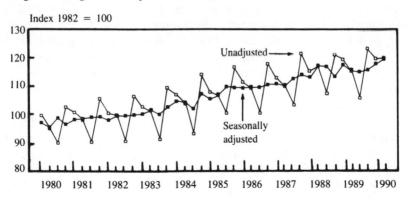

Figure 7. *Production of Processed Foods, 1980–1990*

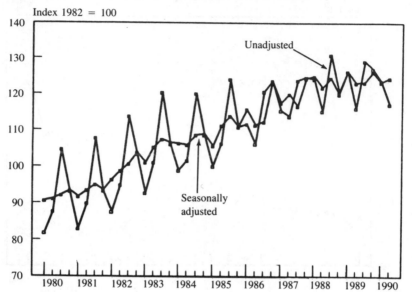

been the failure to stem the rise in money incomes and the sluggishness of housing construction. One can calculate a seasonally adjusted series for the most important component of money incomes of the population—wages of workers and employees in the state sector as illustrated by Figure 10. Although the growth in earnings decelerated slightly after the second quarter of 1989, wages are by no means under control.[29] Meanwhile, housing commissionings (completions) (Figure 11) have exhibited no real growth on a seasonally adjusted basis since 1986.

In the industrial materials sector, ferrous metals output (seasonally adjusted) has remained at roughly the same level since 1986, aside from a sharp spike in output in the fourth quarter of 1989 (Figure 12). The growth of chemicals output (Figure 13) decelerated in 1987, peaked in the third quarter of 1988, and has since declined more in percentage terms than any of the other industrial sectors. The production of forest products, on the other hand, climbed unevenly through the first quarter of 1988 and has basically stayed at the same level since that time (Figure 14).

The performance of the fuels and power sector has been not much different from that of industrial materials. The output of fuels (Figure 15) leveled off in 1988 and the first half of 1989 and then fell because of declining oil and coal production. The production of electric power (Figure 16) rose throughout the 1980s, but at a slower rate in 1989. In the first two quarters of 1989, it

29. The tax on wage increases that was intended to slow the rise in wages reportedly affected only one-fifth of the enterprises that were supposed to be affected by it (*Komsomolskaya pravda*, May 1, 1990, p. 1).

Figure 8. *Consumer Goods Production, 1987–1990 (in Retail Prices and Excluding Alcohol)*

Billion current rubles

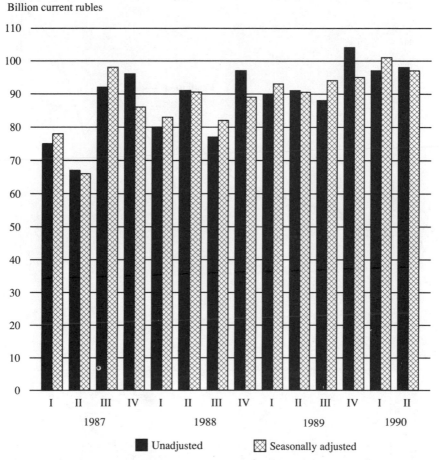

■ Unadjusted   ▨ Seasonally adjusted

declined slightly. Aside from the fall in production of ferrous metals, fuels, and chemicals in the third quarter of 1989 and the failure to sustain sudden increases in ferrous metals output (fourth quarter 1989), and chemicals output (first quarter 1990) Soviet industrial leaders have managed to maintain production of the wide assortment of products for which seasonally adjusted series can be calculated.

A more general indicator of economic activity—tons of rail freight hauled (Figure 17)—declined throughout 1988 and 1989, at least partially because of the unrest in the Transcaucasus. The seasonally adjusted index increased again in the first quarter of 1990 for the first time since the end of 1988, and then fell to its lowest level since the first quarter of 1987, when winter storms and record cold spells snarled the rail system.

Figure 9. *Retail Trade Turnover, 1987–1990*

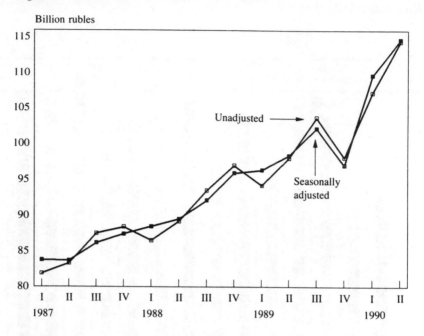

Billion rubles

Figure 10. *Average Monthly Earnings of Workers and Employees, 1986–1990*

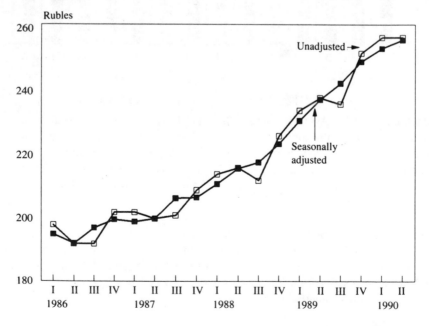

Rubles

Figure 11. *Housing Commissionings from State Resources, 1987–1990*

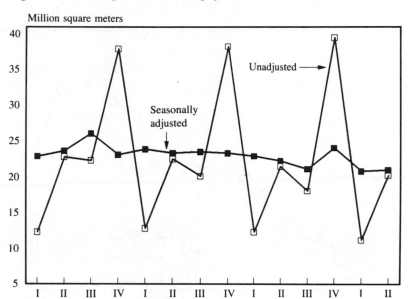

Figure 12. *Ferrous Metals Production, 1980–1990*

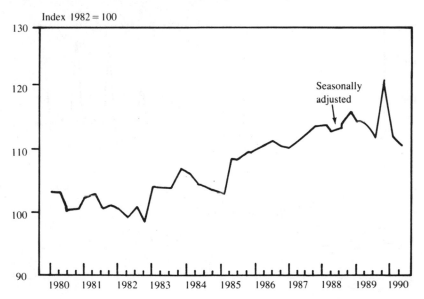

Figure 13. *Production of Chemicals, 1980–1990*

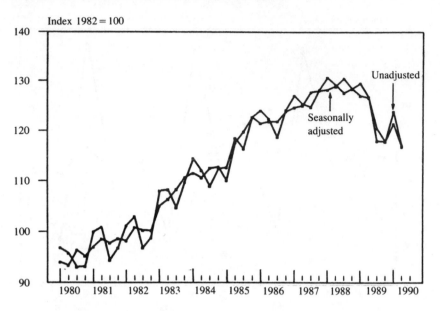

Figure 14. *Forest Products Production, 1980–1990*

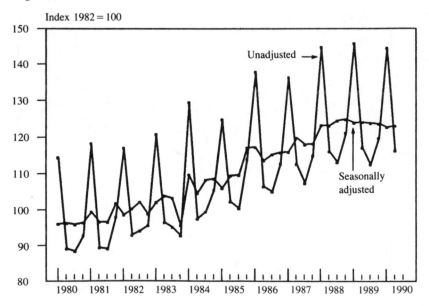

Figure 15. *Fuels Production, 1980–1990*

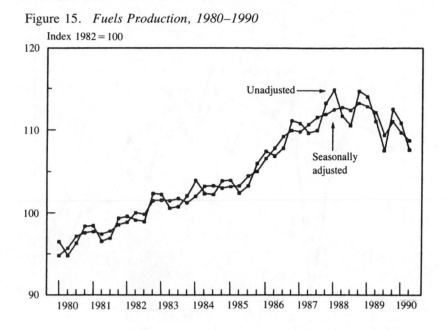

Index 1982 = 100

Figure 16. *Electric Power Production, 1980–1990*

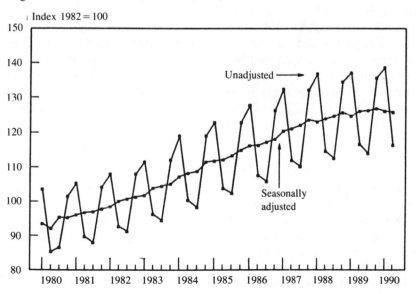

Index 1982 = 100

Figure 17. *Volume of Rail Freight Traffic, 1986–1990*

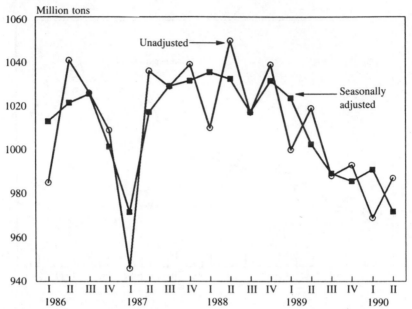

The July–August statistics are too sparse to determine whether there has been any break in trend. Industrial production in January–July was reported to be 0.6 percent less than in January–July 1989. January–June production was 0.7 percent below the January–June 1989 level. But in July total industrial production, production of all consumer goods except alcohol, and livestock purchases were all below the average monthly figures in the first six months of 1990. On the other hand, the June statistics for retail trade turnover, the volume of paid services, freight shipments, and the population's money income all exceeded the average monthly totals during January–June (*Rabochaya tribuna*, September 5, 1990, p. 2). In August, there was an indication that a more severe recession might be at hand. Industrial production for January–August was again 0.7 percent below the level during the comparable period of 1989, and production in August reportedly was 1.7 percent less than in August 1989 even though the number of working days was the same in both months (*Izvestiya*, September 14, 1990, p. 1). However, when Goskomstat's more revealing third-quarter report becomes available, it will be possible—using the physical production statistics and seasonal adjustment—to obtain a better sense of the situation in both industry and agriculture.

Summing Up. This survey of seasonally adjusted indices indicates that Soviet production is not "imploding" or "collapsing," as is sometimes suggested. The trend is upward for most consumer-oriented production and retail sales. Retail sales in state and cooperative trade increased more rapidly than domestic production of consumer goods because of the growth in imports and an element of price inflation. If the statistics included alcoholic beverages and purchases on collective farm markets and from the new cooperatives, the increase in retail sales would be even greater. On the other hand, the reorientation of industrial production from heavy industry to the manufacture of consumer goods, coupled with transportation bottlenecks, strikes, a trend toward greater regional autarky, and ethnic conflict have slowed or halted growth in the output of industrial materials,[30] but there is yet no sign that the heavy industrial sector is unraveling.

For those formulating Soviet economic policy, the most discouraging development is the lack of any substantial progress in slowing the growth in money incomes. The attempts to control wages under Gosbank supervision in the spring of 1988 and by a tax on wage growth introduced last winter have failed. Now the government must hope that the decisions to hold down the growth in aggregate demand by cutting new fixed investment and defense expenditures can be sustained and will—with tighter control over bank credits—be translated into a slower rate of wage growth.

Viewed within the context of these seasonally adjusted series then, the production side of the Soviet economy has coped reasonably well with the reform half-measures, the sudden and sharp shifts of priorities, civil strife, and the government's failure to curb the growth of excess demand in markets for all kinds of goods and services. The government, for its part, has recently corrected—at least partly—some of its earlier policy mistakes. As a result some progress has been made in reorienting the economy toward the consumer:

(1) The reduction of state spending on defense and investment is freeing resources for greater production of consumer goods;

(2) This maneuver is, not unexpectedly, affecting the output of products like steel, construction materials, and producer durables;[31]

(3) Meanwhile, the reduction in defense spending also is reducing demand for the output of heavy industry;

(4) In response, production of consumer durables is beginning to increase at a substantial rate, and there are some signs of increased output of processed foods and soft goods; and

(5) This rise in domestic production is, when augmented by imports and price inflation, beginning to close the gap between the growth of money incomes and retail sales of consumer goods and services.

30. This is partially represented in Figures 12, 13, and 14 by ferrous metals, fuels, and electric power.
31. A calculation based on the 1988 Soviet input-output table (see Treml, 1989), for example, suggests that the 6.5-percent decline in new fixed investment (first half 1990 over first half 1989) would by itself reduce the demand for construction output by 5.6 percent, for building materials by 4.9 percent, for ferrous metals by 3.2 percent, for machine-building output by 3.3 percent, and for electricity by 1.7 percent. Altogether, the decline in new fixed investment results in a 2 percent reduction in demand for output of the sectors of the economy that account for national income produced, which is equal to the 2 percent decline in national income reported by Goskomstat for the first half of 1990 over the first half of 1989 (*Ekonomika i zhizn'*, No. 32, August 1990, p. 15).

The picture which emerges, then, is one of an economy struggling to get out of first gear rather than one in decline.

OUTLOOK

If the state of the Soviet economy described above is accurate—that is, an economy laboring heavily to achieve a fundamental restructuring and one that is not in a free fall—it suggests that the Soviet government and Western countries that wish to aid reform in the Soviet Union can and should make policy choices in a more deliberate, less feverish manner. Many of the wounds sustained by the USSR's economy over the past five years have been self-inflicted. Some have been corrected, whereas others have not. Above all, Soviet leaders at the national level and in the republics should take the time to lay the foundation for further economic reform. Another attempt to introduce ill-considered partial reforms, as in 1987–1989, could, in fact, be the death of reform.

Establishing Preconditions for a Regulated Market Economy

The discussion of recent Soviet economic history in Soviet and Western publications has produced some agreement on measures that should be taken to prepare the economy for a transition to a market-oriented regime. The most important are discussed below.

Restoring Macroeconomic Balance. To stop the growth of excess demand in the markets for consumer and producer goods, the state budget deficit should be cut drastically and bank credit should be rationed more tightly.[32] As noted earlier, the government plans to reduce the budget deficit mainly by paring outlays of investment and defense. According to Nikolay Ryzhkov, the government's program is designed to reduce the deficit to 2.5 to 3 percent of GNP by 1993 (*Moscow Television Service in Russian*, 0605 GMT, May 24, 1990). New legislation on enterprise and personal taxation is about to come into force. There is considerable uncertainty, however, about the budget projections. Budget revenues continue to fall below expected levels, and the implementation of the new tax legislation will require the elaboration of new regulations and the recruitment and training of a new bureaucracy.

This summer's decision to establish a two-level banking system—a central bank subordinate to the national legislature and a lower tier of commercial banks—is a promising step in establishing the monetary controls necessary for a transition toward a market economy (O proyekte, 1990, p. 3ff). But here, too, personnel must be recruited and trained. Meanwhile, the new central bank will require strong leadership in order to withstand the pressures for accom-

---

32. See, for example, the interviews with Nikolay Petrakov (*Rabochaya tribuna*, April 24, 1990, pp. 1–2); Oleg Bogomolov (*Die Zeit*, May 4, 1990, pp. 43–44); and Abel Aganbegyan (1990).

modating credit policies on the part of both the Ministry of Finance and the Supreme Soviet.

While the Soviet economic policy community generally agrees on the need to restrict cash flows to enterprises and households, they disagree on what to do about existing money stocks. The position of the government and many economists has been that it would be unfair to implement a monetary reform that would eliminate some of the cash holdings and bank deposits on savings accounts belonging to enterprises and the population. To those who want to seize the "unearned" incomes of speculators and black marketeers, these economists and state officials reply that speculators and black marketeers have already protected themselves against monetary reform by converting their cash into material assets. Instead they urge that the monetary overhang be immobilized or drawn down by raising interest rates on savings accounts and state bonds and by selling state property to households and enterprises.

The idea of attacking the monetary overhang while beginning the process of "destatification" by selling state assets is attractive but will be extremely difficult to implement until the existing impasse over price reform is resolved. The distortions in existing prices are so large that they do not provide a basis for the valuation of assets. The value of a share of an enterprise will depend on the prices prevailing under a market regime. Many enterprises that are profitable now will then be unprofitable, while others that presently record losses will become profitable.

Despite its repeated rejection of monetary reform, the economic program proposed by the government in May 1990 would erode the purchasing power of existing cash balances while reducing the discrepancy between money incomes and expenditures. The retail price increases in the Ryzhkov proposal (assessed at 199 billion rubles) would raise the population's outlays by 48 percent, and therefore would reduce the purchasing power of cash in hand and savings by 32 percent. The discussion of the program, however, suggests that at least some of this erosion would have been compensated, just as the proposed direct compensation for the price increases (135 billion rubles) amounted to 70 percent of their cost to the population (*Moscow Television Service in Russian*, 0605 GMT, May 24, 1990). Although deferred for the time being, large average increases in retail prices are likely to be an important component of a policy dealing with the monetary overhang.

Price Revisions or Price Reform? The disarray in Soviet thinking on how to address the issue of prices is striking. In the past the USSR has revised wholesale prices at long intervals to reflect accumulated changes in relative average production costs. Another revision of this kind was planned for 1990–1991 as part of the 1987 economic reform package, but has not yet been implemented. The mechanism of price formation remained basically unchanged except for the limited flexibility introduced in 1988 and 1989. Ryzhkov's December 1989 program promised a revision of industrial wholesale prices and agricultural procurement prices in 1991 but postponed a revision of retail prices until 1992—and then only after nationwide discussion. In May 1990, Ryzhkov proposed that the schedule be accelerated—that "at the beginning of 1991 a simultaneous and comprehensive review of the entire price system should be implemented in a centralized manner" (*Moscow Television Service in Russian*, 0605 GMT, May 24, 1990). The ensuing outcry in the Supreme Soviet and in the country regarding the magnitude of the proposed retail price increases illustrated just how divisive the question of price realignment had become.

The government is in a bind. Industrial wholesale prices for energy and basic materials are too low, and the government wants to increase prices for agricultural products. But it cannot raise energy and material prices without reducing the profits of other enterprises, and raising farm prices without adjusting retail prices would result in larger budget deficits and greater macroeconomic disequilibrium. Thus the concept of the need for a comprehensive revision is a sound one.

Much of the argument over price policy centers on the degree of control to be exercised over price changes and their timing. The May 1990 program identifies three basic types of prices: (1) prices established by the state, (2) regulated prices which could vary within certain limits from the official price list, and (3) free or flexible prices. Ryzhkov indicated that in view of the strained marked situation the state should establish prices for important raw materials, fuels and power, the output of monopolies, and prices on compulsory sales by farms to state procurement agencies. Furthermore, the state would retain control over retail prices for most consumer goods and charges for electricity and transportation. He estimated that in 1991, as much as 55 percent of retail trade turnover would be conducted at state-fixed prices, 30 percent at regulated prices, and 10 to 15 percent at free prices. Then, "as market relations are established and the market is filled , the proportion of prices being controlled by the state will gradually be reduced and free prices formation will expand" (*Moscow Television Service in Russian*, 0605 GMT, May 24, 1990).

The indecision on prices stems fundamentally from fear and anxiety about popular reaction to large-scale retail price increases. As Gorbachev said in October 1989 at a Central Committee Conference: "For Selyunin everything is easier. He says that the market itself will sort out everything in a month. . . . I know one thing, within a fortnight this kind of 'market' would make the whole people take to the streets and topple any government" (*Pravda*, November 6, 1989, p. 11). The debate over the winter and spring did nothing to change his mind. In May he declared that "uncontrolled price formation" was "simply impermissible" until a market had been established because "it would strike a grave blow against the people's standard of living" (*Moscow Television Service in Russian*, 1700 GMT, May 27, 1990). Gorbachev's academic advisors apparently reached the same conclusion. At least Ryzhkov told a press conference in May 1990 that he would not list the names of academics who had said six months earlier that "we must definitely change prices, create free prices, and that there would be no sort of market without that. Now we see articles which say that in no event must prices be increased." He then indicated that Petrakov had been one of the offenders, and that six months ago the economist had refused to become Chairman of the State Price Committee (Goskomtsen) because of his disdain for controlled prices, but was now writing that prices should not be increased (*Moscow Domestic Service in Russian*, 1100 GMT, May 25, 1990).[33]

The arguments for a phased transition to market-determined prices appear to be persuasive. First, there are the likely problems inherent in an "all-at-once" approach when relative prices are so distorted. Free prices would result in quite substantial price changes that would be blamed on the reliance on markets rather than viewed as a necessary and overdue measure, even in a planned economy. As Joseph Berliner contends, it would be better to take this medicine in the pretransition stage (Berliner, 1990). With justification, the government also maintains that predicting the impact on living standards will be much easier in a price revision than in a market-price regime. Thus the compensation that the government has promised can be calculated and introduced simultaneously or in advance of the price revisions. The overall rationale for revising wholesale and retail prices in the early stages of the economic reform process is to reduce the possibility that the income, output, and employment adjustments that would occur after controls over prices and output are removed would be so large that they would destroy the reform.

Reducing Rigidities. Another reason for decontrolling prices gradually is that it provides some time to prepare the economy for a market regime. Soviet scholars involved with the economic reform worry greatly about the highly concentrated nature of the economy, especially industry.[34] Legislation to promote small business has been adopted, and the promotion of joint stock companies is intended to create another means of market entry. A more promising approach to stimulating competition is the dismantling of ministries and large associations that assumed the middle tier of management after the main administrations (*glavki*) fell out of favor. At the same time, a revision in wholesale prices should create incentives for enterprises to adjust and expand their production profiles in search of profits. The weakening of ministerial authority over production assignments also should promote competition.

The structural adjustments implied by a transition to a market-oriented economy also would be assisted by measures to increase the mobility of labor and capital. Employment services and retraining programs will have to be developed. For the time being new investment is to be financed mainly out of retained earnings and bank loans. The challenge will be to manage the new monetary

33. In an interview with *Asahi Shimbun* (April 4, 1990, p. 6) Stanislav Shatalin expressed his regret at having advocated administered price reform. He declared that he favored market prices but that the state should continue to control prices for energy, basic industrial materials, heavy machinery, and basic foodstuffs. He maintained that if the prices for those products were freed up in the existing circumstances, the Soviet economy could not be sustained "for even three days."

34. See, for example, the relatively recent pronouncements of Nikolay Petrakov (*Die Zeit*, May 4, 1990, pp. 43–44 and *Rabochaya tribuna*, April 24, 1990, pp. 1–2).

institutions so as to keep the overall demand for investment credit in line with the availability of investment goods.

Near-Term Prospects

In the summer of 1990, the Soviet government was scrambling to prepare a new economic reform program for submission to the Supreme Soviet. Whether it will succeed in developing a plan that will satisfy both the all-Union Supreme Soviet and the several republic legislatures is uncertain. Even Gorbachev's leading economic advisors seem to doubt that a workable program can be fashioned quickly.[35] Moreover, the declaration by most republics (including the RSFSR and the Ukraine) that their laws take precedence over all-Union legislation is certain to impede the adoption of any economic reform devised in Moscow.

President Gorbachev's attempt to have Abel Aganbegyan referee a compromise between the Shatalin proposals and the government's economic reform program illustrates the difficulty of reaching agreement. The compromise gave the all-Union government the right to tax the population and enterprises directly and left out language in the Shatalin plan that asserted the primacy of republican laws. Whether the republics will agree to this is unclear. More important, the Shalatin plan amended is still more an agenda for reform than a program. The stabilization projected in the last quarter of 1990 seems particularly dubious as does the pace of privatization. There is a host of problems to be worked out along the way. Although it is essential to begin a reform, it would be no surprise if the "500 days" turns out to be closer to 5,000 days.

Meanwhile, however, there is some reason to believe that the restructuring that has occurred in the economy in the last year or so will continue. The shifts in investment that have taken place will have an effect on production after a certain time lag. In particular, the conversion of defense-industrial enterprises, which up to now has been proceeding ponderously, seems to be accelerating. The chaos that attended the breakdown in the centralized supply system could well be ameliorated as enterprise and local authorities become accustomed to elaborating alternative arrangements for locating sources of supply and customers. The outlook for the harvest seems excellent, which should improve food supplies and reduce the requirement for grain imports. The USSR's foreign exchange position also should be bolstered by the transition of its trade with Eastern Europe to a hard-currency world-prices basis in 1991, the availability

---

35. Stanislav Shatalin, in a commentary on an article by Vasiliy Selyunin, questioned the existence of obvious solutions to the reform program. Rhetorically he asked, "where are those outstanding people . . . who know the precise formula for success and who possess all the data—the experience, will, the authority and so on—to force 15 republics, hundreds of nationalities, and in general almost 300 million individuals scattered over one-sixth of the globe to act according to that formula" (*Asahi Shimbun*, April 4, 1990, p. 6). Nikolay Petrakov expressed it more succinctly. Citing the lag in Soviet economic thought, he said, "generally speaking, we are beginning from zero." Nor did he think that foreign advice would save the situation, because the Soviet Union has so few of the attributes of a market economy.

of large German credits, and the rise in oil prices precipitated by the confrontation in the Persian Gulf area.

If world oil prices remain at about $30 per barrel[36] and the USSR maintains its exports to hard-currency markets, hard-currency earnings should rise by more than $500 million per month. In addition, increases in gold and natural gas prices will boost export earnings. However, the loss of Iraqi oil received in payment for past debts will offset some of these gains.

In the wake of what appears to be a substantial victory for Gorbachev at the 28th CPSU Congress, the Soviet leader, moreover, may be in a position to effect further cuts in budget outlays. In a May 27 television speech, Gorbachev spoke of "realistic possibilities" for doing so and said "we must have a kind of emergency state budget for the second half of this year" (*Moscow Television Service in Russian*, 1700 GMT, May 27, 1990). He mentioned savings in administrative expenses, but further reductions in defense spending and foreign aid, which politically were untenable before the Congress, may be possible now. For some time prominent economists have been urging additional steps to curb investment, especially for projects of long duration.[37] In sum, the government has not done everything possible to reduce the budget deficit.

While the above represent some positive factors in the USSR's near-term economic outlook, continued progress toward realignment of the USSR's economy must rely upon an uncertain base in agriculture and on an increasingly disgruntled workforce.[38] Almost half of the population's consumption comes directly from agriculture or indirectly through the food-processing industry and part of light industry. The central authorities are attempting, through a combination of higher prices, new labor and property arrangements, and investment in infrastructure to raise productivity and reduce losses. The danger is that the new incentives and investment will raise incomes more than farm output, thus adding to general excess demand. The government's economic strategy also could founder if the morale of the labor force deteriorates to a point that its level of effort falls significantly.

The USSR's energy situation represents another major area of uncertainty. Total energy production fell in 1989 for the first time since the 1940s, and, as noted above, the decline is continuing. The coal industry has been troubled by labor unrest and the increasingly difficult mining conditions in major fields of the western USSR. Oil development has been forced to move farther north in Siberia and offshore, where indigenous technology has not been able to develop new fields fast enough to offset falling output in older producing areas. Insta-

36. The price as of September 1990 when this paper was first published in *Soviet Economy*. [Eds.]

37. At a June 1989 session of the Congress of People's Deputies, Nikolay P. Shmelev suggested the rule should be to invest solely in projects that have a rapid effect on consumption (*Izvestiya*, June 10, 1989). In May 1990 Nikolay Petrakov declared that many construction projects should be frozen without delay and that investment should be redirected toward small- and medium-sized companies (*Die Zeit*, May 4, 1990, p. 43).

38. An article in *Kommunist* highlights the problems created for economic policy by the "revolution of expectations" that has taken place under Gorbachev. With a "reduced level of tolerance" the population "no longer wants to make 'temporary' sacrifices." As a result the probability of a "social outburst" has increased (Kagalovskiy, 1990).

bility in the management of the West Siberian fields, worker dissatisfaction, and an underestimation of investment requirements also have contributed to the decline (CIA/DIA, 1990, p. 25). In the short run, the Soviet Union is striving to adjust to the diminished supply of energy by reducing oil exports to Eastern Europe, but energy shortages already are affecting transportation services, agricultural work, and industrial activity. In the past, the government has been able to mobilize people and equipment in "campaign" fashion in order to avoid an energy crunch. It seems doubtful, however, that Soviet society has the stomach for another campaign.

Assessing the economic future of the territory now included within the USSR is complicated perhaps most of all by the uncertain effects of ethnic unrest and the devolution of political and economic decision making from Moscow to the republics and lower levels of authority. An economic reform encompassing all republics may no longer be feasible. Indeed, the new all-Union treaty that is to be negotiated over the coming months will determine whether there will be a Soviet market or a collection of individual markets. If republican independence is pursued to the point where separate currencies are established, the consequences for interrepublican economic ties are such that the level of well-being for all of the republics in aggregate is likely to be reduced, although some individual republics might be better off than they are now.

Implications for the West

The analysis in this paper will at best support some limited judgments regarding a Western policy to the Soviet Union that reflects a desire to promote democracy and a better life for the Soviet people. Like Soviet policymakers, Western governments must devote the time necessary to reach considered decisions on whether and how to aid the Soviet Union. In a worst case scenario, in which economic linkages fracture in the near term because of general strikes or ethnic-related civil conflict, aid programs probably could not be accelerated quickly enough to make a difference.[39] On the other hand, if ongoing restructuring results in a slow improvement in the consumer situation, there is time for deliberation on how aid might best be channeled into the USSR. This was the approach favored by the G-7 at the Houston summit in June 1990. It may or may not have changed in the aftermath of the brief Helsinki summit in September 1990.

Assuming that it has been decided to give aid to the USSR (as it probably has), such aid would have to be focused to be effective—unless Western nations take the unlikely step of agreeing to provide aid on a massive scale (perhaps 10 to 15 billion dollars per year). Two obvious targets are the food distribution chain and development of energy resources. The potential for reducing losses

---

39. The experience of the past year with the back-up of shipping at ports, the lack of internal transportation, and leakages in the internal distribution system suggest that the USSR is not equipped to handle a sudden surge in imports of food and consumer goods.

of agricultural products as they move from farms to the ultimate consumer is enormous, and Western countries have sufficient expertise and technology to render substantial assistance. In the energy sector, the Soviet Union requires assistance in maintaining oil production in existing fields in order to stave off an energy-induced depression in the economy. Over the longer term, exploitation of Soviet energy resources is the most promising source of the export growth needed to support the USSR's continued economic development. A variety of approaches are possible, the granting of outright concessions representing the most radical.[40]

Should Western aid be conditioned on Soviet behavior? The answer is, of course. One can think of two kinds of conditionality, however—implicit and explicit. Implicit conditionality, for example, should be imbedded in the general expectation that spending on military programs would decline in tandem with reductions in NATO's defense outlays. It also should encompass the expectation that the Soviet Union would work steadily and seriously to develop a democratic society and, in its economy, greater reliance on markets. It would be a bad idea, in this author's opinion, to insist on particular aspects of an economic reform package—whether this involves the measures themselves or their sequencing. Because the experience with the successful reform of centrally planned economies is so limited, Western advisors probably are not prepared to specify a particular reform program as a precondition for aid.

One example of explicit conditionality might be considered, although there certainly are others. The uncertainties inherent in the debate over the relative powers of the central and republican governments are so important for the economic future of what is now the Soviet Union that a Western aid consortium should make it clear that interrepublic economic relations must develop sensibly as a condition of aid. Moreover, as a substantially greater degree of economic independence is likely to result from the new all-Union treaty to be negotiated this fall, some lessons drawn from the Marshall Plan's approach may be applicable. Under the Marshall Plan the aid recipients were required to meet together to discuss requirements for aid and ways of integrating and liberalizing their economies. Something similar to this approach might prove necessary in designing an aid program for a country that may well resemble a collection of independent or semi-independent states rather than become a federal nation like the United States.

---

40. Conservation also has great potential to increase the supply of energy available for export. This potential is likely to be tapped slowly, however, and only after an economic reform realigns energy prices and a competitive environment prevents enterprises from passing increases in energy prices along to their customers.

CHAPTER 21

"Crisis" in the Consumer Sector: A Comment

Gertrude E. Schroeder

MANY OBSERVERS, in the West as well as in the East, are convinced that living standards in the Soviet Union have declined markedly under Gorbachev, especially in the past two years. This belief is buttressed by the commonly expressed observation that there is ''nothing to buy'' in the retail stores. Yet both Soviet official data and CIA measures show that real per capita consumption of goods and services has increased, albeit much more slowly than in the past. This paradox has persuaded many people that the statistical measures are telling the wrong story. The purpose of this paper is to reconcile this seeming contradiction; in doing so, it expands on James H. Noren's analysis of developments in the consumer sector of the economy (Noren, 1990).

THE RECORD FOR CONSUMPTION

Table 1 below, which is based on CIA measures, shows the changes in real per capita consumption in the 1980s. During the five years of Gorbachev's watch, the quantities of goods and services offered to the Soviet people rose at a snail's pace—0.7 percent per year on average. Since Soviet official statistics would show the annual average growth during the period at a level of about 2 percent,[1] both measures indicate that overall improvement in living standards was slower in 1985 through 1989 than in the preceding five years.

A major reason for this outcome is the dramatic impact of Gorbachev's anti-drinking campaign on measures of consumption. As a result of the sharp cutback in state production, per capita consumption of alcoholic beverages (as calculated in the CIA index) fell by 15 percent in 1985, 38 percent in 1986, and 9 percent in 1987. With the reversal of the campaign in 1988, per capita consumption of alcoholic beverages (mainly vodka) rose by 4 percent in that year and by an additional 22 percent in 1989. Alcoholic beverages, which are both highly

First published in *Soviet Economy*, 1990, 6, 1, pp. 56-64. [Eds.]
1. Based on *Narkhoz* (1988, p. 7) and *Press-vypusk* (No. 54, February 1990).

Table 1. *Real Per Capita Consumption in the 1980s*
(rates of growth in percent)[a]

Category	1981–1984[b]	1985	1986	1987	1988	1989	1984–1989[b]
Total consumption	0.9	−0.2	−2.1	0.3	3.0	2.7	0.7
Goods and household services	0.9	−0.4	−2.3	0.1	3.1	2.9	0.7
Goods	0.7	−0.8	−3.1	−0.4	3.0	2.9	0.3
Food, beverages, and tobacco	0.3	−3.5	−7.1	−1.1	2.9	3.1	−1.2
Soft goods	0.8	3.1	2.2	0.5	3.1	3.4	2.5
Durables	2.7	3.5	3.0	0.3	3.0	1.4	2.2
Services	2.2	1.8	1.4	2.7	3.0	2.1	2.2
Goods and services[c]	1.2	2.1	2.4	1.4	3.0	1.5	2.1
Communal services	0.8	0.9	0.2	1.7	2.2	0.9	1.2

Sources: CIA estimates and revised version of estimates presented in Kurtzweg (1990).
a. The concepts and methodology underlying the index of consumption are described in Schroeder and Denton (1982).
b. Annual average.
c. Excluding alcoholic beverages.

priced and highly prized by consumers, have a large weight in the CIA's overall index of consumption—13 percent in the base year (1982). Hence, the spectacular rise and fall of the anti-drinking campaign contributed greatly to the decline in total per capita consumption from 1984 to 1987 and to its upturn in 1988 and 1989. The latter continued in the first half of 1990, when physical sales of vodka increased by 21 percent in comparison with the corresponding period in 1989 (*Press-vypusk*, No. 274, July 19, 1990).

Another factor which significantly contributed to the availability of consumer goods during the period from 1985 to 1989 was the government's decision to curtail imports of consumer goods in 1986 and 1987 and the reversal of that decision late in 1988. Imported consumer goods (valued at retail prices) fell from 48.5 billion rubles in 1985 to 40.5 billion rubles in 1987—from 15 percent to 12 percent of total state retail sales (*Torgovlya*, 1989, pp. 197–198). Imports increased only slightly in 1988, but rose sharply in 1989, perhaps by as much as 8 to 9 billion rubles. This upsurge, coupled with the rebound in production of alcoholic beverages, accounted for most of the overall increase in per capita consumption in 1989. Imports are scheduled to rise significantly in 1990. In comparison with the corresponding period in 1989, they increased by 5.6 billion rubles in the first half of 1990 (*Ekonomika i zhizn'*, No. 32, August 1990, p. 16).

DISINTEGRATION OF THE CONSUMER MARKET

Gorbachev's economic policy initiatives have wreaked havoc in retail markets. True, consumer markets were already in massive disequilibrium in early 1985, when Gorbachev ascended to leadership and power. Random shortages and queues were prevalent, consumer complaints about the quality and variety of products abounded, the government railed about poor labor discipline, and money incomes had been rising more rapidly than the supply of goods and services for many years. Five years later the situation had deteriorated dramatically. Most people in the Soviet Union now are prone to describe their lot after five and one-half years of economic *perestroyka* as being worse than under Brezhnev, or Stalin, or even under the Tsars! How did this terrible situation come about?

Ill-conceived government policies are mainly to blame for the present state of affairs in the consumer sector. The anti-drinking and import policies that contributed so much to decreased supplies of consumer goods during 1985–1987 set in motion processes that have virtually destroyed any semblance of an orderly retail distribution system—turning "trade" into "distribution," to use a currently popular description of what has happened. These two policies deprived the stores of tens of billions of rubles in potential sales (for which the state was unable to provide substitutes), while the population's money incomes continued to rise at rapid rates. These policies also engendered a boom in the moonshine industry and led to runs on stores to purchase sugar and products containing alcohol (perfume, brake fluid, etc). While these particular policies have been reversed, great damage already has been done. The growing malaise in the consumer sector was clearly evident at the beginning of 1988 (Schroeder, 1988).

Government policies connected with the economic reforms hastened the break-down of the retail market in 1988–1990. To begin with, they greatly accelerated the growth of the population's money incomes. Whereas these incomes had risen by a total of 11 percent during 1985–1987 (CIA, 1989, p. 11), they increased by 22 percent in the years 1988–1989 (*Ekonomika i zhizn'*, No. 12, 1990, p. 12). During the first half of 1990 they rose by 13 percent in relation to the corresponding period in 1989 (*Ekonomika i zhizn'*, No. 32, August 1990, p. 15). This acceleration reflected three facets of the reform program. First, a comprehensive wage and salary reform implemented with vigor in 1988 and 1989 mandated large increases in wage and salary rates throughout the economy, with the provision that they were to be financed from enterprise profits obtained from raising labor productivity. But the new Law on the State Enterprise loosened government controls over prices, wages, and profits, enabling state enterprises to raise wages with little regard to productivity. And, finally, new laws permitting private economic activity and encouraging formation of cooperatives resulted in rapid growth of the private sector. At the end of 1989, 4.5 million persons were employed full time and part-time in cooperatives, with an average monthly wage more than double that of the state labor force (*Pravda*, January 28, 1990, p. 1). By mid-1990, employment in cooperatives had reached 5 million (*Ekonomika i zhizn'*, No. 32, August 1990, p. 15), and competition for skilled workers from the private sector gave state firms an added incentive to raise wages. Also, the government itself decided on large wage increases for workers in public services. The government's several measures to curb the growth in incomes proved feckless.

Next, the provisions of the 1987 reform package involving the reform of retail prices unintentionally encouraged the population to begin hoarding goods on a vast scale. The 1987 reform decrees stated that a full public discussion would precede steps to reform retail prices and that such a reform would be carried out without reducing the population's real income. This promise was repeated many times in the speeches of political leaders. The press aired such discussions during 1988 and 1989, along with talk about possible monetary reform to soak up excess purchasing power. The population not only vociferously has opposed both price increases and monetary reform, but its fear of the likelihood that they would materialize led it to hoard goods of all kinds. The resulting shortages were highly publicized, leading to more hoarding and worsening shortages. A Soviet survey conducted in early 1989 found that nine-tenths of all females surveyed were stockpiling goods for future use, compared with one-quarter of all families one year earlier (*Pravitel'stvennyy vestnik*, No. 6, February 1990, p. 6). The survey also reported that the average family had on hand 9 kilograms of sugar and 2 kilograms of detergent and soap. People continued to purchase excess supplies of these products in amounts equivalent to one-fifth of retail sales in 1989, and rationing of detergents prevailed in many parts of the country (*Pravda*, January 28, 1990, p. 2).

In its review of economic performance for the first half of 1990, Goskomstat stated that "despite a significant increase in supplies, the situation in the consumer market worsened. Store shelves became virtually empty, due to the rush demand for food products in the second half of May and early June, especially for pasta, cereals, and flour" (*Ekonmika i zhizn'*, No. 32, August 1990, p. 16). Such was the population's response to the government's proposed price increases for bread products, a measure advocated by Nikolay Ryzhkov that was subsequently postponed.

Another consequence of the population's hoarding has been the rapid decline in retail inventories, to their lowest level (measured in days of turnover) since before 1950. Stocks of almost all consumer goods are below standard levels (*Torgovlya*, 1989, pp. 237-238; *Vestnik statistiki*, No. 4, 1989, pp. 45–51), and the decline has continued through the first half of 1990.

As the pressure of rapidly growing purchasing power on slowly growing supplies increased, various groups of the population took action to protect their interests. Distribution of consumer goods through special channels proliferated. Soviet specialists claim to have identified 20 such arrangements that bypass the ordinary retail outlets. One of the largest and fastest growing of these channels is direct sales of "deficit" goods at workplaces, both in response to advance orders by the workers and by direct allocations of products to enterprises.[2] One Soviet source estimates that one-third of all sales of consumer goods does not pass through the stores (*Pravitel'stvennyy vestnik*, No. 6, February 1990, p. 6). The same source also reports that sales of consumer goods at enterprises and directly from wholesale bases have augmented the supplies

2. During the first nine months of 1989, the following percentages of total supplies of these products were sold in Moscow through "order-sale" to enterprises and organizations: canned meat—59, canned fish—24, vegetable oil—14, cheese—15, tea—31, knitwear—24, shoes—26, television sets—27, and refrigerators—53 (Osipenko, 1990, p. 75).

of speculators, whose needs were thus satisfied on a large scale. Widespread barter arrangements also have proliferated, whereby enterprise employees buy whatever product arrives at the plant (whether or not they need it) and then rely on barter or shadow economy transactions to exchange it for something they want.[3] Another source reports that 14 percent of all furniture was sold through special channels in 1989 and that the share has been growing (*Statisticheskiy press-byulleten'*, No. 12, 1990, p. 52). In its report on economic performance during the first half of 1990, Goskomstat states that "a considerable portion" of consumer durables was sold through workplaces and through special dispatch to designated areas or groups of people (*Ekonomika i zhizn'*, No. 32, August 1990, p. 16).

People without access to such special channels or unable to find what they wanted in the stores have turned to private channels—to "speculators." A Goskomstat survey in the first half of 1989 revealed that 63 percent of families used such sources to purchase a wide variety of goods and paid prices that on the average were nearly one-third higher than those in state stores (*Pressvypusk*, No. 152, April 16, 1990).

As the shortages of consumer goods in relation to purchasing power worsened, local and regional governments began to exercise their newly acquired authority over the consumer sector. Many took measures to reward particular groups or to "protect" their local populations. A decree recently adopted by the RSFSR government stipulates that above-plan produce sold to the state in 1990 will be paid for in special checks that entitle farmers to purchase goods through specially organized channels (*Izvestiya*, July 30, 1990, p. 1). Local rationing of a variety of goods now exists on a scale unheard of in peacetime. In early 1989, sugar rationing was virtually universal. According to one survey, meat and poultry were rationed in 33 of the 146 cities surveyed, butter in 20, and tea and vodka in 16 (Gaydar, 1990, p. 28). A Goskomstat survey found meat, butter, and sausage to be rationed in approximately one-fifth of the 445 cities surveyed (*Pravda*, January 28, 1990, p. 2). In May 1990, the Moscow city council imposed purchase limitations on dozens of products, including cigarettes (*The New York Times*, May 29, 1990, pp. 1, 8).

Another common measure adopted to protect local populations is the requirement that people must present proof of local residence through passports or specially issued cards to make purchases in local stores. Pioneered by the Baltic republics, this measure has spread to Belorussia, Moscow, Leningrad, and some other cities (*Literaturnaya gazeta*, June 13, 1990, p. 2).

Finally, a number of republics and lower-level administrative units have

---

3. Although the magnitude of the shadow economy (*tenevaya ekonomika*) has been assessed by the authors of the 500-day program at 20 percent of the GNP (*Perekhod*, 1990a, p. 126), the validity of such data is at best questionable. Illicit or illegal economic activities are generally known to be nearly impossible to measure. But even if some such activities were assessed with some degree of accuracy, we have no clue how the Shatalin group proceeded to calculate them. There is, therefore, no reason to view their effort to attach ruble values to certain categories (e.g., 5.7 billion rubles of illicit automobile sales, 1.0 billion of spare auto parts, or 1.0 billion paid out by cooperatives to officials as bribes) deemed to comprise the shadow economy (*Perekhod*, 1990a, pp. 125-126) as anything more than a guesstimate.

legislated bans on exports of consumer goods from their territories. In 1989, several republics failed to meet state orders for deliveries of farm products to all-Union stocks, preferring to retain the produce for local needs, but greatly complicating the central government's efforts to increase supplies in state stores in the cities. A Soviet writer describes the developing situation as follows: "Everywhere people are discussing how to prohibit the export of goods from a region, how to prevent sales of above-plan production outside the oblast, or how to force enterprises of all-Union subordination to work for the needs of a rayon, city, or oblast. The bacchanalia of local protectionism is enough to horrify any sensible economist aware of its consequences" (Gaydar, 1990, p. 26).

RESOLUTION OF THE PARADOX

Thus, it becomes apparent that there is no necessary contradiction between the statistical finding that quantities of goods supplied per capita have increased slowly during Gorbachev's watch and the widespread observations of empty shelves in the stores. Goods have been diverted into household hoards, sold through a wide variety of essentially closed networks, and bought up by speculators for resale on the black market. To remedy this situation, the government must curb the growth of incomes and raise retail prices. Its present supply-side approach is doomed to failure, especially in view of the backlog of unsatisfied effective demand, which the government itself estimates at 165 billion rubles (*Pravda*, January 29, 1990, p. 2).

The foregoing recital of evidence pointing to the breakdown in retail markets also shows why people perceive that their lot has deteriorated in the past few years. It has, indeed, deteriorated in a welfare sense. The cost to consumers in toil and trouble to obtain the slowly growing supply of goods and services has increased greatly. Moreover, the processes that have destroyed orderly retail trade also have unleashed inflation, both open and repressed, on a scale not experienced since World War II. While not yet high by Western standards, the inflation has accelerated. By CIA measures, the rate was 6 percent in 1989 (more than double the average in the preceding two years) and threatens to rise sharply in 1990. An indicator of the degree of repressed inflation—the ratio of collective farm market prices to state store prices for food—rose from 2.8 in 1988 to 2.94 in 1989 (*Statisticheskiy press-byulleten'*, No. 10, 1990, p. 27). Overall, collective farm market prices increased by 7 percent in 1989 and by 18 percent in the first 7 months of 1990 relative to those in the corresponding period of 1989 (*Ekonomika i zhizn'*, No. 36, September 1990, p. 12). In view of the rapidly growing incomes and extensive hoarding, black market prices no doubt also are rising sharply.

Accelerating inflation in and of itself makes people feel less well off, even in the face of large supplies of goods. In addition, the Soviet people's sense of worsening living standards under Gorbachev is reinforced by their greater awareness (as a result of *glasnost'*) of what consumer markets are like in the West. They thus perceive greater relative deprivation than they did under Brezhnev. Finally, the advent of *perestroyka* probably raised expectations in the first few years, especially in view of the grandiose programs to increase supplies of consumer goods and services that Gorbachev announced in 1985, supplemented by a blitz of 34 consumer-related decrees in 1985-1987. Although people's hopes have been dashed by events, they do not seem yet to have been rekindled by the latest "lurch" toward the consumer that began in 1989.

In sum, while the Soviet leadership has managed to keep per capita consumption rising, the rate of improvement has been so slow as to be scarcely perceptible to the population and hardly sufficient to maintain, let alone increase, the work effort. But Gorbachev's serious policy mistakes have combined and accumulated to impose enormous welfare losses on the long-suffering populace. It seems that this is the reason why people perceive their living standards to be deteriorating and also why the current mood of the nation is one of fear and despair. Hence the reluctance of Soviet people to buy into economic *perestroyka*. Will they place much hope in the 500-day program devised by the Shatalin group in an effort (among others) to alleviate the crisis in the consumer goods sector? The referendum on land ownership proposed by Gorbachev appears as yet another maneuver to buy time, while the proposal to introduce emergency measures in some regions, allegedly to rescue the reforms (*The Washington Post*, September 22, 1990, p. A1), may tend to signal something different. Mikhail Gorbachev seems unable as yet to forgo reliance on the brisk flow of new reform blueprints, programs, and decrees in favor of a decisive move.

CHAPTER 22

Property Rights in the New Phase of Reforms

Philip Hanson

SOVIET REFORMERS no longer doubt that state ownership of most capital assets is incompatible with a market economy. That relatively simple premise has become the standard point of departure since about the end of the past year. The aim of *razgosudarstvleniye* (literally, destatization) has been incorporated into the Soviet government's plethora of plans for transition to what is now no longer disguised but rather clearly called a market economy. This paper reviews the main measures of destatization now in place or (where the drafts are known) in draft form at the federal (USSR) level. It also takes note of the program of destatization incorporated in the so-called "Shatalin Plan" (*Perekhod*, 1990a; *Perekhod*, 1990b; *Transition*, 1990), and compares it with the federal government's program.[1]

ISSUES IN LEGISLATIVE REFORM

The chaos in present-day Soviet economic policy makes the details of current legislation seem of doubtful interest. It is reasonable to assume that much of it will be revised, and not at all clear which territorial or republican legal jurisdiction will ultimately be responsible for the economic space that is still identified as the USSR. And one is entitled to wonder how much of any of the current legislation will be implemented in practice.

Despite these doubts, the general direction of current legislation on ownership, and the thinking behind it, do matter. The various laws and decrees may not serve as reliable guides to the precise shape of things to come, but it

First published in *Soviet Economy*, 1990, 6, 2, pp. 95–124. Much of the material in this chapter is traceable to discussions with Soviet colleagues, whose collective input is gratefully acknowledged. [Eds.]

1. The text of Gorbachev's compromise plan is given in *Izvestiya*, October 27, 1990, pp. 2–5. It seems consistent with one conclusion of this paper: that differences between the programs identified with Shatalin-Yavlinskiy and Ryzhkov-Abalkin with regard to intended ownership forms (though not on the transition to them) are numerous but mostly minor. Therefore, no compromise program (and there will be some in the future) will add radically new ideas on ownership.

will be argued here that this legislation, with all its ambiguities and lacunae (and all doubts about its chances to survive), reflects a considerable degree of agreement within the Soviet and Russian economic policy elite.

James H. Noren has argued (Noren, 1990) that the Soviet economy may yet muddle through, so that observers should not prematurely dismiss the possibility of that economy's transformation in the future. But Noren, who is not quite as optimistic as the architects of the Shatalin Plan, believes that 5,000 days—more plausible than the 500—might be the timeframe in sight. Let us then make an allowance for thoughts that five to ten years hence observers could look back and say that there had after all been a successful transformation. If that were to be the case, the present thinking on ownership would have contributed to it.

The apparent nexus of economic analysis with what is more frequently examined by legal specialists prompted me to begin with a brief account of the meaning of some of the key terms currently in use in Soviet legislation. This is followed by notes on the evolution of the Soviet public debate on ownership—topics I have dealt with at greater length elsewhere (Hanson, 1989, 1990a, 1990b).

The following sections summarize the major legislative developments at the USSR (federal) level and examine the ownership ingredients of the Shatalin Plan compared to those found in the program advanced as its revision.[2] The last section offers an assessment, taking into account the presidential compromise.

The method of presentation is deliberately attuned to current circumstances. Legislative events are moving so rapidly that one either has to take stock of them with little time to spare or leave the task to the definitive assessment of some future economic historian. Moreover, the legislation is considered only from the point of view of its economic rationale and economic implications. A lawyer would approach it somewhat differently. Most Soviet economic legislation is regarded by Western lawyers as poorly drafted and therefore problematic on technical legal grounds. No doubt some of the gaps and ambiguities that are apparent to an attorney also are apparent to an economist, but others will not be.

Terminology

In English-speaking countries, the term ''public sector'' refers to that part of the economy in which the capital assets are owned and the labor is employed by the state, by agencies of the state, or by corporate bodies established and owned by it as entities with their own legal existence. The latter may be public

---

2. The politics and organizational setting of the two programs are well retraced by Åslund (1990), whereas the anatomy has been crisply exposed in *Foreign Affairs* by Ed A. Hewett (Hewett, 1990).

corporations in the British meaning or commercial concerns in which that state is the sole or majority shareholder.

Whether the state is involved at the national, federal, or some other level, including local or municipal, makes no difference insofar as our use of the term "public sector" is concerned. Conversely, the private sector is everything else, including producer cooperatives.

In the present Soviet debate and legislation there has been a tendency to restrict the scope of the terms "private" *(chastnyy)* and "privatization" *(privatizatsiya)*. This does not apply to some writers like Vasiliy Selyunin[3] but it is true of most.[4]

The attempt to limit the scope of these terms is most pronounced in the speeches and documents formulated by Gorbachev, Ryzhkov, Abalkin, and others associated with the USSR establishment. They generally avoid referring to privatization in a favorable sense.[5] The authors of the Shatalin Plan are more relaxed about it, treating "privatization" as an important part of their agenda. But they also use the terms "private" and "privatization" more narrowly (the latter is treated as a special case of the former) than is normally done in Britain or the United States. "Destatization" is used to mean transformation into so-called "collective" forms of ownership, mainly joint-stock companies. This is treated as the main type of ownership change that is planned for the medium term. From a Western point of view, much of this politically loaded terminology is rather confusing. By and large, however, what most Soviet economists and politicians call destatization is what we would call privatization.[6]

The Ongoing Debate

The Soviet public debate on economic reform has moved quite quickly to confront the issue of property rights. In 1987, the dominant reform view was that "market relations" could and should be combined with state ownership of all land and nearly all capital. Since late 1989, all major policymaking groups have been advocating the sale of a large proportion of state assets and the introduction of small family firms and larger joint-stock companies, with such institutional concomitants as a stock exchange and a network of com-

3. See Selyunin's (1990, p. 2) specific comments on this difference in terminology.
4. This results, among other reasons, from the continuing reliance of the country's legal infrastructure on the legacy of the constitutional framework bequeathed by Stalin (with regard to property rights, the Brezhnev Constitution substantially retains its predecessor's foundation). An informative summary and analysis of the Stalinist legacy is to be found in the as yet unpublished paper by Block (1990), who makes good use of such pre-Gorbachevian sources as Stuchka (1931), Venediktov (1948, 1949), and Genkina (1950).
5. Gorbachev's compromise document of October 27, 1990, comes rather closer to the more "radical" use of language.
6. Admittedly, British usage is not always clear. "Privatization" can mean both the sale of state assets and the device of offering for open, competitive tender contracts to carry out services previously provided in-house by, say, city council employees. The latter producer goes one step further than leasing a state-owned cafe or factory to its existing employees. In their study of privatization in the United Kingdom, Vickers and Yarrow (1988) concentrate on asset sales.

mercial banks clearly separated from the central, state bank. The differences now are over terminology and the pace and final extent of the transformation.

A letter in the literary journal *Novyy mir* in May 1987 marked the most conspicuous shift in the debate (Popkova, 1987). It was written by a young radical economist, Larisa Piyasheva (writing as Larisa Popkova). She argued that the most prosperous economies in the world were market economies, that none of them were socialist, that experiments in combining planning and the market in the West had been written off as failures and that socialism was incompatible with the market. That view was outside the rules of the public debate at the time.[7] It is now regarded as conventional by many of the economists, officials, and elected deputies who are drafting programs for the transition to a market economy.

The route along which the Soviet debate has evolved has not led through an abstract analysis of the economics of property rights. One does not see references to the Western economic literature on principal-agent relations or the market for corporate control.

The emphasis has instead been on two closely linked phenomena widely observed in the Soviet economy. The first is the wasteful use of natural resources and capital assets in the absence of identifiable proprietors with a direct interest in their value. The second is the failure of attempts to induce enterprises to behave independently, short of cutting all links between them and the central authorities.

At the same time, favorable references both to Western and to Hungarian and Polish experience have proliferated. Writings about, and translations of, Hayek and Friedman have begun to appear (e.g., Pinsker and Piyasheva, 1989), but the discussions related most closely to policy tend to appeal to "common sense" rather than theory.

At present, semantic differences, such as those already described, over the meaning of "private," loom large in public discussion. Thus the country's President, Prime Minister, and Deputy Prime Minister responsible for reform (still Leonid Abalkin, at least *de jure*) not so long ago continued to describe their plans for the future as "socialist," while preparing for a stock exchange, foreign direct investment, and the transformation of state enterprises into "joint-stock companies" and "small firms."[8]

More radical policymakers, including Boris Yel'tsin, speak favorably of "private ownership" without displaying an obviously different view of future economic institutions. These differences of terminology are considered by the radical reformers to signal real disagreement—above all, differences in willingness to create an economy composed largely of firms that are genuinely independent of the central authorities (e.g., see Selyunin, 1990).

7. Though earlier somewhat less direct expressions already were on record (e.g., Levikov, 1986, or Strelyanyy, 1986).
8. See Ryzhkov's speech to the Congress of People's Deputies (*Izvestiya*, December 4, 1989, pp. 2–4) and his report to the joint meeting of the Presidential and Federation councils (*Izvestiya*, July 22, 1990, pp. 1–2).

Before this year, the only pieces of legislation that could have facilitated a significant departure from the general rule of state ownership[9] were the 1987 decree on joint ventures on Soviet territory and the 1988 law on cooperatives. The 1988 law on individual labor activity was extremely limited in scope and did little more than clarify the legal status of minor sideline activities already in existence.[10]

The law on cooperatives provided a framework in which firms that were *de facto* private could operate. It allowed cooperative members, who could be as few as three in number, to employ non-members without any ceiling on the number of such non-members. Whether these hired workers could legally both be full-time and long-term employees remains in doubt, even after recent adoption of amendments to the law.[11] In reality many (though probably not most) Soviet cooperatives are for all practical purposes private businesses. But the role of legalized "private" enterprises is small, and the ongoing debate correspondingly crucial in light of the massive share of the pie that remains in the hands of the federal bureaucracy.

Distribution of Capital Assets

The present distribution of fixed capital assets by ownership, according to Goskomstat, is such that around 95 percent are either state or collective-farm property. Table 1 gives data derived from a source published in October 1990 and described as illustrating the position "now" (Goskomstat, 1990). The most plausible interpretation of the time to which the data can be linked leads me to believe that they refer to mid-1990. The values are probably in January 1984 estimate prices, though the source fails to identify them.

Before the privatization program of the Conservative government in the UK began in 1989, the share of state-owned public corporations (of which there were then 47) in the British economy was almost as small as the share of the independent sector in the Soviet economy.[12] The disparity in the scale of British and Soviet "destatization" programs would be hard to overstate. Yet even the comparatively tiny British program, conducted within an existing framework of market institutions, has been problematic and is not yet complete.

9. I follow Soviet reformers' practice in disregarding the largely formal ownership differences between collective farms and state enterprises.

10. And make them liable to licensing fees and taxation.

11. The original law was published in *Izvestiya* on June 8, 1988. The revisions, approved on June 6, 1990, were published in *Izvestiya* on June 24, 1990.

12. Vickers and Yarrow (1988, p. 140) show the following with regard to the public corporations in 1979:

aggregate	percent share of UK total
GDP	10.5
employment	8.1
capital stock	17.2
investment	15.2

Other elements in the UK public sector are not included.

Table 1. *Book Value of Fixed Capital Assets in Mid-1990*

Ownership	Gross of depreciation and net of retirements		Net of depreciation and retirements	
	Billion rubles	Percent	Billion rubles	Percent
Total (all assets)	2971	100.0	1959	100.0
state	2612	87.9	1690	86.3
cooperative	55	1.9	44	2.2
kolkhoz	203	6.8	156	8.0
private	101	3.4	69	3.5
Total (productive assets)	1986	100.0	1198	100.0
state	1771	89.2	1035	86.4
cooperative	28	1.4	21	1.8
kolkhoz	165	8.3	123	10.3
private	22	0.9	19	1.6

Note: Values are at historic cost adjusted to 1984 prices and exclude land, mineral deposits, forests, and purely personal possessions, but not livestock. Productive assets are those used directly in material production, so assets used in some commercial service activities are excluded from the lower half of the table, but included, along with housing and other infrastructure assets, in the top half. "Private" probably includes private-plot assets.
Source: Based on Goskomstat, 1990.

THE MAIN FEDERAL MEASURES[13]

Whoever designs the package of federal economic legislation that finally stays in place is likely to confront the probability that that legislation will not cover several of the present republics. Some of the present conflicts of jurisdiction may well be resolved by outright secession. In other cases, the room for differences in commercial laws between republics that remain within a revised union may also be substantial. Certainly, the relatively advanced legislation of republics such as Estonia is not about to be guided by the federal measures.[14]

Direct Measures

The main federal laws and decrees bearing on property rights that have been approved or are in the form of drafts (either published or circulated) since late

13. The legislation discussed in this section comprises a part of the USSR government's program designed to implement the proposed transition to a market economy. Originally formulated in late 1989, the program was rejected by the parliament and strongly criticized in the Soviet press. For the sake of simplicity, I shall refer to the package as the federal measures (as opposed to the RSFSR measures identified with the Shatalin Plan). A list of planned legislation associated with an early version of the transition program is to be found in *Izvestiya*, September 26, 1989 (p. 1). Legislation associated with the rival team of transition planners operating under the Gorbachev-Yel'tsin agreement of July 27, 1990, but closely linked to the Russian Republic (RSFSR) leadership, is discussed in the subsequent section. Some of that legislation (in draft form, as it is available to me) is intended to be RSFSR legislation but some is would-be federal legislation. All of it appears to emanate from the Shatalin group rather than the Ryzhkov-Abalkin team—a plausible reason for treating it separately (as in Mikhail Berger's "Sosny i sosenki" and "Sosenki bez sosen," respectively, in *Izvestiya*, August 13, 1990, and *Izvestiya*, August 27, 1990.
14. The legislation of Estonia is well covered in the *Byulleten' IME*, published in Tallinn since late 1989 (also in Estonian).

1989 are presented in Table 2. The tabular arrangement reflects the amount of information available to me at the time of this compilation during the first week of December 1990.

Leasing. The legislation constitutes a framework for republic laws that could (as far as federal legislators are concerned) contain some variations. It applies to producer durables, land, and, apparently, minerals rights. The lessor is the owner of the asset in question, and the law envisages all possible owner categories with respect to reproducible capital assets—including foreign citizens or firms and Soviet individuals—but only a state authority with respect to land and natural resources in general.

Leasing may be from some person or juridical person authorized by the owner to act in the capacity of lessor, so a branch ministry could, as in previous practice, act for practical purposes as the lessor. A workforce can lease its enterprise from the state after securing a two-thirds majority (among workers) in favor of such action. A lessee may by negotiation purchase the leased assets outright—though this probably does not apply to land.

Ownership in General. The law on ownership in general has been criticized by radicals. In August, Boris Yel'tsin announced his intent to ask the Russian parliament to abolish it, presumably within Russian territory (*Literaturnaya gazeta*, August 26, 1990, p. 2). It certainly contains some gray areas. Ownership is defined as rights of possession or control *(vladeniye)*, use *(pol'zovaniye)*, and disposal *(rasporyazheniye)*. Article 1.4 seems to open the way to private sector employment by stipulating that an owner can conclude agreements with other citizens to use their labor to exploit the asset owned—subject to federal and republic laws. Yet Article 1.6 states that ownership must not be used for the alienation of the worker from the means of production and the exploitation of man by man—a provision that has been mocked as meaningless by the more secularly minded Soviet commentators, but could still be used to restrict the consequences of Article 1.4.

Ownership (allowable in the USSR) is categorized in the law as citizens' ownership, collective ownership, and state ownership. Citizens' ownership can include shares, but there is no clear statement of a right of individual citizens to own entire businesses employing other people. Joint-stock companies are classified as a collective form of ownership, though Article 15 states that shareholders in such companies do not have to be workers employed by those companies themselves—again with the ambiguous proviso that this must also be allowed by federal and republic legislation.

Land, mineral deposits, and other natural resources are said in Article 20 to be the "inalienable property of the peoples living on the given territory" (Article 20.1), but the same article also provided for the USSR to have the control and use of natural resources needed for federal (all-Union) purposes, including defense, trunk pipeline networks, etc. (Article 20.2). This was an ill-defined compromise between federal and republic claims, leaving open the question of who is to decide what constitutes a necessary federal function. This

Table 2. *Main Federal Laws and Decrees on Property Rights*

Coverage	Type or status	Approving or issuing authority	Dates			Source
			of decree or resolution	of approval	effective as of	
Leasing	Foundations of legislation[a]	Supreme Soviet	n.a.	November 23, 1989	1990	1
Ownership in general	Framework law (on property)	Supreme Soviet	n.a.	March 6, 1990	July 1, 1990	2
Land	Foundations of legislation[a]	Supreme Soviet	n.a.	March 1990	n.a.	3
Intellectual property	Draft law	—	—	—	—	4
Business units in general	Law on enterprises	Supreme Soviet	n.a.	June 4, 1990	January 1991[b]	5
Joint-stock companies	Statute[c]	Council of Ministers	n.a.	June 19, 1990	June 19, 1990	6
Securities	Statute[c]	Council of Ministers	n.a.	June 19, 1990	June 19, 1990	7
Currency market	Resolutions[d]	Council of Ministers	July 20 and 24, 1990	August 4, 1990	January 1, 1991	8
Small business	Decree	Council of Ministers	August 8, 1990	August 8, 1990	August 8, 1990	9
	Draft on activities	Supreme Soviet		—	—	10
State holding company	Presidential decree[e]	President	August 9, 1990	n.a.	n.a.	11
Privatization	Drafts in preparation[f]	—	—	—	—	12
Foreign investment	Presidential decree	President	October 26, 1990	n.a.	n.a.	13
Banking system	Draft law on banks	—	—	—	—	14
	Draft law on Gosbank	—	—	—	—	15

Sources: 1. Osnovy . . . ob arende, 1990. 2. Zakon SSSR o sobstvennosti, 1990. 3. Osnovy . . . o zemle, 1990. 4. Zakon-proyekt, 1990. 5. Zakon . . . o predpriyatiyakh, 1990. 6. Polozheniye . . . ob aktsionernykh, 1990. 7. Polozheniye o tsennykh, 1990. 8. Kommersant, August 13, 1990, pp. 1, 6; Izvestiya, August 7, 1990, p. 1. 9. Kommersant, August 13, 1990, p. 8. 10. Informatsionyy, 1990. 11. Kommersant, August 13, 1990, p. 4. 12. Kur'yer soyuza arendatorov i predprinimateley SSSR, August 23, 1990, p. 1. 13. Ob inostrannykh, 1990. 14. Proyekt zakona . . . o bankakh, 1990. 15. Proyekt zakona . . . o gosudarstvennom, 1990.

Notes: a. Federal as well as union-republic. b. most provisions. c. *polozheniye*. d. *postanovleniya* covering the internal foreign market and shops selling consumer goods for hard currency. e. *ukaz* creating the USSR State Property Fund. f. two rival drafts by the government and by the Union of Leaseholders and Entrepreneurs. Also on record are non-binding procedural recommendations by the government.

has become a major issue between republics, especially Russia, and the USSR since the law was approved.

Land. Legislation on land elaborates what is implicit in the preceeding legislation on leasing and ownership in general. The intention that natural resources remain state property is clear, although the "state" will usually be the union or autonomous republic where the resources are located. Land can be leased, and leases can be heritable and of indefinite duration; the lessee has rights of control and use (usufruct) but not of disposal, i.e., sale. The possibility of a land market seems to be excluded, but that of a market in land-use rights may not be.

Intellectual Property. The draft law affecting inventors has been controversial and its approval long-delayed. The key provision in published drafts with regard to registered inventions is that inventors would have exclusive rights of use (as in most Western patent laws), and therefore could sell (license) such rights to use the invention to others. This is a major departure from the old "inventors' certificate" regime, in which inventions were treated as public property, with no right on the part of the inventor to monopolize their use. Simplifying somewhat, one could say that the traditional system amounted to a giant company suggestions scheme, in which USSR, Inc. exercised a monopolist's power to set the terms of any reward to inventors. The draft would open the way to a Western-style market in intellectual property.

Business Units in General. The Law on the Enterprise was originally scheduled to be that on the socialist enterprise. Dropping of the adjective in the course of parliamentary review of the original draft is one sign of the rapid secularization of thinking among the policymaking elite. The law is general, covering all kinds of business entities: state enterprises, cooperatives, family firms, joint ventures, and others. The general principle is enunciated that all new enterprises (whatever the type) must be registered with the local council and thereupon entered on a national register of business.

Managers are said to be appointed by the owners. This represents a step back from earlier moves toward workforce election of management. Cooperatives and workforce-leased enterprises will be the only types of business in which the workforce is the owner, and even in cooperatives this will not be true where there are non-member employees. The workforce is to be represented on the enterprise council in numbers equal to the representation of the owners— but the enterprise's statute may provide otherwise.

The law specifically states that enterprises can choose their own customers and suppliers, but adds that state enterprises will only acquire this right at the beginning of 1993. That, under the original Ryzhkov-Abalkin transition plan, would be when centralized supply allocation and placing of state orders would begin to be phased out to a more than marginal extent. The state, according to the law, can control some prices, especially those of monopolists, but no operational definition of monopoly is provided. That presumably will be accomplished by specific anti-monopoly legislation, still to come.

Joint-Stock Companies. The statute allows for the establishment of Western-style corporations or public limited companies. Individual Soviet citizens, Western citizens, and Western firms (as well as Soviet juridical persons) can be shareholders. This statute—to be replaced by a law later—should in principle allow the creation of (and the transformation of existing state enterprises into) the kind of business organization that is the core of a Western private sector.

For joint-stock companies, the law sets a minimum size of initial capital, of 500,000 rubles, with shares required to have a minimum nominal value of 100 rubles each. The so-called shares issued by Soviet state enterprises hitherto often have not been real shares: They have paid a fixed return on nominal value, and carried no rights of control (Kitaygorodskiy, 1990; *Izvestiya*, June 21, 1990, p. 2).

Securities. This statute and the associated statute on securities envisage the issuing of recognizable equity shares and the development of a secondary market in shares. Individuals are restricted to holding named shares, i.e., cannot hold bearer shares. This need not prevent a secondary market developing in which individuals could participate.

Currency Market. Detailed regulations on the foreign currency market are still being drafted by Vneshekonombank specialists as well as others. The main ideas are that private citizens should be able to open their own hard-currency bank accounts more freely than at present, and that trading in currencies, including the purchase and sale of freely convertible currencies against rubles, should be widely conducted by enterprises and organizations (but not private citizens) through interbank transactions and currency exchanges. This should allow a market rate to emerge—something that the small and highly controlled Vneshekonombank currency auctions have not achieved. It may be possible for an individual to get around the restriction on private citizens dealing in currencies by using the new small-business legislation to incorporate himself or herself.

Detailed regulations for the (retail) "trading houses" for foreign goods also are still being elaborated. The idea is that enterprises that have foreign currency can import consumer goods and sell them through these shops. Whether anyone who had hard currency would be able to buy in them is not yet clear. Nor is it clear whether restrictions on paying salaries in hard currency will be removed.

Small Business. The resolution on small businesses covers enterprises of all varieties of ownership, but is primarily intended as the framework for private enterprises on a scale smaller than the joint-stock companies covered in earlier legislation. There are size limits on the labor force: 200 in industry and construction, 100 in research and development, 15 in retail trade, and 25 in the remaining areas of the service sector. The small firm can have limited liability, though the exact relationship between the enterprise, as a juridical person, and its founders has not been clearly specified. There are no special tax concessions.

Each firm must register with the local district council but registration is meant to be quick and simple. The first small private firm was registered in the Oktyabr'skiy district of Moscow on August 21, 1990, to market a board game called "Kapital" and perhaps later to go into publishing on the occult (*Kommersant*, August 27, 1990, p. 1).[15] Several more small private businesses have since been set up.[16] Evidently, sympathetic local authorities will readily register private firms without undue delay, prompted by lack of detailed regulations. This is in conformance with the description in recommendations on privatization procedures as nonbinding.

The small-business legislation could be used by existing cooperatives or state enterprises. A cooperative that was in reality a private business could register under this heading and avoid possible legal difficulties over its employment of contract, non-member labor—unless, of course, it was already employing more than the ceiling number of staff. A state enterprise could be privatized by splitting it up into a number of small firms (few state enterprises are small), as an alternative to conversion into a joint-stock company.

State Holding Company. Arrangements pertaining to a state holding company have caused controversy. The USSR State Property Fund, created by the presidential *ukaz* of August 9, 1990, is meant to arrange the privatization of state enterprises, ensuring also that monopoly positions are destroyed. It is apparently meant to cover enterprises subordinate to federal-level ministries only, applying to about 40 percent of the book value of all non-infrastructure capital assets, concentrated in only about 8,500 enterprises (of which one-quarter is to be converted to joint-stock companies by the end of 1990) (*Konnersant*, August 13, 1990, p. 4).

The Fund will itself be a state body, but not subordinate to the government. In principle, therefore, it will not be under the thumb of the branch ministries who have hitherto been the *de facto* owners of these enterprises. Its powers are supposed to be defined by the President and its activities regulated by parliament. The Fund's tasks include the valuation of assets and the protection of "state interests" during the process of valuation and sale.

The main worry expressed by Soviet reformers is that the Fund will try to keep a majority stake in the new companies, in the cause of "protecting state interests." For these critics, the provision that its powers will be temporarily delegated to other state agencies while the Fund and its staff are taking shape— to the Ministry of Finance and possibly the branch ministries—is ominous.

Privatization Program. What is known to the author of the planned privatization program comes only from an independent, market-oriented publication, the *Kur'yer soyuza arendatorov i predprinimateley*. According to the *Kur'yer*, this program has been in preparation in the Council of Ministers (in great secrecy) since June 1990. The *Kur'yer* claims to know, however, that this and other drafts envisage the free distribution of certificates to every Soviet man, woman, and child, representing an equal share of the assets to be pri-

15. The report gleefully describes this firm as the first real capitalist business in Moscow.
16. E.g., as reported by a deputy director of such an enterprise in Moscow (personal communication from A. A. Ponomarev, October 20, 1990).

vatized—which they estimate to be 50 to 60 percent of all non-infrastructure assets.

The Union of Leaseholders and Entrepreneurs (publishers of the *Kur'yer*) is preparing its own, rival draft. The Union wants people to be free to sell their certificates for money as well as to exchange them for shares, and wishes the shares to be sold for certificates *and* money. The Union fears that without these provisions the valuation of assets will have to be managed by the center to fit the total nominal value of certificates, removing all flexibility from the valuation.

The author should also note here the non-binding federal government recommendations to local councils on *procedures* for taking property out of state ownership (Informatsionyy, 1990).

Foreign Investment. At least two drafts of the law on foreign investment are circulating in typescript. The draft the author has seen probably was prepared by USSR Council of Ministers staff. Relatively liberal, its key point can be summarized as follows.

Foreign investment is defined broadly to include the placing of deposits in Soviet banks and the purchase of Soviet shares by foreign firms and individuals, as well as the acquisition of buildings and equipment, and of leases on land and natural resource deposits. Foreign direct investment is explicitly included, so it is made clear that foreign firms can purchase or establish subsidiaries in the USSR. Military enterprises and establishments owned by the KGB or the Ministry of Internal Affairs are not for foreign purchase. Nor can foreigners set up wholly owned banks or insurance companies outside special economic zones, or media or educational concerns anywhere. Everything else can be done. Whether "military enterprises" means those directly under the control of the Ministry of Defense or the much larger category that comes under the Military-Industrial Commission ministries is not clear.

As with existing joint ventures, wholly or majority-owned foreign subsidiaries are to be registered with the Ministry of Finance. Prior to registration, government permission is needed for the creation of wholly new firms: republic government approval where the capital is 100 million rubles or less and USSR government approval for larger values. Tax treatment is to be no less favorable than for domestically owned enterprises, and normally (as for joint ventures) involves 30 percent on profits after a two-year grace period, plus 20 percent on repatriated profits. A list of product groups for which preferential profits tax treatment is provided includes manufactured consumer goods, food processing, electronics, and pharmaceuticals. Foreign-owned firms usually will not be allowed to spend more on convertible currency than can be covered from their own revenue. However, repatriation of profits through a consortium of foreign-owned firms is not ruled out, and in exceptional cases the Soviet or a republic government may provide hard currency to cover the repatriation of ruble profits.

In its operating activities in the USSR, the foreign-owned firm must provide its Soviet staff with standard Soviet social insurance arrangements. There will be no restrictions on pricing for its own products or its choice of currency for settlements. Nor is an import or export license from the Soviet authorities required, except for the export of any item to whose price its own value-added contributions is less than 30 percent.

Banking System. The draft law on banks other than the central bank (Proyekt . . . o bankakh, 1990) is part of an attempted shift from the old monobank system to one that resembles the system that is normal in the West. In other words, the aim is to separate commercial banking functions from those of the central bank (Gosbank), with the latter controlling the money supply.

The draft law on banks in general provides for state-owned "commercial" banks to become joint-stock companies, and requires them to be registered with USSR Gosbank and to abide by reserve ratios and other controls set by the central bank. It restricts operations in foreign currency to Gosbank, Vneshekonombank, branches of foreign banks, joint venture banks—and other banks specifically authorized by Gosbank.

The mimeographed typescript of the Law on USSR Gosbank that the author has seen is (not unlike that on foreign investments) also probably a draft prepared by the USSR Council of Ministers staff. It may be very similar to the draft reportedly accepted in the Soviet parliament on first reading (see above). There was a different draft (a Gosbank version), previously approved by the federal government and then reviewed by relevant parliamentary commissions (*Kommersant*, August 27, 1990, p. 4), which reportedly would have subordinated the central bank to the federal government.

The draft reviewed by the author, and that which received preliminary parliamentary approval, subordinated the Gosbank to the USSR Supreme Soviet. This is in accord with what many reformers have wanted. In any case, this draft is still likely to run into difficulties.

The definition of central bank functions does not seem controversial. It embraces control of the money supply, general powers to regulate other banks, regulation of the reserve ratios required of the commercial banks, functions of lender of last resort, dealing in 3-month bills and other securities, influencing interest rates throughout the system, etc. There has been some criticism of the provisions for direct credit controls by Gosbank (*Kommersant*, August 27, 1990, p. 4). But the strongest objection to the draft seen by this author will probably be political: It envisages a state bank in which USSR federal powers are dominant and republic gosbanks are clearly subordinate.

Another provision of the aforementioned draft calls for a Central Council of the USSR Gosbank, concerned with broad policy, as well as a Board for day-to-day management, with the same person chairing both. The republic gosbanks are to be divisions of USSR Gosbank. Their chairmen are to be on the USSR Gosbank Central Council, but not on the USSR Gosbank Board, which is to be appointed by the USSR Supreme Soviet. It appears that the republic Gosbank boards will be more or less directly subordinated to the USSR

Gosbank Board—an arrangement quite likely to prove unsatisfactory to a number of the republics.

Related Measures

In addition to the foregoing legislative measures, there are those not directly and exclusively concerned with ownership but nevertheless important to the infrastructure of the new economic regime. These measures include the new laws on individual and enterprise taxation and the August 16, 1990, decree on anti-monopoly measures. This paper incorporates under this heading the recently promulgated presidential decrees on foreign investment and the commercial exchange rate for the ruble (*Izvestiya*, October 26, 1990, p. 1).

Taxation. The law on enterprise taxation, approved by the Supreme Soviet on June 14, 1990, is to become effective from the beginning of 1991 (*Izvestiya*, June 29, 1990, pp. 1–3). It covers several different forms of business taxation and deals with USSR taxes as well as some federal-level rules about republic and lower-level taxation. The law envisages a federal profits tax of 22 percent, and a ceiling of 45 percent on the total of federal-plus-lower-level profits taxes. Soviet commentators have assumed that 45 percent would in fact be the overall rate of profits tax, and many have criticized it as "too high."

What is more obviously objectionable is inclusion of a "supertax" of 80 percent on the first 10 percent of enterprise profits (over and above profits that would represent twice the industry-average return on capital) and 90 percent on the next 10 percent. Such rates would be questionable on incentive grounds in an operating market economy. It is true that in an economy still emerging from massive distortions of product prices and asset values, such high rates of return may bear very little relation to enterprise behavior. But controlling the rates so early in the transition is hardly conducive to rapid liberalization.

The presidential decree of October 4, 1990 "On Priority Measures for the Transition to Market Relations" (*Izvestiya*, October 5, 1990, p. 1) only strengthens such doubts. It calls for a substantial shift to "contract pricing" in 1991, but makes it clear that the new prices should be "based on" the central planners' revised wholesale prices worked out in 1988 and 1989. Moreover, an absolute ceiling is to be put on profit rates. Not unexpectedly, the decree was promptly criticized in the liberal Soviet press (e.g., *Izvestiya*, October 6, 1990, p. 2).

Anti-Monopoly Measures. These measures constitute a necessary ingredient for any successful privatization program. Accordingly, the government issued an appropriate decree adopted on August 16, 1990, and published in September (O merakh, 1990).

It provides for the establishment of an anti-monopoly committee under the aegis of the USSR Council of Ministers. Its functions would include fostering small business as well as monitoring and possibly breaking up monopolies.

The exact scope of its powers is not clear, for many provisions of the decree contain instructions apparently addressed to other government agencies.

The principal aim of the decree is to prevent domination of markets by individual producers. This is defined at two levels: a 70 percent market share during the process of transition to the market economy—apparently this degree of concentration is to be avoided or prevented—and a lower level of 36 to 70 percent, where enterprise behavior is to be monitored, but will presumably be treated as not necessarily constituting a *prima facie* case for action.

The committee is to monitor large investment projects for their monopoly effects. It is also to observe the workings of the (increasingly numerous) "associations" and "concerns" *(kontserny)*, which often cover entire sub-branches of industry. Moreover, the committee is specifically charged with investigating market-sharing arrangements, activities that create barriers to market entry, price rings, and the like. It also has a remit to deal with "unfair trading practices." Enterprise actions that create or sustain market dominance (in the above sense) make executives liable to sanctions imposed through the courts.

Among provisions that are not specifically addressed to this committee, one finds a ruling (Point 8) that the sale of state enterprises should incorporate separate disposition (sale) of technologically independent production units within a given enterprise. This is presumably addressed to the State Property Fund and investment funds created by it.

There is also a provision that branch ministries should cease to be responsible for the fulfillment of contracts by enterprises attached to them (Point 6). But this is not to come into effect until after the economy has been stabilized in a macroeconomic sense. The importance of the monopoly power built into the supply system is recognized by a provision (Point 15) that Gossnab offices be turned into independent commercial wholesaling enterprises.

The other points worth noting here are provisions that the statutory monopoly of insurance be ended (Point 20), that foreign trade organizations at present subordinated to the Ministry of External Economic Relations become independent of it (Point 22), and that direct foreign investments encourage desirable competition (Point 23).

Foreign Investments and Revised Exchange Rates. Two presidential decrees *(ukazy)* of October 26, 1990, had implications for foreign investors that seemed at first sight to be favorable (Ob inostrannykh, 1990; O vvedenii, 1990). Both, however, were brief and left a great deal to be clarified in more detailed legislation.

The decree on foreign investment stated in essence that foreign investors could acquire or establish wholly owned subsidiaries in the USSR; that firms with foreign participation (whether with the foreign partner holding a minority stake or a majority or 100 percent stake) could convert ruble profits freely at market-determined exchange rates, and repatriate them, subject to taxation.

The decree on the commercial exchange rate and the creation of a currency market had two main provisions: the establishment of a new commercial rate that devalued the ruble by a factor of three (from about 0.6 rubles per U.S. dollar to about 1.8) and the legalization of free currency exchange, within the USSR, at rates to be determined by the market, for all juridical persons—not, in other words, for private citizens.

On the face of it, these decrees between them promised to make it possible for foreign investors to set up in business in the USSR, selling on the domestic market for rubles, and to repatriate ruble profits. In practice, the retention by the central authorities of a very high proportion of available hard currency could mean that this route could be followed only by paying very high ruble prices for hard currency.

A further presidential decree of November 2, 1990 specified that the federal government would take 40 percent of all hard-currency earnings (in exchange for rubles) as an emergency measure during 1991—apparently in addition to other arrangements by which Soviet enterprises lose control of most of their hard-currency earnings. That reinforces doubts about the scope for a currency market to develop in the near term. Joint ventures and foreign-owned firms are specifically exempted from this measure.

The text of the November 2 decree states that the expropriation of 40 percent of hard currency by the federal authorities is needed to settle Soviet payments overdue to foreign suppliers and restore the USSR's credit rating. There is a depressing and characteristic contradiction here. One of the key principles of reform is that state and enterprise should be at arm's length from one another. Neither of them should be required or expected to bail out the other. That principle is explicitly stated in the 1990 law on enterprises discussed earlier. Yet here the debts of some Soviet enterprises and organizations are being treated as state obligations, regardless of whether any state agency had acted as a financial guarantor of the credit concerned. At the same time, other enterprises are to be required to contribute to paying off this debt through the state. This is precisely the "old thinking."

OWNERSHIP ELEMENTS IN THE SHATALIN PLAN

Privatization (in the broad, Western sense) is treated clearly and prominently as a central element of the so-called Shatalin "500-Day" program (or plan).[17] It is the clear and prominent presentation of this fact that chiefly distinguishes the Shatalin Plan from the various documents that constitute the Soviet government's program, best known as that identified with Ryzhkov and Abalkin.

The preceding section was intended to demonstrate that the privatization envisaged by the federal government is very extensive indeed, and therefore necessarily a central element in its program as well. But Ryzhkov, Abalkin,

17. The program, identified with Gorbachev's economic advisor Stanislav Shatalin, is by now best known in the West as the "Shatalin Plan," though such labels as "500-Day Plan" or "Shatalin Program" are in continued use.

and their associates have nowhere presented this fact in a clear and forceful way.

This section is concerned, however, with differences of substance between the two programs, rather than differences in presentation. It will serve to suggest that these lie chiefly in the clarity of the relevant draft legislation and the role of privatization in the transformation strategy as a whole. Differences in the general character of the institutional changes that are planned are not fundamental.

The Approach and Timing

The short, programmatic statement about the Shatalin group's proposals, entitled "Man, Freedom and the Market," conveys the general approach of the group to property rights (see *Izvestiya*, September 4, 1990, p. 3). In that statement, the Shatalin group declares that their program will achieve reform at the expense of the state, not the people. The Soviet Union, they say, has "a rich state and a poor people." By returning resources to the people, the program will end their poverty.

After the introduction, the relatively brief (ca. 3,500 words) statement comprises six sections, each dealing with some "right." The first two are "Man's Right to Property" and "The Citizen's Right to Economic Activity." The return of property to the people is described as "an act of social justice." The desirability of selling, rather than giving away, state assets is asserted as a general principle although some scope for free distribution of assets is accepted. The underlying theme is the interest of identifiable proprietors in maintaining and increasing the value of their assets, and therefore in using them effectively. No Soviet policymakers in the leadership have ever made such a strong and prominent statement of this philosophy of ownership; this is true not only of Ryzhkov and his associates, but also of Gorbachev.

The documents that set out specific proposals of the Shatalin group deal with ownership primarily in the form of a section in the program itself (*Perekhod*, 1990a, pp. 55–69) and in the supplementary volume covering draft legislation (*Transition*, 1990, pp. 69–157).[18] The two sources will be discussed in that order.

Shatalin's program puts its emphasis on union republic legislation stating that a presidential *ukaz* "On Freedom of and the Defense of Entrepreneurship" provides an all-Union guarantee of equal opportunities for all various forms of ownership.[19] Republic legislation, however, is to provide the specific rules of the game.

Much of what follows refers to a timetable that has already become obsolete since the program was drafted at the end of August 1990. By October 1, 1990,

18. In the Russian-language original the corresponding material is to be found on pp. 61–125 (*Perekhod*, 1990b).

19. This *ukaz*, as best known at the time of this writing, is planned but not yet issued.

a privatization program was to have been drawn up, and by November 1 the USSR State Property Fund (see above) and its republic equivalents were to have prepared lists of state enterprises for privatization. Even before, by October 10, 1990, the republics were to repeal legislation that made various forms of private enterprise a criminal offense, and grant amnesty to offenders jailed under those laws. And by October 15, the division of responsibilities for managing privatization between the center (Union) and the republics was to have been determined.

The general guideline for this Union-republic division is (was) that the federal government (Union) should continue to control (and not destatize) defense plans not subject to conversion, nuclear facilities, trunk pipelines, main railways, "communications" (probably the phone system), and defense facilities. It also should supervise the sale of assets in aerospace electronics, shipbuilding, the merchant marine, and major ports. Enterprises in the aforementioned branches should become joint-stock companies, initially with shares held by the state property funds of the republics. Everything else should be handled at the republic level.

Union responsibilities are therefore restricted to the military-industrial sector, i.e., the enterprises subordinate to those ministries that report to the Military-Industrial Commission (VPK), and to a few other branches in the continued-union-control category that are apparently thought of as either providing public goods or constituting natural monopolies.

That telephone systems and rail networks can be privatized and have competition introduced into at least some of their activities is, in the Soviet context, a minor criticism. Provided that the other category of Union-responsibility industries is meant to be privatized in due course by its republic holding companies, the division of responsibility between the Union and the republic is a reasonable one. Problems are likely to arise, however, when it comes to deciding the precise republic shares, and how to do business with separatist republic leaderships.

Shatalin and his associates have been criticized for proposing an implausibly high pace of privatization. Their imaginative diagram (see Table 3) tends to suggest that they envisaged about 20 percent of industry would be converted to joint-stock enterprises by 1992,[20] while nearly 70 percent would still remain in state hands. At several points in the program the authors in fact acknowledge that state assets simply cannot be sold off quickly. They sensibly point out that it is very hard to sell large blocks of assets before basic capital-market institutions have been created.

The emphasis is on an early declaration of intent and a preliminary listing of enterprises for sale, with an early and rapid start on the privatization of

---

20. It is not at all clear whether "1992" means the beginning or the end of that year. In any event, no resolution in 1992 is in sight for reasons such as the raging disputes among the various federal and republic authorities and jurisdiction over "who owns what."

Table 3. *Projected Ownership of Industrial Assets in the Shatalin Plan,*
1990-2002
(percent)[a]

Year \ Sector	Lease-holds	Collective (group)	Private	Associations and cooperatives	Joint-stock	State
1990	5	2	—	—	—	>90
1991	>5	2	—	2	2	<90
1992	<10	2	—	2	>20	<65
1993	<10	2	neg.	>2	30	55
1994	<10	2	neg.	>5	<40	45
1995	<10	>2	neg.	10	40	>35
1996	<10	>2	2	>10	>45	<30
1997	<10	>2	>2	>10	50	<25
1998	<10	<5	>2	<15	50	>20
1999	<10	<5	<5	<15	50	<20
2000	<10	<5	<5	15	50	<20
2001	<10	<5	<5	15	50	<20
2002	>5	<5	5	15	50	<20

Source: *Perekhod*, 1990a, p. 63.
a. Rounded approximations based on rough calculations from diagram.

assets in road haulage, building, the building materials industry (where work-force leasing of enterprises was first developed), retail trade, catering, other services, and the textiles, clothing, and food-processing industries.

The early-privatization sectors are intended for sale to individuals, families, small cooperatives, and partnerships. The Shatalin group's first target in this area is the sale of one-half of all retail food stores with a workforce of less than eight by the spring of 1991, and half of all retail non-food stores employing fewer than 11 workers. Together, these would apparently account for about 15 percent of present state retail sales in outlets at present employing about 600,000 people. Small-scale privatization would continue rapidly through 1991.

One example of such a program already under way is the Leningrad City Council's sale of an initial tranche of leases on 100 food shops (*Kommersant*, September 13, 1990, p. 4; Yakovchuk, 1990). The aim is to continue for the time being to supply these shops, as before, through centralized supply chan-nels, while encouraging the new independent shopkeepers to supplement the centralized supplies on their own initiative—something the existing managers had little incentive to do under state ownership. The number of bidders for these shop premises comfortably exceeds the number of shops offered.

The Shatalin group assumes that the state's share of industrial-sector assets will fall below 50 percent in the fifth year of the transformation process—i.e., well after the period of 500 days has elapsed. The authors envisage it levelling off at about 20 percent after eight years or thereabouts (*Perekhod*, 1990a, p. 63). Presumably they expected small-scale privatization in other sectors to move somewhat faster.

Table 4. *Proposed Legislative Measures in the Shatalin Plan*

Coverage	Type[a]	Jurisdiction	Source
Joint-stock companies	Law	RSFSR	1
Securities and stock exchanges	Law	RSFSR	2
Management of state property	Regulations	USSR	3
Supervision of securities	Regulations	RSFSR	4
Property liability of enterprises	Law	USSR	5
Bankruptcies of juridical persons	Law	USSR	6
Bankruptcy of enterprises	Law	USSR	7
Foreign investment	Law	RSFSR	8

Sources: *Perekhod*, 1990b (*P*); *Transition*, 1990 (*T*); pp. [1]61-73 (*P*), 68-87 (*P*); [2]74-79 (*P*), 87-96 (*T*); [3]80-82 (*P*), 96-100 (*T*); [4]83-86 (*P*), 100-105 (*T*); [5]87-92 (*P*), 105-112 (*T*); [6]93-99 (*P*), 112-120 (*T*); [7]100-113 (*P*), 120-138 (*T*); [8]114-124 (*P*), 138-157 (*T*).
a. All laws and regulations are presented as drafts.

Legislative Measures

The legislative measures in the Shatalin Plan that merit a comment in this section are tabulated above (Table 4).

Because the parliament of the Russian Republic approved the Shatalin Plan in early September, it is, at least in principle and in outline, committed to the Shatalin drafts intended for RFSFR legislation. Presumably the Russian leadership also is committed to pressing for Union-level adoption of the draft USSR laws and regulations unveiled by the Shatalin group, though it has no official standing with respect to federal legislation.

As time marches on, any discussion of Shatalin's legislative program on ownership is bound to face the problem of rapid obsolescence. In the words of Ed A. Hewett, "as the economy deteriorates, the government will respond with more decrees. Within months, attention will turn to the search for yet another plan" (Hewett, 1990–1991, p. 166). However, for the reasons outlined in the introduction (above), the author will briefly comment on its general character, in comparison with that of the federal program, and then discuss selected points on which specific differences appear to be important.

The drafting of the Shatalin documents looks, at any rate to an economist, to be less ambiguous and rather more purposeful: It had fewer statements of general desiderata and more concentration on matters that might plausibly be regulated by law.

It is at the same time less comprehensive in coverage. There is no general framework law on ownership, and no law on land, on intellectual property, or on foreign currency markets. The reasons for this difference of coverage are presumably some or all of the following: satisfaction with existing USSR legislation on the subject in question, belief that no legislation on it is needed at all, and the existence of RSFSR laws that are either already approved or still being drafted.

The inclusion in the Shatalin Plan of a law on the property liability of enterprises is a definite advantage. It tackles the fundamental question of loan securities and penalties for breach of contract. How successfully it does so, in comparison with Western commercial law, is for learned attorneys to judge. But there is to the author's knowledge no comparably serious attempt at this in the current flow of legislation associated with the federal government's transition program. The drafts on bankruptcy and reorganization also appear more complete and more systematic than any comparable existing USSR legislation.

The draft RSFSR law on joint-stock companies makes it clear that foreign investors are, with some specified restrictions, to be treated on a par with locally based investors. It sets the minimum number of shareholders somewhat higher than the federal statute: three for closed companies and 10 for public limited companies. It also allows a smaller minimum size of initial capital (10,000 and 50,000 rubles, respectively) and tolerates minimal values of shares (10 rubles). There are no restrictions on individual citizens' ownership of bearer shares, and the legal requirements for internal structure do not include the rather elaborate ones involving supervisory boards, as in the USSR statute.

Registration procedures are not much different, except that the RSFSR Ministry of Finance accepts and maintains lists of registrations. The Union statute, finally, has no counterpart to the requirement that purchases (on the secondary market) of more than 10 percent of a company's shares have to be reported to and approved by the republic Ministry of Finance.

The draft RSFSR law on securities markets is clearer on the matter of secondary markets, stating specifically that anyone can buy and sell on them.[21]

The Shatalin securities law is also specific in excluding from its ambit the so-called "enterprise shares" and "workforce shares" issued under USSR Council of Ministers resolution No. 1195 of October 15, 1988 (referred to in the preceding section). And it addresses the question of capital gains tax on the sale of shares by providing for such gains to be treated for tax purposes as income, pending any new legislation on the subject.

In general, it seems fair to say that the Shatalin legislation on companies and securities is more businesslike. One obvious problem is simply that it is in conflict with a number of points in the federal legislation. These may not be very serious matters in and of themselves, but the question of which law has precedence, and where, will have to be addressed, or else one or the other piece of legislation will have to be changed.

The Shatalin version of USSR regulations for a committee to manage the sale of state assets makes it clear that the investment trusts (to be created as state holding companies under the committee) are to do their best to sell off the assets they hold, retaining responsibility for control and management only as an interim arrangement. The presidential *ukaz* of August 9, 1990, setting

---

21. Reliance on the principle that whatever is not specifically forbidden is allowed is still problematic in the USSR, partly because a great deal of conflicting earlier laws and regulations are still on the books.

up the USSR State Property Fund, leaves a good deal of detail to be worked out, and does not exclude the possibility of continued state control.[22]

The draft RSFSR law on foreign investment seems on the whole to be simpler, clearer, and more generous than the USSR law. Registration with the republic Ministry of Finance is required only for firms with majority foreign owners. Other entities can be registered with local authorities, although this is in conflict with the law on companies. A foreign firm can set up a branch in the Russian Republic by a fairly simple procedure, whereby the republic Finance Ministry must respond within 90 days of the application and its negative response can be appealed.

Hard-currency profits can be repatriated, including currency bought for rubles. No export or import licenses are needed. Exemptions from taxation appear to be more generous than in the USSR law. The awkward and unclear distinction between joint ventures and wholly or majority-owned foreign firms that emerges from the USSR draft law is not present. The Shatalin group seems, sensibly, to be assuming that the term "joint venture" will become redundant, as far as their legislation is concerned. Finally, the list of product groups on whose manufacture there are tax concessions for foreign companies is rather more detailed than in the USSR draft. Differences between the two draft laws are probably not too serious, since the USSR legislation specifically allows for republic variations.

This outline comparison will be completed by noting that the Shatalin Program also contains draft USSR and RSFSR bank laws (*Transition*, 1990, pp. 1–53; *Perekhod*, 1990b, pp. 5–45). Here the key difference is that the Russian Republic reform team tends to envisage a USSR central bank modelled roughly on the U.S. Federal Reserve Board (the authors call it the USSR Reserve System). The idea is to give greater authority to republic central banks without departing from monetary union and a single monetary policy.

The Shatalin group's draft legislation on ownership looks on the whole stronger than that of the federal government. It does, however, complicate the situation in several areas where either: (a) conflicts of USSR and RSFSR legislation arise and it is still not clear whose jurisdiction prevails, and (b) the Shatalin group is backing draft USSR legislation that differs significantly from that advanced by the rival team. Again, the drafts should be viewed in light of their historical rather than jurisprudential significance.

PRELIMINARY ASSESSMENT

A first preliminary conclusion is that there is extensive agreement on major issues of principle in the various established and drafted pieces of legislation on ownership. The general objective implicit throughout is the creation of a mixed economy. The thinking behind it is also reasonably clear.

22. See p. 425.

The various teams of establishment reformers all appear to endorse the proposition that the attempt at transforming Soviet economic performance would begin to succeed: (a) if the managers of production units were to conclude that they had to worry more about customers and actual or potential competitors than about higher authorities; (b) if the foregoing was true for investment and market entry and exit decisions as well as for current output decisions; (c) if all such decisions were taken in an environment where prices tended to reflect relative scarcities; and (d) if there were more or less predictable rewards for success and penalties for failure.

Similarly, there seems to be no disagreement that only an economy with identifiable proprietors of capital assets can provide such an environment.[23] The arguments for this second proposition are often implicit rather than explicit. They include the following:

(1) If there is no market in which capital assets are valued, there is no reliable basis for product prices that reflect opportunity costs in production. The existence of a product market is also necessary for the appropriate valuation of capital assets, so the link runs both ways.

(2) The existence of a capital market with competition for asset ownership provides both the possibility of free product-market entry and exit and of a market for corporate control, through which the managers of assets are under pressure to respond to asset-owners' interests in maintaining and increasing the value of assets.[24]

(3) Arrangements of this kind are more conducive to static allocative efficiency, X-efficiency, and technological progress than the existing system of state ownership.

The legislation and draft legislation reviewed in the preceding two sections are widely criticized by Soviet radical reformers as being inadequate.[25] The outside observer, however, is bound to say that both packages of measures are in any event clearly aimed at the creation of the legal framework for a mixed economy. The federal government measures contain their share of bureaucratic traps and half-measures. But these weaknesses seem to be less evident in the more recent than in earlier measures within the package.

For example, the ambiguities in the framework law on ownership in general (see above) are greater than those in the joint-stock company statute or the draft law on foreign investment. And in what I understand to be successive drafts of the law on the central bank, subordination of USSR Gosbank to the federal government has given way to subordination to parliament—in the Soviet context, probably an improvement. On the other hand, conflicts between the

---

23. Interviews in Moscow and Leningrad in August 1990 with more than a dozen reform thinkers have reinforced this interpretation.

24. For a review of Western literature on the relationships between ownership and control, see Vickers and Yarrow (1988).

25. This includes severe criticism of the Shatalin Plan, such as that by Larisa Piyasheva in *Komsomol'skaya Pravda*, October 6, 1990, p. 2.

two programs are not going to help. The Gorbachev compromise program published in the Soviet press (*Izvestiya*, October 27, 1990, pp. 2–5) provides no guidance on how these conflicts of detail would be resolved.

There are also some missing elements and unresolved issues in one or both programs that are quite important. *First*, the question of the future ownership of land is still contentious and far from nearing any apparent consensus. The development of a market in land-use rights may be sufficient to support the general development of such a market, but thus far no clear provision for it is on record. An extraordinary session of the RSFSR Congress of People's Deputies voted on December 3, 1990, to approve an RSFSR land law that included the right of private ownership of agricultural land in the Russian Republic (*Izvestiya*, December 4, 1990, p. 1). This is a historic step. Nonetheless, the outcome was a compromise that stopped short of facilitating a land market. Farm land (but no other kind of land) may be privately owned and inherited, but can only be sold to the state, in the form of the local soviet.

Second, the half-measures, bureaucratic traps, and disabling lower-level countermeasures have not disappeared from the federal legislation. It is not clear, for example, why there should be labor-force ceilings on "small enterprises" when some of the dynamism of mixed economies comes from small firms that succeed in getting big. And there is a real risk that the conversion of state enterprises into companies will be managed in a way allowing the state to keep a majority stake and/or ex-*nomenklatura* managers to become the new owners, leading to undiminished monopoly power.[26]

Third, the implementation of the legislation calls for an infrastructure of skills and institutions that is still only rudimentary. Commercial law and accountancy skills and stock exchanges and similar institutions cannot be built and streamlined overnight. *Finally*, experience in China, Hungary, and Poland already makes it clear that privatization of a large proportion of the economy— in part for the reason just given—simply cannot be rapid.

The ownership measures must also be considered, not merely as a framework to be arrived at, but as part of the transition process toward a new system. In other words, the timing and pace of their adoption and implementation are crucial. Here the Gorbachev "compromise" is helpful insofar as it compresses the official USSR transition timetable to 18 to 24 months, which is not so very different from that of the Shatalin Plan.

On the other hand, that timetable is enormously ambitious and already regarded (even by optimists) as embodying a touch of utopia. And the conflict over the determination of republic and federal powers is probably unresolved.

How should the timing and pace of the Soviet privatization program be determined if the economic transformation is to succeed? This is not the place to embark on the increasingly difficult question of desirable sequencing of the

---

26. This has been a serious problem in Poland and Hungary. Paul Marer, David Stark, Marton Tardos, and others have contributed to the understanding of the issue at the Trento conference on Self-Employment and Entrepreneurship in the Socialist Countries in April 1990.

transformation process. The following remarks, however, address the narrower question of how the timing of the initiation of ownership legislation and the speed of its implementation can affect other elements in that process.

The main groups of policy measures in a transformation of the Soviet economy to a market system are: (a) macroeconomic stabilization; (b) decontrol of prices and quantities; (c) privatization; and (d) opening up to the international economy. The process of structural change is also part of the transformation, but is a consequence of these measures rather than a set of measures in itself.

All of these groups of measures require extended periods of time to design, introduce, and implement. They are more or less certain to overlap one another in time, so that sequencing cannot be reduced to saying: A must be done before B. Moreover, policymakers have to get the sequence "right" in a cardinal, and not merely an ordinal, sense.

In general, the linkages between the various groups of measures run in all directions. There are at least four major linkages between a privatization program and the other components of the transformation process.

First, privatization can contribute to stabilization because it promises to change the prevailing patterns of microeconomic behavior of enterprises that help to generate inflationary pressure. In Kornai's terminology (e.g., Kornai, 1980), the introduction of hard budget constraints (presumably on some critical mass of enterprises) may be a necessary condition of macroeconomic stabilization. This consideration is strengthened by the simple observation that the sale of state assets provides revenue that helps bring the state budget deficit under control.

In other words, it may be futile to wait for purely budgetary and monetary reforms to create a stable monetary environment before embarking on privatization. Some analyses suggest that this has been the case with regard to banking reforms in China (Herrmann-Pillath, 1990).

Second, there is a "which comes first" (chicken and egg) relationship between privatization and decontrol. Assets cannot be sensibly valued while product prices are controlled. Decontrolled product prices, however, will not reliably reflect opportunity costs until there is a market in which capital assets are valued according to their yields in alternative uses.

Third, there is a tricky relationship between privatization and opening up the product market to import competition. If assets are sold while the product market is still heavily protected, and if this protection is not expected to be removed soon, the values of the assets will be greatly different from what they would be if all had to be operated in conditions of strong import competition.

German unification illustrates one extreme solution, in which the value of former GDR assets, at least those used in the production of tradeables, was sharply reduced by the abrupt and complete opening of the product market. Conversely, in less open product-market conditions (say, Skoda rather than Trabant conditions), any initial privatization without the opening of product markets is subject to a threat of substantial losses in asset values later on.

Therefore, if privatization comes first, domestic political pressures are strengthened to maintain protection. Both the early opening of product markets (perhaps step-by-step in a pre-announced program) and early opening to foreign direct investment seem desirable.

Finally, the sequence of privatization itself must be affected by the speed and sequence of other measures. Thus, it makes sense to start first and move fastest with small-scale privatization for several reasons. The estimation of expected returns on assets is likely to be easier, in part because retailing, consumer services, and building are less vulnerable to import competition than manufacturing, and in part because they are already selling to hard-budget-constraint buyers—namely, households. The monopoly problem also is generally smaller in these sectors.

One conclusion, then, would be that the various privatization programs are generally sensible with respect to the branch sequence of assets to be privatized. Another conclusion, however, would be that the relationship to product-market protection seems to have been neglected. And both main programs seem to run the risk of pushing privatization ahead too rapidly while many prices are still controlled—though this seems a more serious problem in the case of the federal government program.

Lastly, with respect to sequencing, the hope of achieving rapid stabilization before significant ownership changes are in place could turn out to be doomed, for the Kornai-type reasons suggested above.

This last conclusion is in conflict, head-on, with the previous one. That merely illustrates the difficulty of the transformation process. The Shatalin Plan seeks to handle such difficulties by early announcement of a complete package of measures and an announced timetable of rapid implementation. Overly precise and ambitious as parts of the Shatalin Plan appear, the serious attempt to influence expectations in this way was a strength when the program first appeared. As time passes, however, it becomes a wasting asset.

For all their deficiencies, the various pieces of ownership legislation may be capable of contributing to an eventual "muddling-through" solution, however hard that may be to imagine at present. The transformation of establishment thinking that these drafts or decrees represent is perhaps the most encouraging aspect, and it is an important one.

CHAPTER 23

The New Half-Measures

Ed A. Hewett

AMONG THE many conflicts in the USSR in the summer of 1990, none was more riveting or important than the clash between Mikhail Gorbachev and Boris Yel'tsin, the chairman of the parliament of the Russian Soviet Federated Socialist Republic. Since last May Yel'tsin has been on the attack, accusing Gorbachev of dragging his feet on the introduction of market reforms and of denying Russia its sovereignty. The demand for sovereignty has been popular among Russians convinced that their lives would improve dramatically if they could only liberate their republic's resources from the hands of Moscow bureaucrats. For other republics it was an immense boost to have Russia—the core of the USSR and Gorbachev's power base—join their side in their battles with the central government. The call for a rapid move toward a market economy also found enormous resonance in a population frightened by the combination of a chaotic economy and a government helpless in the face of the decline of the Soviet Union.

For Gorbachev, skilled politician that he is, Yel'tsin's approach and its appeal could hardly have come as a surprise. The Soviet president must have watched with a tinge of envy as his old rival used his advantage as a leader of the opposition to insist that the problems were easier to confront than the leadership supposed and, in particular, that introducing a market economy need not be painful if only it were handled well.

THE INITIAL BLUEPRINTS

Yel'tsin's message was welcome news to a population already feeling pain long before the government got around to considering a market system. As 1990 unfolded the Soviet economy was sliding downward, with no realistic prospect of a reversal. Official statistics in the spring were already showing a

First published as "The New Soviet Plan" in *Foreign Affairs*, 1990/1991, 69, 5, pp. 146–167. [Eds.]

fall of between 1 and 2 percent of GNP, and a realistic adjustment for inflation would have yielded an even greater decline. Inflationary pressures were building as the government printed rubles at record rates to accommodate a deficit equal to between 5 and 6 percent of GNP and to allow wages to grow at about 9 percent per annum—although labor productivity was actually falling. Consumer savings began to swell as the growth in wages far outpaced real output. The government estimated that consumers held approximately 165 billion rubles (equal to about a half-year's consumption expenditures) in ''hot'' money—so called because consumers were likely to spend it quickly whenever goods appeared. Finally, sheer governmental mismanagement, compounded by the oil-price shock that began in August, left the Soviet Union several billion dollars in arrears on suppliers' credits, leading to a dramatic plunge in the Soviet credit rating in international financial markets.

Prime Minister Nikolay Ryzhkov's government tried to respond, submitting to the Supreme Soviet in May a plan for introducing a market economy. As an economic document this was a major improvement over previous efforts. It recognized the need to create a market economy, and the approach it proposed made sense in many ways. But it was vague on how quickly a market economy would emerge and, in particular, on how property rights would be handled under the new system. As a political document, however, it was a disaster because it led off with a bone-crunching austerity program built around a massive increase in consumer prices. To be sure, the government promised compensation for the price increases and indexation of future incomes. But the population was in no mood to trust the Ryzhkov government, given its previous track record; accordingly, the Supreme Soviet sent the prime minister back to the drawing board with orders to come up with a better plan by September 1990.

In most countries the government would have fallen with the rejection of its plan. But in the USSR today, it remains Gorbachev's decision whether to replace a government. For whatever reason, he chose to hold on to Ryzhkov. As the summer wore on, disintegration of the party and the centralized union accelerated. The government began to lose control over the situation.

This provided an ideal platform on which Yel'tsin could stand tall, promising to bring order from chaos by installing a market economy in 500 days, and at the same time to give substance to the hitherto empty concept of a ''union of sovereign republics.'' Yel'tsin was still essentially powerless, but he was hugely popular and had political momentum—and not only in Russia. Gorbachev, on the other hand, enormously powerful on paper and triumphant on the inter- national stage, was increasingly unpopular at home and was losing momentum, even in Russia.

Under these circumstances Gorbachev moved in late July to cut a deal with Yel'tsin. On August 2 he announced the formation of a working group of 13 members, including both his and Yel'tsin's top advisers, charged with com- bining the Ryzhkov and Yel'tsin plans into a common strategy for introducing a market economy as the foundation for a new Treaty of Union (to replace the previous treaty, which dated from 1922).[1] What came to be called the Shatalin Working Group (after its chairman, Stanislav Shatalin, the only economist on Gorbachev's presidential council) was given one month to complete its work, with the intention that this group's report, and not the Ryzhkov government's revised plan, would be what would go to the Supreme Soviet the first week in September.

The Shatalin Working Group complied with the timetable, and—as best they could—with the mandate. They presented Gorbachev and Yel'tsin with a plan to create a market economy and an economic union in the USSR in 500 days; the proposal also included much of what made sense in the government's plan (see *Perekhod*, 1990a, 1990b). They proposed to present this plan both to the USSR Supreme Soviet and to the supreme soviet of each republic, in the hope that all would approve it by late September, enabling the 500 days to run from October 1990 to March 1992.

Despite Gorbachev's clear directive, the Ryzhkov government cooperated only reluctantly and partially with the Shatalin Working Group. Indeed, Leonid Abalkin, Ryzhkov's deputy prime minister in charge of economic reform and the only direct link between Ryzhkov and the Shatalin Working Group, dropped out early in August. The Ryzhkov government came back to the Supreme Soviet on September 1 with merely a revised version of its May plan, while the Shatalin Working Group—essentially converted into a task force for elaborating Yel'tsin's 500-Day Plan—presented a very clear and radical alternative.

HALF-MEASURES

While the two plans shared much in their details, there were several large issues on which they fundamentally disagreed. The Shatalin Plan began by reconstituting the USSR as a confederation, which would then grant powers to the center. The Ryzhkov Plan retained powers in the center, but granted increased power to the republics.

The two plans also disagreed on sequencing and timing. The Shatalin Plan would have deferred consumer price increases, beginning instead with such measures as a quick sale of state assets to build popular support for the program. The Ryzhkov Plan, on the other hand, would still have led off with price increases, albeit less severe than those proposed in May, and with full monetary compensation to the population. Finally, the authors of the Shatalin Plan called for a rapid dismantling of the government apparatus and "destatization" of assets, while the Ryzhkov Plan (written by the government apparatus) would have moved more slowly on both counts.

1. The original composition of the working group included Stanislav Shatalin (its chairman) and Nikolay Petrakov, both economic advisers to Gorbachev; Leonid Abalkin, the USSR deputy prime minister in charge of economic reform; Grigoriy Yavlinskiy, the RSFSR deputy prime minister in charge of economic reform; Boris Fedorov, the bright young minister of finance for Russia; and a group of mostly young academic specialists.

Gorbachev was unwilling to endorse either plan. His closest economic advisers—Shatalin and Nikolay Petrakov—were authors of the 500-Day Plan, and clearly Gorbachev was drawn to many parts of the scheme. But the most obvious problem for Gorbachev was the federalizing plank, whereby the USSR would be converted into a confederation. Moreover, Gorbachev persisted in supporting Ryzhkov, and his preference for the middle ground led him to ask economist Abel Aganbegyan in early September to develop a compromise. In a very few days Aganbegyan came up with a new document that was basically the Shatalin Plan, but which contained a healthy dose of "blue smoke and mirrors," particularly in its proposals for the structure of authority in the new federation.

By mid-September the parliament of the Russian Republic endorsed the Shatalin Plan, basically on principle, since they hardly had time to digest all 222 pages. The Soviet (all-Union) parliament, on the other hand, had by then only just received the three documents they were being asked to consider: the Shatalin Plan, the Ryzhkov (formally, the Council of Ministers) Plan, and Aganbegyan's rewrite of the Shatalin Plan. Even Aganbegyan's plan, however, failed to receive Gorbachev's explicit support, and the all-Union Supreme Soviet recommended that the president ask yet another group to combine the three plans into one, and report back to it on October 15. In the meantime Gorbachev asked for and received special powers to issue decrees necessary to stabilize the economy and move to a market. Not coincidentally, these powers are valid through March 1992, approximately 500 days later.

On October 16, Gorbachev came back to the Soviet parliament with a "Presidential Plan," which he fully supported. This plan, again authored by Aganbegyan, retains the basic elements of Aganbegyan's earlier draft, and therefore of the Shatalin Plan. But the Presidential Plan is one-third the length of the Shatalin Plan, leaving out virtually all specifics on key points, and eschewing a day-by-day timetable. For example, it drops any mention of 500 days, but retains the four stages of the original Shatalin Plan. It is therefore not so much a plan as it is a statement of intent so general as to be unobjectionable to the various factions in the debate. It easily passed the Supreme Soviet on October 19—with the proviso that the legislators might wish to modify it later—and it was to go into operation on November 1.

At the same time, Gorbachev continued to issue presidential decrees, many of which are not dissimilar to those called for in the first 100 days of the Shatalin Plan—the difference being that the decrees are coming out in absence of an agreement with the republics. Indeed, Russia has announced its intention to go ahead with the 500-Day Plan, which is likely to mean considerable tension with the union. Other republics, while they may not follow the 500-Day Plan, will also tend to go their own ways.

While the Shatalin Plan seems, for the present, to have been shoved into the background, there are good reasons to believe that its significance will nevertheless loom large in the coming months. The fact that the plan was too radical to win approval this fall means little. Given the rapidly deteriorating economic and political situation of the USSR, this month's unacceptably radical proposal can be next month's conventional wisdom. Moreover, the unique strength of the Shatalin Plan, among all the plans under discussion, lies in its serious attempt to come to grips with current political and economic realities; it assumes the union is breaking apart and seeks to construct a viable economic logic to reconstruct it.

Over the next years as the centrifugal forces grow still stronger and the economic crisis deepens, it is the Shatalin Plan that offers the only feasible approach to controlling the disintegration and reversing the economic decline. To understand this plan is to understand the dilemma the Soviets now face, and its possible resolution.

THE SHATALIN PLAN

The origins of the Shatalin Plan lie in a 400-day model drawn up last February in Deputy Prime Minister Abalkin's office by Grigoriy Yavlinskiy and several of his associates. It was designed to guide Gorbachev in using proposed strong presidential powers to stabilize the economy quickly and introduce a market economy, all by decree. Although Gorbachev did, in fact, win his new presidential powers in March, he ignored the plan, relying instead on the Ryzhkov government (essentially Gosplan, the state planning agency) to implement reforms. The plan lay dormant until the spring, when Mikhail Bocharov, a contender against Yel'tsin for the chairmanship of the RSFSR Supreme Soviet, modified and expanded it into a 500-Day Plan. Upon assuming his new post, Yel'tsin adopted the plan as his own, and Yavlinskiy left Abalkin's office to join the Russian government as a deputy prime minister and chairman of the RSFSR State Commission of Economic Reform (the counterpart to Abalkin's post at the union level).

In August Yavlinskiy and his co-authors joined the Shatalin Working Group, along with Yevgeniy Yasin, Abalkin's most senior and best economist. They brought with them the 400-Day Plan, the proposed 500-Day Plan, and other programs they had developed while working for Abalkin that had been rejected as too radical. Under the leadership of Shatalin, Nikolay Petrakov (Gorbachev's personal economic adviser) and Yavlinskiy, the group set out to weave these disparate threads together into a plan for creating an economic union and moving to a market economy in 500 days.

The result is an exciting document, infused with a spirit of liberation from the dogmas of the past and from the bureaucracy that has used those dogmas to retain its oppressive hold over the lives of Soviet citizens. The word socialism never appears; Karl Marx does not even linger in the background. The authors of the plan are pragmatists seeking to create—in less than two years—a market, or what they sometimes call a "normal," economy. Most prices would be determined by supply and demand; enterprises would be primarily in private hands (or at least under the control of the stockholders, only one of which would be a disinterested state "owner"); the ruble would be fully convertible, and the economy would be oriented to meet consumer needs, not those of the military or the bureaucracy.

But the Shatalin group members were pragmatists working against a one-month deadline, faced with a bureaucracy reluctant to give them the necessary data or help. The result, for all its boldness, is a hastily prepared, internally inconsistent, and sometimes vague document supported by only very sketchy quantitative analysis. On some key issues—for example, the rate at which privatization will occur—different parts of the plan offer dramatically different scenarios. The answers to other concerns—the likely magnitude of a decline in economic activity or real living standards, for instance—are either not given or are only implied. This document deserves to be analyzed, however, because the Presidential Plan that was adopted by the Supreme Soviet in October still follows the mainline of the Shatalin Plan, albeit at a slower and more conservative pace.

The First Stage

In Stage One, the first hundred days, of the 500-Day Plan the Soviet Union would be reconstituted as a voluntary economic union, much along the lines of the European Community.[2] The 15 sovereign republics would hold all power in the system, governing through an Inter-republican Economic Committee (IEC), which would supervise the remaining, and much diminished, central bureaucracy. The chairman of that IEC, separate from the president of the USSR, would wield considerable power. The center would serve the republics, enjoying only the powers granted to it. Each of the republics would control the introduction and operation of the market economy within its borders; each could move at a somewhat different pace, although large disparities would cause difficulties.

The plan calls for a unified all-Union market, with no internal barriers to trade, and a single tariff system surrounding the entire country. The unified market would require a single currency and a single central bank, the "Reserve System," modeled after the U.S. Federal Reserve and enjoying independence from the central and republican governments. The Reserve System would be managed by a chairman and assistants appointed by the Soviet president, and by a board composed of those appointees and the heads of the central bank of each of the 15 republics. Macroeconomic stability would be preserved by a firm rule that the central and republican governments could not (with minor

---

2. Republics not prepared to join the union could apply for "associate" or "observer" status. I will assume here, for purposes of exposition, that all 15 would join.

exceptions) finance deficits through the bank, but only through bond sales to the population.

Republics would delegate to the central government responsibility for national defense, internal security, the regulation of prices for key products, environmental policy, and other responsibilities that the republics agree should be managed at a national level. Because republics and local authorities would hold all taxing power, finances for central government activities would be gathered either through contributions from the republics (according to a formula negotiated among them) or—more probably at the beginning—through the granting of specifically delimited taxing powers to the center (for example, a turnover tax or a profits tax).

All foreign exchange would flow either to the republics (for example, receipts from the export of raw materials and fuels, which would be recognized as republican property), or to enterprises within the republics. These enterprises would be required to sell some of their foreign exchange for rubles at the prevailing exchange rate. The republics would then retain some of that foreign exchange, dividing the remainder between contributions to local authorities and a central fund for servicing the Soviet debt.

The plan leaves much unsaid regarding procedures for reaching and enforcing agreements among the 15 republics. It suggests, for example, that contributions by the republics to the central budget could be made either on the basis of relative level of GNP, or on GNP per capita, without belaboring the obvious point that using the per capita formula would cost the rich republics much more than the total GNP formula.

Also, it is clear that this constitutional component of the plan—which the Shatalin Working Group developed in close consultation with representatives of virtually all of the republics—is not fully integrated with the remainder of the document. Many chapters of the plan discuss in detail what economic policy should be without even a passing mention of the fact that such policy could be instituted only after long, presumably heated, debates in the IEC. There is a very clear sense in this document that the economists on the Shatalin Working Group were able or willing to absorb only partially the logic of an economic union in their plans for the introduction and operation of a market economy in the Soviet Union.

The first stage of the Shatalin Plan would also feature a set of quickly executed measures designed to win the confidence of the population by a clean break with the past, combined with an all-out effort to use existing resources to expand the supply of goods while retaining controls over prices and over much economic activity. Then, having done all it could with existing resources, the leadership would turn to the people to ask for patience and some sacrifice during the remainder of the implementation period.

The break with the past would start on Day One, with the Soviet president and the heads of the republics issuing decrees declaring equal rights for all individuals in all forms of economic activity, announcing guarantees of property rights to individuals and eliminating laws punishing entrepreneurial activity. A general amnesty would be given to those arrested in the past for economic crimes that would no longer be illegal in the new system.

Some elements of the past would be temporarily retained in order to preserve a modicum of stability. Prices would remain frozen throughout the first stage. Enterprises would be required to fulfill state orders (a device introduced several years ago to replace obligatory plan targets) but they could negotiate prices with the Union Contractual System, the all-Union body issuing the orders. Moreover, the magnitude of state orders would probably be lower than under the old system. Although price liberalization would begin after the first phase, state orders would be retained until about halfway through the program, in order to retain some semblance of stability during the early, and most tumultuous, phases of the transition.

There would be a quick sell-off of various state assets: a portion of the state-held fleet of autos and trucks; unfinished construction projects, uninstalled equipment, and construction materials; various civilian products (e.g., automobiles) now in the hands of the military; and assets, now held by "social organizations" and other party organizations, that were acquired with state funds. These moves would have the triple advantage of establishing the new system's concern for consumer welfare, of launching the process of privatization immediately and, at the same time, of soaking up some of the 165 billion rubles in "hot" money.

The Reserve System would be up and running within the first two weeks, and within several months the existing specialized state banks (for industry, agriculture, and so forth) would be converted into joint-stock commercial banks. The Reserve System would freeze the money supply in an effort to squeeze out inflation. This, plus a cutoff in subsidies to state enterprises, would put pressure on all enterprises to improve efficiency.

In Stage One the government would balance the budget by cutting various expenditure categories: a 20 percent cut in KGB expenditures, a 10 percent cut in defense (from which a third of the savings would be used to increase salaries for military officers and housing allowances for decommissioned soldiers), a reduction of approximately 15 percent in centrally financed state capital expenditures, and a cutoff in all subsidies to state enterprises.[3] Had these measures been implemented for the fourth quarter of 1990, as originally scheduled, the Shatalin Working Group estimates that the budget would have staged a turnaround, from a projected 15-billion-ruble deficit that quarter to a surplus of four billion rubles. A freeze would be put in place on new budget programs costing over 100 million rubles, save for programs associated with the cleanup of the Chernobyl' nuclear accident site.

During the first stage a multitude of measures would be applied in an effort

---

3. These are all cuts for one quarter, and would be less for the year as a whole.

to stabilize the consumer goods market. The government would move to expand the supply of consumer goods through the asset sales mentioned earlier, and through sales of consumer goods imported with Western assistance. The central government would also sell to the population what I estimate to be $1.5 billion, or approximately 10 percent, of its dollar holdings, and $400 million, or about 1 percent, of its gold bullion reserves, receiving in return 12 billion rubles. Quick sales of 1 percent of the housing stock would bring in five billion rubles during that first hundred days.

These asset sales would continue throughout the four stages of implementation, eventually totaling 143 billion rubles. These measures alone could potentially put a major damper on excess demand, although how much depends on how confident Soviets are that the stabilization program will succeed. Soviet citizens have about 500 billion rubles in cash and savings, and all of that would become "hot" if they became convinced that hyperinflation were imminent, in which case they would become desperate to exchange their cash for goods.

Destatization

In addition to these quick sales of assets, the cornerstone of the Shatalin Plan is a call for the government to get started immediately on the "destatization" and privatization of productive assets. "Destatization" (*razgosudarstvleniye* in Russian) is a very special term that is important to understand in order to avoid confusing it with denationalization. It means, literally, taking the assets out of the hands of the state (read "bureaucrats"), but it does not automatically imply selling or giving those assets to private persons. The assets, for example, could be leased out for a fixed fee; they could be sold to employees or given out on a lease-to-buy basis, or they could simply be transferred to a state-established holding company that would act as an independent owner/investor. Privatization, by sale or auction to private individuals, might then occur either immediately or somewhat later.

The plan stipulates that within the first two weeks the USSR Fund for State Property (which was created this summer to manage assets transferred from branch ministries) and its republican counterparts would agree on who would be responsible for destatizing portions of the state's assets, which have a book value of 2.6 trillion rubles. The center would retain control over several categories of assets: defense contractors; producers in the nuclear power industry; the pipeline, railroad, postal, telegraph and unified energy systems, and all military facilities.

A second set of industries—instrument makers, communications-equipment manufacturers, electronics, shipbuilding, and other national but nonstrategic industries—would be converted into transrepublican joint-stock companies, whose stock would be distributed among the republics.

Republics and local authorities would divide responsibility for destatizing the remainder of productive assets. In the first stage priority would be given to rapid destatization or privatization of enterprises in the construction and construction-materials industries, auto transport, services, trade, light industry, and food processing. The plan recommends total privatization of all small retail outlets and restaurants, if not in the first stage, then shortly thereafter.

It would also be during the first phase that republican and local authorities would begin a massive land reform, along with a privatization of farming and farm-related services. The goal is to reconstitute some of the 60,000 state and collective farms into private or cooperative farms, while breaking up others to free land for the creation of 150,000–180,000 small farms. These farms would be free to grow or raise what they wished and could sell their products at market prices. This new freedom, combined with a privatization in the transportation and food-processing industries, will lead to a rapid improvement in the quantity and quality of food available to the population—or so the Shatalin Working Group hopes.

The working group recognizes that destatization and eventual privatization of the huge state enterprises will take considerable time to implement, although different portions of the report vary greatly on just how much time. Particularly at the beginning, when there is no experience in this area, no capital markets, and a price system in disarray, it would be risky to force the pace of destatization.

The report emphasizes investment funds as a transitional form of ownership, useful in beginning the process of converting to joint-stock companies. State enterprises slated for destatization through conversion to joint-stock companies would be given a book value, for which a packet of stocks would be issued and then passed on to the appropriate investment fund. These funds would act as owners (without participating in the daily operations of the enterprises), and receive dividends, which would be passed on to the budget of the union, republican, or local government that created the fund. Over time the investment funds would dispose of their stock through sales to the population, to workers of the enterprises involved (up to 10 percent of the stock can go to them at a discount), and to foreigners. Most of the proceeds from the sales would simply be taken out of circulation as part of the effort to soak up "hot" money.

There is no effort in the report to estimate the potential value of productive assets sold over the 500-day period, but some magnitudes are discussed. Selling off small retail outlets might raise four billion rubles early on. More significant sums would come from selling off the large enterprises. Here, the authors of the Shatalin Plan offer the suggestive calculation that the population could more or less immediately purchase something in the range of 100–150 billion rubles of assets out of cash holdings (mostly stocks), and another 50–60 billion rubles per year for the first two years out of new savings. That would add up to sales of something approaching 10 percent of the two-trillion-ruble depreciated value of all capital in the USSR over the 500 days.

The arithmetic is clear enough. But the timing would require the instantaneous resolution of all the disputes now raging among various government bodies at all levels over who owns what in the USSR—and such concord seems highly improbable. Moreover, it is unlikely that the population will purchase significant amounts of assets early on, before they are fairly confident that the new economic environment has truly changed, and changed irreversibly in a direction favoring private initiative and enterprise. That, also, will likely take a lot longer than 100 days.

In short, the Shatalin Plan outlines a two-speed approach to privatization. Small enterprises would be sold immediately in a straightforward privatization that would not amount to much in rubles, but would signal a total departure from past practice. Most of the large enterprises now controlled from the Moscow ministries (with the exception of those slated to stay under central control, such as defense plants) would be immediately shifted to state holding companies ("destatized"). Then over an unspecified period extending over years, these enterprises would gradually be sold to individuals, either directly or, more generally, through stock sales. The final result, easily a decade away, would be a mixed economy, probably with a considerably larger state sector than is typical of Western Europe.

The Second Stage

During Stage Two—from Day 100 to Day 250—the pace of destatization and privatization would accelerate, very tight monetary and fiscal policies would continue and the first moves toward price liberalization would be taken. Price liberalization would result in an increase in the price level, leading to pressures for some compensation from those segments of the population that are well organized, or well placed to strike. Layoffs would accelerate, throwing people into the newly created unemployment and retraining system.

The Reserve System would continue to freeze the money supply during this period, and output would fall in many sectors. The national and regional governments would move to balance budgets by continued expenditure cuts, but even more by increasing taxes and finding other new revenue sources. Most notably, dividend income from joint-stock companies is projected to provide an additional 60 billion rubles per year (out of total annual budgetary receipts in the range of 610–677 billion rubles); social insurance rates would be dramatically increased, bringing in an additional 125 billion rubles per year in new revenue, and turnover tax receipts would rise, approximately canceling out the drop in profits tax receipts as enterprise profits fall.

Many enterprises would be forced to cut output under the pressure of falling demand. Those enterprises in the greatest economic difficulty would be targeted for sale, as the destatization and privatization processes accelerated. At the end of Stage Two, between 1,000 and 1,500 state enterprises would be operating as joint-stock companies under investment funds, and approximately half of all small retail outlets would be in private hands.

The liberalization of price controls would be one of the key components of this stage, and the design of these measures will play a critical role in determining the success of the program. For that reason it is unfortunate that the plans for price reform are rather conservative, at times out of step with the radical tone of the remainder of the program. From Stage Two onward, most wholesale prices for manufactured goods would be freely negotiated between buyer and seller, with two exceptions: markets where one or a few producers dominate would be state controlled, and goods produced under state order would be negotiated with central authorities, and could even be imposed by them if no agreement were reached.

Prices of the most important raw materials and fuels, which generally move in inter-republican trade, would be negotiated among the republics, and then administered by union authorities, who would adjust prices over time as costs change. Surprisingly, there is no indication in the plan that these prices should approximate world prices for similar products. This is a dangerous omission, for if prices for these critical commodities differ significantly from world prices, the entire price system will be distorted, leading inevitably to a multiplicity of restrictions on economic activity and foreign trade, in direct contradiction to the spirit of the entire Shatalin Plan.

Retail prices constitute one of the most sensitive areas. The Ryzhkov Plan failed before the Supreme Soviet in May because of its intention to raise consumer prices, and Yel'tsin promised that his plan would be different. The Shatalin program calls for liberalizing retail prices gradually after Stage One, except for a group of approximately 100–150 products whose prices would continue to enjoy subsidization throughout the 500 days. Precisely which products are involved is not clear. The plan does state that toward the end of the 500 days, between 70 and 80 percent of consumer goods should be selling at free prices, and that at the conclusion of the 500 days only a few necessary consumer goods will be sold at controlled prices (some types of bread, meat, milk, cooking oil, sugar, basic medications, school texts, transport fares, and selected consumer services).

Each republic will design the subsidy system for its jurisdiction, the general policy being to subsidize over-the-counter goods directly at the retail outlet. This, it is hoped, will be a major improvement over the existing system, which subsidizes at the wholesale level, allowing black marketeers to take subsidized goods and resell them for huge profits. Nevertheless, it will still be a very difficult matter actually to confirm sales over the counter, as opposed to under it, since the rewards of black market sales will be high for those willing to falsify sales data.

These price controls are an important component of the Shatalin Plan's attempt to win popular support for a quick move to the market. The program offers extensive promises to protect living standards. In addition to controls on consumer prices, the second 150 days would see the introduction of partial indexation of incomes, in order to compensate consumers for whatever inflation did occur. But it is not clear precisely what form this indexation would take, and whose income would be covered. Nor does the plan estimate the total costs of a system of indexation.

Republican and local authorities would be in charge of indexation, and would finance it wherever state money was involved. Indexation would be based on a special consumer price index for nondurable goods. Enterprises would be ordered to increase wages by some portion of the increase in the index, financing the increase out of their own funds if profits permitted. If profits did not permit this, the state would have to pay. This provision appears to apply to all enterprises, including those privately owned, but the report does not comment on the possibility that the state might end up subsidizing unprofitable private firms in order to index wages of their employees. Republican and local governments are to pay directly to subsidize pensioners, students, other state dependents, and government employees.

A minimum wage would provide yet another pillar to this strong safety net. Based on a calculation of a minimum cost of living, and differentiated according to skill levels and difficulties in working conditions, this wage would be phased in over the 500 days as an obligatory floor for wages in all enterprises. Presumably enterprises that could not afford to hire at the minimum wage would go under.

The Shatalin Working Group claims that the joint effect of these price controls and indexation would be to ensure that living standards would first stabilize, and then rise. In real terms (that is, in terms of the goods the population can actually acquire) that may be true, but it is also clear from the few data provided in the report that prices would rise, possibly dramatically, relative to incomes, and therefore that *measured* real incomes would fall.[4]

For 1991 (the bulk of the last 400 days), the Shatalin Working Group outlines three possible scenarios for incomes and prices. Under the two best scenarios (in terms of inflation), prices would rise 55 percent over the year, yet there is no mention of indexation in incomes, and measured real incomes are predicted to fall between 12 and 13 percent. It is only in the third scenario, under which inflation would notch up to 90 percent for the year (because asset sales would be going so slowly that excess demand would keep pressure on markets) that compensation would be paid. But it is only a partial payment, and real measured income in this scenario is forecast to fall by 25 percent over the year.

This decline in measured real income makes sense from the economic point of view, and is one strong point of the program that has received no public attention—for the plan's rhetoric has obscured it. Of course, from a political standpoint, it is understandable that the authors of the plan are not eager to advertise this particular feature.

Finally, during this second 150-day stage, the economy would rapidly begin

---

4. "Measured" real incomes are nominal incomes (not adjusted for inflation) divided by prices. In an economy where prices are fixed and goods are scarce, incomes divided by prices do not measure actual living standards. If prices rise, and more goods become available, measured living standards will fall, while actual living standards rise.

ED A. HEWETT

to open trade with, and to receive investment from, the rest of the global economy. The ruble would be made convertible on the current account, and even (if the plan is to be believed) on the capital account. Its exchange rate would be determined in foreign-exchange markets where 10–15 commercial banks would enjoy full rights to buy and sell foreign exchange. Since most foreign exchange would be in the hands either of republican and local authorities or of enterprises, the supply side of the market would rest on fairly broad foundations. On the demand side, because stringent monetary and budget policies are being counted on to keep down demand for foreign exchange, the plan foresees a fairly stable market in the range of five to eight rubles per dollar.[5] In addition, the Reserve System, which would oversee foreign-exchange markets, could at times buy and sell foreign exchange in order to stabilize the exchange rate.

The general thrust of the new regulations in foreign economic relations would be to foster the rapid integration of the Soviet economy into the world economy, encouraging existing enterprises to export, and foreign enterprises to invest in the Soviet economy. But as long as price controls remain in effect for a significant group of products, and shortages remain, controls on exports, imports, and direct foreign investment would be inevitable.

The Third Stage

Stage Three, Days 250 through 400, should in many ways repeat the previous stage, the major difference being that months of tight money policy would begin to take a serious toll on business—leading to unemployment, especially in areas such as primary products, heavy machinery, and construction. Price liberalization would accelerate during this period, as would the selling off of assets. By the end of this stage, the plan calls for the destatization or privatization of between 30 and 40 percent of industry, of up to 50 percent of construction, and at least 60 percent of retail trade, food, and services.

Unemployment would be the most important feature of this period, rising from an estimated six million on Day One (3.7 percent of the labor force), to eight million (4.8 percent) at the halfway point, to 11.6 million (7 percent) toward the end of the transition period. To cope with what for Soviet society would be a potentially traumatic rise in job insecurity and unemployment, the Shatalin Plan outlines a generous unemployment scheme in which enterprises must provide two to three months' notice to local authorities and workers before a layoff, and must pay one month's severance pay. The local employment office would then provide assistance to laid-off workers in finding further employment, and for the first 18 months of unemployment would provide benefits that could be something like the following: 70 percent of the last wage

---

5. The recently devalued official rate is currently about two rubles to the dollar; the noncommercial (tourist) rate, about six rubles to the dollar; and the black-market rate, 15 to 20 rubles to the dollar and up.

for the first three months; then 60 percent for the next three; and finally 50 percent for 12 months. If a worker still could find no job at the end of this 19 months of support, he or she would go on welfare.

All of these benefits would be financed and administered locally, but according to norms set at the republican level, and coordinated among all the republics. The plan forecasts that toward the end of the 500 days, unemployment benefits could amount to 2.7–3.3 billion rubles per month, about 5–5.5 percent of budget expenditures for the republics and the center combined.

The plan forecasts the beginning of an economic boom during its last stage, the remaining 100 days. The stabilization should have been sufficient to wring out most of the excess demand, permitting the Reserve System to allow interest rates to fall, leading to a recovery in investment. The supply-side effects of the increasing competition among the various new entrants into the market should be filling the shelves with goods.

By Day 500, if all goes as planned, three-quarters of Soviet industry would be operating generally without subsidies, in a competitive environment, managed by bodies independent of any direct state supervision, or directly by private individuals. Eighty to 90 percent of construction, auto transport, trade, food, and other services would be in mostly private hands. The bulk of retail prices would move freely in response to supply and demand, as would the interest and exchange rates.

In short, the Soviet Union would have a market economy. It would be rudimentary by standards of the United States or Western Europe, but it would work. Most important, institutions would be sufficiently in place to allow the further development over the following years of a truly complex and rich set of market institutions.

CONCLUDING COMMENTS

It is easy to pick apart the 500-Day Plan on any number of grounds. Obviously the goals outlined here would take many multiples of 500 days to realize under even the best of circumstances. And the next few years in the USSR will hardly constitute the best of circumstances.

The published quantitative analysis underlying the document is so sketchy that it is difficult even to judge how overly ambitious the plan is. To take just one example, the few tables published do not include any estimates of the course of economic activity over the 500 days, yet many of the most critical variables depend directly on that: the rate of unemployment, the level of subsidies, and the size of government receipts, to name just three.

Moreover, the plan was so hastily assembled that it is riddled with inconsistencies and ambiguities, which would have to be reconciled before implementation began. For example, the nature of destatization remains ill defined, and the pace of privatization is not at all clear. Judging from recent East European experience, it would be a miracle if, over the course of a mere one and one-half years, the new Soviet government managed to reach the goals for destatization it has set for Day 500—70 percent of industry, 90 percent of trade and construction, and so forth. And yet, falling short there means falling short on the targets for asset sales, which will allow excess demand to spill over into the markets for goods, leading to high inflation rates.

Furthermore, while the authors of the plan clearly understand the enormous importance of maintaining fiscal balance, in fact the plan hardly inspires confidence that this important goal will be met. It is fine to say, for example, that the Reserve System will refuse to lend to the union or republican banks. But is it realistic to suggest that the Reserve Bank will have the clout to refuse Yel'tsin or his bank when they need short-term finance and the bond markets are not buying?

Nor does the plan leave much maneuvering room for politicians when the going gets tough. Yel'tsin seemed to promise a virtually painless transition to a market. But come Stage Two, when inflation rates are in the range of 5 to 8 percent a month, the pressure for full indexation will be enormous, and both Yel'tsin and Gorbachev will have to be extraordinary politicians indeed to resist these enormous pressures, waiting patiently for tight money to squeeze inflation out of the system.

The Presidential Plan approved on October 19 is, on the surface, an improvement over the Shatalin Plan, because it seems to make allowances for some of the latter's weaknesses. Although the Presidential Plan retains the four phases of the Shatalin Plan, it drops the numbers of days, and hence the explicit promise of lightning-fast results. Destatization and privatization are to proceed at a slower pace, which implies that "hot" money will remain so for some time. In light of that, the Presidential Plan foresees a longer period of controlled prices, in an effort to avoid a price explosion. Finally, the Presidential Plan extends the period over which subsidies will be withdrawn, so as to give enterprises more time to adjust.

These are a few examples in which the Presidential Plan weakens the Shatalin Plan in ways that it might have been changed anyway. One could argue, therefore, that the Presidential Plan is a politically pragmatic restatement of the Shatalin Plan, providing Gorbachev with much-needed room for maneuver. Following this reasoning, one could imagine that the next 500 days will go as well as Shatalin and his colleagues could hope, as Gorbachev uses his power of decree to establish the market system as quickly as it is feasible to do so.

However, to hope for such a felicitous outcome would be to ignore political realities in the USSR today. The Soviet population is weary of a leadership seemingly helpless in the face of a deteriorating economy; republican leaders find it not only politically profitable but imperative to fight for their sovereignty in an attempt to abandon what appears to them to be a sinking ship.

The Shatalin Plan begins with an all-out effort to restore confidence in the union's leadership, first by reconstituting the union, then presumably by bringing new faces into government, and finally by using the first 100 days to do everything possible to prepare the population for the inevitable pain of the transition. In that situation Gorbachev would be issuing decrees on behalf of a new government that drew its legitimacy from its clear commitment to a new beginning, and from direct support of the union's constituent republics.

Unlike the Shatalin Plan, the Presidential Plan denies this political reality. It relies on the current government to implement new presidential decrees, which will hardly inspire confidence among a population convinced that it is this government that has brought the economy to a crisis. The Presidential Plan proposes to go ahead without the support of the republics, which guarantees conflict not only over particular decrees, but over the legitimacy of all presidential decrees.

All of this suggests that the next few months will be much like the last few: enormous confusion and contention while economic decline and political disintegration intensify. Enterprises will be ordered to fulfill plans (or state orders, as they are now called) and fined when they do not do so, but to no avail. The population, convinced that the leadership is giving them more of the same old policies, will increase its efforts to hoard, and inflation will accelerate. The government will offer to sell off or lease assets, but in the uncertain economic environment it will find few buyers. Republics and even cities will respond to the crisis by seeking to hold onto the scarce products they produce, increasing the fragmentation of the economy. As the economy deteriorates, the government will respond with more decrees. Within months attention will turn to the search for yet another plan.

That plan will most likely be some version of the Shatalin Plan, or at least the framework that plan outlines. If the union is ever to be viable as an economic whole, it will only be after the republics have voluntarily joined to form a new entity, governed by a center enjoying the support of the republics and their populations. The Shatalin Plan, for all its failings, seems like the most plausible strategy for transforming the USSR.

Even the Shatalin Plan, however, may prove to be unworkable, at least in the near term. That plan is a valiant effort to reconstruct the union virtually out of whole cloth, on the basis of economic interests, rather than fear. But years of suppressed anger over nationality issues, combined with the natural instinct of each republic and city to protect itself against the chaos of the system as a whole, may give such force to separatism that there remains little support for even a loose economic union. That is not likely to be the long-term outcome; years of central planning have bound the union republics together in intricate ways that they are only now discovering. They will need each other's markets if they are to prosper. But it could require some time for that logic to overcome the bitter legacy of seventy years of Soviet socialism.

For now, there is not a great deal the West can do except to stand ready with whatever technical expertise might be useful in devising a strategy. Should some version of the Shatalin Plan—more carefully prepared and more thoroughly documented—eventually be adopted as policy, then loans and even aid would be in order to support the process, providing a much-needed boost at the beginning by expanding the supply of consumer goods, thereby reducing the tendency toward hyperinflation. But financial aid of any magnitude will only be justified when, and if, a consensus emerges within the USSR around a plan that makes sense. Until that occurs, no amount of Western goodwill or aid will set things right.

CHAPTER 24

Perestroyka in the Aftermath of 1990

Gertrude E. Schroeder

THE YEAR 1990 was one of major economic milestones. The performance of the economy turned out to be the worst by far in the postwar period. An unprecedented shift occurred in the structure of production and investment. Truly radical programs for reform of the economic system were promulgated and adopted. Laws concerning property ownership and related matters that would have been unthinkable five years ago were enacted at both the federal and republic levels. The role of the union republics in economic affairs escalated dramatically, as did center-periphery tensions in general. Despite these remarkable developments, the year ended on a somber note with growing disorganization in the economy and with a crisis of governance, the resolution of which will decisively influence the nature and pace of economic *perestroyka* in the 1990s.

ECONOMIC PERFORMANCE IN 1990

For the first time in the postwar period, the Soviet government reported a drop in GNP, industrial production, and agricultural output. Official statistics report declines of 2 percent, 1.2 percent, and 2.3 percent, respectively (*Ekonomika i zhizn'*, No. 5, 1991, pp. 9–13). CIA assessments, when available, probably will confirm the decline with figures in the same general range. The fall in industrial production was widespread, with the largest declines occurring in the metallurgical and fuels industries. Crude oil production fell by 6 percent and coal production by 5 percent. In agriculture, although grain production climbed to a near-record level, production of potatoes, vegetables, and fruits and berries fell by 7 to 12 percent. The only bright spots in this otherwise gloomy picture were appreciable gains in the production of consumer durables

First published in *Soviet Economy*, 1991 7, 1, pp. 3–13. [Eds.]

and alcoholic beverages and modest advances in the provision of services to the population.

Thanks to increased domestic output of consumer goods, continued large imports, and a further drawdown of inventories, the government managed to increase real consumption per capita in 1990, but at a markedly slower pace than in 1989. Much of the gain was the result of sizable increases in the supply of alcoholic beverages and a variety of consumer durables produced in defense industries. Consumer services also continued to expand, although at a slower rate. But as in the preceding two years (Schroeder, 1990), these small quantitative gains likely were not felt by consumers, because the imbalances in consumer markets worsened rapidly throughout the year.

The population's money incomes rose by 16.9 percent in 1990, compared with 13.1 percent in 1989. Thus, the gap between money incomes and the supplies of goods and services in real terms continued to widen, adding to inflationary pressures and increasing the money overhang in the consumer sector. According to official estimates, the consumer price index for goods and services rose by 5 percent in 1990—more than double the rate in 1989. Moreover, the rate of increase accelerated throughout the year. Collective farm market prices alone rose by 29 percent, and black market prices continued to climb. The Soviet statistical agency (Goskomstat SSSR) also estimates that unsatisfied demand increased by nearly a third in 1990. The population added 43 billion rubles to its savings deposits, compared with 41 billion rubles in 1989.

With inflationary expectations of the populace being fueled by accelerating price increases and rumors of more to come, the consumer market deteriorated markedly throughout the year. The population continued to hoard on a large scale, with household food stocks rising by 50 to 100 percent, according to Goskomstat. Empty shelves, queues, various forms of rationing, and special distribution systems bypassing the retail stores became widespread. Clearly, the government's supply-side strategy for balancing the consumer market failed, as did its efforts to curtail the growth of incomes.

In contrast to consumption, state investment declined by about 4 percent, the first such decline since World War II. The government also reported that budgetary expenditures for defense dropped by 6 percent. The fall in investment resulted entirely from a large reduction in budgetary expenditures on investment and the mothballing of many projects as part of the government's efforts to cope with the huge budget deficit. But investment financed by enterprises rose sharply as they rushed to start new projects. As a consequence, the disarray and waste in the investment sector worsened. The volume of unfinished construction exceeded that of investment, and state orders for commissionings of new facilities were not fulfilled by huge margins; only 39 percent of such orders were completed for new industrial facilities, and despite ambitious goals to improve matters, the construction of new housing and social facilities was well below the levels achieved in 1989. Attempts to convert defense facilities to civilian production added to the strain on investment resources.

There was no good news on other fronts. The budget continued to be in substantial deficit, and cash emissions increased by more than 50 percent. Foreign trade turnover dropped by 6.9 percent, the balance of payments deficit was 10 billion rubles, and Soviet foreign debt increased by some 38 percent. Nonetheless, despite the growing difficulties in the economy, the reorientation in the structure of production in favor of the consumer sector—a major goal of *perestroyka*—gathered momentum in 1990. Goskomstat reported an unprecedented decline of 3.2 percent in production in heavy industry (Group A) and a 4.4 percent rise in consumer-related industry (Group B). As a consequence, the share of the latter in total production rose from 26 percent to 28.4 percent. The shift from defense to civilian production also appears to have accelerated somewhat, along with the redirection of investment toward consumer goods industries and the development of social infrastructure.

Finally, we note a most unfortunate development in 1990, the growing proclivity of Soviet and many Western observers to describe the USSR's worsening economic plight in apocalyptic language. Frequently, undefined terms such as "collapse," "catastrophe," "chaos" replaced dispassionate analysis and description. Journalists and economists, who should know better, felt free to pull out of the air a wide range of numbers purporting to measure the decline in GNP and the rise in inflation. It seemed that no number was too low to depict the size of Soviet GNP relative to that of the United States and to characterize relative living standards in the two countries. But the relative size and rate of growth of a nation's economy can only be determined by careful measurement using internationally accepted procedures. The casual empiricism that flourished in 1990 neither aided Western understanding of the economic situation in the Soviet Union, nor helped its government, which urgently needed to know its actual situation in order to devise appropriate policies to deal with its obviously growing economic difficulties.

THE RADICALIZATION OF ECONOMIC REFORM

The year 1990 witnessed a major breakthrough in the radicalization of programs for economic reform. For the first time, comprehensive blueprints were adopted that, if implemented, would dismantle the institutions of centrally planned socialism and replace them with those appropriate for a largely private enterprise market economy. Two of these programs have been approved by legislative bodies. The harbinger of this momentous development was the so-called Abalkin Blueprint of October 1989, which for the first time focused on property ownership as the centerpiece of reform (Hewett, 1989c). This theme also figured, albeit in a more subdued way, in the three more conservative

Ryzhkov government programs promulgated in December 1989 and in May and September 1990.

The most radical of the reform programs appeared in August as the much touted "500-day" (Shatalin) Plan, which ultimately was adopted "in principle" by the RSFSR legislature, although the Plan was rejected by the federal legislature. This program was notable both for its stress on property rights and its fast timetable for accomplishing the destatization of property ownership and the speedy decontrol of prices that is essential for a market economy (Hewett, 1990/91). The basic features of the Shatalin program were incorporated in more general form into the so-called Presidential Plan adopted by the federal legislature on October 19, 1990 (*Izvestiya*, October 27, 1990). In addition to provisions for systemic reform per se, all of these programs contained assorted recipes and schedules for "stabilization," i.e., dealing with the massive financial disequilibrium afflicting the economy. They also differed in the relative roles prescribed for the federal and republic governments.

The operational program for economic reform at the national level as of now is the Presidential Plan, entitled "Basic Guidelines for Stabilization of the National Economy and Transition to a Market Economy." In a report to the Supreme Soviet in late November, then Deputy Prime Minister Albalkin detailed a series of actions that the government intended to take to implement the Plan during the coming year (*Ekonomika i zhizn'*, No. 49, 1990, pp. 3–5). While one can fault the Basic Guidelines for the generality of language and the lack of a detailed timetable for actions, this document is truly radical, nonetheless, and especially so when compared with the comprehensive program of economic reforms adopted in July 1987, which Gorbachev at the time labeled "radical" and "revolutionary" (Schroeder, 1987). If it were to be implemented throughout the Soviet Union, that Plan along with a spate of new laws already on the books, would ultimately destroy the venerable institutions of Stalinist central planning and create new ones suited to a market economy with a substantial state sector.

In a marked departure from past reform legislation, the Basic Guidelines state, "There is no alternative to switching to a market," and "The choice of switching to the market has been made, a choice of historic importance to the fate of the country." They call for "resolute measures" to destatize and demonopolize the economy. By past standards, the legislation drastically shrinks the economic domain of the federal government and expands that of the republics. The document envisages that the process it outlines for stabilizing the economic situation and switching over to a market-oriented economy will require 18 months to 2 years, after which the new institutions can be consolidated and the economy can improve. Whatever one may think about that timetable under present conditions, the document itself represents a decisive break with the past. If its prescriptions could be carried out, the Soviet economy finally would be off the 25-year treadmill of reform programs that had failed to "reform" the institutions of socialist central planning.

The year 1990 also marked a watershed in the extent and kind of reform legislation adopted by both the central and republic governments. Merely listing the subjects of the major federal laws and decrees shows their unprecedented nature, even though each one can be faulted in its particulars (Hanson, 1990a). They concern: property ownership in general, ownership and disposition of land, operating rules for all enterprises regardless of ownership, measures to promote small businesses, prevention of monopoly and demonopolization, establishment of a Western-style central bank and a commercial banking system, creation of a uniform system of taxation of business profits, setting up joint-stock companies and a securities market, and general conditions for investment and employment. Some of this legislation took effect during 1990 and other parts on January 1, 1991. Some progress was made during 1990 in business ownership. Goskomstat reports that at the end of 1990, leased industrial units produced 5.2 percent of total industrial output; cooperatives employing 6.2 million persons accounted for about 7 percent of GNP; 40,600 individual peasant farms were operating; and about 1,200 joint-stock companies and 3,000 joint enterprises with foreign partners had been registered (*Ekonomika i zhizn'*, No. 5, 1991, p. 5). The agency also reported that there were about 1,400 cooperative and commercial banks operating and that a stock exchange had been opened in Moscow.

On September 24, 1990, the USSR Supreme Soviet gave Gorbachev the authority to implement economic measures by means of Presidential Decrees until March 31, 1992 (*Pravda*, September 26, 1990). Specifically, he is authorized to issue decrees and "to give instructions on matters of property relations, organization of the management of the economy, the budget and financial system, pay and price formation, and the strengthening of law and order." Gorbachev has acted vigorously to implement his program, focusing first on stabilizing production and consumer markets.

Three Presidential Decrees, adopted on September 27, October 4, and December 14, respectively, seek to deal with the growing disarray in the industrial supply system and halt the slide in production by (1) ordering all enterprises to keep existing contractual ties through 1991, (2) providing for introduction of a new set of wholesale and procurement prices on which 1991 contracts are to be based,[1] and (3) declaring invalid all inter-enterprise and inter-regional arrangements that disrupt existing ties (*Pravda*, September 28, 1990; *Izvestiya*, October 5 and December 15, 1990). Several decrees, supplemented by a Council of Ministers' decree, deal with acute problems in the consumer sector (*Izvestiya*, October 26, 1990; *Pravda*, November 15, 1990, December 1, 1990, January 11 and 23, 1991). These decrees established higher rates of interest to be paid on savings deposits, free prices on designated kinds of luxury consumer goods, authorize worker groups to monitor the distribution of food

---

1. New industrial wholesale prices were introduced on January 1, 1991. The overall level rose by over 50 percent; the prices of oil and gas rose by 130 percent and 100 percent, respectively. Some 40 percent of industrial prices were freed via the mechanism of contract prices.

supplies, outline steps to stabilize the distribution of food supplies and raise their level, remove 50 and 100 ruble notes from circulation, and impose limitations on withdrawals from savings banks.

Three Presidential decrees and an implementing Council of Ministers decree relate to foreign trade (*Izvestiya*, October 26 and November 4, 1990; *Ekonomika i zhizn'*, No. 1, 1991, p. 25). They provide more favorable conditions for foreign investors, establish a new commercial exchange rate, and centralize a larger share of enterprises' hard-currency earnings in a Union-Republic Foreign Currency Fund.[2] Two more decrees, issued on December 29, 1990, levy a nationwide tax of 5 percent on the gross turnover of all enterprises and establish All-Union and Republic Economic Stabilization Funds, to be formed from the confiscation of a portion of enterprises' amortization and various other sources. The stabilization funds are to be used to finance Union-wide programs for investment and research and development, military conversion costs, and grants to enterprises experiencing financial difficulties and to the poorer republics (*Pravda*, December 30, 1990). Meanwhile, the legislation adopted in 1990 presumably continues to be implemented to the extent possible amidst the general economic and political disarray.

Finally, President Gorbachev on January 26, 1991, issued the highly controversial decree entitled "On Measures to Combat Economic Sabotage and Other Crimes in the Economic Sphere" (*Izvestiya*, January 28, 1991). This decree authorizes the police and state security agencies to inspect the premises and records of business units in search of violations of state laws and regulations. This authority extends to firms under all forms of ownership, including foreign-owned firms and joint ventures. Thus, Gorbachev has been implementing his latest program of economic reforms largely through traditional types of administrative measures in a desperate effort to stabilize the financial situation, halt the deterioration in consumer markets, and arrest the decline in production. To bring the federal administrative structure in line with its changed role as outlined in the Basic Guidelines, Prime Minister Pavlov in mid-February 1991 presented to the Supreme Soviet a plan for reorganizing the many central agencies responsible for dealing with the economy (*Pravda*, February 21, 1991).[3]

RISE OF REGIONAL ASSERTIVENESS

The meteoric rise in the assertiveness of republican and lower-level governmental bodies in the economic arena in 1990 not only was breathtaking, but also was of a complexity that almost defies description. The focus here is on the economic dimension, in light of its intricate and critical connection with

2. In addition, the Supreme Soviet on March 1, 1991, adopted a new law regulating hard currency (*Izvestiya*, March 16, 1991). Subsequently, the USSR State Bank established a new tourist rate of exchange and commenced the start of biweekly hard-currency auctions (*Wall Street Journal*, April 4, 1991).

3. Subsequently, the Supreme Soviet adopted a new Law on the Cabinet of Ministers and approved a list of agencies (*Izvestiya*, March 28 and April 10, 1991).

the political dimension. Building on their earlier initiatives to gain "economic sovereignty," all three Baltic republics in 1990 declared their independence or their intention to move toward it. Georgia and Armenia also declared such an intent.[4] By the end of the year, all republics had issued declarations of "sovereignty," a concept intended to include control over their own economic affairs. These declarations, which differed considerably among republics, tend to be quite general in nature, but most of them include statements asserting the primacy of republic laws over federal laws and claims of republican ownership of land and natural resources. Many lower-level autonomous administrative units and other regional bodies also issued declarations of sovereignty, notably those within the RSFSR (Sheehy, 1991).

Early in the year, the USSR Supreme Soviet adopted a law entitled "On the Fundamentals of Economic Relations Between the USSR and the Union and Autonomous Republics" (*Izvestiya*, April 17, 1990). This law, which was slated to take effect on January 1, 1991, lays out in fairly broad terms the areas of responsibility that are reserved for the federal government, prescribes general procedures for forming the all-Union budget, and stresses the primacy of federal laws over those of the republics. A major section of the law deals with the "all-Union market." Republics are forbidden to discriminate against one another in economic matters or to erect barriers to inter-republican commerce. They are authorized to enter into treaties with the federal government and with other republics. The USSR Council of Ministers was instructed to draft implementing documents and procedures.

But events did not wait for orderly implementation of this law. One by one, the republics (and some lower level bodies) began to sign treaties and economic cooperation agreements with one another, a movement that gathered speed in the second half of the year as the overall economic situation deteriorated markedly. By the end of March 1991, the RSFSR and the Ukraine had signed agreements of one kind or another with all other republics, and all the rest (but one) had done so with at least half of the republics. These assorted agreements vary widely in content and specificity, but most of them contain a pledge to maintain existing economic ties at least at the 1990 level during 1991. In some cases, it seems that the republics forged new ties during 1990 that disrupted those in Union-dictated state orders, a development that elicited the Presidential Decree noted above invalidating such arrangements. Most of the republics and many local bodies also moved to establish direct trade ties with foreign countries. A number of localities declared the intention to establish Free Trade Zones on their territories. Finally, moves were made to conclude treaties of cooperation among groups of republics such as the Baltics and the four major central republics (RSFSR, Ukraine, Belorussia, Kazakhstan).

Along with the adoption of economic reform legislation and consideration of ever more radical reform programs at the national level during 1990, republic

4. Georgia declared its independence in April 1991.

legislatures have acted to draft and/or enact their own laws on economic matters that are also the subject of federal legislation, for example, on land reform, property, enterprises, and taxes. The Baltic republics were the most active in this regard. Some of these laws conflict with federal legislation, creating massive confusion in their implementation. Some republics also drafted their own blueprints for economic reform, and the RSFSR legislature voted to endorse "in principle" the Shatalin Plan that was rejected at the national level. This whole process came to be described as the "War of Laws."

Connected with this "war" and the declarations of republic sovereignty were the conflicts that erupted between the center and the republics over the control of individual enterprises. At the end of 1989, enterprises subordinated to all-Union ministries accounted for sizable shares of industrial production in all republics; the shares ranged from 28.4 percent in Moldavia to 69.0 percent in the RSFSR (*Narodnoye khozyaystvo SSSR v 1989 godu*, p. 331). But the all-Union shares in the total industrial capital stock in 1989 in these two republics were 48.2 and 86.8, respectively. The Baltics, in particular, fought battles with Moscow over this issue, as did the Ukraine in regard to the coal industry. This process has come to be described as the "war of jurisdictions" (*Pravda*, February 12, 1991).

Acrimonious debates also erupted over the matter of inter-republic economic dependencies. The argument often was couched in terms of "who feeds whom?" and was related to discussions as to how individual republics would fare economically if they were to leave the Union. All this has prompted Goskomstat to release an unprecedented amount of data depicting the extent of the trade ties that had developed among the republics over the years as the consequence of centrally dictated development policies that had fostered specialization rather than diversity within republic economies. The new data revealed that most of the republics had sizable balance of trade deficits, irrespective of whether domestic prices or so-called world market prices were used to value trade flows (*Vestnik statistiki*, No. 4, 1990, p. 49).

Probably the most revealing set of data are those that relate trade flows to republic production and consumption (*Narkhoz*, 1989, p. 635). They show that in 1988 the shares of exports (including foreign) in the total value of republic production ranged from 12 percent in the RSFSR and Kazakhstan to 27 percent in Belorussia; the shares exceeded one-fifth in most other republics. The shares of imports in total republic consumption ranged from 15 percent in the RSFSR to 31 percent in Armenia, with shares of 22 percent or more for most of the rest. Only four republics were self-sufficient in energy as measured in standard fuel equivalents in 1988 (Goskomstat, *Press-vypusk*, No. 394, 5 September 1989). Revelations such as these no doubt were intended to chill the fevers for independence from the Union.

An unfortunate development that figured heavily in the economic downturn in the last half of 1990 was the growing regional autarky. As the economic situation deteriorated, especially in the consumer sector, more and more republics and local entities took steps to protect their own populations from the endemic shortages of almost everything, but especially of food. Schemes were introduced in many places to restrict purchases to local residents. Various governmental bodies banned the export of designated products from their territories. The Baltic republics attempted to set up customs controls on their borders. Such moves merely exacerbated the economic difficulties and frustrated the efforts of the central government to acquire and distribute centralized food stocks. Some local bodies acted on their own to negotiate barter deals with neighbor territories to secure supplies. All this culminated in the issuance in January 1991 of a Presidential Decree and a Council of Ministers Decree embodying the terms of an "agreement" approved by the newly formed Federation Council to try to augment food supplies and stabilize markets (*Pravda*, January 11 and 19, 1991).

Toward the end of the year and in early 1991, battles also were waged over the formation of budgets for 1991, in particular over the size of republic "contributions" to funding the federal budget. It seems that Gorbachev finally managed to forge some kind of an accord with the republics in regard to budgetary and related matters and coordination of price, wage, and social policies. It was endorsed "in principle" by the Federation Council (*TASS*, Moscow, January 3, 1991). But the failure of some republics (including the RSFSR) to observe this agreement contributed to an accelerating decline in production and a budgetary crisis, as some republics failed to remit the agreed-upon sums to the Union budget. This situation led Gorbachev to unveil an "anti-crisis program," which, among other things, proposes to speed up the implementation of many of the economic reform measures contained in his Presidential Plan (*Pravda*, April 10, 1991).

ENTERING THE 1990S

The new decade begins with a continued decline in industrial production (*TASS*, Moscow, February 14, 1991). Supply difficulties appear to be mounting. At long last, the government seems poised to try to introduce measures to increase retail prices, but evidently with nearly full compensation to the populace.[5] Although 1990 saw a breakthrough in the conceptualization and adoption of potentially radical reform of the economic system, the economy remains unreformed at the start of the new decade and mainly administrative approaches are being used to try to stabilize the economy. But reform measures continued to be adopted in early 1991 at both the national and republic levels. For example, a draft USSR law on destatization of property and privatization of enterprises was published in February (*Ekonomika i zhizn'*, No. 7, 1991, pp. 18–19). In April, the USSR Supreme Soviet adopted a new law on business activity that

5. New retail prices took effect on April 2, 1991 (*Pravda*, March 20, 21, and 27, 1991). Wages and incomes of other groups were raised so as to compensate for most of the increase. At the same time, the government freed roughly one-fourth of all retail prices, allowing them to be set through contractual negotiations.

greatly liberalizes the earlier laws on private and cooperative business activities (*Izvestiya*, April 10, 1991).

The macroeconomy is in massive and growing disequilibrium, with no effective solution on the horizon. The rise of conservative political forces, the continuing ethnic clashes in the republics, and the resort to the use of force to stem the drive for independence in the Baltics all cloud the outlook for vigorous implementation of liberalizing economic and political reform in the near term. Especially unfortunate was the recent decree that employs the security forces to combat "economic sabotage," an action that is more likely to inhibit legitimate economic ventures than to stifle black market activities. But a longer perspective must take into account the remarkable legacy of 1990—a body of systemic reform legislation on the books at long last that is worth trying to implement.

Although nearly six years of economic *perestroyka* have wreaked havoc in the economy, the real crisis in the Soviet Union in the spring of 1991 is one of governance. On the whole the Presidential Plan and related legislation represent a reasonably practical and coherent approach to trying to stabilize the financial situation, while simultaneously moving to create market-oriented institutions and environment. But the Plan and its supplemental legislation, as do the recommendations of the recent study of the Soviet economy made in response to a request by the Houston Summit in September 1990 (IMF, 1990), rest on the existence of a strong central government based on consensus with the authority to carry it out. Thus, the Basic Guidelines state, "Economic relations among sovereign republics will be based on a recognition of the state sovereignty and equality of the republics and, at the same time, of the integrity of the Union as a federation, with the understanding that the enterprise is the foundation of the economy and the task of the state is to create the most favorable conditions for its operation" (*Izvestiya*, October 27, 1990, p. 2). But that assumption is in grave jeopardy at the moment.

In order to implement his program for economic reform, Gorbachev must first forge some kind of a treaty of friendship and navigation with the republics on a consensual basis. Resolution of the crisis of governance also is essential to carrying out economic reform programs that might be undertaken by individual republics, for their economic fortunes are deeply intertwined, whether they like it or not. The present impasse over who is in charge of what is generating massive confusion and uncertainty, fostering a popular sense of despair and even peril, and hampering foreign aid and investment. In seeking a new Union treaty and holding a public referendum on preservation of the Union, Gorbachev seeks to create a federal government with sufficient authority to enforce unpopular macroeconomic policy, manage a nationwide infrastructure, and formulate foreign and defense policy. He has long made it clear that he wants to preserve the union and strengthen a large common internal market within which autonomous business units can operate freely in response to market signals. His program now also implies an unprecedented delegation of decision-making authority to republics and lower level bodies. If he succeeds in forging such a political consensus, economic reform can proceed and could bring about the long sought-after "turning point" in the fortunes of the economy. If he fails, an entirely new situation will emerge in the 1990s. The "Joint Statement" (*Pravda*, April 24, 1991) signed by Gorbachev and the leaders of nine republics in late April is a promising first step toward such a consensus.

References

Abalkin, Leonid I., "Uskoreniye sotsial'no-ekonomicheskogo razvitiya: sushchnost' i istochniki (Acceleration of Socioeconomic Development: Essence and Sources)," *Planovoye khozyaystvo*, 3:9–16, March 1986a.

⸻, "Proizvodstvennyye otnosheniya i khozyaystvennyy mekhanizm (Industrial Relations and the Economic Mechanism)," *Ekonomicheskaya gazeta*, 46:2, 4, 1986b.

⸻, *Kursom uskoreniya (The Course of Acceleration)*. Moscow: Politizdat, 1986c.

⸻, *Politicheskaya ekonomiya sotsializma—teoreticheskaya osnova ekonomicheskoy politiki KPSS (The Political Economy of Socialism—the Theoretical Foundation of the Economic Policy of the CPSU)*. Moscow: Mysl', 1986d.

⸻, "Obnovleniye sotsialisticheskoy sobstvennosti (The Renewal of Socialist Property)," *Ekonomicheskaya gazeta*, 45:10–11, November 1988.

⸻, "Radikal'naya ekonomicheskaya reforma: pervoocherednyye i dolgovremennyye mery (Radical Economic Reform: Short- and Long-Term Measures)," *Ekonomicheskaya gazeta*, 43:4–7, October 1989a.

⸻, "Abalkin Explains Wage Tax Legislation," *Argumenty i fakty*, 41:1–3 (translated in FBIS, *Daily Report: Soviet Union*, October 20, 1989b, pp. 77–81).

Abalkin, Leonid I., (with Ed A. Hewett, Abram Bergson, Gregory Grossman, and Jerry Hough), "The New Model of Economic Management," *Soviet Economy*, 3, 4: 298–312, October–December 1987.

Abalkin, Leonid I., and V. V. Tsakunov, eds., *Proizvodstvennyye otnosheniya sotsializma (Industrial Relations of Socialism)*. Moscow: Mysl', 1986.

Admirin, Itzchok, "A. G. Aganbegjan. Pragmatiker der Wissenschaft und Theoretiker der neuen Wirtschaftspolitik (A. G. Aganbegyan. Economic Pragmatist and Theoretician of the New Economic Policy)," *Osteuropa*, 39, 1:23–35,1989.

Afanas'yev, Yuriy, ed., *Inogo ne dano: perestroyka—glasnost', demokratiya, sotsializm (There Is No Alternative: Restructuring—Openness, Democracy, Socialism)*. Moscow: Progress, 1988.

Aganbegyan, Abel G., "Na novom etape ekonomicheskogo stroitel'stva (At the New Stage of Economic Construction)," *Ekonomika i organizatsiya promyshlennogo proizvodstva*, 16, 8:3–24, August 1985a.

————, "Strategiya uskoreniya sotsial'no-ekonomicheskogo razvitiya (The Strategy of Acceleration of the Social-Economic Development)," *Problemy mira i sotsializma*, 29, 9:13–18, September 1985b.

————, *The Economic Challenge of Perestroika*. Bloomington and Indianapolis: Indiana University Press, 1988.

————, *Inside Perestroika. The Future of the Soviet Economy*. New York: Harper and Row, 1989a.

————, "Pragmaticheskiye dela ekonomicheskoy nauki (Practical Matters of Economic Science)," *Ekonomika i organizatsiya promyshlennogo proizvodstva*, 20, 9:17–29, 1989b.

————, "Ekonomicheskaya nauka—praktika zakonodatel'noy deyatel'nosti (Economic Science—The Practice of Legislative Activity)," *Voprosy ekonomiki*, 62, 2:3–12, 1990.

————, "Ob ekonomicheskikh urokakh perestroyki (On the Economic Lessons of Perestroyka)," *Ekonomika i matematicheskiye metody*, 1:70–81, January–February 1990.

Aganbegyan, Abel G., (with Ed A. Hewett, Abram Bergson, Gregory Grossman, and Herbert S. Levine), "Basic Directions of *Perestroyka,*" *Soviet Economy*, 3, 4:277–297, October–December 1987.

Akodis, I. A., *Finansovyy aspekt upravleniya rentabel'nost'yu i assortimentom (The Financial Aspect of Administration by Profitability and Assortment)*. Moscow: Finansy i statistika, 1985.

Aleksashenko, S., "Partner ili diktator? (Partner or Dictator?)," *Sotsialisticheskaya industriya*, June 15, 1989, p. 2.

Ambartsumov, Ye. A., "Analiz V. I. Leninym prichin krizisa 1921 g. i putey vykhoda iz nego (V. I. Lenin's Analysis of the Causes of and Ways of Resolution of the Crisis in 1921)." *Voprosy istorii*, 59, 4:15–29, April 1984.

Andreyeva, Nina, "Ne mogu postupat'sya printsipami (I Cannot Give Up My Principles)," *Sovetskaya Rossiya*, March 13, 1988, p. 3.

Åslund, Anders, "Gorbachev's Economic Advisors," *Soviet Economy*, 3, 3:246–269, July–September 1987.

————, *Gorbachev's Struggle for Economic Reform*. London: Pinter, 1989.

————, "The Making of Economic Policy in 1989 and 1990," *Soviet Economy*, 6, 1:65–94, January–March 1990.

Ayvazov, L. A., "Tsena: stimul i regulyator (Price: Incentive and Regulator)," *Sel'skaya zhizn'*, September 23, 1987, p. 2.

Ayvazyan, S. N., "O vozmozhnosti ispol'zovaniya bankovskoy informatsii dlya resheniya obespecheniya tovarno-denezhnoy sbalansirovannosti (On the Prospects of Utilizing of Bank Information for the Resolution of Problems of Securing Commodity-Money Balancing)," *Ekonomika i matematicheskiye metody*, 21, 1:139–146, January–February 1985.

Babashkin, L. E., "Finansovyy aspekt ekonomicheskogo eksperimenta v promyshlennosti (The Financial Aspect of the Economic Experiment in Industry)," *Finansy SSSR*, 6: 12–19, June 1985.

Bahry, Donna, *Outside Moscow: Power, Politics, and Budgetary Policy in the Soviet Republics*. New York: Columbia University Press, 1987.

Bannikov, N. A., "Sebestoimost' sel'skokhozyaystvennoy produktsii i puti yeye snizheniya (Cost of Agricultural Output and Ways of Reducing It)," *Obzory po infor-*

matsionnomu obespecheniyu nauchno-tekhnicheskikh programm i programm po resheniyu vazhneyshikh nauchno-tekhnicheskikh problem: Obzornaya informatsiya NII Tsen, 9, 3:1–64, July–September 1986.

"Basic Provisions for Radical Restructuring of Economic Management," *Pravda*, June 27, 1987, pp. 2–3 (translated in FBIS, *Daily Report: Soviet Union*, June 30, 1987, pp. R1–22).

Bazarova, G., and V. Pashkovskiy, "Financial and Credit Levers in the System of Economic Management," *Voprosy ekonomiki*, 2, 1981 (translated in *Problems of Economics*, 25:63–83, May 1982).

Belkin, V. D., P. A. Medvedev, and I. V. Nit, "Sfera obrashcheniya puti radikal'noy reformy (The Sphere of Influence of Radical Reform Measures)," *Kommunist*, 14:35–39, September 1988.

Belokh, N. V., N. Ya. Petrakov, and V. P. Rusakov, "Dokhody naseleniya, predlozheniye i tseny—problema sbalansirovannosti (Incomes of the Population, Supply and Prices—The Problem of Balancing)," *Izvestiya AN SSSR, seriya ekonomicheskaya*, 13, 2:71–77, March–April 1982.

Belokh, N. V., and V. P. Rusakov, "Sbalansirovannost' sprosa i predlozheniya i mekhanizm tsen (Balancing of Demand and Supply and the Price Mechanism)," *Izvestiya AN SSSR, seriya ekonomicheskaya*, 15, 3:68–76, May–June 1984.

Belousov, R. A., "Demokraticheskiy tsentralizm i khozyaystvennaya samostoyatel'nost' (Democratic Centralism and Economic Independence)," *Ekonomika i organizatsiya promyshlennogo proizvodstva*, 1:3–22, 1984.

———, "Vzaimovliyaniye obobshchestvleniya proizvodstva i upravleniya (The Mutual Influence of Socialization Production and Management)," *Voprosy ekonomiki*, 57, 1:3–14, January 1985.

Berliner, Joseph S., *Factory and Manager in the U.S.S.R.* Cambridge, Mass.: Harvard University Press, 1957.

———. *The Innovation Decision in Soviet Industry*. Cambridge, Mass.: MIT Press, 1976.

———. "Planning and Management," in Abram Bergson and Herbert S. Levine, eds., *The Soviet Economy: Toward the Year 2000*. London: George Allen and Unwin, 1983, pp. 350–390.

———. "The Transition Problem." Unpublished paper, April 1990.

Bialer, S., and J. Afferica, "The Genesis of Gorbachev's World," *Foreign Affairs*, 64, 3:609–645, 1986.

Bim, A., and A. Shokhin, "Sistema raspredeleniya: na putyakh perestroyki (The System of Distribution: On the Road to Restructuring)," *Kommunist*, 63, 15:64–73, October 1986.

Birman, Igor, "The Financial Crisis in the USSR," *Soviet Studies*, 32:84–105, January 1980.

Biryukov, Yu., and R. Vantsiyan, "Sovershenstvovaniye tsen v agropromyshlennom komplekse (Refinement of Prices in the Agroindustrial Complex)," *Ekonomika sel'skogo khozyaystva*, 62, 3:40–42, March 1982.

Blejer, Mario I., and Gyorgy Szapary, "The Evolving Role of Fiscal Policy in Centrally Planned Economies under Reform: The Case of China." International Monetary Fund, Asian and Fiscal Affairs Departments, March 31, 1989.

Block, Kevin, "Depoliticizing Ownership." Unpublished manuscript, Harriman Institute, Columbia University, New York, 1990.

Bochkov, V., "Economist's Remarks: Banking Boom?" *Sotsialisticheskaya industriya,* January 26, 1989 (translated in FBIS, *Daily Report: Soviet Union,* February 1, 1989, pp. 79–80).

Bogomolov, Oleg T., "Mir sotsializma na puti perestroyki (The Socialist World on the Path to Restructuring)," *Kommunist,* 64, 16:92–102, 1987a.

———, "Politekonomiya—ekonomike (Political Economy for the Economy)," *Izvestiya,* May 13, 1987b.

———, "*Perestroika* of the Soviet Economy in the Light of East-West Relations." Report prepared for the roundtable conference on "Market Forces in Planned Economies," organized by the International Economic Association jointly with the USSR Academy of Sciences, Moscow, March 28–30, 1989.

Bokov, A., and A. Shmarov, "Prognozirovaniye razvitiya sistemy platnykh uslug (Forecasting the Development of the System of Paid Services)," *Ekonomicheskiye nauki,* 28, 10:14–21, October 1985.

Borkhunov, N., S. Yakovlev, and G. Kaliman, "Ob effektivnosti nadbavok k zakupochnym tsenam (On the Effectiveness of Surcharges on Purchase Prices)," *Ekonomika sel'skogo khozyaystva,* 64, 11:42–46, November 1984.

Bornstein, Morris, "Soviet Price Policy in the 1970s," in U.S. Congress, Joint Economic Committee, *Soviet Economy in a New Perspective.* Washington D.C.: U.S. Government Printing Office, 1976, pp. 17–66.

———, "The Administration of the Soviet Price System," *Soviet Studies,* 30, 4:466–490, October 1978.

———, "The Soviet Industrial Price Revision," in G. Fink, ed., *Socialist Economy and Economic Policy.* Vienna and New York: Springer Verlag, 1985, pp. 157–170.

———, "Soviet Price Policies," *Soviet Economy,* 3, 2:96–134, April–June 1987.

———, "Price Reform in the USSR: Comment on Shmelev," *Soviet Economy,* 4, 4:328–337, October–December 1988.

Borozdin, Yuriy V., "Planovoye tsenoobrazovaniye v novoy sisteme khozyaystvovaniya (Planned Price Formation in the New System of Economic Management)," *Kommunist,* 63, 16:26–37, November 1986.

———, "Problemy radikal'noy reformy sistemy tsen (Problems of the Radical Reform of the Price System)," *Izvestiya AN SSSR, seriya ekonomicheskaya,* 19, 3:45–56, May–June 1988.

———, "Ekonomicheskaya reforma i tovarno-denezhnyye otnosheniya (Economic Reform and Commodity-Money Relationships)," *Voprosy ekonomiki,* 61, 9:13–25, 1989.

Braginsky, Mikhail, *Joint Ventures: Benefit for All.* Moscow: Novosti Press Agency Publishing House, 1988.

Brovkin, V., and D. Gorbuntsov, "Vinovat li ogurets? (Is the Cucumber Guilty?)," *Pravda,* July 14, 1986, p. 3.

Bunich, Pavel G., "Eskiz mekhanisma uskoreniya (An Outline of the Mechanism of Acceleration)," *Literaturnaya gazeta,* February 12, 1986a.

———, "Novyye usloviya khozyaystvovaniya: dostizheniya, problemy, perspektivy (New Conditions of Management: Accomplishments, Problems, Perspectives)," *Ekonomika i organizatsiya promyshlennogo proizvodstva,* 5:3–20, 1986b.

———, "The New Economic Mechanism and Credit Reform," *Ekonomika i organizatsiya promyshlennogo proizvodstva*, 3, 1988 (translated in *Problems of Economics*, 31:80–94, December 1988).

———. Novyye tsennosti (New Prices). Moscow: Ekonomika, 1989.

Bunich, Pavel G., ed., *Khozyaystvennyy mekhanizm upravleniya sotsialisticheskoy ekonomikoy (The Economic Mechanism of Management of the Socialist Economy)*. Moscow: Ekonomika, 1984.

Burlatskiy, Fedor M., "Otkrovenno o trevozhnom (Candidly About a Worrying Matter)," *Literaturnaya gazeta*, 19:1, May 9, 1990.

Burns, James MacGregor, *Roosevelt: The Lion and the Fox*. New York: Harcourt Brace and Company, 1956, pp. 328–336.

Butenko, A. P., "Protivorechiya razvitiya sotsializma kak obshchestvennogo stroya (Contradictions in the Development of Socialism as a Social System)," *Voprosy filosofii*, 10:16–29, October 1982.

Buzdalov, I., "Khozyaystvennyy mekhanizm APK i tsenoobrazovaniye (The Economic Mechanism of the Agroindustrial Complex and Price Formation)," *Voprosy ekonomiki*, 38, 5:124–133, May 1985.

Campbell, Robert W., "Energy Prices and Decisions on Energy Use in the USSR," in Padma Desai, ed., *Marxism, Central Planning, and the Soviet Economy: Economic Essays in Honor of Alexander Erlich*. Cambridge, Mass.: MIT Press, 1983, pp. 249–274.

Chapman, Janet G., "Drastic Changes in the Soviet Social Contract" (mimeo), 1989.

Chekhlov, N. I., "Tseny i tarify v promyshlennosti (Prices and Rates in Industry)," *Ekonomika i organizatsiya promyshlennogo proizvodstva*, 17, 4:180–195, April 1986.

———, "Kto vse-taki vyigrayet? (Who Will Actually Win?)," *Sovetskaya Rossiya*, February 5, 1988, p. 3.

Chernenko, K. U., *Narod i partiya yediny (The People and Party Are United)*. Moscow: Politizdat, 1984.

Chubakov, G. N., "Tsena i plan (Price and Plan)," *Ekonomicheskaya gazeta*, 17:14, March 1986.

———, "Napravleniya sovershenstvovaniya roznichnykh tsen (Directions of Refining of Retail Prices)," *Voprosy ekonomiki*, 59, 1:66–76, January 1987.

Chursin, A. M., K. S. Kameneva, and D. S. Golubitskaya, *Tseny i kachestvo sel'skokhozyaystvennoy produktsii (Prices and the Quality of Agricultural Output)*. Moscow: Kolos, 1984.

CIA, *A Guide to Monetary Measures of Soviet Defense Activities*, SOV 87-10069. Washington, D.C.: Directorate of Intelligence, November 1987.

———, *USSR: Sharply Higher Budget Deficits Threaten Perestroyka*. Washington, D.C.: Directorate of Intelligence, 1988.

———, *USSR: Estimates of Personal Incomes and Savings*, SOV 89–10035. Washington, D.C.: Directorate of Intelligence, April 1989a.

———, Revised estimates of deficit, May 1989b.

CIA/DIA, *The Soviet Economy Under a New Leader*. Paper submitted to Joint Economic Committee, U.S. Congress, March 19, 1986.

———, *Gorbachev's Modernization Program: A Status Report*, DDB-1900–140–87, August 1987.

——, *Gorbachev's Economic Program: Problems Emerge*, DDB-1900–187–88, June 1988.

——, "Gorbachev's Economic Program: Problems Emerge," in U.S. Congress, Joint Economic Committee, Subcommittee on National Security Economics, *Allocation of Resources in the Soviet Union and China—1987*. Washington, D.C.: U.S. Government Printing Office, 1989a, pp. 3–70.

——, *The Soviet Economy in 1988: Gorbachev Changes Course*, DDB-1900–155–89, April 1989b.

——, *The Soviet Economy Stumbles Badly in 1989*, DDB-1900–161–90, May 1990.

Davies, R. W., *The Development of the Soviet Budgetary System*. Cambridge: Cambridge University Press, 1958.

"Delegaty XIX Vsesoyuznoy partkonferentsii na stranitsakh 'Kommunista' " (Delegates of the 19th Party Conference on the Pages of 'Kommunist')," *Kommunist*, 11:3–43, July 1988.

Dementsev, V. V., "Povysit' rol' finansov v razvitii sel'skokhozyaystvennogo proizvodstva (Increase the Role of Finances in the Development of Agricultural Production)," *Finansy SSSR, 60, 4:3–11, April 1985*.

Deminov, A., "Novyye smetnyye normy i tseny (New Estimate Norms and Prices)," *Ekonomicheskaya gazeta*, 15:8, April 1984.

Deryabin, A., "Tsena i nauchno-tekhnicheskiy progress (Price and Scientific-Technical Progress)," *Voprosy ekonomiki*, 38, 9:37–47, September 1985.

——, "Osnovy perestroyki tsenoobrazovaniya (The Foundations of the Restructuring of Price Formation)," *Voprosy ekonomiki*, 59, 1:55–66, January 1987.

——, "U rynka svoi zakony: spros-tsena-predlozheniye (The Market Has Its Own Laws: Demand-Price-Supply)," *Ekonomicheskaya gazeta*, 9:5, February 1988a.

——, "V zerkale defitsita: spros, predlozheniye, tseny (In the Mirror of the Shortage: Demand, Supply, Price)," *Trud*, May 18, 1988b, p. 2.

Desai, Padma, "*Perestroika*, Prices, and the Ruble Problem," *The Harriman Institute Forum*, 2:11, November 1989.

Documents and Materials of the 19th All-Union Conference of the CPSU: Report and Speeches by Mikhail Gorbachev, General Secretary of the CPSU Central Committee. Resolutions. Moscow: Novosti Press Agency Publishing House, 1988.

Doronin, Igor, "Monetary Instruments: Problems of Their Improvement," *Foreign Trade*, 69, 4:33–36, April 1988a.

——, "Monetary Instruments in External Economic Ties of the USSR: Problems of Their Improvement," *Foreign Trade*, 69, 6:25–27, June 1988b.

Duchêne, G., "Place de l'effort de défense dans comptes nationaux de l'URSS," in M. Lavigne and W. Andreeff, eds., *La Réalité Socialiste*. Paris: Economica, 1985, pp. 83–111.

Dyker, David A., *The Process of Investment in the Soviet Union*. Cambridge: Cambridge University Press, 1983.

Ekonomicheskaya gazeta, No. 41, 1986.

——, No. 17, April 1987a.

——, No. 32, August 1987b.

——, No. 38, September 1987c.

——, No. 39, September 1987d.

————, No. 40, October 1987e.

Ekonomicheskiy mekhanizm khozyaystvovaniya sel' skokhozyaystvennykh predpriyatiy (The Economic Mechanism of Management of Agricultural Enterprises), A. N. Mayuk, ed. Moscow: Kolos, 1983.

FBIS (Foreign Broadcast Information Service), *Daily Report: Soviet Union*, daily.

————, *Daily Report: Soviet Union*, August 12, 1987.

Fedorenko, N. P., "Planirovaniye i upravleniye: kakimi im byt'? (Planning and Management: What Should They Be Like?)," *Ekonomika i organizatsiya promyshlennogo proizvodstva*, 15, 12:3–20, December 1984.

Feshbach, Murray, "Issues in Soviet Health Problems," in U.S. Congress, Joint Economic Committee, *Soviet Economy in the 1980s: Problems and Prospects*, Part 2. Washington, D.C.: U.S. Government Printing Office, 1982, pp. 210–212.

————, "Population and Labor Force," in Abram Bergson and Herbert S. Levine, eds., *The Soviet Economy: Toward the Year 2000*. London: George Allen and Unwin, 1983, pp. 79–111.

Finansy SSSR: statisticheskiy sbornik, 1987–1988 gg. (Finances of the USSR: A Statistical Handbook, 1987–1988). Moscow: Finansy i statistika, 1989.

Figurnov, E., "Tovary tseny inflyatsiya (Goods Hold Back Inflation)," *Ekonomicheskaya gazeta*, 5:13–14, January 1989.

Gal'perin, V., "V interesakh potrebitelya (In the Interests of the Consumer)," *Ekonomicheskaya gazeta*, 42:6, September 1986.

Garvy, George, *Money, Financial Flows, and Credit in the Soviet Union*. Cambridge, Mass.: Ballinger Publishing Co. for National Bureau of Economic Research, 1977.

Gaydar, E., "Kursom ozdorovleniya (On the Course of Recovery)." *Kommunist*, 2:41–50, January 1990.

Genkina, D., ed., *Sovetskoye grazhdanskoye pravo (Soviet Civil Law)*. Moscow: Yuridicheskaya literatura, 1931.

Gladkiy, I. I., "Perestroyka sistemy zarabotnoy platy (Restructuring of the Wage System)," *Ekonomicheskaya gazeta*, 43:6–7, October 1986.

Glushkov, N., "Commodity and Price," *Izvestiya*, July 25, 1984a, p. 3 (trans. in *Current Digest of the Soviet Press*, 36, 30:10–11, August 22, 1984).

————, "For the Good of the People," *Pravda*, September 1, 1984b, p. 2 (trans. in *Current Digest of the Soviet Press*, 36, 35:5, September 26, 1984).

————, "Sovershenstvovaniye tsenoobrazovaniya v APK (Improvement of Price Formation in the Agroindustrial Complex)," *Planovoye khozyaystvo*, 62, 9:42–52, September 1985.

Gogoberidze, A., and B. Lakhov, "Tsena i effektivnost' stimulirovaniya (Price and the Effectiveness of Incentives)," *Planovoye khozyaystvo*, 63, 10:88–94, October 1986.

Gonzal'yez, E., "Rubl' iz gosudarstvennoy kazny. Beseda s ministrom finansov SSSR B. I. Gostevym (A Ruble from the State Treasury: Conversation with USSR Finance Minister B. I. Gostev)," *Izvestiya*, March 30, 1989, p. 2.

Gorbachev, Mikhail S., Speech at a meeting on scientific-technical progress held in the Central Committee on June 11, 1985, *BBC Summary of World Broadcasts* SU/7976/C/1 (June 13,1985a).

————, "O sozyve ocherednogo XXVII s''yezda KPSS i zadachakh, svyazannykh s yego podgotovkoy i provedeniyem (On the Convening of the Regular XXVII Con-

gress of the CPSU and the Tasks Connected with its Preparation and Conduct),"
Pravda, April 24, 1985b, pp. 1–2.

———, "Korennoy vopros ekonomicheskoy politiki partii (The Fundamental Question of the Economic Policy of the Party)," *Literaturnaya gazeta*, June 12, 1985c. pp. 1–2.

———, "V interesakh mira i sotrudnichestva (In Interests of Peace and Cooperation)," *Sotsialisticheskaya industriya*, November 28, 1985d, pp. 1–3.

———, "Perestroyka neotlozhna, ona kasayetsya vsekh i vo vsem. Rech' M. S. Gorbacheva na soveshchanii aktiva Khabarovskoy krayevoy partiynoy organizatsii 31 iyulya 1986 goda (Restructuring is Urgent: It Concerns Everything and Everyone. The Speech of M. S. Gorbachev at the Meeting of the *Aktiv* of the Khabarovsk Kray party organization, July 31, 1986)," *Sotsialisticheskaya industriya*, August 2, 1986a, pp. 1–2.

———, "Politicheskiy doklad tsentral'nogo komiteta KPSS XXVII s''yezdu Kommunisticheskoy partii Sovetskogo Soyuza. Doklad General'nogo sekretarya TsK KPSS tovarishcha M. S. Gorbacheva. 25 Fevralya 1986 goda (Political Report of the Central Committee of the CPSU to the XXVII Congress of the Communist Party of the Soviet Union. Report of the General Secretary of the CC of the CPSU, Comrade M. S. Gorbachev)," in *Materialy XXVII s'yezda Kommunisticheskoy Partii Sovetskogo Soyuza*. Moscow: Politizdat, 1986b, pp. 3–97.

———, *Perestroika: New Thinking for Our Country and the World*. New York: Harper and Row, 1988.

———, Address to USSR Congress of Peoples Deputies, Moscow Television Service, May 30, 1989 (translated in FBIS, *Daily Report: Soviet Union*, May 31, 1989, pp. 47–62).

———, "Mir budushchego i sotsializm (The World of the Future and Socialism)," *Rabochiy klass i sovremennyy mir*, 2:3–12, March–April 1990.

"Gorbachev's Economic Reform: A *Soviet Economy* Roundtable," *Soviet Economy*, 3, 1:40–53, January–March 1987.

Goskomstat SSSR, *Kapital'noye stroitel'stvo SSSR: kratkiy statisticheskiy sbornik (Capital Construction in the USSR: A Concise Statistical Handbook)*. Moscow: Informatsionno-izdatel'skiy tsentr, 1988a.

———, "Uskorit' tempy obnovleniya. Ob ekonomicheskom i sotsial'nom razvitii SSSR v pervom polugodii 1988 goda (To Accelerate Rates of Renewal: On the Economic and Social Development of the USSR in the First Half of 1988)," *Izvestiya*, July 24, 1988b, p. 1.

———, "Uskorit' povorot ekonomiki k cheloveku. Sotsial'no-ekonomicheskoye razvitiye SSSR v 1988 godu (To Accelerate a Change in the Economy Toward Man: The Social and Economic Development of the USSR in 1988)," *Pravda*, January 22, 1989a, pp 3–5

———, "Sotsial'no-ekonomicheskoye razvitiye SSSR v pervom polugodii 1989 goda. Soobshcheniye Goskomstata SSSR (The Social and Economic Development of the USSR in the First Half of 1989: A Report of USSR Goskomstat)," *Sotsialisticheskaya industriya*, July 29, 1989b, pp. 1–3.

———, "V zerkale statistiki (In the Mirror of Statistics)," *Ekonomika i zhizn'*, 40:15, 1990.

Gostev, B. I., "On the USSR State Budget for 1987 and on the Implementation of the

Budget During 1985; Report by Deputy B. I. Gostev, USSR Minister of Finance,"
Pravda, November 18, 1986 (translated in FBIS, *Daily Report: Soviet Union*, November 20, 1986, pp. R15–29).

———, "On the USSR State Budget for 1988 and on the Implementation of the Budget During 1986; Report by Deputy B. I. Gostev, USSR Minister of Finance," *Pravda*, October 20, 1987 (translated in FBIS, *Daily Report: Soviet Union*, October 21, 1987, pp. 48–59).

———, "On the USSR State Budget for 1989 and on the Implementation of the USSR State Budget for 1987," *Pravda*, October 28, 1988 (translated in FBIS, *Daily Report: Soviet Union*, October 28, 1988, pp. 52–62).

———, Interview in *Izvestiya*, March 31, 1989 (translated in FBIS, *Daily Report: Soviet Union*, March 31, 1989a, pp. 76–79).

———, News conference reported in *Trud*, April 2, 1989 (translated in FBIS, *Daily Report: Soviet Union*, April 10, 1989b, pp. 78–79).

———, News conference reported on Moscow Television Service, April 17, 1989 (translated in FBIS, *Daily Report: Soviet Union*, April 19, 1989c, pp. 108–110).

Gosudarstvennyy pyatiletniy plan razvitiya narodnogo khozyaystva SSSR na 1971–1975 gody (State Five-Year Plan of the Development of the Economy of the USSR during 1971–1975). Moscow: Politicheskoy literatury, 1972.

Granick, David, *The Red Executive*. New York: Doubleday and Company, 1960.

Gray, Kenneth, and Yuri Markish, "The Russians Have Agricultural Subsidies, Too," *World Agriculture: Situation and Outlook Report*, September 1987, pp. 24–27.

Gribanov, V., and E. Sukhanov, "Pravo i sobstvennost' (The Law and Property)," *Ekonomicheskaya gazeta*, 23:15, July 1989.

Grossman, Gregory, "The Second Economy of the USSR," *Problems of Communism*, 26, 5:25–40, September–October 1977.

Gur'yev, V., and A. Zaitseva, "Stoimost' zhizni, prozhitochnyy minimum, inflyatsiya (metodologiya i analiz) (The Cost of Living, Subsistence Wage, Inflation (Metodology and Analysis)," *Vestnik statistiki*, 6:20–29, June 1990.

Guzhavina, L., "Dogovornaya tsena (Contract Price)," *Ekonomicheskaya gazeta*, 6:6, February 1987.

Hanson, Philip, "Economic Reform: The Cosmetist Platform," *Radio Liberty Research*, RL 63/85, February 26, 1985a.

———, "Economics, Economic Advisers and the Gorbachev Leadership," *Radio Liberty*. Research, RL 308/85, September 16, 1985b.

———, "Gorbachev's Economic Strategy: A Comment," *Soviet Economy*, 1, 4:306–312, October–December 1985c.

———, "Superministries: The State of Play," *Radio Liberty Research Bulletin*, RL 167/86, 30, 18:1–8, April 30, 1986a.

———, "The Shape of Gorbachev's Economic Reform," *Soviet Economy*, 2, 4:313–326, October–December 1986b.

———, "Capitalism or Socialism? A Minor Semantic Problem in the Soviet Reforms," *Detente*, 16:3–8, 14, December 1989.

———, "Ownership Issues in Perestroika," in John Tedstrom, ed., *Perestroika and the Private Sector of the Soviet Economy*. Boulder, Col.: Westview Press, 1990a, pp. 67–90.

———, "Prospects for Reform: Three Key Issues in 1990," *Radio Liberty Report on the USSR*, 2, 4:1–4, January 26, 1990b.

———, "Property Rights in the New Phase of Reforms," *Soviet Economy*, 6, 2:95–124, April–June 1990c.

Harrison, Mark, "The USSR State Budget under Late Stalinism (1945–55): Capital Formation, Government Borrowing and Monetary Growth," *Economics of Planning*, 20, 3:179–205, 1986.

Herrmann-Pillath, C., "Anpassungsprobleme des chinesischen kreditsektors während der Austeritätspolitik (Adjustment Problems of the Chinese Financial Sector During the [Period of the] Austerity Policy)," *Aktuelle Analysen* (Bundesinstitut für ostwissenschaftliche und internationale Studien), 33, June 1, 1990.

Hewett, Ed A., "Foreign Economic Relations," in Abram Bergson and Herbert S. Levine, eds., *The Soviet Economy: Toward the Year 2000*. London: George Allen and Unwin, 1983, pp. 269–310.

———, "Gorbachev's Economic Strategy: A Preliminary Assessment," *Soviet Economy*, 1, 4:285–305, October–December 1985a.

———, *The Energy Situation and Politics in the USSR*. Paper delivered to the Seminar on Soviet Energy, Soderfors, Sweden, June 5–7, 1985b.

———, "Reform or Rhetoric: Gorbachev and the Soviet Economy," *Brookings Review*, 4, 3:13–20, Fall 1986a.

———, "Gorbachev at Two Years: Perspectives on Economic Reforms," *Soviet Economy*, 2, 4:283–288, October–December 1986b.

———, *Reforming the Soviet Economy: Equality vs. Efficiency*. Washington, D.C.: Brookings Institution, 1988a.

———, "Economic Reform in the Wake of the XIX Party Conference," *PlanEcon Report*, July 22, 1988b, p. 20.

———, "*Perestroyka* and the Congress of People's Deputies," *Soviet Economy*, 5, 1:47–69, January–March 1989a.

———, "Economic Reform in the USSR, Eastern Europe, and China: The Politics of Economics," *American Economic Review: Papers and Proceedings*, May 1989b, pp. 16–20.

———, "Perestroika-Plus: The Albalkin Reforms," *PlanEcon Report*, 5:48–49, December 1, 1989c.

———, "The New Soviet Plan," *Foreign Affairs*, 69, 5:146–166, Winter 1990–91.

Hewett, Ed A., Bryan Roberts, and Jan Vanous, "On the Feasibility of Key Targets in the Soviet Twelfth Five-Year Plan (1986–90)," in U.S. Congress, Joint Economic Committee, *Gorbachev's Economic Plans*, Vol. 1. Washington, D.C.: U.S. Government Printing Office, 1987.

Holzman, Franklyn D., *Financial Checks on Soviet Defense Expenditures*. Lexington, Mass.: D.C. Heath and Co., 1975.

Hough, Jerry F., "The Gorbachev Reform: A Maximal Case," *Soviet Economy*, 2, 4:302–312, October–December 1986.

———, "The Politics of Successful Economic Reform," *Soviet Economy*, 5, 1:3–46, January–March 1989a.

"How to Overcome the State Budget Deficit," *Trud*, April 2, 1989 (translated in FBIS, *Daily Report: Soviet Union*, April 10, 1989b, pp. 78–79).

Hutchings, Raymond, *The Soviet Budget*. London: Macmillan Press Ltd., 1983.

IMF, International Monetary Fund, International Bank for Reconstruction and Development, Organization for Economic Cooperation and Development, European Bank for Reconstruction and Development, *The Economy of the USSR* (Study undertaken in response to a request by the Houston Summit). Washington: IMF, December 1990.

"Informatsionyy kommercheskiy vestnik (Commercial Information Herald)," supplement, *Ekonomika i zhizn'*, 1990.

Ivanov, Ivan D., "Restructuring the Mechanism of Foreign Economic Relations in the USSR," *Soviet Economy*, 3, 3:192–218, July–September 1987.

Ivchenko, L., "Platnaya poliklinika: za i protiv (The Paid Polyclinic: For and Against)," *Izvestiya*, July 11, 1986, p. 3.

JEC, Joint Economic Committee, U.S. Congress, USSR: *Measures of Economic Growth and Development, 1950–80.* Washington, D.C.: U.S. Government Printing Office, 1982.

Kagalovskiy, Konstantin G., "Podzhatsya! Nabolevshiye problemy gosudarstvennykh finansov (The Pressing Problems of State Financing)," *Kommunist*, 11:66–73, 1988.

―――, "Ekonomicheskiy krizis. Gde iskat' vykhod? (The Economic Crisis. Where is the Way Out?)," *Kommunist*, 4:60–67, 1990.

Kalnyn'sh, A., "Puti sovershenstvovaniya khozyaystvennogo mekhanizma APK (Ways to Improve the Economic Mechanism of the Agroindustrial Complex)," *Voprosy ekonomiki*, 39, 10:64–72, October 1986.

Katsenelinboigen, Aron, "Coloured Markets in the Soviet Union," *Soviet Studies*, 29, 1:62–85, 1977.

―――, *Soviet Economic Thought and Political Power in the USSR.* Oxford: Pergamon Press, 1979.

Katsenelinboigen, Aron, and Herbert S. Levine, "Market and Plan; Plan and Market: The Soviet Case," *American Economic Review*, 67, 1:61–66, February 1977a.

―――, "Some Observations on the Plan-Market Relationship in Centrally Planned Economies," *The Annals of the American Academy*, 434, 6:186–198, November 1977b.

Kazakevich, D. M., "K sovershenstvovaniyu potrebitel'skikh tsen (Toward the Improvement of Consumer Prices)," *Ekonomika i organizatsiya promyshlennogo proizvodstva*, 17, 1:33–43, January 1986.

Kellogg, Robert L., *Modeling Soviet Agriculture: Isolating the Effects of Weather*, SOV 88-10054. Washington, D.C.: CIA Directorate of Intelligence, August 1988.

Khozyaystvo i pravo, No. 11, November 1985.

Khubiyev, K., "Kooperativy, arenda, sobstvennost' (Cooperatives, the Lease, and Property)," *Ekonomicheskaya gazeta*, 2:8, January 1989.

Kim, V., "Zakupochnyye tseny sel'skokhozyaystvennoy produktsii (Purchase Prices for Agricultural Output)," *Voprosy ekonomiki*, 35, 6:60–71, June 1982.

―――, "O sud'be tsenovoy reformy (On the Fate of Price Reform)," *Ekonomicheskaya gazeta*, 52:8, December 1988a.

―――, "Problemy tsenovoy perestroyki (Problems of Price Restructuring)," *Ekonomicheskiye nauki*, 31, 5:25–35, May 1988b.

Kirichenko, Vadim N., "Perestroyka sistemy upravleniya i tsentralizovannoye planirovaniye (Restructuring of the System of Management and Centralized Planning)," *Kommunist*, 63, 13:10–19, September 1986.

————, "Nuzhen ne proryv a strategicheskoye nastupleniye (A Strategic Offensive Rather Than a Breakthrough Is Needed)," *Pravitel'stvennyy vestnik*, 19:3, May 1990.

Kirillov, A., "Eksport: rezervy povysheniya konkurentosposobnosti (Exports: Reserves to Increase the Ability to Compete)," *Ekonomicheskaya gazeta*, 44:21, October 1986.

Kitaygorodskiy, I., "Kak sozdavat' aktsionernyye obshchestva (How to Create Joint-Stock Companies)," *Ekonomika i zhizn'*, 27:15, 1990.

Komin, A., "Tekhnicheskiy progress i tseny (Technical Progress and Prices)," *Planovoye khozyaystvo*, 62, 10:13–20, October 1985.

————, "K vysshemu kachestvu—cherez mekhanizm tsen (Toward Higher Quality—Through the Price Mechanism)," *Ekonomicheskaya gazeta*, 8:16, February 1986a.

————, "Tsenoobrazovaniye v usloviyakh planovoy ekonomiki (Price Formation in the Conditions of the Planned Economy)," *Planovoye khozyaystvo*, 63, 5:59–65, May 1986b.

————, "Perestroyka tsenovogo khozyaystva (Reconstruction of the Pricing Economy)," *Voprosy Ekonomiki*, 41, 3:107–114, March 1988.

Kontorovich, V., "Can the Tightening of Discipline Accelerate Soviet Economic Growth?" Command Economies Research, Inc., October 1985 (mimeo).

Kornai, Janos, *The Shortage Economy*. Amsterdam: North Holland, 1980.

————, "The Hungarian Reform Process: Visions, Hopes and Reality," *Journal of Economic Literature*, 24:1687–1744, December 1986.

————, "The Affinity Between Ownership and Coordination Mechanisms: The Common Experience of Reform in Socialist Countries." Report prepared for the Round Table Conference on "Market Forces in Planned Economies" organized by the International Economic Association jointly with the USSR Academy of Sciences, Moscow, March 28–30, 1989.

Korotkov, P., "Inflyatsionyy 'vsplesk': masshtaby i prichiny (The Inflationary "Splash": Extent and Causes)," *Ekonomicheskaya gazeta*, 13:12, March 1989.

Korovyakovskiy, D., "Kolkhoznyy rynok i snabzheniye naseleniya prodovol'stviyem (The Collective Farm Market and the Supply of Food to the Population)," *Voprosy ekonomiki*, 39, 9:80–89, 1986.

Koryagina, Tat'yana I., "Uslugi tenevyye i legal'nyye (Legal and Shadow Services)," *Ekonomika i organizatsiya promyshlennogo proizvodstva*, 20, 2:60–65, 1989.

————, "Tenevaya ekonomika v SSSR (The Shadow Economy in the USSR)," *Voprosy ekonomiki*, 62, 3:110–120, 1990.

Kostakov, V. G., "Zanyatost': defitsit ili izbytok? (Employment: Shortage or Surplus?)," *Kommunist*, 2:78–79, 1987.

Krasnopivtsev, A., "Sovershenstvovaniye planirovaniya sel'skogo khozyaystva (Improvement of the Planning of Agriculture)," *Ekonomicheskaya gazeta*, 4:19, January 1981.

Kufakov, V., "Sovershenstvovaniye tsenoobrazovaniya v APK (Improvement of Price Formation in the Agroindustrial Complex)," *Ekonomika sel'skogo khozyaystva*, 64, 2:26–32, February 1984.

————, "Sebestoimost' sel'skokhozyaystvennoy produktsii i tsenoobrazovaniye (Cost of Agricultural Output and Price Formation)," *Ekonomika sel'skogo khozyaystva*, 66, 3:59–64, March 1986.

Kurashvili, B. P., "Gosudarstvennoye upravleniye narodnym khozyaystvom: perspektivy razvitiya (State Management of the National Economy: Prospects for Development)," *Sovetskoye gosudarstvo i pravo*, 56, 6:38–48, June 1982.

———, "Kontury vozmozhnoy perestroyki (Limits of a Possible Restructuring)," *Ekonomika i organizatsiya promyshlennogo proizvodstva*, 16, 5:59–79, May 1985.

———, *Ocherk teorii gosudarstvennogo upravleniya (Outline of the Theory of Management by the State)*. Moscow: Nauka, 1987.

Kurenkov, P., and G. Zhuravleva, "Tsena kak faktor sbalansirovaniya sprosa i predlozheniya (Price as a Factor in Balancing Demand and Supply)," *Ekonomicheskiye nauki*, 28, 11:71–76, November 1985.

Kurtzweg, Lauri, "Trends in Soviet Gross National Product," in Joint Economic Committee, U.S. Congress, *Gorbachev's Economic Plans*. Washington, D.C.: U.S. Government Printing Office, 1987.

———, *Estimates of Soviet Gross National Product in 1982 Prices*. Washington, D.C.: U.S. Congress, Joint Economic Committee,1990 (forthcoming).

Kushnirsky, Fyodor, "Methodological Aspects in Building Soviet Price Indices," *Soviet Studies*, 37, 4:505–519, October 1985.

Kuznetsov, Vladimir, "Domestic and Foreign Trade Prices: Their Interconnection in the New Economic Management Conditions," *Foreign Trade*, 69, 7:42–46, July 1988.

Lazutin, V., "Rezervy snizheniya sebestoimosti sel'skokhozyaystvennoy produktsii (Reserves for the Reduction of the Cost of Agricultural Output)," *Planovoye khozyaystvo*, 62, 2:99–106, February 1985.

Levchuk, I., "Share Holding Banks Linked to Tighter Credit Policy," *Pravitel'stvennyy Vestnik*, No. 22, November 1989, p. 8 (translated in *JPRS Report, Soviet Union: Economic Affairs*, December 20, 1989, pp. 8–9).

Levikov, A., "Remeslo (Craft)," *Novyy mir*, 1986, 4:180–199.

Levin, A. I., and A. P. Yarkin, *Ekonomika potrebleniya: Voprosy teorii, upravleniya prognozirovaniya (The Economics of Consumption: Problems of Theory, Administration, and Forecasting)*. Moscow: Nauka, 1984.

Lisichkin, Gennadiy, *Plan i rynok (Plan and Market)*. Moscow: Ekonomika, 1966.

———, "Mify i realnost' (Myths and Reality)," in *Osmyslit' kul't Stalina (Comprehending the Cult of Stalin)*. Moscow: Progress, 1989, pp. 247–283.

———, "Kak zarabatyvayem—tak i zhivem (What We Earn Is How We Live)," *Delovyye lyudi*, February 1990.

Lokshin, R., "Stoimost' i struktura roznichnogo tovarooborota (Value and the Structure of Retail Trade Turnover)," *Voprosy ekonomiki*, 34, 10:81–92, October 1981.

Lopatnikov, L., "Chto naydem, chto poteryayem? (What Will We Gain, What Will We Lose?)," *Literaturnaya gazeta*, January 20, 1988, p. 10.

Lukinov, I., "Tsenovoy paritet (Price Parity)," *Ekonomicheskaya gazeta*, 27:22–23, July 1988.

L'vov, Dmitriy, "Obnovleniye fabrik i rynok (Renewing the Factories and the Market)," *Pravda*, April 5, 1990.

Malakhov, K., "Material'no-tekhnicheskoye obespecheniye narodnogo khozyaystva (Material-Technical Supply of the National Economy)," *Planovoye khozyaystvo*, 10:3–15, October 1989.

Mann, Dawn, "Gorbachev Sworn in as President," *Radio Liberty Report on the USSR*, 2, 12:1–4, March 23, 1990.

Maslyukov, Yuriy D., "O Gosudarstvennom plane ekonomicheskogo i sotsial'nogo razvitiya SSSR na 1989 god i o khode vypolneniya plana v 1988 godu. Doklad kandidata v chleny Politbyuro TsK KPSS, pervogo zamestitielya predsedatelya Soveta Ministrov SSSR, predsedatel'ya Gosplana SSSR deputata Maslyukova Yu. D. (On the State Plan for the Economic and Social Development of the USSR for 1989 and Plan Fulfillment in 1988: A Report by Candidate Member of the Politburo of the CPSU Central Committee, First Deputy Chairman of the USSR Council of Ministers and Chairman of USSR Gosplan, Deputy Yuriy D. Maslyukov)," *Pravda*, October 28, 1988, pp. 2–4.

———, "O novykh podkhodakh i parametrakh proyekta Gosudarstvennogo plana ekonomicheskogo i sotsial'nogo razvitiya SSSR na 1990 god. Vystupleniye Yu. D. Maslyukova na sessii Verkhovnego Soveta SSSR (On New Approaches and Parameters of the Draft State Plan of the Economic and Social Development of the USSR for 1990: A Speech by Yuriy D. Maslyukov at a Session of the USSR Supreme Soviet)," *Sotsialisticheskaya industriya*, August 5, 1989, pp. 1, 3.

"Maslyukov Addresses Supreme Soviet," Moscow Television Service, August 3, 1989 (translated in FBIS, *Daily Report: Soviet Union*, August 4, 1989, pp. 38–45).

Materialy Plenuma Tsentral'nogo Komiteta KPSS, 23 aprelya 1985 godu (Materials of the Plenum of the Central Committee of the CPSU, April 23, 1985). Moscow, 1985.

Materialy XXVII s"yezda Kommunisticheskoy Partii Sovetskogo Soyuza (Materials of the 27th Congress of the Communist Party of the Soviet Union). Moscow, 1986.

Matosich, Andrew J., and Bonnie K. Matosich, "Machine Building: *Perestroyka*'s Sputtering Engine," *Soviet Economy*, 4, 2:144–176, April–June 1988.

Mayorets, A. I., "Otrasl' na puti k polnomu khozraschetu (Branch on the Road to Full Economic Accountability)," *Ekonomicheskaya gazeta*, 50:4, December 1988.

McKinnon, Ronald I., "The Order of Liberalization for Opening the Soviet Economy." Report prepared for the International Task Force on Foreign Economic Relations, New York, April 1989a.

———, "Stabilizing the Ruble." Paper prepared for the Atlanta meetings of the American Economic Association, December 28, 1989b, pp. 1–20.

Medvedev, Zh., "Innovation and Conservatism in the New Soviet Leadership (interview)," *New Left Review*, May–June 1986, pp. 5–27.

Metodicheskiye ukazaniya k razrabotke gosudarstvennykh planov ekonomicheskogo i sotsial'nogo razvitiya SSSR (Methodological Guidelines for the Development of Government Plans for Economic and Social Development of the USSR). Moscow: Ekonomika, 1980.

"Metodika opredeleniya optovykh tsen i normativov chistoy produktsii na novyye mashiny, oborudovaniya i pribory proizvodstvenno-tekhnicheskogo naznacheniya (Method of Establishing Wholesale Prices and Normatives of Net Output for New Machinery, Equipment, and Instruments for Use in Production)," *Ekonomicheskaya gazeta*, 6:11–14, February 1983.

"Metodika opredeleniya optovykh tsen na produktsiyu proizvodstvenno-tekhnicheskogo naznacheniya syr'yevykh otrasley tyazheloy promyshlennosti (Methodology for Determination of Wholesale Prices on Output of Producer Goods of the Raw Material Branches of Heavy Industry)," *Ekonomicheskaya gazeta*, 3:19, January 1988.

Milner, Boris Z., "Problemy perekhoda k novym formam organizatsii upravleniya (Problems of Transition to New Forms of Management Organization)," *Voprosy ekonomiki,* 61, 10:3–14, 1989.

Ministerstvo finansov SSSR, *Byudzhetnoye upravleniye, Gosudarstvennyy byudzhet SSSR i byudzhety soyuznykh respublik (The State Budget of the USSR and the Budgets of Union Republics).* Moscow: Finansy i statistika, various years.

Ministerstvo vneshney torgovli (Ministry of Foreign Trade), *Vneshnyaya torgovlya SSSR v ___ . Statisticheskiy sbornik (Foreign Trade of the USSR in ___ . Statistical Compendium).* Moscow: Finansy i statistika, annual.

Moskaleva, N. I., "Tsena uslugi, ee funktsii i puti sovershenstvovaniya (The Price of Services: Its Functions and Ways of Improving It)," *Finansy SSSR,* 57, 4:39–43, April 1982.

Mostovshchikov, S., "Tenevaya ekonomika (Shadow Economy)," *Trud,* August 12, 1988, p. 4.

"Nachalo kontsa monopolii (The Beginning of the End of the Monopoly)," *Sotsialisticheskaya industriya,* July 8, 1989, p. 1.

Narodnoye khozyaystvo SSSR (National Economy of the USSR). Moscow: Finansy i statistika, various years.

Narodnoye khozyaystvo SSSR v 1982 g.: Statisticheskiy yezhegodnik (National Economy of the USSR in 1982: A Statistical Yearbook). Moscow: Finansy i statistika, 1983.

Narodnoye khozyaystvo SSSR v 1984 g.: Statisticheskiy yezhegodnik (National Economy of the USSR in 1984: A Statistical Yearbook). Moscow: Finansy i statistika, 1985.

Narodnoye khozyaystvo SSSR v 1985 godu.: Statisticheskiy yezhegodnik (National Economy of the USSR in 1985: A Statistical Yearbook). Moscow: Finansy i statistika, 1986.

Narodnoye khozyaystvo SSSR za 70 let: yubileynyy statisticheskiy yezhegodnik (National Economy of the USSR over 70 Years: Anniversary Statistical Yearbook). Moscow: Finansy i statistika, 1987.

Narodnoye khozyaystvo SSSR v 1987 g.: Statisticheskiy yezhegodnik (National Economy of the USSR in 1987: A Statistical Yearbook). Moscow: Finansy i statistika, 1988.

Narodnoye khozyaystvo SSSR v 1988 g.: Statisticheskiy yezhegodnik (National Economy of the USSR in 1988: A Statistical Yearbook). Moscow: Finansy i statistika, 1989.

Narodnoye khozyaystvo SSSR v 1989 g.: Statisticheskiy yezhegodnik (National Economy of the USSR in 1989: A Statistical Yearbook). Moscow: Finansy i statistika, 1990.

Nazariyan, Sh. G., *Sebestoimost' i effektivnost' proizvodstva v pishchevoy promyshlennosti (Cost and Effectiveness of Production in the Food Industry).* Moscow: Agropromizdat, 1986.

Nemchinov, V. P., *Kachestvo, effektivnost', tsena topliva (The Quality, Effectiveness, and Price of Fuel).* Moscow: Nedra, 1983.

Nikiforov, Lev V., "Arendnyye otnosheniya: problemy stanovleniya (On Leaseholding: Problems of Formation)," *Voprosy ekonomiki,* 61, 11:3–16, 1989.

Nikitin, D., and V. Kabankov, "Tseny i kachestvo tovarov narodnogo potrebleniya (Prices and the Quality of Consumer Goods)," *Planovoye khozyaystvo,* 61, 8:86–91, August 1984.

"1987 Panel on the Soviet Economic Outlook: Perceptions on a Confusing Set of Statistics," *Soviet Economy,* 3, 1:3–39, January–March 1987.

Noren, James, "The New Look at Soviet Statistics: Implications for CIA Measures of the USSR's Economic Growth," in *The Impact of Gorbachev's Economic Policies on Soviet Economic Statistics*. CIA, Directorate of Intelligence, SOV 88-10049, July 1988, pp. 69–81.

————, "The Soviet Economic Crisis: Another Perspective," *Soviet Economy*. 6, 1:3–55, January–March 1990.

Nove, Alec, *An Economic History of the USSR*. Harmondwood, England: Pelican, 1972.

————, " 'Radical Reform', Problems and Prospects," *Soviet Studies*, 39, 3:452–467, July 1987.

"The Novosibirsk Report," *Survey*, 28, 1:88–108, 1983.

"Novyye ofitsial'nyye materialy (New Official Materials)," *Ekonomicheskaya gazeta*, 44:17, 1986.

Nuti, Domenico Mario, "Hidden and Repressed Inflation in Soviet-Type Economies: Definitions, Measurements, and Stabilizations." Unpublished manuscript, 1985.

————, "Remonetization and Capital Markets in the Reform of Centrally Planned Economies," Working Paper No. 88/361, European University Institute, Santa Domenico, Italy, 1988.

"O dal'neyshem sovershenstvovanii ekonomicheskogo mekhanizma khozyaystvovaniya v agropromyshlennom komplekse strany (On the Further Improvement of the Economic Mechanism of Management in the Agroindustrial Complex of the Country)," *Pravda*, March 29, 1986, pp. 1–2.

"O Gosudarstvennom plane ekonomicheskogo i sotsial'nogo razvitiya SSSR na 1986 god i vypolnenii plana v 1985 gody (On the State Plan for Economic and Social Development of the USSR in 1986, and the Fulfillment of the Plan for 1985), *Ekonomicheskaya gazeta*, No. 48, November 1985, insert.

"O Gosudarstvennoy komissii Soveta Ministrov SSSR po ekonomicheskoy reforme (On the State Commission of the USSR Council of Ministers on Economic Reform)," *Ekonomicheskaya gazeta*, 31:16–17, July 1989.

O korennoy perestroyke upravleniya ekonomikoy: sbornik dokumentov (On the Radical Restructuring of the Management of the Economy: A Collection of Documents). Moscow: Gospolitizdat, 1987.

O merakh po ozdorovleniyu ekonomiki, etapakh ekonomicheskoy reformy i printsipyal'nykh podkhodakh k razrabotke trinadtsatogo pyatiletnogo plana (On Measures for Economic Recovery, Stages of the Economic Reform, and Fundamental Approaches to the Compilation of the Thirteenth Five-Year Plan). Moscow, November 29, 1989.

"O merakh po demonopolizatsii narodnogo khozyaystva (On Measures for the Demonopolization of the Economy)," *Ekonomika i zhizn'*, 38, supplement (pp. 2–3), 1990.

"O nalogooblozhenii fonda oplaty truda gosudarstvennykh predpriyatiy (ob'yedineniy) (On Taxation of the Wage Fund of the State Enterprise (Association))," *Izvestiya*, August 11, 1989, p. 1.

"O plane podgotovki zakonodatel'nykh aktov SSSR, postanovleniya Pravitel'stva SSSR po sovershenstvovaniyu zakonodatel'stva SSSR na 1986–1990 gody (Concerning a Plan for the Preparation of Legislative Acts of the USSR and Decrees of the Government of the USSR on the Improvement of Legislation for 1986–1990)," *Vedo-*

mosti Verkhovnogo Soveta Soyuza Sovetskikh Sotsialisticheskikh Respublik, 37:730–736, September 10, 1986.

"O proyekte zakona SSSR o gosudarstvennom banke SSSR (Draft of the USSR Law on the State Bank)," *Dengi i kredit*, 3:3–12, March 1990.

"O shirokom rasprostranenii novykh metodov khozyaystvovaniya usilenii ikh vozdeystviya na uskoreniye nauchno-tekhnicheskogo progressa (Concerning the Broad Expansion of New Methods of Economic Management and Strengthening Their Influence in Accelerating Scientific-Technical Progress)," *Ekonomicheskaya gazeta*, 32:11–14, August 1985.

"O variantnosti i al'ternativnosti sotsial'no-ekonomicheskogo razvitiya (On Variation and Alternatives of Social and Economic Development)," *Voprosy ekonomiki*, 62, 3:3–17, 1990

"O vvedenii kommercheskogo kursa rublya k inostrannym valyutam i merakh po sozdaniyu obshchesoyuznogo valyutnogo rynka (On the Introduction of a Commercial Exchange Rate for the Ruble and Measures to Create an All-Union Currency Market)," *Izvestiya*, October 26, 1990, p. 1.

"Ob inostrannykh investitsiyakh v SSSR (On Foreign Investment in the USSR (presidential decree)," *Izvestiya*, October 26, 1990, p. 1.

"Ob osnovnykh napravleniyakh vnutrenney i vneshney politiki SSSR (On the Basic Directions of Domestic and Foreign Policy of the USSR)," *Pravda*, June 25, 1989, pp. 1, 2.

"Ob uluchshenii planirovaniya, ekonomicheskogo stimulirovaniya i sovershenstvovanii upravleniya proizvodstvom tovarov narodnogo potrebleniya v legkoy promyshlennosti (On Better Planning, Economic Incentives, and Improvement of Administration of Production of Consumer Goods in Light Industry)," *Ekonomicheskaya gazeta*, 2:2, 15, 16, January 1986.

"Obmenyayemsya myslyami pered S"yezdom . . . (Exchanging Ideas Before the Congress . . .)," *Sotsialisticheskaya industriya*, May 20, 1989, p. 2.

OECD, *Social Expenditure 1960–1990: Problems of Growth and Control*. Paris: OECD Social Policy Studies,1985.

Ofer, Gur, "Soviet Economic Growth: 1928–1985," *Journal of Economic Literature*, 25, 4:1767–1833, December 1987.

———, "The Welfare State in Soviet Economic Reform: Also Converging?" Paper presented at the Allied Social Science Associations Annual Meeting, December 28–30, 1989a, Atlanta, Georgia, pp. 1–3.

———, "Budget Deficit, Market Disequilibrium and Soviet Economic Reforms," *Soviet Economy*, 5, 2:107, April–June 1989b.

———, "Fiscal and Monetary Aspects of Soviet Economic Reform." Paper presented at the IX Latin America Meeting of the Econometric Society, Santiago, Chile, August 1–3, 1989c.

———, "Issues in the Macroeconomics of Soviet Reforms," 1990.

Ofer, Gur, and Joyce Pickersgill, "Soviet Household Saving: A Cross-Section Study of Soviet Emigrant Families," *Quarterly Journal of Economics*, 95, 1:121–145, August 1980.

Ofer, Gur, and Aaron Vinokur, "The Distributive Effects of the Social Consumption Fund in the Soviet Union," in Gail W. Lapidus and Guy E. Swanson, eds., *State* *and Welfare USA/USSR: Contemporary Policy and Practice.* Berkeley, Calif.: Institute of International Studies, University of California, Berkeley, 1988.

Okhapkin, A., and M. Ratgauz, "O sovershenstvovanii tsenovogo mekhanizma sel'skogo khozyaystva (On the Improvement of the Price Mechanism of Agriculture)," *Ekonomika sel'skogo khozyaystva,* 65, 7:34–38, July 1985.

"On Measures to Eliminate Shortcomings in the Practice of Pricing," *Pravda,* February 4, 1989 (translated in FBIS, *Daily Report: Soviet Union,* February 6, 1989, pp. 86–89).

"On Measures for State Regulation of Foreign Economic Relations," Decree of the USSR Council of Ministers, March 7, 1989, No. 203.

"Organizatsiya vypolneniya godovogo plana (Organization of the Fulfillment of the Annual Plan)," *Planovoye khozyaystvo,* 2:3–18, February 1989.

Orlov, A., and N. Fonareva, "Obespecheniye sootvetsviya sprosa i predlozheniya tovarov (Securing Correspondence of Demand and Supply for Goods)," *Planovoye khozyaystvo,* 61, 1:34–40, January 1984.

Orlov, Ya., "Rol' promyshlennosti i torgovli v udovletvorenii sprosa naseleniya (The Role of Industry and Trade in the Satisfaction of the Demand of the Population)," *Voprosy ekonomiki,* 38, 6:127–136, June 1985.

Osipenko, O. V., "K analizu fenomena 'Chernogo rynka' (Toward an Analysis of the Black Market Phenomenon)," *Ekonomicheskiye nauki,* No. 8, 1990, pp. 71–80.

"Osnovnyye napravleniya ekonomicheskogo i sotsial'nogo razvitiya SSSR na 1986–1990 gody i na period do 2000 goda" (Basic Guidelines for the Economic and Social Development of the USSR for 1986–1990 and for the Period to 2000), *Sotsialisticheskaya industriya,* November 9, 1985, 1–6.

"Osnovnyye polozheniya o primeneniyu skidok s optovykh tsen na produktsiyu podlezhashchiyu snyatyu s proizvodstva (Basic Provisions for the Application of Discounts from Wholesale Prices on Output Subject to Removal from Production)," *Ekonomicheskaya gazeta,* 3:19, January 1986.

"Osnovnyye polozheniya korennoy perestroyki upravleniya ekonomikoy (Basic Provisions for the Radical Restructuring of Economic Management)," *Pravda,* June 27, 1987.

"Osnovnyye polozheniya korennoy perestroyki upravleniya ekonomikoy (Basic Provisions for the Radical Restructuring of Economic Management)," *Ekonomicheskaya gazeta,* 27:11–14, July 1987.

"Osnovy zakonodatel'stva SSSR i soyuznykh respublik ob arende (Principles of Legislation of the USSR and Union Republics on Leasing)," *Izvestiya,* December 1, 1989, p. 3.

"Osnovy zakonodtel'stva SSSR i soyuznykh respublik o zemle (Principles of Legislation of the USSR and Union Republics on Land)," *Ekonomika i zhizn',* 11:17–20, 1990.

Otsason, Rein, and I. Raig. "Ne 'del'tsy', a pomoshchniki (Not 'Wheelers Dealers,' but Helpers)," *Pravda,* September 5, 1987.

"Panel on Growth and Technology in *Perestroyka,*" *Soviet Economy,* 3, 4:332–352, October–December 1987.

Parkhomovskiy E., "Tovary, tseny, my . . . (Goods, Prices, Us . . .)," *Izvestiya,* November 19, 1987, p. 2.

Pavlov, V., "Vazhnaya sostavnaya chast' perestroyki (An Important Component of Restructuring)," *Kommunist,* 64, 13:14–26, September 1987.

"Pavlov's 25 September Report on State Budget Published," *Izvestiya*, September 27, 1989, pp. 4–6 (translated in FBIS, *Daily Report: Soviet Union*, September 28, 1989, pp. 37–49).

PER. *PlanEcon Report*, weekly.

Perekhod k rynku. Chast' 1. Kontseptsiya i programma (Transition to the Market. Part 1. Concept and Program). Moscow: Arkhangel'skoye, 1990a.

Perekhod k rynku. Chast' 2. Proyekty zakonodatel'nykh aktov (Transition to the Market. Part 2. Drafts of Legislation). Moscow: Arkhangel'skoye, 1990b.

PETFR-SU. *PlanEcon Trade and Finance Review: Soviet Union*, yearly.

Petrakov, Nikolay Ya., "Prospects for Change in the Systems of Price Formation, Finance and Credit in the USSR," *Soviet Economy*, 3, 2:135–144, April–June 1987a.

————, "Ukrepleniye denezhnogo obrashcheniya i strategiya uskoreniya (The Strengthening of Money Circulation and the Strategy of Acceleration)," *Voprosy ekonomiki*, 59, 8:3–11, August 1987b.

————, "Zolotoy chervonets vchera i zavtra (The Gold Ruble Yesterday and Today)," *Novyy mir*, 63, 8:205–221, 1987c.

Petrakov, Nikolay Ya., and D. L'vov, "Kachestvo tempov (The Quality of Growth Rates)," *Ekonomicheskaya gazeta,* 3:14, January 1987.

Petrakov, Nikolay Ya., and Ye. Yasin, "Ekonomicheskiye metody upravleniya (Economic Management Methods)," *Ekonomicheskaya gazeta*, 47:12, November 1986.

Pickersgill, Joyce, "Recent Evidence on Soviet Households' Saving Behavior," *Review of Economics and Statistics*, 62, 11:628–633, November 1980.

Pinsker, Boris, and Larisa Piyasheva, "Sobstvemost' i svoboda (Ownership and Freedom)," *Novyy mir*, 1989, 11:184–199.

Pinzenik, V. M., "Usileniye stimuliruyushchey roli limitnykh tsen v povyshenii effektivnosti novoy tekhniki (Strengthening the Incentive Role of Limit Prices in Raising the Effectiveness of New Equipment)," *Vestnik Moskovskogo universiteta, seriya 6:ekonomika*, 41, 2:23–28, February 1986.

Pipes, Richard, *U.S.-Soviet Relations in the Era of Detente*. Boulder, Col.: Westview Press, 1981.

Piskotin, M. I., *Sotsializm i gosudarstvennoye upravleniye (Socialism and State Management)*. Moscow: Nauka, 1984.

Planirovaniye tsen (The Planning of Prices), V. E. Esipov, ed. Moscow: Vysshaya shkola, 1982.

"Polozheniye o poryadke ustanovleniya dogovornykh optovykh tsen na produktsiyu proizvodstvenno-tekhnicheskogo naznacheniya i uslugi proizvodstvennogo kharaktera (Statute on the Procedure for Establishment by Enterprises of Contract Wholesale Prices on Output of Producer Goods and Producer Services)," *Ekonomicheskaya gazeta*, 5:23, January 1988.

Popkova, L., "Gde pyshneye pirogi (Where the Pies Are More Sumptuous)," *Novyy mir*, 63, 5:239–241, 1987.

Popov, Gavriil Kh., *Effektivnoye upravleniye (Effective Management)*. Moscow: Ekonomika, 1985a.

————, *Upravleniye ekonomikoy—ekonomicheskiye metody (Economic Methods for the Management of the Econmy)*. Moscow: Ekonomika, 1985b.

————, "S tochki zreniya ekonomista (From the Viewpoint of an Economist)," *Nauka i zhizn'*, 4:54–65, 1987.

Popov, Yu. D., "Kachestvo sistemy kachestva (The Quality of the System of Quality)," *Ekonomika i organizatsiya promyshlennogo proizvodstva,* 7:70–83, 1986.

Press-vypusk (Press Release). Moscow: Goskomstat (various issues).

Primakov, Yevgeniy, Paper presented at the Brookings Institution, October 27, 1989.

"Primernyy ustav kooperativa po zagotovke i pererabotke vtorichnogo syr'ya pri territorial'nykh organakh Gossnaba SSSR (Model Charter of a Cooperative for Processing Secondary Raw Materials Under Territorial Organs of Gossnab, USSR)," *Ekonomicheskaya gazeta,* 43:15–16, October 1986.

"Priotitet—novym pokoleniyam tekhniki (Priority to New Generations of Equipment)," *Ekonomicheskaya gazeta,* 3:19, January 1986.

Problemy mira i sotsializma, No. 7, July 1987.

"Programma Kommunisticheskoy partii Sovetskogo Soyuza ("Novaya" redaktsiya) (Program of the Communist Party of the Soviet Union [New Edition])," *Sotsialisticheskaya industriya,* October 26, 1985, pp. 1–6.

Rahr, Alexander, "Gvishiani Leaves Gosplan," *Radio Liberty Research,* RL 455/86, December 5, 1986.

———, "From Politburo to Presidential Council," *Radio Liberty Report on the USSR,* 2, 22:1–5, June 1, 1990.

Rakitskiy, Boris, "Puti k konsolodatsii: uchast' nomenklatury i lichnyye sud'by byurokratov (The Roads to Consolidation: The Lot of the Nomenklatura and the Personal Destinies of Bureaucrats," *Voprosy ekonomiki,* 61, 12:56–68, 1989.

Rayevskiy, V. A., "Povysit' deystvennost' ekonomicheskikh rychagov proizvodstva tovarov narodnogo potrebleniya (Raise the Influence of Economic Levers on the Production of Consumer Goods)," *Finansy S.S.S.R.,* 60, 6:3–9, June 1986.

"Reflections on Technology in Postwar Reconstruction," *Soviet Economy,* 3, 4:353–359, October–December 1987.

"Resursy dlya tekhnicheskogo perevooruzheniya (Resources for Technical Reequipment)," *Ekonomicheskaya gazeta,* 18:23, April 1986.

Rostowski, S., and P. Auerbach, "Storming Cycles and Economic Systems," *Journal of Comparative Economics,* 10:293–312, September 1986.

Roze, V., "Spros i potrebleniye uslug passazhirskogo transporta (Demand and Consumption of Passenger Transport Services)," *Voprosy ekonomiki,* 38, 8:131–135, August 1985.

Rozenova, L., "Rol' tseny v upravlenii tekhnicheskim progressom (The Role of Price in the Administration of Technical Progress)," *Voprosy ekonomiki,* 38, 5:113–123, May 1985a.

———, *Tsena i novaya tekhnika (Price and New Equipment).* Moscow: Ekonomika, 1985b.

———, "Tsena i kachestvo tekhniki (Price and the Quality of Equipment)," *Voprosy ekonomiki,* 39, 4:28–37, April 1986.

———, "Nauchno-tekhnicheskiy progress i tsenoobrazovaniye (Scientific-Technical Progress and Price Formation)," *Planovoye khozyaystvo,* 65, 9:64–72, September 1988.

Rumer, Boris, "Some Investment Patterns Engendered by the Řenovation of Soviet Industry," *Soviet Studies,* 36, 2:257–266, April 1984.

————, "The 'Abalkinization' of Soviet Economic Reform," *Problems of Communism*, 39, 1:74–82, 1990.

Rutgayzer, V., "On a Paying Basis or Free of Charge?" *Pravda*, December 19, 1985, p. 3 (transl. in *Current Digest of the Soviet Press*, 37, 51:22–23, January 15, 1986).

————, "Kollektivnaya sobstvennost' (Collective Property)," *Ekonomicheskaya gazeta*, 27:4, 6, July 1989.

Rutgayzer, V., Yu. Shevyakhov, and L. Zubova, "Sovershenstvovaniye sistemy planovykh pokazateley dokhodov naseleniya (Improvement of the System of Planned Indicators of the Incomes of the Population)," *Voprosy ekonomiki*, 41, 1:31–41, January 1988.

Rutland, Peter, "Abalkin's Strategy for Soviet Economic Reform," *Radio Liberty Report on the USSR*, 2, 21:3–6, May 25, 1990.

Ryzhkov, N. I., "O gosudarstvennom plane ekonomicheskogo i sotsial'nogo razvitiya SSSR na 1986–1990 gody (On the State Plan for Economic and Social Development of the USSR for 1986–1990)," *Pravda*, June 19, 1986.

————, Address to Congress of People's Deputies, June 7, 1989, Moscow Television Service, June 7, 1989 (translated in FBIS, *Daily Report, Supplement: USSR*, June 8, 1989a, pp. 15–30).

————, Speech to Supreme Soviet, December 13, 1989, *Stroitel'naya gazeta*, December 14, 1989b, pp. 1–3.

Sagers, Matthew J., and Milford B. Green, "The Freight Rate Structure of Soviet Railroads," *Economic Geography*, 61, 4:305–322, October 1985.

Salimzhanov, I., and V. N. Alpeyev, "Problemy vzaimodeystviya optovykh tsen i finansov v novykh usloviyakh (Problems of Interaction of Wholesale Prices and Finances in New Conditions)," *Finansy S.S.S.R.*, 61, 7:19–26, July 1986.

Sapilov, E., "Otsenka kachestva produktsii (Evaluation of Product Quality)," *Planovoye khozyaystvo*, 62, 8:49–55, August 1985.

Schmemann, Serge, "Soviet Prices Up on Consumer Items," *New York Times*, February 10, 1983, p. 4.

Schroeder, Gertrude E., "Soviet Economic Reforms: A Study in Contradictions," *Soviet Studies*, 20, 1:1–21, July 1968.

————. "The 1966–67 Soviet Industrial Price Reform: A Study in Complications," *Soviet Studies*, 20, 4:462–477, April 1969.

————, "Soviet Economic Reform at an Impasse," *Problems of Communism*, 20, 41:36–46, July–August 1971.

————, "The Soviet Economy on a Treadmill of Reforms," in U.S. Congress, Joint Economic Committee, *Soviet Economy in a Time of Change*, Vol. 1. Washington, D.C.: U.S. Government Printing Office, 1979, pp. 312–240.

————, "Soviet Economic Reform Decrees: More Steps on the Treadmill," in U.S. Congress, Joint Economic Committee, *Soviet Economy in the 1980s: Problems and Prospects*, Part I. Washington, D.C.: U.S. Government Printing Office, 1982, pp. 65–88.

————, "Gorbachev: 'Radically' Implementing Brezhnev's Reforms," *Soviet Economy*, 2, 4:289–301, October–December 1986.

————, "Anatomy of Gorbachev's Economic Reform," *Soviet Economy*, 3, 3:219–241, July–September 1987.

————, "Consumer Malaise in the Soviet Union: Perestroika's Achilles' Heel?" *PlanEcon Report*, 4, 11:1–12, March 10, 1988.

————, "Soviet Economic Reform: From Resurgence to Retrenchment," *The Russian Review*, 48, 3:305–319, July 1989.

————, " 'Crisis' in the Consumer Sector: A Comment," *Soviet Economy*, 6, 1:56–64, January–March 1990.

————, "*Perestroyka* in the Aftermath of 1990," *Soviet Economy*, 7, 1:3–13, January–March 1991.

Schroeder, Gertrude E., and Elizabeth M. Denton, "An Index of Consumption in the USSR," in U.S. Congress, Joint Economic Committee, *USSR: Measures of Soviet Economic Growth and Development.* Washington, D.C.: U.S. Government Printing Office, 1982, pp. 317–401.

Seleznev, A., "Sobstvennost': gosudarstvennaya i kooperativnaya (Property: State and Cooperative)," *Ekonomicheskaya gazeta*, 6:14, February 1989.

Selyunin, Vasiliy, "Posledniy shans (The Last Chance)," *Literaturnaya gazeta*, 18:9, May 2, 1990.

Selyunin, Vasiliy, and Grigoriy Khanin, "Lukavaya tsifra (The Sly Number)," *Novyy mir*, 63, 2:181–201, February 1987.

Semenov, V. N., "Finansovo-kreditnyy mekhanizm agropromyshlennogo kompleksa (The Financial-Credit Mechanism of the Agroindustrial Complex)," *Finansy SSSR*, 58, 7:8–19, July 1983.

————, "Ukrepleniye ekonomiki kolkhozov i sovkhozov (Strengthening the Economy of Collective and State Farms)," *Finansy SSSR*, 60, 9:3–11, September 1985.

————, "Finansovyy mekhanizm APK i puti yego sovershenstvovaniya (The Financial Mechanism of the Agroindustrial Complex and Ways of Improving It)," *Voprosy ekonomiki*, 39, 8:63–72, August 1986a.

————, "Sovershenstvovaniye finansovo-kreditnykh otnosheniy v APK (Improvement of Financial-Credit Relations in the Agroindustrial Complex)," *Planirovaniye i uchet v sel'skokhozyaystvennykh predpriyatiyakh*, 13, 7:1–7, July 1986b.

Senchagov, V. K., "Relative Proportions of Tax Revenues Examined," *Pravitel'stvennyy Vestnik*, 22:4–5, November 1989 (translated in *JPRS Report, Soviet Union: Economic Affairs*, December 20, 1989, pp. 4–8).

Shapkina, G., "Khozyaystvennyye dogovory na dvenadtsatuyu pyatiletku (Economic Contracts in the Twelfth Five-Year Plan)," *Khozyaystvo i pravo*, 11:19, 1985.

Shastiko, V., "Rasshireniye funktsii khozrascheta (Widening the Functions of Economic Accountability)," *Ekonomicheskaya gazeta*, 42:20, September 1986.

Shatalin, Stanislav S., "Sotsial'noye razvitiye i ekonomicheskiy rost (Social Development and Economic Growth)," *Kommunist*, 63, 14:60–70, 1986.

————, "Khochu priznat' svoyu oshibku (I Want to Acknowledge My Own Mistake)," *Sotsialisticheskaya industriya*, October 30, 1988, p. 2.

Sheehy, Ann, "The State of the Multinational Union," *Report on the USSR* (RFE/RL Research Institute), 3, 1:16–19, January 4, 1991.

Shmarov, A., and N. Kirichenko, "Inflyatsiya, reforma rozhnichnykh tsen; narodnoye blago sostoyaniya (Inflation, Reform of Retail Prices, and National Well-Being)," *Voprosy ekonomiki*, 8:25–36, August 1989.

————, "Inflyatsiya v potrebitel'skoy sfere i sotsial'naya naprazhennost' (Inflation in the Consumer Sphere and Social Tension)," *Voprosy ekonomiki*, 1:36–45, January 1990.

Shmelev, Nikolay P., "Avansy i dolgi (Advances and Debts)," *Novyy mir*, 63, 6:142–158, 1987.

———, "Novyye trevogi (New Alarms)," *Novyy mir*, 64, 4:160–175, 1988a.

———, "Rethinking Price Reform in the USSR," *Soviet Economy*, 4, 4:319–327, October–December 1988b.

———, "Interconnection Between World Markets and Planned Economies." Report prepared for roundtable conference on "Market Forces in Planned Economies," Moscow, March 28–30, 1989a.

———, Address to Congress of People's Deputies, June 8, 1989, *Pravda*, June 9, 1989b (translated in FBIS, *Daily Report, Supplement: USSR*, June 9, 1989b, pp. 26–29).

Shmelev, Nikolay P., and Vladimir M. Popov, *The Turning Point*. New York and London: Doubleday, 1989.

Shprygin, V. I., "Kak sozdat' protivozatratnyy bar'yer (How to Create a Cost-Containment Barrier)," *Ekonomicheskaya gazeta*, 32:9, July 1986.

Simakov, Anatoliy, "Konkurentsiya ili sorevnovaniye ([Antagonist] Competition or [Emulative] Competition)," *Sotsialisticheskaya industriya*, July 16, 1988, p. 3.

Simonyan, Rair R., "Korporatsiya—ot igolki do rakety (The Corporation—From Needle to Rocket)," *Sotsialisticheskaya industriya*, January 8, 1988, p. 3.

Sitaryan, S. A., "Kontseptsiya uskoreniya—politiko-ekonomicheskiye aspekty (The Concept of Acceleration—Political-Economic Aspects)," *Kommunist*, 64, 7:13–24, May 1987.

Smirnitskiy, Ye. K., *Ekonomicheskiye pokazateli promyshlennosti (Economic Indicators of Industry)*. Moscow: Ekonomika, 1980.

———, *Odinatsataya pyatiletka (The Eleventh Five-Year Plan)*. Moscow: Politizdat, 1982.

———, *Dvenadtsataya pyatiletka: slovar'-spravochnik, 1986–1990 (The Twelfth Five-Year Plan: A Handbook, 1986–1990)*. Moscow: Politizdat, 1986.

"Snabzheniya—gibkost', ekonomichnost', ritm (For Supply—Flexibility, Economy, Regularity)," *Ekonomicheskaya gazeta*, 17:6, 1986.

Sobraniye postanovleniy pravitel'stva SSSR.

———, No. 25, 1985.

———, No. 18, 1986a, pp. 305–308.

———, No. 27, 1986b.

———, No. 25, 1986c, pp. 435–444.

———, No. 33, 1986d.

———, No. 34, 1986e.

———, No. 36, 1986f.

———, No. 10, 1987a.

———, No. 11, 1987b.

———, No. 15, 1987c.

———, No. 26, 1987d.

———, No. 7, 1989a, Article 19.

———, No. 18, 1989b, Article 59.

————, 1989c, Articles 103 and 108.

Solodkov, M. V., ed., *Material' no-tekhnicheskoye snabzheniye v usloviyakh intensifikatsii proizvodstva (Material-Technical Supply Under Conditions of Intensified Production).* Moscow: Ekonomika, 1986.

Sorokin, D., "Perestroyka otnosheniy sobstvennosti: Sotsialisticheskiy vybor (Restructuring Property Relations: The Socialist Choice)," *Ekonomicheskaya gazeta*, 52:15, December 1988.

Sotsialisticheskiy trud, No. 2, 1987a.

————, No. 3, 1987b.

"Soviet Military Budget: $128 Billion Bombshell," *New York Times*, May 31, 1989.

"Soviets Boost Prices on Some Consumer Goods," *Wall Street Journal*, February 10, 1983, p. 30.

Spravochnik po tsenoobrazovaniyu (Handbook for Price Formation). Moscow: Ekonomika, 1985.

SSSR v tsifrakh v 1988 godu (USSR in Figures in 1988). Moscow: Finansy i statistika, 1989.

SSSR v tsifrakh v 1989 godu (USSR in Figures in 1989). Moscow: Finansy i statistika, 1990.

"State Bank Chairman Denies Rumors of Monetary Reform," U.S. Foreign Broadcast Information Service, *Soviet Union*, February 28, 1986, S1.

Statisticheskiy press-byulleten' (Statistical Press Bulletin). Moscow: Goskomstat (various issues).

Stepanenko, V., "Novyye tarify na perevozku gruzov (New Freight Rates)," *Ekonomicheskaya gazeta*, 50:17, December 1988.

Strelyanyy, Anatoliy, "Rayonnyye budni (Days in the Countryside)," *Novyy mir'*, 1986, 12:231–241.

Stuchka, P., *Kurs sovetskogo grazhdanskogo prava* (Course in Soviet Civil Law). Moscow: Yuridcheskaya Literatura, 1931.

"Supporters and Opponents of *Perestroyka*: The Second Joint *Soviet Economy* Roundtable," *Soviet Economy*, 4, 4:275–318, October–December 1988.

Sutela, Pekka, *Socialism, Planning and Optimality. A Study in Soviet Economic Thought.* Helsinki: The Finnish Society of Sciences and Letters, 1984.

Tardos, Marton, "The Hungarian Banking Reform." Report prepared for roundtable conference on "Market Forces in Planned Economies," Moscow, March 28–30, 1989.

Tedstrom, John, "New Draft Law on Income Taxes," *Radio Liberty Report on the USSR*, 1:8–10, May 26, 1989.

Teague, Elizabeth, "Philosophy Journal Under Fire for Unorthodox Views," *Radio Liberty Research*, RL 436/84, November 15, 1984a.

————, "Further Polemics over Economic Reform," *Radio Liberty Research*, RL 437/84, November 16, 1984b.

————, "The Powers of the Soviet Presidency," *Radio Liberty Report on the USSR*, 2, 12:4–7, March 23, 1990.

Telen', L., "Kakim byt' sorevnovaniyu? (What Kind of Competition?)," *Sotsialisticheskaya industriya*, August 17, 1988, p. 4.

Tenson, Andreas, "More Leeway for the Private Sector?" *Radio Liberty Research,* RL 16/83, January 10, 1983.

"The Aftermath of the 19th Conference of the CPSU: A *Soviet Economy* Roundtable," *Soviet Economy,* 4, 3:181–222, July–September 1988.

"The 19th Conference of the CPSU: A *Soviet Economy* Roundtable," *Soviet Economy,* 4, 2:103–136, April–June 1988.

"The Novosibirsk Report," *Survey,* 28, 1:88–108, 1983.

Torgovlya SSSR: Statisticheskiy sbornik (Trade in the USSR: A Statistical Handbook). Moscow: Goskomstat, 1989.

Treml, Vladimir G., *Agricultural Subsidies in the Soviet Union.* Washington, D.C.: U.S. Department of Commerce, 1978.

―――, "The Inferior Quality of Soviet Machinery as Reflected in Export Prices," *Journal of Comparative Economics,* 5, 2:200–221, June 1981.

―――, "Subsidies in Soviet Agriculture: Record and Prospects," in U.S. Congress, Joint Economic Committee, *Soviet Economy in the 1980s: Problems and Prospects.* Washington, D.C.: U.S. Government Printing Office, 1983, Part 2, pp. 171–185.

―――, "The Most Recent Input-Output Table: A Milestone in Soviet Statistics," *Soviet Economy,* 5, 4:341–359, October–December 1989.

Tretyakova, Albina, "Sources of Investment Financing in the USSR," *CIR Research Note,* Center for International Research, U.S. Census Bureau, 1986.

Trotsenko, I., "Khozyaystvennyy mekhanizm knigoizdaniya" (The Economic Mechanism of Book Publishing)," *Voprosy ekonomiki,* 39, 8:82–91, August 1986.

Tsena v khozyaystvennom mekhanizme (Price in the Economic Mechanism), N. T. Glushkov and A. A. Deryabin, eds. Moscow: Nauka, 1983.

Tseny i tsenoobrazovaniye (Prices and Price Formation), A. A. Deryabin, ed. Moscow: Finansy i statistika, 1985.

Tsipko, Aleksandr, "Istoki Stalinizma (Sources of Stalinism)," *Nauka i zhizn',* Nos. 11 and 12, 1988; Nos. 1 and 2, 1989.

Tsypkin, Mikhail, "The Committee for Defense and State Security of the USSR Supreme Soviet," *Radio Liberty Report on the USSR,* 2, 19:8–11, May 11, 1990.

Ulanovskiy, V., "Razumnoye potrebleniye material'no-bytovykh uslug (Reasonable Consumption of Material Everyday Services)," *Voprosy ekonomiki,* 39, 7:85–95, July 1986.

U.S. Congress, Joint Economic Committee, *USSR: Measures of Economic Growth and Development, 1950–80.* Washington, D.C.: U.S. Government Printing Office, 1982.

U.S. Department of Agriculture, Economic Research Service, *USSR: Agriculture and Trade Report,* RS-89-1, May 1989.

U.S. Department of Commerce, Bureau of Economic Analysis, *Survey of Current Business,* 68, July 1988.

U.S. Department of Commerce, Bureau of the Census, *Statistical Abstract of the United States, 1989.* Washington, D.C.: U.S. Government Printing Office, January 1989.

"USSR Law on State Enterprise (Association)," *Pravda,* July 1, 1987 (translated in FBIS, *Daily Report: Soviet Union,* July 6, 1987, pp. R1–33.

"V kommissii po sovershenstvovaniyu upravleniya, planirovaniya, i khozyaystvennogo mekhanizma (In the Commission on Improving Management, Planning, and the Economic Mechanism),'' *Ekonomicheskaya gazeta*, 8:10, 1986a.

————, *Ekonomicheskaya gazeta*, 11:31, 1986b.

————, *Ekonomicheskaya gazeta*, 47:17, November 1986c.

"V osnovnom zvene obnovleniya: 'Kruglyy stol' 'Kommunista' na novolipetskom metallurgicheskom kombinate (In the Basic Links of Renewal: A Round Table of *Kommunist* on the Novolipetsk Metallurgical Combine),'' *Kommunist*, 11:14–32, July 1986.

"V presidiume Soveta Ministrov SSSR (In the Presidium of the USSR Council of Ministers),'' *Voprosy ekonomiki*, 3:3–4, 1989.

"V Tsentral'nom Komitete KPSS (In the Central Committee of the CPSU),'' *Pravda*, June 3, 1986.

Val'tukh, K., and B. L. Lavrovskiy, "Proizvodstvennyy apparat strany: ispol'-zovaniye i rekonstruktsiya (The Country's Production Apparatus: Utilization and Reconstruction),'' *Ekonomika i organizatsiya promyshlennogo proizvodstva*, 2:17–32, February 1986.

van Brabant, Jozef M., "Socialist Economics and Disequilibrium—Kornai versus Portes.'' Paper presented June 24, 1988 (mimeo).

Vedomosti Verkovnogo Soveta SSSR, No. 22, May 1986a.

————, No. 37, September 10, 1986b.

————, No. 17, 1987.

Venediktov, A., *Gosudarstvennaya sotsialisticheskaya sobstvennost' (State Socialist Property)*. Moscow: Akademiya nauk, 1948.

————, "Voprosy sotsialisticheskoy sobstvennosti v trudakh Iosifa Vissarionovicha Stalina (Issues of Socialist Ownership in the Works of Joseph Vissarionovich Stalin),'' *Sovetskoye gosudarstvo i pravo*, 12:53–74, 1949.

Vestnik statistiki, 68, 9:80, September 1985.

Vickers, John, and George Yarrow, *Privatization. An Economic Analysis*. Cambridge, Mass.: MIT Press, 1988.

Vid, L. B., "1989-y kachestvo tempov rosta (1989: Quality of Rates of Growth),'' *Ekonomicheskaya gazeta*, 36:1, September 1988.

Vinokur, Aaron, and Gur Ofer, "Inequality of Earnings, Household Income, and Wealth in the Soviet Union in the 1970s,'' in James R. Millar, ed., *Politics, Work, and Daily Life in the USSR: A Survey of Former Soviet Citizens*. Cambridge: Cambridge University Press, 1987.

————, "Poverty in the Soviet Union.'' Paper presented at the Twentieth Annual AAASS Convention, Honolulu, Hawaii, November 18–21, 1988.

Volkonskiy, V. A., and Yu P. Solov'yev, "Modelirovaniye denezhnykh sberezheniy naseleniya (Modeling Monetary Savings of the Population),'' *Izvestiya AN SSSR, seriya ekonomicheskaya*, 16, 2:75–85, March–April 1985.

Vologzhin, V. M., "Utro sovetskikh aktsiy (The Dawn of Soviet Stocks), *Ekonomika i organizatsiya promyshlennogo proizvodstva*, 20, 1:41–50, 1989.

Voronin, L. A., "Ekonomicheskiy eksperiment—pervyye itogi i puti razvitiya (The Economic Experiment—the First Results and Ways of Development),'' *Planovoye khozyaystvo*, 61, 12:9–18, December 1984.

————, "Sovershenstvovaniye khozyaystvennogo mekhanizma—nepremennoye usloviye perevoda ekonomiki na intensivnyy put' razvitiya (Perfection of the Economic

Mechanism—a Requisite for Switching the Economy to an Intensive Course of Development)," *Planovoye khozyaystvo*, 62, 8:9–17, August 1985.

———, "On the State Plan for the USSR's Economic and Social Development in 1990," *Pravda*, September 26, 1989, pp. 2–4 (translated in FBIS, *Daily Report: Soviet Union*, September 27, 1989, pp. 49–64).

Voznesenskiy, L. A., "Vperedi-krutaya stupen' (A Drastic Stage Lies Ahead)," *Pravitel'stvennyy vestnik*, 15:1, 3, April 1990.

"Vremennaya metodika: opredeleniye optovykh tsen na novuyu mashinostroitel'nuyu produktsiyu proizvodstvenno-tekhnicheskogo naznacheniya (Temporary Methodology: Determination of Wholesale Prices on New Machinery Output for Producer Use)," *Ekonomicheskaya gazeta*, 51:15–16, December 1987.

Weickhardt, G. G., "Gorbachev's Record on Economic Reform," *Soviet Union/Union Sovietique*, 12, 3:251–276, 1985.

Wolf, Thomas A., "Economic Stabilization in Planned Economies: Toward an Analytical Framework," *Staff Papers*, 32:78–129, International Monetary Fund, 1985.

———, "Macroeconomic Adjustment and Reform in Planned Economies." Report prepared for conference on "Economic Reforms and the Role of Planned Economies in the Global Economic Reforms," Helsinki, Finland, June 12–16, 1989.

Wyzan, Michael L., "Soviet Agricultural Procurement Pricing: A Study in Perversity," *Journal of Comparative Economics*, 9, 1:24–45, March 1985.

Yakovchuk, N., "Leningrad, fondovaya birzha (Leningrad, the Stock Exchange)," *Ekonomika i zhizn'*, 41:7, 1990.

Yanowitch, M., *Work in the Soviet Union*. Armonk, N.Y.: M. E. Sharpe, 1985.

Yarovikov, A., "Trebovaniya potrebiteley i assortiment tovarov: problemy sbalansirovannosti (The Requirements of the Consumers and the Assortment of Goods: Problems of Balancing)," *Planovoye khozyaystvo*, 62, 7:52–59, July 1985.

Yasin, Ye., "Sotsialisticheskiy rynok: problemy i vozmozhnosti (The Socialist Market: Problems and Possibilities)," *Ekonomicheskaya gazeta*, 26:10, June 1988a.

———, "Tseny i dokhody (Prices and Incomes)," *Trud*, July 14, 1988b, p. 2.

Yastrebova, O., "Zakupochnyye tseny i stimulirovaniye proizvodstva (Purchase Prices and the Stimulation of Production)," *Ekonomika sel'skogo khozyaystva*, 64, 11:47–51, November 1984.

Yel'tsin, Boris, *Bekannelsen* (Against the Current). Stockholm: Forum, 1990.

Yezhov, A. N., and A. K. Yershov, *Teoriya i praktika tsenoobrazovaniya na bytovyye uslugi (Theory and Practice of Price Formation for Everyday Services)*. Moscow: Legkaya promyshlennost' i bytovoye obsluzhivaniye, 1986.

Yevstigneyev, R. N., and V. K. Senchagov, eds., *Predpriyatiya v usloviyakh intensifikatsii: opyt yevropeyskikh stran (Enterprises Under Conditions of Intensification: Experience of European CMEA Countries)*. Moscow: Ekonomika, 1987.

Yun', O., "Razvivaya planovoy mekhanizm khozyaystvovaniya (Developing the Economic Planning Mechanism)," *Kommunist*, 13:41–51, September 1985.

———, *Intensifikatsiya ekonomiki (Intensification of the Economy)*. Moscow, 1986.

Yureyev, R., "We Reveal Budget Secrets," *Pravitel'stvennyy Vestnik*, 18, September 1989, p. 6 (translated in FBIS, *Daily Report: Soviet Union*, September 22, 1989, pp. 83–85).

Zakharov, V., "Credit and Banks in the Economic Management System" *Voprosy ekonomiki*, 3, 1982 (translated in *Problems of Economics*, 26: 3–19, May 1983.

"Zakon Soyuza Sovetskikh Sotsialisticheskikh Respublik: O Gosudarstvennom Pred-priyatii (Ob"yedinenii) (Law of the Union of Soviet Socialist Republics: On the State Enterprise (Association))," *Pravda*, July 1, 1987, pp. 1–4.

"Zakon Soyuza Sovetskikh Sotsialisticheskikh respublik: O neotlozhnykh merakh po uluchsheniyu pensionnogo obespecheniya i sotsial'nogo obsluzhivaniya naseleniya (Law of the Union of Soviet Socialist Republics: On Urgent Measures to Improve Pensions and Social Services to the Population)," *Sotsialisticheskaya industriya*, August 4, 1989, p. 1.

"Zakon-proyekt SSSR ob izobretatel'stve v SSSR (Draft USSR Law on Invention in the USSR)," *Izvestiya*, April 7, 1990, pp. 2–3.

"Zakon SSSR o predpriyatiyakh v SSSR (USSR Law on Enterprises in the USSR)," *Izvestiya*, June 12, 1990, pp. 2–3.

"Zakon SSSR o sobstvennosti (USSR Law on Ownership)," *Izvestiya*, March 10, 1990, pp. 1–2.

Zaslavskaya, T. I., "Social Factors of Speeding-up the Development of the Soviet Economy." Novosibirsk, 1986a (mimeo).

———, "Chelovecheskiy faktor razvitiya ekonomiki i sotsial'naya spravedlivost' (The Human Factor in the Development of the Economy and Social Justice)," *Kommunist*, 63, 13:61–73, September 1986 (translated in *Current Digest of the Soviet Press*, 38:41, 1986b).

———, *Sotsial'no-demograficheskoye razvitiye sela. Regional'nyy analiz (The Social and Demographic Development of the Countryside: A Regional Analysis)*. Moscow: Statistika, 1980.

Zaslavskaya, Tat'yana I. (with Abram Bergson, Jerry Hough, Gregory Grossman, Thane Gustafson, and Herbert S. Levine), "Socioeconomic Aspects of Peres-troyka," *Soviet Economy*, 3, 4:313–331, October–December 1987.

Zhelesko, S. N., B. V. Sazonov, and A. E. Chirikova, "Peremeny v khode peremen (Changes in the Course of Change)," *Ekonomika i organizatsiya promyshlennogo proizvodstva*, 11:79–88, 1985.

Zhukov, Yu. V., "Kachestvo izdeliya i yego tsena (The Quality of an Article and Its Price)," *Kommercheskiy vestnik*, 14, 17:2–5, September 1985.

Zhuravlev, S., "Investitsionnaya politika: granitsy manevra (Investment Policy: The Limits of Maneuver)," *Planovoye khozyaystvo*, 12: 30–41, December 1989.

Zoteyev, G., "Ob otsenke valovogo natsional'nogo produkta (On Estimating Gross National Product)," *Ekonomicheskaya gazeta*, 42:10, 1987.

———, "Perestroyka kak strategiya perekhodnogo perioda: Vzglyad iznutri (Peres-troyka as a Strategy of the Transitional Period: A View from Within)." Paper presented at the Allied Social Science Associations Annual Meeting, December 1989, Atlanta, Georgia, pp. 1–41.

Zwass, Adam, *Money, Banking, and Credit in the Soviet Union and Eastern Europe*. White Plains, N.Y.: M. E. Sharpe, 1979.

Chronology of Major Economic Reform Legislation in the USSR, April 1985–May 1991

1985

April

  14 On measures relating to the development of   Decree (CC/CM)
services for the repair and construction of
housing, structures for horticultural associations,
garages, and other dwellings during 1986–1990,
and through the year 2000

  18 On measures for the development of local   Decree (CC/CM)
industry in 1986–1990, and through the year
2000

May

  17 On measures for overcoming drunkenness and   Decree (CC)
alcoholism

  17 On measures for overcoming drunkenness and   Decree (CM)
elimination of illegal distillation of alcohol

July

  12 On the broad dissemination of new methods of   Decree (CC/CM)
economic management and the strengthening and
acceleration of scientific-technical progress

September

  12 On the introduction of workplace certification in   Decree
industry and other sectors of the economy   (CM/VTsSPS)

October

  17 On measures for improving the management of   Decree (CC/CM)
the machine-building sector

November

  23 On the improvement of management in the agro-   Decree (CC/CM)
industrial complex

498

December

    12 On the creation of intersectoral scientific-   Decree (CC/CM)
          technical complexes, and measures for supporting
          their activities

1986

March

    14 On measures for continuing improvement in the   Decree (CC/CM)
          management of the country's fuel-energy complex

    29 On continuing improvement of the economic   Decree (CC/CM)
          mechanism in the country's agro-industrial com-
          plex

May

    6 On the improvement of planning, economic in-   Decree (CC/CM)
         centives, and management in the production of
         consumer goods in light industry.

    15 On radical improvements in the utilization of raw   Decree (CC/CM)
          materials, fuel-energy, and other resources under
          conditions of intensive development of the econ-
          omy during 1986–1990, and through the year
          2000

    28 On measures for strengthening the struggle   Decree (CC/CM)
          against non-labor incomes

June

    5 On measures for increasing the responsibility of   Decree (CC/CM)
         associations, enterprises, and organizations for
         the fulfillment of contracts for delivery of prod-
         ucts

    19 On the state plan for economic and social devel-   Law
          opment during 1986–1990

July

    2 On measures for radical improvement in the qual-   Decree (CC/CM)
         ity of production

    30 On measures to accelerate social-economic devel-   Decree (CC/CM)
          opment in light of decisions of the Twenty-sev-
          enth Congress of the CPSU

August

    5 On the improvement of planning, economic in-   Decree (CC/CM)
         centives, and management in state trade and con-
         sumer cooperatives

19 On measures to improve the management of eco-   Decree (CC/CM)
nomic and scientific-technical cooperation with
socialist countries

19 On measures to improve the management of for-   Decree (CC/CM)
eign economic relations

28 On measures to improve the organization of   Decree (CC/CM)
wages and to introduce new salary scales for
workers in the productive sectors of the economy

September
13 On continuing improvement of management of   Decree (CC/CM)
the country's construction complex

October
16 Model statute of cooperatives for the procurement   Decree (CC/CM)
and processing of secondary raw materials under
the territorial organs of *Gossnab*

November
21 On individual labor activity.   Law

1987

January
13 On the procedure to create joint ventures on So-   Decree (CC/CM)
viet territory and the activity and participation of
organizations and firms from capitalist and developing countries

13 On the procedure to create joint ventures on So-   Decree (CM)
viet territory and the activity of international associations and organizations from the USSR and
other CMEA member countries

February
12 On the formation of cooperatives for the produc-   Decree (CM)
tion of consumer goods and services licensed by
local *ispolkomy*

27 On double-shift and triple-shift work and social   Decree (CC/CM)
services in enterprises

March
23 On the granting of credit to privately employed   Decree (CM)
persons

April
3 On the procedure for payment of pensions to pri-   Decree (CM)
vately employed persons

June

27 Basic provisions (*Osnovnye polozheniya*) for the   Decree (CC/CM)
radical restructuring of management of the econ-
omy

30 On the state enterprise (association)   Law

July

17 On improving the national banking system and   Decree (CC/CM)
strengthening its influence to increase economic
efficiency

17 On measures for the radical improvement of na-   Decree (CC/CM)
tional statistical services

17 On restructuring planning and enhancing the role   Decree (CC/CM)
of USSR *Gosplan* under new conditions of eco-
nomic management

17 On restructuring the activity of ministries and de-   Decree (CC/CM)
partments in the sphere of material production
under new conditions of economic management

17 On restructuring the financial mechanism and en-   Decree (CC/CM)
hancing the role of the Ministry of Finance under
new conditions of economic management

17 On the basic provisions for restructuring the pric-   Decree (CC/CM)
ing system under new conditions of economic
management

September

30 On the transfer of scientific organizations to full   Decree (CC/CM)
economic accounting and self-financing

December

22 On the provision of effective employment, im-   Decree
provement of the job placement system, and   (CC/CM/VTsSPS)
strengthening of social guarantees for labor

1988

May

26 On cooperatives in the USSR   Law

December

2 On the foreign trade activity of state, cooperative,   Decree (CM)
and other enterprises

1989

February

4 On measures to eliminate shortcomings in pricing   Decree (CM)
practices

March

7 On measures for state regulation of foreign eco-   Decree (CM)
nomic relations

15 On measures for financial normalization and the   Decree (CC/CM)
strengthening of monetary circulation in the econ-
omy in 1989–1990 and during the 13th Five-Year
Plan

April

1 On the economic and organizational fundamentals   Decree (CM)
of leasehold relations

12 On the radical restructuring of economic relations   Decree (CM)
and management in the agro-industrial complex

August

2 On the endorsement of the decree of the Presid-   Law
ium of the Supreme Soviet on income tax from
cooperatives

3 On the introduction of amendments and supple-   Law
ments to the law on the state enterprise (association)

3 On the taxation of wage fund of the state enter-   Law
prise (association)

3 On the endorsement of the decree on regulations   Law
about trade representations of the USSR abroad

October

9 On the procedure for the resolution of collective   Law
labor disputes (conflicts)

16 On the introduction of amendments and supple-   Law
ments to the law on cooperatives in the USSR

November

20 On additional measures to stabilize the consumer   Decree (SS)
market and strengthen state control of prices

23 Fundamentals of all-union and union-republican   Law
    legislation on leasing

27 On the economic independence of Lithuania,   Law
    Latvia, and Estonia

27 On urgent measures to improve the environment   Decree (SS)

1990

February

28 Fundamental legislation of the USSR and the   Law
    union republics on land

March

6   On ownership in the USSR   Law

April

9   On the general principles of local self-government   Law
    and the local economy in the USSR

10 On the fundamentals of economic relations be-   Law
    tween the USSR and the union and autonomous
    republics

23 On the phased repeal of tax on single men, single   Law
    women, and childless couples

May

21 On the rights, duties, and responsibilities of the   Law
    state tax inspectorates

30 On pensions of Soviet citizens   Law

June

4   On enterprises in the USSR   Law

14 On the taxation of enterprises, associations, and   Law
    organizations

August

8   On measures to encourage the establishment and   Decree (CM)
    development of small enterprises

9   On the formation of the USSR State Property   Presidential
    Fund   Decree

16 On measures for the demonopolization of the na-   Decree (CM)
    tional economy

September

24 On additional measures to stabilize the economic   Law
    and socio-political life of the country

October

4 On priority measures for transition to market rela-   Presidential
   tions   Decree

12 On measures to preserve the inviolability of prop-   Presidential
   erty rights in the USSR   Decree

19 Basic guidelines for stabilization of the national   Decree (SS)
   economy and transition to a market economy

23 On the introduction of amendments to the law on   Law
   the general principles of local government and local economy in the USSR

23 On special procedures for the utilization of for-   Presidential
   eign currency reserves in 1991   Decree

25 On increasing citizens' interest in keeping savings   Presidential
   in the institutions of the USSR savings bank   Decree

26 On foreign investment in the USSR   Presidential
                                                          Decree

26 On the introduction of a commercial exchange   Presidential
   rate for the ruble and measures to create an all-   Decree
   union currency market

31 On increasing responsibility and penalties for   Law
   speculation, illegal trading activity, and abuses in
   trade

November

2 On mutual relations of state enterprises and co-   Decree (CM)
   operatives created under their aegis

2 On special procedures for the utilization of for-   Presidential
   eign currency reserves in 1991   Decree

30 On the strengthening of workers' control and or-   Presidential
   der in the storage, transportation, and trade in   Decree
   food and consumer goods

December

10 On trade unions, their rights, and guarantees for   Law
   their activity

10 Principles of legislation on investment activity in   Law
   the USSR

11 On banks and banking activity in the USSR and   Law
   the *Gosbank* of the USSR

14 On measures to prevent the disorganization of   Presidential
   production in connection with unsatisfactory ful-   Decree
   fillment of supply contracts

24	On the state of the country and priority measures to overcome the socio-economic and political crisis	Resolution (CPD)
29	On setting up additional budgetary funds for the stabilization of the economy in 1991	Presidential Decree
29	On the introduction of a tax on sales	Presidential Decree

1991

January

5	On priority tasks to implement the land reform	Presidential Decree
10	On urgent measures to improve the food situation in 1991	Presidential Decree
12	Forecast on the functioning of the country's economy and state plan for 1991 under USSR jurisdiction	Decree (SS)
15	Fundamental legislation for the USSR and union republics on employment	Law
19	On rates of turnover tax for joint ventures	Decree (CM)
22	On discontinuing acceptance of 50 and 100 ruble *Gosbank* banknotes issued in 1961 and limiting cash withdrawals from citizens' deposits	Presidential Decree
26	On measures to carry out the struggle against economic sabotage and other economic crimes	Presidential Decree

February

19	On measures to stabilize the consumer market, pricing policy, and social security of the population	Decree (CM)

March

1	On hard-currency regulation	Law
19	On the reform of retail prices and social security	Presidential Decree
19	On the reform of retail prices	Decree (CM)
21	On the miners' strikes	Decree (SS)
23	On compensation for savings	Presidential Decree
24	On taxation	Presidential Decree

28	On the USSR Cabinet of Ministers	Law

April

8	On urgent measures in agriculture	Presidential Decree
12	On emergency measures to secure the supply of material resources to enterprises, associations, and organizations	Presidential Decree
12	On the general principles of private enterprise in the USSR	Law
23	On the anti-crisis program	Decree (SS)
29	On the situation in the country and ways to extricate the economy from crisis	Decree (CC)

May

6	On compensation for losses incurred as a result of depreciation of citizens' financial savings under long-term contracts with USSR state insurance	Presidential Decree
13	On compensation for retail price increases	Presidential Decree
16	On stability in basic industries	Presidential Decree

Note: CC = Central Committee of the CPSU; CM = Council of Ministers of the USSR; CPD = Congress of Peoples' Deputies; SS = Supreme Soviet of the USSR; VTsSPS = Central Trade Union Council. All republican and local legislative enactments are excluded; all laws are enacted by the Supreme Soviet of the USSR.

Sources: Hewett (1988a, pp. 360–364); CREES Database, University of Birmingham as amended and revised by Gertrude E. Schroeder, University of Virginia.

Name
Index

Abalkin, Leonid I., 58, 61, 63–64, 71–72, 79–81, 85–88, 94, 122–135, 164–166, 229, 231–233, 263–264, 270, 273, 296, 298, 305, 309–311, 314–315, 330–331, 333–334, 336, 341–343, 349–356, 358–360, 364, 415, 417–418, 420, 430, 443, 445
Admirin, Itzchok, 341
Afanas'yev, Yuriy N., 246–248, 256–259
Afferica, Joan, 65
Aganbegyan, Abel G., 9, 28, 58, 61–62, 68, 71–72, 78, 80, 85–88, 91, 94, 104–111, 113, 115–120, 122, 134, 230, 314, 320, 331, 333–334, 336–337, 339, 341–342, 350, 353, 355, 358–359, 377, 379, 404, 444
Akodis I. A., 190–191
Aleksandrov, A. P., 80
Aleksashenko, Sergey, 310, 358
Alpeyev, V. N., 191
Ambartsumov, Yevgeniy A., 80, 90, 343
Anchishkin, Aleksandr I., 79, 85–87, 344
Andreyeva, Nina, 260
Andropov, Yuriy V., 3, 14, 16, 22, 26, 37, 84–85, 88, 343, 366, 368
Antonov, Mikhail, 341, 346
Arbatov, Georgiy A., 87, 312, 348
Åslund, Anders, 71, 74–94, 331, 335–359, 416
Assekritov, S. V., 351
Auerbach, P., 59, 62
Ayvazov, L. A., 199
Ayvazyan, S. N., 193

Babashkin, L. E., 40
Bahry, Donna, 271
Baily, Martin N., 72
Bannikov, N. A., 182
Baranov, Aleksandr, 92
Batalin, Yuriy, 234
Batkin, Leonid M., 252
Baybakov, Nikolay K., 6–7, 26, 39, 81, 84
Belkin, Viktor D., 268–269, 295, 303–304, 342
Belokh, N. V., 193
Belousov, Igor', 234
Belousov, Rem. A., 62, 81
Belyakov, Vitaliy D., 62
Berger, Mikhail, 420
Bergson, Abram, 72, 113–114, 126, 143
Berliner, Joseph S., 47, 67, 176, 403
Bialer, Seweryn, 65
Bim, A., 193–194
Birman, Igor, 270–271
Biryukov, Yuriy, 180
Biryukova, Aleksandra, 234
Blejer, Mario I., 273, 275, 284–286, 288
Block, Kevin, 417
Bocharov, Mikhail, 332–333, 357, 445
Bochkov, V., 293, 295
Bogomolov, Oleg T., 71, 77, 80, 84–89, 111, 248, 263, 296, 304, 330, 336, 343–345, 349–351, 353, 400
Bokov, A., 194
Borkhunov, N., 180–182
Bornstein, Morris, 95, 153, 163–164, 167–203
Borozdin, Yuriy V., 90, 202, 345

507

Bortnik, Ivan M., 314
Boyev, V. R., 89
Boyev, Yuriy P., 314
Braginskiy, Lev, 241, 345
Brezhnev, Leonid I., 4, 13, 25, 37, 49,
    53, 78, 91, 253, 352, 368, 410, 414,
    417
Brovkin, V., 195
Bukharin, Nikolay I., 259
Bunich, Pavel G., 83, 85, 93, 165, 235,
    246–249, 259, 268, 277, 285, 293, 294,
    345–346, 349, 351
Burns, James McGregor, 233
Butenko, Anatoliy P., 80, 90, 343
Buzdalov, I., 180

Chapman, Janet, 288
Chekhlov, N. I., 171, 178, 202
Chernenko, Konstantin U., 6, 38, 78, 88,
    91, 337, 366, 368
Chubakov, G. N., 90, 172
Chursin, A. M., 180
Cooper, Julian, 26

Daniloff, Nicholas, 56
Dashishev, Vyacheslav, 343
Davies, R. W., 270
Dementsev, Viktor V., 182
Deminov, A., 167
Deryabin, Anatoliy, 79, 90, 175, 178–
    179, 198, 202
Dobbs, Michael, 387
Doder, Dusko, 88
Doronin, Igor, 198
Duchene, Gerard, 27
Dyker, David A., 14
Dzerzhinskiy, Feliks E., 259

Eban, Abba, 47

Fedorenko, Nikolay T., 78, 80, 87
Fedorov, Boris G., 332–333, 358, 443
Feshbach, Murray, 9, 289
Friedman, Milton, 418
Frolov, Konstantin, 80

Gal'perin, V., 175, 178
Garvy, George, 268
Gavrilov, B. N., 65
Gaydar, E., 412–413
Genkina, D., 417
Gladkiy, Ivan I., 63, 193, 202
Glushkov, Nikolay T., 184–185, 189, 192

Gogoberidze, A., 178
Gonzal'yez, E., 321
Gorbachev, Mikhail S., 3–7, 9, 12–26,
    29–33, 38, 43, 46–58, 64–65, 67, 71–
    81, 83, 86–89, 92–94, 108, 120, 128,
    140, 163–165, 207, 213–215, 217–218,
    223–237, 242–245, 248, 257, 260–263,
    265, 286, 289, 304, 312–315, 318–
    321, 331–333, 335, 337, 339, 347, 350–
    369, 372, 377, 379–380, 384, 386–
    387, 402, 404, 408–409, 413–414, 417,
    431, 438, 441–445, 456–457, 462–464,
    467–468
Gorbuntsov, D., 195
Gostev, Boris I., 76, 84, 265, 271, 273,
    278, 283, 285, 307, 321
Granberg, Aleksandr G., 80, 85, 342
Granick, David, 47
Gribanov, K., 310
Grigor'yev, Leonid, 358
Grossman, Gregory, 72, 114–115, 129–
    130, 148, 238
Gur'yev, V., 371
Gustafson, Thane, 72, 146, 229, 245
Guzhavina, L., 190
Gvishiani, Dzhermen M., 58, 82, 84–85,
    344

Hanson, Philip, 3, 23–33, 57–68, 78, 263,
    273, 333, 415–440, 463
Harrison, Mark, 268, 270–271
Hayek, Friedrich A., 418
Herrman-Pillath C., 439
Hewett, Ed A., 3–35, 57, 71–73, 110–
    115, 120–121, 133, 163–166, 225–238,
    242–254, 256, 260–262, 264, 284, 308–
    334, 351–353, 377–378, 416, 434, 441–
    458, 461–462
Holzman, Franklyn D., 268, 270
Hough, Jerry F., 4, 30–34, 47–56, 72,
    128, 140
Hutchings, Raymond, 270

Ivanchenko, Vasiliy, M., 79
Ivanov, Ivan D., 90, 213, 314, 350
Ivchenko, L., 194

Kabankov, V., 190
Kadar, Janos, 67
Kagalovskiy, Konstantin G., 273, 289,
    301, 405
Kaliman, G., 180–181
Kalnyn'sh, A., 194

Kamemtsev, Vladimir, 234
Kantorovich, Leonid, 78
Kapustin, Yevgeniy, 79, 80, 87
Katsenelinboigen, Aron, 78, 86, 238, 240
Katsura, Pyotr, 336, 351
Kazakevich, David M., 193–194
Kebich, Vyacheslav, 381
Kellogg, Robert L., 377
Keynes, John Maynard, 233
Khachaturov, Tigran S., 79
Khanin, Grigoriy I., 93, 244, 347
Khasbulatov, Ruslan I., 346
Khrushchev, Nikita S., 25, 49, 141, 247, 257, 260–261, 372
Khrushchev, Yelena N., 247
Khubiyev, K., 310
Kim, Vladimir V., 180, 200, 203
Kirichenko, Vadim N., 82–83, 263, 314, 336, 349–350, 371, 385
Kislinskaya, L., 382
Kitaygorodskiy, I., 424, 479
Klyamkin, Igor, 259
Kolmogorov, Georgiy D., 60
Komin, A., 174–175, 177–179, 197
Kontorovich, Vladimir, 26, 57
Kornai, Janos, 57, 59, 293–294, 302, 439–440
Korovyakovskiy, Dmitriy Z., 195
Koryagina, Tat'yana I., 240, 346, 353
Kostakov, Vladimir G., 82, 91, 112, 346
Kosygin, Aleksey N., 36, 47–49, 79, 82
Krasnopivtsev, A., 180
Kufakov, V. A., 181–182, 184–185
Kunel'skiy, L. E., 63
Kurashvili, Boris P., 24, 91
Kurenkov, P., 190–191
Kurtzweg, Lauri, 360
Kushnizsky, Fedor, 39

Lakhov, B., 178
Latsis, Otto, 91, 343, 380
Lavrovskiy, B. L., 364
Lawrence, Bruce, 360
Lazutin, V., 181–182
Lemeshev, Mikhail, 346
Lenin, Vladimir I., 36, 46, 121, 164, 218, 250, 257, 259, 357
Levchuk, Igor V., 293–295
Levikov, Aleksandr, 91, 418
Levin, A. I., 194
Levine, Herbert S., 72, 113–114, 150, 164, 227–228, 230–233, 238–240, 245

Ligachev, Yegor K., 58, 80, 87, 224, 348–349, 357
Lisichkin, Gennadiy S., 89–90, 343, 349
Lokshin, Rafail A., 189
Lopatnikov, L., 202
Lukinov, I., 200
Lukyanenko, Vladimir, 85
L'vov, Dmitriy K., 90, 345
Lynev, Ruslan, 92

McKinnon, Ronald I., 301, 303
Makarov, Valeriy M., 78, 85–86, 345
Malakhov, K., 381
Mann, Dawn, 353
Marchuk, Guriy I., 39, 80, 84
Marer, Paul, 438
Marx, Karl, 258, 445
Martynov, Vladlen A., 350
Mashchits, Vladimir, 358
Maslyukov, Yuriy D., 234, 284–285, 294, 298, 310, 315, 317, 321–324, 326–327, 338–339, 348–350, 352–356, 359
Matosich, Andrew J., 366
Mayorets, Anatoliy I., 197
Medvedev, Zhores, 65, 67
Mel'nikov, Aleksandr G., 83, 85
Mikhaylov, Aleksey, 357–358
Milner, Boris Z., 343, 350
Milyukov, Anatoliy, 336, 348, 351, 357
Moore, Barrington, 47
Morgachev, A., 66
Moskaleva, N. I., 192, 194
Mostovoy, Pavel, 381
Mostovshchikov, S., 240
Mozhin, Vladimir P., 76, 226, 230, 337, 348
Murakhovskiy, Vsevolod S., 17, 234

Nazarbayev, Nursultan A., 320
Nazarenko, Viktor I., 89
Nazariyan, S. G., 181
Nemchinov, V. P., 17!
Nikiforov, Lev V., 90, 343
Nikitin, D., 190
Nikonov, Viktor, 234
Noren, James H., 263, 332, 360–408, 416
Nove, Alec, 65
Nuti, Domenico M., 297
Nyers, Reszo, 67–68

Ofer, Gur, 165, 229, 263–307, 318–319, 370

Okhapkin, A., 182
Orlov, A. V., 351
Orlov, Ya., 189
Osipenko, O. V., 411
Otsason, Rein, 89, 349

Palm, Victor, 248
Parfenov, Vasiliy I., 91
Parkhomovskiy, E., 202
Pasternak, Boris, 257–258
Pavlov, Valentin S., 197, 201, 264–265,
    271, 273, 283, 289, 291, 295, 307,
    314, 349, 464
Perlamutrov, Vilen, 90, 345
Petrakov, Nikolay Ya., 71, 79, 85, 90,
    95–103, 193, 231, 331, 336, 340–341,
    345, 349, 351, 353, 355, 400, 403–
    405, 443
Pickersgill, Joyce, 297
Pinsker, Oleg, 347, 418
Pinzenik, V. M., 176
Pipes, Richard, 48
Piskotin, Mikhail, 91
Piyasheva, Larisa, 346, 418, 437
Podgornyy, Nikolay V., 49
Ponomarev, A. A., 425
Popkova, Larisa, 347, 418
Popov, Gavriil Kh., 41, 85, 91, 248, 346,
    349, 351
Primakov, Yevgeniy, M., 380
Putilov, N. I., 252

Rahr, Alexander, 82, 353
Rakitskiy, Boris, 345
Rasputin, Valentin, 353
Rayevskiy, V. A., 190
Remnick, David, 334
Rimashevskaya, N. M., 340
Roberts, Bryan, 284
Romanyuk, V., 92
Roosevelt, Franklin D., 52, 233
Rostowski, S., 59
Roze, V., 194
Rozenova, Lira I., 177–178, 195, 197
Rumer, Boris, 15, 341–342, 356
Rusakov, V. P., 193
Rutgayzer, Valeriy M., 194, 201, 310
Ryabov, Yakov P., 62
Ryzhkov, Nikolay I., 32, 76–77, 80, 83,
    85, 93, 206, 208–210, 217, 234–235,
    247, 264–265, 271, 283–285, 289–291,
    294–295, 298, 303–305, 308, 313, 317–

319, 321–322, 324, 331–333, 336, 338,
    341, 348–350, 352–356, 359–360, 364,
    376–377, 385, 387, 401–402, 411, 415,
    417–418, 420, 430, 442–444
Ryzhkov, V., 66

Sagers, Matthew J., 167
Sakharov, Andrey D., 165, 246, 248
Salimzhanov, I., 191
Sapilov, E., 179
Schmemann, Serge, 189
Schroeder, Gertrude E., 4, 30–33, 36–
    46, 131, 164, 168, 197, 204–224, 229,
    233–238, 240–241, 244, 331, 334, 366,
    374, 408–414, 459–468
Seleznev, A., 310
Selyunin, Vasiliy I., 92, 243–244, 283,
    341, 347, 402, 404, 417–418
Semenov, Viktor N., 182–183, 185, 192
Senchagov, Vyacheslav K., 85, 273, 285,
    301, 314–315, 349
Sergeyev, Aleksey A., 346, 352
Serov, V. M., 314
Shapkina, G., 44–45
Shastiko, Vladimir M., 90, 195
Shatalin, Stanislav S., 71, 79, 82, 85, 91,
    193, 202, 296, 331, 333–334, 336, 340–
    342, 344–345, 353, 355, 358, 361, 403–
    404, 415, 420, 430, 432, 437, 443–
    444, 456, 462
Shcherbakov, Vladimir I., 314, 380
Shcherbitskiy, Vladimir V., 89
Shelepin, Aleksandr N., 49
Shelest, Petr Ye., 49
Shevardnadze, Eduard A., 243
Shimko, Vladimir, 348
Shmarov, A., 194, 263, 371
Shmelev, Nikolay P., 73, 153–160, 163–
    165, 196, 198, 200–202, 231–233, 246–
    248, 252, 254–256, 258, 260, 270, 294,
    296, 300, 302, 304, 324, 346, 349,
    358, 381
Shokhin, A., 193–194
Shprygin, V. I., 178
Silayev, Ivan S., 17, 234
Sillaste, Yu., 89
Simakov, Anatoliy, 311
Simonyan, Rair R., 311
Sitaryan, Stepan A., 82, 314, 336, 338–
    339, 344, 350–351, 356, 380
Skorov, Georgiy Y., 58

Slyun'kov, Nikolay N., 76, 93, 226, 230, 234, 243, 337, 348, 352, 357
Smirnitskiy, Yevgeniy K., 83, 172, 235
Solodkov, M. V., 211
Solomentsev, Mikhail S., 92
Solov'yev, Yuriy P., 193
Stalin, Joseph V., 17, 25, 36, 46–47, 54, 410
Stark, David, 438
Starodubtsev, V. A., 321
Strelyanyy, A. S., 91, 418
Stuchka, P., 417
Sutela, Pekka, 78
Systov, A. S., 382
Szapary, Gyorgy, 273, 275, 284–286, 288

Talyzin, Nikolay V., 7, 17, 26, 39, 58, 60, 81–82, 84–85, 234, 336, 338
Tardos, Marton, 294, 438
Teague, Elizabeth, 57, 353
Tedstrom, John, 288
Telen', L., 311
Tenson, Andreas, 90
Tikhonov, Nikolay Z., 84
Tikhonov, Vladimir I., 346, 349
Tolstov, V., 92
Treml, Vladimir G., 184, 195, 307
Tretyakova, Albina, 283
Trotsenko, I., 192
Tsakunov, V. V., 88
Tsipko, Aleksndr, 343
Turgenev, Nikolay, 230–231
Turysov, K., 350

Ukrainskiy, Dmitriy V., 82
Ulanovskiy, V., 194

Valovoy, Dmitriy V., 81, 92
Val'tukh, K., 364
van Brabant, Josef M., 297
Vanous, Jan, 72, 229, 284–285, 290, 319
Vavilov, Andrey, 358
Venediktov, A., 417
Vickers, John, 417–418, 437
Vid, Leonard B., 82, 297, 338
Vilkas, Edvardas I., 349
Vinokur, Aaron, 296–297, 301
Vladimirov, Boris, 92
Vladislavlev, A. P., 350
Volkonskiy, V. A., 193
Vologzhin, V. M., 349

Vol'skiy, Arkadiy I., 247–248, 337
Voronin, Lev A., 40, 61, 81–82, 84, 234, 289, 298, 352, 356
Vorotnikov, Vitaliy I., 92

Weickhardt, George G., 65
Winston, Victor H., 3–5, 71–73, 163–166, 232–233, 236, 238–242, 245, 331–334
Wolf, Thomas A., 268–270, 294–295, 297
Wyzan, Michael L., 180

Yakovlev, Aleksandr N., 71, 77
Yakovlev, Sergey V., 180–182
Yanowitch, Murray, 64
Yaremenko, Yuriy V., 344
Yarin, Venyamin, 353
Yarkin, A. P., 194
Yarovikov, A., 190
Yarrow, George, 417–418, 437
Yasin, Yevgeniy, 90, 198, 202, 311, 345, 351, 358, 445
Yastrebova, O., 182
Yavlinskiy, Grigoriy A., 332–333, 357–358, 445
Yegyazaryan, Gevork A., 346, 350
Yel'tsin, Boris N., 246, 248, 332–334, 344, 346, 353, 357–358, 360, 418, 420–421, 441–443, 445, 452, 456
Yemel'yanov, Aleksey M., 346, 349
Yershov, A. K., 186
Yevstigneyev, Ruben N., 85, 344, 350
Yevtushenko, Yevgeniy, 331
Yezhov, A. N., 186
Yun', Oleg M., 82, 85
Yureyev, R., 265, 271, 291, 298, 307

Zadornov, Mikhail, 357–358
Zaslavskaya, Tat'yana I., 24, 28, 71–73, 80, 85–86, 88–89, 91, 111, 136–152, 193, 248, 302, 340, 345, 351
Zaykov, Lev N., 76–77, 93, 357, 364, 383
Zhelesko, S. N., 40
Zhukov, Yuriy V., 190, 495
Zhuravlev, S., 379
Zhuravleva, G., 190–191
Zoteyev, Gennadiy N., 265, 271, 275, 307, 341, 346

Subject
Index

Abalkin Commission. *See* Commission on Economic Reform, USSR

Academy of Agricultural Sciences, 89

Academy of the National Economy, 83, 85, 235, 247, 259

Academy of Sciences of the USSR, Economic Department of, 78, 81, 336, 341–342, 344; influence of, 77, 340; institutes of, 58, 72–73, 77–80, 82–83, 86–90, 99, 246–247, 310–312, 336, 340, 343–346; prices and, 90, 154, 194; reform orientation of, 86, 92–93

Academy of Social Sciences, 81

Afghanistan conflict, 318

Agricultural prices: decree on, 463; reform of, 97, 101, 116–117, 153, 157–160, 179–186, 198–200, 401–402; revisions of, 180–184; zonal differentiation of, 180–182, 199

Agriculture sector, 270; Basic Provisions and, 214–215, 224; China and, 111, 116, 125; cooperatives and, 63; deemphasis of, 114; energy and, 406; expenditures for, 15, 23, 298, 301; growth of, 8, 27, 105, 115–116, 365, 367–368, 369, 373, 377, 459; investment in, 20, 21; leasing and, 299; popular support and, 113; privatization of, 28, 303; reform in, 31, 33, 39, 42, 54, 55, 65, 89, 125–126, 234, 334, 339. *See also* Brigade system

Alcoholic beverages: consumption of, 238, 390, 408–410; production of, 247, 286, 364, 367, 399, 460; taxes on, 101, 200, 211, 266, 280–281, 292, 306. *See also* Anti-alcohol campaign

Allocation of Petroleum Products, State Committee for, 210

All-Union Central Council of Trade Unions (AUCCTU), 211, 350, 352; wages and, 65, 212

All-Union industrial associations (VPOs), 18, 208

All-Union ministries. *See* Ministries

All-Union treaty. *See* Union treaty

Anti-alcohol campaign, 14, 24, 38, 106, 187, 226–228, 236, 364–365, 367, 379, 408–410; budget revenues and, 254, 286, 301, 318, 379

Anti-monopoly law, 312, 423, 428–429, 463

Armenia, 262, 342, 385, 464, 466; earthquake and, 292, 318–319, 350, 376–377

Asset valuation, 311, 401, 426, 428, 439, 450

Azerbaijan, 342, 385

Balance of payments, 320, 382, 461; competition and, 312; import cuts and, 323 .

Baltic republics, 261, 343, 464–467; food supply in, 374; special economic zones and, 254

Bank credits, 102–103, 223; interest on, 207, 212–213; investment and, 223, 283; ministries and, 209

Banking system: absence of, 270; Basic Provisions and, 212–213; budget deficits and, 276, 369–370; control over wages, 269, 370; independence of, 277; plenum (*1987*) and, 108; profits and, 130; reform of, 22, 72, 91, 102–103, 109, 165, 264, 283, 292–293, 302, 366, 370,400–401, 422, 427–428, 463; republics and, 427–428, 436; resources of, 102; Shatalin Plan and, 446–447

Bankruptcy, 112, 121, 137, 150, 434–435; Law on the State Enterprise and, 206; prices and, 219–220; private sector and, 145

Banks: cooperative, 293, 304; financing capital investment, 223; foreign economic, 424, 427; foreign trade, 270

Barter trade, 338, 362, 381–382, 412, 466

Basic Guidelines (*Osnovnyye napravleniya*) for Twelfth Five-Year Plan, 5, 6

Basic Provisions (*Osnovnyye polozheniya*) for the radical restructuring of economic management, 74, 108, 204–223, 231, 293, 308

Belorussia, 374, 385, 465–466

Black market, 238–240, 331–332, 372, 401, 413, 452, 467

Bonuses, managerial, 40, 55, 65, 206, 212, 219, 222

Brigade system, 28, 54, 64, 125, 218

Budget deficit, 271, 307; defense spending and, 290–291; definitions of, 272; inflationary effects of, 264, 276–277, 292, 294, 369; price reform and, 155, 158–160, 402; reduction of, 160, 165–166, 235, 263, 301, 304, 321, 325, 331, 359, 388, 400, 405, 439, 460–461; Shatalin Plan and, 447–448, 451, 454, 456; size of, 237, 254, 263, 265, 266, 273, *274*, 275, 298, 299, 300, *317*, 318–319, 339, 369–370, 379

Budget, state, 264, 266, 306–307, 387; enterprises and, 36, 39, 40, 44, 132; expenditures of, 169–170, 184, 248, 265, 271–274, 277, 282–284, 287–291, 299, 318; foreign trade and, 270, 318–319, 376; investment and, 319, 370, 379, 460; prices and, 100, 265, 268; republics and, 210, 334, 465, 467; revenues of, 62, 101, 265, 271–274, 277, 280, 287, 292, 400; Shatalin Plan and, 447–448, 451. *See also* Subsidies

Bureau for Chemical and Timber Complex, 208

Bureau for Machinery, 208

Bureau for Social Development, 208

Bureau of Fuel and Energy Complex, 208

Capital-output ratio, 11

Capital productivity, 10, 12, 284, 364

Capital stock: agricultural sector and, 179, 420; enterprises and, 222, 370, 419–420; growth of, 9, 12–13, 15, 19, 29, 234; prices and, 169–170, 179; renovation of, 18; republics and, 466; retirements of, 364; tax on 197; technological level of, 36, 114–115

Center for Study of Public Opinion, 340

Central Asia, republics of, 146–148, 464; food supply in, 374

Central Committee of the CPSU, 6–7, 16, 350; economic decisions and, 75–78, 80–84, 163, 243, 335, 351; Economic Department of, 76–78, 84, 336; influence of, 347–348, 355; interference of, 134; new leader and, 53–54, 67; plenum (*1983*) of, 78; plenum (*1987*) of, 74, 86, 93; Nineteenth Conference of the CPSU and, 226, 347; prices and, 117; science and, 87; Secretariat of, 76; Socioeconomic Department of, 358. *See also* Communist Party of the Soviet Union; Party congresses; Party plenums; Politburo

Central Economic Mathematical Institute (TsEMI), 72, 77–80, 90, 99, 246, 340, 344–346

Central planning: Basic Provisions and, 205–206, 218–220; criticism of, 351–352; fiscal-monetary aspects of, 264, 268–269, 292, 296; introduction of, 36; investment and, 272, 293, 298; maintenance of, 22, 31, 303; prices and, 153–154; reduction of, 255, 309, 366; streamlining of, 16, 29, 35, 37, 39; strengthening of, 43, 57, 66, 299; supply system and, 109

Chernobyl' nuclear disaster, 39, 292, 385, 448; cost of, 318–319, 376

Chinese economic reform, 16, 31–32, 51, 243; agricultural sector and, 34, 55, 111, 113, 116, 125; banks and, 439; budget deficit and, 275, 284; currency and, 256; enterprises and, 285; prices and, 160, 202; privatization and, 344, 438; production growth and, 264; success of, 250, 387

CIA, 331, 365, 372, 377, 459; estimates of cash holdings, 295; estimates of consumption, 408–409; estimates of defense spending, 290–291; estimates of GNP, 8, 25, 316–318, 361–363; estimates of inflation, 413; estimates of monetary overhang, 292; estimates of personal income, 410; estimates of savings rate, 297

Coal industry, 21, 392, 405, 466; prices and 169, 172, 197; profitability of, 173

Collective farm markets: disequilibrium and, 269, 373–375; prices in, 186–187, 189, 194–195, 375–376, 413, 460; statistics and, 399

Collective farms, 270; autonomy of, 214–215, 234; brigade system and, 64; capital stock of, 419–420; cooperatives and, 63; costs of, 181; CPSU and, 134; interactions of, 238–242; prices and, 179, 200, 372–373; privatization of, 450; profitability of, 182–185, 200; revenues of, 183; rights of, 116; taxes on, 101

Commission on Economic Reform, RSFSR, 445

Commission on Economic Reform, USSR, 298, 308, 310, 313–315, 326, 341, 350–357

Commission for the Improvement of Management, Planning and the Economic Mechanism, 39, 85, 93, 314, 336

Commission for the Study of Productive Forces, 87

Communist Party of the Soviet Union (CPSU): Armenia and, 377; control of, 7; Democratic Platform and, 248; demoralization of, 383; economic reform and, 75–78, 92, 142, 260, 331–332; General Secretaryship and, 337; influence of, 35, 258, 347–348, 357; local officials of, 133–135, 140; wage policy and, 212. *See also* Central Committee of the CPSU; Nineteenth Conference of the CPSU; Party congresses; Party plenums; Politburo

Competition, 120–121, 137, 165, 302, 311–313; prices and, 219–220, 403; privatization and, 326, 437, 439–440

Congress of People's Deputies, 165, 308, 318, 320, 325, 340, 344, 347, 352, 355, 381; budget deficit and, 405; equity and, 321–322; members of, 246–248, 349; populism of, 309, 312, 356; reform economists and, 351

Construction sector, 42; growth of, 8, 365; investment in, 20–21, 25, 284; Politburo and, 233; reform of, 39; State Committee for, 208

Consumer cooperatives, 194–195

Consumer goods: distribution of, 268, 270, 372, 375, 411; imports of, 236–238, 244, 247, 286, 302–304, 323–324, 376, 384, 390, 398–399, 409–410, 449, 460; Politburo and, 233; prices of, 198; production of, 107, 223, 228–229, 234, 269, 286, 294, 323, 362, 372, 380–381, 384, 388, 390–393, 398–399, 414, 460; rationing of, 239–242, 374, 375, 379, 412; republics and, 385; shortages of, 155, 166, 202, 237, 320, 371, 379, 386, 409–412; subsidies for, 192, 194

Consumer prices. *See* Retail prices

Consumer sector, 237–238, 244, 408–414; emphasis on, 383–384, 399; growth of, 26–27, 29, 367, 372; Hungarian reform and, 59, 65; Shatalin Plan and, 446, 449, 458; state interference in, 229

Consumer welfare. *See* Living standards

Contract prices, 55, 191, 197, 211, 428

Contracts, fulfillment of, 41 44–45, 463

Conversion, defense. *See* Defense sector

Convertibility. *See* Ruble convertibility

Cooperatives, 250–253, 292–294, 299, 417, 425; approval for, 42, 45–46, 55; banks and, 293, 304; Basic Provisions and, 214, 218; control on wages in, 323, 410; foreign trade and, 382; growth of, 55, 63–65, 67, 108, 121, 254, 261, 463; income inequality and, 144–146; interactions of, 240–241; prices of, 372; property relations and, 124, 128–129, 311, 423; radical reform and, 58; statistics and, 399; taxes on, 266, 300

Copyrights. *See* Intellectual property

Corruption, 38, 42, 251, 364

Council for Mutual Economic Assistance (CMEA), 12, 84, 121, 213, 386

Council of Ministers, USSR, 16–17, 39, 76; anti-monopoly committee of, 428–429; circumvention of, 92; cooperatives and, 42; economic decisions and, 75, 83, 85, 321, 356; foreign investment and, 426; pace of reform and,

215–217; planning and, 205; plenum (*1987*) and, 108; privatization and, 425; reform commissions of, 335–336, 339, 350–351, 354–355, 358; wage policy and, 212, 323

Credit system: Basic Provisions and, 212–213; central planning and, 268–269, 292–293; control of, 303, 331, 399–401, 427; expansion of, 263; investment and, 62, 283, 379, 404; market and, 90, 270, 302, 304; price reform and, 100, 366; reorganization of, 102–103; savings rate and, 297

Crime prevention, 251, 386

Cuba, 247, 354

Currency. *See* Foreign currency

Currency market, 422, 424

Czechoslovakia, 49, 243

Decrees, various, on economy. *See* Chronology

Defense sector, 332–333; basic guidelines for Twelfth Five-Year Plan and, 6–7, 9, 26–27; burden of, 23, 290–291; conversion of, 323, 362, 372, 383–384, 387, 404, 432, 461, 464; expenditures for, 56, 101, 229, 265–266, 289–291, 298, 300, 306, 322, 372, 377, 387–388, 399–400, 405, 407, 460; Shatalin Plan and, 448, 451

Democratization, 72–73, 104, 107–110, 128, 133–134, 142, 152, 257–260, 407; bureaucracy and, 252, 383; state property and, 136, 258, 309

Depreciation funds, 98, 103, 278, 283; prices and, 168, 170

Destatization, 298, 302, 310, 326, 401; Britain and, 419; Shatalin Plan and, 333, 358–359, 415, 417, 443, 449–451, 456, 462

Discipline campaign, 14, 18, 20, 22, 24, 26, 37–38, 363–365; growth and, 66, 378; private enterprise and, 67; productivity and, 379

Disequilibrium. *See* Economic disequilibrium

Eastern Europe: exports to, 406; industrial modernization and, 20; monetary policy and, 293; reforms in, 32, 387, 455; revolutions in, 330–331, 376, 385–386

East Germany, 31, 51, 384, 439; *kombinate* and, 24, 61–62; reform in, 65–68

Economic disequilibrium: consumer sector, 263, 264, 294, 298, 302, 305, 331, 409, 467; household sector, 269

Economic Scientific Research Institute, 82

Economic zones, 254, 343–344, 465

Education, economic, 340; emphasis on, 106, 372; level of, 140; price of, 150; share of national income, 120; subsidies on, 192, 318

Energy sector: cost of, 10, 15, 37, 169; foreign prices and, 254, 286, 376, 405; growth of, 390, 392, 397, 459; investment in, 20–22, 25, 226, 322, 406–407; organization of, 39; prices in, 95, 154, 157, 172, 378, 402, 459; profitability of, 173; rental payments in, 197; republics and, 332, 466

Enterprises: bank accounts of, 103, 268–269, 277, 295, 369–370, 401; Basic Provisions and, 217–220; foreign trade and, 40; hard budget constraints of, 285, 293–294, 298, 302, 305, 439; Hungarian reform and, 59; independence of, 18–19, 22, 24, 37–40, 42, 55, 57, 62, 121, 126, 130, 206–207, 263, 270, 272, 302–305, 309, 366, 381, 410, 445–446, 467; indexation and, 453; investment by 283, 293; *kombinate* and, 61–62; labor and, 119, 132; interactions of, 238–242; management in, 108–109, 124, 127, 222; price control and, 255, 294, 371; republics and, 465–466; resources of, 102; taxes and, 170, 273; statistics and, 362; water charges and, 170, 197, 199

Environment, 114–115, 197, 211, 333, 372, 385

Estonia, 89, 109, 420. *See also* Baltic republics

Ethnic unrest. *See* Nationalities

European Community, 446

Exchange rates, 286, 429–430, 454, 464

Exports: to Eastern Europe, 12, 385–386, 406; enterprises and, 49, 213–214, 382, 430; increases of, 12, 17, 55; joint ventures and, 64; oil and gas, 10–11, 286, 291, 404, 406, 447; prices and, 198

Federation Council, 466–467

Fiscal system: Basic Provisions and, 212–
213, 222–223; bonds and, 295, 447;
centralization of, 271; disorganization
of, 263–264, 298; foreign trade and,
270; prices and, 268; Shatalin Plan and,
333, 447–448, 451, 454, 456; stabilization of, 264, 298–305, 400. See also
Budget, state; Taxation
"500 Day" Plan. See Shatalin Plan
Five-Year plans: investment and, 284;
quality and, 41; stability of, 32, 44,
59–60, 62, 67, 219. See also Thirteenth Five-Year Plan; Twelfth Five-
Year Plan
Food Program (1982), 214
Food supply, 105, 164, 228, 236, 365,
367, 372–375, 390, 392, 404–405, 409;
distribution of, 406, 463; Politburo and,
233
Foreign currency, 304, 376, 404, 430.
See also Balance of payments
Foreign debt, 317, 320, 324, 447, 461;
state budget and, 265, 291
Foreign Economic Commission, 39, 90,
208, 213, 349
Foreign investment, 55, 406–407, 418, 422,
426–427, 429–430, 434, 436, 440
Foreign policy, 52, 55–56, 333, 346, 468
Foreign trade: Basic Provisions and, 213–
214; growth of, 64, 461; law on, 241;
reforms in, 90, 366, 464; ruble devaluation and, 203; state budget and, 265–
266, 270, 280–281, 286, 300–301, 306,
318–319, 376; Shatalin Plan and, 453–
454; state monopoly of, 40, 270, 381;
windfall losses in, 29, 318, 376. See
also Exports; Imports; Ruble convertibility
Free trade zones. See Economic zones

Georgia, 385, 464
German Democratic Republic (GDR). See
East Germany
Glasnost', 134, 141–142, 152, 259, 261–
262, 265, 309, 327, 383; reform econ-
omists and, 345–346
Glavki (sectoral sub-branches), 25, 208,
403
Gosagroprom (State Agroindustrial Com-
mittee), 208, 214
Gosarbitrazh (State Arbitration Commit-
tee), 210

Gosbank (State Bank), 85, 103, 332, 437;
budget deficit and, 271, 275, 369–370;
Commission on Economic Reform and,
315; inconsistency of, 60; Ministry of
Finance and, 270; money supply and,
427; plenum (1987) and, 108; production sector and, 268; wages and, 388,
399
Goskomstat (State Committee for Statistics), 211, 315, 349, 361, 388, 390,
398, 411–412, 419, 460, 463, 466; inflation and, 371; labor productivity and,
319, 386
Goskomtsen (State Committee for Prices),
72, 78, 85, 90, 349, 351; Basic Provisions and, 216; budget deficit and,
159; CPSU and, 134; parametric prices
and, 175; price reform and, 156–157,
177–178, 191, 197, 203, 211, 227–
229, 256, 403
Gosplan (State Planning Committee), 17,
75, 77, 215–216, 349; Basic Provisions and, 205; circumvention of, 92–
93; Commission for the Improvement
of Management, Planning and the Economic Mechanism and, 336, 339;
Council of Productive Forces of, 76;
Economic Research Institute of, 83, 346;
goszakazy and, 205–206, 381; inflation
and, 371; influence of, 351–353, 355–
356, 366, 445; interest rates and, 323;
investment and, 377; Law on the State
Enterprise and, 255; leadership of, 81,
84, 310, 315, 338, 351; orthodoxy of,
78, 82, 113, 349; price reform and,
156, 228; privatization and, 310; quality and, 37; reorganization of, 208, 235;
supplies and, 41; Twelfth Five-Year Plan
and, 6–7, 26
Gospriyemka (state quality inspection
system), 41, 107, 112, 118, 223, 362,
366, 379–380; machine-building and
metal working and, 107
Gossnab (State Committee for Material
and Technical Supply), 26, 40–42, 44,
84–85, 113, 228, 381, 429; Basic Provisions and, 210–211, 216; plenum
(1987) and, 108; producer goods and,
61
Gosstandart (State Committee on Standards), 41, 59, 366
Goszakazy (state orders for fulfillment of
its highest priority needs), 209, 215–

216, 219, 227, 235, 293, 298, 303, 457; consumer goods and, 229, 384; importance of, 205–206; Law on the State Enterprise and, 255; reduction of, 325, 423; republics and, 413, 465; Shatalin Plan and, 448

Gross domestic product (GDP), 300, 307; budget deficit and, 273–275, 280–281, 298–299; defense spending and, 290–291; investment and, 279, 283–284; personal income taxes and, 288; profits and, 285; social welfare and, 301; subsidies and, 287, 301; taxation and, 289; turnover taxes and, 286, 301

Gross national product (GNP), budget deficit and, 237, 400; defense spending and, 290; growth of, 8, 25, 52, 253, 317, 361–363, 365, 367–369, 373, 387, 442, 459, 461; planning and, 255, 316, 318

Health care, 106, 115, 229, 372; price of, 150; subsidies for, 192, 318

Hoarding, 331–332, 410–411, 413, 457, 460

Horizontal interactions, 238–242; black market and, 238–240; collective farms and, 238–242; cooperatives and, 238–242; enterprises and, 238–242; matrix of, 238–242; rationing and, 239–242

Household sector: monetary balances and, 268, 270, 295, 303–304; production sector and, 238–242, 269; savings of, 272, 292

Housing, 105, 228, 236, 372, 390, 392, 395; in Armenia, 377; cooperatives and, 55; enterprises and, 207; investment in, 20–21, 25, 115, 284; prices of, 150, 154, 198; privatization of, 304, 449; state spending on, 98, 263, 289, 291, 296, 301; subsidies for, 192, 194

"Human factor," 12, 14, 54, 364

Hungarian reform, 16, 31–32, 35, 51, 68, 74, 243; bankruptcy and, 137; cooperatives and, 253; investment and, 217; lessons of, 224, 250, 344; outside support and, 116; prices in, 112, 160; privatization and, 310, 418, 438; radicalism of, 58–59; services and, 34, 53, 55, 65; taxes in, 222, 326; transition in, 114, 119–120, 245

Imports, 11–13, 20; budget revenues and, 254, 286, 302; competition from, 121, 312, 439–440; of consumer goods, 236–238, 244, 247, 286, 302–304, 323–324, 376, 384, 390, 398–399, 409–410, 449, 460; from Eastern Europe, 12, 385–386; enterprises and, 49, 59, 64, 213–214, 382; of food, 105, 404; of machinery, 323, 376; prices and, 198; technology of, 56

Incentive funds, 36, 39–40, 44, 98, 205, 207; prices and, 169

Incomes, personal: differentiation of, 139–140, 143–146, 186, 202, 222, 326; growth of, 331–332, 370–371, 373, 388, 390, 392, 394, 398–399, 409–410, 413, 460; indexation of, 442, 452, 456

Industrial output: enterprises and, 120; ethnic unrest and, 385; growth of, 8–9, 25, 60, 116, 330, 365, 368–369, 373, 388–389, 398, 467

Industrial prices, 96–100, 196–198, 401–403; *1982* revision of, 168–173; 195; *1966–67* revisions of, 37, 185, 195; reform of, 157–160, 163, 167–168, 401–403, 439

Industry: modernization of, 12, 14–15, 19–22, 52, 107, 115, 226, 236, 347, 363–365, 367, 369, 377–378; prices of, 172; profitability of, 173; reform in, 31–32, 34, 37, 51, 62; reorientation of, 399; transition period and, 114

Inflation: control of, 305, 370; fixed incomes and, 322; interest rates and, 293; Law on State Enterprise and, 209; origins of, 263, 276, 292, 294–299, 302; rate of, 156, 201, 187–189, 265, 371, 373, 413, 442, 460; repressed, 22, 25, 264, 319, 371; Shatalin Plan and, 452–453, 456–458; significance of, 116, 255, 325, 331–332; statistics and, 316, 362, 390, 399; wages and, 319

Institute for Agricultural Economics, 89

Institute for Systems Analysis, 82, 344

Institute of Economic Forecasting of Scientific and Technical Progress, 344

Institute of Economics, 77, 79, 87, 90, 246, 310–311, 336, 340, 343

Institute of Economics and Organization of Industrial Production (IEiOPP), 77, 79–80, 86, 88, 148–149

Institute of Economics of the World So-
cialist System (IEMSS), 77, 79–80, 84,
88–90, 247, 336, 343–344
Institute of Socio-Economic Problems of
the Population, 340
Institute of State and Law, 91
Institute of the Market, 340
Institute of the USA and Canada, 58, 73,
247, 312, 346
Intellectual property, 422–423, 434
Interest rates: enterprises and, 102, 212–
213, 223, 293, 303–304; *Gosbank* and,
427; on savings, 248, 270, 323, 401,
463
International Monetary Fund (IMF), 467
Inter-Regional Group of Deputies, 246,
248, 344
Interrepubican Economic Committee, 333,
446
Inventories, 39, 44, 224, 411
Investment: allocation of, 217; basic
guidelines for Twelfth Five-Year Plan
and, 6, 14–15; budget funding for, 223,
266, 274, 282, 299, 300, 306, 319,
379, 387–388, 400, 405; commissionings of, 316, 367; consumer goods and,
155; decentralization of, 283, 292; in
energy sector, 406; financing of, 44,
62, 95, 98, 205, 207, 213, 272–273,
275, 277, 283, 285, 370, 380, 403,
464; growth of, 8–10, 19–22, 25–27,
29, 107, 278, 364–365, 367, 377–378,
460; inflationary pressures of, 283, 380,
399; local control of, 210; machine-
building and metal working and, 14–
15, 21–22, 25, 107, 114, 284, 322,
364; prices and, 199; reduction of, 284,
298, 322, 325, 460–461; return on, 36,
66, 226, 404; Shatalin Plan and, 448;
Twelfth Five-Year Plan and, 316–318;
wages and, 252, 272, 293

Joint-stock companies, 252, 403, 417,
421–422, 424–425, 427, 432, 434–435,
463; Shatalin Plan and, 333, 448, 450–
451
Joint ventures, 64, 240–241, 254, 419,
422, 426, 430, 436, 464
Jurisdictional conflicts. *See* Regionalism

KGB, 244, 426, 448, 464, 467
Khozraschet, 102, 235, 366; bankruptcy
and, 121; banks and, 103; Basic Pro-

visions and, 212, 217–218, 224; democracy and, 134; enterprises and, 43,
62, 108–109, 111–112, 124, 378, 381;
labor and, 137, 139; ministries and, 37,
40; prices and, 111, 116–117, 126, 128;
profits and, 131, 362; republican, 308,
327
Kosygin reforms (*1965*), 32, 43, 45, 47–
49, 217, 221

Labor collective, 127, 132, 207–208, 212,
217, 219
Labor force: cost of, 154; growth of, 9,
12, 29, 378; incentives for, 193; redistribution of, 223; reduction of, 112,
118–119, 132, 137–138; strikes and,
244, 322, 331, 384, 386, 399, 405; tax
on, 197, 222. *See also* Wages
Labor productivity, 8, 13, 27–28, 37, 106,
124, 294–295, 305, 312, 364, 386; discipline campaign and, 14, 18, 379; plan
and, 316–317; wages and, 319, 410,
442
Labor and Social Issues, State Committee
for, 85, 118; plenum (*1987*) and, 108;
wages and, 212, 380
Land, 333, 438, 450, 465; draft law on,
352, 422–423, 434, 463; referendum
on, 414; rent on, 199
Law on Cooperatives, 63, 238, 241, 337,
419
Law on Individual Labor Activity, 63, 90,
108, 236, 238, 241, 337, 419
Law on Labor Collectives, 207
Law on the State Enterprise, 88, 108, 111,
129–133, 204, 217–220, 241, 277, 337,
423; agricultural sector and, 215; criticism of, 338; foreign trade and, 213–
214; ministries and, 216, 226, 255; state
intervention and, 112, 206–207, 209,
366; wages and, 319, 410
Laws, various, on economy. *See* Chronology
Leasing, 129, 236, 299, 304, 310–311,
333, 421, 449, 463; draft law on, 352
Light industry, 40, 42, 44, 298, 405; capital stock in, 234; growth in, 390–391;
independence of, 62; prices in, 172,
198; profitability of, 173; privatization
of, 303
Living standards, 7, 8, 42, 73, 138–139,
141; comparative, 120, 461; level of,
105, 225; per capita consumption and,

317, 331–332, 367, 408–409, 460; poverty and, 322; pressure to improve, 309, 339, 364, 413–414; prices and, 151, 211, 402–403; Shatalin Plan and, 446, 452–453

Machine-building and metal working (MBMW): burden on, 378; growth of, 8–9, 19, 367, 380; investment in, 14–15, 21–22, 25, 107, 114, 284, 322, 364; ministries and, 17, 39; pricing in, 95, 99, 172; profitability of, 173
Marshall Plan, 407
Marxism-Leninism, 48, 54, 81, 231, 245, 258
Maslyukov Commission, 350–351
Media, reform bias of, 91–92
Military-Industrial Commission (VPK), 26, 426, 432
Ministries: All-Union, criticism of, 86; Basic Provisions and, 216; control of funds, 40, 103, 285; heavy industry and, 209; interference of, 16, 46, 209, 381; local CPSU and, 133; personnel of, 349, 365; reorganization of, 24, 39, 61, 66, 208–209, 338, 403; role of, 126–128; Twelfth Five-Year Plan and, 6
Ministry of Defense, 41, 372, 426
Minisitry of External Economic Relations, 382, 429
Minisitry of Finance, 76, 85, 211–212, 256, 349, 425–426; budget deficit and, 339, 401; control of *Gosbank*, 270
Minisitry of Foreign Trade, 213
Minisitry of Internal Affairs, 426
Moldavia, 374, 466
Monetary overhang, 263–264, 292, 299, 442, 460; effect of, 270, 375; elimination of, 165, 302–304, 323, 326, 401, 448–450
Monetary system: budget deficits and, 272, 276, 299, 370; dichotomy of, 295; growth of money supply and, 263, 271, 273, 296, 369–371, 379–381, 427, 461; NEP and, 256; parallel currency and, 343–344; republics and, 436; ruble notes and, 463; Shatalin Plan and, 359, 436, 446–448, 451, 454, 456; stabilization of, 72, 264, 298–305, 325, 338–339, 400–403; statistics, reliability of, 265, 268

Monopolies, 121, 270, 294, 302, 311–312, 333, 423, 425, 428–429, 440, 462–463; Hungary and, 59; prices and, 157–158, 198, 255, 402

National income: consumer sector and, 372; cooperatives and, 63–64; defense and, 27; education and, 120; growth of, 7–10, 28, 60, 249, 316–317, 322, 368, 373, 377; of Hungary, 34
Nationalism, 49, 385
Nationalities, 343, 384–386, 399, 406; Crimean Tatars, 262; Nagorno-Karabakh, 342
NEP, 36, 47, 54, 164–165, 248, 250, 257–260; Basic Provisions and, 218; currency and, 256
Nineteenth Conference of the CPSU (*1988*), 109, 155, 164, 225–226, 229, 232–233, 244, 261, 339, 372; economic policymaking and, 347–349, 351
Nuclear power, 21, 449

OECD, 228

Party congresses: 26th Congress of the CPSU (*1981*), 84; 27th Congress of the CPSU (*1986*), 6, 16, 27, 30, 53–54, 72, 85, 89, 101, 104; 28th Congress of the CPSU (*1990*), 335, 348, 356–359, 387, 405
Party plenums: (*1985*), 104, 110; (*1988*), 164; (*1989*), 339. *See also* Plenum of the Central Committee of the CPSU (*1987*)
Patents. *See* Intellectual property
Pensions, 269, 288–289, 296, 301; increases in, 106, 155, 318, 321; military, 290; poverty and, 322; private sector and, 145; social insurance taxes and, 169
Planning. *See* Central planning
Plekhanov Institute of Economics, 346
Plenum of the Central Committee of the CPSU (*1987*), 110, 120, 164, 230, 233–236; agriculture and, 215; basic guidelines for Twelfth Five-Year Plan and, 108, 204, 243; confusion from, 244, 365–366; preparation for, 337; prices and, 227; results of, 337, 341
Poland, 49, 116, 119, 344–345; crisis and, 360; inflation in, 305; living standards

and, 120; prices and, 160; privatization in, 310, 418, 438

Politburo, 7, 17, 54, 353; cooperatives and, 42; economic reform and, 67–68, 74, 84, 233, 321, 335; personnel changes in, 336, 347–349, 354–355, 357

Presidential Council, 335, 345, 353–355, 357, 360

Presidential Decrees, various on economy. *See* Chronology

Presidential Plan, 334, 444, 446, 456–457, 462–464, 467

Prices: Basic Provisions and, 211, 220–221; budget and, 287, 302–304; central control of, 16, 22, 58–60, 265, 298–300, 369, 380; competition and, 120; consumer goods and, 154; contract, 55, 191, 197, 211, 428; credit system and, 90, 100; deformation of, 154–155; demand and, 53, 145, 173; destatization and, 401, 450; effectiveness of, 123, 176–178; enterprises and, 263; Law on the State Enterprise and, 226–227; marginal, 98; parametric, 175–176; stabilization of, 72, 102, 309; stepped, 174–175; temporary, 174, 190. *See also* Agricultural prices; Industrial prices; Retail prices; Wholesale prices

Private sector, 62, 67, 90, 214; income inequality and, 143–146. *See also* Cooperatives

Privatization, 244, 247–248, 301–304, 310, 326–327, 344, 425–426, 437–440; republics and, 431–432; Shatalin Plan and, 333–334, 357–358, 404, 417, 430–436, 449–451, 454–456

Production sector: budget deficits and, 277; central planning and, 268, 292–295, 298; household sector and, 269, 270, 272; inflationary pressure of, 302–304

Productivity, 9, 23, 38, 367–368, 378–379; prices and, 157, 177, 405. *See also* Capital productivity; Labor productivity

Profits: banks and, 130; Basic Provisions and, 205; importance of, 36, 62, 363; incentives and, 43–44, 98; *kombinate* and, 130; prices and, 97, 157, 168, 172, 176–177, 196, 219–220, 313, 401–402; rate of, 172, *173*; repatriation of, 426, 429–430, 436; size of, 37, 279, 284–285, 292, 306; state control of,

265, 270, 272, 286; taxes on, 40, 43, 266, 292, 299–300, 428

Property ownership, 309–311; draft law on, 352; enterprises and, 54, 302–303, 305; importance of, 235–236, 253, 325, 344–345, 437–440, 461; multiple forms of, 73, 124, 128–129, 137, 333, 343; popularity of, 254; reform economists and, 345; Shatalin Plan and 333, 416–419, 430–436, 446; union policy on, 420–428

Protectionism, 49–50, 55; local, 413, 457, 466

Quality control, 9, 19–20, 24, 33–34, 40–41, 45–46, 217, 364, 368; growth and, 112, 117–118, 226, 230, 378–380; Hungarian reform and, 59–60; prices and, 37, 52, 99, 176–178; statistics and, 362–363

Radicalism in reform, 30–35, 48, 52, 58, 111, 123–124

Rationing. *See* Consumer goods

Raw materials, 10–12, 320; prices for, 197–198, 219, 402, 452; savings on, 37, 378

Regional agricultural production associations, 214, 234

Regionalism, 464–468; autarky and, 399, 412, 457, 466; Basic Provisions and, 208–210, 216–217; control of budgets, 271, 334; economic autonomy and, 261, 308, 327; jurisdictional conflicts, 332–333, 465; property and, 420–421, 436

Resolutions, various, on economy. *See* Chronology

Retail prices: compensation and, 155–157, 193, 201–202, 331, 401, 403, 442–443, 451, 453, 467; increase in, 467; indexes of, 187, 188, 189, 201; reform of, 73, 96–97, 109, 112, 116–117, 150, 160, 186–195, 200–202, 331, 334, 342, 401–403, 411, 439, 442–443; Shatalin Plan and, 452

Ruble convertibility, 198, 213, 454

RSFSR, 404, 412, 434–436, 465–466; food supply in, 374; land law of, 438; leadership of, 332, 441–443; Ministry of Finance of, 435–436; sovereignty of, 322, 385; Supreme Soviet of, 332, 334, 357, 445, 462, 465

Ryzhkov program (*1990*), 331, 333, 352–354, 360, 385, 400–402, 442–444, 462

Savings, household, 269, 270, 273, 292, 295–297, 401; bonds and, 274, budget deficit and, 276, 370; interest rates and, 248, 270, 323, 401, 463; price reform and, 156, 201; size of, 237, 278, 295, 297, 317, 320, 442, 460
Science and technology: assimilation of, 124–126, 368; budget funding for, 99, 266, 282, 306; development of, 5, 15–16, 22, 45, 62, 104, 106, 364; lag behind West, 37, 49–50, 224; imports of, 13; prices and, 99–100; property relations and, 437; state control over, 205
Science and Technology, State Committee for, 84–85, 108, 208, 229
Scientific Research Institute for Prices, 90
Scientific Research Institute of Finance, 246
Second economy, 238, 269
Securities, 424, 434–435, 463
Self-financing. *See Khozraschet*
Sequencing of reforms, 55, 111–112, 115–116, 125–126, 295, 299, 331, 342, 438–440; in Eastern Europe, 55; Shatalin Plan and, 443
Service sector, 365, 367, 398, 460; China and, 125; Estonia and, 89; labor force and, 132; reform in, 31, 54–55, 114, 119
Shadow economy, 73, 148–150, 238–242, 412; prices and, 187
Shatalin Plan, 331, 333–334, 414, 462; destatization and, 415–417, 449–451, 455; fiscal policy and, 447–448, 451, 454, 456; foreign trade and, 454; monetary policy and, 436, 447–448, 451, 454; presentation of, 357–359; prices and, 448; privatization and, 430–436, 438–440, 449, 451, 454–456; republics and, 404, 447, 465; sequencing of, 443
Siberia, 147–148, 405
Small business, 111, 403, 422, 424–425, 438, 463
Social insurance, 269; prices and, 173, 197; safety net, 312–313, 361, 453; taxes, 101, 169, 266, 280–281, 288, 300, 302, 306, 321, 451
Sovereignty of republics, 332–334, 360, 385, 404, 406, 456, 464–468

Soviet Sociological Association, 148
Stabilization funds, 464
Stalinism, 247, 249, 257–261
State orders. *See Goszakazy*
State Property Fund, 422, 425, 429, 432, 436, 449
Statute on Socialist Enterprise, 42
Stock exchange, 463
Strikes. *See* Labor force
Subsidies: agriculture sector and, 184, 192; budget funding for, 101, 158–160, 211, 282, 285–291, 299–300, 301, 306; consumer, 263, 266; defense, 290; enterprises and, 43, 132, 199, 313, 322; retail prices and, 154–156, 158–160, 186, 191–194, 200–201, 203, 265; Shatalin Plan and, 448, 452–453, 455; wholesale prices and, 184–185
Summit meetings, 406, 467
Supreme Soviet of the USSR, 261, 308, 349, 355, 463; economic programs and, 322, 404; *Gosbank* and, 427; populism of, 356, 401–402; private activity and, 42; Ryzhkov program and, 352, 354, 360; Shatalin Plan and, 333–334, 443–444, 446
Sweden, 342–343

Talyzin Commission, 58, 86, 89, 92, 336–337
Taxation, 266; on cooperatives, 45, 101; draft law on, 352; on excess wage growth, 322–323, 326; indirect, 285; on private enterprise, 63; retail prices and, 265; republics and, 465; sales tax and, 464; Shatalin Plan and, 333, 359, 451; value-added tax and, 301. *See also* Social insurance; Taxes on enterprise profits; Taxes on personal incomes; Taxes on turnover
Taxes on enterprise profits: budget revenues and, 101, 273, 277, 284, 292, 306, 400, 451; capital gains and, 435; excess, 275, 299; law on, 400, 428, 463; localities and, 210; size of, 279–280, 300; rate of, 39–40, 43
Taxes on personal incomes, 55, 101, 280–281, 288, 291, 300, 302, 306, 400, 428; progressivity and, 140, 214, 326
Taxes on turnover, 266, 269, 284–286, 300, 301; budget revenues and, 101, 280–281, 286, 306, 379, 451; reform of, 101, 154–155; retail prices and, 186,

200–202; wholesale prices and, 167, 171
Thirteenth Five-Year Plan (*1991–95*), 58, 109, 204, 220, 227, 298, 327, 366; *Gosplan* and, 215
Time series, seasonal adjustment of, 388–390
Transition theory, 115–117, 125–126, 236–244, 438–440
Transportation sector, 365; in Armenia, 377; bottlenecks in, 263, 365, 384, 399; energy and, 406; growth in, 389–390, 393, 398; investment in, 20–21; *khozraschet* and, 108; management of, 42, 322; prices in, 154
Twelfth Five-Year Plan (*1986–90*), 5–7, 9, 17–23, 25–26, 29, 38, 316–317, 364, 384; abandonment of, 322; Basic Guidelines for, 5–6; democratization and, 108; feasibility of, 230–233, 324, 378; growth and, 249, 320–321, 363; investment and, 13–15, 25–26, 95, 107, 109, 377; prices and, 227; services and, 119

Ukraine, 374, 385, 404, 465–466
Unearned incomes, 38, 45–46, 55, 401
Unemployment, 73, 206, 298, 403, 451, 454–455
Unified Fund for the Development of Science and Technology, 174, 176–177
Union Contractual System, 448
Union of Leaseholders and Entrepreneurs, 247, 422
Union-Republic Foreign Currency Fund, 464
Union treaty, 360, 406–407, 443, 468

United Workers Front of Russia, 353
Uskoreniye, 72, 104, 106, 341, 362–363, 367
Uzbekistan, 385

VAZ/Sumi experiment, 40, 62, 83, 85
Vneshekonombank, 424, 427
Vneshtorgbank, 270

Wages: banking system and, 269; Basic Provisions and, 212, 224; growth of, 263, 294, 338, 388, 392, 394, 410, 442; incentives and, 44, 132, 193, 221–222; investment and, 252, 272, 293; *khozraschet* and, 131, 139, 235; prices and, 168–171, 193, 202, 319, 380, 442; reforms of, 344, 366, 410; revision of, 65; state control of, 39–40, 154, 272, 288, 303, 305, 370, 388, 399; tax on excess growth, 322–323, 326, 388, 399. *See also* Incomes, personal
War Communism, 259–260
Wholesale prices: decree (*1990*) on, 463; of energy, 378; reform of, 73, 96–100, 112, 167–179, 401–403, 439; Shatalin Plan and, 452
Wholesale trade, 60; Basic Provisions and, 210–211, 220; plenum (*1987*) and, 108, 366; prices and, 227–228, 381–382; reform of, 109, 216; shadow economy and, 149–150; transition and, 245, 255–256
World Economics and International Relations Institute (IMEMO), 90

Yugoslavia, 119, 122, 132, 235, 250; investment in, 217; taxes in, 222